501

MUST-BE-THERE EVENTS

501

MUST-BE-THERE EVENTS

Bounty Books

Publisher: Polly Manguel

Project Editor: Emma Beare

Designer: Ron Callow/Design 23

Picture Researcher: Vickie Walters

Production Manager: Neil Randles

First published in Great Britain in 2009 by
Bounty Books, a division of Octopus Publishing Group Limited

This paperback edition published in 2014 by Bounty Books,
a division of Octopus Publishing Group Limited
Endeavour House, 189 Shaftesbury Avenue, London WC2H 8JY
www.octopusbooks.co.uk

An Hachette UK Company
www.hachette.co.uk

Copyright © 2009, 2014 Octopus Publishing Group Limited

A CIP catalogue record is available from the British Library

ISBN: 978-0-753726-95-2

Printed and bound in China

Please note: We now know that political situations arise very quickly and a city or country that was quite safe a short time ago can suddenly become a 'no-go' area. Please check with the relevant authorities before booking tickets and travelling if you think there could be a problem.

Please check dates of the events before you travel as these may be subject to change.

Contents

INTRODUCTION   **6**

NORTH AMERICA   **8**
Kieran Fogarty and Joe Toussaint

CENTRAL AMERICA & THE CARIBBEAN   **56**
Arthur Findlay

SOUTH AMERICA   **74**
Arthur Findlay

AFRICA   **100**
Sarah Oliver, Jackum Brown, Janet Zoro and Roland Matthews

EUROPE   **152**
Janet Zoro, Jackum Brown, Joe Toussaint, Sarah Oliver, Roland Matthews, Kieran Fogarty and Arthur Findlay

EASTERN MEDITERRANEAN & MIDDLE EAST   **364**
Sarah Oliver and Arthur Findlay

ASIA   **378**
Joe Toussaint, Kieran Fogarty, Sarah Oliver, Jackum Brown, Arthur Findlay and David Brown

AUSTRALASIA & OCEANIA   **500**
Roland Matthews and Arthur Findlay

INDEX   **540**

Introduction

We humans are sociable creatures: we have always lived in family groups, joining forces with other family groups in order to share food, to work and, of course, in the defence of our common "interests". We have always celebrated special occasions – a fruitful harvest, a successful hunt, worshipping, thanking or asking favours from the gods or recognizing a birth, a marriage or a death. We also have an instinctive need to come together with others, to share experiences and let our hair down.

Today, when it's relatively easy to travel almost anywhere in the world, it is possible to experience any number of amazing events that take place all year round, all over the globe. Many of the events in this book are ancient, such as the Pasola festival in Sumba, with its origins back in the mists of time; yet there are others, like Singapore's already immensely popular ZoukOut dance festival, that are only a few years old.

Whether it's eating seafood, story telling, throwing tomatoes at one another, watching puppet theatre, listening to jazz or dancing the days and nights away – there are innumerable different themes to these festivals and events and you're bound to find some that appeal to you.

There are famous sports meetings and other annual sporting events: cycling, golf, motor racing, football, cricket, marathon running, sailing, cross country skiing, tennis and more. Some events feature animals – there are wonderful festivals dedicated to elephants in Thailand, camels in India and Australia, and eagles in Mongolia. If you love horses you can go to events in Britain, America, Tibet, Portugal or Ireland to mention just a few. Other festivals seem to be plain silly, like the World Bog Snorkelling Championships in Wales, or the World Wife Carrying Championships in Finland, or boating without any water at the Henley on Todd Regatta and cockroach racing in Australia.

Many of the world events featured are religious in

nature, drawing believers and visitors from all over the world: the Easter Mass led by the Pope in Rome, the celebration of Eid in Damascus and the Sikh festival of Holla Mohalla in Anandpur Sahib in the Punjab are just a few. There are events that are restricted in some way, such as the Hajj in Mecca, while there are others, like the Sami people's Jokkmokk Winter Market in Swedish Lapland, that are really primarily for the local population. Some are family orientated, such as Thanksgiving in the USA, or Chahar Shanbeh Suri in Iran or the Famadihana in Madagascar. The majority of events and celebrations, though, welcome all comers; indeed there are a few that have been created principally to attract visitors and to put their town or region 'on the map'.

And of course, there is music: from opera in Verona, classical music in Prague to electronic music at KaZantip in Ukraine, from jazz in Monterey to rock at Exit in Serbia or world music in Sarawak and at Mali's Festival in the Desert – whatever your taste in music, someone, somewhere will be celebrating it. The arts have given rise to a great many annual events – as well as musical events there are festivals of theatre, literature, painting and photography described here too.

As with all travelling, when visiting events in foreign countries it helps if you can speak even just a little bit of the local language, although it has to be said that shared smiles, laughter and dancing are universal languages understood by all. It's a good idea to plan festival trips rather further ahead than you might plan other trips – accommodation may have to be booked at least twelve months in advance for very popular events.

So from kite festivals in China to beer festivals in Germany, from film to fashion, from bull fighting to camel wrestling, from carving chocolate in Italy to carving ice in Central Asia, from celebrating the victory of good over evil during Galungan in Bali to the Festival of the Dead in Mexico, you can travel the world, meet new people, enjoy unusual festivities in foreign lands, deepen your knowledge of other cultures and religions – and have a great time!

NORTH AMERICA

Quebec Winter Carnival

WHEN:
Starts late January or early February
and lasts for 17 days
WHERE:
Quebec City, Quebec
BEST FOR:
Sport, music and spectacle
YOU SHOULD KNOW:
If you have never been inside an
igloo, then head for the Igloo Village.
The wonderful and often elaborate
ice structures provide welcome
respite from the biting cold of the
Quebec winter.

Nobody does winter quite like Canadians, but that is probably due in part to the fact that no one has winters quite like Canada. In true Arcadian spirit they make the best of it and the Carnaval de Québec is the biggest and best of its kind in the world.

There has been a winter festival of sorts in Quebec since 1894; however most were low-key affairs and often postponed for reason of war or economic privation. In recent years astute marketing and generous corporate sponsorship have seen the event grow to one that now attracts over a million participants. The Plains of Abraham, a large park on the banks of the St Lawrence River, plays host to many of the events as visitors from around the globe are welcomed by the festival's totem – Carnaval Bonhomme, a jolly, giant snow figure.

The visual highlight of the celebration is the night-time parade, when the Québecois wrap up warm to watch a procession of elaborately decorated floats. Music, street theatre and a firework finale, set against the backdrop of the marvellous walled city of Quebec, make this a real night to remember. As for the sporting events, lovers of hibernal high jinks should head for the Grand Viree – a hair-raising dog-sled race – or its motorized equivalent, the Raid des Braves, an off-piste snowmobile race. If medals were given out to the hardiest competitors, then those who compete in the canoe race across the ice floes of the St Lawrence River would win hands down. More artistic recreation can be enjoyed at the International Snow Sculpture Event as creators produce astounding ephemeral works of art. The Place du Palais is the centre for music and dance and is often the scene of giant conga dances across its snow-covered grounds.

The festival features buildings created from ice blocks, like this magnificent castle.

Le Festival du Voyageur

The snow sculptures at the festival are superb.

If you are looking for the archetypal Canadian scene, then head for St Boniface – Winnipeg's French Quarter – in mid-February. The place springs to life with historical re-enactment and jollity, all in the deepest mid-winter setting. This is Canada at its purest and rawest. Established in 1969, Le Festival du Voyageur celebrates the pioneering spirit of East Coast French Canadians who, over 300 years ago, ventured west to make contact with First Nations bands to buy fur. Now home to western Canada's largest French-speaking community, Winnipeg stages one of North America's most spectacular winter festivals.

Le Festival du Voyageur is the perfect blend of Gallic exuberance and New World ruggedness. There is ample good food and much fiddle playing, interspersed with dog-sled races, sporting challenges and snow sculpting. Live theatre, juggling and firework displays help to shake off the winter blues, as the whole town wraps up warm and turns out to party. The historical heart of the ten-day festival is the faithfully recreated early 19th century Fort Gibraltar, where many of the events take place. Throughout the whole carnival there is plenty to stimulate the mind, body and taste buds, but the two must-see events occur towards its end. The spectacular torchlight parade and free-to-enter gala are followed the next day by the hottest ticket in town – the Governor's Ball. In this evening of five-course feasting, dancing and gaiety, the townsfolk dress in 19th century garb, let their hair down and party as though it were 1820.

Although the theme of the festival is historical, there is little in it that feels stuffy. In reality it provides the residents of Manitoba with a vital link to an important period in their past, while offering relief from the harsh realities of winter on the Canadian Plains.

WHEN:
Over ten days in mid February
WHERE:
Winnipeg, Manitoba
BEST FOR:
History, culture and sport
YOU SHOULD KNOW:
If you want to stay in the French Quarter be sure to book well in advance as rooms are at a premium during Le Festival. Travel into town can be disrupted by fresh snowfall.

A local Inuit builds an igloo.

Toonik Tyme, Iqaluit Spring Festival

Like Mardi Gras, Toonik Tyme is essentially a celebration of the arrival of spring. Each year since 1965 the mainly Inuit inhabitants of Iqaluit, on Baffin Island, have turned out to celebrate the traditions of their ancestors and generally to have fun. The festival is the most eclectic and eccentric of events, where giant bingo sits alongside seal hunting and skinning contests, while ice sculpting is featured together with last-man-standing game shows.

The event attracts visitors from all across Nunavut and competition is keen, right from the junior hockey tournament to the fishing Derby. Prize money is just one factor that draws in talent from far and wide; there is also much inter-band rivalry, as old skills and new are put to the test. The diet during the gala is definitely 'low-carb', as at almost every turn you are greeted by the delicious smell of cooking meat and fish.

One of the most keenly contested events is the snowmobile race which, though clearly not traditional, shows how people have adapted to this harsh environment. It may be spring, but there is still enough thick sea ice to drive on. The centrepiece of each festival is the Community Feast, held at the Parish Hall. The food is free and plentiful and the atmosphere is joyful. The evenings are filled with concerts and dances, culminating in a last-night bash with a headline act, usually held at Nakasuk School. The true significance of Toonik Tyme is to re-engender a civic pride that was almost lost through centuries of persecution, and to hone traditional skills that were all but wiped out. It may have been going only since 1965, but it is rooted in traditional Native North American celebrations throughout the ages.

WHEN:
Mid April
WHERE:
Iqaluit, Baffin Island, Nunavut
BEST FOR:
Music, sport, Inuit culture, food and giant bingo
YOU SHOULD KNOW:
The only practical way of reaching Iqaluit is by air. The most regular services are from Yellowknife, Montreal and Ottawa.

Canada Day in Ottawa

Canada Day marks the founding of Canada as an entity by the British in 1867 and is celebrated throughout the world with varying degrees of exuberance. In London, England, a musical extravaganza is laid on in Trafalgar Square, while in west coast Vancouver the festivities take the form of laid-back mid-summer fun. In Montreal residents use the holiday to move house (June 30 is the traditional end of tenancy) before they have their fun, but nowhere is the day more fulsomely celebrated than in the nation's capital, Ottawa.

Large swathes of the downtown area are blocked to traffic as Canadians cover themselves with anything sporting the red maple leaf and take to the streets. The theme is multicultural as things get underway before noon at the World Exchange Plaza, where performers from Canada's different ethnic groups strut their stuff. The French half of town enters into the spirit of things in Jacques-Cartier Park, across the river in Gatineau, where a variety of child-friendly events are laid on, including a circus and lots of participatory games. Majors Hill Park is the preferred hangout of locals. Offering great views of Parliament and close to many food outlets, it is the perfect place to go if you just want to relax and soak up the atmosphere. Buskers, street artists and face painters vie for your attention, while music booms out from a large stage.

As the evening approaches the focus of attention switches to Parliament Hill. At 18.00 a 'pre show' is followed by the main event around 21.00, when modern entertainment blends with performances by the Army and the Royal Canadian Mounted Police. All eyes then turn skyward as this most pleasant of days ends with a spectacular firework display.

Everyone is out for fun on Canada Day.

WHEN:
July 1
WHERE:
Ottawa, Ontario
BEST FOR:
Culture and music
YOU SHOULD KNOW:
Canada Day provides a great opportunity to explore Ottawa at very little cost. Museums and galleries throw open their doors for free, while much of the street food is of good quality and affordable. As long as you like the taste of maple syrup you should be okay.

Merrymakers perform on the streets during Montreal's Just For Laughs Festival.

Just For Laughs Festival

With over a thousand artists drawn from across the globe and over a million paying patrons, Montreal's Just For Laughs (*Juste pour rire*) festival may be far removed from its humble origins as a two-day Francophone festival in 1983, but its emphasis on all things comedic remains the same. It is now the premier comedy festival in the world, pulling in Hollywood A-listers, as well as top comedy acts from Europe. While headline acts draw in huge crowds in the city's leading venues, away from them the whole town has the feel of a comedic Olympic village as merrymakers perform on any stage possible and even on the street.

Such has been the importance of Just For Laughs that just about anybody worth their salt in the field has performed here. The atmosphere at times has the feel of a school reunion, as fellow comedians sit in the audience, guffawing at their mates. Now stretching over a full month, the festival reflects Canada's bilingual status, as the first two weeks are dominated by French language acts, while the last fortnight is reserved for English-speaking comedians.

As it has evolved the festival has broadened its remit to include mime, acrobatics and theatre. The 1990s saw the inauguration of the Just For Laughs Film Festival, which provides a platform for short independent film makers as well as showcasing new work from top animators. Stand-up comedy may have come a long way since its 19th century vaudeville origins as risible politicians and the comedians who bait them come and go, but one thing remains true – the mantra Just For Laughs.

WHEN:
Throughout July
WHERE:
Montreal, Quebec
BEST FOR:
Comedy, culture and film
YOU SHOULD KNOW:
There are broadly two ways to approach the festival. If you want to play it safe (and pay more money) then you can stick to the more established acts on the headline stages. However if you want to take a risk, head for the smaller venues where the atmosphere is more rough and ready and every now and then a true gem is uncovered.

Royal Nova Scotia International Tattoo

With a cast of thousands, the Royal Nova Scotia International Tattoo, held annually in Halifax since 1979, celebrates Canada's fighting men and women in a special partnership between civilian and military performers. Each year has a new overall theme, but the underlying purpose throughout the years has been to form a 'bond of friendship' between Canada and the rest of the world. Great feats of dancing, gymnastics and athleticism are on show, all backed by pipes and drums, military bands, solo singers and choirs. Traditional marching is overlaid with more modern artistry and old-time music is augmented by interpretations of current classics.

While modern circus can provide much of the spectacle seen here, it cannot match the sheer effort of those who display their skills and vigour, mixing essential training programmes with manoeuvres that leave you astounded by the precision of their execution. The Tattoo has grown in stature and now attracts performers from across the world, so you can expect to see Cossack dancing, French mime and Beefeaters alongside the tartan and maple leaf of the hosts.

Mock battles and recreations of the theatre of war remind you that the Tattoo has a purpose and that the Canadian military is a fighting force that has been, and still is, involved in many conflicts around the globe. Part of this generally upbeat evening is given over to remembering the, mainly young, men and women who have died in the service of their country. The Tattoo is a two-and-a-half hour family show that provides a most memorable and often moving evening's entertainment. Breathtaking in its magnitude and dynamism, it leaves the audience with a genuine sense of awe.

WHEN:
Over nine days, around the beginning of July
WHERE:
Halifax Metro Centre, Halifax, Nova Scotia
BEST FOR:
Spectacle, music and theatre
YOU SHOULD KNOW:
The tickets for the best seats sell out quickly, so if you are planning to take in the Tattoo as part of a visit, be sure to book well in advance.

A cast of thousands takes part in the Tattoo.

The Calgary Stampede

Founded in 1886 to promote and celebrate the Old West and the cowboy way of life, the Calgary Stampede has grown to earn its status as 'The Greatest Outdoor Show on Earth'.

For ten days in July the inhabitants of this bustling Albertan oil town squeeze into jeans, don stetsons and go out to party. The whole thing starts with a lavish parade through the centre of town, where locals line the route from around 07.00 in keen anticipation. Nowhere is the Calgarian's famous hospitality more in evidence than at the parade, where free pancakes are laid on to warm spectators' hands in the early morning chill. Once underway, the parade is great fun, with marching bands, floats, horses, clowns and a carnival queen.

After the parade attention switches to Stampede Park where a whole

The breathtaking chuck wagon race is a highlight at the Calgary Stampede.

host of stalls, funfair rides, livestock shows, art exhibitions and live bands surround the main arena. Horsemen and women come from across the world to compete for bountiful purses at the rodeo. Bareback riding, bull riding, steer wrestling and tie-down roping are among the hair-raising events that thrill the crowd. The most spectacular event is the chuckwagon derby, where two pairs of horses tow a rider and carriage at breakneck speeds around a tight circuit. Each day sees heats, building up to a grand finale and a prize fund of over a million dollars. Unfortunately there is a downside to all this. The derby has been the cause of considerable controversy, as it has taken a heavy toll on both horses and riders, resulting in several deaths over the years.

Away from the park, the whole town has a real party atmosphere as bars, restaurants, theatres and clubs take up the Western theme.

*Each team puts on a fantastic
display of fireworks in this
competition.*

Celebration of Light Festival

Each year towards the end of July the skies above the city of
Vancouver are filled with the bursting and crashing of fireworks for
the annual Celebration of Light Festival. Three or occasionally four
teams from around the world compete in a fantastic show of sound
and light, as music is played to accompany each presentation.

The show itself is centred on English Bay, but such is the layout
of Vancouver that it makes a perfect amphitheatre for such events,
and the show can be viewed from far and wide (the accompanying
music can be heard via local radio stations). Vancouver has a skyline
to rival that of any city in the world – it's backed by mountains and
set in a wonderful natural harbour. The fireworks start at 22.00 but
the whole evening is about enjoying yourself before the big crescendo.
Much of the city is made traffic-free as the evening draws on, and
each section of Vancouver society moves towards what it considers
to be the best seat in town. Yale Town and Robson Street apartment
blocks positively hum with partying sophisticates, while English Bay
is lined with boats of all shapes and sizes. Stanley Park and Sunset
Beach offer the closest vantage points, but the best seat in the house
and the best atmosphere is to be found at Kitsilano Beach, where the
views across the bay are tremendous. The competition itself
comprises three (or four) individual displays, each separated by two
days, culminating in a final that takes the form of three (or four)
nine-minute displays, before the champion is announced. Different
teams compete each year, but the quality of display is always top
class, especially if a Chinese team is invited to participate.

WHEN:
Over eight days, starting towards
the end of July
WHERE:
Vancouver, British Columbia
BEST FOR:
Music and spectacle
YOU SHOULD KNOW:
All restaurants which offer a good
view of the fireworks are booked up
well in advance, so perhaps the best
way to enjoy the evening is to picnic
on the beach. Be warned, though,
that public drinking is not allowed in
Vancouver and while the city police
might turn a blind eye to the odd
covered can or bottle early in the
evening, they clamp down hard on
anything they consider to be
anti-social behaviour.

Cape Breton Celtic Colours International Festival

Nowhere in the world are the autumn colours more vibrant than along the eastern seaboard of North America. It is this wonderful tapestry that forms the backdrop to the Celtic Colours International Festival. Founded in 1997, it has grown in size, attracting hundreds of performers and tens of thousands of visitors, to become one of the world's foremost Celtic gatherings. Over a period of ten days, Cape Breton Island becomes home to a matchless carnival of music and culture. Crowds flock to dozens of concert halls the length and breadth of the island and are entertained both day and night by art exhibitions, workshops, impromptu street performances and more formal concerts.

The theme is always the music that the islanders' forebears brought across the Atlantic from the western fringes of Europe. More recently, however, the festival has broadened its remit to include performers from Cuba and Germany. The larger concerts, featuring more established artists, usually take place at the bigger venues in the island's capital, Sydney. However, more intimate events are to be found almost anywhere on the island and there is a lively fringe, where dancers, musicians, storytellers and other tradition-bearers perform in small venues at little or no cost.

All in all, the festival succeeds in its twin aims of preserving Celtic culture while promoting one of the most beautiful landscapes in the world. While the festival is reason enough to visit Cape Breton, you should allow time to explore this island that is the inspiration for many of the fabulous performances which the festival delivers.

WHEN:
Over ten days each October – check ahead for the exact dates.
WHERE:
Cape Breton, Nova Scotia
BEST FOR:
Culture and music
YOU SHOULD KNOW:
Public transport on Cape Breton is poor at the best of times and comes under particular strain during the festival. If you want to travel to events outside of Sydney, it is recommended that you hire a car.

Performers take part in a concert at the Cape Breton Celtic Colours Festival.

Niagara Falls Festival of Lights

WHEN:
From November to early January
WHERE:
Niagara Falls, Ontario
BEST FOR:
Culture and spectacle
YOU SHOULD KNOW:
Such is the popularity of the area
that it's probably a good idea to
leave the car at home. A regular
shuttle service links the rail station
and bus terminal at Niagara Falls
Town to the Falls themselves.

The twin cataracts of the American and Horseshoe Falls that make up Niagara Falls provide one of the most astounding natural spectacles on earth. Stunning all year round, they have a special aura in winter, when the surrounding hillsides are covered with snow and the spray from the torrent of water freezes in the air. The outstanding natural beauty of the Falls is augmented by illuminations and pyrotechnic displays during the annual winter Festival of Lights. Things get underway in early November at Queen Victoria Park, with a huge free firework display and the turning on of the illuminations, which comprise over three million twinkling lights.

With one eye on marketing and pleasing the kids, many of the

illuminations are themed, often recreating scenes from popular children's animation films. More grown-up fun can be had in the form of the many classical music concerts put on during the festival. For those who can't wait for Christmas, there is a Santa Claus parade at the end of November and, if you want to lose a few calories in the lead up to Yuletide, there is a 5-km (3-mi) fun run which is open to all.

December sees more concerts and a few Broadway plays, and a huge party heralds the build up to Christmas, a few days before the big day. Christmas Day and Boxing Day in Canada are all about being with the family, and the festival takes a well-earned break before laying on an unforgettable New Year's Eve celebration, where fireworks once again light up the skies above the iconic waterfalls.

As if the falls were not spectacular enough on their own, they have added lights!

Pasadena Rose Parade

WHEN:
New Year's Day every year
(unless January 1 is a Sunday, when
it takes place on January 2)
WHERE:
Pasadena, California
BEST FOR:
US folklore and culture; and sport
YOU SHOULD KNOW:
No doubt seeking an holistic
approach to the Rose Parade, in
1998 the Washington Township High
School Minutemen Marching Band
from Sewell, New Jersey, chose to
decorate/clothe all of its musicians
entirely in real, fresh flowers – like
the parade floats. The hallucinatory
image of a bouquet of gardenias
with a fuchsia hat, blowing a
trombone or banging a drum, is
authentically Californian.

In 1890, when the countryside round Los Angeles was still a paradise of green fields and orange groves, Pasadena's Valley Hunt Club instituted a festival to celebrate the fact that on New Year's Day, when New York was freezing and snowbound, Pasadena looked out on flowers blooming in the warm sunshine. The Tournament of Roses rapidly became a New Year tradition. The actual Rose Parade starts the day. Every surface of the floats must be covered in real flowers and greenery, whatever technical wizardry is also used. The floats are interspersed with a selection of the world's finest marching bands, who audition fiercely for coveted places. Equestrian formations of unsurpassed splendour and dazzling professional excellence also join the parade and feature a wide variety of horse breeds. It takes more than two hours for the regal procession to pass its familiar 9 km (5.5 mi) route down Colorado Boulevard, Pasadena's main thoroughfare (and originally part of US Route 66). Afterwards, the floats park up like some mobile botanic garden so that the tens of thousands of admirers can get a close look at the floral subtleties and intricate construction.

Eventually, most of the million-odd visitors turn their attention to the day's other abiding tradition: the Rose Bowl college football game. It's the most prestigious game of the college circuit, and the Rose Parade is its fairy godmother. Ever since it was invited to share the billing (previous post-parade entertainment included racing between an ostrich and an elephant and Ben Hur-style chariot races), the Rose Bowl game has been brushed with the stardust created by the atmosphere of the Rose Parade. You can't help glowing in the unfeigned warmth created by a community at genial play, doffing its hat to the High School Rose Queen of the year, proud of what it is, what it can do and what it can give back to the country of which it is resolutely proud. The professionalism of the Tournament of Roses is driven by civic pride of rare sincerity. The more you see, the more you enjoy being part of it – and the flowers are fabulous.

The Rose Queen and her court ride down Colorado Boulevard.

Sundance Film Festival

Not since Charlie Chaplin and Douglas Fairbanks started United Artists has an actor influenced the US Film industry so strongly. From 1978 Robert Redford's support for the fledgling Utah & US Film Festival helped attract the stellar participation it now enjoys; and by association in the public consciousness, his Sundance Ranch gave it (only in 1990) its official name. But it was the director Sidney Pollack who in 1981 foresaw that, by moving it from September to high-season January in the Rocky Mountains' Utah ski resort of Park City, the festival would have 'Hollywood beating down the door to attend'. They flooded in. Now the Sundance Film Festival is the biggest and most important celebration of independent artists and audiences – a provocative taste-making forum for discussion between the industry and the people whose judgements may make or break them.

Film buffs complain that Sundance is getting unwieldy. You can see perhaps 100 US and world premieres (selected from around 3,500 submissions) in ten drama and documentary categories as well as a range of panel discussions addressing every cranny of film culture. It's true, too, that the strict intellectual savvy of the festival's early days seems diluted by the glitz and glamour that commands international headlines. But very few film festivals are as democratic and faithful to their roots. You can get into literally everything on the programme (and local Utah residents still get subsidized priority), if you only apply early enough. Sundance still reflects the integrity of its earliest aspirations – which means removing the barrier between the stars of movie production and their fiercest critics and champions.

And Sundance isn't just film. It's the mountains in winter glory, live music in big and small venues, packed bars full of lively discussion with new friends, and a priceless feeling of communal exhilaration that such a sophisticated event should be so accessible.

WHEN:
Ten days in mid to late January, each year
WHERE:
Park City, Utah. Festival screenings, panels and other events are also scheduled in the nearby towns of Ogden, Sundance and Salt Lake City.
BEST FOR:
Seeing films, celebrity spotting, intense cultural and political discussion, and dedicated partying
YOU SHOULD KNOW:
For a festival of such genuine substance and international chic, the atmosphere throughout Sundance is refreshingly Western American – down-home, can-do and welcoming.

Crowds gather around the Egyptian Theatre on Main Street, Park City.

The Arizona Cardinals celebrate a touchdown in the 2009 game.

The Super Bowl

The Super Bowl is the championship football game of the National Football League (NFL). Every year it's played on a Sunday at the end of January or the beginning of February in a stadium (bowl) in one of the warmer, southerly States, neutral to both teams. Since the first contest in 1967, sporting status and the excitement it generates have made Super Bowl Sunday an unofficial US national holiday second only to Thanksgiving. Everyone gives or goes to a party. That includes a host of corporately sponsored charity events like the Super Bowl Cheerleaders Party, the Body Doubles Party and Hawaiian Tropic Party, among dozens held close to the actual stadium. Super Bowl Sunday is the one day of the year when everyone is determined to be sociable and have fun, but it's also big business.

The game itself would be smothered by the showbiz glitz, superstar glamour and huge corporate spending that envelop it (the half-time show alone costs millions and takes months to plan), except that the hoopla almost always inspires the competing teams to extraordinary heights. Year after year, fresh laurels are added to the legendary sporting achievements on the field, and the season's heroes throw further, run faster and leap higher. There are Davids and Goliaths, and pairs matched like Achilles and Hector, but the occasion raises them all to their peak. High drama, real courage and total commitment guarantee brilliant entertainment – at its very best inside the stadium, if ever you could get a ticket. But most people enjoy Super Bowl on television, and that's the way to make the most of it as an American festival. It's a sporting event of the first magnitude, to be enjoyed in the company of a nation in no-holds-barred party mode.

WHEN:
Sunday at the end of January or beginning of February
WHERE:
In a major stadium chosen for its local climate, typically in Florida, Louisiana, Texas, Arizona or California
BEST FOR:
Sport and cultural understanding
YOU SHOULD KNOW:
It's widely believed that the outcome of Super Bowl can influence the US stock market.

The American Birkebeiner

The annual Birkebeiner cross-country ski race, known affectionately as the Birkie, is the largest event of its kind in North America. At 51 km (32 mi) long, it attracts some 8,000 skiers of varying ability and 20,000 spectators to a three-day marathon of events in Wisconsin, of which the Birkie and the shorter Kortelopet races are the climax.

The Birkie was founded in 1973, its name commemorating a famous event in Norway's history. In 1206, during the Norwegian civil war, a group of soldiers, known as Birkebeiners for their birch-bark protective leggings, smuggled the illegitimate 18-month-old son of King Sverresson from Lillehammer to the safety of Trondheim on skis, saving his life and enabling him to grow up and take the throne himself.

Set in the glorious Chequamegon-Nicolet National Forest that covers much of northwest Wisconsin, the race starts in Cable and ends in Hayward, two towns with a combined population of less than 3,000. The race is the biggest date in the local calendar, as thousands of enthusiasts pour into the area from around the world.

Competitors set off in waves on a course that climbs and rolls to the high point of Firetower Hill, 120 m (400 ft) above the start point. From here there are many tricky descents and arduous climbs before crossing the frozen Lake Hayward into town, past thousands of cheering spectators lining the finishing point on Main Street.

The Birkie is not just for professional athletes; it is for everyone who loves cross-country skiing. Some have raced it many times; others have never participated in a marathon ski journey in their lives. All who cross the finishing line not only feel a tremendous sense of achievement but also receive a medallion to remind them of this beautiful course and the camaraderie of skiing through the forest with thousands of like-minded people.

Skiers in 'the Birkie' face tricky descents and arduous climbs.

WHEN:
The last weekend in February
WHERE:
Northwest Wisconsin
BEST FOR:
Cross-country skiing through a pristine National Forest
YOU SHOULD KNOW:
The American Birkebeiner is one of the Worldloppet Ski Federation's worldwide cross-country ski marathons. At Norway's Birkebeinerrennet race, skiers traditionally carry backpacks weighing 3.5 kg (7.5 lb), roughly the weight of an 18-month-old child.

St Patrick's Day, Boston

WHEN:
Usually on the Sunday closest to
March 17
WHERE:
Boston, Massachusetts. Southie's
Parade begins at 13.00 (but the fun
begins much earlier with the
assembly at 11.00 of bands, floats and
marching formations at the Broadway
MBTA station by Gillette Park). Best
views are on E Broadway, or E 4th St
before the Grand Marshals' reviewing
platform at Thomas Park.
BEST FOR:
Cultural shenanigans of an
uproarious nature
YOU SHOULD KNOW:
The traditional menu for St Patrick's
Day in Boston is corned beef
and cabbage.

Not even Ireland is as Irish as Boston, Massachusetts, on St Patrick's Day. Boston first celebrated St Patrick's Day in 1737, and since 1901 its parades, dinners, parties, marching bands, concerts and community get-togethers have established themselves as an annual event, usually held on the Sunday closest to March 17, the saint's actual feast day. Boston is dressed in green. So are the 850,000 residents and visitors who crowd the streets for 'Southie's (South Boston's) Parade' from Gillette Park to Andrew Square, a 5.1 km (3.2 mi) festival of music, song, dancing, prancing and high spirits. The parade is the heart and soul of St Patrick's Day, and people spend all year planning spectacular floats, dance routines, and *coups de theatre* that draw collective gasps from the excited crowd. You might well see 50 black-and-white 2 m (7 ft)-high pints of Guinness bopping in co-ordinated rumba, a hundred leprechauns 'voguing' or break-dancing along the margins, and dozens of exotic, even interactive, floats whose unstuffy but commercial origins are smothered in shamrocks and rendered attractive by their sheer goodwill.

The noise can be deafening as over 35 marching bands – fife and drums, cheerleading, rock, jazz, military and traditional Irish – succeed each other. All are draped in the tricolour, and positioned to emphasize the inclusion of more dignified formations like the veterans, firefighters and other services honoured by the city. But St Patrick's Day in Boston measures respect by the amount of fun people are having, and the traditional mythology of 'Irishness' dictates letting yourself go. As the parade disperses, it spreads its excitement so that all Boston glows with communal cheer – and it's a feeling you'll take away with you, too. On St Patrick's Day in Boston, everyone has the right to be Irish and get away with it.

The 'St Patrick' float adds to the fun.

Iditarod Dog Sled Race

Often called the 'Last Great Race on Earth', Alaska's Iditarod is run in March every year between Anchorage and Nome. As many as 80 teams of 12 to 16 dogs, each with their 'musher', race across 1,840 km (1,150 mi) of central Alaska's most unforgiving mountains, forests, rivers and tundra. The race has alternating northern and southern routes, both of which commemorate the supply route from the coast to the mining villages established during Alaska's 19th century Gold Rush, and include Iditarod village itself. Since its first running in 1973, experience and technological improvements have massively decreased the Iditarod's duration. The slowest winner (1974) took over 20 days to triumph over the blizzards and frozen deprivation; recent winners take ten to 12 days, and in 2002 the record of eight days 22 hours 46 minutes and two seconds was set.

The Iditarod is professional only in its organization, mushing skills, and attitudes. The volunteers who organize it raise money for charity and to help participants, not themselves. This spirit of community goodwill and encouragement extends all the way along the race route, with whole villages turned out day and night in the sub-zero howling winds. The volunteers, like the mushers, might be fishermen, teachers, lawyers, preachers, oilmen, housewives or students – a wondrous mix of age, gender and background reminiscent of the settlers who originally founded the trail. Part of the Iditarod's allure is that it poses exactly the same demands on courage, endurance and old-fashioned guts as it did in the 1890s; outside the brightly lit communities, Alaska's wilderness – through Finger Lake, over the Alaska Range to the Yukon, Shaktoolik and Nome – is as vicious, spiteful and beautiful as ever. Iditarod mushers and dog teams challenge nature as well as each other. There has never been a better recipe for drama, heroism, sportsmanship and high-adrenaline thrills than this.

WHEN:
March
WHERE:
In Alaska – from Anchorage to Nome on the Bering Strait
BEST FOR:
Extreme sports using arcane skills and community culture in an extreme environment
YOU SHOULD KNOW:
Dog sled teams usually consist of either Alaskan malamutes or Siberian huskies. The last musher to finish extinguishes a red lantern next to the finish line, and keeps it as a prize. The red lantern carries great honour – its winner has usually had to overcome injury or exceptionally difficult circumstances to finish at all.

An all-white dog team heads off.

Over 500 American Indian nations attend the Pow Wow.

Gathering of Nations Pow Wow

Native American tribal culture was almost overwhelmed by centuries of European immigration and technological advantage, but the increasing flood of civil rights legislation since the 1970s has encouraged even the smallest tribal groups to reassert their claim to ancestral culture as well as land. The Gathering of Nations is the umbrella organization of more than 500 Federally recognized American Indian nations, from the Sioux, Cheyenne, Navajo and Apache to the less-well-known Ossahatchee or Athabascan. The organization offers practical legal, educational and social help – but it celebrates its inclusiveness at its annual Pow Wow, a three-day cultural feast of singing, dancing, drumming, story-telling and traditional entertainments. It's where Native Americans bare their cultural souls to each other. Non-Indians are most welcome both to look and even participate – all you need is a sense of fun, an ear for rhythm, and respect for the fine details of other people's ancestral voices.

At the Gathering of Nations Pow Wow, ritual and etiquette are paramount. You need to know a little about the role of the 'Host Drum', the tones of the 'Northern Style' (high) and 'Southern Style' (low), and the precedence of age, gender and family relationship among guest drummers and singers. You'll see Grass, Fancy and Traditional dances for men, and Shawl, Buckskin and Jingle dances for women – and when they are competitive, the more you understand about the use of feathers and regalia in their outfits, the more you'll appreciate the whirling kaleidoscopes of colour of a 'smoke' or 'gourd' dance.

You can't help but notice a less attractive, commercial aspect to the fringe of the Pow Wow and perhaps some of the newly revived tribes take themselves a bit seriously – but the Gathering of Nations has a core of purity that is itself the most eloquent guardian of the tribes' ancestral cultures.

WHEN:
Over three days (Friday to Sunday) in late April
WHERE:
University of New Mexico's Arena ('The Pit'), Albuquerque, New Mexico
BEST FOR:
Native American culture and folklore
YOU SHOULD KNOW:
If at any time (during a dance, procession, dressing or any other kind of ritual) an eagle feather falls to the ground, you and everything else must stop until the appropriate 'returning of the feather' ritual is performed.

Old Settler's Music Festival

Established back in 1987, the Old Settler's Music Festival is renowned throughout the USA for presenting the best of roots and Americana music, a genre sometimes labelled 'alternative country music'. This family-orientated gathering offers a wide selection of great sounds along with numerous stimulating activities. Better yet, the whole thing happens in lush Central Texas hill country near state capital Austin, at the height of the spectacular Bluebonnet and wildflower season. The four-day festival (from Thursday to Sunday) takes over a regular camping ground with all the usual facilities, plus a music stage erected for the occasion. Camp Ben McCulloch provides a beautiful setting, complete with meadows and a creek, and OSMF regulars know that the whole camping scene complete with late-night jam sessions around camp fires is an essential part of the whole festival experience. Right across from the camp, Salt Lick Pavilion offers three more sound stages that operate on Friday and Saturday and together the four stages showcase the talents of at least two dozen bands and artists, famous and upcoming, along with special events like a Youth Talent Competition for Under-18s.

Quite apart from the music, this vibrant event offers a huge arts and crafts section featuring fine hand-made work, plus a large area selling music-related items. A good selection of food outlets favours healthy eating and alcoholic drinks are available (proper ID required). Kids can have a ball, too. Family-friendly possibilities start with the fact that children under 12 get in free and encompass delights like a monster slide, petting zoo, pony rides, climbing wall, playground, face painting, recycling projects, a parade, kite making and much more. You get the picture! This unique annual festival takes place at the heart of the super-patriotic Lone Star State, and is a quintessentially American experience.

Langhorne Slim perform in 2011.

WHEN:
Thursday to Sunday, late April
WHERE:
Driftwood, Texas, just outside Austin
BEST FOR:
The traditional acoustic music of rural America, with spicy international seasoning
YOU SHOULD KNOW:
To enjoy the full OSMF experience (including the famous 'overnight vibe') no day visitors are allowed to sample the range of activities at Camp Ben McCulloch from Thursday to Saturday. These are reserved for campers only, though day visitors are admitted on Sunday. The camping wristband also allows entry to concerts at the Salt Lick Pavilion on the Friday and Saturday.

Kentucky Derby

WHEN:
The first Saturday in May, every year
WHERE:
Churchill Downs, Louisville, Kentucky
BEST FOR:
Sporting excellence and
no-holds-barred partying
YOU SHOULD KNOW:
The Kentucky 'Bluegrass Country' is
the heart of the American horse
breeding and racing community; and
the Mint Julep (bourbon, mint, sugar
syrup and ice) is its drink. The long
grass of the region's rolling hills
really is blue, too.

*Jockey Calvin Borel brings
home* Mine That Bird.

The Kentucky Derby is the pinnacle of American horse racing, and the jewel of its 'Triple Crown' (the others are the Belmont and Preakness Stakes). Technically, it's a Grade One stakes race for three-year-old thoroughbreds, held in May, in Louisville, Kentucky – and the climax of the two-week-long Kentucky Derby Festival. Originally run over 2.4 km (1.5 mi) to match England's Derby and France's Grand Prix de Paris, in 1896 the race became the 2-km (1.25-mi) sprint known as 'the most exciting two minutes in sports'. Many of its winners become equine legends and over the years the phenomenal standard of racing has attracted presidents, royalty and every kind of celebrity keen to share the adrenaline rush. In turn, they have made the Kentucky Derby one of the most glamorous occasions in the American social calendar, fraught with mystique and traditions played out by the 150,000 people who come to party, bet, parade and let their hair down on race day.

The elegant beauty of the 19th century hexagonal twin towers above the grandstand sets off the gorgeous dresses and scintillating, often bizarre hats of the fragrant 'fashionistas' on Millionaires Row. There's a different party humming in each of these private boxes along the finishing straight – but nothing to match the antics of the Infield. The 40 acres inside the track is crammed with 80,000 determined revelers. At one end Turn One is a family picnic area, roped off from the decadence of the Third Turn, where a younger crowd gathers. The late journalist Hunter S. Thompson described this younger crowd as '. . . staggering drunk. It's a fantastic scene – thousands of people fainting, crying, copulating, trampling each other, and fighting with broken whisky bottles'. It's a proud tradition, like mint juleps – Kentucky Derby Day is a truly great American party, with something for everyone.

Cinco de Mayo in Los Angeles

Everywhere in the USA boasting two or more people of Mexican origin celebrates the Cinco de Mayo. Los Angeles, once the capital of Mexican California, just does it bigger and better. It's a strange fiesta. May 5 1862 was the day a small but stubborn Mexican formation took on regular French troops at Puebla, east of Mexico City, defeating the superior odds and starting the process that led to France's withdrawal from its colonial ambitions in Mexico, and to the Emperor Maximilian losing his head. These are very good republican reasons for partying, except that in Mexico nobody thinks the date is significant. In Los Angeles, however, the historical fact that the Battle of Puebla was beneficial to both Mexico and the USA means that Angelenos are motivated to their biggest annual celebration of Mexican culture.

One of the biggest parties is Fiesta Broadway, held on the weekend closest to Cinco. As many as 500,000 revellers crowd into 24 blocks of specially rigged and decorated booths. Many are commercial (cynics have been heard complaining that US business has subverted a Latino occasion into an American one – but Latinos love it), though they ply bystanders with delicious finger food, interesting fruit drinks (possibly laced with tequila), and a blast of mariachi or salsa to keep the spirits flying. Major Mexican and American artists perform on a series of huge stages. The hot tang of chili in the air, vibrating from the irresistible dance rhythms, creates a surreal intensity for all your senses. Fed and watered at every turn, you can only follow the music with the rest of the crowd. Cinco de Mayo is nothing more or less than a first-rate US-Mexican shindig.

WHEN:
The weekend closest to May 5
WHERE:
Throughout Los Angeles, with the greatest concentration of events, exhibitions and performances in the historic district around El Pueblo and Olvera Street
BEST FOR:
Mexican-American food, drink and music at their best and most raucous
YOU SHOULD KNOW:
The three essentials for a Mexican fiesta are 'menudo, margaritas y Mariachi' – food (a kind of spicy soup), drink (tequila based) and music (traditional).

Cinco de Mayo is the USA's biggest annual celebration of Mexican culture.

Indianapolis 500

One of the oldest events in motor sports, the Indianapolis 500 has been pre-eminent among all classes of American motor races since 1911. It's the most demanding of the traditional (and exclusively American) oval races and is acknowledged by all the US motor-racing organizations as the flagship of their sport. Every year the very best drivers battle at more than 322 kph (200 mph) over 805 km (500 mi) of the historic 'Brickyard'.

The track's nickname derives from its original construction, when the dangerously uneven cinder track of 1909 was resurfaced with 3.2 million special bricks. Now only a 0.91-m (3-ft) section, track-wide, remains – the 'yard of bricks' set into the brand-new asphalt track as the start/finish line. It's the kind of tradition motor fans like, and nearly half a million of them come to celebrate the upcoming 'Greatest Spectacle in Racing' for days before the event. They come for the '500 Festival Parade', the balloon releases, 'Bump Day' qualifying laps, 'Carb (short for 'carburetion') Day' when drivers practise in racing trim, and 'Community Day' when members of the public can actually do a lap of the steeply banked track in their own cars.

The Indy 500 is the excuse for rock concerts, fairs, pageantry and constant hoopla. Then, after the fly-past and *Star-Spangled Banner*, the command 'Gentlemen, start your engines' unleashes the roaring, tyre-screeching, oil-streaked finale. From a rolling start, 11 rows of three-abreast, snarling automotive tigers ratchet up the tension relentlessly. Spectacular crashes make survival look miraculous; and the constant, droning whine and your own adrenaline make you feel slightly ill in the hot fumes: this, too, is traditional – the sensory overload that makes the Indianapolis 500 race itself such consummate entertainment.

Scott Dixon captures his first career win at the 'Brickyard'.

WHEN:
Memorial Day weekend (late May). The 'Indy 500 Festival' events and concerts take place over the two to three weeks preceding the race.
WHERE:
Indianapolis Motor Speedway, 4790 West 16th Street, Indianapolis, Indiana
BEST FOR:
Traditional US (oval) motor racing, and cultural Americana
YOU SHOULD KNOW:
One of the most cherished traditions of the race is for the winner to take a drink of milk immediately on returning to the paddock. One winner who drank orange juice first was booed wherever he travelled for the next few weeks.

The Stanley Cup

For aficionados of professional ice hockey, international contests are soulless compared to North America's annual club championship. Throughout the sport, the Stanley Cup is known as 'The Holy Grail'. It is the trophy to which every ice hockey club in North America aspires. The beautiful silver bowl and its colossal mount embody the history, tradition and rugged ethos of ice hockey with a symbolism unmatched by any other sporting trophy. It's the oldest professional sports trophy in North America, and the only one which is not made afresh each year. Instead, it grows rings – inscribed with the names of the winning players, the coaches, management and club staff of every year. That makes it personal to generations of fans as well as players. It also symbolizes the bond between Canadian and US hockey players. In 1892, the then Governor-General of Canada, Lord Stanley, presented it as a prize for Canada's top amateur team. When the US and Canadian Leagues united as professionals in 1915, The Stanley Cup was confirmed as a votive fetish for everyone who loves the game, and that feeling has grown stronger ever since. Indeed, after the National Hockey League (NHL) players' strike in 2004-05, public indignation about NHL Management's abuse of the Stanley Cup showed just how closely identified it is with ice hockey's soul.

    Add that emotive power to the frosty-foetid air of the crowd-crammed rink-side at the first of the best-of-seven Stanley Cup matches: club players are peoples' champions, and the atmosphere is snorting with their testosterone and physicality. They smash together with the speed and grace of dancers, and aggression of grizzly bears. The Stanley Cup inspires games of outstanding drama and skill. Players and fans perform out of their skins; and that's the denominator that makes the Stanley Cup one of the greatest events in North American sport.

*Detroit Red Wings captain,
Nicklaus Lindstrom, lifts the cup.*

WHEN:
May/June, annually
WHERE:
The seven games are split between the home venues of the opposing finalists. The team with the highest win-lose record in their league has initial home advantage. Typically, the venues will be among the best-known ice hockey arenas in North America.
BEST FOR:
Sporting excellence
YOU SHOULD KNOW:
The Stanley Cup presentation (viewing) tours have raised millions for charity just by giving people a chance to express their affection for it. In May 2007 and March 2008, the Cup was taken to front-line combat troops in Kandahar, Afghanistan, to boost the morale of US and Canadian personnel.

US Open Golf Championship

WHEN:
The four days ending on the third Sunday in June, annually. Playoffs are deferred to the Monday.

WHERE:
At golf courses throughout America: 2010 – Pebble Beach Links (Pebble Beach, CA); 2011 – Congressional Country Club (Bethesda, MD); 2012 – Olympic Club Lake Course (San Francisco, CA); 2013 – Merion East Course (Ardmore, PA)

BEST FOR:
World-class sport and healthy, outdoor exercise

YOU SHOULD KNOW:
The winner of the US Open Golf Championship receives a purse of about $1.25 million, automatic qualification for the following ten US Open tournaments, automatic invitation to the other three majors for five years, automatic invitation to the Players Championship for five years, and membership of the PGA Tour for five seasons.

Tiger Woods celebrates a 'birdie' that sent him through to a play-off for the US Open.

The US Open Golf Championship is a four-day annual tournament for men, played in June on one of America's finest golf courses. It really is 'open'. Though roughly half the field of 156 players qualifies automatically as proven winners on the US or European circuits, any amateur or professional with a current USGA handicap of 1.4 or less is eligible. In practice, the US Open brings together the world's best golfers to compete in one of only four majors among the thousands of tournaments played around the globe throughout the year. The courses are always chosen for their variety of technical difficulties, which change from day to day under the influence of weather patterns and the placings of the pins on the greens. There's no rule about it, but roughly half the US Open courses are links – arranged along a coastal strip of typically sandy scrub, open to the vagaries of sudden storms and constantly changing wind speed and direction. Far inland, course designers provoke similar effects by placing thick stands of trees so that every shot requires exhaustive computation of wind effect at different heights.

For fans, the players' focused anxieties provide joyous opportunities for vigorous support. The US Open is always packed with drama, which intensifies day by day. Should no clear winner emerge after the regulation 72 holes, the Open is the only major to require a play-off of the full 18 holes on the course. Since 1895 there have been 33 such instances, but the most momentous was in 2008, when Tiger Woods finally vanquished Rocco Mediate at the sudden-death 19th playoff hole. You can be part of that fever-pitch excitement, any year you go. About the only thing the US Open guarantees is the pure thrill of golf at its best.

Independence Day

Independence Day, the fourth of July, is America's birthday. It's the date on the Declaration of Independence in 1776, when the 13 original States (still represented on the US flag by the 13 stripes) took the leap into the unknown of rejecting their status as British colonies. The magnitude of the fourth of July's political and civic significance was foreseen from the beginning. One of the signatories to the Declaration, the Founding Father John Adams, described it as 'the great anniversary festival. It ought to be commemorated as the day of deliverance . . . It ought to be solemnized with pomp and parade, with shows, games, sports, guns, bells, bonfires and illuminations, from one end of the continent to the other, from this time forward forever more'. He must be clapping his hands with glee to see his prediction so gloriously fulfilled in the most prosperous nation on the planet.

Patriotism, deeply unfashionable in many parts of the world, is still prized in America, and there's nothing Americans enjoy more than to include visitors in this highest of all American holidays. You might be invited to a Solar Egg Frying Contest in Arizona, an Old Appalachia Anvil Shoot in Tennessee, Bed Races in Idaho, or a Duelling Barges Fireworks Extravaganza on the Mississippi in New Orleans – but these and the tens of thousands of parades, fun runs, picnics and barbecues arranged as holiday entertainment also include moments of serious reflection. It's refreshing to see whole communities stop to salute the flag and renew their collective pledge of allegiance; and awesome to see how sharing their brief acknowledgement of patriotic duty both moves and energizes those communities. The big cities mount the most spectacular shows – but you'll find the real meaning of Independence Day, and have most fun, in the smallest towns and villages.

WHEN:
July 4, every year
WHERE:
Throughout the 50 States, in US Embassies all over the world, and almost anywhere on earth where there are two or more Americans
BEST FOR:
Spectacular displays and parades, moving ceremonies, and unabashed folk culture
YOU SHOULD KNOW:
Be prepared to demonstrate – with a song, a quotation, or brief story – how and why your own country celebrates its national holiday. It's the best and most appreciated way to honour the fantastic spirit of generosity in which Americans bathe you on July 4.

Fireworks at the Washington Monument mark Independence Day.

Oshkosh Air Show

The Oshkosh Air Show is shorthand for 'EAA AirVenture Oshkosh'. Founded as a fly-in convention for members of the Experimental Aircraft Association (EAA) in 1953, the show is now a forum for grass-roots aviation enthusiasts from all over the US and the world. During a week in late July, more than 500,000 visitors and between 10-15,000 aircraft of every age, style, size or quirk crowd into Wittman Regional Airport on the shores of Wisconsin's Lake Winnebago. Pilots just camp under the wings of their aircraft, ready to talk up a design or technical storm to interested bystanders. At Oshkosh, the planes are everything, and you can see wonderful futuristic shapes, created and flown by their owners. Some of them may even offer flights – but curiously, the spirit of Oshkosh is more about getting close to aircraft than actual flying. Sharing technology, tips and altitude experience reinforces the feeling of the Oshkosh Family, fostered from the start to keep commerce from overpowering its juiciest target demographic.

If you've ever looked up when a plane passes overhead, you'll love Oshkosh. Get yourself a spot on the Flight Line – the runway over and on which all the big fly-pasts, aerial trick competitions, aerobatic devilry, and experimental flight displays take place. Every year you can see the best of aviation innovation, from warplane transports to helicopters and ultralites; enjoy hundreds of vintage, military and civil planes; and try your own skills (with or without instruction) on a variety of the most vivid simulators in the world. If you bring a kit, you'll even find expert volunteers delighted to get the chance to help you build it while you get flying lessons. At Oshkosh, you can arrive on foot, but fly away!

WHEN:
Seven days beginning on the last Monday in July
WHERE:
Wittman Regional Airport, Oshkosh, Wisconsin
BEST FOR:
Flying and all things aviation
YOU SHOULD KNOW:
FAA air traffic controllers actually compete to be on the air traffic control teams working Wittman Field – during the show, it's the busiest air control tower in the world. Their reward is as precious as the Yellow Jersey in the Tour de France or the Augusta Masters' Green Jacket. The chosen experts get a neon-pink polo shirt that tells the aviation world they are their peer group's elite.

Bi-planes perform precision flying stunts at the show.

Riders power up the hill.

Pikes Peak International Hill Climb

Like Mount Fuji in Japan, Pikes Peak is an American icon. South of Denver, Colorado, it is the easternmost of the big Rocky Mountain peaks, and legendary in the folklore of first the pioneers, and then of the 1859 Colorado Gold Rush. The prospectors' mantra then was 'Pikes Peak or bust!' – and that's the attitude of the drivers in the annual Pikes Peak International Hill Climb, first run in 1916 and after the Indianapolis 500, the oldest road race in the USA.

The Hill Climb, known as 'the Race to the Clouds' starts a few miles up Pikes Peak Highway, where the tarmac pretty well runs out. The race is over 19.87 km (12.42 mi) of dirt road, with a vertical rise of 1,435 m (4,708 ft), climbing throughout on a gradient that averages seven degrees, twisting and turning through 156 bends including several series of 180-degree hairpins. Many different classes of vehicle race against each other: all of them wrenched screaming and at maximum power into blind corners with a vertical cliff on one side and a 600-m (2,000-ft), unfenced and unprotected drop-off on the other.

You watch with your heart in your mouth as drivers battle the unforgiving granite mountain. Crashes are frequent and brutal; and the chain of vicious dust-devils whipping up clouds of grit above the nodding aspens marks little miracles of survival, as the cars get higher and higher. Even when the vehicles may be tuned to Formula One standards, and driven by some of the world's best, the race exposes an elemental challenge. The majesty of Pikes Peak, towering into the blue with the Rockies stretching away, turns mere motor racing into high adventure.

WHEN:
July
WHERE:
Pikes Peak Highway, Colorado Springs, Colorado
BEST FOR:
Extreme motor sports in a spectacular natural setting.
YOU SHOULD KNOW:
Race classes differ from year to year, but you can expect races between trucks, buggies, stock cars, quads, 4WD, vintage, electric and supercharged Indy-style vehicles, with about 10 motorbike categories.

Cheyenne Frontier Days

A cowboy wrestles down a steer

For all the pomp of being state capital and Wyoming's biggest city, Cheyenne (population 55,000) is still an authentic cowboy town. Created by the cattle barons who built their mansions around the Union Pacific railhead in 1867, the city held its first Frontier Days celebration in 1897 to revitalize the area when the silver boom went bust. Even as it began, Frontier Days blurred the distinctions between the myth and reality of 'the Old West'; now you'd be forgiven for the impression that cowboys are supermen, but that farmers, cowboys and, indeed, Indians, can all be friends at the rodeo, concerts, parades, pow wows and side shows that justify Frontier Days' claim to be 'the Daddy of 'Em All' on the rodeo and 'Western heritage' circuit. It is, and it's very, very exciting.

The Cheyenne Frontier Days rodeo is one of the 'majors' on the rodeo circuit, with the difference that in addition to the best professionals, you'll see far more action in more categories than anywhere else, with less predictable results. Outside the rodeo, Cheyenne lays on a huge variety of free and subsidized entertainment. The Indian Village has its own agenda of dancing and storytelling; cowboy poets and range balladeers tell of people and events brought vividly to life by parades including pioneer covered wagons and the buggies of church-bound farming families; 40,000 people eat over 100,000 free pancake breakfasts over three days; country music stars break off tours to come and play at night. That might sound like the usual format for a cultural celebration. At Cheyenne Frontier Days, sheer enthusiasm and local goodwill make you realize that this rodeo and these sideshows are for once genuinely drawn from the same warp and weft of Western heritage. It is beyond price.

WHEN:
Ten days at the end of July
WHERE:
Frontier Park, Cheyenne, Wyoming
BEST FOR:
Cultural revisionism, historical insight and the most exciting bull riding in the USA
YOU SHOULD KNOW:
Worried that their rodeo bulls couldn't be relied on to be 'ornery', 1920s Wyoming contractors bred a Brahma bull from India into the local stock.

Pageant of the Masters

WHEN:
For eight weeks in July/August
WHERE:
Irving Bowl, Laguna Canyon Road,
Laguna Beach, California
(at the junction of Laguna Canyon
Road and Pacific Coast Highway)
BEST FOR:
Spectacular theatrical extravaganza
YOU SHOULD KNOW:
Bring a cushion to sit on, and a picnic
basket (it's allowed). Renting
binoculars is expensive, so try to
bring your own. Cameras are not
permitted.

*Participants pose motionless in
a* tableau vivant *(living painting)
of an 18th century scene.*

Demonstrating that often the old ways are best, Laguna Beach's Pageant of the Masters revives a medieval entertainment with spectacular modern effects. It consists of a series of *tableaux vivant*, each of which uses real people to recreate a famous picture, posed within a giant frame. Your senses of proportion get an electrifying shock: dwarfed by *The Last Supper*, for example, crammed with people gradually resolving from one carefully planned pose to another, your vision is sharpened, and perception of detail much keener. At best, a presentation can make you feel you really understand the original picture.

It's theatre with a terrific degree of circus showmanship, too. The pageant evolved from the 1932 Arts Festival, which turned Laguna Beach into an enormous art gallery. In the excitement of the festival's success, a local artist persuaded her friends to dress up and pose in a makeshift picture-frame. The idea was a smash; and the participants were as fascinated and pleased by the aesthetic novelty as the audience. The organic spirit remains: although the pageant is staged, lit, and arranged with Broadway professionalism, it's still local volunteers who dress up and rehearse the fantastic routines. You can see representations of the works of Titian, Michelangelo, Degas, Renoir and Andrew Wyeth among many others. The tableaux are part of a whole programme of performing arts chosen to enhance them. A Pageant might include scenes from a ballet, the slapstick knockabout of Italian Comedia dell'Arte, Chinese Lion Dancers, or a high-stepping showstopper with a hint of burlesque.

It could only happen in California. The pageant is sensitively artistic and literate, but it's also capable of wit and irreverence. It can't help but include some expression of California body-beautiful beach culture – in the sure knowledge that the appreciative whistles are from *bona fide* art connoisseurs, who are there to see the pictures.

Maine Lobster Festival

The Maine Lobster Festival gives visitors the chance to eat one of the great delicacies of the world by the shovelful!

If ever a determinedly local festival deserved an international reputation it's the Maine Lobster Festival. For five days in late July or early August, the little fishing port of Rockland – sheltered by a granite headland among the hundreds of rugged fjords of Maine's northern coast – dresses up to welcome a total of more than 100,000 guests to a programme of parades, contests and games designed to entertain them in between gorging on several tons of the finest soft-shell lobster in the world. Lobsters are so plentiful in the area that the festival began in 1947 as a way for fishermen to dispose of their catch. Too fragile to be shipped to Boston or New York, the lobsters cost $1 for all you could eat. These days, $20 will get you three whole lobsters (with a plastic bib and some chips)!

This isn't the Maine of gentle, sandy coves, hauteur and Kennebunkport mansions. Rockland's grandeur is the honesty of its democratic, blue-collar inclusivity. The lobsters are cooked in the world's biggest lobster broiler – capable of holding 545 kg (1,200 lb) at a time – endearingly disguised as a 'lighthouse' and eaten on a series of long benches inside a marquee, which can feel like a Turkish bath. It's so extraordinary to be eating one of the great delicacies of the world by the shovelful, tearing exquisite morsels with your bare hands in circumstances more like a very cheerful canteen than fine dining. That's when you realize that there are just as many locals as visitors present – and it's their strength of identity that makes being at the Lobster Festival feel like a privilege.

Between lobsters, parades, bands and more lobsters, check out the Lobster Crate Racing: you have to 'walk on water' by running across 50 bobbing lobster crates tethered across a neck of the harbour. Most people get a chilly Atlantic ducking after ten crates; the record, back and forth without stopping, is over 3,000!

WHEN:
Late July/early August
WHERE:
Harbor Park, Rockland, Maine
BEST FOR:
Gastronomy (at low, low prices) and New England local traditions
YOU SHOULD KNOW:
The local obsession is summarized by the sole neon sign displayed in the community of Ogonquit. It reads: 'Rooms. Cable. Air-con. Lobster.'

Flushing Meadow:
the US Tennis Open

WHEN:
August/September, during the week
before and the week after Labor Day,
annually.
WHERE:
The USTA Billie Jean King National
Tennis Center, Flushing Meadows-
Corona Park, Queens, New York City
BEST FOR:
Top-quality sporting entertainment

The fourth and last of the annual Grand Slam tennis tournaments, the US Open is contested over two weeks in August and September at the National Tennis Center in Flushing Meadows, Queens, New York City. More than 600 male and female professionals compete for some of the sport's richest prizes. The top seeds perform in the 23,000-seater Arthur Ashe Stadium – but during the tournament's first week you can often see them up close, in action on the many field courts that surround the three principal arenas; or in their daily practice and warm-up sessions. The courts are floodlit, so throughout the early part of the tournament there are matches from 11.00 until fairly late in the evening. Unlike the other Grand Slam tournaments, US Open matches cannot last indefinitely: it's the only one in which the final set can be

decided by a tie-break. That may sound like a minor difference, but if the match is a nail-biting seesaw, a deciding tie-break can raise the tension to palpable levels even in the tournament's early stages.

The US Open was once a high-society event, and in its second week it still feels like it might be. The matches retreat to the main arenas and the tickets, food, drink and all other amenities grow increasingly expensive. The atmosphere becomes competitively corporate and 'social'. Ordinary fans – especially families with tennis-mad kids – have the best time at the beginning. Two days before it begins, the Arthur Ashe Kids Day celebrates the sport by throwing open the Tennis Center with free tennis clinics and autograph sessions with the stars. One day before, you can see the world's best players for free during Open Practice Day. Outside the final rounds, you'll never get a better chance to see great tennis – and you'll be nearly as close as the umpire.

Airforce jets fly overhead as the national anthem is sung to open the tournament.

YOU SHOULD KNOW:
There's no shade at Flushing Meadows, and the weather can be very hot and/or humid. Take an umbrella for shelter from the sun and potential thunderstorms. Sunny days bring out huge crowds – avoid getting stifled in the crush by heading away from Louis Armstrong Stadium to the west side of the complex, where fewer people means you get better access to the tennis on the field courts.

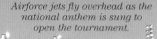

Sturgis Motorcycle Rally

WHEN:
Seven days at the beginning
of August
WHERE:
Sturgis, South Dakota
BEST FOR:
Motor sports, grand touring, and
quintessential Americana
YOU SHOULD KNOW:
Proposals for site expansions to cope
with the rally's ever-growing success
have caused disquiet to Native
Americans (principally Lakota and
Cheyenne) for whom the local
landmark of Bear Butte is a Sacred
Mountain, where prayer feathers
and other markers demonstrate
regular worship.

The Black Hills of South Dakota are emblematic of pioneer America – where the farmer and the cowboy eventually became friends at the expense of the Cheyenne and Lakota. The little town of Sturgis developed next to old Fort Meade, synonymous with historic episodes involving legends like Red Cloud, Crazy Horse, Sitting Bull and George Custer; but it's still a small community in a vast prairie.

Pioneer spirit underwrites the Sturgis Motorcycle Rally, which began in 1938 as a single-race challenge between nine members of the local Jackpine Gypsies Motorcycle Club. Now, roughly 500,000 bikers roar into Sturgis (population 6,426) for seven days every August, to celebrate their freedom of the road and to worship every aspect of the machines themselves. Many travel huge distances, and they come in beards, studs, bikinis, denims, eye-popping tattoos and exotic leathers; rumbling and snorting down dusty Main Street on big Harley-Davidsons, transcontinental scooters, ancient rebuilds, extra-long front forks like stooping chrome giraffes, and futuristic space-age inventions swooping and curving to ingenious technological demands.

Age cannot wither bikers' spiritual vision, and Sturgis belongs to families as much as to Hell's Angels – but their commitment-in-common is to hard-rock biking, the camaraderie of the Endless Grey Ribbon, and a shared vision of 'America Unlimited' in perpetuity. You get entertained by the biggest rock stars (Bruce Springsteen, Aerosmith, etc); track and dirt racing in all their forms; the Wall of Death; and the greatest trick and stunt riders in the world. Yet it's the mass rides through buffalo country, to the Mt Rushmore Memorial carved in the Black Hills, Deadwood, the Badlands or the Crazy Horse Memorial that you'll remember – the exaltation of the mighty, chrome-glinting 'wagon-train' of bikes, the (temporary) community of outlaws, and the prairie wind in your hair.

*Over half a million bikers
attend the rally.*

The burning ceremony takes place on the seventh day.

Burning Man Festival

Burning Man is a hardcore festival of self-reliance, survival and creative self-expression. For the eight days leading up to America's Labor Day holiday around 40,000 celebrants gather in Black Rock City – a temporary city rebuilt from scratch each year – on the dried salt-pan of Nevada's Black Rock Desert. Each of them brings everything he or she needs to survive this inhospitable place. There are no shops and no barter system for exchange. Instead, there is a 'gift economy' in which you give with no expectation of return; and primarily this means giving your imagination, in whatever fantastic form takes your fancy.

Submarines 'surface' from the desert sand; the nave of a skeleton cathedral rises in the middle of windswept nowhere, suggesting a locale for body-painted phantasmagoria (improbably riding bicycles decorated with wings) to hold an impromptu 'service' of dance and group expression. Over a huge area, sculpture, music, colour and invention offer inspiration to 'seekers' with no particular agenda: the only limits of response are self-imposed. The enormity of realizing you don't have to explain or excuse your behaviour can be an emotional bombshell. Typically, you come for several days, if not the whole eight, to participate in a community whose only common purpose is to wing it through the uproarious exhibitionism and posing to whatever genuine aesthetic emerges from the event as a whole. By the time the Burning Man goes up in flames on the seventh day, everyone feels like the 12-m (40-ft)-high emblem is expiating their former selves, and they leave the festival feeling renewed.

Burning Man is not for everyone. It can be dangerous – physically in the desert wilderness; and psychologically, if you're unwilling to embrace your potential for change. Be brave enough to accept its challenging invitation and you'll have the most exciting and fulfilling adventure of your life.

WHEN:
Eight days ending on American Labor Day, every September

WHERE:
Black Rock City, on the playa of the Black Rock Desert, Nevada. The site is about 150 km (90 mi) NNE of Reno, Nevada.

BEST FOR:
Self-expression, creative participation and transcendental adjustment

YOU SHOULD KNOW:
In order to exist, Burning Man does have to satisfy minimum public order codes. Otherwise, the festival allows no advertising, on-site sales, or commercial exploitation. And when it's over, thanks to volunteers who stay behind, the desert shows no trace that it ever took place.

Monterey Jazz Festival

WHEN:
The third weekend of September
WHERE:
Monterey Fairgrounds, Monterey, California
BEST FOR:
Music, jazz conversations, and all things jazz; history and culture
YOU SHOULD KNOW:
Despite Monterey's links to iconic literary figures like John Steinbeck, Henry Miller, Jack London and Robert Louis Stevenson, its proximity to the artists' colony of Carmel, and to 'America's Last Hometown' of Pacific Grove (world famous for its colony of Monarch butterflies as well as its charm) – your festival ticket does not allow you to leave and re-enter the Fairgrounds site.

Maceo Parker giving his all at 'jazz heaven'.

The Monterey Peninsula is both the most beautiful reach of the north California coast and one of the United States' oldest and most historic sites. The Jazz Festival, one of America's and the world's oldest, is integral to that history. Since 1958, when it was inaugurated by Dizzy Gillespie, Louis Armstrong, Max Roach, Billie Holliday and other galactic musicians, Monterey has attracted the best of the best to blow wild and free among the shady oaks of the Monterey Fairgrounds. Musicians wander the grounds, making friends with fans for whom jazz is lifeblood, demonstrating how good the festival makes everyone feel by stepping off stage from their official Arena concert to busk with musicians on the smaller stages, where fans can get up close to stellar jazzmen and women.

To create this kind of ambience, Monterey has had to evolve. Jimmy Lyons, planning the event back in 1956, imagined 'a sylvan setting with the best jazz people in the world' – but sheer popularity has expanded the on-site venues to nine. The five (three evening, two afternoon) headline Arena concerts are all simulcast to the Jazz Theater next to the First Aid post; so if you can't be in the Arena, a 'Grounds Only' ticket enables you to hear those concerts, and in any case to give you access to most of the 500-700 musicians playing during the festival. It's a supremely 'Californian' weekend. There are dozens of booths trading music (and food and drink) and memorabilia – but no 'stiffnecks' boasting superior musical knowledge or capping gig stories. In fact, if you know nothing about jazz, and you never heard it before, there is no better place on earth to hear and learn about it. If you're already lucky enough to be an aficionado, Monterey is certainly 'jazz heaven'.

Halloween in New York City

New York City celebrates Halloween like Rio's Carnival or New Orleans' Mardi Gras. For weeks leading up to October 31 in Queen's, Brooklyn, the Bronx and Staten Island, there are dozens of parades in which children (and pets) get elaborately dressed in the most ghoulish ways, to enjoy ghost stories, graveyard walks or anything that can be haunted, spookily lit or decorated with pumpkins. City authorities throw open every park and facility for family fun. However, on Halloween night itself, the only real show is in Manhattan – New York's Village Halloween Parade.

The parade is an explosion of colour and sound and creative ingenuity. In one of the world's capitals of communications and pop culture, the creative talent pool is bottomless, and the parade is its chosen, collective expression. Fifty thousand costumed revellers form a pageant over a mile long, snaking through Greenwich Village. Circus performers, artistes of every exotic and erotic persuasion, huge articulated puppets, dancers and anyone else in a costume who chooses to do so, form rhythmic entities between floats bearing delirious confections proclaiming the theme of the year. Others carry rock, reggae, jazz bands or orchestras, their music intensified by hypnotic strobes and lasers pulsating into the dark shadows outside the brilliant river of light. Anything goes; and for the two million people cramming the route, jaw-dropping amazement is the universal norm. But the parade is infectious, and as it passes you feel the ripple of energy coursing along the sidewalks, summoning you to the giddy dance.

Halloween Night in the Village is a Dionysian revel. The New York Times calls it 'the best entertainment the people of this city ever give the people of this city'. On this night, New Yorkers generously offer all comers a glimpse of their city's magnificently surreal and grotesque soul. It's enchanting.

Halloween parades in Manhattan create an explosion of colour and sound.

WHEN:
Two to three weeks leading up to October 31 (Halloween Night), every year. Costumed participants in the parade assemble between 14.00 and 18.00 and the parade moves off at 19.00 on October 31.

WHERE:
Halloween events of all kinds take place in every New York City borough. The parade runs along 6th Avenue from Spring St to 21st St in Greenwich Village, Manhattan.

BEST FOR:
Sensory overload, exotic partying and a unique cultural insight into New York City

YOU SHOULD KNOW:
The Halloween Village Parade genuinely reflects the quintessential spirit of New York City. After the tragedy of September 11 2001, the parade went ahead on the improvised theme of 'Phoenix Rising'. Ever since, Dancing Skeletons always lead the march, because 'they know better than anyone what they have lost; and so they dance this one night of the year to celebrate life'.

Tampa Bay Rays batter Evan Longoria hits a single against the Philadelphia Phillies.

The World Series

Saul Steinberg, a cartoonist for *The New Yorker* magazine, famously said 'Baseball is an allegorical play about America, a poetic, complex and subtle play of courage, fear, good luck, mistakes, patience about fate, and sober self-esteem'. The World Series is the play's annual dramatic climax, and the highest expression of Steinberg's truth. Every October, anywhere in the USA, you can share the same sequence of emotions, each of them fine-tuned to maximum pitch.

The World Series is a best-of-seven contest between the divisional winners of baseball's American League and National League. Home-ground advantage goes to the team whose league won the mid-season All Stars exhibition game – but the venue switches every two games. You can't underestimate the fans' influence. At all times individual shouts, groans or sighs are magnified to a roar capable of deflecting a pitcher's throw. Recently, fans have developed idiosyncrasies (like clicking metal castanets or waving a handkerchief) peculiar to specific teams, so the noise acquires extra meaning as well as strength. As the series progresses, even watching on television from a neutral US city, you can't help favouring one of the teams.

Part of the World Series' unique appeal is that you embrace its passion in the middle of your own and everyone else's ordinary lives. The probable outcome changes with every inning of every game, and baseball's ability to surprise and amaze creates sudden, super-intense highs and lows of ever-greater piquancy. If you want your team to win, you have to share the players' emotional dedication throughout. It's exhausting, draining and almost cruelly protracted – yet perhaps the most exciting and rewarding sporting final of any.

WHEN:
Mid to late October
WHERE:
In the two US cities the competing teams call 'home'
BEST FOR:
Sport
YOU SHOULD KNOW:
Describing baseball's democratic, domestic and fundamentally American character, Humphrey Bogart (smiling sardonically) pointed out 'a hot dog at the ball park is better than steak at the Ritz'.

Albuquerque International Balloon Fiesta

As if a Christmas tree had shed its decorations, the sky above Albuquerque fills with hundreds of technicoloured shapes, a flying armada of giant toys wafting upwards in a slow-motion kaleidoscope. The Mass Ascension of the Albuquerque International Balloon Festival is one of the most glorious sights on earth, and with over 700 balloons, unique. This huge number is only made possible by the steadfast predictability of the 'Albuquerque Box', a wholly reliable local system of winds at different heights that enables pilots to maintain close contact with 148-ha (365-acre) Balloon Fiesta Park. The Park, including a launch area the size of 54 football fields, is dedicated primarily to the annual fiesta and includes a museum of its history since 1972, and of ballooning in general. Crammed with pilots and ground crews preparing for different events, Fiesta Park is where obsessive 'tekkies', poets of romantic vision, extreme sports buffs and aficionados of dramatic spectacle get to talk, question and enthuse about ballooning before and after events; and of course, to take off, if not also to land.

Reveille comes before dawn in Albuquerque. The gold and orange slashes on the horizon of New Mexico's daybreak bring the legendary Dawn Patrol – night-flying experts who assay the day's meteorology on behalf of their peers – back to earth. Moments later, the hissing roar of hundreds of balloons powering up surges and slowly fades as they rise, daubs of yellow and red in the intensifying blue. It is truly beautiful. Later there will be world championships for distance and navigation, for hot air and for gas balloons; 'Special Shapes' (a cow, a railway loco, twin bees, cola cans, the Taj Mahal, etc) bringing laugh-out-loud whimsy to an already fantastic delight; and the evening 'Balloon Glow' and 'Special Shapes Glowdeo' – ground-level, *coups de théâtre* of stunning originality.

WHEN:
Nine days in early October
WHERE:
Balloon Fiesta Park, Albuquerque, New Mexico
BEST FOR:
Extreme sports, family activities, photography and aesthetic recharge
YOU SHOULD KNOW:
In autumn Albuquerque generally has near-ideal conditions for ballooning – but to take advantage of the clear skies and low winds you need to arrive as early as possible, especially for the mass ascents and big races. Depending on the first event, the park gates open between 03.00 and 04.30. That means breakfast at 02.00!

Dozens of ballons take to the sky during the festival.

The New York Marathon

WHEN:
09.30 on a Sunday in early
November, each year
WHERE:
All categories start from designated
areas at Fort Wadsworth, Staten
Island, but follow different
(approximately parallel) routes until
mile eight, after which routes merge.
For watchers, Manhattan's Upper
East Side is the best location – and
seating can be reserved (at a high
price but it goes to charity) at the
finish line at Tavern on the Green
in Central Park.
BEST FOR:
Sport and entertainment
YOU SHOULD KNOW:
The New York City Marathon has
different commercial sponsors, but is
always administered by the New
York Road Runners (NYRR), an
organization dedicated to promoting
the sport of distance running and
community fitness programmes. One
of these provides running for some
30,000 New York schoolchildren who
would otherwise have no fitness
opportunities at all.

The New York City Marathon is one of the world's big four (with London, Boston and Chicago), and it sets the city alight. More than 40,000 runners, attended by tens of thousands of friends and families, bring their tensions and anxious hopes to the early-morning rendezvous in Staten Island.

Across the five boroughs, some two million people negotiate the best viewing spots, while hundreds of bars and cafés open early to fuel their enthusiasm with coffee and donuts. Giant screens at strategic locations ensure that nearly everyone can follow the race in all its phases and modes. The first two hours are dominated by the elites – the best international and club runners, super-athletes of other-worldly talent and endurance. Then the real fun starts with 1001 great and small dramas captured by vigilant cameras following the 'fun-runners' dressed in absurdist fancy dress, running alone or in teams, their brave imaginations focused on the intense pain they must all survive to earn as much as possible for the charities they hope to benefit.

The course is a classic. Across the Verrazano-Narrows Bridge, through Brooklyn and Queen's with amazing views of the Empire State and Chrysler buildings across the East River, the race turns at mile 15 and crosses the Queensboro Bridge. As they enter Manhattan, the runners hear a mighty roar of encouragement. This is where you'll come for one of the best views of the race – it's only a short walk across midtown to the finish at Tavern on the Green in Central Park. Like a huge river, the runners wheel back from the Bronx, each with a story worth telling, and 1,000 watchers to listen. The New York Marathon is a dramatic city's most dramatic entertainment. Run it or watch it if you want to understand the democratic generosity in New York's soul.

Runners cross the George Washington Bridge.

Macy's Thanksgiving Day Parade®

What began in 1924 as a light-hearted promotion for one of New York City's most popular stores is now one of the biggest, most glamorous and most colourful parades in America. Its superlative fun and entertainment has earned it iconic status as the jump start to the holiday season: although in ambience and execution it's pure New York, it belongs to the tens of millions of Americans, tenderized by the spirit of Thanksgiving Day, who watch it on TV. Macy's Thanksgiving Day Parade® has matured into 'America's Parade'.

In composition, the parade doesn't change much. Marching bands, cheerleaders in glittering syncopation, fabulous floats, dazzlingly inventive balloons, clowns, acrobats, and dance groups come from inner cities and retirement communities, schools and factories across the country to team up with Broadway and Hollywood professionals. Any group, of any age, can apply to join the parade if they can walk the walk; and the 2.5 million New Yorkers and visiting families who line the route cheer themselves hoarse for their 10-15,000-strong, random but representative 'sons and daughters'. By the time the parade's Grand Marshal, Santa Claus, enters Herald Square in his magnificent, beribboned sleigh, attended by elves distributing gumdrops and gifts from the reindeer's shoulders, you get an almost tangible sense of the shared ritual bringing friends and families together all over America.

But look closely. Each year the minor differences – the novelty balloons, the choice of cartoon characters for giant puppets, and the participating celebrities – provide a cultural snapshot of New York City and the USA. Macy's got big by correctly sensing the popular pulse, and though their generous sponsorship is materially confined to providing the know-how to turn fabulous ideas into witty and dramatic parade statements, their parade is a faithful reflection of what matters to folk in this city and this country.

WHEN:
09.00 to 12.00, Thanksgiving Day (the 4th Thursday in November), annually

WHERE:
There is a new route for 2009. The parade starts at 77th Street and Central Park West and runs through Columbus Circle, east onto Central Park South. When it reaches 7th Avenue it turns south to 42nd Street. It then continues along 42nd Street to 6th Avenue where it veers south to 34th Street. From here it heads west to Herald Square, ending at 34th Street and 7th Avenue.

BEST FOR:
Family entertainment, New York City chutzpah, and (after the parade) Christmas shopping

YOU SHOULD KNOW:
Get there early for a good vantage point, and be prepared for crisp weather.

Dancers make their way through Columbus Circle on the route of the parade.

Rayne Frog Festival

WHEN:
The main events are in November but there are pageants and a run in August, September and October.

WHERE:
Rayne, off Interstate 10, 24 km (15 mi) west of Lafayette, Louisiana

BEST FOR:
Authentic Cajun culture, cuisine and music

YOU SHOULD KNOW:
Rayne features in *Ripley's Believe It Or Not* – not for frogs, but because St Joseph's Church has the only known Judaeo-Christian cemetery in the USA in which the graves face north-south instead of the usual east-west.

When the French colonists called 'Acadiens' were exiled from Nova Scotia in 1755, they came to Louisiana's coastal 'prairie' of freshwater swamps and moss-draped bayous. Their tradition of *joie-de-vivre* and hospitality is the soul of what is now called Cajun culture, and Rayne, in south Louisiana's Acadia Parish, is Cajun heartland. These days Cajun is defined by cuisine and music – but it's part of a cultural gumbo inextricably wedded to Creole, so the influences include French, German, Spanish, African, Native American, Scots and Irish. The popularity of the Rayne Frog Festival is a tribute to the uncomplicated appeal of Cajun culture at its lip-smacking, foot-stomping best. Rayne has been famous as the 'Frog Capital of the World' since 1880, when it began supplying frogs' legs by the barrel to the country's finest gourmet restaurants. Walls in the town are covered in elaborate frog murals, and 'ribbitt, ribbitt!' is a term of endearment.

The festival is an uproarious celebration of its most famous residents, be they giant ouaouaron, grenouie or crapaud. There are frog races and jumping contests, a Grand Parade to show off the Festival Queens, carnival rides, booths and even a Diaper Derby. Most of all there's Cajun food and an array of Louisiana's finest Cajun and Zydeco bands to keep hips twitching and the spirits way high. There's no pretension or slick commercialism. It's a working-man's festival bubbling with good humour, befitting a town still divided by the railway tracks that brought it prosperity, and with what must be America's only surviving five-and-dime store. Park your vanities with the RV (Rayne is proud of its state-of-the-art RV Park with 622 hookups) and get involved. The Frog Festival is an eldorado of rural Americana, made irresistible by Cajun charm.

Festival goers celebrate Rayne's most famous residents!

National Finals Rodeo

Every year in early December the Professional Rodeo Cowboys Association (PRCA) tops off its annual programme of nearly 700 sanctioned rodeo events with the National Finals Rodeo (NFR) in Las Vegas. Only the best of the best may compete – the top 15 money-winners in each of the seven core rodeo disciplines. These are: bareback bronc (bronco riding), saddle bronc, bull riding, tie-down roping, team roping, steer wrestling and barrel racing (exclusive to women). Winners are effectively world champions, and the traditional rodeo prize fancy belt-buckles are, here, made of gold. But all the participants are stars of the rodeo genre as a whole, and within that pyramid of razzmatazz glamorizing an almost entirely mythical 'West', their high-buttoned, sober focus and laconic joshing can make you forget that the entertainment they provide is in every case at least as dangerous as the most extreme sport.

The NFR is as close as you'll ever get to the atmosphere of a Roman circus. The clatter of the stockhouse rails, the thumping kicks of furious animals in wooden stalls, the snorting, the thick smell of caged energy and the sudden explosion into the arena of beast and rider, arcing half-twists, rolls and corkscrew gybes for the eternity of eight full seconds until one or the other gets a scraped cheekbone and a mouthful of sand – go very well with a beer and a chili dog in the shade of the patriotic bunting. The NFR's supreme irony is that in 'Sin City', world capital of insincere glitz and great showmanship, the rodeo events themselves are deadly serious; and for all the rodeo clowns and sequined Western beauty queens on parade, the contest, like no other in the USA, is stripped of fancy presentation. Each ride is a fresh drama; each day racks up the competitive thrills. In an ambience that intense, just a hint of soaring pedal-steel guitar is enough to put a halo round the moon.

WHEN:
Ten days in early December
WHERE:
Thomas & Mack Center at the University of Nevada, Las Vegas, Nevada
BEST FOR:
Thrills, spills and going cowboy/girl
YOU SHOULD KNOW:
The NFR uses tons of special dirt to cover the arena floor, making softer landings. Visitors and Las Vegas residents alike are eerily fascinated by the fact that the dirt is stored after the rodeo, and re-used again and again.

The idea is to hang on for dear life!

Boston Tea Party

WHEN:
As close to December 16 as possible
WHERE:
Old South Meeting House, Boston,
Massachusetts
BEST FOR:
History and human rights
YOU SHOULD KNOW:
'No muskets, swords or weapons of
any kind can be worn or carried' –
even by those in period costume.

On December 16 1773, a physical act of rebellion against Britain took place in Boston, igniting the flame that blazed into the American Revolution of 1776. Following a meeting of 5,000 Colonial Americans to protest about 'taxation without representation' (in Britain's Parliament), a group of men calling themselves the Sons of Liberty (supposedly disguised 'like Mohawk Indians', but really just wrapped in blankets and with muddied faces) stormed three ships, and threw their combined cargo of 342 chests of valuable Bohea tea into Boston harbour. It was to become a defining moment in history, and witnessing it in re-enactment, is both spectacular and inspirational.

Every year, volunteers in period costume re-enact the events of that dramatic night, in the buildings and streets where they actually took place. You can join them, but you need to pre-register to gain access to the Old South Meeting House, the beautiful mid-18th century Puritan hall where the protest grew so heated. Inside, every pew is boxed and as you gaze upon the mobcaps, tricorne hats and beaver skins, weskits, frock coats and powdered wigs crowded into the formal black-and-white severity of the building, you enter a time warp. Actors declaim the original arguments, deriving genuine passion from the eloquence of the shocked colonials of 1773. You can't help getting swept up in democratic righteousness and the desire to shake their smug British oppressors out of their complacency – and you do get the chance to follow the 'Mohawks', axes in hand, to the harbour (and popular justice!).

Hindsight makes the Boston Tea Party much more than a costumed entertainment. Great men spoke in 1773; and great were the consequences of what they said and did. Participating in this re-enactment returns lustre to the rights of men everywhere, and you will take away something very special and enduring.

New Year's Eve in Times Square

Times Square isn't. It's a huge triangle where Broadway's theatre quarter – the original 'Great White Way', nicknamed for the brilliance of its electric illuminations – crosses 7th Avenue above 42nd Street. When *The New York Times* moved in at No.1 in 1904, the paper threw a street party as a New Year's Eve 'housewarming' for the vibrant, expanding city. By 1907 it was already a tradition, and the celebration of renewal was marked by a huge illuminated ball that slid, lights blazing, down a 23 m (77 ft) pole in synchronization with the

final countdown to midnight. 'Dropping the ball' derives from old-time harbour time-signals, but these days the ball is covered in Waterford crystals that spill a million shafts of laser-split light across several city blocks – and across the upturned, wide-eyed faces of around a million New Yorkers, friends and visitors crammed shoulder to shoulder in exuberant communion, to welcome in the optimism of a new year by baying at a notional moon.

The New Year's Eve Party in Times Square is delirium itself. The dropping ball is just the climax to several hours of concerts, addresses, dancing, light shows and whooped-up conviviality. Even to be in it you have to take your place in the afternoon, equipped with warm clothes, food and water (alcohol isn't allowed – so be discreet). You'll lose your vantage point if you leave for a minute: police are expert at corralling crowds and refusing re-entry. Be prepared, and be steadfast, and during the firework displays, the garish strobing of rainbow colours, the ton of confetti filling the sky and the company of smiling strangers, you'll ascend the ladder of cathartic rapture. Anticipation, participation, satisfaction and fulfillment – seek them and find them in the symbolic centre of New York City, where New Yorkers breathe joyous life into their collective commitment to the New Year.

A couple see in the New Year with a kiss.

WHEN:
December 31
WHERE:
Times Square, New York City, New York
BEST FOR:
Popular culture, extravagant spectacle and New Year resolutions
YOU SHOULD KNOW:
Times Square is, by tradition and in fact, one of New York City's liveliest, quirkiest, and most entertaining areas, even with its rough edges. In 2005, the women's world chess championship was played behind a ground-level plate-glass window there; and you see local 'characters' like the 'Naked Cowboy' (who likes to pose in his underwear and accoutrements), and 'Reverend Billy' of the 'Church of Stop Shopping'.

CENTRAL AMERICA & THE CARIBBEAN

Mazatlán Carnival

WHEN:
The week before Lent, so usually in February
WHERE:
Mazatlán, Sinaloa State
BEST FOR:
Red-hot spectacle tempered by ice-cold Pacifico beer
YOU SHOULD KNOW:
Mazatlán's Plazuela Machado used to be the focal point for carnaval, but has now become the scene of a wonderful food fair held from Friday evening to Tuesday – the camarones con mango (mango shrimp), marlin ahumda (smoked marlin) and pescado zarandeado (char-grilled fish) are to die for.

Like many celebrations in Catholic countries, Mazatlán's carnival is held in the run-up to Lent. One of the world's largest fiestas, it's a Mardi Gras extravaganza that rivals those in Rio and Trinidad, with visitors from all over Mexico and beyond pushing attendance towards the half-million mark. There's plenty of room for everyone, for the 'Pacific Pearl' offers 11 km (7 mi) of beachfront Malécon that can accommodate countless celebrants, together with bands to entertain, food sellers to sustain and bars to lubricate from Thursday night to the following Tuesday. Avenida del Mar on Playa Norte is the main focus of street action, where an assortment of stages and other temporary structures appear and music plays non-stop.

When the main events begin the city is ablaze with colourful decorations. On Friday evening the baseball stadium hosts the juegos florales (floral games), where the Flower Queen is crowned and Mexican poets read flowery verse in the hope of winning prestigious prizes. El Rey Feo (The Ugly King) is crowned in the Teodoro Mariscal Stadium. Here, too, an effigy of some unpopular character is hanged and burned in the Quema de Mal Humor (Burning of Bad Humour) ceremony. It ends with a magnificent firework display.

Sunday is another big night, with a huge costume parade (pelted with confetti and streamers by spectators) featuring fantastical characters and newly crowned carnival 'royals'. This time the fireworks are off shore – creating a mock battle that glories in a 19th century victory over a French fleet. Monday's for the fellas – El Día del Marido Oprimido (Day of the Hen-pecked Husband) allows married men a brief spell of unsupervised freedom. There's another big parade on Tuesday afternoon, after which the streets come alive with music and excited revellers – a thundering ending to a very special event.

Dancers contribute to the fun at the carnival.

Equinox at Chichen Itza

Crowds gather to observe the serpentine shadow that falls on the north side of El Castillo during equinox.

Nowhere is the advanced pre-Colombian heritage of Central America more clearly demonstrated that at Chichen Itza, the Maya city in the northern Yucatán Peninsula that reached its zenith in the three centuries following AD 600. This amazing site with its great variety of remains – including many well-preserved stone buildings – is well worth a visit in its own right, but also serves as an attraction for many thousands of visitors drawn to this atmospheric place at particular times: for the vernal and autumnal equinoxes.

The object of their fascination is the Temple of Kukulkan – the Maya equivalent of the Aztec god Quetzalcoatl, The Plumed Serpent. The imposing structure known as El Castillo (The Castle) is a square, stepped pyramid with stairways up each side to the temple. For some time around each equinox, at the rising and setting of the sun, the structure's corner tiers cast a serpentine shadow in the shape of Kukulkan that slithers down the northern side of the pyramid with the sun's passage.

This moving representation of The Plumed Serpent is a tribute to the knowledge of the Mayan astronomers, who succeeded in creating a phenomenon that has become one of the great wonders of the world. Although it is possible to see and appreciate this symbolic shadow in the weeks leading up to and following the equinoxes, it's at its clearest for five days either side of each equinox and most impressive at dawn on the actual day. Crowds gather in darkness, filling the great courtyard beside the pyramid and awaiting the first rays of red light that signal the serpent's coming. It's an eerily moving moment – and in spring the locals still gather in force to pray for an abundant year free from inclement weather, much as their forebears must have done.

WHEN:
March 20-21, September 21-22
WHERE:
Chichen Itza, Yucatán State
BEST FOR:
Connecting present with past
YOU SHOULD KNOW:
The Cenote Sagrada (Sacred Well) at Chichen Itza was used for offerings to the rain god Chaac . . . and for human sacrifices.

Assumption of the Virgin

The Assumption of the Virgin Mary is celebrated across Mexico in mid August. There are special masses everywhere and many towns and villages mount processions, parade statues and honour Our Lady in song and dance. Some of these festivities are famous, providing spectacles that attract both foreign tourists and visitors from other parts of the country. For instance, in Mexico City there is a huge mass at the Basilica de La Virgen de Guadalupe, home to an image of the Virgin that is nationally revered.

But the most famous event of all takes place at Huamantla, in the east. The town starts preparing early and on the second Saturday in August flower blossom, fresh moss and dyed sawdust are carefully laid in the streets, forming intricate multicoloured patterns as the locals prepare a magical carpet for their patron saint, the Virgin of Charity. At midnight on August 15 the fireworks start (literally) as a girl representing the Virgin leads a procession through the lavishly decorated town to Huamantla's main church, where mass is celebrated before bands play, the people dance and splendid sand paintings are examined and admired.

The following Saturday there is a Pamplona-style 'running', where cape-wielding young men test their courage by sharing the streets with rampaging fighting bulls loosed when two huge rockets are fired at noon – that's just one example of what makes this particular 'Assumption' so special. It's not only the extraordinary devotion that goes into the festival itself, but also the accompanying Huamantla Fair that lasts for over two weeks, providing an annual draw for hordes of people from the surrounding rural areas. Hereabouts, all the fun of the fair includes traditional rides, a rodeo, donkey racing, cockfights, craft exhibitions, concerts, livestock shows, a large market, car racing and much riotous eating and drinking.

A statue of the Virgin Mary is carried in a street procession.

WHEN:
August
WHERE:
Huamantla, Tlaxcala State
BEST FOR:
That truly memorable night-time parade led by the Virgin of Charity
YOU SHOULD KNOW:
There are relatively few hotels in Huamantla, so most visitors stay in Puebla, 40 km (25 mi) to the southwest as the crow flies, and travel to the festivities by bus.

Day of the Dead

To be in Mexico at the beginning of November is to experience moving festivals that combine Christian beliefs with pre-Colombian ideas, taking place on the holy days of All Saints and All Souls. The first of the month is Día de los Angelitos – the 'Day of the Little Angels' dedicated to all the children who have died. The following day is Día de los Muertos – the actual 'Day of the Dead' that remembers deceased adults. This may sound morbid . . . and some of the accompanying rituals reinforce that thought. The customs vary from place to place but the centrepiece will often encompass offerings to the dead at decorated altars representing nature's four elements – earth, wind, water and fire.

But this is a culture that believes in a vibrant afterlife and in truth these activities joyously celebrate the lives of the departed rather than mourning their loss, supported by a belief that spirits of the dead return for this brief period to be with their loved ones. Elaborately decorated shrines in private homes are adorned with flowers, pictures of deceased relatives and candles that burn throughout the period. Families visit cemeteries to clean graves and place more flowers and candles and often mount night vigils.

Yet these formal ceremonies are often complemented by lively street festivals, usually accompanied by lavish feasting. Any number of edible horrors – like skulls and coffins made from sugar – are produced, but this apparent frivolity has a serious purpose. The Day of the Dead becomes Hanal Pixan in the Mayan language, which translates as 'a feast for the souls'. Thus the very best of food is prepared – and whilst the spirits are nourished by its essence, the living happily get to eat it – and also take the opportunity to drink and be merry.

WHEN:
November 1-2
WHERE:
Throughout Mexico (though the most colourful festivals tend to be in the south of the country)
BEST FOR:
Turning sorrow to joy
YOU SHOULD KNOW:
Many Mexican children know a good thing when they see one – and have started dressing up in costumes to go trick-or-treating at this time of year, though the local version is somewhat morbidly called pedir muertos (asking on behalf of the dead).

Installations of skeletons are created by artists to celebrate the Day of the Dead.

National Day

WHEN:
For a week either side of
September 10 and 21
WHERE:
Belize City – but the party takes place
throughout the country with much
the same abandon
BEST FOR:
Wild socializing, dirty dancing,
hypnotic music and cultural insight
YOU SHOULD KNOW:
Unlike Mardi Gras, Belize's September
celebrations have no counterweight
period of restraint (like Lent). Since
Belize City officials are willing to close
whole blocks of streets at the drop of
a hat if just a few people and a band
want to have a street party, National
Day only 'ends' when the population
can't take any more.

National Day in Belize is September 10. Specifically, it commemorates the Battle of St George's Caye in 1798, when the 'Baymen' (British settlers descended from pirates) of the then-British colony defeated an armed Spanish incursion in the waters of Belize's barrier reef. Metaphorically, of course, it represents a 'colonial' victory – and since independence in 1981, Belizeans have begun to show greater enthusiasm for Independence Day on September 21, as more representative of their Creole, Hispanic, Maya Indian and Garifuna roots. True to their reputation as 'the smiling face' of the Caribbean, they have solved potential conflict by extending both celebrations. Now, the whole of September is a party time of carnival, pageants, parades, competitions, shows and festive good cheer. Given a general disposition to have a good time, Belize's talent for raising the ante on fun is nothing short of extraordinary, and often extremely witty.

Belize City has always treated National Day like others treat Mardi Gras. They spend months preparing for themed parades that begin with an official carnival in early September. Dazzling colour, pounding drums and the irresistible rhythms of Punta music stir your senses into an electrifying cocktail of helpless motion. It's intoxicating, driven by tropic intensity and the wildly uninhibited clamour of the gorgeous crowds, foremost among whom are dozens of pretty girls, the multiple carnival queens and princesses. September 10 itself is only slightly more sedate. There's a 'citizen's parade' and speeches, greatly enlivened by a wicked parody of the once colonial power: the 'Queen of the Bay' (invariably addressed as 'her Graciousness') boogies through her coronation at the head of a laughing, dancing, jubilant throng, processing to the National Stadium.

Waxing with goodwill and waning with exhaustion, Belize spends September days on the beach or in the crystal water, recharging for the afternoon and evening. Try and keep up. This party lasts a month.

*National Day is treated more
like a Mardi Gras in Belize.*

Festival of St Thomas

Guatemala has festivals and parades galore but the daddy of them all takes place at a small white-walled town with strong Mayan roots that perches precipitously in mountains above mysterious mist-filled valleys. Chichi experiences an extraordinary transformation in the run-up to Christmas, when tens of thousands of people arrive from every corner of Guatemala to join seven days of uninhibited festivities as the Fiesta de Santo Tomás celebrates both the upcoming saint's day of the town's patron on December 21 and also the imminent arrival of Olentzero, a mythical Christmas messenger.

This oh-so-traditional town is always full of vibrant life and elaborate local ritual, centred on the bustling market and historic Church of St Thomas (dating from 1540). But Chichi goes into overdrive for the fiesta – the whole place is swathed in bunting, flags and streamers before erupting into one long street fair that culminates in a massive parade on the saint's day (which also happens to coincide with the year's best market). Throughout the week the town becomes a rowdy riot of copious drinking, colourful costumes, grotesque masks, marimba music, energetic dancing and loud fireworks.

Here, too, it is possible to witness the amazing *palo volador* (flying pole) ritual in front of the white-painted church, where two acrobats spin impressively from ropes fastened to their ankles as they spiral outwards and downwards from a tall pine pole that has been consecrated as a continuing tribute to the Mayan *yaxche* (tree of life). Other highlights include another historic tradition – the Baile de la Conquista (Dance of the Conquest) in which masked dancers portray the invading Spanish conquistadors who arrived back in the 16th century. The whole extravaganza might have been staged for tourists, but isn't – instead representing the soul of Guatemala.

'St Thomas' is paraded through the streets of Chichi.

WHEN:
December
WHERE:
Chichicastenango (Chichi)
BEST FOR:
A unique blend of Mayan and Christian traditions
YOU SHOULD KNOW:
Before swinging into the Fiesta de Santo Tomás, the locals (along with the rest of the country) warm up on December 7 with the Quema del Diablo (Burning of the Devil).

*Maroons gather under the trees
to celebrate the birthday
of Cudjoe.*

Accompong Maroon Festival

In most places maroons may be rockets fired by distressed mariners, but in Jamaica the word means something very different – the descendents of slaves who fled their Spanish masters when the British invaded, disappearing towards the island's wild west and south coasts over three centuries ago. They formed a fearsome guerrilla army in the harsh Cockpit Hills that the Brits never defeated, and their special heritage and unique sub-culture have long been celebrated at the Accompong Maroon Festival.

This takes place just after New Year, honouring the Maroon's founder Kojo and famous warrior Colonel Cudjoe – whose great achievement was to beat a British army after years of on-off strife and conclude a peace treaty in 1738 that guaranteed the Maroons freedom from slavery and their land, where they live to this day as a nation within a nation – largely self-governing and paying no tax.

Though visitors are welcome, the Accompong Festival is very much a Maroon affair that incorporates folk memories descending from the former African and Arawak Indian slaves who escaped Spanish bondage in the 1600s. There are several formal ceremonies such as feeding the dead, when the menfolk cook unsalted pork. Others involve the blowing of the wailing Abeng and the playing of Gumbay drums at the Kindah Tree, an ancient mango tree beneath which Cudjoe held meetings that united the three Maroon tribes – Ashanti, Coromante and Congo. Each tribe has its ancient burial ground and there are four sealed grounds where traditional religious ceremonies are held.

This being the Caribbean, after a march to the Peace Cave where Cudjoe's treaty was signed, the festival erupts into uninhibited song and dance, lavish feasting and the rapid consumption of rum – a blow-out that often continues unabated for several days.

WHEN:
January 6
WHERE:
Accompong, St Elizabeth
BEST FOR:
Insight into a distinctive Caribbean culture that is a fascinating historical survivor . . . and a genuinely traditional event that is celebrated with enormous gusto
YOU SHOULD KNOW:
The Maroons acquired their name from the Spanish word cimmaron, meaning untamed or wild . . . a grudging compliment from grumpy colonial powers that entirely failed to subdue these independent people.

Reggae Sumfest

Appropriately billed as 'the heart-throb of summer' (or less modestly 'the greatest reggae show on earth'), Reggae Sumfest is the world's finest festival dedicated to Jamaica's unique contribution to popular music. This pulsating genre was developed on the island in the late 1960s, as bands like Bob Marley's Wailers transformed local ska and rocksteady styles into compulsive reggae music that was destined to take the world by storm.

Reggae Sumfest attracts tens of thousands of music lovers each year – both islanders and visitors – by presenting an extensive programme of concerts featuring local and international reggae stars, plus related dancehall sounds and some hip hop and R&B. Delicious Jamaican cuisine and the best of arts and crafts from all parts of the island are available on the festival grounds.

The event kicks off in mid June with a massive party at the Rose Hall Beach Club, but the main musical action takes place at Montego Bay's Catherine Hall entertainment complex on Howard Cook Boulevard (from Sunday to Saturday, with a break on Tuesday and Wednesday). The impressive list of performers is finalized by the middle of May, with tickets going on sale shortly thereafter (season tickets are offered, or individual events may be booked). Out-of-town show goers can take a shuttle bus from Kingston or Ocho Rios. No seating is provided but portable chairs, blankets or mats may be taken (though no food or drink, as this would tread on the toes of the many in-venue suppliers).

For the best of everything, visitors can enjoy the classic Caribbean holiday delights of Montego Bay by day (sun, sand and the hip seaside strip) . . . and join passionate crowds for the best of reggae music as the stars come out. Chill!

WHEN:
Mid July
WHERE:
Montego Bay
BEST FOR:
The authentic sound of reggae
YOU SHOULD KNOW:
If you wish to attend Reggae Sumfest it's advisable to book accommodation in January, to be sure of securing the hotel room of your choice – those who leave it too late may not be able to find anywhere.

St Lucia Jazz

WHEN:
The first two weeks in May
WHERE:
All over the island (including Castries, Pigeon Island, Soufrière, Vieux Fort and Laborie)
BEST FOR:
The best international jazz music . . . with brilliant local colour
YOU SHOULD KNOW:
St Lucia has a traditional carnival in July and two major cultural festivals – La Rose (also July, representing the Rosicrucian Order) and La Marguerite in October (representing Freemasonry).

Caribbean festivals fall into two broad categories – traditional carnivals reflecting the unique culture and heritage of these island nations and events dreamed up to attract visitors and boost the key local industry: tourism. Although this mountainous Windward Island has several of the former, St Lucia Jazz is undoubtedly an example of the latter, becoming an established annual event after being founded in 1992 to raise the island's profile in a situation where competitors for the all-important tourist dollar had bigger marketing budgets and higher profiles, even though St Lucia is blessed with exquisite natural beauty.

This imaginative move proved to be inspirational, to the point where St Lucia Jazz takes over the island for a couple of weeks and has become recognized as one of the Caribbean's leading music events and one of the world's 'top five' jazz festivals. A wide spectrum of sounds shakes loose from the beginning of May, with the presentation of multiple shows that include trad, acoustical/straight-ahead jazz, new-age jazz and fusion (plus calypso and R&B), stylishly delivered by acts from the Caribbean, USA, Latin America and Africa . . . a truly international pantheon of jazz artists that draws aficionados from all corners of the globe, growing to the point where it simply can't expand further owing to practical constraints.

This being the West Indies, the irrepressible locals soon made this impressive artificial creation their own. In addition to a wide variety of shows – formal stage concerts, late-night open-air events, club evenings and *al fresco* picnic occasions – numerous fringe activities have sprung up, enhancing the festive atmosphere and providing all sorts of free entertainment. Even if jazz isn't your special thing, St Lucia in May is a great place to have fun.

Saxophonist Rob Taylor entertains pupils from a local school.

Trinidad Carnival

Is Trinidad's annual carnival 'the world's greatest', as organizers claim? It hardly matters, because participants and spectators alike enjoy a fabulous experience in the five days running up to Ash Wednesday. After all that excitement and a stimulating overdose of calypso, soca, steelpan and mas (masquerade), some sober contemplation on the first day of Lent can bring blessed relief.

As with many Caribbean festivals, carnival reflects diverse influences – West African slave culture, European colonial, Spanish and Asian. There are many colourful characters drawn from this heritage, including black wandering minstrels wearing white face paint, the braggart Midnight Robber, ample French aristo Dame Lorraine and Pierrot Grenade who comments on contemporary issues in rhyme.

The motto of Trinidad and Tobago reads 'Together we aspire, together we achieve' – and whilst carnival is indeed a wonderful co-operative effort, there is also ferocious competition for prizes and honours. Each day of this ritual pageant has a special focus, though Port-of-Spain is in festive mood throughout with action all over town. Everything kicks off on Friday with the King and Queen contest. Saturday sees the Panorama. Sunday's highlight is Dimanche Gras, Monday starts early with J'Ouverte and it all comes to a pounding peak on Tuesday with Parade of the Bands. There is some stunning performance art, notably masquerades that are both eye-popping entertainment and powerful social or spiritual statements.

The cornerstone of carnival is music. Though parades of complex floats, elaborate costumes, masked revellers and dancing play an essential part, it is band music that dominates. If you doubt that this massive festival plays a hugely important part in Trinidadian life, note the following pearl of wisdom stating that at any point in time islanders are either (a) preparing for carnival or (b) celebrating it with all their energy or (c) reminiscing over the delights of the latest event.

WHEN:
Normally in February, occasionally early March
WHERE:
Port-of-Spain, Trinidad
BEST FOR:
Sounds of the Caribbean
YOU SHOULD KNOW:
Carnival is part of the school curriculum and children not only join the processions almost as soon as they can walk, but also take part in preliminary 'Kiddies Carnival' shows.

Fantastic costumes abound at the carnival.

Crop Over

WHEN:
July to early August
WHERE:
Everywhere (Bridgetown for
the festival)
BEST FOR:
Calypso capers
YOU SHOULD KNOW:
All is not quite as it seems – the
traditional Crop Over withered as
sugar production declined in the
1940s but was astutely revived in
1974 as an off-season tourist
attraction . . . an opportunity to have
fun that Barbadians have embraced
with enthusiasm.

Barbados is a dream holiday destination and tourism is the economy's mainstay – but sugar production remains a significant activity. The island was once the world's most important producer of the sticky commodity and – in a tradition established back in the 1780s – Barbados celebrates the end of each season's cane cutting at the literally named Crop Over. This takes place over many weeks and encompasses a variety of activities including thanksgiving services, musical events and a series of cavalcades all over the island, enlivened by the uninhibited verve that is a delightful Caribbean characteristic.

It all leads up to the Crop Over Festival in Bridgetown – several days of frantic action beginning with the crowning of Crop Over's King and Queen, proudly ennobled as the season's most productive male and female cane cutters. The opening gala sees the last canes being blessed by the Spiritual Baptists before the place explodes into a riot of sound and colour. The Crop Over King and Queen aren't the only new rulers – there's keen competition to become party, calypso or costume band monarchs. It all comes to a thumping crescendo on Grand Kadooment Day. This national holiday sees a cart parade, processions, dancers and assorted bands filling the streets until the evening sky blazes with fireworks and the all-night party begins.

Meanwhile, Bridgetown Market street fair in the capital's Spring Garden and along Spring Garden Highway beside the sea is a key part of the celebrations, offering a wide range of events and activities representing local Bajan culture. An official element ensures that all aspects of island life are showcased – agricultural produce, artistic output, crafts, music, poetry, dance, folk theatre, food and drink. This is augmented by beach games, all creating a lively carnival.

*Stilt walkers parade on
Grand Kadooment Day, the last
fun-filled day of Crop Over.*

Fiesta de Merengue

WHEN:
July/August
WHERE:
Santo Domingo (recently also in nearby Boca Chica and Juan Dolio)
BEST FOR:
Very fit dancers
YOU SHOULD KNOW:
After dictator Rafael Trujillo came to power in 1930 he commissioned endless merengues that extolled his virtues (and virility) then imposed the music on all levels of society – though he never uttered the phrase 'merengue is the opiate of the people', no doubt the thought was there.

No, merengue isn't a Spanish dessert but the national music of the Dominican Republic – a music and dance style in rapid 2/4 time that has spread far beyond its roots, becoming increasingly sophisticated and complex with the passage of time as new forms are pioneered.

It may have taken much of the Latin world by storm but this hot, spicy music is the birthright of every Dominican and originated in plantation slave culture that made the island of Hispaniola a rich sugar producer and typical Caribbean cultural melting pot. So for two weeks every year the New World's oldest city gets a new lease of life when the Fiesta de Merengue engulfs the place, attracting vast crowds intent on enjoying unremitting music and dance beside the ruined walled town and fabulous limestone palace that Christopher Columbus built five centuries ago.

The nominal venue is Santo Domingo's wide palm-lined El Malecón, a long boulevard that stretches lazily beside turquoise sea and white beaches. And in this incomparable setting the country's finest bands gather to strut their stuff on numerous stages, simultaneously competing with massive sound systems manned by fast-talking DJs and any number of strolling players. Sooner or later virtually every act that's performed merengue in the past three decades reappears, along with a host of hopefuls who fully intend to make it big.

It's a case of music, music everywhere. This being the Caribbean, the rum-soaked action tends to spread to every side street and bar . . . whilst wild beach parties to 160-beat-a-minute merengue are *de rigeur*. There are few in the Dominican Republic who can resist a good fiesta, especially if it involves gyrating to music. Things can get pretty wild . . . but up-for-it visitors are always welcome to join the fun.

Pirates Week

Anyone thinking Captain Jack Sparrow and Disney movies when the words 'Pirates' and 'Caribbean' are put together in the same well-known phrase or film title might be missing the opportunity to have a buccaneering adventure of their own. For the mistitled Pirates Week (celebrations actually last for nearer a fortnight) in the famously hospitable Cayman Islands is a West Indian carnival like no other.

Of course it does have all the usual well-loved ingredients – explosive firework displays, toe-tapping music, street dancing, amazing costumes, grotesque masks, glittering parades, pageants, fun fairs and fancy dress competitions, with the action continuing into the small hours as rich food and strong drink a-plenty are consumed. But nowhere else on earth can offer the spectacle of two old-style sailing ships packed with pirates making a 'surprise' attack. They enter the bowl-shaped George Town harbour and pirates storm ashore on Saturday, to be greeted by thousands who are lining Harbour Place and surrounding streets after just happening to anticipate the raid (which happily ends not in plunder and pillage but with everyone having an uproarious street party).

Both visitors and locals join in heartily, and it's not always easy to tell the two groups apart. It's almost mandatory to dress up in pirate paraphernalia, with complete costumes available for hire, or that subtle touch like a hook or temporary tattoo for those who don't want to go the whole hog but are determined to enter into the spirit of things.

Subsequently, the whole country has an extended celebration at local heritage days, assorted sporting occasions, children's events and various family-orientated activities, all combining to create one long national party. It all comes to an extraordinary end with a cardboard boat race in George Town harbour – don't try that one at home, folks!

WHEN:
November
WHERE:
Grand Cayman (principally George Town) with supporting events on Little Cayman and Cayman Brac
BEST FOR:
Roistering swashing and buckling
YOU SHOULD KNOW:
It is advisable to book early to secure rooms in George Town for 'invasion' and parade weekend, and be aware that hire cars are in short supply at festival time.

If dressing-up as a pirate is your thing – this is for you.

71

World Creole Music Festival

WHEN:
October/November
WHERE:
Mainly at the new Windsor Park national stadium, Roseau.
BEST FOR:
Authentic fusion music from the Creole-speaking world – like Bouyon, Cadence-lypso, Zouk, Soukous, Zydeco and Kompas. Listen and all will become clear!
YOU SHOULD KNOW:
Although Creole culture is French-based and Dominica was originally a colony of France, the island was grabbed by the British in the 18th century – but old habits die hard, and many islanders still speak a Creole patois.

Suitably stimulated by the success of St Lucia Jazz in raising that island's profile – and boosting tourist income – Dominica came up with its own distinctive musical extravaganza in 1997, with considerable success. The World Creole Music Festival is billed as the eastern Caribbean's most authentic showcase for indigenous music and doesn't disappoint.

From modest beginnings, it now attracts tens of thousands of visitors to an event that was initially intended as a platform for home-grown Dominican talent and also to promote Creole music generally as a major art form. It has now become one of the biggest music events in the West Indies, providing a platform for bands and solo artists from all over the Creole-speaking universe (which is mainly the wider Caribbean and Louisiana in the USA) and establishing Dominica as the Creole music capital of the world.

To add another dimension to the festival's concert-style 'three nights of pulsating rhythms', Creole in the Park was added to the festivities in 2003 to create a laid-back daytime event. It extends music into the verdant Botanic Gardens of Dominica by the Roseau River and adds Creole cuisine and local craft products to the evocative sounds of Steelpan, Cadence and Bouyon music.

Visitors to the Botanic Gardens will soon see why this enchanting island in the Lesser Antilles is nicknamed 'The Nature Isle' for its largely unspoiled natural beauty, but those who appreciate some excitement and local colour with their West Indian holiday should definitely aim to be in Dominica when annual independence celebrations, Creole in the Park and the World Creole Music Festival are making the whole place shiver 'n' shake with typical Caribbean gusto.

Junkanoo

This one's for strictly for night birds with unlimited stamina. Uniquely, the stunning climax of this Bahamian festival takes place during the hours of darkness, beginning a couple of hours after midnight and continuing until dawn. It consists of a colourful (and noisy) double whammy – after partying through the night to greet the day after Christmas, Junkanoo reignites a few days later to celebrate the arrival of a new year. As with many Caribbean festivals, the origins of Junkanoo lie in slave culture, for plantation slaves in the Bahamas were allowed a moment of joyful exuberance each year with a brief holiday around Christmas.

Today, the main venue is Nassau's Bay Street, in the heart of town. As the lights come up and Junkanoo begins, the noise and colour generate an almost palpable force field. The vast crowds become a sinuously moving sea of bright colours as spectators gyrate to the pounding rhythms of goatskin drums, horns, whistles and cowbells. At the same time balconies and rooftops are packed with dancing spectators, with every possible vantage point occupied by excited revellers.

The main parade consists of organized groups that may contain up to a thousand participants, each group having spent months preparing to present a theme that is dramatically highlighted by the chosen costumes, masks, music and dance. There are real incentives to put on a top performance, with cash prizes awaiting those groups judged to have delivered the best costume, music and presentation.

The result? A truly awesome cavalcade and entertaining nights that will never be forgotten. Mardi Gras and Rio Carnival eat your hearts out – Junkanoo is up there challenging for the title of one the world's most impressive (and exciting) street festivals.

Elaborate and brightly coloured costumes are the order of the night.

WHEN:
December 26 and January 1
WHERE:
Nassau (with secondary events in Grand Bahama, Abaco, Bimini and Eleuthera)
BEST FOR:
The ultimate carnival experience . . . by night
YOU SHOULD KNOW:
To best appreciate the majestic passing of the Junkanoo parade, you should arrive early and reserve a place on the roadside bench seats – or even better one of the upstairs viewing points in Bay Street.

SOUTH
AMERICA

SOUTH AMERICA/ARGENTINA

Boca Juniors v River Plate

WHEN:
The match date varies within Argentina's soccer season (two round-robin competitions each calendar year).
WHERE:
Alberto J. Armando Stadium (better known as La Bombonera), Buenos Aires
BEST FOR:
Awesome sporting passion
YOU SHOULD KNOW:
The return derby at River Plate's Monumental de Nunez stadium is an even grander occasion, with over 75,000 fans present – but it somehow lacks the raw excitement of the match at Boca's more intimate ground.

At least half of Argentina's soccer fans support one of the capital's leading football teams – Boca Juniors and River Plate. These deadly rivals have been doing battle on (and sometimes off) the pitch for over 70 years . . . and the annual derby match between the two clubs at Boca's extraordinary La Bombonera (Chocolate Box) ground is one of the world's great sporting occasions – a football match like no other.

The excitement as El Superclasico looms grips the country for days, given added spice by what each team represents. Both were founded in the deprived La Boca dockland area of Buenos Aires, but whilst Juniors stayed true to their humble roots River Plate moved to the smart Nuñez district in the 1930s. So now there's nothing fans of the 'people's team' like better than putting one over on the 'millionaires', as social class and money ignite volatile emotions.

The atmosphere within the ground has to be experienced to be believed, as anyone who has ever bought, begged or stolen a ticket will testify. Some 60,000 *barras bravas* (fanatical fans) occupy towering tiers of moving colour – blue and yellow for Boca, red and white for River. Banners wave, streamers stream, fireworks explode, dancers dance, spectators surge . . . and there's a wall of deafening noise as hard-core fans scream tribal chants and roar hysterically as the on-pitch contest unfolds.

The 'people's team' have an edge over 'the millionaires' – it's close, but Boca have won more of these epic contests. Passions always run high – Boca fans accuse their River counterparts of being *gallinas* (scared chickens) whilst River fans retort by calling Boca supporters *los puercos* (smelly pigs). Be warned – things sometimes get out of hand at El Superclasico time, with bitter rivalry spilling over into violence.

The Monumental stadium is engulfed in smoke as the teams get ready for combat.

Buenos Aires Tango Festival

Couples take to the floor and tango.

Grip that flower between flashing white teeth and stand by to tango. After all, Argentina is the spiritual home to the world's sexiest dance, personifying the very height of yearning erotic tension that can exist between a man and a woman. If anyone doubts that fact, they will soon be persuaded should they attend the pulsating week-long Buenos Aires Tango Festival.

During this sexy event the whole city throbs with passion. There is a host of events organized by the Ministry of Culture – including magnificent opening and closing night extravaganzas, live concerts, films, world-famous dancers giving free exhibitions and shows, an international tango fair and competitions for couples at all levels of expertise. And for those who want to learn the tango (or hone their skills), the festival has numerous free classes for beginners and experienced dancers alike.

But official involvement and set-piece spectaculars merely formalize the fact that evocative music and sensual dancing have taken over the town, with every barrio coming alive as the working people of Buenos Aires celebrate their very being to the lively beat of piano music and the atmospheric sob of the bandoneon, partying into the small hours.

It all began with the *milonga*, a traditional Spanish dance that originated in Andalusia. In Argentina the porteños (natives of Buenos Aires) transformed it into the tango, which became the powerful symbol of working-class defiance of staid bourgeois society. Today, the festival focuses that raw energy with the action hotting up in clubs, dance halls, cafés, *milongas* (dance studios, also formal dance evenings) and spilling onto the streets as night falls after the heat of the day. Being there is to come close to understanding the very soul of this sprawling city on the banks of the Río de la Plata.

WHEN:
February/March
WHERE:
Buenos Aires
BEST FOR:
Sensual rhythms
YOU SHOULD KNOW:
The old tradition of *cabeco* still applies, whereby potential partners exchange meaningful glances to establish their willingness to tango, thus avoiding the embarrassment of possible rejection . . . so be careful who you look at, and how!

Gauchos display their skills.

Day of the Gaucho

Just as the tango symbolizes city living, so the Día de la Tradición highlights another aspect of Argentina. This annual event takes place in the Pampas, that vast area of grassland south of Buenos Aires which is home to the gaucho (cowboy), a cultural symbol every bit as potent in Argentina as his counterpart in America's Wild West. In best 'singing cowboy' tradition the gaucho is famed for song and – more unusually – dance, which makes for the liveliest of celebrations.

Native gauchos with outstanding skills and dexterity spread their influence far beyond the Pampas in the 19th century, as many migrated to cities in search of work. They took melancholic folk songs and the wild payada dance with them, to become an essential part of the nation's heritage. This is remembered in the run-up to the Día de la Tradición, with horse parades, singing, dancing and extended feasting. Other activities include folk dance demonstrations and classes, a local arts and crafts week and a variety of interesting events showcasing Creole culture.

It all comes to a pulsating head at the regional capital of San Antonio de Areco, when the Day of the Gaucho starts with mass in the Church of San Antonio. Thereafter things get less formal, with music and traditional dancing taking over – feet moving almost too fast for the eye to follow, spurs jingling and sparks literally flying. A colourful parade of gauchos and *tropillas* (work horses) progresses through the streets, before a lavish lunch for dignitaries and the public. Then there's more music and dance in the park, accompanied by an afternoon of breathtaking displays of horsemanship and other country skills. It's a memorable experience for those who are lucky enough to share the exuberance that characterizes Argentina's rural life.

WHEN:
Early November
WHERE:
Centred on San Antonio de Areco
BEST FOR:
The world's tastiest barbecued beef
YOU SHOULD KNOW:
With suitable pragmatism, all open-air activities on the climactic Day of the Gaucho are postponed for a week if the weather is bad – though the official lunch still goes ahead!

Argentine Polo Finals

Argentina is not only the land of tango, gauchos and the finest beef cattle, but also the world's premier polo-playing country. This fast-moving sport is a dramatic spectacle, and the very pinnacle of sporting excellence is witnessed by crowds of up to 30,000 people drawn by the most prestigious polo tournament on the planet, held in Buenos Aires since 1893. This annual event takes place in the upmarket barrio of Palermo, at a stadium popularly known as 'The Cathedral of Polo' – a nickname emphasizing the importance of polo in Argentinian tradition.

Polo is a game that sees teams of four skilful riders on highly trained ponies do battle, attempting to drive a white ball into the opposition goal using a long-handled mallet. Each game is divided into chukkas, usually seven minutes long, with six chukkas being the norm. Riders change ponies between chukkas. The sport operates on a handicap system that enables teams of differing ability to compete fairly with one another – though handicaps are invariably low at The Argentine Polo Finals, which feature the world's best players.

Fierce though competition may be, these finals are about much more than sporting excellence – as befits a sport where participants require considerable resources. This is also the social occasion *par excellence*, with jet-setters joining international celebrities and well-heeled locals to enjoy the exciting action on the field of play . . . and participate in an endless whirl of clubbing, parties and serious socializing off it. When the circus rolls into Buenos Aires just before Christmas each year this heady combination provides great entertainment for those who are as interested in having fun, urban chic and people-watching as polo-playing – all adding to a unique occasion not to be missed!

A player wheels away after scoring.

WHEN:
December
WHERE:
Campo Argentino del Polo,
Buenos Aires
BEST FOR:
Top competitive sport surrounded by glamour and glitz
YOU SHOULD KNOW:
Polo originated in Persia (Iran) over two thousand years ago as a training exercise for mounted soldiers, sometimes with a hundred or more combatants on each side – but it soon became a game reserved for the nobility, establishing a cachet that remains to this day.

SOUTH AMERICA/BRAZIL

Rio Carnival

WHEN:
Normally in February, occasionally early March
WHERE:
Rio de Janeiro
BEST FOR:
Being the best!
YOU SHOULD KNOW:
This is a hot event – literally. Rio Carnival takes place at the warmest time of year, which explains why some of the liveliest action takes place after nightfall.

Carnival time!

If there's one 'must do' event in Latin America it's Carnival in Rio – one of the world's great shows, perhaps the greatest. Everyone's heard of it and over half a million visitors arrive to swell the ranks of celebrating locals each year. This uninhibited four-day festival begins 40 days before Easter and leads up to the start of Lent on Ash Wednesday, finishing on Fat Tuesday – a glorious opportunity to eat, drink and be merry for those about to take Lenten abstinence seriously.

Carnival begins with the crowning of King Momo (the Fat One), who receives a giant key from the mayor. That's the signal for the city to go carnival-crazy and a host of activities involving euphoric excess to erupt – with street bands stopping traffic, endless parties, dancing, singing and costumed fun-seekers crowding squares and bars.

Despite that wild revelry the event's true heart may be found at the Sambodromo (Sambadrome). This purpose-built new venue is where 70,000 enchanted spectators gather to watch the fiercely competitive Samba Parade – an extraordinary contest between samba schools that is unique to Rio Carnival and makes it so special. Tickets are not cheap, but demand still exceeds supply on key nights (Sunday and Monday); so early booking is advisable for those who wish to see the finest schools.

Each samba school is an organized group of up to 5,000 performers who create a meticulously choreographed parade; pre-planning and rehearsals begin many months before carnival. Each school chooses an imaginative theme and communicates its vision to the audience by means of richly decorated floats, brilliant costumes and specially written samba tunes. The action starts in the early evening and a memorable show continues until dawn. It's an old cliché but, when it comes to the pulsating Carnival in Rio, seeing really is believing.

Salvador Carnival

The city of Salvador on Brazil's northeast coast is notable for culture and fine cuisine. It's also known as 'The Capital of Happiness' because the famously easygoing inhabitants can't resist a party . . . and the best party of all is the annual carnival. Unlike Rio Carnival, which is built around the spectacular formal performances of the samba schools, Salvador's riotous version is entirely unscripted, though equally eye-catching.

Actually, that's not quite true as there are thousands of practised performers who parade around three circuits in the days following the crowning of Rei Momo, the Carnival King, on the Thursday before the start of Lent. Armed with deafening sound systems, long *trios elétricos* (huge trucks) proceed slowly through streets, avenues and squares, each carrying scantily-clad dancers and a trio that blasts out Salvador's favourite sounds. They are supported by dazzling carnival floats and colourfully costumed marching bands.

The three circuits are the Campo Grande circuit, the ocean-side Barra-Ondina circuit and the Pelourinho circuit. There are *camarotes* (temporary grandstands) on each for those who simply want to watch the pageant go by . . . but the real action is down on the tarmac or road-side beaches, where uniformed *blocos* (groups of hyped-up fans) pack tightly around their favourites, whilst outside the *cordão* (security cordon) thousands more press in. And what crowds! It is estimated that some two million people attend carnival, with local revellers joined by nationwide incomers and foreign visitors galore.

To reinforce carnival's informal character, the city is full of *barraccas* (venues offering non-stop entertainment, food and drink), turning Salvador into a city of pulsating six-day parties – literally thousands of them. If you dreamed of getting into *Guinness World Records* it's easy – join the world's biggest street party. And that's official!

Salvador offers the world's biggest street party.

WHEN:
Normally in February, occasionally early March
WHERE:
Salvador, Bahia
BEST FOR:
Uninhibited frolic and fun, Brazilian style
YOU SHOULD KNOW:
Beware of overdosing on *batidas* – these tempting fruit-juice cocktails may seem to be the ideal way to slake that healthy carnival thirst, but they invariably contain a generous measure of *cachaça* (sugar-cane spirit) and pack a lethal punch.

81

Boi Bumbá

This festival combines tribal ritual, an amazing theatrical and musical extravaganza, religious procession and the sort of epic public celebration for which Brazil is famous. As with the Rio Carnival, this event in the River Amazon's island city of Parintins involves highly skilled teams recounting a traditional tale for an enraptured audience that follows every nuance. Unlike Rio's samba schools, who choose their own themes, the *bois* performers of Parintins use the same story – that of Boi Bumbá.

This tells of Pai Francisco, who kills a harsh master's favourite ox to satisfy his pregnant wife's craving for ox-tongue. A priest and doctor fail to revive the beast, leaving Pai facing prison . . . until a *pajé* (shaman) performs a ritual that brings the ox back to life, providing the perfect excuse for a party to hail rebirth and life.

Competition between teams is fierce. Each *boi* (there are two – Caprichoso and Garantido) has its *galeras* – fanatical supporters who cheer every intricate move and watch the opposition in stony silence. The Bumbódromo where nightly performances take place is divided into opposing halves and the interactive contribution of each set of *galeras* is taken into account by the jury and plays an important part in determining the winning *boi*.

The festival presents the best of performance folk art, telling this symbolic tale in music and dance with the help of fabulous costumes, parade carts, giant puppets and a narrator who explains every move. The *bois* do battle over three nights – giving six magnificent performances, though no two are ever the same, with dances, rituals, puppets and costumes changing each time. Announcement of the winning *boi* leaves half the city in ecstasy and the other half in despair . . . until the prolonged party that ensues engulfs friend, foe and visitor alike.

A spectacular procession impresses the crowd during Boi Bumbá.

WHEN:
Late June
WHERE:
Parintins, Tupinambarana Island, Amazonas
BEST FOR:
Being one of the *bois*
YOU SHOULD KNOW:
The depth of passion aroused by tribal rivalry between supporters of each *boi* may be judged by the fact that most houses in Parintins are painted in colours representing one or other of the *bois*.

Círio de Nazaré

The port city of Belém in northern Brazil is built on islands in the Pará River, part of the Amazon system. It's a steamy place, with a humid equatorial climate and high rainfall. But at least the great 15-day festival of Círio de Nazaré takes place outside the rainy season.

The highlight comes on the second Sunday in October when there is a huge procession, preceded on the Saturday by Romaria Fluvial, when an effigy of the Virgin of Nazaré is brought from Vila de Icoaraci across the water to Belém's waterfront, accompanied by hundreds of boats. From there, the Virgin is taken to the Igreja de Sé (Metropolitan Cathedral). She is accompanied on her travels by a small band of followers, but the story is very different the next day.

For on Sunday the saint is conducted around the city by a vast company of devout pilgrims, carried on a flower-strewn *berlinda* (litter) during a stately five-hour progression to the Basílica de Nazaré, where she subsequently lies in state for two weeks as an endless line of devotees file by. She is followed by floats carrying worshippers, clergy and children dressed as angels. As it proceeds, the litter is surrounded by barefooted men and women who hold a rope symbolizing the link between the Blessed Virgin and her people. Despite this honour guard, people crowd in hoping to touch the Virgin and vie for the privilege of carrying the litter.

It is an uplifting experience which creates a sense of well-being amongst the legion of participants. This soon translates into high spirits and there's a collective decision to have some fun, Brazilian style – so the day invariable ends in music and dancing, with the revelry continuing during the Virgin's lying in state. The festival's eventual conclusion is marked by another parade and a firework display.

WHEN:
October
WHERE:
Belém, Pará
BEST FOR:
Stupendous religious spectacle without commercial trimmings
YOU SHOULD KNOW:
This is almost certainly the world's largest celebration honouring the Virgin Mary, attracting up to two million pilgrims each year.

The Círio de Nazaré is the largest Catholic festival in Brazil and has been celebrated for over 200 years.

Iemanjá in Olinda

WHEN:
December
WHERE:
Olinda, Pernambuco
BEST FOR:
That unique Brazilian mix of complex religious festival and lively fiesta
YOU SHOULD KNOW:
There is a similar event in Salvador, down the coast. It takes place in early February when there is a procession to the mouth of the Red River where the image of Iemanjá and offerings are set adrift in All Saints Bay.

Floral offerings pay tribute to Iemanjá.

The beautiful city of Olinda on Brazil's northeastern Atlantic Coast not only occupies a stunning location, but also serves as a magnificent monument to the country's past, with some of the best-preserved colonial buildings in South America (now a UNESCO World Heritage Site). In common with most Brazilian cities and towns, Olinda has a carnival – in this case a lively street festival. There is also a Holy Week with numerous religious processions after Lent, collective Christmas celebrations take place and there is a wonderful firework party on the beach to greet New Year.

But Olinda has one special event that is very different. The Iemanjá ceremony is a local festival that plays tribute to Orixá, a spirit that reflects one of the manifestations of God in the Yoruba spiritual system brought to South America by slaves. Their Yemanja has become Brazil's Iemanjá – the Mistress of Earth and Heavens, a goddess who personifies

84

the sea, motherhood and the protection of children. A street procession known as The Blue Walk is a cortege that transports the figure of Iemanjá down steep cobbled streets on an allegorical vehicle, accompanied by her Holy Sons, solemn white-garbed acolytes and a crowd of thousands. When the procession finally reaches the sea, a Pot of Offerings is reverently deposited into the water.

Amidst all the jollity to be found at Brazil's innumerable fiestas, Iemanjá serves as a moving reminder that this is a country that has seamlessly blended the beliefs and traditions of indigenous peoples and slaves imported from Africa with the Catholic doctrine of the Portuguese colonial masters – in a devout country where the unique religious festivals that result still play an important part in national life.

Festival of Kings

The Folia de Reis (Festival of Kings) maintains a tradition that came to Brazil from Portugal in the mid 17th century. There, this religious festival became a secular event allowing people to let down their hair and have fun after Christmas, but the Brazilian version has remained a religious celebration preserving a precious ritual that has travelled down many generations through oral tradition, especially in country areas.

Between Christmas Eve and Epiphany, groups of musicians and singers perform in towns, villages, farms and at isolated homesteads. They carry flags bearing images of the Three Kings and Holy Family, giving thanks for the birth of Jesus. Along the way, they collect food and money for charitable purposes in return for a blessing. Group members are often low-income workers, who are nonetheless skilled performers.

They dramatize the birth of Christ, recounting tales of Balthazar, Gaspar and Melchior's visit to baby Jesus, guided by the Star of Bethlehem, and telling of the gifts borne by these wise men. They also follow the Three Kings of the East back to their homeland and describe the Flight to Egypt. Characters are brought to life, like the Three Kings themselves (boys), Shepherds (girls), Angels (girls) and Patience (boys). Clowns in animal-skin masks distract Herod's soldiers, provide light relief and collect offerings. The whole show is accompanied by the playing of drums, tambourines, cow bells and cavaquinhos (small guitars). The structure of a genuine group is highly formalized and its conduct must follow a well-established set of rules.

These soulful performances are at the opposite end of the spectrum from Brazil's lively street carnivals, showing another, more spiritual side of the country's culture. To see the Folia de Reis at its most authentic, it's worth visiting the vast rural state of Minas Gerais in southeastern Brazil.

WHEN:
December 24 to January 6
WHERE:
All over Brazil (but mainly in small backwoods communities)
BEST FOR:
A spiritual journey in song
YOU SHOULD KNOW:
The Folia de Reis varies considerably from region to region, depending on local custom and the preferences of its all-powerful master (leader) of the troupe – but the Three Kings always remain central to the performance.

85

SOUTH AMERICA/BOLIVIA

Fiesta de la Virgen de la Candelaria

WHEN:
February 2-5
WHERE:
Copacabana, La Paz Department
BEST FOR:
The extraordinary Basilica with its soaring Baroque altarpiece containing the venerated dark-wood statue of the Virgin – below her a silver ship representing the moon, above her a gold statue symbolizing the power of the sun. There is also a fascinating museum.
YOU SHOULD KNOW:
Rio de Janeiro's famous Copacabana Beach was named in honour of the Dark Virgin of the Lake after she miraculously saved some Brazilian fishermen.

The Festival of the Virgin of Candelaria is celebrated in several South American countries, including Chile, Peru, Uruguay and Venezuela. But nowhere does it have more significance than Bolivia – for the Virgin is the country's revered patroness. She is also known as the Dark Virgin of the Lake or Our Lady of Copacabana. This revered icon attracts pilgrims to the important lakeside town of Copacabana from all over Bolivia and Peru, with high points at Easter and during Bolivian independence celebrations in August – but her dedicated event takes place in February each year.

Supplicants gather as the festival approaches, praying to the Virgin using a unique mixture of native and Catholic beliefs. Her statue is said to have been sculpted by Inca craftsman Tito Yupanqui in 1576 after some local fishermen were caught in a terrible storm on Lake Titicaca, whereupon the Virgin appeared and led them to safety – the first of many miracles with which she is credited.

As the festival proper begins, the Virgin herself is confined to the magnificent white Basilica, as local superstition has it that calamity will ensue if she's taken outside. But a finely dressed replica is allowed to parade through the town and many thousands of celebrants don colourful costumes, jam the streets and enjoy extended bouts of singing, dancing and feasting – everything a joyous festival should be.

New vehicles are brought to Copacabana from all over Bolivia to be garlanded with flowers and receive an elaborate *cha'lla* (blessing) in the name of the Virgin . . . before being anointed with beer and launched into a hopefully safer working life. Another popular activity is burning incense and purchasing tiny replicas of coveted material possessions, in the hope that the Virgin will grant the real thing in the year ahead.

Celebrants accompany a replica of the Virgin in a colourful parade.

Tinku Festival

Aymara Indian women fight one another at the Tinku Festival.

Old traditions die hard in South America, where pre-Hispanic rituals remain ingrained. Nowhere is this better demonstrated than at the annual Tinku Festival when thousands of indigenous Bolivian Quechuas trek to the remote town of Macha with one objective . . . to engage in combat. Nobody fights to the death any more though sometimes accidental death still results, deemed a price well worth paying for additional benefits that are likely to accrue from the ultimate sacrifice. But everything still gets pretty violent and blood must be spilt for the ritual to have meaning. There's no discrimination – after much chanting and ceremonial dancing men fight men, women fight women and community fights community. Many participants still wear colourful hats modelled on the helmets of Spanish conquistadors – folk memories are long in these parts.

The word *tinku* translates as 'encounter'. The purpose of the rite is to release tensions, allowing scores to be settled and disputes to be resolved whilst also making a blood offering to the Earth Goddess, Pachamama, in an attempt to ensure that she will deliver a good harvest in the forthcoming year. This is a vital aspiration for people who rely on a subsistence economy for survival.

Inevitably, the existence of such an event finally came to the attention of the outside world, and it is now a spectacle that attracts backpackers, filmmakers and adventurous tourists bold enough to make the trek up into the remote Bolivian Andes. The advent of tourism has resulted in a dilution of the very festival they come to see, with numerous policemen on hand to ensure that fighting never gets out of hand (a tear-gas grenade tends to restore order if a riot threatens). The extraordinary Tinku Festival is fascinating, but not for the faint-hearted.

WHEN:
May
WHERE:
Macha, Potosi Department
BEST FOR:
Observing (but not joining in) ancient local customs that have resisted the march of time
YOU SHOULD KNOW:
Participants are not always happy to be the focus of attention from outsiders – at best simply looking surly or demanding money to be photographed, at worst taking a swing at anyone deemed too intrusive.

A portrayal of Christ is paraded through the streets of Cusco.

Semana Santa

For the devout people of the Andes, Semana Santa (Easter Week) represents the pinnacle of their faith and generates intense religious sentiment. Although this special time is celebrated all over Peru, nowhere is this holy week greeted with more fervour than in the Ayacucho Region. Here, in towns and villages high in the Andes, one of the world's most significant collective portrayals of the passion, death and resurrection of Christ takes place.

The most famous Semana Santa event takes place in Ayacucho and involves the whole town in an extended celebration. On the Friday before Palm Sunday the meeting of Christ and his mother, the Virgen Dolorosa, is re-enacted. On Palm Sunday Christ enters Ayacucho on a donkey and festive palm fronds are waved as excitement starts to build up. There are various processions each day and evening during the following week, in which participants seek to display their undying devotion. Good Friday itself is occupied with solemn rites during which sadness at the death of Christ leads to an outpouring of grief.

But this is also an affirmation of life, and on Saturday the atmosphere changes dramatically. It is a traditionally held belief that while Christ is dead and not yet risen, there is no such thing as sin – the perfect rationale for a party, which duly ensues. A large all-day market is held, catering for every need. Music plays while people dance, drink, feast, chew coca leaves and generally have fun. Anything goes!

On Easter Sunday sanity returns, along with solemnity. Religious rituals resume, building up steadily to a joyous celebration of Christ's resurrection. This comes to a climax with an extraordinary amalgam of prayer, music, song and fireworks lasting far into the night, until Semana Santa is finally over for another year.

WHEN:
Easter Week
WHERE:
Ayacucho, Huamanga Province, Ayacucho Region
BEST FOR:
A truly spiritual experience
YOU SHOULD KNOW:
A large number of visitors come to share Ayacucho's Semana Santa celebrations and accommodation is limited – so if you wish to join them it's wise to book accommodation well in advance.

Inti Raymi

Some traditions in South America managed to survive the arrival of Spanish conquerors and their imposed faith. One such is Inti Raymi, though in truth this moving event has been re-orchestrated in modern times to ensure that it reflects Inca ritual of times long past, when such pagan activities were banned by the Spaniards and the festival went underground.

This revived survivor is a celebration of the Southern Hemisphere's winter solstice and the Sun God Inti, rendering homage to the all-powerful giver of life and offering prayer for a good harvest. The event's enduring appeal may be judged by the fact that it has become one of the largest festivals in South America, attracting hundreds of thousands to the city of Cusco for a week-long jolly that sees music and dancing in overflowing streets.

The main event takes place on June 24 when hundreds of players act out a day-long ceremony before a vast crowd. It begins in front of the church of Santo Domingo, built over the ancient Temple of the Sun. The Sapa Inca calls for a blessing from the Sun, before being carried with his wife Mama Occla to the old fortress of Sacsayhuamán as part of an elaborate costume procession along flower-decked streets swept clear of evil spirits. Once there, the Sapa Inca makes a speech, as do the Snake (for the devils below), the Puma (life on earth) and the Condor (the gods above). A white llama is sacrificed to ensure fertility and a bountiful crop – bloodstains being read to foretell the future.

As dusk falls stacks of straw are set ablaze and dancers honour the Empire of the Four Wind Directions, before the procession returns to Cusco and the people are blessed at the start of a new year.

WHEN:
June 24
WHERE:
Cusco, Cusco Province, Cusco Region.
BEST FOR:
Ancient ritual
YOU SHOULD KNOW:
The sacrifice of the white llama and holding aloft of its bloody heart by the high priest are – despite appearances to the contrary – an extremely realistic simulation. No animals are harmed during the making of this particular production number!

Men in traditional dress perform during the Inca winter solstice festival.

Virgen del Rosario Festival

WHEN:
End of September and early October
WHERE:
Cajabamba, Cajabamba Province,
Cajamarca Region
BEST FOR:
The extraordinary Devils' Dance
YOU SHOULD KNOW:
There are other well-known
celebrations dedicated to the
Virgin of Rosario at Cajatambo in
Lima Province and all over the
large Ancash Province in the
northern Andes.

The Dominican Order was in charge of the slave brotherhoods during the colonial era, and this work seems to have attracted the approval of the Virgen del Rosario (Virgin of the Rosary) – for she was the order's patron saint and her worship in these parts dates back to 1536. Today, the Virgin's association with the former slave population is acknowledged when her image is accompanied by an icon consisting of a letter S attached by a nail, symbolizing the plight of Peru's black slaves.

The Virgin is also the patron saint of Cajabamba and this pleasant mountain town with its old-fashioned atmosphere pays tribute during a ten-day celebration that sees the place come alive with locals in regional costume, displays of handicrafts like ceramics and textiles, music, folk dancing competitions, fireworks, visiting bands, bullfighting, markets offering the best of local food and general carousing. The climax of this lively event always comes on the first Sunday of October, with festivities centred on a solemn mass in the Church of St Nicholas Tolentino followed by a procession through the streets (first held in 1668). The day's highlight is the famous Danza de los Diablos (Devils' Dance) centred on the Plaza de Armas.

This ancient tradition has its roots way back in 13th century Hispanic culture, where the characters first appeared at the religious feast of Corpus Christi to represent the ugliness of mankind compared to God. In Cajabamba, the dance is dedicated to the Virgen del Rosario by men making an act of devotion and seeking symbolic forgiveness for human sin. They dance in pairs wearing monstrous masks, fringed costumes, tights and white gloves, carrying a plaited leather whip, sword and bouquets of carnations and roses.

La Diablada

WHEN:
The first week of November
WHERE:
Puno, Puno Province, Puno Region
BEST FOR:
More devilish antics
YOU SHOULD KNOW:
If you don't want to stand out from the crowd, wear red – it's definitely the colour of choice at La Diablada.

On the banks of Lake Titicaca in Peru, the annual La Diablada festival at Puno appears to be a celebration of the devil incarnate, with satanic costumes everywhere and people dancing in the streets as if possessed. But worry not, there's no devil worship afoot in this attractive lakeside city, just thousands of locals having a thoroughly good time for a riotous week in November.

Admittedly, their idea of a good time is rather bizarre, and the origins of La Diablada are somewhat obscure. Is it joyous acknowledgement of freedom gained from Spanish colonial masters in the 19th century; perhaps some primitive instinct to honour the

A child folk dancer – or is it a little devil?

gods of the lake; or maybe the folk memory of trapped miners who were being transported to the fires of hell by an army of demons until they appealed to the Blessed Virgin of Candelaria and were rescued? Nobody is quite sure – but there can be no doubt that the ensuing carnival is most impressive.

After several days of serious preparatory revelling (round up the usual ingredients – music, dancing, drinking and feasting), it all comes to a spectacular head on November 5 with a fabulous parade. The local version of the devil leads the cavalcade, in a stunningly rich outfit, followed by capering townsfolk in monstrous costumes. This frantic Danza la diablada (Diablo dance) is very much part of the event, and also an essential part of Puno's great Feast of the Virgin of Candelaria at the beginning of February. It's perhaps not surprising that Puno hosts two such extraordinary events – the place rejoices in the title of Capital folklorica del Peru y Sud America (The folklore capital of Peru and South America) and certainly lives up to its billing.

Fiesta de la Patria Gaucha

Argentina may have a higher profile when it comes to the raising of beef cattle and cultural awareness of the gauchos who look after them, but in truth this macho rural industry is equally important – and well respected – in Uruguay. The annual Fiesta de la Patria Gaucha (Festival of Gaucho Culture) reflects the fact. Held in the northern part of the country in March, it is one of the biggest such events in South America and lasts for around five days.

As the festival gathers pace over 3,000 horses and their riders congregate in Tacuarembó to honour 'the soul of the gaucho'. This influx serves as a powerful magnet both for country people in traditional garb who travel in from a wide area and interested visitors who journey from all parts of Uruguay and beyond to experience the unique festival atmosphere. The town comes alive with costume parades and becomes the scene of endless rodeos and other competitions designed to challenge the legendary abilities of the proud gauchos and their horses. These include gaucho-style dressage (no black coats and top hats!), bareback riding and lassoing events. There are also demonstrations of equestrian skills, often with adept riders as young as five or as old as 80 performing tricks like riding backwards, to appreciative applause.

As darkness falls, the night fills with the sound of music, folk tales or poetry being recited and the delicious aroma of the finest organically produced meat cooking in numerous *parrillas* (barbecue pits) and on large racks. Although this is a festival built around cowboys and their way of life, it represents much more than that, here as in Argentina. For the Fiesta de la Patria Gaucha is a heart-felt tribute to a traditional rural life that is deeply embedded in the national psyche.

A gaucho is unseated by an unbroken horse during the Fiesta de la Patria Gaucha.

WHEN:
Early March
WHERE:
Tacuarembó, Tacuarembó
Department
BEST FOR:
Local colour and tradition . . .
including superb barbecued beef
YOU SHOULD KNOW:
Many of the fiesta's main events are
held on the shores of Tacuarembó's
Laguna de las Lavanderas
(Laundrywomen's Lake) – and
sometimes in it.

Jan/Feb/**March**/April/May/June/July/Aug/Sept/Oct/Nov/Dec

Quema de Judas

WHEN:
Easter Sunday
WHERE:
All over Venezuela
BEST FOR:
Banishing the blues with a bang
YOU SHOULD KNOW:
Legend has it that the first 'Judas'
was burned around the year 1500
when the effigy represented the
Italian explorer Amerigo Vespucci,
after he arrived on his first voyage to
South America and attempted to
trade with the natives, before sailing
away and never returning.

As in many Catholic countries in South America and beyond, the treacherous apostle Judas Iscariot continues to pay a heavy price for his 30 pieces of silver – as year after year on Easter Sunday the Quema de Judas (Burning of Judas) ceremony sees his effigy hanged and burned by the jeering mob. This is very much an occasion when devout believers hope to achieve a specific purpose by following the ancient ritual – cremating negative feelings like anger, resentment or envy along with the symbolic representation of Judas and hopefully ending bickering within the community and uniting everyone around dislike of a common enemy.

But of course Venezuelans will seize any excuse for a good knees-up so Quema de Judas also provides a great excuse for general merrymaking at this sad-happy time of year. It is very much a local event that – whilst no longer as common as once it was – remains an important part of Venezuelan folk tradition and may be found anywhere in the country, from remote country village to deprived shanty town. The Judas effigy must always be as grotesque as possible; it's often crafted to resemble a suitable hate figure like an unpopular politician or harsh landlord and is always stuffed with fireworks – so the final conflagration is always an explosive affair. But this is delayed until the unfortunate miscreant has been dragged through the streets as a salutary reminder of the wages of sin.

At one recent Quema de Judas event in Caracas the bad guy was dressed up as 'Mister Exxon', complete with slick hair, pink face, snappy suit and aviator dark glasses, after the oil giant lost a legal battle over disputed revenues with the Venezuelan government – that particular Easter ritual must have ended in quite a blaze!

Los Diablos Danzantes

WHEN:
May/June
WHERE:
San Francisco de Yare, Miranda State
BEST FOR:
Authentic Venezuelan culture at its
most uninhibited
YOU SHOULD KNOW:
When exactly? Corpus Christi is on
the Thursday following Trinity Sunday
which is the first Sunday after
Pentecost which is the 49th day
(or 50th, inclusively) after Easter
Sunday. Simple!

The feast of Corpus Christi (Body of Christ) honours the Eucharist (Holy Communion) and as such does not celebrate any particular event in the life of Jesus – but that doesn't stop it being celebrated. Indeed, it is one of Venezuela's biggest festivals, where Catholic doctrine and African traditions combine to create an extraordinary occasion. Originating in Spain and embroidered by African slaves, one of its most spectacular manifestations involves Los Diablos Danzantes (Dancing Devils) who strut their stuff before churches, in town squares and on streets all over Venezuela during the eve and day of Corpus Christi.

There are notable performances everywhere in the country, but one of the best outings of the Dancing Devils may be seen in the sleepy colonial town of San Francisco de Yare, southeast of Caracas.

Appearances can be deceptive – Los Diablos Danzantes have been active here since 1742 and the locals prepare for months ahead of each renewal. At festival time they are joined by thousands of visitors, with residents and incomers alike bent on enjoying frenzied revelry.

After carousing in the streets on Corpus Christi Eve, the Devils proceed to El Calvario (Stations of the Cross) for an all-night vigil. The following morning they pay their respects at the cemetery before performing a joyful pageant in the church square. A procession brings the bishop, and mass is held. Dancers are blessed, junior devils inducted and an afternoon of whirling dancing concludes back at El Calvario.

The profane Devil Dancing symbolizes the eternal struggle between good and evil. The former eventually triumphs as the Devil Dancers submit themselves to the Eucharist at church. The exercise has strong echoes of pagan ritual and is thought to ensure an abundant harvest, prosperity and general wellbeing, also offering protection against natural disasters. It's an impressive way of asking!

One of the many masks worn by the Dancing Devils.

Barranquilla Carnival

WHEN:
Normally in February, occasionally early March
WHERE:
Barranquilla, Atálantico Department
BEST FOR:
Carnival excess as it's meant to be
YOU SHOULD KNOW:
Visitors to Barranquilla Carnival experience 'A Masterpiece of the Oral and Intangible Heritage of Humanity' (that's UNESCO's rather long-winded way of awarding Five Stars for Fun).

This is Colombia's spirited entry in the extensive lexicon of South American carnivals that explode to life in the run-up to the beginning of Lent on Ash Wednesday. And what an entry – for the Carnaval de Barranquilla is one of the world's largest fiestas. Although outdone by Rio Carnival in terms of sheer size, the Barranquilla Carnival is recognized as taking the top prize for being less commercial and more authentic than its Brazilian counterpart. Throughout four days of feast and frolic that build up with true Caribbean spontaneity to the final splurge on Fat Tuesday, the city is gridlocked as street dances, marching bands and masquerades bring traffic to a standstill.

Many types of Colombian music are performed, especially *cumbia*, and the atmospheric sound of drums and wind instruments is to be heard at every corner. Dances like the indigenous *mico y micas*, the African congo and Spanish *paloteo* are but three among many styles on display, whilst colourful costumes are everywhere – often adorning masked revellers who criss-cross the city engaging in *la burla* (poking of fun). Larger-than-life puppets make stately progress with red-nose clowns capering about. Popular comedy performances maintain the carnival's oral traditions, whilst folkloric theatre and local choirs all add to the extraordinary atmosphere that infuses the city.

Highlights include the coronation of Rey Momo (Clown King) and Carnival Queen of Queens, a beauty pageant, Battle of Flowers (on Saturday) and a Grand Parade (on Sunday). Official processions use a rather run-down avenue in the port area, but the floats often proceed to the town centre where the locals really cut loose – spray foam, party poppers and flying flour are constant hazards as excitement reaches fever pitch. There can be no argument – Barranquilla Carnival truly is the people's festival.

The carnival marches through the streets of Barranquilla.

Día del Descubrimiento de Dos Mundos

The day that Christopher Columbus arrived as the first documented European to reach the New World was celebrated throughout the Americas as the Día de la Raza (Day of the Race). It is of fairly recent origin, becoming established throughout Latin America in the 1920s as an attempt to commemorate the Spanish community's establishment and stress its continuing importance – especially in face of the USA's growing strength and influence.

But over time that aspect faded and Día de la Raza became an affirmation of the distinctive culture that evolved as Hispanic influence melded with the practices of indigenous peoples, African slaves and successive waves of assorted immigrants. In keeping with the change of emphasis away from Spanish exclusivity there were moves to rename Chile's public holiday on October 12 – altering Día de la Raza to something more appropriate like Día de la Resistencia Indígena (Day of Indigenous Resistance, Venezuela's change) or Día de la Diversidad Cultural Americana (Day of Diverse American Culture, Argentina's new version). In the end, Chile's choice was Día del Descubrimiento de Dos Mundos (Discovery of Two Worlds Day). That said, the old name is still widely used by traditionalists.

Whatever the name, the celebration's the same – a fiesta of local culture with music and parades through cities, towns and villages throughout the country. The main event in Santiago sees colourful processions with revellers in traditional costumes, marching bands, dancing, much flag-waving and symbolic historical re-enactments in churches and impromptu venues – it's all tremendous fun with everyone, including enthusiastically performing children, taking part. To outsiders it may seem like one of many typical South American fiestas, but to the locals it is a true celebration of their unique heritage – the process of *mestije*, the mingling of races that created the population of today.

WHEN:
October 12
(or on the nearest Monday)
WHERE:
Santiago
BEST FOR:
An awesome display of
South American pride
YOU SHOULD KNOW:
In English-speaking countries
(notably the USA) October 12 is
known more prosaically as Columbus
Day, which simply celebrates the
discovery of the Western Hemisphere
. . . and all that followed.

97

Fiesta de la Cultura

WHEN:
Late December
WHERE:
Valparaiso
BEST FOR:
Highbrow entertainment
YOU SHOULD KNOW:
Valparaiso is renowned for its vibrant nightlife, with a high percentage of young people and many clubs, bars and restaurants that remain 'open all hours'.

The important seaport of Valparaiso clings to over 40 steep hillsides overlooking the Pacific Ocean and with its labyrinth of streets and cobbled alleys the historic quarter is a UNESCO World Heritage Site. This rapidly regenerating city is known as 'The Jewel of the Pacific' and has become a significant political and cultural centre, housing Chile's National Congress and recently officially named as the country's Capital of Culture. This newly minted reputation is underlined by the presence of Chile's new Ministry of Culture and annual festivals galore – of song, Chilean music, film and the major Fiesta de la Cultura (Cultural Festival) after Christmas.

The latter was established as recently as 2001 to support Valparaiso's successful bid for World Heritage status, but already draws large and enthusiastic crowds, playing an important role in Chile's relatively recent drive to preserve and enhance the nation's cultural life. But in that context the Cultural Festival is less about celebrating local traditions than promoting international status.

Each year, a different country is selected as the festival's focal point and a programme is built around the chosen national theme. This lively end-of-year 'culturefest' sees the city buzzing with diverse action, with a flurry of events covering a wide spectrum of the arts. There are gallery exhibitions, music concerts, theatrical performances, literature readings in bars and cafés, film shows . . . even gastronomic fairs.

Both the Cultural Festival and Valparaiso's year come to an explosive climax on December 31 with a spectacular fireworks display beside the sea, watched by over a million people who pack the shoreline, hillsides surrounding the bay and boats on the water. Not a bad turnout for a city with a population of around 250,000 people!

Fiesta de la Mama Negra

The Mama Negra herself is a symbol of Ecuador's most extraordinary cultural event. The 'Black Mother' is a combination of the Virgin Mary with African deities, reflecting the local version of Catholicism. Conquering Spaniards imposed their religion upon arriving to exploit rich mineral resources, but it was modified by a continuing native belief in spirits – and subsequently other indigenous ideas as slave workers were imported from elsewhere in South America and Africa. The Fiesta de la Mama Negra is therefore a melting pot that combines differing traditions – Spanish, Mayan, Aymaran, Incan and African. Oh, and it provides an ideal opportunity for some thoroughly uninhibited revelry.

The thriving market town of Latacunga lets its hair down with parades featuring all sorts of colourful characters that underline the event's diverse roots – such as the Moorish King, Angel of the Stars, Camisonas (gaudy transvestites) and Los Huacos (representing pre-Colombian heritage), Spanish Conquistadors and white-masked Spirits. It's all held together by endless clowns, costumed dancers, musicians and marching bands, together creating a splendid spectacle as the crowds sway rhythmically and consume alcohol as though it's going out of fashion.

Large quantities of the local delicacy are eaten during the celebrations – *chugchucaras* consist of deep-fried pork, pork rind, potatoes, maize and plantain. Another staple is *cuy* (guinea pig) – not for the squeamish. Sweetmeats and containers of wine are thrown to spectators as the processions pass by.

The highlight of the fiesta sees the Mama Negra arrive on horseback, bearing dolls representing her children. Don't get too close – she squirts milk and water over the crowd from a capacious 'breast' *en passant*. Worse still, the capering clowns are liable to spray mouthfuls of raw alcohol over unwary spectators without warning. Last but not least, there's the inevitable display of spectacular pyrotechnics.

WHEN:
Officially September 23-24
(but can vary slightly)
WHERE:
Latacunga
BEST FOR:
Local culture – with bells, whistles and fireworks
YOU SHOULD KNOW:
The official title of the fiesta is the Festival de la Madonna de la Merced, in recognition of the Merciful Virgin's role in saving Latacunga when the nearby Cotapaxi volcano erupted violently in 1742.

The 'Black Mother' rides through the streets of Latacunga.

AFRICA

Abu Simbel Festival

WHEN:
February 22 and October 22
WHERE:
Abu Simbel
BEST FOR:
Ancient science and crowds
YOU SHOULD KNOW:
The sun lights the statues of Ramses, Amun-Re and Re-Herakhte but does not reach Ptah, 'the hidden one', the god of darkness.

More than 3,000 years ago, the great pharaoh Ramses II marked the southern extent of his kingdom with four rock-hewn *colossi* – portraits of himself – to gaze sternly at travellers entering Egypt at Abu Simbel. He also had temples cut into the cliffs: one as a monument to his favourite wife Nefertari and the other, the great Sun Temple, essentially as a monument to himself. Not until the 19th century did archaeologists finally manage to shift the sands of time that had drowned the site. In the 1960s the waters of Lake Nasser, rising behind the Assam dam, threatened Abu Simbel and UNESCO led a daring rescue operation – sandstone was stabilized, the temples were literally cut out in huge blocks and then re-inserted into a newly built mountain.

Abu Simbel is now one of Egypt's most spectacular sites. Past the façade with its 20-m (65-ft) figures, the Hypostyle Hall is carved and painted with detailed scenes of Ramses' achievements. The Sanctuary, deep inside the mountain, houses four statues, once cased in gold, which wait for the sun. So sophisticated were ancient Egyptian scientists and engineers that the temple was aligned to allow the rising sun to reach the Sanctuary on just two days each year: February 21 and October 21. These dates – the birthday and coronation of Ramses and also the days when the passage of the sun marks spring and autumn – changed by one day with the relocation of the temple.

The little town of Abu Simbel celebrates the biannual festival with music, dance and feasting. Visitors must travel by night, and thousands arrive in darkness at about 03.00 for the event. A lucky few enter the temple but the majority watch on a screen outside for the moment when the pale sunlight finally illuminates the statues of the deities.

Dancers perform outside the Great Temple of Ramses II.

Moulid of Abu El Haggag

Egyptian *moulids* (birthdays) are lively affairs. They often celebrate a holy man, but reverence is combined with much revelry. The streets are packed with funfair rides, food stalls and sideshows, and the residents – dressed up to the nines – watch the noisy processions. In the evenings, *zikrs* (remembrances) are held; long lines of Sufi followers sway and chant to rhythmic clapping, which may continue for hours. In Luxor, the *moulid* of Abu el Haggag is held in honour of the town's 12th century patron sheikh, whose mosque is built into a corner of Luxor Temple.

This big, boisterous celebration lasts for five days and includes traditional stick fights and some very wild horse races. Riders may join the cavalcade, along with decorated camels and *calèches*. Parades in Luxor include a large boat, sometimes linked with the solar barque procession of Pharonic times. Other floats represent the sheikh himself, and the town's trade guilds; live or canned music accompanies each. Into the pandemonium of the parade weave the sounds of itinerant preachers, the ever more frenzied chants from the *zikr*, the laughter and shrieks of children in party hats with ear-splitting whistles, and exploding fire-crackers.

For tourists, dizzied by the scale and extent of the remains of ancient Thebes, the Moulid is an extraordinary experience. Outsiders (who should dress conservatively) are welcomed at an occasion which shows visitors that there is life outside ancient Egypt and allows them a chance to experience the vibrant culture, beliefs and traditions of the people who live in this, the 'world's greatest open-air museum'.

Crowds gather for the birthday celebration.

WHEN:
Two weeks before Ramadan. The Islamic calendar is lunar-based and Ramadan begins 11 days earlier each Western year.
WHERE:
Luxor
BEST FOR:
Egyptian popular culture
YOU SHOULD KNOW:
Holiday companies often herd visitors around the sights and direct them to 'tourist friendly' shops. *Moulids* (there are several smaller ones in the area) are also well worth visiting.

Ghadames Festival

WHEN:
Usually three days in mid October
WHERE:
Ghadames, 640 km (400 mi)
southwest of Tripoli
BEST FOR:
Celebrations and dates
YOU SHOULD KNOW:
The Imazighen (named Berbers by
the Romans) inhabited Libya for
centuries before the arrival of the
Arabs. Modern government policy
has encouraged integration and the
speaking of Arabic, but several
communities retain their strong
identities and traditions, including the
Ghadames Imazighen, the Berbers of
Ghadames. The Tuareg are a distinct,
though distantly related, group.

With superb, uncrowded classical sites, extraordinary landscapes and a people who, while calm and reserved, are helpful and welcoming, the vast desert country of Libya has many attractions. Near the borders with Tunisia and Algeria, on a well-tended oasis settled since pre-history, lies the fascinating town of Ghadames, where Arabs, Berbers and Tuaregs live and work harmoniously. Its position made it an important and independent town until trade across the Sahara declined in the 19th century, and now it stands empty. In the 1980s a government modernization initiative resulted in the population moving to a purpose-built housing area (with amenities) outside the old town, though in hot weather many return to enjoy its vernacular 'air conditioning'. To ameliorate the heat, Ghadames was built with narrow covered alleyways, with gaps for light and ventilation, and built-in seats for the men to rest and chat; the roofs of the white houses are linked by terraces to allow women free movement in their domain. This lovely ghost town is now a favourite with visitors and guides are mandatory – the town is truly labyrinthine and, more importantly, the fees boost an economy based, as it has been for centuries, on dates.

The date harvest is the occasion for a festival, when the old town comes joyously to life. The first day's celebrations are centred on the new town, but on the second day householders don brilliant traditional costumes and many of the beautifully decorated houses in the old town are opened for music, feasting and the enactment of Berber ceremonies. The activities on the third day take place in the Tuareg area of town where, after more entertainments and the consumption of date-based delicacies, an evening of dancing among the dunes of the surrounding desert brings the festival to a close.

Evala Festival

The friendly people of tiny Togo believe ardently in a Supreme Being but, though Christianity and Islam are firmly established, at family altars it is the many intermediate divinities of voodoo, fetishism and animism that are worshipped. Most of the country's lively festivals mark harvests, but the most important event of the Togolese calendar is the week-long Evala Festival in the northern Kabye lands. In recent years, this event has been largely centralized from individual Kabye village ceremonies to an arena outside Kara. The town, in wonderfully festive mood, is full of music, dancing and story telling, but at the heart of Evala remain long days of fierce wrestling.

The fighters are young males and Evala is not only a sporting event but also a coming-of-age ritual that all must undertake before manhood and marriage. Initiates fight here for three years; after this they are men, and do not wrestle again. Evala is the penultimate event of the initiation rites – the last is circumcision – and comes after a week of isolation and physical and mental exercises. The Evalos, who start training as young boys, come from the entire Kabye diaspora. On the first day of wrestling, bodies slicked with talc, they fight family and neighbours; the next two days see larger and larger groups pitted against each other until, after a rest day, huge groups composed of fighters from several villages battle in front of an enormous crowd. Winners, festooned with coloured scarves, are borne aloft by supporters at the end of the fighting, though all who wrestle are initiated, and winners and losers join the rest of the community in the joyful festivities.

WHEN:
July, usually coinciding with the second Saturday of the month
WHERE:
Kara, northern Togo
BEST FOR:
Traditional wrestling
YOU SHOULD KNOW:
The Evala is followed in August by the Akpema, a festival of initiation for girls.

Men of the Kabye tribe are ready to wrestle.

Festival in the Desert

WHEN:
Three days in early January
WHERE:
Essakane, 65 km (40 mi) north
of Timbuktu
BEST FOR:
Tuareg culture, world music,
the Sahara
YOU SHOULD KNOW:
Beware the *cram cram*; the sands
are full of these tiny spiky burrs
which cling and can work their way
under the skin; avoid open sandals.

Under a vast blue sky, high white sand dunes shelter tents and an impromptu stage of spread carpets where dancers sway and chant, and musicians play to an international audience of music lovers. Later, the temperature drops and spectators move to the main stage, to be enraptured by a dazzling sequence of sounds – throbbing drums, plaintive instrumentals, hypnotic chants and tumultuous bands – under a heaven pale with stars. Around campfires, gossip and jam sessions continue late into the night.

This is the Festival in the Desert. Participants have made their way deep into the Sahara by sand road from Timbuktu. Their hosts, the Tuareg, may have ridden miles to set up camp in family and clan groups; for them this is, importantly, an old-style social and business meeting as well as a celebration of their culture. Following the 1996 'Flame of Peace', a symbolic pyre of weaponry after years of fighting in the Sahara, the festival was conceived partly as a means to re-establish the traditions of the Tuareg. Since 2001 it has been held

*Tuareg riders show off
their camels.*

at the oasis village of Essakane and has grown in scope and scale. Here, local acts perform to global audiences – the hugely popular Tinariwen 'went electric' at the 2003 event. The late, great Ali Farka Touré was an ardent supporter of the event, and stars of the Arab and African world appear alongside musicians from Europe and America – regulars who have worked with Malian musicians include Robert Plant, Markus James and Lo'Jo.

Vivid memories of the Festival in the Desert are not only of outstanding performances but of silent, camel-mounted Tuareg and the flashing smiles of unveiled women, limitless sands, flickering fires in the blackness of a desert night, and companionship.

Festival on the Niger

The lifeblood of Mali, the mighty River Niger winds through the southern fringes of the Sahara. The pleasant town of Segou, once the capital of an ancient Bambara kingdom, lies in a relatively fertile basin, greened by the symbol of the area – the *Balanzan* tree. With its wide tree-lined avenues, faded colonial buildings and river trips, Segou is a friendly, charmingly slow-paced and relaxing place – except for a week in winter when the riverbank rings with the sounds of the Festival of the Niger.

Segou and the surrounding villages take pride in their traditional arts and this festival is a spirited expression of the region's unique cultural heritage. This is, however, more than a scaled-down version of the Festival in the Desert, for each year Segou hosts a forum on a theme relevant to Malian society, offers training to promising youngsters and runs a wide range of workshops. Here, traditions are passed on, skills and knowledge exchanged. At a large fair, craftwork and traditional regional agricultural products are displayed and traded. Work by Malian and international artists is exhibited, and competitions encourage adults and children to take part in the festival.

During the week both town and riverbank – the *Quay des Arts* – are packed with performers. Local, inexperienced acts appear on the 'discovery stage' while the 'giant concerts', set against the wonderful backdrop of the Niger, feature famous Malian musicians and stars from further afield. Storytelling is an important aspect of African culture and one of the highlights of the festival is the 'Evening under the *Balanzan*', when storytellers, musicians and puppeteers bring local myths and epics to life and allow visitors a glimpse of Segou's glorious past.

WHEN:
Late January/early February
WHERE:
Segou
BEST FOR:
Malian history, traditional arts and culture
YOU SHOULD KNOW:
The Segou area is proud of *Bogolan*, a local technique of decorating fabric by painting it with mud. Workshops are offered and expert practitioners can be seen at the festival.

107

Everyone celebrates once the cattle have been herded back to Diafarabe after the floods.

Deegal – the Crossing of the Cattle Festival

In the Mopti region of Mali the Niger divides and splits, forming a huge area of small streams and rich pastures. This is the Niger Central Delta, and the little mud town of Diafarabe at its heart is home to farmers, fishermen and cattle herders. When the rains come, streams swell to raging torrents and Diafarabe, like several other communities in the Delta, becomes virtually an island for several months. Before this happens, the cattle must be moved to drier lands and the semi-nomadic Fula people drive the herds north over the still-shallow river. The floods start to abate in November, and in December herdsmen and cattle return from the parched southern Sahel. There are several cattle crossing points, but at Diafarabe the waters recede earliest and so it is here that villagers from all over the Delta gather to celebrate Deegal – a huge, exuberant party and the most important Fulani festival.

The town puts on its glad rags: people dress in their finest and the houses are beautified – doorways picked out in white paint, floors darkened and pattered with white clay, walls hung with woven hangings. Splendidly dressed young people seek marriage partners in the Promenade des Jeunes. Now the precious herds are judged – herdsmen decorate their favourite cows – and prizes are awarded for the fattest and healthiest. For some of the young men, this can also be a rite of passage: those who have gained experience away from home may be granted positions in their communities.

This is a joyful occasion for singing, dancing and merry making, but also an emotional one. After these few days with families, friends and future brides, the Fulani disperse – some back to their homes, the young men south to the newly rich grazing.

WHEN:
December, though the exact date is never set until a few days before the crossing – check with the Tourist Office in Mopti.
WHERE:
Diafarabe, 113 km (70 mi) west of Mopti
BEST FOR:
Traditional festivities
YOU SHOULD KNOW:
For the marriageable girls of Diafarabe, the Cattle Crossing is the highlight of the year. They buy special, brightly coloured seating mats, which are for the sole use of suitors when they pay calls, and make great efforts with their hair, dresses and jewellery to impress the young men.

Bissau Carnival

Guinea-Bissau is a small, low-lying country of rainforests and rivers with an indented, sandy coastline and a sheltering archipelago – the remote Bijagos islands. Like much of West Africa, a long, bitter struggle for independence and years of dictatorships and military rule left the economy in tatters. One legacy of Portuguese rule the people have embraced and made their own is the Bissau Carnival. Only a small proportion of the population is Christian, but members of the country's many distinct ethnic groups flock to the capital to represent their unique cultures at this friendly and marvellous four-day pre-Lent party.

There are no massive set pieces, motorized floats or expensive costumes at this parade but, as in Rio and Venice, much time and energy goes into preparations. Costumes are made from anything salvageable – villagers and islanders use animal horns and vegetation, flotsam and shells; town dwellers recycle packaging and cast-offs. The streets echo to the music of different communities – the sweet song of *kora* and *balafon*, the hypnotic beat of talking drums, the rattling gourds, groaning cow horns and reverberating wooden drums, which accompany the islanders' dances.

The cavalcade of extraordinary masks, carried on the heads of young men, is competitive, with a large cash prize for the winning group. Each year the government sets a theme, usually reflecting political issues and social reforms such as gender equality and anti-drug-trafficking campaigns; masks are made, using mud and stick armatures and papier maché, by enthusiastic groups of children.

Bissau is a poor, run-down city, but remarkably easy-going and sociable, and its carnival is a proud and joyful display of the culture and customs of these resilient people.

WHEN:
Pre-Lent, usually February/March
WHERE:
Bissau
BEST FOR:
Music and masks
YOU SHOULD KNOW:
The mask makers are children from different backgrounds and neighbourhoods who come together to work around the city. They produce amazingly elaborate masks, caricatures and whole scenes on the year's theme – though the influence of cartoon characters and foreign videos is also evident.

Young men carry highly colourful masks on their heads.

Durbar Festival

WHEN:
Around the time of the Eid festivals after the month of Ramadan. Eid al Fitr marks the end of Ramadan, Eid al Adha comes 68 days later; Ramadan, because the Islamic calendar is lunar, is 11 days earlier each Western year. For example, the two Eid festivals occur around September 10 and November 17 in 2010 and August 30 and November 6 in 2011.
WHERE:
Katsina, northern Nigeria
BEST FOR:
Pageantry and horsemanship
YOU SHOULD KNOW:
Niger state Ministry of Tourism and Culture now courts visitors and corporate funding by arranging 'Grand Durbars'. These are massive affairs on sports grounds, with 'cultural displays of all sorts' supplementing the traditional elements.

The wealth of the powerful Hausa cities of northern Nigeria derived from trans-Sahara trade routes; later, they became centres of Islamic scholarship. Their rulers, the Emirs, in times when horses were used in warfare, introduced the Durbar, a military parade to demonstrate the loyalty of the people. Once or twice a year the various regiments mustered outside the Emir's palace in an impressive display of horsemanship and readiness for battle.

The tradition of Durbar continues to this day, now chiefly as a local addition to the Muslim festivals at the end of Ramadan. They take place in several places, but that in Katsina, near the Niger border, is one of the most traditional. Though little remains of the massive 11th century city walls, the old town, with its mud architecture and alleyways bustling with robed traders, is an interesting, if rarely visited, place. The central square is lined on three sides by old colonial buildings; the fourth is occupied by the Emir's palace.

The modern festival starts with prayers; then long lines of horsemen, each representing a different village, town, region or noble house, parade through town accompanied by drummers and

dancers and musicians with feather headdresses to take their place in the square. Riders are magnificent in gorgeous robes, lofty turbans and copper armour; horses, caparisoned with fringed and tasselled harnesses, are no less resplendent. Last to arrive, the Emir and his splendid entourage position themselves in front of the palace. Each group of horsemen gallops at full tilt across the square, stops dead, and salutes the emir, ceremonial swords raised and flashing in the sun. The Emir's own regiment brings the thrilling display to a close, after which the Emir retires to his palace and his loyal subjects celebrate late into the night.

A Katsina drummer

Argungu Fishing Festival

Modern Sokoto, one of the hottest cities in the world, is a huge, congested and polluted town in the savannah of northern Nigeria. In 1934, Sultan Hasan dan Mu'azu Ahmedu, paid a visit to the river town of Argungu, west of Sokoto. A grand fishing festival was promptly organized in his honour, and hundreds of men and boys dived into the water to catch fish, the largest of which was presented to the Sultan. Nile Perch are the biggest fish in these waters – they can grow to over 60 kg (130 lb)!

Now held annually in February or March (the end of the growing season and harvest), the Argungu Fishing Festival has become a major week-long affair, where the many visitors enjoy not only fishing but a variety of events on land and water. In the lead up to the finale, traditional arts and crafts, music and dance, wrestling and archery all take place alongside camel, donkey and bicycle races on shore, while on the river there are wild duck hunts, canoe and swimming races and diving competitions.

The highlight is the enormous ' bare-handed' fishing contest. In preparation, fishing is banned on a stretch of river to preserve stocks, and on the great day, the fish are driven towards the shallows by canoes laden with drummers and gourd-rattlers. Thousands of competitors with hand-nets (and gourds for buoyancy) leap into the river and do battle for the best catch. After about 45 minutes, the fish-laden rivals leave the river, fish are weighed (the heaviest is still traditionally offered to the local rulers), prizes awarded and the friendly merrymaking of this very welcoming traditional celebration continues long into the night.

The contestants search for the biggest fish in the Sokoto River.

WHEN:
February or March
WHERE:
Argungu, about 100 km (60 mi)
from Sokoto
BEST FOR:
A joyful fishing frenzy
YOU SHOULD KNOW:
If the year's rains have been poor and water levels are low, the Fishing Festival does not take place.

111

Sidi Ben Aissa Moussem

WHEN:
April/May (The date is fixed according to the Islamic lunar calendar.)
WHERE:
Meknes
BEST FOR:
Sufi mysticism and Berber horsemanship
YOU SHOULD KNOW:
Meknes was once the capital of Morocco and is a UNESCO World Heritage Site with a 17th century palace and exquisite mosaics.

A number of *moussems* or festivals for saints are held all over Morocco but the Sidi Ben Aissa Moussem in Meknes is the most spectacular. Held on the day before the birthday of the Prophet Mohammed, the festival is firmly rooted in Sufism, a mystical branch of Islam that is frowned upon by orthodox Sunni Muslims, although still tolerated in Morocco.

Sidi Ben Aissa Moussem is traditionally a time for the gathering of the Aissoua Sufi cult, renowned for their ability to fall into trances in which they can perform extraordinary death-defying feats and acts of self-mutilation, apparently completely inured to pain. The Moroccan government has clamped down on the wilder excesses of their rituals, pronouncing them 'un-Islamic'; nevertheless the atmosphere is remarkably unrestrained in comparison with the respectable everyday conventionality of Sunni Islam culture.

The *moussem* lasts for two days and is a cross between a religious pilgrimage and a fair. Much of the action happens around the tomb of Ben Aissa, where the Aissoua pitch their white conical tents. These lend a medieval air to the festival – a feeling that grows as the day progresses and you witness more and more amazing events. Inside the tents jugglers, illusionists, glass-swallowers and contortionists perform mind-boggling feats. There is an incredible *fantasia* display, a popular Moroccan entertainment in which riflemen on horseback perform a group charge and fire a blast of gunpowder into the air in a formidable show of synchronicity. Men wearing brilliantly coloured, embroidered robes line the street, swaying sinuously to the accompaniment of cymbals, horns and drums, occasionally being transported into a religious ecstasy under the influence of the throbbing beat. The whole festival is the stuff of legend – so extraordinary that you would not believe it if you had not seen it with your own eyes.

Horse riders take part in a fantasia display.

Fes Festival of World Sacred Music

Tokyo drummers performing at the festival.

The 1,200-year-old city of Fes is Morocco's spiritual capital and musicians come from all over the world to participate in a ten-day festival of devotional music and dance. Every year the programme gets broader. You may hear everything from mesmerizing Sufi chants to haunting gypsy songs, Sephardic Jewish laments to Gospel choirs; watch whirling dervishes and Balinese temple dance. There are also fascinating *rencontres* – musical encounters in which musicians of different nationalities and faiths play together in a synthesis of genres (with varying degrees of success).

From its inception in 1994, the festival has grown to encompass not only music but also art exhibitions and cultural debates. Performances take place mainly within the walls of the old city and the inspirational settings add a whole extra dimension to the music. One-man recitals are held on the ground under the branches of a huge Barbary oak tree in the tranquil garden of the Batha Museum, moonlight concerts are staged in the 14th century courtyard of the Bab Makina Palace and Sufi nights begin at midnight among the mosaics of the Dar Tazi garden in the heart of the medina.

Fes is one of the most romantic cities in the world with a magical atmosphere. Its medieval architecture and winding alleyways make you feel that you have been transported back in time; it is no wonder at all that people gather here from far and wide to experience the first stirrings of their spirituality. The festival has an intensely serious purpose at its core – to emphasize the common values that unite the world's faiths and to promote cultural and religious understanding through the transcendent power of music. It is a unique multi-cultural event that cannot fail to touch the soul of even the most hardline secularist.

WHEN:
June
WHERE:
Fes
BEST FOR:
Devotional music and spiritual uplift
YOU SHOULD KNOW:
A certain amount of unease has been expressed that, as it grows, the festival is becoming too commercialized, with the cost of tickets being far beyond the reach of the average Moroccan.

113

AFRICA/MOROCCO

Gnawa World Music Festival

WHEN:
June
WHERE:
Essaouira
BEST FOR:
Gnawa music
YOU SHOULD KNOW:
Essaouira has a wonderful beach.
The town was a hippy hang out in
the 1960s and Jimi Hendrix owned a
house in the medina.

The charming 18th century port town of Essaouira on Morocco's Atlantic coast has long been a hip holiday haunt. Since 1998, when the first Gnawa Music Festival was held here, it has become even more popular, attracting hordes of visitors for five days of non-stop music.

The Gnawa (Gnaoua) are a distinct ethnic group, easily recognizable by their colourful robes and tasselled hats. The descendants of slaves from sub-Saharan West Africa, they established themselves around Essaouira and Marrakesh, making a living as musicians and spiritualists. They are famed as healers, cannily combining Islamic traditions with a hotch-potch of pre-Islamic Berber, Arab and African rituals based on a belief in possession and the casting out of evil spirits (*djinn*). Their musical tradition dates back to the 16th century and makes use of only three instruments – lutes (*guenbri*), castanets (*qraqeb*) and drums (*tbel*) – with which they produce complex, hypnotic music that has become increasingly popular among aficionados of world music. As a result, Gnawa bands are beginning to distance themselves from their traditional religious and spiritualist role, becoming more closely associated with the alternative music scene.

The festival not only celebrates the African roots of the Gnawa brotherhood but also freedom and unity through music. It has become increasingly international over the years and an eclectic mix of performers appears on the various stages around town. Jazz, pop and rock musicians often join in impromptu collaborative concerts with the Gnawa bands, sometimes with inspirational results. The beautiful setting and architecture of Essaouira provides the perfect backdrop for this melting pot of musical creativity. Festival visitor numbers are already creeping up to the half-million mark, so it's probably best to go soon.

*The Gnawa create complex,
hypnotic music.*

Imilchil Marriage Moussem

The annual Berber marriage festival held at the village of Imilchil in the Atlas Mountains has become the best-known *moussem* (Muslim festival) in Morocco and, even though it has turned into a tourist spectacle, it is still a vibrant affair, including a huge street market, where you can see tribespeople in traditional costume and be seduced by the charm of the Berber culture.

Dancers beat up a storm at the festival.

The semi-nomads of the Ait Haddidou tribes pitch their tents around two beautiful mountain lakes near the tomb of their patron saint, Sidi Mohamed el Maghani. By tradition, a marriage arranged here is blessed and will turn out happy. Tourists are regaled with a tear-jerking legend of epic proportions, which ends in a pair of forcibly separated young lovers drowning themselves in lakes of their own tears. Supposedly, this tragedy resulted in the tribal elders granting girls the freedom to marry whomever they choose at the *moussem*. The tale is most likely eyewash invented to assuage Western sensibilities regarding women's rights. In a society in which marriage is a matter of economics rather than romance, it is hard to believe that any self-respecting Berber father would let his daughter decide something so important.

But suspend your cynicism and enjoy the privilege of your encounter with Berber culture. For the *moussem* serves a serious purpose – an opportunity to negotiate business transactions, reinforce kinship ties and inject new blood into a family – vital for the survival of an ancient way of life under constant threat from the pressures of global capitalism. The festivities are thrilling: elaborately costumed brides are introduced to potential grooms, some hard bargaining takes place, then celebratory singing and dancing before the newly married girl is bundled up on horseback and carried off to her husband's home to start a new life – hopefully a happy one.

WHEN:
August/September (date fixed according to the Islamic lunar calendar)
WHERE:
Imilchil
BEST FOR:
Traditional Berber costumes and festivities
YOU SHOULD KNOW:
The Marriage Festival was once exclusively a Berber affair and it was only the bait of the tourist dollar that persuaded the tribesmen to tolerate public scrutiny. Be discreet and don't ogle, in case it causes offence.

Tissa Horse Festival

WHEN:
September/October (date varies according to the harvest moon)
WHERE:
Tissa, 50 km (30 mi) northwest of Fes
BEST FOR:
Traditional displays of horsemanship known as *fantasia*
YOU SHOULD KNOW:
The Arab-Barb horse is a crossbreed between the indigenous Barbary horse, known for its endurance and strength, and the Arab, a horse universally admired for its lightness, speed and good looks.

On a normal day, Tissa is a nondescript town set in the rolling treeless countryside northwest of Fes. Nowadays, the people of this region are settled farmers but not so long ago they were semi-nomadic warrior horsemen wandering through the plains with their herds. Tradition dies hard – horses have been bred here for centuries and during the Horse Festival the town could be a scene out of *A Thousand and One Nights*. Men in spotless white robes mill around discussing business. Drummers and pipers march behind teams of horsemen like medieval troubadours, while raggedy children run and dance excitedly behind them and riders in elaborate costumes show off their horses. The festival is ostensibly held in honour of a 15th century local saint, Sidi Muhammed ben Lahcen, but it is also an annual opportunity for Berber horse-breeders from around the region to show their Arab-Barb horses, make deals and, most importantly, compete in the spectacular *fantasia* competitions that are held here.

A rectangular arena is enclosed by tents, each flying the
Moroccan national flag, their plain white walls belying luxurious
interiors of red and green hangings and richly coloured kelim rugs.
The tension mounts as the crowds gather to watch the horsemen
prepare to test their cavalry skills in the *fantasia*, hair-raising
displays of martial art that are a symbolic re-enactment of the
Berber tribes' allegiance to the King. The riders charge
simultaneously with thundering hooves, kicking up a great cloud of
dust, suddenly pulling up and shooting a volley of gunfire from
ancient rifles so that the air grows thick with the smell of cordite.
The teams are judged on the fitness of the horses and the riders'
costumes as well as speed and co-ordination, prize money is
awarded and the show comes to an end with a huge parade.

*Horsemen test their skills
in the* fantasia.

Erfoud Date Festival

WHEN:
October
WHERE:
Erfoud
BEST FOR:
Traditional dancing and a
dromedary race
YOU SHOULD KNOW:
Dates play an important part in
Moroccan culture. They are
associated with good luck and are
given as offerings on ceremonial
occasions and as tokens of esteem.

The Tafilalt Oasis in the Moroccan Sahara is one of the largest oases in the world, renowned for the lusciousness of its produce. The date-palm is the mainstay of the local economy and there are more than a million date-palms around the sleepy old trading town of Erfoud. This is a great place to use as a base for unforgettable excursions into the desert and if you go at the right time of year you can participate in the annual festival that celebrates the date harvest and brings good luck for future crops. The dusty desert town bursts into life with three days of celebrations, street processions, singing and dancing and, not least, a dromedary race through the Merzouga Dunes.

As you wander through the souk of this picturesque town, you can watch Berber traders with great heaps of dates piled up, bartering and haggling over the price and quality. You will be charmed by Berber hospitality and will find no shortage of enthusiastic bystanders prepared to explain the finer points of the harvest festival and educate you in the subtleties of sweetness, stickiness, juiciness and size that combine to make the perfect date. Food plays a central part in the festival. Apart from being eaten on their own as delicacies (the Moroccan equivalent of sweets), dates are used in numerous recipes. You will get plenty of opportunity to savour the local tagines (stews), which carry a delicious underlying fruity sweetness from the addition of a few dates. And you can wash down your meal with a glass of refreshing mint tea as your Berber hosts press gifts of yet more dates upon you.

Tribesmen tread the dates.

International Festival of Carthage

Phoenician Carthage, founded in 814 BC, was a major power in the Mediterranean until eventually sacked by the Romans, whose own rebuilt city was in turn laid low. What little remains of the vast and legendary city – traces of the Punic quarter and ancient ports, Roman circus, amphitheatre and baths are included in the UNESCO World Heritage Site – are scattered over what is now a suburb of Tunis. But Carthage remains a powerful symbol and in 1964 became the location of an arts festival which is one of the longest running in Africa and the Arab world.

In its early years this was a truly international festival, with stars such as Louis Armstrong, Miriam Makeba and Joe Cocker appearing alongside big names from around the Mediterranean. All genres and styles of the arts were represented and audiences were international. But the festival lost its lustre and for some time was not only very localized but also almost exclusively commercial in its programming. Fortunately in recent years, driven by the vision of new directors, it has started to recapture excellence and public interest, attempting once more to combine performances by fine Tunisian artists with appearances by international stars. Recent programmes have included theatre, international film, readings by famous poets, classical Arabic music and traditional Tunisian music and dance.

Shows take place in venues in and around Carthage, but the most exciting place to see a performance is in the reconstructed Roman theatre, where the original tiered seating accommodates over 7,000. Caressed by the balmy night air and enjoying the benefits of the magnificent ancient acoustics, the audience feels the magic of the past.

A performance in the Roman theatre.

WHEN:
July/August
WHERE:
Carthage
BEST FOR:
A variety of events in a spectacular setting
YOU SHOULD KNOW:
Theatre and spoken word performances are usually in French; most shows start at 22.00, when the air is cooler.

Festival of the Sahara

WHEN:
December or January, though the date may sometimes be altered because of Ramadan
WHERE:
Douz, southern Tunisia
BEST FOR:
Bedouin traditions
YOU SHOULD KNOW:
Douz's interesting museum of aspects of life in the Sahara is organized by a popular 'desert' poet, Abdellatif Belgzcem, who also runs the festival poetry contest.

Festival goers at Douz wear traditional Berber dress.

South of Chott el Djerid – a vast, mirage-filled saltpan – and within sight of the great dunes of the eastern edge of the Sahara, lies Douz, Tunisia's largest desert oasis and 'Gateway to the Desert'. This unassuming, friendly place is also the centre for the traditionally nomadic Mrazib people. Though most are now settled here, many still keep flocks and their still-nomadic kinsfolk migrate with the animals in spring, returning in winter to camp around the town. South of the centre with its lively cafés and souk (there is an excellent market on Thursdays), a walk through thousands of deliciously shady trees in the *palmeraie* leads to the sands and the Great Dune, where visitors can enjoy a taste of the desert. Here the Place du Festival, with its racetrack and grandstand, is the location for the four-day Festival of the Sahara.

Originally a camel fair, this festival is now a glorious celebration of the arts and traditions of the desert people. The population of

Douz doubles as tribes-people, performers and spectators arrive from across Tunisia and the Sahara, and further afield. In the tented town, goods are traded, stories told, and tempting food prepared over open fires. By day, the varied and spectacular main events take place. Bedouin horsemen and their dazzling displays, camel races, Salukis chasing rabbits over the sands, jugglers' astonishing acts, all prompt wild cheers from the huge audience; a hush falls for the enactment of Bedouin traditional ceremonies and the breathtaking exploits of acrobats; appreciative cries accompany the hypnotic music and graceful movements of the dancers. By night, around the campfires and in the town, dancing, story telling, poetry reading and music continue in this magnificent showcase for traditions that are very much alive.

Tunisian folk dancers perform at the opening ceremony of the festival.

Tuareg men perform for appreciative young women.

Wodaabe Geerewol and the Cure Salée Festival

WHEN:
Late September
WHERE:
In-Gall, 110 km (68 mi) west
of Agadez
BEST FOR:
Spectacle
YOU SHOULD KNOW:
Dazzling white teeth are vital to the
Wodaabe; they use special herbs to
keep them bright and when teeth are
lost in old age, they are happy to
spend large sums on a brand-new,
gleaming false set.

During the rains, when the lush, salt-rich pastures can support the enormous herds of cattle, thousands of nomadic herdsmen – mainly Tuareg and the Wodaabe, a branch of the largely settled Fulani people – gather among the salt flats and pools around the northern Niger town of In-Gall before once more setting off for fresh pastures. This gathering, the Cure Salée (Salt Cure), provides rest and health-giving refreshment for animals and men, and is for them the most important event of the year. It is a time when families meet, social bonds are strengthened and animals traded. More importantly, it is the time when marriages are arranged.

Tuareg men perform displays of traditional skills and spectacular riding tricks for the audience of appreciative young women who court their attention. For the Wodaabe, two days of remarkable, formalized peacockery constitute the male beauty contest – Geerewol. The Wodaabe maintain a strict code of behaviour – their name means 'people of the taboos' – and in their culture physical beauty, *boodal*, is crucial to the extent that a man may share his wives with more handsome men to ensure attractive offspring. The first day of tireless, bark-liquor-fuelled dancing (the *yaake*) is a 'charm' contest. After a long and elaborate make-up session, the dancers make a series of extraordinary facial contortions – crossed eyes, grimaces, gnashing teeth – all accentuated by pale faces and blackened eyes and lips. The Geerewol dance is a measure of beauty; preparations include shaved foreheads, red-ochre face paint and hair dressed elaborately with ostrich feathers and shells. Marriageable girls watch both dances intently and indicate winners – whom they may marry – with a light touch or a gesture. Losers are simply mocked.

Though the Government now fixes the date of the Geerewol and treats it as a tourist attraction – to the disgust of the Wodaabe – the Cure Salée remains a traditional nomad festival, which may last for weeks.

National Vodun (Voodoo) Day

The small West African country of Benin is the heartland of Vodun, the ancient animist religion of coastal West Africa. Vodun is thought to be at least 6,000 years old and is still practised by most of the inhabitants of the region, albeit often combined with a surface veneer of Islam or Christianity. In Benin, Vodun Day is a national holiday and it's just as important as Christmas or the Eid celebrations of Islam.

People travel from as far away as the USA, the Caribbean and Brazil to the seaside town of Ouidah on the 'Slave Coast', the spiritual home of Vodun, to participate in the dramatic festivities here. Priests and priestesses enveloped in voluminous, brilliantly coloured costumes process through exuberant crowds to the mesmerizing rhythm of rattles and drums; incantations are uttered as sacrifices of chickens and goats are offered up to the elemental spirits of fire, earth, air and water; everywhere people are singing, chanting and dancing. The vibrant atmosphere is infectious: every so often someone will dance themselves to a frenzied pitch, fall into a trance and fling themselves to the ground where maize meal is ritually scattered about them as they writhe around exorcizing their demons in a spiritual catharsis.

Hundreds of people gather at 'La Porte de non Retour' (Gate of No Return), a memorial arch that stands on the beach as a poignant reminder of man's inhumanity to man – more than a million prisoners were transported from this stretch of coast to be sold as slaves across the Atlantic. In the New World, the colonialists sought to break the spirit of their victims by weakening ancestral and family ties and the practice of Vodun was proscribed. So Vodun Day is as much a celebration of cultural continuity as it is a day of worship.

WHEN:
January 10
WHERE:
Ouidah
BEST FOR:
Vodun religious rituals and beliefs
YOU SHOULD KNOW:
The word voodoo is a Western corruption of the West African Vodun or Vodou. Ouidah was colonized by the Portuguese in 1580 and grew to be one of Africa's largest slave-trading ports. Travel writer Bruce Chatwin wrote *The Viceroy of Ouidah*, a fictionalized account of the life of the infamous Francisco Felix de Sousa, who made a fortune out of the slave trade.

AFRICA/GHANA

Homowo Festival

WHEN:
Last week of August/first week
of September
WHERE:
Accra
BEST FOR:
Traditional food, dance-drumming
and rituals
YOU SHOULD KNOW:
The Ga is an ethnic group occupying
the coastal region around Accra,
comprising about three per cent of
the total population of Ghana.

According to tradition, Homowo has its origins in a terrible famine. The Ga people, worn out by starvation, managed by a supreme effort of will to gather themselves together for a last-ditch attempt at sowing a huge crop. Completely exhausted by this exercise, they could do nothing else but pray. Their prayers were answered; the rains came, providing them with a bumper harvest which saved them from certain death. Ever since, at harvest time, they have celebrated Homowo or 'Hooting at Hunger'. It is the most important date of the Ga calendar – a feast that is the culmination of a month of rituals commemorating their ancestors' great victory over famine.

You can hear drumming every day all over Accra as the excitement mounts in the week leading up to Homowo. The morning before the festival, ritual wailing emanates from behind closed doors as families mourn loved ones who have died during the course of the year. Later in the day, pairs of twins (regarded as special blessings in Ga culture) parade through the city accompanied by bands of dancers, singers and drummers. On Homowo Day itself, as hordes of people dance-drum their way through the streets, a traditional meal is prepared at home – *kpokpoi* (steamed fermented corn meal), palm-nut soup and smoked fish – and *kpokpoi* is sprinkled around in propitious places as offerings to the spirits. The smell of food wafts through the air and everyone holds open house, inviting friends and strangers alike to share in the family feast. Between noon and six in the evening all the women must accept hugs from men, a tradition that enables the young to further their romantic attachments and find marriage partners. Jubilant celebrations continue right through the night to welcome in the start of the Ga New Year.

A Ga woman 'hooting the hunger'.

Hogbetsotso

Hogbetsotso or 'Festival of the Exodus' is celebrated by the Anlo-Ewes people who live around the Keta Lagoon in the River Volta wetlands of southeastern Ghana. A series of complex ceremonies is associated with the festival – purification and peacemaking rituals designed physically and spiritually to renew the community, strengthen kinship ties and commemorate ancestors. In the days leading up to Hogbetsotso everyone sets about clearing their villages of rubbish, sweeping their houses and settling any outstanding disputes with their family and neighbours.

A young queen of the Ewe tribe is surrounded by young girls.

The highlight of the festival is the *durbar*, a formal gathering at the coastal town of Anloga. The tribal chiefs, dressed in magnificent regalia and mounted on ornate palanquins shaded by brightly coloured umbrellas, parade through the crowd to receive homage from their people. The Ewes are renowned for their sophisticated dance-drumming techniques and the musicians beat out an amazingly complex, poly-rhythmic accompaniment to the animated dancing and singing with which everyone celebrates their heritage.

The tribes of the Ewes ethnic group have a history of migration. It is not certain where they originated but by the 15th century the Anlo-Ewes tribe had settled peacefully in the ancient walled city of Notsie (in what is now Togo), integrating with the local inhabitants. However in the late 16th century, the tyrant King Agokoli embarked on a policy of persecution and attempted to enslave the tribe. A wise old man, seeing what was happening, hatched a daring escape plan and the Anlo-Ewes left the city *en masse* by secretly breaching part of the wall and sneaking out under cover of darkness. The last people to leave walked backwards so that Agokoli's guards would be confused as to what direction the tribe had taken. At Hogbetsotso, the walking-backwards exodus is re-enacted to commemorate the Anlo-Ewes' great escape to freedom.

WHEN:
First Saturday of November
WHERE:
Anloga in southeastern Ghana
BEST FOR:
Spectacular dance and *misego* drumming.
YOU SHOULD KNOW:
Hogbetsotso is celebrated by the Anlo-Ewe diaspora all over the world, even as far away as Canada and the USA.

Young girls carry reeds at the royal residence.

Umhlanga

WHEN:
Late August/early September
WHERE:
Lobamba
BEST FOR:
Traditional dance and costumes
YOU SHOULD KNOW:
Some observers have objected to Umhlanga on the grounds that it is demeaning and disempowering for the girls who take part. Others, including many participants, argue the reverse: that it gives the girls confidence in their bodies at the same time as encouraging them to retain their virginity until they are ready to marry.

Thousands of girls from all over Swaziland take part in Umhlanga, the annual ceremony of the Reed Dance. It is one of the most important cultural events of the year, a highly organized mass dance exhibition in celebration of maidenhood. Girls of all ages can participate, from children to young women, the only stipulation being that they are still virgins.

In the days leading up to the ceremony, the girls gather at the Queen Mother's village outside Lobamba where they are registered, split into groups according to age and region, and allocated to camps. They are then sent off to the riverside to cut reeds. Each girl gathers a bundle of the strongest and tallest reeds she can find, way taller than she is herself. The bundles are then heaped into piles to be used later for repairing the fencing of the Queen Mother's village.

On the day of Umhlanga, the Royal Princesses, decked in red

feathers to denote their status, lead a procession of around 20,000 girls into a public arena to perform their dances in front of a huge audience, including the King. The girls all wear traditional costumes consisting of an intricately beaded belt around their loins and a sash slung across one shoulder from which brilliantly coloured wool tassels trail. Some of them wield reeds or knives to symbolize their labour in the reed beds, and although they dance *en masse*, each group performs its own particular steps and songs. The arena becomes a whirl of colour, and the pleasure and sense of pride the girls derive from their performance can be seen in their animated faces. As well as being a spectacular display, Umhlanga serves a useful social purpose – in recent years the King has used the occasion as an opportunity to raise AIDS awareness.

Ncwala

Swaziland is one of the last remaining monarchies in Africa, ruled by King Mswati III. It is a country steeped in tradition and Ncwala (First Fruits) is the most important celebration of the year – a unique harvest festival that is essentially a kingship ceremony, confirming loyalty to the crown and honouring ancient customs.

Ncwala lasts for three weeks and involves a series of complicated preparatory rituals. On the night of the full moon in November, the Bemanti or 'Water People' set off on their travels to the rivers of Swaziland and the Mozambique coast to collect water and the foam of the Indian Ocean waves. This water is invested with curative powers and is collected for the King's use in the ceremony of Little Ncwala at the December New Moon.

Big Ncwala starts a fortnight later, at the Full Moon, and lasts for six days. The first three days are taken up with ritual preparations for the highlight of the festival at the Royal Kraal in Lobamba, 20 km (12 mi) from the Palace. Here, on the fourth day, crowds gather to take part in the Ncwala festivities. The king's warriors look stunning, draped in leopard skins and animal pelts, decorated with feathers and great tufts of cow hair. They dance and chant to call the King out from behind a brushwood enclosure until he finally emerges, magnificently attired in full regalia, and performs a sacred dance. He is offered the first gourd of the harvest and, as he bites into it, he blesses his people and their ancestors. This is the signal for the party to start. The following day is a much-needed day of rest. Finally, on the sixth day, Ncwala is brought to a close with a huge bonfire and yet more celebratory dancing, singing and feasting.

WHEN:
December/January – the exact date changes each year but the main day of Ncwala is the fourth day after the full moon nearest the longest day, December 21.
WHERE:
Lobamba
BEST FOR:
Impressive traditional costumes and ritual dancing.
YOU SHOULD KNOW:
Although visitors are allowed to attend most of the Ncwala festivities, photography is restricted so make sure you get permission unless you want to risk having your camera whipped away from you. Recording of the sacred singing is not permitted under any circumstances.

Famadihana

WHEN:
July to October
WHERE:
Central Highlands
BEST FOR:
Traditional ritual
YOU SHOULD KNOW:
Famadihana is a family religious ritual not a public entertainment. It is *fady* (forbidden or taboo) to point at the tomb and will meet with a shocked reaction. Don't take photographs without permission and wait to see what the protocol is before you go too close; or, better still, get to know a family personally and they might invite you to share in the ceremony.

Families carry the bodies of their dead relatives.

The Famadihana or 'turning of the bones' is a traditional ritual among the Merina people of the central highlands of Madagascar. It derives from ancestor worship and is a festive occasion in which corpses are exhumed from the family tomb, brought out into the fresh air and wrapped in fresh shrouds. The dead participate in a family feast, are entertained with music and held in the arms of the living for a dance, before being returned to their resting place.

Although this ceremony sounds horribly ghoulish, it has its own spiritual rationale that makes it seem perfectly sensible and not in the least macabre. It is based on the ancient belief in the existence of close ties between living and dead: all life flows from God through the *razana* (spirits of the ancestors) who act as intercessors between the living and God and are therefore prayed to in their own right; a person only joins the eternal world of their ancestors when their body has completely decomposed; in the meantime, their spirit needs perking up – hence the Famadihana. From this point of view, the living are merely temporary extensions of the dead – in its way a far more realistic attitude to life and death than that in more technologically advanced cultures.

Family tombs are built next to people's houses and are more important buildings than the family home, often wonderfully decorated and built at great expense. The Famadihana is a costly affair: everyone in the family must be fed, musicians must be hired, and expensive cloth for new shrouds bought. Everyone is expected to hold Famadihana rites as soon as they are able to afford it, and every weekend throughout the dry months you will hear drum music and see families dancing and feasting as they perform this extraordinary ritual.

Lake of Stars Music Festival

Lake of Stars is the brainchild of a British DJ who lost his heart to Malawi during his 'gap year' travels. Moved by the material poverty of this breathtakingly beautiful country, he set about promoting Malawi's music at the same time as raising money for UNICEF. A festival seemed a good idea, so he organized one – just like that. Even though Lake of Stars has only been going since 2004, it has already achieved renown as an ultra-cool event, quite unlike anything else in the world.

The three-day festival is held at Senga Bay on the western shore of Lake Malawi, a beautiful stretch of coast with miles of immaculate white sandy beaches. The audience is an unlikely mix of trendsetters, globetrotters, expatriate workers and students, joined, as the weekend progresses, by more and more of the local youth, seduced by the revelry. The crowd grows to about 1,500, gathered around a couple of bamboo stages, small enough to give a joyful sense of camaraderie so that by the end of the festival the motley horde appears to have transmuted into a strange sort of multi-ethnic tribe, bonded through their shared experience.

Apart from an amazing range of performers, from African jazz players to English DJs, the unique magic of Lake of Stars lies in its incredible ambience and exquisite natural setting: the constantly changing mood of the lake – one minute a shimmering turquoise sheet, the next, whipped up by the wind into a frenzied, wave-belching monster; the energizing beat of the music in the enervating heat of the African sun; the shaded palm-fringed shore and the soft deep sand. At nightfall, people gather round campfires on the beach, jamming and dancing until dawn when the fishermen return with their catch. It doesn't get any more chilled than this.

WHEN:
October
WHERE:
Senga Bay on Lake Malawi
BEST FOR:
Chilled atmosphere and beautiful lakeside setting
YOU SHOULD KNOW:
The campsite at the festival is surprisingly well organized with excellent sanitary facilities. While the waters of Lake Malawi look very inviting, you should probably resist the temptation to swim here due to the presence of the *bilharzia* parasite. Though it's easily cured once diagnosed, *bilharzia* has serious consequences if left untreated.

Singers and dancers celebrate Malawian music.

Women celebrate the anniversary of Namibia's independence.

Maherero Day

Once a German Christian mission station, Okahandja is a provincial market town north of Windhoek, known for its historical sites. Every year, on Maherero Day, there is a massive gathering of the Herero tribal clans to commemorate their past leaders and all those killed in the territorial wars of the 19th century.

The Herero are a pastoral people, cattle-breeders of Bantu origin who measure their wealth in terms of the number and quality of cattle they own. Reputed to be courageous fighters, they are thought to have migrated to Namibia from the East African Lakes in search of fresh pastures during the 17th century. By the mid 19th century they had come under increasing territorial pressure from northward-migrating Nama tribes, which led to the Bloodbath of Okahandja on August 23 1850. The Germans took advantage of this inter-ethnic strife to gain a foothold in Namibia; from 1884 to 1914 they held it as a colony, subjugating both Nama and Herero peoples by brute force, causing yet more loss of life.

The paramilitary march-past of the clans is an utterly surreal spectacle in which the costume and ceremonial of 19th century

WHEN:
Last weekend in August
WHERE:
Okahandja
BEST FOR:
Unique national costume and local history
YOU SHOULD KNOW:
Namibia is the second most sparsely populated country in the world after Mongolia. By 1900 nearly 75 per cent of the Herero population had either been killed or forced to flee to Botswana. Today the population stands at some 100,000 and is increasing, as the Herero continue to return from Botswana to their homeland pastures.

130

Europe have been assimilated with the traditions and rituals of Africa. Squads of men kitted out in vintage army uniforms parade past their clan chiefs in disciplined military formation. But it is the women who steal the show. They are an amazing sight, all immaculately dressed in Victorian crinoline skirts, layers of petticoat and fitted jackets, a costume that is topped-off by an extravagant headdress of rolled-up cloth fashioned to resemble the horns of a cow. They carry off this rather bizarre attire with such aplomb that, despite it being wholly unsuitable for the climate, one can only gaze in admiration as they parade down the road.

Maitisong Festival

Maitisong is the highlight of the year in Gaborone, the capital of Botswana. It's a week-long performance arts festival in which the whole city comes alive in a vibrant atmosphere of round-the-clock bonhomie and merriment. The festival always has an eclectic programme of spectacle and sound: performances of traditional and modern dance and drama, music of every genre, acrobatics, stand-up comedy and films. As well as the shows that take place under the roof of the Maitisong Theatre, for which you must buy a ticket, there are numerous outdoor performances in and around Gaborone where you can just roll up and join the crowd for a free show.

The word *maitisong* translates literally as 'place of entertainment'. It is the equivalent of the domestic hearth or fireside, where traditionally family and friends gather to share stories and sing songs, passing down oral culture from one generation to the next. The festival of the same name emerged out of the vision of the headmaster of Maru a Pula School, a community school opened in 1972. He initiated the idea of having a *maitisong* incorporated into the school and started a fund-raising campaign for a hall to be built. It took him some years and a lot of persuasion to raise sufficient money, but eventually in 1987 an auditorium with a stage and seating for 400 was opened as a community *maitisong* for plays and concerts. It was named the Maitisong Theatre and a festival was organized for the opening ceremony. The community response was so enthusiastic that Maitisong became an annual event. The festival has grown bigger by the year and today attracts some of the most famous names in African entertainment.

WHEN:
March/April
WHERE:
Gaborone
BEST FOR:
Marimba music, theatre and dance
YOU SHOULD KNOW:
The Maitisong Theatre stages cultural events all year round – from Shakespeare plays to traditional dance performances.

Splashy Fen Music Festival

WHEN:
Easter (March/April)
WHERE:
Near Underberg, Kwazulu-Natal
BEST FOR:
Popular and contemporary South African music, and the spirit of Woodstock
YOU SHOULD KNOW:
The festival is set in spectacular countryside; you can swim in the river which passes through the site, and Easter is a great time for hiking in the Drakensberg Mountains.

In 1990 a trout farm owner and former journalist decided to stage a music festival on his land in the gently rolling foothills of the southern Drakensberg mountain range. With conscious echoes of Woodstock and Glastonbury he launched the first Splashy Fen Music Festival, which has been held annually ever since. From small beginnings focusing on folk and folk-rock, the festival has expanded to take in all shades of popular and contemporary music, including rock, blues, indie, house and techno. Bands and musicians come from all over South Africa, and occasionally from abroad, and the festival is one of the best places to catch the hottest new talents of the music scene. Black music, both traditional and contemporary, plays a big part, including *mbaqanga*, the up-tempo jive music of the townships, and the wonderfully distinctive Zulu style of *iscathamiya*, the a cappella choral singing made famous by groups such as Ladysmith Black Mambazo.

Splashy, as the festival is affectionately known to its fans, takes place over the Easter weekend when a packed four-day programme features non-stop live music on two main marquee stages and various smaller arenas. All the ancillary features you would expect

A juggler entertains festival goers with fire sticks.

are there too, including arts-and-crafts stalls, clothes markets and a diverse array of food outlets. The organizers take safety and security seriously and there is a designated area for children. The regular festival goer sleeps under canvas (camping included in the festival ticket), but the autumn weather in this part of the Highveld is as unpredictable as it is at Glastonbury. So if you don't fancy getting down and dirty with rain and mud you might consider trying out the on-site Tent Hotel, which does the hard work of camping for you, or you could stay off-site in the small town of Underberg, 19 km (12 mi) away.

Addo Elephant Trail Run

Addo Elephant National Park, which lies some 75 km (47 mi) inland from Port Elizabeth, covers 164,000 ha (405,000 acres) of characteristically thick bushveld in the Sundays River region of the Eastern Cape. Addo's original elephant section was designated a national park in 1931 in order to protect the local population of these majestic animals which had declined to dangerously low levels. Protection and judicious eco-management have led numbers to increase to nearly 500 and to Addo being home now to one of the densest concentrations of African elephants on earth.

The runs can be epic struggles for the participants.

If you have trained to be part of that elite band who are extreme-distance runners, then a very special way to experience this magical environment is to take part in the annual Addo Elephant Trail Run. First held in 2005 the Addo Run is a relatively 'new kid on the block' of ultra-marathons but one that has already carved out a distinctive profile. You can sign up for either the 50-mile run (80 km) or the 'mere' marathon length of 25 miles (40 km); for the ultimate test there is the full 100-mile run (160 km) which starts at 06.00 and has to be completed within 30 hours. This truly is an event for serious runners: only nine finished the 100-mile course in 2008 and 50 the 50-mile run.

The Trail Run starts just outside the park boundary in Kirkwood and takes you mainly along tracks through the mountains and valleys of the national park. Addo is home to all the 'big five' (lion, leopard, buffalo, elephant, and rhino) and there is a good chance of occasional sightings along the course, although park rangers are on hand to ensure that encounters don't become uncomfortably close.

WHEN:
Early May
WHERE:
Eastern Cape
BEST FOR:
Extreme sport and wildlife
YOU SHOULD KNOW:
The race date is chosen each year for its proximity to the date of the full moon so as to provide the 100-mile (160-km) entrants with better light when running through the night.

More than 12,000 runners compete in the marathon.

Comrades Marathon

WHEN:
Sunday in mid June
(but late May in 2010)
WHERE:
Kwazulu-Natal
BEST FOR:
Sport and humans pushing
themselves to their limits
YOU SHOULD KNOW:
The Marathon has been a non-racial
event since 1975, with the first
black South African winning the
race in 1989.

South Africa's biggest single sports event, the annual Comrades Marathon in Kwazulu-Natal, is one of the world's great long-distance running events. The name is a misnomer since this is much more than a simple marathon; in fact, at a distance of 89 km (56 mi) it is more than twice as long and is closer to a pedestrian version of the Tour de France in terms of the gradients tackled. Athletes come from all over the world to test their mettle and endurance on a course that runs between the inland city of Pietermaritzburg and the coastal city of Durban. The direction of the course alternates each year between the two cities, the so-called 'up' and 'down' races.

The event was started by a veteran of World War I, Vic Clapham, as a way of honouring his fallen comrades, and the first Comrades Marathon was run in 1921 with just 34 entrants. Held every year since (except for the war years 1941–1945), this supreme trial of stamina and strength has a legendary and fearsome reputation amongst road runners across the globe and it now attracts some 15,000 runners. To enter you must be over 20 on race day and have run a qualifying time in an approved prior race. To qualify as an official finisher you have to complete the course inside 12 hours; the first ten men and ten women finishers each receive a gold medal.

If ultramarathons and extreme endurance events are not your chosen activity, there is plenty of excitement still to be had from being a spectator at the Comrades Marathon – and many good viewing points along the spectacular course, such as the upland villages of Camperdown and Cato Ridge.

Stellenbosch Wine Festival

Lying just 46 km (29 mi) east of Cape Town and easily accessible by road and rail, the elegant provincial city of Stellenbosch is South Africa's second oldest settlement with a history going back to 1679. The early European settlers were quick to realize that the climate and soils of the area provided perfect conditions for the cultivation of the vine and Stellenbosch remains to this day at the heart of the country's wine industry. Not surprisingly, the region surrounding the city is known as the Winelands and now includes over 100 estates. Stellenbosch itself was the first place to recognize the commercial opportunities in wine tourism and established South Africa's first (and still largest) wine route in 1971.

You can visit the wineries and sample their products at any time of year but for one hectic long weekend at the end of July or beginning of August Stellenbosch throws its somewhat conservative image to the winds and gives itself up to a wholehearted celebration of the noble grape. The annual Wine Festival draws enthusiasts and connoisseurs from all over the country who gather for the chance to taste over 500 wines, to meet the winemakers and to watch related activities such as cookery competitions. Nor do you have to know your Syrah from your Pinotage to appreciate this event as tutored wine-tasting sessions are offered throughout the festival.

You should certainly aim to take in a historic tour or two during the weekend and admire the graceful early-settler architecture and the broad streets with their avenues of mighty oaks, many dating back to Stellenbosch's origins in the late 17th century. And for those looking for a physical challenge to burn off the consequences of any over-indulgence, the Wine Festival also features a hotly contested mountain bike challenge.

WHEN:
Late July/early August
WHERE:
Stellenbosch, Western Cape
BEST FOR:
Wine and food
YOU SHOULD KNOW:
As well as wine tasting many wineries have their own restaurants and offer other activities such as horse riding.

135

The eggman cometh!

Grahamstown National Arts Festival

WHEN:
Early July
WHERE:
Grahamstown, Eastern Cape
BEST FOR:
Culture, especially the arts of Africa –
both contemporary and traditional
YOU SHOULD KNOW:
Booking opens two months before
the festival. It can be quite cold here
in July so you should dress
accordingly.

For ten frenetic days at the start of July each year the small Eastern Cape city of Grahamstown becomes the focus of the nation's attention as it plays host to Africa's largest arts festival. Every art-form is represented: theatre, jazz, classical and folk music, dance, art, crafts, comedy, street entertainment, literature, film. With more than 500 events packed into this short period the city is well and truly taken over by culture, and every hall and open space is pressed into service as a venue. Although the festival always features a number of artists and groups from overseas, the emphasis is very much on celebrating the creativity and cultural diversity of Africa, and Grahamstown is one of the best places to capture the pulse of this dynamic continent.

Although dating only from 1974, the National Arts Festival is

136

now regarded by many as the world's second biggest arts festival after Edinburgh, a claim based in large part on the existence, as with Edinburgh, of a huge and flourishing fringe festival that runs in parallel to the official programme. The festival operates an 'open door' policy for its fringe whereby any performer or artist can present their work if they can raise the funds and take the financial risks required. Most festival visitors come for a few days, if not the whole duration, so they can immerse themselves in the heady atmosphere of non-stop creativity and entertainment. There are plenty of free events around town, too, so you don't have to have deep pockets to enjoy what the festival has to offer.

For the rest of the year Grahamstown is a quiet, dignified place which, with its cathedral, university and rows of well-maintained colonial-era buildings, has a distinctly English air about it.

Cape Town International Comedy Festival

You don't really need an excuse to visit South Africa's most beautiful and cosmopolitan city, but September is a particularly good time to find yourself there in order to sample what's on offer at the International Comedy Festival. In little over a decade this annual festival has established itself on the international circuit of funny men and now bills itself as 'Africa's largest and funniest comedy festival'. For two weeks the art of making people laugh is celebrated in all its forms: stand-up, slapstick, satire, vaudeville, farce, street performance and physical comedy. The festival features comedians from around the world who are invited to share stages with home-grown talent. As with all the best humour nothing is sacred, but amidst the daring and the provocative there are also shows to keep the whole family entertained.

The Comedy Festival's main performances take place at the Baxter Theatre complex in Rondebosch. Here, on the three Sundays of the festival, in addition to the headline artists you will find Best of the Fest – when the most popular acts of the previous week are showcased in a single evening. New talent is encouraged through the Comedy Showdown, a contest run during the festival to find the country's hottest new comedians.

If you want to experience the atmosphere without paying to see a show, there is also a comprehensive programme of free outdoor performances at the V&A Waterfront. There can be few more uplifting experiences than to watch a skilled street entertainer going through his paces in warm sunshine against the iconic backdrop of Table Mountain.

WHEN:
September
WHERE:
Cape Town
BEST FOR:
Comedy
YOU SHOULD KNOW:
It is advisable to avoid public transport in Cape Town after dark and to use metered taxis instead.

137

Trumpeter Hugh Masekela

Macufe – Mangaung African Cultural Festival

WHEN:
Beginning of October
WHERE:
Bloemfontein, Free State
BEST FOR:
African arts and culture
YOU SHOULD KNOW:
Pervasive as the international music scene may still be, music derived from home-grown traditions and influences is enjoying a marked resurgence in South Africa.

The Mangaung African Cultural Festival, or Macufe as it is popularly known, is one of the most significant of the plethora of festivals that have sprung up in post-apartheid South Africa to celebrate the arts and culture of this dynamic new nation. Launched in 1997, the festival is held annually over ten days in and around the Free State capital of Bloemfontein. The emphasis is very much on music, and the organizers make sure that the full spectrum of contemporary African music is represented in its programmes, from gospel and classical through folk and jazz to r&b, hip-hop, rock and *kwaito*, the distinctive youth sound of the townships. The festival provides a platform for artists from all over the African continent; recent years have featured performers with international reputations of the calibre of neo-soul singer/songwriter Angie Stone, steel drum maestro Andy Narell and the dance music collective Soul II Soul.

Other art-forms play their part in what was designed from the outset to be a showcase for the very best in African arts. There are drama and dance performances, literature and poetry readings and a large and colourful arts-and-crafts market running for the duration of the festival in the centre of town. A particular feature of Macufe is that it also organizes smaller community festivals in a number of the outlying districts of Bloemfontein in the run-up to the main festival; some performers from these events are then invited to present their work at Macufe itself. A few days spent at Macufe and you cannot fail to be amazed by the sheer depth of creativity and artistic talent in the local population.

Mardi Gras – São Vicente

With its overwhelmingly Catholic population the tradition of carnival is alive and flourishing in the Cape Verde islands. This small group of islands in the North Atlantic was formerly a Portuguese colony and gained its independence in 1975. It is now one of the world's most isolated nation states, lying some 500 km (310 mi) off the West African coast. Today's population of around half a million is spread over ten volcanic islands and is largely descended from the African slaves whom the Portuguese traders originally imported to work the arid lands. Cultivation was an uphill struggle, however, and the lack of reliable rainfall has been a constant obstacle to major development.

Life is often harsh and unrelenting for the Cape Verdean islanders, but once a year carnival affords a welcome release from more pressing concerns. The popular celebration of feasting and dancing in the three days leading up to the start of Lent and its period of fasting is nowhere promoted with greater gusto than on the island of São Vicente and its main settlement of Mindelo. Called Mardi Gras (Fat Tuesday), as in New Orleans and many other places, after the day preceding Lent, Mindelo's carnival has its roots in Portuguese traditions but also displays much of the exuberance and flair of Brazil, reflecting Cape Verde's strategic position on the trading routes across the Atlantic. Three days of spectacular costume parades and open-air parties fill the streets of this attractive port town. In bars and restaurants all around Mindelo's fine natural harbour live bands play the gently swaying rhythms and plaintive melodies of *morna*, the indigenous music of the Cape Verde islands which has been brought to the world in recent years by the enchanting 'barefoot diva' and native of Cape Verde, Cesaria Evora.

WHEN:
February or March
(the three days before Lent)
WHERE:
Mindelo, São Vicente Island
BEST FOR:
Dancing, music, costumes, folklore
YOU SHOULD KNOW:
Cricket is a popular game on the island, a legacy of a British settlement and coaling station in the 19th century.

One of the many ornate floats in the carnival parade to delight the crowds.

AFRICA/TANZANIA

Festival of the Dhow Countries

WHEN:
Early July
WHERE:
Stone Town, Zanzibar
BEST FOR:
Film, music, African Arab culture
YOU SHOULD KNOW:
It is considered good manners to always ask permission before taking photographs of people and street scenes.

Mention the name Zanzibar and a world of spices and exotic fruits, of palm-fringed beaches and turquoise seas, is instantly evoked. It is a world that seems to belong more to the realm of fable and imagination; yet this island off the coast of Tanzania is all too real a presence and a visit is a richly rewarding experience for all the senses. Surprisingly small for its reputation at just 85 km (53 mi) long and 20 km (12 mi) wide, Zanzibar packs in a lot of history and culture. Zanzibar may have been a British protectorate for 70 years but it is the influence of the Arabs, who governed here for several centuries, which is everywhere apparent in the architecture and the culture.

This culture, the product of a once-formidable trading power with links to every corner of the Indian Ocean and beyond, is celebrated each year in the week-long Festival of the Dhow Countries. The festival is named after the traditional Arab sailing ships with their triangular lateen sails, the profiles of which provide such a distinctive image of this region. It celebrates the arts and culture not just of Africa but of all the countries bordering the Indian Ocean – India, Pakistan, the Gulf States and Iran. The festival is officially known as the Zanzibar International Film Festival (ZIFF) and film is very much at the heart of the programming. Many films are shown in competition and a jury awards the Golden Dhow each year for the best of them. There are live performances, too, and a full schedule of workshops and seminars, with dedicated sections for children and women. Venues with resonant names like the Old Fort, House of Wonders, Palace Museum and the Mambo Club are mostly near the seafront.

A concert ouside the clocktower of the Zanzibar House of Wonders is free for all.

Mwaka Kogwa

One of the oldest and most interesting traditional festivals in the country, and one unique to Zanzibar, is Mwaka Kogwa. The festival celebrates the arrival of the New Year, or *Nairuz*, according to the ancient Persian or Iranian calendar. Shirazi Persians were the first foreigners to settle in Zanzibar in significant numbers during the early medieval period. Many aspects of their culture were absorbed by the indigenous Swahili inhabitants of the island and subsequently given a distinctive local flavour. The Mwaka Kogwa festival is a typical example of this assimilation with its combination of tribal ritual and elements of Zoroastrian fire-worship.

Young women celebrate the Persian new year.

Mwaka Kogwa is celebrated all over Zanzibar but nowhere as spectacularly as in Makunduchi, at the southern end of the island, which attracts visitors from all over Tanzania. Men and women have clearly defined roles in the ceremony: the men are involved in a ritual fight which initially sets two pairs of brothers from opposite ends of the village against one another, using banana stems as weapons instead of the earlier sticks and cudgels. The fights usually expand to involve supporters from the rival camps; in this way past resentments and bad feelings are released and this in turn means that the New Year will be free from conflict.

Meanwhile the womenfolk, dressed in their finest, watch the fighting and sing songs about life and love, many containing messages for the combatants. A small thatched hut is then built and set alight as a symbol of good fortune. Once the rituals are completed, an enormous banquet is held to which visitors are warmly welcomed, followed by traditional dancing on the village field and the nearby beach.

WHEN:
Mid July
WHERE:
Makunduchi, Zanzibar
BEST FOR:
Traditional ritual
YOU SHOULD KNOW:
This is a predominantly Muslim community so you should dress respectfully and appropriately at all times.

141

Jan/Feb/March/April/May/June/**July**/Aug/Sept/Oct/Nov/Dec

An oarsman at the ceremony in traditional dress ready to make the journey to Limulunga.

Kuomboka

WHEN:
February, March or April – the precise date is decided upon by the Litunga, about one week in advance.
WHERE:
Lealui and Limulunga, western Zambia
BEST FOR:
Local culture and music
YOU SHOULD KNOW:
In the Lozi language the word Kuomboka literally means' to move out of water'. In the past, if one of the Litunga's oarsmen appeared to be slacking, he would be tossed overboard and left for the crocodiles.

The landlocked Central African country of Zambia holds over 20 traditional festivals annually. Of these, the most significant is the Kuomboka ceremony – a tradition that has taken place for over 300 years and occurs during February, March or April. The Lozi people live in the far west of Zambia, on the flood plains of the Zambezi. Each rainy season the river floods and Kuomboka is a celebration of the moment when the Litunga (King) moves from his compound in Lealui, on the eastern shore, to higher ground at Limulunga.

The day before Kuomboka, the royal war drums can be heard all over town, heralding the move. The day dawns and the ceremony begins with a procession of people carrying possessions from the palace to the royal barge. This magnificent vessel, painted with vertical black-and-white stripes, carries the Litunga, all his goods, attendants and musicians, plus 100 oarsmen in traditional dress. The cabin is topped with a statue of an elephant and inside a fire billows smoke, signalling all is well. The Queen has her own barge, topped by a white egret, and following on is the Prime Minister.

Two white canoes set off first, checking for enemies, while the drumbeat is pounding, music is playing, and the crowds lining the bank are cheering and waving. Finally the barges begin their six- to eight-hour voyage, and everyone else gets set to follow.

At Limulunga, thousands more eagerly await the first sight of the black elephant, cheers and drumming ripping the air. The canoes have scoped the shore, but the Litunga's barge still lunges at the bank three times, playing war songs to scare off any opponents before landing. The Litunga walks slowly to the palace, shaking many hands as he goes and relishing the enthusiastic welcome. After addressing the crowd, the Litunga's party enters the palace and the next few days are party time.

Lamu Dugong Festival

The dugong is a large marine mammal which is found in the warm tropical waters of the Indian and Pacific oceans. Its size – dugongs can grown up to 3 m (10 ft) in length – and unusual appearance are thought to have given rise to sailors' tales of sighting mermaids at sea, half-fish, half-human. Whatever its origins the dugong, or sea cow as it is popularly known, is now an endangered species. Each year a festival takes place on the Lamu archipelago off the north Kenyan coast dedicated to raising awareness of the plight of this shy and gentle giant. Dugongs favour shallow coastal areas so if you take a boat trip during your visit you might just be fortunate enough to spot one in the crystal-clear waters.

The Dugong Festival is centred on Lamu Town, an ancient trading port from whence ivory, rhino horn and slaves were once exported. Lamu is regarded as Kenya's oldest living town, with a record of settlement stretching back over a thousand years. Its ancient stone buildings display a distinctive fusion of native styles and traditional Arab architecture (the ornate doorways are a special feature to look out for), which has given Lamu UNESCO World Heritage status as 'the oldest and best-preserved Swahili settlement in East Africa'. The festival is a genuine community event with something of the atmosphere of a village fete; here you will find familiar activities such as lucky dips, raffles, face-painting and a none-too-serious dog show.

The festival is at its liveliest when the donkey races are held. As only one car is allowed on Lamu, donkeys are the main means of conveyance through its narrow streets. Once a year these humble beasts of burden take centre stage as they are egged on their way by the enthusiastic and highly partisan local crowds.

WHEN:
May
WHERE:
Lamu Island
BEST FOR:
Community fun
YOU SHOULD KNOW:
This is a mainly Muslim community so you will often see women dressed from head to toe in the black *bui-bui* robe.

143

Maralal Camel Derby

WHEN:
Early August
WHERE:
Maralal, northern Kenya
BEST FOR:
Sport and fun
YOU SHOULD KNOW:
Camels can move at speeds of up to 40 kph (25 mph), though you are unlikely to experience this unless you can convince the handler of your competence in the saddle!
A notable resident of Maralal until 1994 was the British travel writer and Arabist Wilfred Thesiger.

Associated in most people's minds with the deserts of Arabia and the Sahara, the camel, or more precisely the single-humped dromedary, actually originated in East Africa; a fact which is commemorated annually in the Camel Derby at Maralal, a small town in the remote north of Kenya. For three days in August this normally quiet town explodes into life as serious camel racers, thrill-seekers and enthusiasts for the unexpected turn Maralal into one huge party. There are serious points to this jamboree as well, which involve promoting better camel husbandry practices amongst the region's communities and raising awareness more widely of the dangers of increasing desertification in this part of Kenya.

Camels are a vital part of life for the nomadic communities of northern Kenya and, although they are used mainly as pack animals, when it comes to derby time many of the beasts are shrewdly assessed for their speed and stamina. The main race is taken very seriously and attracts professional riders and handlers as well as the finest animals themselves. It is considered a great honour to win the derby, which starts in the town centre and takes the form of a 42-km (26-mi) marathon through the arid scrub surrounding Maralal. There is also a 10-km (6-mi) novices' and amateurs' race which is open to all-comers, so if you fancy getting more involved than as a mere spectator you could consider hiring your own camel and handler and saddling up for a ride which you are unlikely to forget. Be warned, though; camels are notoriously strong-willed beasts with a propensity to head off in whatever direction the mood takes them, which is probably not the one you have in mind!

The camels line up for the start of the derby.

Mombasa Carnival

Even if you find it hard to tear yourself away from Mombasa's fabulous beaches you won't want to miss the city's annual carnival. This is everything a carnival should be: a riotous and heady mix of colour, sounds and spectacle as giant decorated floats make their way in procession to the pulsating rhythms of the streets. Kenya's second city has been a trading port since ancient times and a true melting-pot of different cultures. Artists and performers come to strut their stuff from all over Kenya. Nowhere is the country's rich diversity of tribes and ethnicities more evident than at carnival; Maasai warriors rub shoulders with brass bands, and street entertainers weave their way in and out of artists sporting the most extravagant costumes.

The carnival provides a setting for all kinds of events, including an arts-and-crafts market, food and fashion shows and a number of sporting fixtures such as an offshore sailing regatta. It is also a great place to catch the different music styles of East Africa; in bars all over the city as well as on the parade itself you will hear live music showcasing everything from hip-hop and the latest urban sounds to *Taarab* bands playing traditional Swahili music with its infectious, foot-tapping rhythms.

The climax of the carnival is the enormous street parade which features the city's many different cultures and faith communities. This starts as two smaller processions, which converge on Moi Avenue for the grand finale. If you come through this assault on the senses still wanting more, there are plenty of impromptu parties where you can then dance the night away under the stars.

A dance troupe performs at the carnival.

WHEN:
November
WHERE:
Mombasa
BEST FOR:
Folklore and music
YOU SHOULD KNOW:
Taarab music shows the influence of Zanzibar down the coast, to which Mombasa belonged until it was ceded in 1963 to the newly independent Kenya.

Orthodox Christians celebrate Timket.

Timket

The festival of Timket is a major date in the Ethiopian Orthodox Tewahedo Church calendar. Religion is deeply important to Ethiopians, and with believers numbering some 40,000,000 souls, it is the largest of the Oriental Orthodox churches. Timket, the celebration of Epiphany, here commemorates Christ's baptism in the Jordan – rather than the Magi's visit to the baby Jesus, as celebrated by Western Christians.

Ethiopia is a land of churches, and Timket is celebrated everywhere. However, probably the best places in which to see it are Addis Ababa, Lalibela or Gondar. The central tenet of Ethiopian Christianity is that the Ark of the Covenant is safely housed in a church in the town of Axum – but every other church in the country has its own replica.

On Timket Eve, the celebrations begin with these replicas, covered in silk cloths, being carried by the priests from the churches to the closest body of water. Behind them, accompanied by the sound of chanting, rattling *sistras*, horn-blowing, incense billowing and drummers drumming, process thousands of white-robed believers.

Vigil is kept all night, with people enjoying lamp-lit picnics by the

WHEN:
January 19
WHERE:
All across Ethiopia, though best in Addis Ababa, Lalibela or Gondar
BEST FOR:
Culture
YOU SHOULD KNOW:
Only a specially named guardian monk can see the original Ark of the Covenant, in accordance with the bible. Unsurprisingly this has led scholars to doubt its existence. The guardian, appointed for life by his predecessor, must stay in the chapel of the Ark for the rest of his life. It is claimed that many of these guardians die quickly, mainly because of the cataracts that have formed in their eyes due to the glorious light that the Ark emits.

waterside. Mass is said during the early hours and, at sunrise, the priest blesses the water and numerous people jump in, splashing and shouting. Sometimes the Ark is carried back to its church later that day in another huge procession, but sometimes not until the following day, itself dedicated to the Archangel Michael.

While this festival is basically religious, the celebrations are totally accessible. Sheep are slaughtered and roasted and special, spicy bread, *Ambasha*, is baked. *Tej*, an alcoholic mead, and *Tella*, the local beer made of maize or *teff*, are brewed and vast quantities enjoyed. The scenes are exhilarating and unforgettable, even if you are an unbeliever.

Ethiopian Music Festival

An exciting initiative for the 21st century with historic roots, the Ethiopian Music Festival (Festival de Musique Ethiopienne) was founded in 2001 and now boasts an impressive list of sponsors that includes UNESCO, Ethiopia's National Theatre and the Goethe Institute of Addis Ababa. This strong cultural support is entirely justified, for the festival's original aims were to promote, protect and encourage the performance of Ethiopia's distinctive music. Those aims remain unchanged, but as the festival has grown in size and profile it has expanded to include overseas performers who have been influenced by Ethiopian musical tradition, many of whom come from France.

The result is a festival like no other, held in a country like no other, featuring music (and dance) like no other. There is ample opportunity to hear traditional instruments such as the *kirar* (acoustic harp), *mesengo* (single-string fiddle), *washint* (Ethiopian flute) and *kebero* (Ethiopian drums). The ethnic diversity of this populous country is reflected by vocals in several languages, including Tigray, Somali and Waliyta, while tributes are invariably paid to Ethiopian musical legends like Sahle Degago and Lemma Demissew. Another distinctive, if more modern, Ethiopian sound to be heard at the festival is the ethiojazz developed from the early 1960s, notable for raw funkiness and a haunting quality created by combining Ethiopia's pentatonic scale with Western chords . . . and more than a dash of American influence absorbed after locals heard the records of artists like Sam Cooke and Nat King Cole, brought to the country by Peace Corps volunteers. Ethiojazz inspires many of the overseas ensembles invited to attend, whose spirited performances in a variety of styles electrify locals and visitors alike. And enjoying this special music festival's many and varied sounds won't break the bank, because all performances are free of charge.

WHEN:
Around 10 days in mid March (but check, it can vary)
WHERE:
Various venues in Addis Ababa, Ethiopia's capital city
BEST FOR:
The opportunity to set a visit to this fascinating landlocked country to compelling music
YOU SHOULD KNOW:
In recognition of the dynamic fusion of Ethiopian traditional music with American jazz 'n' blues, the country's Medal of Honour was presented to jazz great Duke Ellington by Ethiopia's Emperor Haile Selassie in 1973.

Kreole Festival

The Republic of Seychelles is made up of more than 100 islands lying northeast of Madagascar, in the Indian Ocean. Originally unpopulated, the islands now have some 80,000 inhabitants: the smallest population of any African state. The Seychellois are mainly descended from slaves, imported by the French from East Africa and Madagascar, and the vast majority are Creole. People here are proud of their heritage – indeed, Creole has been made an official language, alongside French and English.

The Kreole Festival is the major event of the year. First mooted in the 1980s by Creole academics from other parts of the Indian Ocean and the Caribbean, its purpose is to raise the profile of Creole languages and cultures, and to bring scattered Creole societies closer together. Taking place on the three main islands during the course of a week are scores of different events, as well as a seemingly never-ending party.

All sorts of activities go on during the week and most of them are free. The opening ceremony, at 18.00, is timed so that by the time the street party gets going, it'll surely last all night. There are special competitions and quizzes for children, a great street procession, *pirogue* and raft races, coconut tree climbing competitions, a fantastic night of Creole music, singing competitions, a Creole language conference, fashion shows and much, much more. There are also all sorts of special dinners where Creole cuisine from around the world is on offer.

The final night of the festival is celebrated with a traditional, night-long ball, the Bal Asosye. There is fabulous live music, scrumptious food, drinks galore and dancing. At midnight, soup is consumed to re-energize the revellers and at dawn the last dance, the Krayon, plays the festival out.

WHEN:
Late October
WHERE:
The islands of Mahé, Praslin and La Digue
BEST FOR:
Culture
YOU SHOULD KNOW:
Time your trip so you have a few days to relax on the beach after the festival – you'll need it!

There's dancing on the beach at the Kreole Festival.

EUROPE

Westman Islands Festival

WHEN:
The first weekend of August
WHERE:
Heimaey
BEST FOR:
Music and partying
YOU SHOULD KNOW:
This is now the biggest festival in Iceland. It began in 1874 when celebrations for the 1,000-year anniversary of the settlement of Iceland were organized on the mainland and the Westman islanders were unable to travel because of bad weather conditions. They decided to stage their own celebration, and have continued to do so ever since. Ironically, thousands of mainlanders now make their way to Heimaey each year.

Heimaey is the largest of the remote Westman Islands that lie off Iceland's southern coast. With a population of just over 4,000, it is also the only one that is inhabited. The Westmans are part of a young, active, underwater volcanic system and in 1973 there was a dramatic eruption on Heimaey when a new cone, Eldfell, appeared where once had lain a meadow. Lava flowed, buildings were buried or burned by red-hot ash, and the whole world focussed its attention on Iceland.

Heimaey is also famous for its festival. Held each summer, when the days are 21 hours long, thousands of people travel from the mainland and wider Europe to party 24/7 for three days on this beautiful island. There are hotels, but most choose to camp at the centre of the action – the locals in large, white tents. This is a music festival, but it is also a 'drinkathon' and a love-in – many couples happily make out in the most surreal of locations: a natural, grassy amphitheatre in the hollow of a volcano.

There are three highlights during the weekend. At midnight on Friday a gigantic bonfire is lit, warming those who have not yet consumed sufficient vodka to feel no pain at all. The drinking of vodka is utterly stupendous, but it enables people to roll *en masse* down the hill without breaking any bones, and timid foreigners to test out the local delicacy – smoked puffin.

Saturday night's treat is a fantastic firework display, and the Sunday night special features a glorious singsong for the whole audience, who join Heimaey's beloved Arni Johnsen in renditions of traditional folksongs. At midnight the site glows with a ring of red torches, symbolizing the volcanic eruption. The audience go wild, dancing and drinking the night away for the third night running.

A huge bonfire is lit at midnight to start the festival.

Holmenkollen Ski Festival

The Holmenkollen Ski Festival is Norway's number one visitor attraction. Holmenkollen itself is a hill that rises just to the north west of Oslo, about 30 minutes on the metro from the city centre. This is a not only a hugely popular recreational area, but also home to the famous Holmenkollen ski jump, visible from wherever you are in the city, and the location of the second oldest ski jumping event in the world.

Opened for competition in 1892, it was an immediate success and attracted some 10,000 spectators. Since then it has hosted nine world championships, the 1952 Winter Olympics, and has been awarded the 2011 Nordic World Ski Championships. Today, more than 50,000 spectators come to the festival, including members of the Norwegian royal family – some of whom have taken part in the past. In 1923 the Ski Museum was opened. Situated inside the ski jump, it has been part of the 2009 rebuilding programme and is due to be reopened in April 2010. It provides a wonderful virtual experience, which enables you to 'be' the jumper or the downhill racer that you are in your dreams and illustrates 4,000 years of skiing history. The equipment used on the polar expeditions of Nansen and Amundsen is also on display. If you go up to the starting platform, the views of forests, Oslo and the fjord are inspiring.

This is lovely country: deep, green pines cover the hill, through and around which are miles of cross-country trails. The whole area is a national and World Cup venue for cross-country skiing, ski jumping and rifle shooting. A large number of winter sports events are held here, all leading to the ski festival, held each March, that marks the end of the Nordic Tournament.

The 2010 FIS World Cup competition will be the first major event after the rebuilding of the Holmenkollen ski jump and arena. However it is well worth a trip to Holmenkollen, whether you go to the festival or not.

WHEN:
March
WHERE:
The outskirts of Oslo
BEST FOR:
Sport
YOU SHOULD KNOW:
No World Cup competitions took place at the ski jump during 2009 because it was being rebuilt. Prior to this, the only times it had been unavailable for competition was during World Wars I and II.

155

Flag-waving crowds gather around the Royal Palace.

Norwegian National Day

Held during May, Norway's National Day is its most important holiday, honouring the signing of the constitution declaring Norway's independence at Eidsvoll in 1814. At the time, Denmark had ceded Norway to Sweden after defeat in the Napoleonic wars, although this union was not finally dissolved until 1905.

One delightful aspect of National Day is that, in typically liberal style, the celebrations strongly feature children of all ages – Norway's future – rather than the military, as is so often the case. It also focuses on the royal family not the government. The largest parade, in Oslo, involves 100,000 people passing the palace, showing their affection for the royal family, who are all there to be seen. However, it merely skirts the side of the parliament building, where the president waves from his small balcony. The Royal Guard perform the sole military parade in central Oslo, displaying their renowned drilling skills – they have taken Firsts at the Edinburgh Tattoo several times. Their marching band joins the children's parade, alongside all the school bands, and is always roundly applauded.

The children's parades are central to the celebrations. Every school district plans its own strategy, often wearing local national dress decorated with red, white and blue ribbons. Flags and banners are waved, whistles blown enthusiastically, and songs sung to accompany the local marching band as hordes of children troop through their localities, stopping in front of war memorials, hospitals and retirement homes.

Almost everyone parades, including the 'russ' – school leavers – who wear jazzy clothes, play practical jokes and parade in multi-coloured vehicles playing very loud music. Speeches are given, games played, and quantities of sweets, hot dogs and ice cream consumed, as well as more traditional food such as lutefisk (dried or salted white fish prepared with lye), lefse (a traditional flatbread), and sour-cream porridge.

WHEN:
May 17
WHERE:
Throughout Norway
BEST FOR:
Culture
YOU SHOULD KNOW:
Norwegian communities across the world celebrate National Day. In Canada and the United States, the Sons of Norway organization arranges the festivities. Stockholm has its own dedicated May 17 marching band, who parade with thousands of people, and in Orkney, The Orkney Norway Friendship Association celebrates its historic links with Norway.

Ekstremsportveko

Extremsportveko is the largest extreme sport and music festival there is, and it takes place each year in western Norway. During the past 15 or 20 years, as our personal freedom has become ever more confined by health and safety laws, hygiene laws and more, it is interesting to note that young people have become exponentially more interested in extreme and dangerous sports. Nowadays, it seems that those who are driven to school when they could easily walk and are forbidden to climb trees for fear of falling, are drawn towards the undisputed adrenaline highs of mountain climbing, paragliding, ice diving, kite surfing and base jumping.

Voss, in western Norway, is perfectly positioned. It lies on a beautiful lake and is surrounded by snow-topped peaks, fast and furious white-water rivers and thick forest. For some years it has been a centre for adventure sports and in 1998 began to host the extreme-sports week. Today over 1,000 competitors from some 30 countries, as well as more than 20,000 spectators, arrive here each year. The festival is not just for serious athletes, however: there are beginner sessions for many of the sports, where you can learn the basics from experts. For those with no desire to risk their lives or limbs, a vicarious thrill can be had just from watching others participate.

Try not to tire yourself out during the daytime – the night life in Voss is almost as spectacular as the sporting events. Apart from visiting the bars and restaurants – where the local speciality is *smalahove*, a sheep's head complete with eyes and tongue – a large festival tent is set up for the duration and you can dance until you drop to one of the many bands that come to play here during festival week.

Voss is the place to be for the ultimate adrenaline rush.

WHEN:
Late June
WHERE:
Voss
BEST FOR:
Sport and music
YOU SHOULD KNOW:
Athletes from Voss itself have represented Norway at every Winter Olympic Games since 1948, except in 1972, and between them have won six gold, five silver and seven bronze medals. In 2007, Ekstremsportveko itself won five awards: Best Sponsor Object of the Year, Tourism Prize of the Year, Tourism Prize of Hordaland Region, Explore Prize and Lldsjelprisen (awarded to organisations who contribute to society based on help from volunteers).

St Olav's Day

Although festivities take place over the course of ten days, St Olav's Day itself is on July 29 each year and it is marked all over the country. As the patron saint of Norway, St Olav is held in esteem here, and on Olsok, as the day is known, his life is celebrated. The saint himself was a Norwegian king who was determined to unite the whole country through Christianity, using the sharp end of his sword. According to the Norse sagas, he cheerfully lopped off limbs, killed women and children and confiscated land to this end. After being killed at the Battle of Stiklestad in 1030, several miracles occurred and the King was quickly canonized.

St Olav is believed to be buried at Nidaros (Trondheim) Cathedral, and this is a great place to enjoy the festivities which begin with a vigil held at the Cathedral during the previous night. But this festival is not solely about religion. Instead, it is one of Norway's major cultural festivals, with several hundred different events taking place. There is great live music to enjoy, ranging from rock and country music to jazz and classical performances. Some concerts are held outside, where of course the daylight goes on and on. There is traditional food and drink to try, exhibitions to visit, pilgrims' walks, children's activities and a fabulous medieval market. Many people wear traditional dress – you can rent a costume if you want to blend in.

In Stiklestad, one of the major events that takes place on St Olav's Day is the St Olav Drama, enacted out of doors at the National Cultural Centre. Written by Olav Gullvag in 1954 and performed every year since then, it commemorates the Stiklestad battle.

Nobel Peace Prize Concert

The awarding of the annual Nobel prizes is a significant event throughout the world, and the Peace Prize is undoubtedly the one that catches the public imagination. The award ceremony takes place on December 10, the anniversary of Nobel's death, and the Peace Prize concert, inaugurated in 1994, is held the following day. This has become a major event in the Norwegian calendar, and every year some 7,000 spectators, as well as the prizewinner and other eminent guests, arrive for the show.

Alfred Nobel was born in Sweden in 1833. His father was an inventor and engineer whose career veered several times from bankruptcy to great success and influence. Alfred was brought up in St Petersburg and by the age of 17 he spoke five languages and was fascinated by chemistry, physics, literature and poetry. After choosing

a career in chemical engineering, Nobel patented dynamite in 1867 and rapidly became a hugely successful industrialist and entrepreneur, forming many companies around the world. On his death in 1896 it was discovered that he had left his huge fortune to fund five annual prizes: physics, chemistry, medicine, literature and peace, reflecting his own abiding interests, despite his involvement with weapons technology.

Tickets for the concert, held at Norway's top venue, the Spektrum Arena, go on sale in October and they sell like hot cakes. Each year a number of international stars appears and different genres of music feature. Planning begins in January, when most of the artists are invited, but as the prizes are not announced until October, there are usually a few last-minute bookings that reflect the Peace Prize winner. During the event, the winner and his or her work are introduced, a filmed interview is screened, and he or she gives a speech. The whole event is filmed and broadcast to over 100 countries.

The Nobel Peace Prize Concert takes place the day after the Peace Prize is awarded.

159

Kiruna Snow Festival

WHEN:
January
WHERE:
Kiruna
BEST FOR:
Culture
YOU SHOULD KNOW:
Due to mining-related subsidence, the whole town is to be moved bit by bit to the edge of Lake Luossajärvi, to the northwest. Most buildings will be rebuilt there, but the town hall is to be cut in four, transported and reassembled. In 2007 Virgin Galactica signed an agreement with Spaceport Sweden to carry tourists from Kiruna into space. The first group should take off in 2012, if everything goes to plan.

Way up in northern Sweden, 140 km (87 mi) north of the Arctic Circle, is the town of Kiruna. Situated amidst stunning scenery, this area encompasses some of Europe's last surviving wilderness. Beautiful at any time of year, Kiruna comes into its own in January, when the annual Ice Festival is held – a wonderful winter celebration which even the night sky seems to applaud with occasional displays of the Aurora Borealis.

Kiruna is home to Sweden's space station, set up to study the Aurora, and the Ice Festival was first organized in 1985 to mark the launch of a rocket. Taking place over the course of a week, a daily programme of events and competitions is planned, and guided tours, lectures and exhibitions at the space station can be enjoyed during this time. If you are an 'outdoorsy' person, you'll love it here. You can ski, skate, watch dog-sleigh or reindeer racing, and enjoy the exhibition of customized 'arks' – small shelters in which to spend the night when fishing on frozen lakes.

Alternatively, just enjoy the party – there's no shortage of vodka. Grab the chance to stay in an ice hotel – there's one built every autumn in nearby Jukkasjärvi, on the River Torne. During winter, the Torne is covered with a metre of ice, which is beautifully clear due to the water's purity and the steadiness of its flow. The Ice Hotel is absolutely astonishing – its design changes every year, depending on who creates it. As well as a reception area and uniquely styled bedrooms, it includes an ice bar and a church.

The highlight here is the ice sculpting championship: in a park near the centre, about 60 artists from different countries across the world create magical sculptures from large blocks of compressed snow. It is a delightful privilege to see these transient beauties.

The coolest venue in town is the Ice Hotel at Jukkasjärvi.

Jokkmokk Winter Market

Jokkmokk is the cultural heart of Swedish Lapland. Situated just inside the Arctic Circle, the population is usually a mere few thousand but it swells for three days each February when an extra 30,000 or 40,000 people, mainly Sámis (Lapps), rock up for the premium event of the year – the Winter Market.

There have been winter markets here for over 400 years. The Sámi, indigenous northern reindeer herders who recognized no boundaries, are spread across Russia, Finland, Sweden and Norway. Today, a significant area of land – 9,400 sq km (3,629 sq mi) – named Laponia has been listed as a UNESCO World Heritage Site. Traditionally people came to trade, collect taxes, exchange news with distant friends and meet their future spouse. Apart from tax collection, nothing much else has changed.

This is a unique event. The day before the official opening vendors begin to arrive, and by the evening many have already set up their stalls. The big day opens with a short speech and a parade of white reindeer pulling sleds – expect to see a great many reindeer, moose and elk during the next few days. As well as all the usual items, these stalls sell fabulous Sámi handicrafts – wonderful knives, jewellery, wooden caskets, cups and sculptures, fur-lined leather hats and gloves, hand-knitted goods, homemade lingonberry and bilberry preserves and, of course, furs. Here you'll see pelts as well, but watching indigenous people wearing furs in –25 °C (–13 °F) feels quite different from seeing wealthy ladies wearing fur to the opera.

Try reindeer stew, steaks and burgers, salmon and shrimp – no freezers needed here – washed down with cloudberry schnapps. Watch reindeer racing on the frozen lake, visit Ajtte, the Sámi museum, enjoy a torchlight procession, the taxidermy championships, dog-sled expeditions and the Sámi music and dancing that takes place in a complex of heated tepees at night.

WHEN:
Three days starting on the first Thursday in February
WHERE:
Jokkmokk, Norrbotten County
BEST FOR:
Culture
YOU SHOULD KNOW:
By early February, there are several hours of daylight every day, but at night it is still possible to see the Aurora Borealis. Don't forget, it's really very cold here – it's not unusual for the temperature to be –30 °C (–22 °F) at Winter Fair time, and it can be as low as –40 °C (–40 °F). You need to come as warmly dressed as possible.

Reindeers race across the ice towards the finishing line.

Valborgsmassoafton (Walpurgis Night)

WHEN:
April 30
WHERE:
All over Sweden – it's especially worth celebrating in Gothenburg
BEST FOR:
Culture
YOU SHOULD KNOW:
St Walpurgis was born in Devon in AD 710, but although this is a religious day, celebrated by Catholics, it is also a day celebrated by pagans and Satanists. Early Christians frequently took over pagan festivals, and Walpurgis Night originates in ancient rites of spring. On the night of April 30, ghosts and mischievous spirits were said to walk the earth, before being banished once more at sunrise, with the coming of May Day.

Crowds warm up around the bonfire on Walpurgis Night.

Walpurgis Night, celebrated across much of northern and central Europe, falls on April 30, the day before the public holiday of May Day and, as such, it is often treated as a half-holiday. Although the form of the celebrations varies from area to area, some are set in stone – the lighting of large bonfires, for example, which began during the 1700s, and the singing of traditional songs of spring. An older, rural tradition was for young people to decorate local cottages with leaves and branches collected from the woods at dusk. Payment for their efforts was in eggs.

Students in Sweden's oldest university cities are fervent in their upkeep of these traditions. In Lund and Uppsala, both current and past students take part in festivities that begin early in the morning, continue through the day and well into the small hours. In Gothenburg, the students at Chalmers University have a special tradition: The Cortege. Prior to 1909, not only did the students change their black, winter caps to white, summer caps on April 30, but they also spent the day walking about the city with one foot on the sidewalk and the other in the gutter.

In 1909, students organized every carriage in Gothenburg to take them in style along the route they usually walked, and within two years this had morphed into a wonderful procession that has taken place every year since, save for 1940. The most bizarre collection of vehicles makes its way through the streets, accompanied by marching bands, people in costume, and thousands of spectators. Splendidly inventive, students ride bicycles made for four, cars that are upside down, sofas with wheels and motors – just about anything you can think of. There's no doubt about it – this is Sweden shrugging off its long, hard winter and welcoming summer with open arms.

Gotland Medieval Week

Some 90 km (56 mi) east of mainland Sweden, in the Baltic Sea, lies Gotland – Sweden's largest island. Occupied since prehistoric times, Gotland was a major trade centre for the Vikings and later for the Hanseatic League. However, in 1361, the Danish king Valdemar Atterdag and his well-equipped army invaded Gotland, slaughtering 1,800 people before entering the city of Visby. It is in commemoration of this event that Gotland Medieval Week is held.

Knights joust at the medieval games in Visby.

Visby is Gotland's major city, and it has one of the best-preserved medieval ramparts in the world. The wall that surrounds the inner city, built during the 12th and 13th centuries, is over 3 km (2 mi) in length, and boasts 36 towers. Within, lovely cobbled lanes twist and turn, lined with over 200 fabulous medieval houses, warehouses and ancient churches. During Medieval Week some 150,000 people come here, many dressed in costumes as historically correct as possible, to enjoy the fun.

Gotlanders take it all pretty seriously – some even attend evening classes during the long winter evenings in order to get their costumes just right, and throughout the week of the festival there are lectures and history courses to attend as well as re-enactments of various important historical dates, including the 1361 invasion itself.

The Medieval Market is colourful and eye-catching – crowded with stalls selling jewellery, clothes and armour. You can eat delicious and authentic medieval food, listen to medieval music, watch street theatre, applaud the jugglers and jesters, gasp at the fire eaters, try your hand at archery and feel your pulse race as you watch knights in armour joust for the hearts of their beloveds and the entertainment of the crowd.

WHEN:
August
WHERE:
Visby, Gotland
BEST FOR:
Medieval culture
YOU SHOULD KNOW:
Gotland is renowned for its 94 medieval churches, built in Romanesque and Gothic style between AD 1150 and 1400 when the island was at the height of its wealth and influence.

Readers are spoiled for choice at Gothenburg's Book Festival.

Gothenburg Book Festival

The city of Gothenburg, on Sweden's west coast, lies at the mouth of the river Gota alv, where it feeds into the North Sea. Strategically located roughly halfway between Copenhagen and Oslo, Sweden's second city has a history of both trade and industry, and has the largest seaport of all the Scandinavian countries. It also has a large student population, being home to Sweden's largest university, and Chalmers University of Technology.

Gothenburg was founded in 1641 by King Gustavus Adolphus. Because of its situation at a marshy river mouth, the Dutch, with their special skills in this area, were brought in to plan and oversee the project, which of course involved canals. In the 18th century trade with Asia flourished thanks to the Swedish East India Company, but trade with North America grew increasingly important and the port became the main embarkation point for Swedish emigrants to the New World.

Nowadays Gothenburg is an attractive, modern city, trying to diversify. It hosts a number of festivals during the course of the year, including the Book Festival, which takes place each September. Launched 25 years ago, this has grown to be the largest literary festival in Scandinavia, and in Europe second only to the international book fair at Frankfurt. Whilst Gothenburg's festival started life as a trade fair, aimed at teachers and librarians, it now attracts publishers, authors – including Nobel Prize winners – poets and thousands of bibliophiles. About 100,000 visitors enjoy readings, book signings, workshops and discussion groups, as well as wandering around looking at what's on offer at some of the 1,000 exhibitor stands.

WHEN:
September
WHERE:
The Exhibition Centre,
Gothenburg
BEST FOR:
Literature
YOU SHOULD KNOW:
Gothenburg was named after the Goths, who were the inhabitants of Gothia, now southern Sweden. The blueprint for the city's canals are exactly the same as those used for Indonesia's capital, Jakarta – another city where you can still see a strong Dutch architectural influence in the older areas.

Sankt Hans Bonfires

Nothing lifts the spirits and warms the cockles like sitting around a bonfire, and no one does bonfires quite so stylishly as the Scandinavians. In Denmark, midsummer is marked by a multitude of intimate alfresco fireside gatherings in gardens, parks and, most traditionally, on beaches. Although this ritual stretches back to pagan times, its current manifestation centres on the feast of Sankt Hans (John the Baptist). In early Christian times the year was split in two, with Jesus being worshipped in the first half and then John taking centre stage in the latter half. Sankt Hans is held on the eve of the transition.

It was not only the early Christians who attempted to claim midsummer as their own. In the 19th century the festival became a time for singing patriotic songs. Pagan elements remained, as it was believed by farmers that fire would ward off the evil spirits that caused illness amongst their livestock. What at first seems a benign gathering has accrued so many different meanings that it has caused much controversy down the years.

The tradition was so rooted in Danish culture that an edict in 1743 by the dominant Protestant church to ban it went largely unheeded and the law was rapidly withdrawn. A more controversial element of the celebration is the tradition of burning the figure of a witch. The ritual recalls a dark time in the country's history when many thousands of mainly women were burned at the stake by religious fanatics in the 16th and 17th centuries. Many people now choose to forgo this element of the festivities. Today, the Sankt Hans bonfire is regarded as a pleasant custom where people gather with friends and family to sing traditional midsummer songs around a bonfire.

WHEN:
June 23
WHERE:
All over Denmark – the people of Fjordmarken in the western part of Aalborg throw what is considered to be one of the best parties in Denmark.
BEST FOR:
Culture
YOU SHOULD KNOW:
The most charming tradition associated with Sankt Hans is a ritual whereby a single woman picks two herbs and hangs them under the ceiling joist in her room. The herbs represent her and the young man she has designs on. If she awakes to find that the herbs have grown together, then her prayers will be answered. If they have grown apart then she must wait another year before trying again.

A typical beach bonfire marks the feast of Sankt Hans.

Roskilde Festival

WHEN:
Over eight days (including the warm up) which starts late July or early August
WHERE:
Roskilde
BEST FOR:
Music
YOU SHOULD KNOW:
It is hard to believe, but this enormous festival is put on by a full-time staff of just 25. This helps to maximize income for the Roskilde Foundation which does much good charitable work at home and abroad.

One of the by-products of declining music sales is that performers have to get up on stage and earn their money. The music calendar is now so crammed with festivals there is probably soon going to be a new illness called 'chronic festival fatigue syndrome'. However, if you are looking for a festival that is innovative yet established, massive yet intimate and crammed with headline acts and up-and-coming talent, rush to book your place at Roskilde.

Founded by two students in 1971 and now run by a not-for-profit foundation, the festival has always had the right credentials to be popular without being overly commercial. Most musical tastes are catered for and the organizers seem to delight in juxtaposing musical styles. Where else would you find Ray Charles and the Velvet Underground sharing top billing, as they did here in 1993? Bob Dylan also seems to love the place and has strutted his stuff at Roskilde on numerous occasions in his many manifestations.

Like a Cecil B. DeMille movie, Roskilde has a cast of thousands. An astonishing 25,000 volunteers staff the stalls, build the stages and provide guidance and security. This atmosphere of general goodwill pervades the whole festival as up to 80,000 paying guests join them to turn the 80-ha (200-acre) site into a giant jamboree of a campsite. Once you are firmly encamped it is time to take your pick of the performances on offer. Those who love the stadium-rock feel can head for the Big Stage, to join with up to 60,000 others to see the headline acts. A more intimate experience can be had at the Green Stage (capacity 17,000). A lively fringe complements the main attractions, with hip-hop, dance and indie rock fans well catered for as well as those of opera, theatre and film.

Swedish band Bob Hund performs at Roskilde festival.

Aarhus Festival

The emphasis is on the intellectual and the atmosphere is distinctly highbrow, as culture-vultures from around the globe descend on Denmark's charming second city for the annual Aarhus Festival. This is a truly multi-media event: cutting edge exhibitions and film are regularly on the menu and musical offerings include jazz, opera and classical concerts. Stretched over ten glorious days, the festival utilizes just about every possible venue in town. The more traditional concert halls are supplemented by municipal buildings, museums, churches and libraries and the city's parks also become hives of activity.

Over 300 separate events combine to make this one of Europe's premier artistic events and each year much thought is put into finding a new and original theme with which to frame the festival. Past themes have included such diverse topics as Hans Christian Andersen, Women in Culture, and Asia. But whatever theme is chosen, the selections and performances are always first rate. Invited guests from come from far and wide to perform alongside local talent and the festival has recently attempted to broaden its appeal to the young by including more progressive music.

A lively fringe has grown up around the festival and it is here that hidden gems can be uncovered. In the past South American rainmaker bands, Japanese drummers and African gospel choirs have all performed. Culture is a difficult word to define; it can often boil down to a matter of taste. One thing is certain, however – the Aarhus Festival has grown to be such a 'big tent' that there will always be something to suit every interest.

Cuban jazz drummer Ignacio Berroa entertains the crowds.

WHEN:
Late August into early September
WHERE:
Aarhus
BEST FOR:
Theatre and music
YOU SHOULD KNOW:
The days and nights are filled with performances, so it is impossible to see everything and careful planning is required. Tickets should be bought in advance for the main concerts and some of the events are quite expensive to get into. There is, however, enough free entertainment – particularly in the parks – to ensure an enjoyable time, even on a tight budget.

European Medieval Festival, Horsens

WHEN:
The last weekend in August
WHERE:
Horsens, eastern Jutland
BEST FOR:
Culture and music
YOU SHOULD KNOW:
The medieval period lasted for about 700 years from AD 800. The organizers have chosen to focus on the period between 1350 and 1536, when the Danes were more benign, thus avoiding the need for too much pillaging in order to maintain authenticity.

It was very unlikely, towards the end of the 1st millennium, that the Danes would invite you to a party. In fact it was more probable that they would turn up unannounced at yours, raze the place to the ground and make off with anything they could carry. Such was their fearsome reputation that it was deemed preferable to pay them vast sums of silver, in the form of Danegeld, to stay away. Thankfully the years have mellowed them and they are now the most agreeable of hosts.

First held in 1995, the European Medieval Festival was founded to spread knowledge of the importance of the medieval period to the city of Horsens. The festival fulfilled a need in Scandinavians to re-engage with their past, and participants come from all over Europe to dress up and revel in all things ancient. Costumes and props are laid on by the town council and even telephone booths and lamp posts are adorned with garlands of twigs. A cast of over 5,000 locals tog up as characters from the full range of medieval Horsens society. People shed their modern personas to become lords and ladies, knights and maidens, beggars, fortune tellers and monks, in what must be one of the biggest and most authentic fancy dress parties on earth.

The centre of town is transformed into a fiery landscape as beacons are lit and oil lamps and candles are burned all along its streets and in its open spaces. Local taverns open their doors and serve up traditional fare such as hog roast, washed down by mead (honey wine) and ale. Period song, theatre and music are all on offer, as is the unique sport of flag throwing.

Local girls are dressed for the event, with a little help from the town council.

168

Finlandia Hiihto Ski Marathon

In Finland, skiing is second nature. Archaeologists have unearthed skis dating back to 2,000 BC, so clearly this means of getting around has a long history. Towards the end of the 19th century cross-country skiing started to be taken up seriously as a sport, and in recent years it has become increasingly popular as more and more people have discovered that it is a thoroughly effective and enjoyable means of keeping fit.

The first Finlandia Hiihto was held in 1974 and it was at one time the biggest ski event in the world. The race was originally a 75-km (47-mi) dash across several frozen lakes between the towns of Lahti and Hämmeenlinna, but the ground conditions were so variable from year to year that the course was changed into a circular route through the countryside around Lahti. You can participate in races of varying distances, depending on your age and experience, ranging from 20 km (12 mi) to the classic 62-km (40-mi) marathon.

The race attracts more than 5,000 contestants to Lahti, beside Lake Vesijärvi in southeast Finland. On the day of the marathon, the participants gather in the town's stadium to be sent off in staggered waves. The course starts with a daunting uphill climb – a serious fitness test – but soon eases to follow a rolling path with only one or two really steep sections. There are refreshment stops *en route* for flagging skiers to pep themselves up and crowds of enthusiastic bystanders to cheer them onwards. Everyone who completes the course receives a medal, so even if you are not among the frontrunners, you will have a permanent memento of achievement – not just the next morning's obligatory aching limbs to prove that you took part.

WHEN:
February
WHERE:
Lahti
BEST FOR:
Cross-country skiing in beautiful scenery
YOU SHOULD KNOW:
The Finlandia Hiihto is part of the Worldloppet series of races which includes the US Birkebeiner and the Sapporo in Japan. The logistics of the Finlandia make it a particularly appealing event for participants: you can register for the marathon online and from Helsinki airport there is a bus that takes you directly to Lahti in less than an hour.

They're off!

Jutajaiset Festival of Nightless Nights

WHEN:
June
WHERE:
Rovaniemi, Finnish Lapland
BEST FOR:
Breathtaking natural scenery, midnight sun, Sámi culture and reindeer
YOU SHOULD KNOW:
Rovaniemi is best known for being the supposed hometown of Santa Claus and as the venue for the Ounasvaara Winter Games.

In the sub-Arctic wilderness of northern Scandinavia, where for six months of the year the sun barely peeps above the horizon, the arrival of the long summer days signals the festival season. Jutajaiset is the Arctic Circle's biggest summer solstice festival, an annual cultural celebration for the Sámi, the indigenous pre-Viking people of Lapland. The traditional Sámi way of life, based on the pastoral pursuits of reindeer herding and forestry, is inevitably under threat in the post-modern world, swamped by the cultural influence of Lapland's Scandinavian neighbours and the effects of globalization. Jutajaiset is a reminder to the world that Sámi folk culture is by no means moribund and that Yoik, their unique tonal voice music, is an integral part of today's Nordic music scene.

When Jutajaiset was first conceived some 35 years ago, the idea behind it was simple enough: to use the traditional summer solstice celebrations as a basis for passing on the rich Sámi heritage of music, dance and folklore to the younger generation. Over the years it has far exceeded the expectations of its organizers, burgeoning into a huge artistic and musical cross-cultural festival with a growing number of international performers attracting an increasingly diverse audience to the remote town of Rovaniemi, the 'Gateway to Lapland'.

The festival arena is scenically situated on the bank of the Kemijoki, the longest river in Finland, beside the brilliantly illuminated Lumberjack's Candle Bridge, a striking architectural homage to the region's foresters. Among the picturesque Sámi folk trappings – performers got up in national costume, colourful crafts stalls and the ubiquitous reindeer – there are contemporary world music bands, modern art exhibitions and international dance troupes. Since it stays light all night, the four-day party is pretty well continuous; sleep is the last thing on anyone's agenda – there's plenty of time for that when summer's gone.

Savonlinna Opera Festival

Ping, Pang and Pong appear in Puccini's Turandot.

Savonlinna is a lively spa town on Lake Saimaa, famous for its medieval monument – the 15th century Olavinlinna Castle. Perched on a rocky island in the lake and surrounded by breathtaking natural scenery, the Castle is a spectacular venue for the annual Savonlinna Opera Festival. Over the years the festival has grown to be one of Finland's most important cultural events, attracting a cosmopolitan audience of around 60,000 people. The repertoire includes classic masterpieces, works by lesser-known composers, premieres of new compositions and concerts.

The Savonlinna Festival was dreamt up by a famous Finnish soprano, Aino Ackté. She was frustrated that Finnish opera was not more widely appreciated and that she rarely got to perform her favourite pieces. On a visit to Savonlinna, she was struck – as everyone always is – by the magical ambience of Olavinlinna Castle and suddenly had a brainwave: the central courtyard with its medieval stone staircases, alcoves and high surrounding walls was a perfect stage, and such a remarkable setting would be certain to imprint Finnish opera in the minds of an audience as a unique experience. She set about turning her vision into reality and in 1912 her ambition was realized when she co-ordinated and sang at the first Savonlinna Festival.

Only five years after its inception, the festival had to be ditched because of World War I. The following decades of political turmoil resulted in a 50-year hiatus – such a long interlude that it is a wonder that the Savonlinna Opera Festival was ever revived in 1967. It has been held every year since then, and although the centre of Finnish Opera is the National Opera House in Helsinki, the Savonlinna Festival is by far the most important operatic event of the year.

WHEN:
July
WHERE:
Olavinlinna Castle, Savonlinna
BEST FOR:
Brilliant opera performances in an idyllic setting
YOU SHOULD KNOW:
Olavinlinna Castle is the best-preserved, most northerly medieval castle in Europe and is open to visitors all year.

World Wife-Carrying Championship

WHEN:
July
WHERE:
Sonkajärvi, northern Savonia
BEST FOR:
Athletics, fancy dress and beer
YOU SHOULD KNOW:
In 2008, the Wife-Carrying Championship attracted competitors from ten countries and more than 5,000 spectators. An Estonian called Margo Uusorg, has won five of the past eight competitions and is generally acknowledged as World Champion.

Does such an absurd-sounding competition really exist? And can anyone take it seriously? The answer on both counts is, unbelievably, 'Yes'. What started as a light-hearted attraction designed to put the little town of Sonkajärvi on the map, has graduated to become a serious contest with competitors in deadly earnest about winning. The 'sport' has proved so popular that it has not only spread to other countries but even across continents.

Nobody really knows how the Wife-Carrying Championship originated but it appears to have been inspired partly by the practice of wife-stealing, once commonplace in the villages of eastern Finland, and partly from the exploits of a notorious local robber called Rosvo Ronkainen who made potential gang members complete an arduous obstacle course as an endurance test. It is not clear whether he had a reputation for robbing men of their wives along with their valuables, but it seems likely.

The contestants are kitted out in the style of Olympic athletes and the women wear protective helmets in case of misadventure. A man may partner any woman over the age of 17, whether she's his wife or not. Egged on by a huge crowd of spectators, each contestant has to sling a woman across his back and carry her over a gruelling 253.5-m (831-ft) obstacle course with log hurdles, rough terrain and deep water. There are various carrying styles, ranging from piggy-back to upside-down-sack-of-potatoes, and anyone who drops his woman gets penalty-time added. The winner is the man who completes the course fastest. He gets to take home his woman's weight in beer.

However idiotic and/or sexist wife-carrying may seem in theory, you only have to be in Sonkajärvi when the championship is on to change your mind as you get caught up in the festive atmosphere and the excitement of the moment.

Contestants take it very seriously indeed – there is beer to be won!

Helsinki Festival

The Helsinki Festival is Finland's biggest cultural festival, a melting pot of theatre, music, dance, visual arts and film. At the end of the summer holidays, after everyone has flocked back to the city, the festival is a chance to have one last fling before the long, dark nights set in. Although Finns are best known for their somewhat dour taciturnity, an ebullient streak in the national character is revealed as the capital city celebrates the last of the summer. The festival's motto is 'Art Belongs to Everyone' and its programme lives up to its promise with something here for old and young alike, from world music to the circus, with outdoor art events and free rock concerts thrown in.

The festival emerged out of Sibelius Week, an annual music event which some people considered elitist. In 1968, attempts were made to broaden the programme, but to no one's satisfaction. The following year students at the Institute of Applied Arts led a protest, demanding that a city-wide festival should include jazz, folk music, street theatre and cinema. As a result, the Helsinki Festival was 'democratized' and every year becomes more eclectic in its appeal. The Huvila Tent has become the unofficial symbol of the festival. Erected every summer in the waterside park in the heart of the city, an immense billowing awning provides cover for a restaurant area and concert arena. Here, international artists perform cutting-edge music from all over the world.

Taiteiden Yö! (Night of the Arts) is the highlight of the festival. For one night in the last week of August, all Helsinki's art institutions, libraries and bookstores stay open with free entry for exhibitions, performances and films, and a hedonistic atmosphere permeates the city's bars and cafés with people eating, drinking and partying until dawn.

The high point is reached in a stickwalking ballet show.

WHEN:
Late August to early September
WHERE:
Helsinki
BEST FOR:
An eclectic mix of drama, music and the arts
YOU SHOULD KNOW:
Helsinki is one of Europe's fastest growing cities and is well known as a major centre for music of all genres.

173

Casimir's Fair

WHEN:
March 4
WHERE:
Vilnius
BEST FOR:
Medieval atmosphere and
authentic folk art
YOU SHOULD KNOW:
The EU designated Vilnius as
European Capital of Culture 2009.
The Old Town is one of the largest
surviving medieval towns in Europe
and is a UNESCO World Heritage Site.

*Stalls spill out from
Cathedral Square in Vilnius.*

Casimir's Fair (Kaziuko Muge) dates back to the 17th century when market traders spotted the opportunity to make some money from the pilgrims who swarmed into the city of Vilnius on Saint Casimir's Day. Every spring, people would come from far and wide to commemorate their patron saint, a 15th century prince who had died tragically young, renowned for his piety, kindness and good works. He was buried in Vilnius and prayers made at his tomb regularly resulted in miracles, not least the routing of Russian invaders. After this, the name of Casimir became so revered among the Lithuanian populace that the Pope had little choice but to canonize him in 1522. Over the centuries, his name became identified with Lithuanian nationalism and anti-Russian sentiment; and hence for the greater part of the 20th century, while Lithuania was part of the USSR, all Casimir's Day festivities, including Kaziuko Muge, were banned by the ruling authorities.

On the day of the fair, traders, peddlers and buskers take over the medieval Old Town of Vilnius, the stalls spilling out from Cathedral Square piled with folk arts and crafts: traditional hand-knitted clothes, gaudily painted toys, glitzy paintings and home-made food and beer. There are two traditional must-buys: dried herbs and grasses woven into the shape of a lily and tied to a stick, known as verbos, which are saved to be taken to church on Palm Sunday; and muginukas, heart-shaped name-cookies made with honey and decorated with coloured icing to be given to family and friends as tokens of affection. This is definitely not the time to plan a sightseeing tour of Vilnius – you will be frustrated by the crowds. Better to relax and enjoy the vibrancy of living Lithuanian folk culture, saving the city's stunning World Heritage architecture for another day.

St John's Eve

In countries where winters are long and bleak, it's not surprising that the arrival of midsummer should be cause for a feverish outbreak of festivity. St John's Eve, two or three days after the summer solstice, is celebrated with tremendous gusto all over the Baltic. The sun barely sets at this latitude and the short night is whiled away drinking, dancing and singing until after sunrise. In Estonia especially, where it is called Jaanipäev, it is regarded as the most important celebration of the year since it is on the same day as Victory Day, the commemoration of a historic defeat of the German Army in 1919 during Estonia's War for Independence.

Despite its name, the festival has remarkably little to do with St John. It is a thoroughly pagan tradition, celebrating the summer break in the agricultural year, hijacked by the Church in order to give the festivities some Christian credence. However, despite the priests' best efforts, there has always been a marked reluctance on the part of Estonians to go anywhere near a church service on St John's Eve.

The most important part of Jaanipäev is the atavistic ritual of lighting a bonfire then jumping over it, to bring prosperity and keep the demons away. The bonfire has added significance because the practice was suppressed for many years by the USSR government and it became a covert expression of anti-Soviet political views. Shortly after independence in 1992, the President declared Jaanipäev a national holiday; he customarily lights the first fire of the day. Whether in the beautiful medieval capital city of Tallinn or in the depths of the countryside, the Jaanipäev festivities are equally boisterous. All over Estonia bonfires are lit, musicians play and everyone gets increasingly merry as the night progresses, dancing, singing, flirting and generally letting their hair down until dawn.

WHEN:
June 23
WHERE:
Tallinn, or anywhere in Estonia
BEST FOR:
Folk rituals, drinking and music
YOU SHOULD KNOW:
It is traditional for girls to pick seven different kinds of flower on Jaanipäev to put under their pillows so that they will dream of their future husband.

Maslenitsa in Moscow

WHEN:
March/April (date varies according to Russian Orthodox Easter)
WHERE:
Moscow and throughout the Russian Federation
BEST FOR:
Folk-culture displays, fireworks and sleigh rides
YOU SHOULD KNOW:
Under the Soviet communist regime, folk traditions and the Russian Orthodox Church were suppressed. So, for the better part of a century Maslenitsa was not celebrated (at least not in public). It is only since 2002 that the authorities have actively sponsored the Moscow Maslenitsa festival.

Maslenitsa or Pancake Week is the Russian Orthodox equivalent of Carnival in Roman Catholicism, a Christian pre-Lent party before the penance of fasting begins. In fact the festival is rooted in the much more ancient pagan rites performed to welcome the imminent arrival of spring, the little pancakes or blinis being symbols of the sun. Like so many pagan ceremonies, Maslenitsa simply got assimilated into Christianity as people converted.

Each day of Maslenitsa Week has its own special purpose, from the Monday Greeting through to Forgiveness Sunday, when everybody asks for redemption from the past year's sins, bows to each other and says 'God will forgive you' so that they can start Lent with a clear conscience. Meat is forbidden all week so, to make up for it, everybody gorges on pastries and blinis. Every day is celebrated with traditional activities – masquerades, sledging, wrestling and snowball fights. Lady Maslenitsa, a straw effigy decked in brightly coloured clothes, is paraded around until the night of Forgiveness Sunday when she is chucked on a fire and her ashes buried in the snow, a tradition that is said to make the earth fertile for the spring sowing of the crops.

Maslenitsa is a huge event all over Moscow, especially around Red Square where, in the shadow of the magnificently gaudy, fairytale onion domes of St Basil's Cathedral, a Maslenitsa Village is set up for the festival. Among the plethora of pancake stalls and pastry counters there are folk music performances, troika sledge rides and firework displays. Stuffing yet another delicious blini into your mouth as you cheer Lady Maslenitsa through the street on her way to the stake, you can't help getting caught up in the exuberant atmosphere and being completely charmed by this inimitable display of Russian folk culture.

An effigy of Lady Maslenitsa is taken to the stake.

Stars of the White Nights Festival

In the far north, the long twilights of summer, when the sun barely dips below the horizon before popping up again, are aptly known as 'white nights'. St Petersburg makes the most of this natural phenomenon by holding the Stars of the White Nights, an annual festival of ballet, opera and music at the world-famous Mariinsky Theatre, home of the Kirov Opera and Ballet, and the Mariinsky Concert Hall, renowned for its superb acoustics. The diversity of productions, both classical and contemporary, is simply staggering, as is the roll of famous names who have performed here. Since 1993, when the first White Nights was held, the festival has gone from strength to strength, its length extended from ten days to three months, with performances that invariably push back artistic boundaries and thrill audiences year after year.

The Scarlet Sails is the highlight of the festival. It is a massive free public concert and water show with flotillas of sailing ships on the River Neva re-enacting historic battles to a *son et lumière* of live music and spectacular fireworks. It is held to celebrate the end of the school year in June so hordes of teenagers and students show up; the huge crowd that gathers along the riverside regularly reaches more than a million.

Any night of the festival is a remarkable experience. Emerging from the historic Mariinsky Theatre at midnight after a soul-stirring performance, you anticipate the dark outdoors only to find yourself instead propelled straight into another theatre: St Petersburg looks completely artificial in the weird milky light. Wandering through the 18th century streets, passing the impossibly beautiful buildings of the Neva embankment, you get a surreal sensation that this haunting city is a giant theatrical set with you at stage centre as the star of the 'white night'.

The actors of the Mariinsky Theatre, here seen performing at the monastery in Tikhvin.

WHEN:
May to July
WHERE:
St Petersburg
BEST FOR:
World-class ballet, opera and music performed by international stars
YOU SHOULD KNOW:
The famous Russian writer Dostoevsky wrote a short story called *White Nights*, which contains vivid descriptions of the experience of walking the streets of St Petersburg.

Dancers at the fertility festival dress in traditional costume.

Sabantui

The great plains on the furthest edge of Eastern Europe are the lands of the Tatars, descended from the 12th century 'Golden Horde' of nomadic Turkic tribes who swept across the Ural Mountains into the Russian steppe bringing their eastern shamanic spiritual practices with them. Despite being superseded by Islam, these ancient mystical beliefs are still very much alive among the rural communities of Tatarstan. The summer fertility festival of Sabantui or 'Great Plough' is perhaps the most important, especially as it loosely coincides with the founding of the Russian Tatar Republic on June 25.

Sabantui has grown to be a major cultural occasion in Tatarstan's ethnically mixed capital, Kazan. A legendary city of minarets and spires, more Asian than European in character, Kazan is strategically sited at the confluence of the Rivers Volga and Kazanka and for over 1,000 years has absorbed immigrants from both east and west with a remarkable degree of harmony. The festival of Sabantui, being neither Christian nor Muslim in origin, is all-inclusive and in the weeks leading up to it everyone gets involved in the preparations to turn the whole city into a giant fairground. Colourful awnings are hung along the streets and tents erected in the public squares, where on the day of the festival neighbours will gather to hold contests, play games, dance and eat outdoor food. The festival is an ebullient celebration of Tatar culture, highly athletic in nature: küräsh or Turkic wrestling, tug-of-war competitions, ping-pong and pole climbing are among the many different events. But the unquestionable highlight is the incredible equestrian show, held at the city's racetrack, where you can see thrilling horse-plough races and marvel at the dizzying exploits of the dzhigits or trick riders – a truly memorable display of Tatar horsemanship.

WHEN:
June
WHERE:
Kazan, or anywhere in Tatarstan, Russian Federation
BEST FOR:
Tatar horsemanship and folk culture
YOU SHOULD KNOW:
The Sabantui festival has been nominated for listing as UNESCO Intangible Heritage of Humanity.

178

Humorina

Every country in Europe has some sort of tradition of making mischief on All Fools' Day, but nowhere is it marked on quite such an epic scale as in Odessa. Best known for its impressive *belle époque* architecture, cosmopolitan culture and sophisticated seaside charm, 'The Pearl of the Black Sea', Ukraine's third-largest city shows itself in an altogether different guise on April 1 when it devotes itself to a day of anarchic partying.

The city is packed with revellers taking part in spoof contests and satirical masquerades, driving cars decorated with slogans and launching themselves down the Potemkin Stairway, Odessa's iconic 192-step landmark, on skis, skates and any other bizarre means they can dream up. A boisterous procession weaves its way from the Cathedral down Deribasovskaya Street, a cobble-stoned road lined with cafés and bars, to Kulikovo Field where Humorina ends with a bang in a pop concert and fireworks display.

Humorina has been celebrated for more than 30 years. The festival was the brainchild of the presenters of KVN, a satirical television game show, which was one of the Eastern bloc's most popular cult programmes. When the show was axed by the authorities in 1972 for making too many anti-Soviet jokes, its presenters responded by organizing a live 'Day of Laughter' in its place. The festival only lasted three years. Threatened by its popularity, the government banned it and for more than a decade it was held furtively behind closed doors in the city's clubs. The advent of glasnost (liberalization of the censorship laws) in 1987 enabled the organizers to revive Humorina in public; since then it has become an institution, attracting locals and visitors alike to take part in making mayhem and cocking a snook at authority.

WHEN:
April 1
WHERE:
Odessa
BEST FOR:
Eastern European hospitality and humour
YOU SHOULD KNOW:
Nobody knows the origin of All Fools' Day. It is possible that it is derived from the Hilaria, an Ancient Roman festival of laughter to celebrate the vernal equinox.

Good humour prevails on the streets of Odessa for Humorina.

Ivan Kupala

WHEN:
July 6-7
WHERE:
Kiev, or any town or village in
Ukraine or Belarus
BEST FOR:
Pagan rituals, fortune telling
and flirtation
YOU SHOULD KNOW:
Gogol wrote a story called *The Eve of
Ivan Kupala* in which the protagonist
finds the elusive fern flower but is
cursed by it.

In Ukraine, the summer solstice signals Ivan Kupala, an ancient midsummer fertility festival celebrating young love. With the arrival of Christianity, Kupala (The Bathing) was assimilated into the official Church calendar and identified with the birthday of John (Ivan) the Baptist or St John's Day, in a futile attempt to inject some Christian piety into the midsummer revelry. But paganism has always been deeply ingrained in the Ukrainian psyche and Ivan Kupala is an occasion to express superstitions handed down through generations, a complex web of folklore and Slavic mythology – a paean to the ancient Slavic sun god Dazhbog and an entreaty to the magical elements of fire and water to ensure a prosperous harvest, and by implication human fecundity.

It is a night of erotic magic when the normal rules governing the world are turned topsy-turvy: a night when trees can walk around, witches cast spells, and ferns spontaneously burst into a blossom that glows in the dark – a great excuse for courting couples to slip away to 'look for a fern flower'. The girls weave willow wreaths in which they place lighted candles. They float these on the nearest stretch of water, telling their fortunes from the direction the wreath takes. According to tradition, any youth who retrieves a wreath will marry the girl to whom it belongs.

Jumping the fire is a traditional pagan ritual of fertility and self-purification.

In Kiev, 'Mother of Cities', Ivan Kupala is a night of spectacular revelry. The girls dress in embroidered peasant costumes, entwine flowers in their hair and set out to ensnare the boy they've had their eye on. Children run through the streets having water fights. And supposedly the witches gather for a Sabbath on the city's Lysa Gora Hill. More mundanely, Ivana Kupala signals the start of the swimming season, the date that Ukraine's bracing waters have warmed up enough to bathe.

KaZantip

If you regret the passing of the rave scene, you need yearn no more. For six weeks every summer a beautiful stretch of beach on the Crimean peninsula becomes a huge outdoor dance floor for aficionados of techno, trance and house music where you can party for 24 hours a day.

KaZantip is the spin-off from an annual Black Sea windsurfing event that always ended with a party. Every year the party got bigger and carried on for longer, until it eventually morphed into the biggest electronic music event in the world. More than 150,000 young people gather here every year, mostly from the former Soviet Union but increasingly from the rest of the world too. For young Ukrainians the existence of KaZantip is symbolic of a hard-won freedom from the repressive grip of totalitarian government. The purported philosophy of the festival is to be beyond politics and, although it is more tightly controlled than appears at first sight, there is at least a temporary illusion of freedom – an extraordinary occurrence in a country where any form of individual expression was rigorously curtailed for so long.

For the duration of the summer KaZantip is an independent 'republic' with its own sub-cultural laws and a special watchword 'schastie' – a neologism which loosely translates as 'be happy and have fun'. There is little in the way of a programme; the organizers rely on the hundreds of amateur DJs who rock up with their record collections to take part in a more or less spontaneous line-up. Although the music pumps continuously, in practice most people rent rooms in the nearby village of Popovka, spend the days hanging out on the beach and hit the dance floor at night – for a new generation of ravers, an idyllic way to spend the summer.

The ultimate beach party awaits visitors to KaZantip.

WHEN:
Mid July to end August
WHERE:
Popovka, Black Sea Coast
BEST FOR:
Sun, sea and . . . raving
YOU SHOULD KNOW:
Entry to KaZantip is with a pre-paid pass, a one-off fee that entitles you to go in and out as many times as you want for the duration of your stay.

Cheltenham Festival

WHEN:
Tuesday to Friday in the second week of March
WHERE:
Prestbury Park Racecourse, Cheltenham, Gloucestershire
BEST FOR:
Connoisseurs of jump racing (and lovers of the craic)
YOU SHOULD KNOW:
Irish eyes not only smile because their well-backed horses invariably snaffle several top prizes, but also because the meeting usually coincides with St Patrick's Day, which helps the celebrations along nicely.

The unique Grand National may be looming, but for dedicated followers of National Hunt Racing the winter season comes to a climax at the splendid Cheltenham Festival – a succession of top races featuring the very best thoroughbred jumping horses, many of them raiders from the 'Emerald Isle' accompanied by thousands of Irish enthusiasts who convert the whole event into one non-stop party.

Every trainer in Great Britain and Ireland (and one or two in France and Germany) prays to have horses worthy of a Cheltenham Festival entry – and then has no higher ambition than actually winning one of the 25 races held over four days. Among other prestigious contests, these include the Champion Bumper (run on the flat), Triumph Hurdle, Arkle Challenge Trophy, Champion Hurdle, Queen Mother Champion Chase and the Cheltenham Gold Cup.

There are no people like jump-racing people when it comes to sheer enthusiasm for the sport they love. With important feature races to appreciate on every day, the famous 'Cheltenham Roar' that greets the thundering hooves of the leading horses as they leap the last jump and start up the long run-in towards the winning post almost lifts the grandstand roof. The highlight of the entire jump-racing season is Friday's challenging Gold Cup, with the finest steeplechasers vying to win it once, or perhaps even join the roll of famous multiple winners like Golden Miller, Arkle and Best Mate.

But – stimulating though the racing may be – there's more to a day out at Cheltenham than that. There's Ladies Day on the Thursday and a wealth of other entertainment to be found, with trade stands, music and almost endless hospitality options on offer. For the uninitiated, simply spending a day at the Cheltenham Festival and enjoying the extraordinary atmosphere will be an experience to savour.

Top horses in action at the Cheltenham course.

Crufts Dog Show

Welcome to the cut-throat world of top dog shows! Actually, despite rumours of vicious rivalry between breeders and sharp practice amongst competitors out to sabotage rivals, none of this is apparent to 160,000 eager visitors to the world's greatest dog show.

At Crufts, all seems sweetness and light. Pedigree dogs that have won qualifying events in the previous year are judged by breed, with winners proceeding into seven final groups (toy, gundog, utility, hound, working, pastoral and terriers). The group winners (and their high-stepping handlers) then compete to become 'champion of champions' by winning the coveted title of Best in Show.

Whilst this blue-riband event may grab headlines and lots of TV coverage, it is just the tip of a wonderful canine pyramid, with all sorts of interesting activities taking place in various rings (not to mention the opportunity to buy each and every accessory known to dog). For many visitors, the supporting events are as interesting as the main show classes – or more so.

There are entertaining competitions that present dogs at their most exuberant and (yes!) obedient. The Agility event sees them attempt to complete an obstacle course against the clock, urged on by equally animated handlers in individual and team competitions. Fly Ball is even more frantic as relay teams of four dogs each jump hurdles before catching a flying tennis ball and racing back to send the next dog on its way. Obedience and heelwork-to-music competitions arouse the envy of every owner with a disobedient mutt, and special demonstrations further underline the extraordinary abilities of well-trained dogs.

But for many, the highlight of Crufts is Discover Dogs, where every breed recognized by the Kennel Club is on display. Most can be petted even as strengths and weaknesses are discussed with a knowledgeable owner.

A Lhasa Apso struts its stuff.

WHEN:
Four days in early March
WHERE:
The NEC (National Exhibition Centre), Birmingham
BEST FOR:
Dazzled dog-lovers
YOU SHOULD KNOW:
The speed with which many Crufts winners appear in dog food advertisements serves as a reminder that Charles Cruft, who founded the event in 1886, worked for . . . a dog biscuit manufacturer.

The crews power under Hammersmith Bridge.

The Boat Race

WHEN:
Late March or early April
WHERE:
River Thames – between Putney and
Mortlake, West London
BEST FOR:
Die-hard Light and Dark-Blue
adherents
YOU SHOULD KNOW:
Despite appearing not to be the
largest of hunks, actor and writer
Hugh Laurie rowed for Cambridge in
1980 . . . and lost.

Sixteen large men and two small people doing battle for 15 minutes
sounds like a major brawl, but in the case of The Boat Race it's a
remarkably civilized (though punishing) encounter. There has long been
healthy rivalry between the ancient universities of Oxford and Cambridge,
nowhere more keenly expressed than in sport where students vie for the
award of a coveted 'blue' (dark for Oxford, light for Cambridge) for
sporting excellence. Using a course upriver from Putney to Mortlake that
is four miles and 374 yards (6,779 m) long, the race was first held in 1829.
Honours are roughly even – though the Light Blues currently hold a
slender overall lead.

This national institution is televised and attracts a viewing audience
out of all proportion to the sporting drama as the eventual winner is often

apparent after a few moments of frantic rowing and the best that can be anticipated is a clash of oars as diminutive coxes both seek the best water. The course is lined with spectators and perhaps the real draw is sheer admiration for the extreme physical effort put in by heavyweight rowers who have trained relentlessly for months.

Both crews finish totally exhausted, but the contrast between jubilant winners and dejected losers is almost too painful to watch.

To be part of this Great British day, it's possible to join the crowds anywhere along the riverside embankments, though this only allows limited sight of the long race. For those who want a TV-style overview of the race coupled with the excitement of a live atmosphere, the ideal solution is to join large crowds that gather in Bishops Park near the start and Furnival Gardens by Hammersmith Bridge to watch on big screens.

The branches fly as horses tackle the fearsome fences.

The Grand National

Without doubt, it's the globe's most-watched horse race, with a worldwide television audience of over 600 million – and adherents of jump racing would have no hesitation in declaring that the Grand National is also the most thrilling.

This famous old steeplechase was first run at Aintree in 1839, though some claim it began three years earlier. It involves a formidable 7,242-m (23,760-ft) race with 30 jumps – the four miles and four furlongs that appears at the top of the race card. The horses undertake two circuits of the course and every fence except the water jump and the notorious Chair have to be crossed twice.

The excitement amongst the 60,000-strong crowd reaches fever pitch as the 40 runners line up at the start and the roar that greets the first horse over the last fence has to be heard to be believed. There always seems to be a great story associated with each race or winner. In 1956 the Queen Mother's Devon Loch slipped up on the flat after the last fence with the race all but won, one year the race was abandoned after a false start that saw many runners continue, another year it was run on the Monday after a bomb scare. The great Red Rum ran in five consecutive Nationals, winning three times and coming second twice. After a long and happy retirement the equine hero was buried by the winning post at Aintree.

Animal rights activists don't approve and their efforts have ensured that some of the fences are now less fearsome. For everyone else, the Grand National is an incomparable spectacle – and whilst most of the audience will enjoy it from the comfort of their armchairs, there's nothing quite like experiencing the drama first hand in the company of tens of thousands of excited race goers.

WHEN:
The Grand National Meeting is staged on three days in April, with the big race on the last day, Saturday, starting at 16.15.
WHERE:
Aintree Racecourse, near Liverpool
BEST FOR:
Those who appreciate the ultimate horseracing thrill
YOU SHOULD KNOW:
The sport of steeplechasing is so named after reckless 18th century English gentlemen who raced each other on horseback from one church to the next, jumping every obstacle in their path.

Knutsford Royal May Day

May Day festivities take place in many communities throughout the British Isles, but nowhere are they more elaborately celebrated than in the small Cheshire market town of Knutsford. The practice of heralding the arrival of summer at the start of the merry month of May has its roots in pagan times and can be traced back to the Celtic festival of Beltane. Knutsford's present revels were first recorded in 1864 although there would almost certainly have been celebrations of some kind in medieval times. For nearly 150 years May Day has been marked annually in Knutsford (except for the war years) on the first Saturday of the month. Along streets festooned in bunting the May Day procession winds its colourful way, led by the distinctive character of Jack-in-the-Green, an ancient fertility symbol and embodiment of summer. Jack plays the part of King of the May and is traditionally surrounded by a wickerwork frame covered in greenery and flowers.

Brightly decorated horse-drawn floats make up the bulk of the procession and these provide an opportunity for the town's children to dress up in costumes illustrating different themes and periods of history. They are accompanied by bands, Morris dancers, the Town Crier and honorary dignitaries for the day, such as the Sword Bearer and the Marshal of the Procession. The festivities reach their climax with the appearance of the May Queen, chosen each year from the young girls of the town. Following her crowning on the town's Heath, the party continues with a huge funfair and other entertainments.

A unique feature of the Knutsford celebrations is the practice of 'sanding the pavement' on May Day morning, where coloured sands are used to decorate the town's pavements with elaborate patterns.

WHEN:
The first Saturday in May
WHERE:
Knutsford, Cheshire
BEST FOR:
Folklore
YOU SHOULD KNOW:
Knutsford May Day acquired its Royal title in 1887 following a visit by the Prince and Princess of Wales.

Morris men bring colour to Knutsford on May Day.

Cooper's Hill Cheese Rolling

WHEN:
Late May
WHERE:
Cooper's Hill, near Brockworth,
Gloucestershire
BEST FOR:
Those with a love of quirky folk
traditions (and a head for heights)
YOU SHOULD KNOW:
The heaviest cheese ever rolled was
a monster 18-kg (40-lb) Cheddar
presented by New Zealand to mark
the resumption of 'real' cheese
rolling from 1954 (a wooden
'cheese' was used during
post-war food rationing).

How do you catch (on foot) a large round of cheese that's travelling at a speed of up to 110 kph (70 mph)? Answer – you don't, but you can have some fun trying . . . and less energetic entertainment by simply watching (an occasional wayward cheese crashes into onlookers, who are also prone to slipping down the precipitous hill – so even spectating can be hazardous!).

The ancient tradition of pursuing a Double Gloucester cheese down Cooper's Hill in the Cotswolds was originally confined to inhabitants of the local village, Brockworth, with contestants pursuing the wheel-like cheese downhill and the first to cross the winning line receiving the fast-rolling dairy produce as their prize. But the fame of this quirky event has spread, attracting competitors and spectators from far and wide, with a thoroughly good day out to be had by all.

The fearsome course is rough and uneven, plunging down the 200-m (655-ft) slope of Cooper's Hill – which has a gradient as steep as 1-in-1 and a concave face, so those on the start line can see the finish far below, but not the course itself. This inevitably leads to casualties such as grazed elbows, sprained ankles or occasionally broken limbs as competitors tumble down the hill. Races are sometimes delayed until ambulances return from ferrying victims of the previous contest to hospital.

The format can vary, but there are usually five downhill races (including a ladies' race), each begun with the traditional cry of 'One to be ready, two to be steady, three to prepare and four to be off!' There are also four lung-bursting uphill races, including one for women and one for children. Though Double Gloucester cannot defy gravity and roll uphill, the prize for each winner is still a cheese. Yummy!

Competitors head off in pursuit of their runaway cheeses.

Glyndebourne Festival Opera

Festival goers mingle on the lawns at Glyndebourne.

An opera lover can find no more magical setting to enjoy an aria than Glyndebourne – the summer Festival Opera season that offers performances of the highest quality in a fabulous setting that combines the advantages of a fine modern theatre with superb acoustics and the timeless atmosphere of a classic English country house.

In 1920, John Christie inherited the 500-year-old house at Glyndebourne that had been extensively remodelled by his forebears in Victorian times, and he immediately added a large music room and installed a full-size organ therein. His love of music led to regular amateur opera evenings for invited guests being staged in this rather grand setting and thus he met his future wife, a Canadian professional singer. Together, they hatched a plan to create an annual opera event at Glyndebourne and set about constructing a theatre annexe to the organ room, complete with orchestra pit.

The first six-week season was launched in 1934 and (with an interruption for World War II) the festival has continued ever since. The original theatre was constantly enlarged, then was finally replaced by a brand-new auditorium which opened 60 years on to the day with a repeat of Glyndebourne's first-ever performance (Mozart's *The Marriage of Figaro*) in 1994. This was doubly appropriate, as the festival has a reputation for staging definitive performances of Mozart's operas.

A visit to Glyndebourne is an essential part of the English summer season, with many people travelling down from London for performances that start in the afternoon, with a long interval that allows for the activity that makes Glyndebourne unique – the ability to combine top-class opera with a leisurely picnic in a country-house garden, or a lingering meal in one of the fine restaurants within the grounds. It truly is a feast of opera like no other!

WHEN:
The festival runs from mid May to the end of August.
WHERE:
Near Lewes in East Sussex
BEST FOR:
Dreamy opera buffs
YOU SHOULD KNOW:
It may not quite compare with the all-round experience of visiting home base, but a touring ensemble called the Glyndebourne Touring Opera brings operatic excellence to the provinces each summer.

189

The soaring arch is the crowning glory of this stunning new stadium.

FA Cup Final

The world's oldest soccer competition is the Football Association Challenge Cup. It has lost a little lustre in recent years, as a Premier League and European competitions with huge financial rewards have seduced the nation's leading clubs. They often field weakened teams in FA Cup matches, but that opens the door to lesser lights – adding to the competition's drama by ensuring that headline-grabbing David and Goliath performances occur.

The FA Cup pyramid is broadly based, with an entry of over 700 clubs and 'minnows' from non-league football contesting preliminary rounds from August. Senior clubs join subsequently, until the biggest guns enter the fray for the Third Round proper in January. Then the fun really starts, with players and supporters of winning small clubs eagerly watching the televised draw for the next round and whooping with joy if they get a mega-opponent like Manchester United, guaranteeing a financial bonanza.

Sadly, whilst Premier League managers may have other priorities, their weakened FA Cup sides are still a match for everyone else and – despite alarms and excursions along the way – the Final is almost always contested by two of England's top clubs. No matter – it's a huge occasion, with demand for tickets from exultant fans of the finalists far exceeding supply as they dream of striding down Wembley Way to a dramatic date with destiny.

Still, quite a few of the tickets are reserved for corporate sponsors and the like, so the neutral can aim to experience the FA Cup Final's very special atmosphere at first hand. It isn't easy, but with sufficient determination (and perhaps a deep pocket), it's usually possible to find a way of saying 'I was there' when the match is subsequently discussed by those mere mortals who could only watch on television – along with the rest of the world.

WHEN:
A Saturday towards the end of May
WHERE:
Wembley Stadium, London
BEST FOR:
Football fans
YOU SHOULD KNOW:
The record FA Cup attendance is estimated at 200,000, when eager spectators gatecrashed the first Wembley Final in 1923 – the crowded pitch was patiently cleared by a mounted policeman on a white horse, creating the lasting soubriquet 'White Horse Final'.

190

Chelsea Flower Show

Fancy following in the footsteps of the Monarch and most of the Royal Family? They rarely appear collectively in public, but one event that attracts them is the fabulous Chelsea Flower Show. This highlight of the traditional English summer social season also draws hordes of gardening enthusiasts to the nation's most famous flower show.

Actually, that description belittles delights to be found at Chelsea. The Royal Horticultural Society's spring show was first held in 1862, and when the RHS flagship finally berthed at Chelsea in 1913 it became a national institution that not only featured the best horticulture but also a whirl of society tea parties.

Nowadays much of the event is devoted to spectacular show gardens created by the world's top garden designers. They are competitive, striving for a coveted gold medal (lesser grades are silver-gilt, silver and bronze) and (in their secret dreams) the ultimate accolade of 'Best in Show'. With reputations on the line, even the most famous admit to acute nervousness as forensic RHS judges evaluate their best efforts.

But Chelsea Flower Show is about much more than cutting-edge garden design. There are also medals for four more categories on display in the marquee: trees; vegetables and herbs; educational and scientific exhibits; pictures, photographs, flower arrangements and floristry. Visitors are always fascinated to see whether their own preferences coincide with those of the judges. In addition, it has become traditional to introduce new varieties at Chelsea, giving visitors 'I saw it first' bragging rights. Numerous stands sell garden accessories.

Don't expect to find much elbow-room at Chelsea – visitor numbers are restricted to 157,000 each year, with all tickets sold well in advance (early pre-planning advised if you mean to be there). The first two days are restricted to RHS members with the general public admitted thereafter.

WHEN:
Five days in May
WHERE:
In the grounds of The Royal Hospital in Chelsea, London
BEST FOR:
Gardening addicts who crave a massive fix
YOU SHOULD KNOW:
There are bargains galore as the exhibits are broken down on Saturday afternoon, with the often-exotic component flora and 'gardenalia' sold at knockdown prices.

Glorious Chelsea flowers in 2009

A wide range of work from both established and emerging artists is on show.

Royal Academy Summer Exhibition

The independent Royal Academy of Arts was founded by George III in 1768 and receives no public subsidy, so one of the august society's chief sources of revenue is the annual Summer Exhibition . . . itself something of an institution. First presented in 1769 and held annually ever since, its primary objective is not financial gain, but to maintain a founding principle – the staging of a major annual public art exhibition that is open to all artists of merit.

Each year, around 1,200 works are carefully chosen by the somewhat long-winded Summer Exhibition Selection and Hanging Committee, formed from the RA's governing body, The Council of Academicians. As many as 10,000 works are submitted by hopeful artists, who may offer no more than two pictures each and must pay a fee designed to deter timewasters. Each of the RA's 80 Academicians is also entitled to enter up to six of their own works in the Summer Exhibition, which usually includes a special gallery with works chosen and arranged by an Academician.

The exhibition is held at the magnificent Burlington House mansion and always has a general theme. A series of events broaden the appeal of this great show, including free talks, family workshops, children's activities and entertainment in the courtyard. There may also be complementary events like a photographic exhibition or a memorial show.

The end result is the world's largest open contemporary art exhibition that draws together a huge variety of new work by living artists, both famous and unknown. Almost all the works in the Summer Exhibition are for sale, with a third of the purchase price going to the Academy. Tickets for the Summer Exhibition may be booked in advance on line or bought at the ticket kiosk in the foyer of Burlington House.

WHEN:
Mid June to mid August
WHERE:
Burlington House, Piccadilly, Central London
BEST FOR:
Figurative art that generally includes recognizable subject matter
YOU SHOULD KNOW:
The great J M W Turner worked so fast that he sometimes painted his entries from a standing start on Varnishing Day, normally reserved for finishing touches after the exhibition is hung. The famous *Rain, Steam and Speed* was one such exhibit.

192

Trooping the Colour

The ceremony of Trooping the Colour has taken place since the 17th century, when it had a practical purpose – soldiers had to be able to recognize their regiment's flags in the heat of battle because the 'colours' were a rallying point, so they were constantly shown to assembled troops.

Today's famous display of pomp and pageantry to mark the Monarch's official birthday dates from 1805. Over 1,400 officers and men turn out, together with 200 horses, supported by bands and corps of drums. They are the Monarch's personal troops, the Household Division, whose colourful dress uniforms are very different from the battledress that is their more usual garb – these are not ceremonial troops, but fighting soldiers who may recently have returned from (or will shortly be posted to) combat zones.

The sound of shot and shell seems a long way away as the clock on the Horse Guards Building strikes eleven and the Royal Procession arrives (though a 41-gun salute will later be fired in nearby Green Park). The Monarch takes the salute and inspects the troops, who then perform the intricate traditional manoeuvres of the Trooping the Colour ceremony with perfect precision, before following the Royal carriage back to Buckingham Palace.

The full parade route extends from Buckingham Palace along The Mall to Horse Guards Parade, then back to the Palace. Those not lucky enough to be on Horse Guards for the main event gather to see the passing pageant at Buckingham Palace, in The Mall or around the Victoria Monument. But there's one thing nobody can miss, however dense the crowds. After the parade the Royal Air Force stages a formation flypast, watched by the Royal Family from the balcony of Buckingham Palace. It marks the end of a very British occasion, stirring memories of the nation's proud history.

WHEN:
On a Saturday in mid June
WHERE:
Horse Guards Parade,
Whitehall, London
BEST FOR:
Pageantry at its very best
YOU SHOULD KNOW:
There is a ballot for seats in the stands erected around Horse Guards Parade – apply early and hope!

The massed band of the Guards marches off down The Mall towards Buckingham Palace.

Royal Ascot

WHEN:
Five days in mid June
WHERE:
Ascot Racecourse, Berkshire
BEST FOR:
Thoroughbreds
YOU SHOULD KNOW:
Thursday (day three) of Royal Ascot is Ladies' Day – a fashion parade that must surely be a ruinous drain on many a platinum credit card.

Competition is of the highest quality, with top horses galloping after some of the most sought-after prizes in the racing calendar – but there's much more to Royal Ascot than that. There are other courses that stage important race meetings, but none has greater social cachet than the annual event held in the Royal Borough of Windsor and Maidenhead every summer.

There are long-standing connections with the Crown, which owns the course. The first race was run in 1711 for a purse of 100 guineas at the instigation of Queen Anne. Nowadays, prize money is somewhat greater (over £3 million) and the Royal Ascot Meeting is attended by the current Monarch, members of the Royal Family and honoured guests who drive along the course after arriving by horse-drawn carriage from nearby Windsor Castle each day.

They are not alone – over 300,000 people are attracted every year, making Royal Ascot Europe's best-attended meeting. However, racing is the last thing on the minds of many – this is a major highlight in the social calendar and a large proportion of those present are drawn for that reason. Dress code is formal and strictly applied in the exclusive Royal Enclosure – morning dress and top hats for the men, proper dresses (no flesh!) and mandatory hats for the women. Many who can only aspire to the Royal Enclosure follow the dress code anyway, and press and television coverage sometimes seems more interested in people and fashion than horse racing.

This is probably true of many visitors who throng less formal areas of Ascot racecourse, to enjoy being part of a great occasion and subscribing to the party mood by quaffing liberal quantities of champagne. But plenty of serious types do actually come to watch some of the best horse racing in the country.

Hats reign on Ladies Day!

Derby Day

Open-top buses are a traditional feature of Derby Day.

Since the late 18th century, Britain's (and latterly Europe's) finest thoroughbred racehorses have thundered across the undulating turf of Epsom Downs in pursuit of the world racing's most coveted prize – The Derby Stakes, generally known as The Epsom Derby or simply The Derby.

But for the fickle finger of fate it would be known as The Bunbury – the Earl of Derby and Sir Charles Bunbury tossed a coin for the honour of having the inaugural race in 1780 named after them (Bunbury lost the toss but won the race). The Derby is one of five English Classics, the others being the One and Two Thousand Guineas run previously at Newmarket, The Oaks on the day before The Derby and the subsequent St Leger at Doncaster.

The staging of the prestigious Epsom Classics takes place at the two-day Derby Festival. Day one is designated as Ladies Day. This is because The Oaks is restricted to fillies and it gives dedicated followers of fashion an excuse to strut their stuff – and strut it they most definitely do, with a spectacular display of millinery and eye-catching summer dresses.

It's a pukka social occasion, but unlike that other top race meeting – Royal Ascot – which takes place a week or so later, Derby Day has long been a traditional day out for ordinary Londoners, who find the broad expanses of Epsom Downs transformed into a lively fiesta to be enjoyed by all. The course is situated amidst wonderful scenery, but that's all but obscured by the temporary tented town that springs up offering all sorts of delights.

Some 40,000 pack into various official enclosures, with another 60,000 occupying The Hill – a sloping vantage point overlooking the course where leisurely picnics are *de rigueur* (and barbecues are known to appear). It really is a terrific occasion.

WHEN:
Usually the first Saturday in June
WHERE:
Epsom Downs, Surrey
BEST FOR:
Fun and frolics to the sound of valuable hooves
YOU SHOULD KNOW:
The most famous non-racing incident associated with the Derby came in 1913, when suffragette Emily Davison threw herself in front of the King's horse Anmer to publicize her cause, bringing him down – she died four days later but gained immortality.

195

Leonard Cohen performs on the Pyramid stage.

Glastonbury Festival

Mud, mud, glorious mud . . . that's not actually the motto of the Glastonbury Festival, but it might as well be. Every year seems to produce pictures of sodden revellers who have braved playful elements to experience the magic of Glastonbury – a music festival so compelling that everyone regards the near-inevitable soaking as part of the fun, with a wild time had by all.

After intermittent beginnings in the 1970s and occasional fallow years since, the Glastonbury Festival of Performing Arts (more commonly simply Glastonbury or Glasto) has become the world's largest green-field festival, attracting around 175,000 visitors annually. Held beneath the benign eye of Glastonbury Tor in the mystical Vale of Avalon, the festival has long espoused alternative values stemming from hippy culture of the 1960s, becoming an annual pilgrimage for those who crave the coming of a New Age. The first festival started on the day after the late, great Jimi Hendrix died, and Glastonbury has continued to champion the spirit of musical energy and innovation embodied in the great guitarist's inspiring work.

A vast tented city appears on pastureland, with the festival offering something for every taste, from the whirl of excitement around the main Pyramid, Other and Dance stages to the spiritual atmosphere of the Sacred Space, a stone circle that harks back to prehistory where sunrise is greeted with fiery torches, chanting and joy. In between are chilled-out scenes like the Acoustic and Jazzworld areas, Kidz Field for families, Circus and Theatre Fields. And many simply head for more peaceful and contemplative places – Tipi Field, Green Fields or the Field of Avalon.

Visitors willingly queue to get in, because once inside devotees enter a unique world where society's rules suddenly seem less constrictive and life is freer for three brief but stimulating days – whatever the weather!

WHEN:
Around the end of June (takes place in most but not all years)
WHERE:
Worthy Farm near Pilton, 10 km (6 mi) east of Glastonbury
BEST FOR:
Waterproof music lovers
YOU SHOULD KNOW:
Glastonbury's 1,500 stewards and helpers are mostly volunteers supplied by a number of charities that (together with others) receive substantial donations from the festival's profits.

Wimbledon Tennis Championships

The perennial question is 'will this be his year or not?' It refers to the current British hero's chances in the men's singles at the Lawn Tennis Championship Meeting (aka Wimbledon Championships) – and the fact that the answer invariably turns out to be 'or not' does nothing to dampen the nation's enthusiasm for this famous fortnight.

Wimbledon is the world's oldest and most prestigious tennis tournament, the third of four Grand Slam events that represent the pinnacle of professional tennis — and the only one remaining faithful to the grass courts that encourage fast power play. The first Gentlemen's Singles in 1877 was won by old Harrovian Spencer Gore from a field of 22, watched by 200 spectators who were each charged a shilling – expect to pay a bit more today and be in the company of rather more people.

Demand for tickets far exceeds supply. Those not lucky enough to enjoy debenture status or corporate hospitality may enter a ballot for tickets to show courts. This closes six months in advance and applicants cannot specify a particular date or court. It's possible to get a limited number of show court tickets 'on the day', but this involves overnight queuing. For ground passes giving access to all outside courts and Number Two Court standing enclosure, it's possible to get away with queuing for four or five hours. Is it worth it? You bet!

That's because spectators not only see great tennis being played, but also get to enjoy the atmosphere of this wonderful event and experience the excitement it generates. From top pros on show courts to up-and-coming stars or fading favourites on outside courts, strawberries and champagne to picnics on the hill in front of the big screen, sunshine to showers, Wimbledon Fortnight is a highlight of London's summer season.

WHEN:
Two weeks at the end of June and beginning of July
WHERE:
Church Road, Wimbledon, London SW19
BEST FOR:
Strawberries and cream, with top sport thrown in
YOU SHOULD KNOW:
The Wimbledon Lawn Tennis Museum is open all year round (to spectators only, during the Championships), providing an opportunity to visit the famous stadium and gain fascinating hi-tech insight into the world of tennis.

Serena and Venus Williams battle it out on Centre Court in the 2009 Ladies Final.

EUROPE/ENGLAND

Stonehenge Summer Solstice

WHEN:
The summer solstice is on June 21 (it's not Midsummer's Day, which is three days later on June 24).
WHERE:
Just west of Amesbury, Wiltshire
BEST FOR:
Those seeking spiritual uplift
YOU SHOULD KNOW:
Special access to Stonehenge is also granted for those who wish to greet the winter solstice, plus spring and autumn equinoxes.

Once upon a time (until 1977, actually) it was possible to turn up and wander around the world-famous prehistoric monument of Stonehenge, touching ancient stones and experiencing wonderment at being in such an atmospheric place, often alone. Not any more – all those hands were contributing to erosion and today's multitudinous visitors may look but not touch.

Stonehenge began as a circular ditch and earth bank constructed around 3100 BC, with the standing stone circle erected some nine centuries later. Research suggests that Stonehenge marked an important burial site, but this prosaic explanation is not accepted by everyone. The purpose of Stonehenge has long been passionately debated with diverse theories mooted – these include religious ritual, astronomical observation and assorted complex and often outlandish supernatural notions. Was it really a landing site for space travellers? Probably not.

Whatever the truth, the place retains an aura of mystery. It was the site of the Stonehenge Free Festival between 1972 and 1984, when revellers gathered to celebrate alternative culture at the summer solstice. That laid-back era came to end in 1985 when the police did battle with 'New Agers' bent on reaching Stonehenge after the festival was banned.

Guardians English Heritage relented in 1999, and those who wish to experience the summer solstice in the company of like-minded people are now permitted to do so – without charge. Many thousands who gather to do just that invariably experience powerful emotion at the moment when the sun rises over the mystical circle on solstice morning, and find themselves amidst all sorts of alternative believers like neo-pagans and druids in fantastic garb who are conducting esoteric ceremonies. It's a magical moment, but reality soon intrudes – the site must be cleared by 08.00 so Stonehenge can revert to lucrative 'tourist business as usual'.

The crowds greet the dawn.

Appleby Horse Fair

James II certainly started something when he granted a charter for a horse fair near the River Eden in the 17th century. The Appleby Horse Fair was the result, held since 1685 at Appleby-in-Westmorland (now called Cumbria, though Appleby has stuck by its traditional name).

Hundreds of horseboxes, trucks, vans, caravans, traditional horse-drawn bowtop wagons and vardos appear, forming a vast and bustling temporary encampment. Gypsies and travellers gather on Fair Hill outside Appleby (once the rather more macabre Gallows Hill where public hangings took place) to buy and sell horses, meet and greet family and friends . . . and sometimes settle old scores. There are horses everywhere – tethered along roadside verges, being washed in the river so they may be shown to best advantage and racing or trotting along Flashing Lane all day (though never allowed across the bridge into the thronged town).

There will be horses of all sorts, but the predominant type is the black-and-white cob. Plenty will change hands, but sales are rarely witnessed – dealers don't want an audience in case they resell the same horse later. Some horses arrive with the travellers whilst dealers bring others in each day.

After suffering a decline after World War II, Appleby Horse Fair has grown in size and popularity and is again similar in scale to the great 19th century events. It is now one of the largest horse fairs in Europe. This colourful gathering includes numerous palm readers, fortune tellers and more than two hundred stands selling everything from saddlery to footwear (including 'wellies' for those who've overlooked the fact that the site can be muddy after rain). Thousands of tourists arrive at the weekend to enjoy the lively atmosphere of this unique event held in the fabulous countryside of the beautiful Eden Valley.

Harness racing adds to the excitement of the lively Appleby Horse Fair.

WHEN:
For a week, ending on the second Wednesday in June
WHERE:
Fair Hill, Appleby-in-Westmorland, Cumbria
BEST FOR:
Assorted horseflesh and colourful characters
YOU SHOULD KNOW:
If you actually buy a horse, expect to be given 'luck money', a small sum returned by the seller to ensure that good fortune smiles on the transaction.

199

World Stinging Nettle Eating Championship

Competitors tuck into their feast of nettles.

They say that strange things happen down on the farm, and they don't come much stranger than this event in rural West Dorset. One weekend in mid June, the pub in the tiny village of Marshwood becomes the focus for international interest when it hosts the World Stinging Nettle Eating Championship during an annual charity beer festival. The humble stinging nettle, scourge of many a country walk, is propelled into the limelight as the raw material for a feeding frenzy, when competitors come from far and wide to test their mettle on the nettle. The object is simple: to consume as many nettles as your stomach can bear in one hour, the winner being judged by the total length of stalks stripped of their leaves. Contestants are not allowed to use their own nettles nor any mouth-numbing substances, though this stricture does not extend to the prodigious quantities of beer consumed which help to take away the rancid taste.

Unlike many unusual country pursuits whose origins are lost in the mists of time, the Nettle Eating Championship dates back merely to 1997, when the enterprising publican of the 16th century Bottle Inn challenged all-comers to take on the pub's resident nettle-eating champion. Some years previously this gentleman had had to deliver on a rash promise to eat any nettle produced that was longer than his own 4.7 m (15.5 ft) specimen. The sight of blackened tongues, some decidedly pallid complexions, and grown men and women chomping their way through piles of raw green stuff may not be one for queasy stomachs, but it provides much merriment in an event that is as good-natured as it is hotly contested. And if you fancy your own chances you might ponder the current world record of nettles consumed, which stands at a sobering 24 m (76 ft)!

WHEN:
Mid June
WHERE:
Marshwood, Dorset
BEST FOR:
Unusual country pursuits
YOU SHOULD KNOW:
Apparently the technique to avoid getting stung is to roll up the leaves before popping them in the mouth.

The Ashes Series

The needle that characterizes international cricket's most celebrated rivalry dates back to 1882, when (shock, horror!) Australia's colonial upstarts humbled England's finest practitioners with willow and leather for the first time in the Mother Country. A spoof obituary was duly published in *The Sporting Times*, lamenting the death of English cricket and adding that 'the body will be cremated and the ashes taken to Australia'.

The message was received Down Under. When England toured Australia in 1882-83 (ironically beating the Aussies) England captain Ivo Bligh (later Lord Darnley) was presented with a small terracotta urn said to contain appropriate ashes (possibly burnt remains of bail or ball). Although the urn did not come to light until Darnley's death in 1927, it soon became cricket's most famous icon and clearly cemented the popular description of test matches between England and Australia as 'Ashes Series'.

These massive tours are biennial, alternating between England and Australia. As they are in different hemispheres and cricket is a summer game, this means gaps between series are 18 or 30 months. English cricket lovers keenly support all test cricket, but there's nothing like the rivalry of an Ashes Series to stir their passions. Anyone who wishes to attend one of (usually) five test matches in England is advised to apply for tickets well in advance – they are on sale for the first four days of each match, with tickets available 'at the gate' for any match that goes into a fifth day.

Tickets for the Lord's test in London are most keenly sought, but matches are also rotated around grounds in Manchester (Old Trafford), Leeds (Headingley), Birmingham (Edgbaston), Nottingham (Trent Bridge), Cardiff (Sophia Gardens) and London again (the Oval). An Ashes series in England may not happen very often, but it's always worth waiting for!

WHEN:
July to September
WHERE:
Test match grounds around the country
BEST FOR:
Masochistic Poms (who occasionally actually win) and crowing Aussies (who usually emerge victorious)
YOU SHOULD KNOW:
Whilst waiting impatiently for the next Ashes Series to come around again, it's possible to visit the real thing – the Darnley Urn is on display in the MCC Museum at Lord's Cricket Ground.

Australian captain Ricky Ponting looks on as England superstar Andrew Flintoff hits out lustily.

EUROPE/ENGLAND

Henley Royal Regatta

WHEN:
Five days over the first weekend
in July
WHERE:
Henley-on-Thames, Oxfordshire
BEST FOR:
British traditionalists (and
interested observers)
YOU SHOULD KNOW:
For a long time, the Stewards barred
'menial' rowers (i.e. manual workers)
– one such was John B Kelly in 1920,
but his son got revenge by winning
the 1947 Diamond Skulls and his
daughter was Hollywood star
Grace Kelly.

Jolly boating weather – at least, that's what competitors and spectators at the Henley Royal Regatta always hope for. This annual extravaganza is held on the upper reaches of the River Thames, and involves rowing races in various classes – including those for women (a recent innovation). Even more recent is abolition of the long-standing requirement that all competitors should be true amateurs. The most prestigious event is the Grand Challenge Cup for Men's Eights.

The racing is competitive, but there's more to the Regatta than that. Despite modern razzmatazz, it remains a grand reminder that the English Establishment is alive and well. It's possible for all and sundry to view the racing and enjoy a wide range of facilities that appear to service the crowds. But the general public is effectively confined to the south (Berkshire) bank. The north bank is occupied by expensive private residences, corporate hospitality sites and (opposite the winning post) the exclusive Phyllis Court Club.

Even across the river there's no absolute 'right to roam' – an area adjacent to the winning post is occupied by the zealously guarded Stewards' Enclosure. This consists of covered grandstands and a full range of tented facilities, all set on immaculate lawns. It is open only to Stewards, members and their guests. Along with various other exclusive enclaves on the Berkshire bank, the Stewards' Enclosure maintains the Regatta's most distinctive characteristic – an old-fashioned formal dress code that sorts out the wheat from . . . well, the rest.

Many of those superior beings have no interest in the rowing, but are there for purely social reasons. Many members of the general public also have no interest in the racing, but are there to watch the great and the good at play and be part of a great occasion. It's all tremendous fun!

The Harvard University crew throw their cox into the water as they celebrate winning the Ladies' Challenge Plate.

The Proms

It's party time at the Last Night of The Proms.

The world's most extensive festival of classical music is The Henry Wood Promenade Concerts presented by the BBC – but there's no need to be formal, because this annual summer concert season at London's Royal Albert Hall is simply known by one and all as The Proms.

The 'Promenade' of the title comes from the late 19th century idea that a new audience could be attracted to classical music if admission prices were low and people could wander about during performances (and also eat, drink and smoke). It was a classical version of the popular musical entertainment that was staged on bandstands for strollers in the Victorian parks.

The great Henry Wood picked up the concept and ran, expanding the classical repertoire and conducting Promenade Concerts for nearly 50 years, during which time The Proms became established as a national institution. Of course there are seats at concerts, but 'Promming' (less the food, booze and cigarettes) has remained an essential part of the concept. Promenade season tickets valid for standing areas of the Royal Albert Hall may be purchased in advance, but the vast majority of these sought-after cheap tickets are reserved for those who buy on the day, often leading to queues for the most popular concerts.

Naturally, the longest queue of all is for the iconic Last Night of the Proms, when the whole series comes to a thunderous climax in an explosion of patriotic fervour and uninhibited appreciation of this great musical occasion. If you can only spend a single day at The Proms, try to make it this one – but those who can't make it to the Albert Hall can now enjoy something of the same excitement and the Last Night atmosphere at Proms in the Park events held simultaneously across the United Kingdom.

WHEN:
Mid July with the Last Night in mid September
WHERE:
Mainly at The Royal Albert Hall, South Kensington, London
BEST FOR:
True 'Prommers' – classical music enthusiasts with a limited budget
YOU SHOULD KNOW:
A bronze bust of Sir Henry Wood (owned by the Royal Academy of Music) is placed in front of the Royal Albert Hall's organ throughout each season of The Proms.

203

Flags fly at the WOMAD festival.

The WOMAD Festival

What exactly is WOMAD when it's at home? The acronym stands for World of Music, Arts and Dance and this movement, founded in 1982 with an inaugural festival at Shepton Mallet in England, has become an international movement that holds festivals all over the world with events in over 25 countries. The declared objective is to allow audiences to gain real insight into cultures other than their own. To underline this point many include informative adult and children's music and dance workshops alongside the performance spectacle.

The WOMAD Festival has been so successful that the annual UK event has moved from its old home at Riverside, Reading, to a new and larger site on a classic country estate owned by the Earls of Suffolk since the 16th century near the delightful market town of Malmesbury.

The festival is designed to create awareness of the potential and worth of multicultural society, aiming to inform and stimulate in a relaxed, family-friendly atmosphere, with overnight camping included in the ticket price. And then of course there are fantastic acts from all over the world performing on various stages around the site, to ensure that there's something for everyone.

Indeed, anyone needing a break from the main music scene can enjoy extras like comedy events, the cabaret tent, DJ sessions, the ever-popular Irish Ceilidh, intimate late-night shows in Club WOMAD, live music playing in the Taste Café as the food cooks, international cuisine in Taste the World, saunas, World of Wellbeing massages, markets selling high-quality ethnic crafts and more in the same alternative vein.

It truly adds up to the festival's boast that – for three days in an English summer – this quintessential world music festival does indeed become a (rather large and loud) global village.

WHEN:
Late July
WHERE:
Charlton Park near Malmesbury
in Wiltshire
BEST FOR:
Adventurous world music lovers
(and families)
YOU SHOULD KNOW:
The special flags that feature
prominently at WOMAD Festivals
have become a symbol of
internationalism used by other
events like the Glastonbury Festival.

Cowes Week

The world's oldest-established regatta (first held in 1826) is based at Cowes on the Isle of Wight, off England's South Coast. A flying visit when the yachting fraternity is in town provides fascinating insight into the fast-changing British social scene as recently mega-rich entrepreneurs rub shoulders with the old establishment, amateur crews mingle with sun-bronzed full-timers from all over the world . . . and expensive ocean racers piloted by top professional skippers share the water with more modest self-skippered cruising yachts.

Cowes Week sees around 40 race starts a day, with over a thousand boats and some 8,500 sailors participating. There are a number of prestigious trophies at stake including The Queen's Cup (presented by Queen Victoria in her Diamond Jubilee Year, 1897), The Britannia Cup and The New York Yacht Club Challenge Cup. With numerous prizes to be won in a wide variety of classes, there's glory to be chased by every yacht, large or small.

But there is also a large influx of visitors who never take to the water, but are sailing enthusiasts who want to be part of this great event – or simply holidaymakers drawn by the incredible buzz generated by Cowes Week, in the town itself and throughout the entire island. A free shuttle bus service connects all the key points and – though many elite functions take place behind the closed doors of exclusive clubs – there is still a wonderful social whirl to be enjoyed by the general public, with parties, events, activities and attractions designed to appeal to people of all ages and walks of life.

After watching a forest of multi-coloured spinnakers criss-crossing the crowded seascape all day, there's nothing better than enjoying the vibrant night life for which Cowes Week is renowned, lasting into the wee small hours. The atmosphere is electric!

WHEN:
Early August, with a complicated formula determining the exact dates – from the first Saturday after the last Tuesday in July until the following Saturday (unless the tides are unfavourable . . . in which case don't ask!)
WHERE:
Cowes, with racing in the Solent, the tricky stretch of water between the Isle of Wight and the mainland
BEST FOR:
Dedicated yachties
YOU SHOULD KNOW:
Those who get confused about what's happening out on the water find that Cowes Radio is awash with information on FM (also broadcast over the public address system).

Spinnakers ahoy!

Notting Hill Carnival

WHEN:
Late August (on a Sunday and the
following Bank Holiday Monday)
WHERE:
Notting Hill, West London
BEST FOR:
Uninhibited calypso capers
YOU SHOULD KNOW:
The National Competition of Steel
– a keenly fought contest between
traditional Caribbean steel bands –
takes place in Hyde Park on the
previous Saturday.

If you think the world's biggest street carnival is in Rio, you're right. But – perhaps surprisingly – second prize goes to London, with the Notting Hill Carnival attracting up to two million people each year. It has grown from an indoor community event aimed at improving race relations after the Notting Hill Riots of 1958, moving outside in 1964 as a gathering for local folk. But it soon acquired the Caribbean character that has become a hallmark – plus a large and ever-expanding annual audience.

After trouble when youths and police did battle in the late 1970s, leading to calls (happily resisted) for the event to be banned, it has gone from strength to strength as a peaceful but dynamic celebration of Britain's multicultural society, though the emphasis remains firmly Afro-Caribbean.

The narrow streets of Notting Hill are the carnival's focal point, though recent years have seen the introduction of a 'savannah' area in Hyde Park where related events occur. Children's Day on Sunday sees a shorter parade tailored to families and kids, complete with appropriate entertainments mounted by under-21s supported by floats, elaborate costumes . . . with painted faces all round.

On Monday, the colourful main parade of decorated floats and flamboyant dancers follows a 6.5-km (3-mi) route along the Great West Road, Chepstow Road, Westbourne Grove and Ladbroke Grove. Officially, the carnival consists of four disciplines – costume masquerade, steel band, calypso and SOCA (the fusion Sounds of the Caribbean and Africa). So the all-pervasive feature is the sound of (loud) music, with static sound systems competing lustily with mobile brethren and bands on passing floats. 'Official' music gets keen competition from just about every other style under the sun, resulting in joyful cacophony. The supercharged result is the most vibrant of events – once experienced, never forgotten!

*A fiery costume lights up
the Notting Hill scene.*

Lewes Bonfire Night

As they dance around leaping flames, children still chant the mantra 'Remember, remember the fifth of November – gunpowder, treason and plot'. And remember Britain certainly does – annual bonfire night celebrations still recall the foiling of 1605's Gunpowder Plot, when Catholic conspirators failed by a whisker to kill King James I, his family and the nation's most prominent aristocrats by blowing up the House of Lords during the State Opening of Parliament.

But Guido Fawkes was found in the Palace of Westminster's cellars as he was about to light the fuse that would have sent the great and the good to Kingdom Come, and ever since that narrow escape has been commemorated by burning a Guy (an effigy of the unfortunate Fawkes), accompanied by fireworks. Thousands of such celebrations take place up and down the land, but nowhere is the tradition more vigorously upheld than in the Sussex town of Lewes.

And what a spectacle the townsfolk put on! Seven bonfire societies hold torchlight costume processions through Lewes. Effigies are drawn through the streets, including those of Guy Fawkes and Pope Paul V, supplemented by topical hate figures and effigy heads on pikes of 'Enemies of Bonfire' (often officials seeking to place restrictions on the festivities, which tend to be ignored).

Additional activities include tableaux, the carrying of 17 burning crosses to remember Protestant martyrs burnt at the stake in Lewes in the 1550s and the throwing of a burning tar barrel into the River Ouse – symbolizing the watery fate of magistrates who tried to read the Riot Act to boisterous bonfire night revellers in 1847. The whole event culminates in five different bonfires where the effigies are consumed by flame amidst spectacular firework displays. No wonder around 50,000 people turn up each year to be part of this extraordinary event.

WHEN:
Guy Fawkes Night – November 5
WHERE:
In the streets and at various sites in the town of Lewes, East Sussex
BEST FOR:
Families with a penchant for pyrotechnics
YOU SHOULD KNOW:
Guy Fawkes wasn't actually burned alive, but sentenced to be hung, drawn and quartered – boldly cheating his grizzly fate by leaping from the scaffold and breaking his neck before he could be drawn and quartered.

Local bonfire societies parade with burning crosses during the annual Lewes bonfire and procession in memory of the town's Protestant martyrs of 1556.

London to Brighton Veteran Car Run

First, the rule that required 'light locomotives' to be preceded by a man carrying a red flag was abolished. Then, in 1896, came the repeal of the 6.5 kph (4 mph) speed limit, which was raised to a reckless 22.5 kph (14 mph). A symbolic red flag was burned and 30 new-fangled automobiles set off on the 'Emancipation Run' down the 97-km (60-mi) road from London to Brighton in celebration. Fewer than half made it, but a tradition was born.

A tribute run was made in 1927 and the event has been held annually ever since, except during World Wars I and II and in 1947 when there was petrol rationing. It is restricted to veterans – three- or four-wheeled vehicles made in or before 1904 – though occasional 'guest runners' that do not meet this criterion are invited for the enjoyment of spectators, of whom there are many.

The run is preceded by a Concours display in Regent Street on Saturday. On Sunday the runners leave Hyde Park, staring at 06.54 (sunrise) and continue to leave in pairs until around 08.30. First arrivals (ancient engines permitting) arrive in Brighton's Preston Park around 10.00, before proceeding to Madeira Drive. Naughtily, runners travel at an average of 32 kph (20 mph), well above the new speed limit the original run celebrated. Cars remain on display in Preston Park until darkness falls.

These colourful veterans, born in the dawn of the motor age, are a wonderful sight as they strut their stuff after more than a century of active life. There are ample opportunities for viewing them before, during and after the race. The route follows the A23 road out of London, with diversions through Croydon and into Crawley, where the runners stop in the market square for a comfort break (for the cars). Thereafter, the route diverts onto minor roads before rejoining the A23 for the final leg into Brighton.

Entrants in the annual London to Brighton Veteran Car Run depart on the 60-mile journey from London's Hyde Park.

WHEN:
The first Sunday in November
WHERE:
London via Croydon, Redhill, Gatwick, Crawley, Cuckfield, Burgess Hill and Clayton Hill to Brighton
BEST FOR:
Nostalgic 'petrolheads' (and their families – it's a great day out)
YOU SHOULD KNOW:
Human nature never changes – it is thought that one runner in the inaugural 1896 run took his vehicle to Brighton on a train, had it splashed with mud . . . and triumphantly became one of the lucky 13 finishers.

Viking Fire Festival

The most northerly part of the British Isles, Shetland is actually closer to the Arctic Circle than it is to London. It is quicker to get there from Norway than from the UK's capital and, appropriately enough, many of Shetland's historical and cultural ties are with Scandinavia rather than Britain. Place names are often of Viking origin, reflecting the pervasive influence of the fearsome Norsemen who ruled over the Shetland Islands for more than 500 years. This legacy is commemorated most spectacularly in Up-Helly-Aa, the annual Fire Festival held on the last Tuesday in January in Shetland's capital, Lerwick. Organizers claim this to be the largest fire festival in Europe and boast proudly that it has never been cancelled due to bad weather.

Up-Helly-Aa harks back to the Viking festival of Yule which celebrated the rebirth of the sun after the winter solstice. The head of the festivities is the Guizer Jarl, or Earl, a local man who is granted the freedom of the town for the day, and whose appearance as a character from Norse history or saga is a closely guarded secret beforehand. He and his Jarl Squad, consisting of some 40 'guizers' (men 'in disguise') magnificently arrayed in full Viking warrior dress, gather to escort a full-size replica of a Viking longship down to the harbour where it remains on view for the day.

The highpoint of the celebrations comes once darkness has fallen when upwards of a thousand guizers take to the narrow streets of Lerwick. With flaming torches borne aloft they accompany the longship in procession to the playing fields. Here the torches are hurled on to the galley and four months of building work goes up in an enormous blaze, thus echoing ancient pagan rituals in which mighty Norse chieftains would be cremated in their longships.

WHEN:
The last Tuesday in January
WHERE:
Lerwick, Shetland Islands
BEST FOR:
Folklore and pageantry
YOU SHOULD KNOW:
If you don't feel like braving the mid-winter weather, an exhibition in Lerwick open during the summer months gives a good flavour of the Fire Festival.

A Viking long boat burns.

Riders maintain the tradition of common ridings.

Common Ridings

During the 13th and 14th centuries many local clans exploited the prevailing instability of the Scottish Borders caused by the long-standing territorial struggle between England and Scotland. With law enforcement effectively non-existent, these families operated with impunity and grew rich and powerful raiding and plundering neighbouring communities and stealing their cattle – a practice known as reiving. The lawlessness of these times is remembered today in the tradition of common ridings, which takes place during the summer months each year in 11 towns along the Scottish Borders. Common ridings take the form of massed ride-outs, in which hundreds of townsfolk 'ride the marches' on horseback, checking that the ancient town boundaries are secure against potential invaders.

The first of the year's ridings takes place at the beginning of June in Hawick and the sequence of pageants finishes in early August in Coldstream. The sights and sounds of hundreds of horses racing along the town streets, multi-coloured banners held high, are unforgettable, and any visitor will be quickly caught up in the excitement and passion of what is still a genuine community celebration. Every year a local person is elected to lead the ride-out and their title varies from town to town; in Hawick, for example, they are known as the Cornet, whilst Kelso has the Laddie and West Linton the Whipman. On the eve of the riding the ceremony of 'colour bussing' takes place, when a local lass ties ribbons to the staff of the town standard or Burgh Flag, recalling the days when a knight's lady attached her ribbon to his lance before battle. Needless to say, the town is full of party spirit in the days surrounding the event itself.

WHEN:
June to August
WHERE:
Scottish Borders
BEST FOR:
Community spectacle
YOU SHOULD KNOW:
In some towns the festivities associated with the annual riding last for up to two weeks.

Edinburgh Festival

Actually, the Edinburgh Festival as such doesn't exist – but anyone who has a mind to visit this extraordinary culturefest needn't panic. The austere but beautiful Scottish capital does indeed come alive with creative frenzy each summer – it's just that there are many events going on at once, each with different organizers.

The Edinburgh International Festival was the first one, founded in 1947 with the lofty objective of 'providing a platform for the flowering of the human spirit'. This is undoubtedly the class act – focusing on the best of mainstream classical and contemporary opera, music, dance and theatre, it still provides the traditional core of the festivities.

By far the most famous companion event is The Fringe. From the beginning, resourceful gatecrashers appeared, appreciating the opportunity to stage their own performances alongside the 'real' thing. Ever since, The Fringe (now officially organized) has presented the very best (and sometimes very worst!) of alternative, experimental and challenging work. It covers – and constantly seeks to expand – the full spectrum of performance art and has outgrown its big brother to become the largest arts festival in the world.

But like Topsy, the range of Edinburgh summer happenings has just growed and growed. Into the eclectic mix have plunged additional specialist festivals – covering areas like books, contemporary art, politics, spirituality, South Asian culture, the internet and various events dedicated to particular music styles like jazz, blues and swing. The British Army has even waded in with the spectacular annual parade known as The Edinburgh Tattoo.

Those who subscribe to the stereotype of 'dour Scotland' will be shocked if they visit Edinburgh at festival time. The whole place explodes into a joyous mixture of crowds and creativity, fun and frolic, unlike anything that can be experienced anywhere else in the world. See and enjoy!

Dramatic street performances abound at The Fringe.

WHEN:
August to September each year
WHERE:
In just about every nook and crannie in Edinburgh that can hold an audience of ten or more people
BEST FOR:
Culture vultures
YOU SHOULD KNOW:
There may be a wealth of entertainment to choose from, but accommodation is almost impossible to find unless booked in advance.

The Glorious 12th

WHEN:
August 12
WHERE:
Heather moors in Scotland and the
north of England (there is also a
small grouse population in the
Welsh uplands)
BEST FOR:
Well-heeled traditionalists
YOU SHOULD KNOW:
The Glorious 12th sometimes
becomes the Glorious 13th
(if the 12th falls on a Sunday,
when no game may be shot).

*A loader walks back at the end
of a successsful drive with a full
game bag.*

The date that coincides with one of the most expensive events that
country sports enthusiasts can enjoy is August 12 – ringed on many
a posh calendar as the celebrated opening day of the red grouse
shooting season. Every game shooter aspires to testing his skills on
fast-moving grouse as they skim the heather, ideally on the first day
of a new season when a plentiful supply of birds may be anticipated,
though few can actually enjoy the privilege.

Unfortunately, *Lagopus lagopus scoticus* is an unpredictable
creature, subject to local conditions and the prevalence of parasites.
Unlike pheasants and partridges, grouse cannot be reared and
released. Consequently, populations fluctuate from moor to moor
and season to season, and if numbers are low that year's shooting
may be cancelled – to the acute disappointment both of those who
were hoping to experience the
Glorious 12th and those who
were expecting to profit from it.

But when everything goes
well, the Glorious 12th is
awesome – first the anticipation,
then the excitement as the great
day dawns, followed by the
pleasure of being part of the
long-established ritual of 'going
to the hill' as part of a large team
of companionable fellow guns,
gamekeepers and beaters whose
objective is pursuit of that most
elusive and challenging quarry –
red grouse. During the day, with
luck, coveys speed towards most
butts, to be gone in an instant
with perhaps a couple left behind
if the shooter is quick of eye and
fleet of hand. Think of it what
you may, nobody can deny that
it's exciting.

For those who can't
participate but wish to salute this
notable British institution, many
top restaurants take pride in
having fresh grouse on the menu
before the sun sets on the
Glorious 12th.

Highland Games

Events that celebrate Celtic – and especially Scottish – culture are held all over the globe, in places where emigrants have begun new lives but still wish to acknowledge historic roots. But similar celebrations still take place in the Old Country, as they have for many centuries.

Physical challenges that tested strength and endurance were once the rationale, with games meetings also used as an excuse for practising warrior skills when Highlanders were banned from carrying weapons. Heavy events – tossing the caber, stone putting, hammer throwing, weight throwing and sheaf tossing – remain an essential part of the entertainment, as are track and hill races.

But since their revival in Victorian times the games have acquired added dimensions – notably music, including massed pipe bands, solo bagpiping and drumming, Celtic bands, fiddling and harp circles. There is also dance – Scottish country dancing and highly skilled Highland dancing. The latter is for individuals, is very competitive and takes two forms – traditional (Sword Dance and Highland Fling) and national (with Scottish Lilt, Flora MacDonald, Highland Laddie, Village Maid, Blue Bonnets and Earl of Errol being the best-known dances).

Up, up and away!

The largest event in Scotland is the Cowal Highland Gathering, held at Dunoon every August. But the most historic Highland Games are those held at Braemar, said to originate from a race organized by King Malcolm Canmore in the 11th century, with the fleet-footed winner becoming his personal messenger. The Braemar Gathering and Highland Games in the beautiful setting of Royal Deeside are also the most famous and prestigious of all as they are traditionally attended by the Royal Family.

Every games is a vibrant occasion, with the word 'gathering' serving as a reminder that these events are famous for people coming together to have a great time, with a warm welcome extended to all.

WHEN:
The Braemar Games are held on the first Saturday in September.
WHERE:
The Princess Royal and Duke of Fife Memorial Park, Braemar
BEST FOR:
Those who appreciate cultural traditions, enjoy a lively day out or want a close look at Royal Family members
YOU SHOULD KNOW:
The world's largest Highland Games has been hosted annually since 1865 by the New Caledonian Club of San Francisco.

213

Hogmanay

WHEN:
December 31 (usually extending until
the morning of January 1)
WHERE:
The biggest Hogmanay gatherings
are in Edinburgh and Glasgow,
though many towns and villages in
Scotland hold their own celebrations.
BEST FOR:
Uninhibited revellers
YOU SHOULD KNOW:
Don't try first-footing in Scotland if
you're a carrot top as the visitor
should ideally have dark hair (as a
fellow Scot) rather than red hair (an
unwelcome Norse intruder) – as
Hogmanay proves, old traditions die
hard in Scotland!

Did the Scots actually invent New Year's Eve? Even if they didn't, they win the gold medal when it comes to seeing out the old and chiming in the new. The uninhibited nature of Scottish Hogmanay revelry is famous the world over – and everyone should experience the real thing at least once.

Hogmanay takes place on the year's last evening, poetically described in Scotland as Auld Year's Night, which is followed by Ne'erday (New Year's Day). The origin of Hogmanay is lost in the mists of time, but it harks back to the Norse tradition of celebrating the winter solstice. Hogmanay customs vary from place to place in Scotland, with the most general being 'first footing', when friends and neighbours visit each other after midnight with the first to cross the threshold bearing a small gift like salt, coal, shortbread or whisky, designed to bring luck for the rest of the year.

Some strange Hogmanay rituals survive. One famous example takes place at Stonehaven, where locals greet the New Year by swinging fireballs around their heads as they march up and down the High Street before casting any balls that are still burning into the harbour. The spectacle draws a large number of visitors and attractions like a pipe band and fireworks have been added. This underlines a modern trend towards organized Hogmanay celebrations that are essentially free public entertainments where people can let their hair down and greet the New Year in the company of thousands of like-minded fun seekers.

One thing's for sure – wherever Hogmanay is observed (and at most New Year's Eve celebrations), the old Scottish custom of linking arms and singing *Auld Land Syne* as the clock strikes midnight will mark the end of an old year and the start of the new.

A palm tree effect wows the crowds during a pyrotechnic display at Edinburgh Castle.

Isle of Man TT Races

The first Isle of Man Tourist Trophy Race took place on May 28 1907. This acorn grew into a mighty annual event that brings top motorcycle road racers and tens of thousands of enthusiastic followers (mostly bikers) to this delightful island in the Irish Sea.

Happily for them, Isle of Man authorities ignore the risk assessments and health and safety concerns that would see the end of such a reckless enterprise were it to be attempted on the mainland. TT Races are held on public roads (prudently closed for the duration) and premier racing bikes hurtle around each lap at an average speed in excess of 200 kph (125 mph). And risky it is, with a number of riders (and spectators) killed in action over the years – though this dangerous edge merely seems to add to the attraction as far as the devil-may-care motorcycling fraternity is concerned.

Riders often lift off at Bray Hill.

The famous Snaefell Mountain Course is a 61-km (38-mi) circuit, from Douglas in the southeast up to Ramsey on the northeast coast and from there returning to the start. There are over two hundred bends and corners, with the course going from sea level to a height of 395 m (1,300 ft) and back. It's a demanding circuit that provides a true test of rider and machine.

There are a number of classes, the most prestigious being the Senior TT Race. Its winner receives the rather long-winded Marquis de Mouzilly St Mars Trophy, originally awarded to the winner of the first TT Race in 1907.

Although no longer part of the official motorcycle racing scene for safety reasons, the very qualities that led to international exclusion ensure that today the Isle of Man TT Races remain an extraordinary and exciting spectacle that is unequalled anywhere else in the world.

WHEN:
Two weeks at the end of May and beginning of June
WHERE:
The Isle of Man
BEST FOR:
Bikers seeking the ultimate thrill
YOU SHOULD KNOW:
The greatest-ever champion was Joey Dunlop, a modest Ulsterman who won 26 TT races – he was sadly killed during a race in 2000 that took place in Estonia rather than his beloved Isle of Man.

EUROPE/WALES

Hay-on-Wye Festival of Literature and Arts

WHEN:
Over ten days at the end of May and beginning of June
WHERE:
Just outside Hay-on-Wye, Powys
BEST FOR:
Serious lovers of creative writing with a social conscience
YOU SHOULD KNOW:
With a neat turn of phrase, ex-President Bill Clinton described the Hay Festival in 2001 as 'The Woodstock of the Mind'.

Anyone visiting for the day will think that Hay-on-Wye is a delightful small town within the stunning Brecon Beacons National Park in the Welsh Borders. They may note that it once punched above its weight, with not one but two medieval castles. But it will soon dawn on them that there are bookshops everywhere – indeed, they have reached bibliophile heaven, with millions of second-hand and antiquarian books to be browsed through in some 30 emporia.

It all began in the 1960s when bookseller Richard Booth opened a shop in Hay's old fire station. Others followed, and by the 1970s Hay had become known as 'The Town of Books'. Booth's brilliant stunt in 1977 was to declare Hay an independent kingdom, with himself as King and his horse as Prime Minister. The ensuing publicity gave added impetus to the town's status and generated a large number of visitors, transforming the local economy.

One impressive spin-off has been the Hay Festival of Literature & Arts, first held in 1988 and now sponsored by *The Guardian* newspaper. Each summer a tented village springs up just outside the town. The festival has expanded over the years to include film previews, musical performances and a host of interesting on-site extras in a beautiful natural environment. In addition there is an associated event for children, aptly called Hay Fever.

A girl reads in front of larger-than-life literature at the Hay-on-Wye Festival.

Such is the scope of this annual event that it is not only able to present top authors but also leading figures from the world stage. The festival's boast is that it is about much more than the arts, being both local and global and engaging with issues that fuel conflict around the world. The comprehensive programme ensures that the Hay Festival remains a prestigious international gathering that manages the trick of combining intellectual excellence with having fun.

The Eisteddfod

The ceremony at the annual Gorsedd of Bards of the Isle of Britain – sitting in the background are novice Druids, dressed in green.

The National Eisteddfod is the oldest, largest and most important celebration of Welsh culture and heritage. Traditionally held in August, the festival moves alternately from North to South Wales, each time to a different venue. Thousands of Welsh people, from over the globe, return to their native land for this essentially bardic competition. Altogether 150,000 visitors support Eisteddfod every year, many of them camping for the week.

Thought to date back to 1176, when Lord Rhys ap Gruffudd held a tournament of poets and musicians at his Cardiganshire castle, Eisteddfod gradually became a huge folk festival. After a subsequent period of decline it was revived and since 1880 has taken place almost every year.

The festival is closely associated with the Gorsedd of Bards. Members of this order – known as Druids – are writers, poets, artists, musicians and others who have contributed to the Welsh nation, language and culture. They wear coloured robes which denote their rank. It is the Archdruid's task to 'crown the bard' – the best free-meter poet – to 'chair the bard' and to award the prose medal. Druidic ceremonies take place in a stone circle – if there isn't one in the vicinity, it is created from local stones. Since 2005 temporary circles of plastic stones have been erected on site, enabling everyone to watch.

Six thousand competitors enter the competitions held in the main pavilion, but there is plenty more to see and do. There are pavilions for literature, science and technology, a theatre, a dance hall, a live-music tent, a learners' tent for those studying and teaching Welsh, hundreds of stalls, food and, since 2004, alcohol. Welsh is the only language spoken here so non-Welsh speakers have to rely on simultaneous translations, but they are still made welcome.

WHEN:
Early August
WHERE:
Different venues every year, decided upon two or three years in advance
BEST FOR:
Welsh culture
YOU SHOULD KNOW:
There are other Eisteddfods, including a youth eisteddfod and an international music eisteddfod, in Wales as well as in Australia and Argentina, where there are large Welsh populations.

*A brave (or crazy?) competitor
takes to the Welsh bog water.*

World Bog Snorkelling
Championship

It is likely that you will want to be a spectator rather than a participant at this event. Every August for the past 20 years crowds have gathered on an undistinguished peat bog outside the small town of Llanwrtyd Wells in mid-Wales to watch the World Bog Snorkelling Championship. Locals are joined by holidaymakers and dedicated fans of eccentric pursuits to follow the fortunes of a random but hardy bunch of contestants who don snorkel and flippers to swim two lengths of a 55-m (180-ft) channel cut in the bog. Propelling themselves is probably a more accurate description since conventional swimming strokes are not permitted, nor is lifting your head out of the water unless for orientation purposes.

The prospect of total immersion in murky, foul-smelling water does not seem to deter some 150 doughty souls from entering the contest each year for the chance to be hailed Bog Snorkelling Champion of the World. The event now brings in competitors from various parts of the globe, many of whom return year after year attracted by the camaraderie and an atmosphere that is as warm and relaxed as the water is chilly. As a humanitarian gesture the organizers do allow wetsuits to be worn if desired, for in spite of this being summer the water temperature in an upland Welsh peat bog does not rise appreciably. Nor are you guaranteed a dry experience as a spectator; you should come prepared for the notoriously unpredictable weather in these parts.

If you are someone who will consider doing anything to make a name for yourself, you might like to know that in 2008 a woman became the world-record holder at 1 minute 35 seconds!

WHEN:
Late August
WHERE:
Powys
BEST FOR:
Light-hearted sport
YOU SHOULD KNOW:
Llanwrtyd Wells lays claim to being the smallest town in Britain, with a population of just 600.

The Orange Day Parades

Orange Order supporters march along the Ormeau Road in Belfast.

Every year, a series of summer parades, known as Orange Walks, takes place across Northern Ireland, as well as further afield. The Orange Order was founded in Loughgall, County Armagh in 1795. With some 75,000 members, the Orange Order is the largest of the Loyal Orders, as they are known.

What is commonly referred to as 'the marching season' culminates in July, when celebrations are held to mark the victory of Prince William of Orange over King James II in 1690, at the Battle of the Boyne. William was a Protestant, born in Holland, who became King William III of Great Britain and Ireland in 1688. His victory over James II's Catholic army promoted the Protestant cause in a land which was predominantly Catholic.

Always political, the Order was strongly opposed to Irish Home Rule and the influence of Catholicism, and this opposition finally led to the six counties of Ulster (Northern Ireland) remaining part of the United Kingdom. Down the centuries the parades have sparked violence, as Protestant marchers sometimes deliberately chose routes through predominantly Catholic areas of Ulster's towns and cities, triumphantly defending both Protestant rights and the rule of a Protestant monarch. Today, after much hard work on all sides, the parades are largely peaceful.

The major parades are often fronted by a figure riding a white horse, representing William of Orange. Crowds gather on the streets to watch as representatives of the various different Lodges march with their individual banners and flags. Usually accompanied by a marching band of fife and drum, flutes and accordions, the dark-suited Orange Order members, their orange 'collars' sporting regalia, some wearing bowler hats, walk in step to the solemn sound of the drumbeat. Difficult for outsiders to fully comprehend, these parades are hugely significant, and carry a weight of history impossible to deny.

WHEN:
July 12, with lesser parades taking place between April and August
WHERE:
Marches take place across Northern Ireland.
BEST FOR:
Culture
YOU SHOULD KNOW:
The only membership requirement is to be a Protestant. Parades still also take place in Eire (one), Scotland, the United States, Canada and Liverpool.

Fun and fishy frolics are on offer during the fast-developing West Belfast Community Festival.

West Belfast Community Festival

Few current festivals can be born out of such recent heartache. Féile an Phobail (West Belfast Community Festival) draws its strength from two connected killings which came to epitomize the troubles that so afflicted this corner of Ireland. The first of the two tragically symbolic events was the shooting of three unarmed IRA volunteers by British Special Forces in Gibraltar. The resulting funeral saw the kidnap and murder of undercover police by IRA members. While both sides of the divide grieved, some resolved that they could no longer live like this and no matter how bitter recent memories were, something now had to be done. It was in this atmosphere of determination to change that Féile an Phobail was first launched in 1988.

The first festival was a relatively low-key affair with a few floats and marching bands, watched by a small but curious crowd. The real triumph, though, was the organization of several street parties in West Belfast, where the pent-up need for some form of public celebration led to a large turnout. It was as if someone had released the cork from a long-forgotten bottle of wine.

Féile an Phobail has now grown into one of the largest community festivals in Britain and has a range of events for young and old alike, which now span the whole calendar. Most people still know it for the August Féile, which is a festival of music, drama, dance and literature. That it can attract the best names across many fields of the arts stands as testament to both the organizers' skills and to how far Northern Ireland has come in such a relatively short space of time. Community cohesion is an ongoing project as Belfast moves towards a brighter future and Féile an Phobail provides opportunities for locals to learn new skills as well as providing a window to the world.

WHEN:
All year round with a week-long festival, including a parade, in August
WHERE:
Belfast
BEST FOR:
Culture, music and theatre
YOU SHOULD KNOW:
For those wanting to get an early taste of the event, the festival has its own radio station – Féile FM. As well as giving information on up-coming events, it has become a training ground that has propelled local talent on to the national stage.

The Ould Lammas Fair

Ballycastle is a sleepy little seaside town on the Antrim coast of Northern Ireland. It has a population of just over 5,000, but on a cold winter's day when one man and his dog are all that can be seen on the beach, this figure seems a gross exaggeration. The town's diminutive size is much of its charm, but for two days in August it becomes a hive of activity as people come from all over the land to revel at the Ould Lammas fair.

The Fair, which dates back to the 17th century, has an uninterrupted history of over 300 years. Fruit and flowers used to be offered as gifts to God at holy wells to mark the end of summer and the onset of harvest time. Nowadays the event has more the feel of a large village fete crossed with a country fair. Stalls line the narrow streets selling toys, bric-a-brac and local crafts, while traditional music rings out from every tavern. Local delicacies are also on offer in the form of dulse, a seaweed unique to the waters of Lough Neagh, and Yellow Man, a chewy candy strip.

If there were one word to describe the Ould Lammas fair and its host town, it would be unpretentious. It does not claim to be the biggest or best of its kind, it is simply people out having a good time and the mood is infectious. People sing, dance, eat and drink in a friendly atmosphere, preserving an age-old custom that still has a place in modern Ulster.

WHEN:
The last Monday and Tuesday of August
WHERE:
Ballycastle, County Antrim
BEST FOR:
Culture and music
YOU SHOULD KNOW:
The fair has been immortalized in song and it is well worth learning at least the chorus as impromptu sing-a-longs are a big feature of pub-going in these parts. You never know, as the song goes you might get to 'treat your Mary Ann, to some Dulse and Yellow Man, at the Ould Lammas Fair in Ballycastle-O!'

This old-style country fair maintains a long-standing tradition.

EUROPE/REPUBLIC OF IRELAND

St Patrick's Day Parade in Dublin

WHEN:
March 17
WHERE:
Dublin
BEST FOR:
Culture and spectacle
YOU SHOULD KNOW:
Because St Patrick's Day has been designated a feast day by the Vatican, every now and then, when Easter falls early, there is a clash of dates. In 2008 a compromise was reached whereby the feast day was moved, but the secular celebrations – including the parade – were held on March 17 as usual.

To say that the Irish were slow off the blocks to embrace their patron saint is something of an understatement. Those with long memories can recall a time when the celebrations involved a morning service, followed by a low-key parade. They would then shuffle off home to watch the more raucous festivities of their American cousins being beamed across the Atlantic on their televisions. The fact that pubs were closed further dampened the mood. Today the Irish celebrate as if they are making up for lost time, having cast aside any lingering doubts about who St Patrick was and turning the celebration into a five-day carnival of all things Irish.

For those who are unfamiliar with Dublin and wish to gain an uninterrupted view of the centrepiece parade, it is probably advisable to pay for a grandstand seat. The real vibe, however, takes place among the assembled hoards who behave much like the wildebeest of the Serengeti migrating from one watering hole to another. It is said that 'Everyone wants to be Irish on St Patrick's Day', but even the casual observer cannot help but be struck by the multi-cultural make-up of the parade. Traditional marching bands are joined by inflatable dragons and steel drums. Costumes take the form of elaborate moving sculptures and the whole day feels like a Mardi Gras festival.

Right from the opening ceremony at Dublin City Hall, through to the evening fireworks over the River Liffey, it is a day crammed full of fun. Children are well catered for by a giant funfair, while grown-ups can enjoy music, street theatre and of course the focal point of modern Irish life, the pub. The true identity of St Patrick is still the source of great debate among Irish scholars, but what cannot be doubted is the gusto with which half a million locals celebrate their patron saint.

Fun along the way as an unusual spectator observes the crowds.

222

Bloomsday

Few books can divide opinion like James Joyce's *Ulysses*. Its modernist stream-of-consciousness style has been described as unfathomable by some and sheer genius by others. It seems impossible just to like the book; you have to love it or hate it and those who love it embrace it with a passion. The book describes events on one ordinary day, June 16 1904, and records the experiences of Leopold Bloom as he wanders around Dublin – hence Bloomsday.

The celebration starts a week prior to the big day with street theatre, guided walks and several exhibitions and literary events around town. Whether you are an avid re-reader of the book or completely new to it, Bloomsday provides a wonderful way to explore the landmarks and the hidden corners of Dublin. It has become a tradition to rise early, dress in Edwardian garb and start the day with a full Irish breakfast. Having scoffed the sausages, bacon, fried bread, beans, and blood pudding on offer (vegetarian option: beans), it is time to retrace the footsteps of our hero Leopold Bloom. You can do this on your own or with a group of friends but, if you are unfamiliar with Dublin, staff at the James Joyce Centre will gladly assist you, and escorted tours are available.

Joyce afforded some of the city's hostelries legendary status by declaring in the book that 'Dublin's pubs offered dependable comforts to men at all troubled in mind or spirit' and you will probably find yourself drawn towards Davy Byrne's pub, among others, at several points in the day, whatever your mood. Roddy Doyle declared that '*Ulysses* could have done with a good editor' and in some senses Bloomsday is that edition. It strips away the language of the book, turning it instead into a series of journeys.

On Bloomsday people trace the route of the fictional Leopold Bloom through the real city of Dublin, as described in James Joyce's Ulysses.

WHEN:
June 16
WHERE:
Dublin
BEST FOR:
Culture and sightseeing
YOU SHOULD KNOW:
Bloomsday has grown to be a worldwide phenomenon. The day is now celebrated in such diverse places as America, Hungary, Italy and Australia. However none of these can match the authenticity of the celebrations in the book's hometown of Dublin.

The Galway Races

WHEN:
Starts towards the end of July
WHERE:
5 km (3 mi) from Galway City,
County Galway
BEST FOR:
Sport
YOU SHOULD KNOW:
You will need to book early if you
require a hotel room in Galway
City, as the festival now attracts
combined crowds of over
200,000. Outside the city
accommodation is often cheaper,
but you will have to travel to and
from the racecourse under your
own steam.

The prize money may be greater at Cheltenham, more champagne may be quaffed at Royal Ascot, but nothing beats the Galway festival for charm and atmosphere. Dating back to 1869, this test of horses and riders now extends over a full week and includes flat, hurdle and steeplechase races. All over Ireland people of all ages and backgrounds prepare for the Galway Races with a passion that borders on the religious in its intensity. Holidays are planned and desks are cleared to make way for the annual pilgrimage to Ballybrit race course, to have a punt and enjoy the craic.

The bars and restaurants ring with racing talk. There are stories, often incomprehensible to the uninitiated, of horses being 'laid out' for certain races, of stallions 'catching pigeons' on the gallops at home and of trainers in and out of form. The best horses and riders from across the British Isles turn up – some more in

hope than expectation. The roar of the crowd can make the hairs stand up on the back of your neck, as the white flag that heralds the start of every race is raised. Thursday is the busiest day of the meeting, being both Ladies' Day and the day of the richest and most eagerly anticipated race on the whole card – The Galway Plate. Betting turnover goes through the roof for this two-and-three-quarter mile handicap chase and the tightness of the course and closeness of some of the fences ensure that it is a race of many thrills and spills.

The race meeting has now cemented its place in the Irish social calendar and is very much the place to be seen. Politician and celebrity guests come to demonstrate their 'street-cred', but the real festival crowd party well into the night, long after the whirring of the VIPs' helicopter blades has stopped.

Horse racing is the excuse for a massive party!

Rose of Tralee Festival

WHEN:
The end of August
WHERE:
Tralee, County Kerry
BEST FOR:
Spectacle and music
YOU SHOULD KNOW:
A parade with decorative floats was introduced in 1967 and the first float was designed around a giant scallop shell. As the design took shape a sharp-eyed helper noticed that it closely resembled the logo of a large oil company. Not wanting to give free advertising to a multi-national, the design was shelved and the floats are now based around a floral design.

Unashamedly old fashioned, the annual Rose of Tralee Festival sets out to find a woman whose grace and beauty most closely resemble the spirit of Irish womanhood. Drawing inspiration from a song, the festival was the brainchild of accountant Billy Clifford and local newspaper man Dan Nolan and quickly grew into an Irish institution. Although there was a previous festival, with at its centre the crowning of Tralee's Carnival Queen, this fell by the wayside after World War II. Its repackaging as the Rose of Tralee Festival was a masterstroke and it soon outgrew the small cinema that housed it.

It was originally open only to women from County Kerry, but as its appeal grew the rules were relaxed to include all women of Ireland and eventually all those of Irish stock. Recent entrants have included a mixed-race woman of Jamaican and Irish descent and several contestants from America, Australia and New Zealand. Most Irish people know it from watching it on television and in its heyday it drew in the largest audience of any event in the country. Top presenters like Gay Byrne would host the gala and first-rate music was laid on by world-famous acts. In 1986 the Taoiseach, Charles Haughey, opened the event. While the festival still pulls in a large crowd, it commands a TV audience that is a fraction of what it once was. It has become too easy to parody in the Ireland of today, most notably in the sit-com *Father Ted*, where the eponymous priest judges a farcical 'lovely girl' competition. More cerebral criticism comes from journalist Claire Byrne who questions why Irish women 'still want to don the dress and impress as shy, bashful, Jane Austen types who will represent a non-existent version of Ireland abroad'.

A band plays at this unashamedly old-fashioned festival.

All-Ireland Hurling Final at Croke Park

Fast and furious action is the hallmark of the hurling final.

The fast and furious game of hurling is Ireland's national game. It has probably been played for over two millennia, but its present incarnation as a countrywide competition dates back to 1884, when the newly formed Gaelic Athletic Association instigated an All-Ireland competition. After a series of regional elimination rounds, the two best teams head to Dublin for the final, held at the magnificent Croke Park. With a capacity of over 82,000, it is one of Europe's biggest stadiums. That it is filled to bursting point for the hurling final is all the more remarkable, given Ireland's size and the fact that few outside of the island play the sport.

In the immediate build-up to the game the streets of the surrounding Dublin 3 area throng with rival supporters. Colourful flags and intricately embroidered banners are carried by both sets of fans, who sing themselves hoarse. Once inside the stadium rivalry is set to one side at the singing of the National Anthem. Then the two teams of 15 men peel away from a huddle and do their final warming-up exercises.

To the uninitiated hurling can seem confusing and if you don't know the rules someone in a local bar will gladly enlighten you. Briefly, the object of the game is to propel a hard ball (sliotar) over or under some H-shaped posts – chiefly with the aid of a stick called a hurley. One point is awarded for hitting the ball over the posts and three for the more difficult task of hitting it under them into the guarded net. A team's score is shown with their 'goals' (three points) tally first and then 'overs' total – so a score of 3-9 would mean they had scored 18 points. Fitness, bravery and skill are displayed in equal measure as for the next 70 minutes warrior-like action takes place on the field.

WHEN:
A Sunday in early September
WHERE:
Dublin
BEST FOR:
Sport
YOU SHOULD KNOW:
Before 1930 no detailed records of the finals were kept. Often the only thing reported was the winning score. This led to some fanciful claims by players about their scoring feats. A certain Jimmy Kelly, representing Kilkenny, claimed to have scored seven goals in half an hour during the 1905 final. The records show that his team did put seven past Cork on that day, but he may have exaggerated his own part in that total.

Storytelling Festival on Cape Clear Island

WHEN:
The first weekend in September
WHERE:
Cape Clear Island, West Cork
BEST FOR:
Culture and music
YOU SHOULD KNOW:
Lack of knowledge of the language of the storyteller should provide little barrier to one's enjoyment of the tale. Rather like listening to a song in a foreign tongue, the style, rhythmic structure and strength of delivery can transfix in a way that mere words usually cannot.

The Irish have many ways to describe those who talk a lot. Those blessed with great verbosity are said to have the 'gift of the gab' or to have kissed the Blarney Stone. The art of storytelling, however, transcends this everyday chatter and there is much more to Irish storytelling than first meets the ear. A good storyteller must demonstrate calmness, wisdom and brevity; they must be able to hold an audience, to display and impart knowledge and to construct narrative pathways from the past through the present and into the future.

Cape Clear is Ireland's most southerly inhabited Gaeltacht (Gaelic speaking) island and its stark beauty is reason enough to visit at any time of the year. In September each year it plays host to a remarkable oral gala, as storytellers from around the globe descend on this corner of Ireland in a celebration of the spoken word. Founded in 1994, the event has grown into one of the most important of its kind. The line-up usually has at its core Irish artists, both Gaelic and English speaking, with a goodly sprinkling of invited guests from such places as North America, the Caribbean and India as well as the Celtic fringes of Britain.

The mythical tales spun with supreme oral dexterity are greatly enhanced by the island's immense natural beauty and, weather permitting, many of the events take place in the open air. Musical accompaniment and even the odd puppet show have also been added to widen the festival's appeal to the young. The festival now has educational and participatory components to reflect the recent renaissance of the Irish language amongst the middle classes. Many audience members will be storytellers themselves, eager to continue this long and noble tradition.

Galway International Oyster Festival

If sitting at a bar, with half-a-dozen freshly shucked oysters laid out on a bed of ice before you and a glass of bubbly to wash them down is your idea of heaven, then head down to Galway in the autumn. Originally the brainchild of hotelier Brian Collins to extend the holiday season and bring in a better class of customer, the Galway International Oyster Festival has grown to become one of Europe's top food events.

Much music and merriment surrounds the occasion, but it is the humble bivalve mollusc that always takes centre stage. The event commences with the Irish Oyster Opening Championship, where

exponents of this specialized craft from around the country gather to compete in a test of agility and speed. The large assembled audience applauds the shuckers' endeavours, while helpfully scoffing the fruits of their labours. The winners of this event progress to the world championship, which takes place two days later. An official free-to-enter opening ceremony takes place on the Saturday, where a symbolic first oyster of the season is presented to the town's mayor to kick off the festivities. A parade of musicians, vintage cars and colourful floats then wends its way through the streets of the city towards the giant red-and-white Oyster Marquee, where all things oyster are back at the top of the menu. Tastings, the world opening championship and an 'elegant lady' competition are worthy accompaniments to the main dish.

The place to be seen, however, is the Oyster Festival Gala Ball – an exclusive black-tie event where the champagne flows and the cuisine and cabaret are top drawer. The festival is then given a fitting farewell at Nimmo's Pier where musicians serenade the climax of a brilliant weekend of first-class gastronomic indulgence.

Women in traditional dress offer their tasty wares.

WHEN:
Late September
WHERE:
Galway City, County Galway
BEST FOR:
Oysters and pearls
YOU SHOULD KNOW:
The oyster has come a long way since it was used as cheap filling for meat pies. The festival and the concomitant eating of the 'humble bivalve' come with a hefty price tag. Other than the opening ceremony, all the other events are quite pricey. But most who attend think it is worth every penny.

229

Lisdoonvarna Matchmaking Festival

Each year, after the crops have been gathered in the tranquil little town of Lisdoonvarna, on Ireland's west coast, there is the buzz of romance. Matchmaking is an ancient tradition in Ireland and those charged with the duty of bringing people together still hold great status in the community, with the title often being passed down through generations. The land has always been the biggest source of income in these parts, and this led to a demographic imbalance between young men who worked the land and women who would seek employment in the towns and cities. For generations landed families from miles around would gather to dance, drink and frolic and to find a suitable partner for their sons.

The Lisdoonvarna festival dates from the mid 19th century, when the Great Irish Famine and mass emigration so depleted the population that marriage and reproduction were essential for economic survival. Large dowries were paid to successful matchmakers and the festival brought much-needed money to the town. Today it is a much more light-hearted affair, though the challenge remains the same – to find the perfect partner. Dances and festivities take place mainly at weekends, but even by Thursday evening the town throngs with partygoers. What at first may seem like a disorganized barn dance is in fact an elaborate play of manners. It is usually up to the woman to make the first move by approaching the matchmaker and expressing an interest in a particular man. It is then that the art of the matchmaker is called into play. If he or she judges it a good match, then a formal introduction is made. Many marriages are still arranged in this way. Even if at the end of the festival you do not find Mr or Ms Right, you can console yourself with the fact that you have attended a great party.

Matchmaker, matchmaker make me a match!

WHEN:
September and October
WHERE:
Lisdoonvarna, County Clare
BEST FOR:
Singing, dancing and marriage
YOU SHOULD KNOW:
One of the most popular recent additions to the festival is a speed-dating weekend. Each person has three minutes to convince the other of their worthiness before repeating their patter to someone at the next table. Quite what the matchmakers think of this hasty way of approaching true love, one can only imagine!

The Ballinasloe Horse Fair

The Ballinasloe Horse Fair is one of the oldest expositions in Ireland and was at one time the biggest of its kind in the world. While now almost exclusively associated with the horse, in the early 19th century it was more famous for its cattle. There is very little documentary evidence detailing the origins of the fair, but it is probable that, due to the strategic location of Ballinasloe, a fair has taken place on this site since ancient times. Its Irish name of Béal Átha na Sluaighe (literally: crossing point of the crowds) clearly marks it as a place of great importance to trade.

Over nine days, spanning two weekends, the emphasis is now on all things equine and having survived tricky economic times after World War II, the fair has cemented its place in the Irish social calendar. Horses are still bought and sold, but the main attractions are show jumping and steeple chasing, as well as competitions for youngsters and their ponies. An agricultural show, a dog competition and a Festival Queen of the Fair contest all give the event the feel of a giant village fete. Stout farm hands compete in a tug-of-war, while street theatre performers and magicians entertain children and adults alike. Away from the showground, the whole town comes to life, with music and dance fuelled by innumerable pints of the 'dark stuff'. Considerable stamina is required to last out the full nine days and, with this in mind, the festival ends with a conveniently quiet family day. However, those nursing hangovers should put earplugs in, as the party ends with a spectacular firework display. The motorcar may have superseded the horse as a mode of transport, but in this part of Ireland the horse is still king, for a couple of weekends anyway.

WHEN:
October
WHERE:
Ballinasloe, County Galway
BEST FOR:
Horses, culture,
sport and music
YOU SHOULD KNOW:
Thousands of horses and ponies are still sold at the fair. It is a strictly cash-only business and no paperwork is ever produced. If you are tempted to buy a horse, be sure you know what you are doing. Rarely does the term *caveat emptor* have more meaning.

All the fun of the horse fair!

Queen's Day

WHEN:
April 30 (or 29 if the 30th falls on a Sunday)
WHERE:
Amsterdam and throughout the Netherlands
BEST FOR:
Street parties
YOU SHOULD KNOW:
It's a good idea to go equipped with small change so you can buy that little something you never knew you wanted from a vrijmarkt trader.

April 30 is Koninginnedag, or Queen's Day, in the Netherlands, the closest thing the Dutch have to a national day. Queen's Day is a public holiday which marks the birthday of former Queen Juliana, the much-loved monarch who reigned for over 30 years until abdicating in 1980 in favour of her daughter Beatrix. Queen Beatrix herself was born in chilly January, so wisely decided to leave the date of Koninginnedag unchanged. The result is a day on which the Dutch belie their image of sober respectability and let their hair down in the late-spring sunshine.

Queen's Day sees the whole country *en fête* with celebrations in communities throughout the land, two of which are favoured each year with a Royal visit. Unsurprisingly, the biggest and most intense party of all takes place in the capital, Amsterdam, which regularly attracts hundreds of thousands of locals and visitors who throng the streets, squares, parks and quaysides of the city to enjoy all manner of free outdoor entertainment, including live bands, folk dancing, street theatre, and the inevitable boat parade on the canals. One colour alone rules on this day: orange. Revellers colour their hair, paint their faces, wear wigs and generally disport themselves in the colour that commemorates the House of Orange, the Dutch royal family.

A particular feature of Queen's Day is the custom of the vrijmarkt or 'free market', when normal trading regulations are suspended for the day and the Dutch honour their history as a proud trading nation by turning out on the streets in force to sell redundant possessions and anything else that takes their fancy. This may be commerce, but it is a relaxed affair and children especially are encouraged to practise their emerging mercantile skills.

Thousands of people celebrate Queen's Day on boats on the canals of Amsterdam.

International Sand Sculpture Festival

It's amazing what can be created with (quite a few) grains of sand!

The largest coastal town in the country, Scheveningen is the seaside resort for Den Haag; nowadays, indeed, the two communities more or less run into one another. Although it still draws plenty of holidaymakers in the summer months, Scheveningen, like many a North Sea resort, has known better times; buildings like the monumental Kurhaus on the seafront, built as a grand hotel in the late 19th century, are powerful reminders of past glories.

Scheveningen's principal attraction is its long expanse of golden sand. In early summer every year the northern end of the beach is transformed into a huge sculpture park when the International Sand Sculpture Festival is held. Teams comprising between three and five sand sculptors come from different countries to create original and highly elaborate works of art using no more than sand and water. This is a competitive event and at the end of five days a jury decides on the winning design. The carvers have to work to the particular theme chosen for that year: in 2005, for example, the theme was the Queen, while the following year it was Mozart, in honour of the 250th anniversary of the composer's birth.

Sand carving is taken very seriously and the sculptures are considered genuine artworks. Apparently the raw material, which is obtained from the silt of the River Maas (Meuse), is reckoned to be some of the best sculpting sand in the world. The sculptures remain on view for three weeks after the competition so you have plenty of time to inspect them at close quarters and arrive at your own verdict. For maximum enjoyment stop first on the promenade and pick up a couple of *poffertjes*, the delicious little Dutch pancakes.

WHEN:
April to June
WHERE:
Scheveningen
BEST FOR:
Seaside art
YOU SHOULD KNOW:
The Netherlands is home to the World Sand Sculpting Academy, which is based at Zoetermeer, a short distance inland from Scheveningen.

Iggy Pop performs at Holland's answer to Glastonbury.

Pinkpop Festival

Held over the Whitsun weekend, Pinkpop is the country's premier rock music festival. It takes place on a green-field site known as Megaland at Landgraaf, which is in the far south of the Netherlands, near Maastricht and sandwiched between the German and Belgian borders. The open-air event showcases the very best in contemporary rock and pop with three days of non-stop action. From small beginnings in 1970 when 10,000 music-lovers turned up for a one-day festival, Pinkpop has grown to become a major player on the music scene and now attracts some 70,000 fans who come to listen to 40 bands perform on three separate stages. Unlike Glastonbury in the UK, Pinkpop has never missed a year and has an entry in the *Guinness Book of Records* as the oldest continuous rock festival in Europe.

With its leanings towards the more progressive end of the rock music spectrum, Pinkpop has tended to serve as a trendsetter for many other festivals in Europe. Even so, whilst it may not operate on quite the scale of Glastonbury, Pinkpop's pedigree still gives it sufficient clout to bring in the biggest acts of the day: from the early seventies, which featured bands like Fleetwood Mac, Status Quo and Steve Harley and Cockney Rebel, to the present when the headlining acts in 2007 included the Arctic Monkeys, Smashing Pumpkins and Snow Patrol and in 2008, Metallica, Foo Fighters and Rage Against The Machine.

Like Glastonbury there is a huge dedicated campsite for the festival, with all the facilities you would expect. Pinkpop is also similarly prey to the vagaries of the northern European summer so you should come prepared for most types of weather, especially if you are camping.

WHEN:
Late May
WHERE:
Near Maastricht, Limburg province
BEST FOR:
Rock music
YOU SHOULD KNOW:
Weekend tickets for the whole three-day event tend to sell out early so you should book well in advance (tickets go on sale in mid February).

The Four Days Marches

The Dutch may be inextricably linked with the bicycle in the popular imagination but they are also energetic and enthusiastic walkers. This pastime is honoured most strikingly in the eastern town of Nijmegen, close to the border with Germany and the oldest town in the Netherlands. For nearly one hundred years the town has organized an annual mass walking festival in mid July. Attracting some 40,000 entrants every year it is now officially recognized as the world's largest walking event. This is a strictly non-competitive occasion where taking part is all, and it caters for walking enthusiasts of all kinds. Participants register for a distance of either 30 km (19 mi), 40 km (25 mi) or 50 km (31 mi), depending on age and gender. This distance must be walked on each of four consecutive days, the route on each day being different and taking walkers into the beautiful countryside surrounding Nijmegen.

Calling these walks 'marches' reflects the event's origins in the military, and it is without question a test of fitness and stamina; it should not, however, be beyond the capabilities of anyone in good health who is a reasonably experienced walker and who has trained appropriately beforehand. Those who complete the required distances over the full four days are awarded the coveted Four Days Medal, a five-armed cross to acknowledge 'proven marching ability'. There is a truly festive atmosphere on the final afternoon when crowds of spectators fill the specially erected grandstands lining St Anna Straat to cheer and encourage the weary walkers down the home straight. The street is renamed Via Gladiola for the occasion, to honour an endearing tradition in which every participant carries a bunch of orange gladioli with them across the finishing line.

WHEN:
Mid July
WHERE:
Nijmegen and surrounding area
BEST FOR:
Participation sport
YOU SHOULD KNOW:
The Four Days Cross is a decoration that has royal approval which Dutch servicemen are permitted to wear on their uniforms.

Walkers old and young have their gladioli at the ready.

Flamboyant is fun on the canals of Amsterdam during the annual Gay Pride festival.

Amsterdam Canal Parade

When the staid and prosperous merchants of 17th century Amsterdam established themselves along the quaysides of the newly created Grachtengordel, the belt of canals encircling the medieval city, they can have had no conception of the sights their handsome town residences would be countenancing today. Without doubt the most flamboyant is the Canal Parade, which is held on the first Saturday in August and forms the centrepiece of Amsterdam's annual Gay Pride festival. A flotilla of more than 70 flat-bottomed boats and barges, extravagantly decorated and filled with dancers, musicians and partygoers in various states of fancy dress and undress, makes its exuberant way from the Westerdok along the length of the Prinsengracht canal to the Amstel River and thence via the Oude Schans to finish at the Oosterdok.

Floats cannot be built up to the heights of their counterparts in street parades because of the many low bridges the vessels have to clear; decorators also plan their displays to take account of the fact that many of the best vantage points for spectators are from above, from the upper floors of houses and from the bridges themselves.

Nearly half a million people are reckoned to watch the Canal Parade, a non-stop riot of colour, frenetic action and high-volume music pumped out by DJs from any number of sound systems. This may not be the time to visit if you want to enjoy the tranquil beauty of this most elegant and harmonious of urban environments, but you will find it hard to resist being drawn into the party atmosphere, which continues through the night with parties on the streets and in the city's bars and clubs.

WHEN:
The first Saturday in August
WHERE:
Amsterdam
BEST FOR:
Costumes, music and partying
YOU SHOULD KNOW:
The Canal Parade is the only Gay Pride event in the world to take place on water.

Aalsmeer Flower Parade

The Dutch love affair with flowers is well known; everywhere you go in the country you will see evidence of the pride they take in their floral displays, whether in grand municipal parks, suburban gardens or a simple window box. The cultivation of flowers and plants is a huge business, accounting for a quarter of the country's export revenue from agricultural products. The figures are staggering: some nine billion bulbs are grown annually in the Netherlands and more than 11,000 ha (27,000 acres) are devoted to modern greenhouse production, most of this in the area between Amsterdam and Rotterdam. Each year on the first Saturday in September Aalsmeer, a small town 20 km (12 mi) southwest of Amsterdam and close to Schiphol Airport, plays host to the Bloemencorso, Europe's biggest flower parade. A procession of spectacular carnival floats extends for some 3 km (2 mi) as it makes its boisterous way to the centre of Amsterdam, accompanied by bands, dancers and all manner of street performers.

It is worth being in Aalsmeer a couple of days before the parade to watch the feverish preparations as hundreds of flower arrangers work away to create their floral extravaganzas. At the end of the parade there is a free music festival and in the evening an illuminated boat show and a huge firework display.

Aalsmeer is also the site of the world's largest flower auction. Auctions take place on weekday mornings and deal in fruit and vegetables as well as flowers and plants. They are open to visitors and are definitely worth seeing for the unique Dutch 'clock' auction system, where prices start high and go down as the clock pointer turns. Bidders stop the clock at the price they are willing to pay.

WHEN:
The first Saturday in September
WHERE:
Aalsmeer, southwest of Amsterdam
BEST FOR:
Flowers and colourful street entertainment
YOU SHOULD KNOW:
Half a million flowers are used each year in the parade.

The band leads the parade.

EUROPE/LUXEMBOURG

Dancing Procession of Echternach

WHEN:
May or June
WHERE:
Echternach
BEST FOR:
Pageantry
YOU SHOULD KNOW:
You should check beforehand if you wish to take part as, in order to preserve the festival's integrity as a religious event, the Church issues strict guidelines for participating pilgrims.

Echternach is a charming little town in the east of Luxembourg and the gateway to the ancient forests of the Müllerthal, a veritable walkers' paradise where deep hidden ravines carved out of the sandstone plateaus wait to be explored. Echternach's most famous building, and the most important religious edifice in the country, is the enormous basilica, built on the site of a Benedictine abbey founded by St Willibrord in 698 AD. Born in Northumbria, Willibrord was an Anglo-Saxon monk who came to the continent to spread the Christian message, settling eventually in Echternach where he died in 739. His tomb in the crypt of the abbey church duly became a great centre of pilgrimage in the Middle Ages.

Echternach is the venue for one of Europe's more unusual religious festivals, when on the Tuesday following Whit Sunday the so-called Dancing Procession takes place in honour of St Willibrord. Dressed in white shirts and flourishing white handkerchiefs, pilgrims take to the cobbled streets accompanied by a variety of bands and musical groups, all of whom play the same jaunty tune. To this simple melody participants execute a distinctive dancing step, as they move forward with a swaying movement to the left and right.

St Willibrord's Procession is a joyous occasion.

The traditional gait was even more distinctive, consisting of three steps forwards and two backwards, but the sheer numbers involved nowadays has made this particular sequence no longer practical.

Although anyone can take part, this remains very much a religious festival rather than a piece of folklore, colourful and entertaining as it is. The origin of the Dancing Procession is unclear, but it is likely that it developed as part of the rites petitioning the Saint's deliverance from the plague and other medieval illnesses that ravaged the land, especially the disease known as St Vitus's Dance.

Binche Carnival

Once a year the citizens of the small Walloon town of Binche, situated midway between Mons and Charleroi, forget their current worries and throw themselves wholeheartedly into the extravaganza of dressing up, parading, music and revelry that is carnival. There has always been a strong tradition of pre-Lenten festivities in this staunchly Catholic country, and Binche provides one of the most authentically bizarre carnival celebrations of all, a fact recognized by UNESCO in giving the event World Heritage status.

Preparations begin many weeks beforehand, with costume-making, rehearsals for the musicians and drumming groups, and with balls hosted by different carnival societies. Fancy dress in the streets gets under way in earnest on the Sunday preceding Lent when the men of the town traditionally dress as women. Monday is young people's day, which is followed by Shrove Tuesday and the climax of the carnival. Long before first light the men and boys are being dressed by their families (this remains a robustly male-only affair) in the characteristic clown-like Gille costumes: a straw-coloured smock decorated with motifs in the red, yellow and black of the Belgian national colours, topped with a white bonnet and ruff. Gradually the Gilles gather in the town centre, where to persistent drum-beats and wearing strange wax masks with small green spectacles they stomp around menacingly, shaking bundles of sticks to ward off evil spirits.

After lunch the Gilles congregate again to dance through town, this time wearing huge head-dresses of ostrich feathers and accompanied by local boys carrying baskets of oranges. If you haven't yet got caught up in the proceedings, you certainly will be now as the Gilles hurl oranges into the watching crowds. The long day is rounded off by dancing in the main square and a spectacular illuminated procession.

Traditional masks feature prominently at the Binche Carnival.

WHEN:
February
WHERE:
Binche, Wallonia
BEST FOR:
Folklore
YOU SHOULD KNOW:
Do not be tempted to toss any oranges back; they are distributed as gifts so it is regarded as rude if you seem to reject them.

239

Pistes de Lancement Circus Festival

WHEN:
March
WHERE:
St Gilles, Brussels
BEST FOR:
Circus
YOU SHOULD KNOW:
Ticket prices are very reasonable. The main venue for performances is the Maison du Peuple in St Gilles.

If you enjoy the sight of humans performing unbelievable feats then the Brussels district of St Gilles is the place to be in March. A popular haunt of artists and students, this vibrant, up-and-coming area just south of the city centre plays host to the annual Pistes de Lancement Circus Festival. 'Pistes de Lancement' translates as 'Launch Pads' and, true to its name, the festival offers a showcase for young circus artists in the early stages of their performing careers. What they may lack in experience, however, is more than compensated by the sheer imagination and vitality in their dazzling displays of tricks, stunts and skills.

Promoted by an organization with the colourful name Espace Catastrophe (Catastrophic Space), Pistes de Lancement is where you will encounter the cutting edge of contemporary circus performance. All the traditional elements of the circus repertoire are present – trapeze, tightrope, acrobatics, trampoline, juggling – but here they are given fresh twists. The resulting acts combine visual poetry with jaw-dropping spectacle, presented by young artists who come from all over Europe to learn from one another and to test the limits of human ability and ingenuity.

Nor are the more earth-bound antics of the clown overlooked. The rough-and-tumble and slapstick routines that are the circus clown's stock in trade are dusted down and re-presented with new angles for modern audiences. A local clown called Monsieur Clément (actually a woman!) has become a popular feature of the festival over the years and presides over proceedings with a suitably anarchic attitude. Whilst the young performers take their art very seriously, they never forget that their principal object is always to entertain.

La Flèche Wallonne

Apart from football, which is followed in Belgium as avidly as anywhere in the world, cycling comes closest to being the country's national sport; and in Eddy Merckx, who won the Tour de France a staggering five times in the 1970s, Belgium has a true sporting immortal. Every spring the elite of the world's professional road racers gather in Wallonia, the French-speaking area of the country, to compete in La Flèche Wallonne (the Walloon Arrow), a one-day event over a gruelling 200-km (125-mi) course. The Flèche is one of a trio of Belgian races known as the Ardennes Classics, which are held every April and are seen by many riders as key staging-points in their preparations for the Tour de France.

Starting in the old mining city of Charleroi in the heart of the country's Pays Noir (Black Country), the race route follows an eastward course towards the smaller town of Huy, where riders complete three laps of a circuit that includes the race's most famous feature, the notorious Mur de Huy (Wall of Huy), a 1-km (0.6-mi) climb with an average gradient of nearly 10 per cent; in places the slope is more than twice as steep. Mention of the Wall, as it is referred to in the business, strikes fear into the heart of the most seasoned professional cyclist who knows that he must tackle it three times, including at the very end with the finish in Huy itself. Many are the races which have been decided only in that final agonizing push to the summit.

The Flèche was first raced in 1936 and has been held every year since, except for 1940. A separate women's race was introduced in 1998.

WHEN:
April
WHERE:
Wallonia
BEST FOR:
Endurance sport
YOU SHOULD KNOW:
Eddy Merckx is one of only three riders to have won the Flèche three times.

The going gets tough as the cyclists head up a hill.

241

Ommegang Pageant

WHEN:
Late June/early July
WHERE:
Brussels
BEST FOR:
Historical pageant
YOU SHOULD KNOW:
You can view the procession for free, but you will need to buy tickets well in advance to see the display in the Grand Place.

In 1348 the wife of a simple Brussels cloth worker had a vision in which she was told to bring a statue of the Virgin Mary from Antwerp to reward the local crossbow-men's guild for having erected a chapel in her honour. The task duly completed, the statue became the object of such popular devotion that a grand new church had to be built to house it; the church of Notre Dame du Sablon still stands today, although without the original statue. In former times this statue was paraded through the city streets, and thus developed the tradition of the Ommegang (meaning 'walk around' in Flemish). From these humble beginnings it has grown to become the capital's most famous annual celebration.

The Ommegang has long since lost its original religious associations. It owes its contemporary grandeur rather more to the visit of the Emperor Charles V in 1549. Charles wished to present his son and heir, the future Philip II, to the people of Flanders, which then formed part of the Spanish Netherlands. The procession you see today winding its way through the streets from the Sablon church is a recreation of that period, with participants dressed in elaborate costumes of the time. The procession of civic and religious leaders and representatives of the medieval guilds of crafts- and tradesmen arrives in the Grand Place where it is presented to the Emperor and his court, who are 'played' by modern aristocrats, many of whom can trace their ancestry back to the real nobility of the 16th century.

The climax of the Ommegang is the evening pageant held in the illuminated Grand Place, Brussels' magnificent main square. Fourteen hundred performers in Renaissance dress present a colourful display featuring music, dancing, acrobatics, banner-waving, crossbowmen, horsemanship, and stilt-walking.

The pageant comes to a stirring climax in the Grand Place.

Pukkelpop

Now one of Belgium's biggest music festivals, Pukkelpop started in 1985 with just 3,000 fans attending a one-day event on a Sunday in July to hear Ostrogoth. Bands strutting their stuff in those early years included the Ramones, Buzzcocks, Jesus and Mary Chain, and Nick Cave and the Bad Seeds. Since then Pukkelpop has grown to join the elite among European festivals, cultivating along the way an enviable reputation for supporting the more progressive and alternative sectors of rock. Techno, punk and metal feature regularly in the festival line-ups and Pukkelpop has developed a particular name for its dance scene, with the Dance tent receiving rave reviews in recent years.

The crowds enjoy good music and weather at Pukkelpop.

Pukkelpop moved to its present site, a spacious park in Kiewit on the outskirts of Hasselt in eastern Flanders, in 1992. In 1995 the first two-day festival was held, featuring Radiohead, Prodigy and the Smashing Pumpkins, and in 2001 it expanded yet again to its current three-day format. The 2008 festival saw more than 200 bands playing on eight separate stages to a crowd of 150,000 over the three days. Headline acts included The Killers, Metallica, Sigur Ros, Manic Street Preachers and the Flaming Lips. Aside from the music there are lots of other activities, including a stand-up comedy programme and the Cinemaaah! Tent showing non-stop music and cult films. The 2008 event also featured a live 'wall of fame' created by artists from materials found on the site, and an authentic Balkan circus troupe.

Most festival goers come for the full three days, sleeping under canvas in a well-organized campsite. Pukkelpop takes place in the middle of August, so if you are looking for a music festival but are wary of the uncertainties the early summer weather might visit on Glastonbury or Pinkpop, this could well be the event for you.

WHEN:
Three days in mid August
WHERE:
Hasselt, Limburg province
BEST FOR:
Rock music
YOU SHOULD KNOW:
The festival ticket includes free return train or bus travel from anywhere in Belgium.

Paris Fashion Shows

As the clothing industry continues to go global, fashion weeks may now be found in many parts of the world – but the big four centres (New York, London, Milan and Paris, in that chronological order) still stage by far the most important events. These grand occasions take place months ahead of the season in question (January to March for autumn, September to November for spring) and provide an opportunity for influential trade buyers and fashion journalists to check out the next 'in' look and assess the creations of famous *haute couture* designers. Interested members of the public can join the fun, either in person or through extensive press coverage.

The formal twice-a-year 'weeks' are at the fashion pinnacle, showcasing the imaginative talents of famous designers whose every stitch will be studied and analysed by industry pros – designers whose gorgeous (and often outrageous) creations will be bought and worn only by the fabulously rich, yet whose clothing may well set the trends that determine the future direction of the mass market that mere mortals rely on. These are the fabulous catwalk shows surrounded by a luxurious aura of theatrical glitz and glam, where everyone who's anyone in the world of international high fashion must see . . . and equally importantly be seen.

But an important fashion centre like Paris has much, much more to offer than top-designer shows during the main fashion weeks. As well as these headline-grabbing *haute couture* spectaculars, there are also dedicated events for important market sectors like ready-to-wear, men's fashions, lingerie, young fashions and children's clothing, providing a constant round of interesting happenings from January to December. Paris is always delightful (especially in spring!), but for serious 'fashionistas' it can seem like sheer heaven all year round.

Models from Christian Dior on the catwalk add yet more glamour to Paris Fashion Week.

WHEN:
January to March for autumn, September to November for spring
WHERE:
Paris
BEST FOR:
Getting ahead in the fashion game
YOU SHOULD KNOW:
It is possible to buy tickets for many Paris fashion shows – but be aware that the best seats at the most high-profile shows can be very expensive.

La Fête des Gardiens

The historic city of Arles in Provence is located where the River Rhône forks to create the enchanting Camargue delta. The city hosts many annual events, including spring and autumn encierros (bull-running in the streets), bullfighting corridas, an international photography festival, nude photography festival, music and film events. But the most authentic expression of local culture is La Fête des Gardiens.

This appealing festival is built around the long-established parade of the *gardiens* – those hardy and independent custodians of the Camargue's legendary white horses who also breed sheep and fearsome black fighting bulls for local use and export to Spain. After strutting their stuff through ancient streets every May Day, they elect a new Captain for the Guardian Guild, founded in 1512.

The event begins with a parade of women and children dressed in costumes worn only in Arles, complemented by intricate jewellery. Married women have brightly coloured outfits, whilst unmarried women are distinguished by white scarves and headdresses. Next come men in colourful shirts, ties, black coats and distinctive black hats. Musicians deftly play flutes with one hand and drums with the other. Finally the gardiens themselves appear on splendid white horses, often with a woman seated behind, skirt fanned out across the horse's rump.

The procession pauses for a blessing (in Provencal) in front of the Romanesque Notre Dame de Major, then files into the Roman amphitheatre for an incredible display of traditional skills – mock bullfights for boys, games where athletic riders test their abilities to the limit, women dancing and riding side-saddle to music and finally an impressive demonstration of cattle-herding skills where horsemen ride in ever-decreasing circles until the bulls are penned in a tight bunch. It's a vibrant affirmation of a traditional way of life that refuses to be submerged in the modern world.

WHEN:
May Day
WHERE:
Arles, Bouches-du-Rhône
BEST FOR:
A fascinating encounter with the Provence of old
YOU SHOULD KNOW:
When in Arles, be sure to take in the open-air market (held on Wednesday and Saturday mornings) – it's one of the best in France.

Gardiens *herd the bulls.*

Gypsies parade their patron saint, the black servant Sarah.

Roma Pilgrimage and Festival

Every spring the Roma journey from all over Europe to the seaside village of Saintes-Maries-de-la-Mer in Provence for one of France's most colourful and original annual events. This long-standing pilgrimage and festival honours the Gypsy patron saint Sarah, known as Sara-la-Kali (Black Sarah), who will be saluted in prayer and music.

The area has a long tradition of myth and legend. The ancient boat-shaped church contains three statues – two white, one black, the latter being venerated by the Roma. Legend has it that two represent Mary Jacobé and Mary Salomé, who landed at Saintes-Maries-de-la-Mer after coming by boat from Palestine following Christ's crucifixion. The third is their black Egyptian servant Sarah (their travelling companion, Mary Magdalene, has somehow got lost in the mists of time).

Whatever the truth of it, 'Egyptians' (Gypsies) were making pilgrimages here in the 15th century, just 400 years after they first migrated from India. Today, the two Marys are carried into the sea by Catholic pilgrims, whilst the Roma fast overnight; they worship their 'Black Virgin' the following day. Candles are lit, flowers placed at Black Sarah's feet and the clothing of sick Romas placed on the statue to encourage a cure, along with requests from supplicants. She is the protectress who cures sickness, grants fertility and brings good luck, and the ceremony involves carrying her into the sea on a flower-strewn platform.

Traditionally, the Roma gathered in advance to exchange news and arrange marriages, play music and dance, eat and drink together. Today, this ancient festival has become a major tourist attraction. It all still happens but nowadays camera-wielding tourists tend to outnumber Romas. The Gypsies still play music and dance, but business is business – it may prove necessary to cross palms with silver to see the full production number.

WHEN:
May 24-25
WHERE:
Saintes-Maries-de-la-Mer,
Bouches-du-Rhône
BEST FOR:
The best collective display of traditional Gypsy culture . . . anywhere
YOU SHOULD KNOW:
Sadly, there has been recent controversy surrounding the festival after the local mayor banned the playing of music in the streets.

Jan/Feb/March/April/**May**/June/July/Aug/Sept/Oct/Nov/Dec

Cannes Film Festival

Ask the question 'what is the world's most prestigious film festival?' and the answer from industry insiders and public alike is sure to be 'Cannes'. No other festival can match the sheer style, glamour and chutzpah of this must-be-seen-there gathering on the French Riviera, which has been grabbing headlines since 1946.

The opening ceremony of Cannes draws crowds hoping to catch a glimpse of their favourite stars.

Of course there's plenty of serious cinematographic activity taking place around the Palais des Festivals et des Congrès, Théatre Lumière and Salle Debussy, with intense competition for the coveted Palmes d'Or for best film and short film. Other sections include original works from cultures near and far, film school entries, out-of-competition movies, special screenings and Cannes classics.

Cannes at festival time is also home to Directors' Fortnight, International Critics' Week and the Marché du Film. The latter is the world's busiest movie market, with wheelers and dealers brokering everything from distribution rights to finance for big projects, often involving star packages. It provides the perfect excuse for players whose films have not been invited to attend despite the snub, look busy and be seen on all the right super-yachts in the harbour even if they haven't actually got deals to discuss or films on the big screens.

If the word that springs to mind is 'incestuous', that's not quite fair. Cannes is not only for feverish film folk but also tremendous fun for outsiders, with film music and public film screenings at the famous Cinéma de la Plage on Macé Beach for movie buffs, whilst those who like to crowd the red carpet at the Palais will see a galaxy of international stars. Meanwhile, the whole town fills with beautiful people and is infused with an electric atmosphere and manic energy. Sorry Venice, Berlin and Sundance, but when it comes to film festivals there's nothing remotely like Cannes!

WHEN:
May
WHERE:
Cannes, Alpes-Maritimes
BEST FOR:
International movie glamour
YOU SHOULD KNOW:
Accommodation should be booked well in advance if you want to see the stars at work and play – ideally within easy reach of, rather than in, Cannes where prices during the Festival can provide a serious test for most credit card limits.

247

Jan/Feb/March/April/**May**/June/July/Aug/Sept/Oct/Nov/Dec

Le Mans 24

WHEN:
Mid June
WHERE:
Le Mans, Sarthe
BEST FOR:
Brits – Britain not only tops both the 'races won' and 'winning drivers' lists, but also provides a high percentage of each year's spectators.
YOU SHOULD KNOW:
The famous Le Mans start where drivers raced across the track when the French Tricolore dropped, leapt into their cars, started up and roared wildly away was abandoned for safety reasons after 1969. The race now has a rolling start.

The 'Grand Prix of Endurance' has been held at Le Mans since 1923 on a demanding Circuit de la Sarthe course that partly consists of temporarily closed public roads. The 24 Heures du Mans (Le Mans 24) is the ultimate challenge that pushes drivers and their machines to the limit with a non-stop test of flat-out day-and-night driving.

Actually, it's not quite non-stop, as the high-powered sports cars do pause to refuel, change tyres and rotate drivers (three share each car). But stops are brief, because an important rationale behind this unique race has been the development of fuel-efficient engines. There are four classes divided on the basis of speed, weight and power output – LMP 1 and LMP 2 (LMP = Le Mans Prototype, designed specifically for the race) and GT1 and GT2 (GT = Grand Tourer, a modified production car). Class prizes are awarded but the overall race winner almost always comes from the LMPs, unless poor reliability unexpectedly lets in a GT.

The meeting starts with testing the weekend before the race. On Monday and Tuesday entrants are minutely examined for compliance with the rules. Wednesday and Thursday are practice days, with sessions in the evenings and at night. On one of these days spectators can enjoy the Le Mans Legend race, when cars from a nominated era that have previously competed in the Le Mans 24 do battle. The entire field growls through the centre of Le Mans on the rest day (Friday) before the race begins in mid-afternoon on the Saturday . . . and continues for (surprise!) 24 hours. It's a grand occasion for serious motor-racing fans that lasts for nearly a week, lets them see tomorrow's automotive technology in action today and comes to a sustained (and sometimes thrilling) climax.

The race serves as the climax of a major motorsport occasion.

Tour de France

The pack hits the Champs-Elysées during the final stage of the tour.

To the uninitiated spectator, the Tour de France can seem like a futile experience. Days of preparation may be rewarded with only fleeting glimpses of cyclists hurtling along at astonishing speeds. However, to see Le Tour simply as a cycle race is to miss the point. It is a gladiatorial contest surrounded by the biggest carnival in the sporting world. Millions line its route and a worldwide audience of over two billion tune in to watch its daily ups and downs.

Conceived in 1902 by Géo Lefèvre and Henri Desgrange, the race has always had one eye on marketing and all along its 3,000-km (1,875-mi)-plus route it attracts great gatherings, both official and impromptu. It is also common for the race to start outside France to widen its appeal; however it always ends with a traditional sprint down the Champs-Elysées in Paris where the champion is crowned.

In its modern form the race is a team event, with 20 or so invited teams competing for a surprisingly broad range of titles. Different-coloured jerseys are awarded for Sprint Champions, King of the Mountains, Highest Placed Young Rider and the most coveted of all, the Yellow Jersey worn by the overall race leader. It is the job of each team to assist its number-one rider in any way possible around the demanding course, even if it means stopping and waiting for him.

At times the rigours of the course make the task of completing it seem almost superhuman and, like other sports, Le Tour has in recent years been tainted by some competitors seeking an advantage through the use of drugs. This however has not diminished the appeal of the race, and it has served to enhance the reputations of the great champions of the past who won their titles fair and square.

WHEN:
Over three weeks in July
WHERE:
All around France with some stages in neighbouring countries
BEST FOR:
Sport, culture and food
YOU SHOULD KNOW:
The best places to enjoy the Tour are at either the start or finishing points of the legs. Each town celebrates the Tour's arrival with a gala of music, food and much partying. The best place to see the actual cycling is on the up-slopes of the Pyrenees where the pace of the race is slower.

Avignon Festival

WHEN:
July
WHERE:
Avignon, Vaucluse
BEST FOR:
A heady overdose of culture in the sun
YOU SHOULD KNOW:
The world-famous song *Sur le pont d'Avignon* refers to the medieval Pont St-Bénezet. Of huge importance as a Rhône crossing in its day, only four of the old bridge's original 22 spans now remain.

One of the most beguiling cities in the South of France, Avignon has a long and fascinating history – and hosts the thoroughly modern Festival d'Avignon (Avignon Festival), one of the world's most prestigious arts gatherings. Founded by Jean Vilar in 1947, it has gone from strength to strength ever since. As with the Edinburgh Festival a month later, there is both an official programme and an *avant-garde* fringe. In Avignon the first is called the 'Festival In' and the second 'Festival Out'.

It all began with heavyweight theatre performances in the grandiose setting of the main courtyard of Avignon's Palais des Papes (Popes' Palace). From the 1960s this basic element was augmented by the introduction of new venues and additional theatrical productions, music and dance. This was swiftly followed by film, literary readings, arts workshops, debates and children's theatre. The end result is a wonderful all-round take on contemporary culture that is enjoyed by a discerning audience of well over 100,000 people each year.

The fringe is altogether more anarchic, vibrant and exciting. Every wall is covered in gaudy posters extolling shows put on in any venue, however small or unlikely, that can hold anything from one performer and an audience of five, on upwards. Those who can't find (or afford) houseroom perform for free in streets and parks. Hundreds of established performers and talented amateurs converge on the city, determined to gain public recognition for their work and go on to greater things. This surge of passionate creative energy supercharges the atmosphere and makes Avignon a stimulating place to visit at any time during July.

The official festival may provide the serious artistic claret, but the fringe supplies the fizzing champagne. Together, they create a wonderful summer high point in the cultural life of France.

Actors perform in the Palais des Papes.

Festival of Giants

History throws up some strange customs, none more so than Les Fêtes de Gayant. The three-day Festival of Giants in Douai has its origins back in 1530, when northern France was occupied by Spanish rulers of Flanders. After defeating the French they ordered that a grand pageant should take place and Douai's guild of basket makers obliged by constructing a huge wickerwork *gayant* (the Picardy dialect's version of the French *géant*) as a centrepiece. The following year, Monsieur Gayant was joined in matrimony to Marie Cagenon and a tradition lasting five centuries (thus far!) was born.

There were ups and downs along the way, with the lofty ramblers banned periodically for religious or political reasons. But the festival was reinstated after Napoleon's fall and has thrived ever since. Nowadays, there are around one hundred effigies, led by the Gayants and their children (Jacquot, Fillon and baby Binbin), followed by a motley assortment of towering figures up to 7 m (23 ft) tall that include local legends, a fool on a hobby horse, dragons and devils.

Each is propelled by up to six men during a Sunday procession and each has its band of loyal adherents in local costume, including women wearing traditional tall round hats made of lace in tribute to the giants. At the town hall the parade pauses while brass bands play, pigeons are released, sweets handed out and the mayor makes a speech. Until Tuesday evening Douai is alive with musical concerts, drama performances, further processions by folklore groups and numerous tempting food stalls. Don't miss delicious Gayantines, rich caramels named after the giants – though the less romantically inclined may be tempted by Les Boulets du Ch'ti, praline chocolates made to look like lumps of coal in tribute to Douai's more recent mining heritage.

Towering figures form part of a procession during the Festival of Giants.

WHEN:
July
WHERE:
Douai, Nord
BEST FOR:
Raucous carnival-lovers who don't easily suffer from a cricked neck
YOU SHOULD KNOW:
Visiting politicians (and others) should resist the temptation to kiss baby Binbin for luck . . . this is a privilege strictly reserved for the inhabitants of Douai.

Saint Cyr cadets march down the Champs-Elysées.

Bastille Day

In 1789, the feared Bastille gaol in Paris was almost deserted, containing only a handful of prisoners. But arms and gunpowder were stored there, and on July 14 (after several days of street disturbances) an angry mob of thousands stormed the lightly defended fortress-prison, overwhelming the defenders after a sporadic exchange of gunfire, seizing munitions, freeing seven prisoners and parading the heads of the governor and some of his men on pikes. Demolition of the feared and hated establishment symbol began immediately and was completed by the end of the year, whilst the Storming of the Bastille became established as an event that marked the start of the French Revolution.

Consequently, the Fête National on July 14 (universally known as Bastille Day) commemorates the Fête de la Fédération, held in 1790 to mark the first anniversary of the historic event. This important national holiday is greeted with patriotic fervour all over France, but the most impressive celebration takes place in Paris on the morning in question, on the famous Champs-Elysées down from the Arc de Triomphe, suitably draped in flags for the grand occasion.

It is here that the French President stands with honoured guests to take the salute from a visually stunning parade of the Republic's armed forces, with bands playing and military jets screaming overhead. In recent years, acknowledging France's pivotal role in the European Community, military representatives from allied countries have joined in, including British troops and the famed RAF Red Arrows formation display team.

Paris pageantry may be the impressive formal face of Bastille Day, but bands play and proud people parade the French Tricolore flag in hundreds of cities, towns and villages all over the country on this most important of national occasions. The message everywhere is simple – *Vive la France!*

WHEN:
July 14
WHERE:
All parts of France and her overseas Departments
BEST FOR:
French patriotism at its most intense
YOU SHOULD KNOW:
Bastille Day always falls during the Tour de France cycle race, and French riders make a superhuman effort to ensure that one of them wins that day's stage.

Lorient Inter-Celtic Festival

The bustling seaport of Lorient on Brittany's southern coast makes a good living from fishing, cargo handling, recreational yachting and tourism. The latter is hugely boosted each summer by the Festival InterCeltique Lorient (Lorient Inter-Celtic Festival), founded in 1971. As the name suggests, it celebrates Celtic culture, attracting performers and spectators from the Celtic heartlands – Brittany, Cornwall, Ireland, Wales, the Isle of Man, Scotland, Cape Breton Island, Asturias and Galicia. They are joined by the Celtic diaspora – heritage-conscious people from all over the world who take pride in Celtic ancestry – and non-Celts attracted by this fascinating event.

There are venues throughout the city for events large and small. It all kicks off on Saturday evening in the Port de Pêche (Fishing Harbour) with the Cotriade. This traditional Breton supper is accompanied by the spirited rendition of sea shanties and stirring maritime music. Next day a Grand Parade of Celtic Nations makes lively progress through Lorient, featuring thousands of dedicated Celts – dancers, singers, musicians and pipe bands – many wearing national costume. Thereafter, the Parc de Moustoir hosts National Bagadoú (bagpipe) Championships, where Brittany's many pipe bands and individual pipers compete.

During the following week the Village Celtique operates in the city centre, providing information, literature, music, crafts, clothing, food and drink. Master classes take place each morning for fiddlers, harpists, accordionists and pipers. There are numerous performances of said instruments (and more) every afternoon, offering dance, folk and traditional music. Evenings are reserved for major rock and orchestral concerts plus the spectacular Nuits Magiques (Magic Nights) featuring a striking combination of dancers, choirs, pipe bands and fireworks. There's a vibrant fringe, with numerous musicians performing in bars and clubs until late. Saturday's climax comes with the Nuit de Port de Pêche, an amazing concert featuring Brittany's finest rock and folk musicians.

WHEN:
Late July/early August
WHERE:
Lorient, Morbihan
BEST FOR:
Authentic Celtic capers
YOU SHOULD KNOW:
Believe it or not, one of the world's largest St Patrick's Day concerts (put on by the Celtic Festival's organizers, featuring 150 Celtic musicians and bands) attracts an audience of 70,000 in . . . Paris.

Local dancers wear traditional Breton dress at the Inter-Celtic Festival.

Médoc Marathon

WHEN:
September
WHERE:
Pauillac, Gironde
BEST FOR:
Being part of the world's tastiest marathon, as participant or spectator
YOU SHOULD KNOW:
The Marathon du Médoc has become so popular that entry is now restricted to around half the would-be 17,000 runners (8,500 are accepted), a fifth of whom must be foreigners – entry forms are available on line from mid February.

Finely tuned athletes need not apply, for the Marathon du Médoc is one race where fleetness of foot is a distinct disadvantage, as the last thing anyone wants to do is actually win. That would be a grave mistake, for this bibulous progression is about wine, wine, glorious wine.

It starts at Pauillac, not far from Bordeaux. Participants (many wearing outlandish costumes) are entertained by nearly 60 châteaux that offer a taste of fine wine to passing runners at tasting stations. Snacks like raisins and fruit are available along the way and there are also refreshment stops that serve tasty food like grilled beef, oysters and cheese. Meanwhile, musicians serenade passing competitors.

A not insubstantial entry fee is required, plus a medical release, but the effort is worthwhile. The watchwords of 'The Médoc' are health, sport, conviviality and fun – with special emphasis on the latter, with the entry form specifically discouraging speed merchants and anyone who is sad, unfriendly or stressed out. Those who fail to gain entry (or are medically unfit!) can watch, enjoy the general razzmatazz and stay on for the grape harvest that follows.

Perhaps it's just as well that this event really is more about the taking part than the winning, or even managing to finish. Sadly, many runners get distracted by temptation – not only failing to get round inside the six-and-a-half hours that earns a medal and loads of goodies (including a bottle of Médoc wine), but failing to finish at all. The number of dropouts is undoubtedly swelled by the fact that it seems mandatory to eat excessively on the previous evening – with Pauillac mounting a Soirée Mille Plâtes (Thousand-dish Evening) and numerous smaller dinners hosted by individual vineyards. It's all delightfully French – and simply delightful.

The Médoc Marathon is about fabulous food and wine as well as running!

Icarus Cup

They fly through the air with the greatest of ease – in all sorts of weird and wonderful costumes. Yes, the highflight of the four-day Coupe Icare (Icarus Cup) is undoubtedly the series of daring, exciting and hilarious Masquerade Flights that feature fancy-dressed paraglider and hang-glider pilots competing for handsome prizes in the Icarnaval contest.

The event was started in 1973 as an offbeat tourist attraction by the commune of St-Hilaire, situated high in the Rhône-Alpes of southeast France, but now the Icarus festival has become a major annual occasion that has far outgrown its humble beginnings. A legion of enthusiasts for flight sports now ascend to this splendidly appropriate venue every autumn, not only to enjoy watching those spectacular Masquerade Flights but also to attend the International Free Flight Film Festival and browse through a wide selection of specialist merchandise on offer at the Icare Expo air sports trade fair.

Then there's an extraordinary selection of performances, demonstrations and displays. These include amazing aerobatics by leading paraglider and hang-glider pilots, parachuting, speed gliding, microlight and paramotor flying, girocopter and light helicopter flights, wingsuits, conventional gliders and more. Every year sees the addition of more related activities such as kite flying, boomerang throwing, model aircraft and birds-of-prey shows. Hot-air balloons are there too, with an international meet seeing dozens of these colourful behemoths taking to the skies. If it flies in an amusing or entertaining context, expect to find it here.

There are numerous attractions for children, built around the Icare Momes facility for youngsters – paper-plane contests, the construction of identified flying objects, gyroscopes, a wind garden, bungee trampoline and falconry demonstrations. There's also a Children's Book Fair, the Icarus Cinema for young people, kite-flying areas, modelling workshops and music, street shows and animation. Fantasical!

The Eiffel Tower takes to the sky!

WHEN:
September
WHERE:
The combined sites of St-Hilaire du Touvet-Lumbin, Isère
BEST FOR:
High-flying families
YOU SHOULD KNOW:
Icarus is not the most reassuring title for a festival of human flight – in Greek mythology Icarus fell to his death when attempting to escape from exile on Crete using artificial wings . . . sadly flying too close to the sun, at which point his wax-and-feather wings melted with disastrous consequences.

255

Cucurbitades Festival

WHEN:
Early October
WHERE:
Marchiennes, Nord
BEST FOR:
None-too-serious shivers down the spine and sensational pumpkin pie
YOU SHOULD KNOW:
Why Marchiennes, of all places? Simple – the festival commemorates the fact that the last sorcery trial in France took place here in 1679, after which five accused women were burned at the stake.

The Scarpe-Escaut area of northern France was once a benighted place – stripped of trees by German invaders in World War I and thereafter a bare, marshy plain seriously polluted by continuing coal mining – until the 1960s, when mining stopped and tree-planting and land reclamation started recreating an area of attractive countryside where nature could flourish once more. At the new nature park's heart is the tranquil village of Marchiennes, with its ancient Sainte-Rictude Abbey gatehouse.

But all is not always quite as peaceful as it seems, for the first weekend in October sees an early start to the Hallowe'en season, with Marchiennes being dramatically transformed into something unexpected – the scene of a scary two-day festival of witchcraft, sorcery and all things spooky called Cucurbitades which is a hugely popular annual event that attracts around 30,000 spectators. This bizarre occasion is named for the members of the Cucurbitaceae family (pumpkins, marrows, cucumbers, courgettes, squashes and the like). These tasty vegetables all feature prominently in the celebrations, firstly by being turned into frightening candle-lit faces and then being included in all sorts of sustaining dishes that will subsequently feed hordes of hungry revellers.

But they're not the main course – as night falls a legion of witches comes out to terrorize the people (in the nicest possible way, scattering thousands of chocolate coins that occasionally turn to gold as if by magic!), whilst lively performances against the picturesque backdrop of the Benedictine Abbey include thunderous music and dance, with plenty of capering characters in outrageous costumes contributing to the fun. There are magical roundabouts to delight younger children, who attend in their thousands and often seem less alarmed by the grotesque disguises and general mayhem than their parents.

Prix de l'Arc de Triomphe

Is this Europe's most prestigious horse race? Those who promote English Classic races may argue, but there can be no doubt that the Prix de l'Arc de Triomphe provides a resounding climax to the year's flat-racing season. Generally known simply as 'The Arc', this is one of the world's richest turf races and is open to three-year-old (or older) thoroughbred horses of either sex. In fact, The Arc is a mere stripling compared to the English Classics – the race was inaugurated as recently as 1920 whilst the first Epsom Derby was run in 1780.

The Arc takes place in the elegant surroundings of Hippodrome de Longchamp on the banks of the River Seine in the Bois de Boulogne –

Kieren Fallon, left, pilots Dylan Thomas to victory in the 2007 race.

France's premier horseracing venue ever since the first contest was staged in 1857 with Emperor Napoleon III and his wife Eugénie in attendance. This set a trend whereby the cream of French society turned up for racing at Longchamp, and today the international set joins them for the Arc meeting, which offers a high-quality card with seven races classified at the highest level (Group 1) and an impressive supporting cast of Group 2s.

Entries are international, too, giving visitors from Europe's top racing countries (France, Great Britain, Ireland, Italy and Germany) the chance to support national favourites. But home cheers ring out most often for The Arc winner, France having won three times more often than the rest put together. But that doesn't stop the trainers of overseas raiders and their fans hoping for a big race win, while victories in lesser races usually provide some consolation.

This creates a wonderfully cosmopolitan atmosphere at Longchamp during Arc weekend, which has all the drama, excitement and colour to be expected of one of the most famous occasions in international sport.

WHEN:
The first Sunday in October
WHERE:
Longchamp Racecourse, Paris
BEST FOR:
People-watching with some splendid horseracing thrown in
YOU SHOULD KNOW:
Eager status seekers should be aware that one of The Arc's modest Gallic slogans is *Ce n'est pas une course, c'est un monument* (Not so much a race, more a monument).

257

Paris Motor Show

WHEN:
October 2010, 2012, 2014, etc.
WHERE:
Paris Expo, Porte de Versailles, Paris
BEST FOR:
Star cars
YOU SHOULD KNOW:
For those who can't wait for the next Mondial de l'Automobile and can get by with a mere two wheels, there's an equally impressive motorcycle event in alternate years when the Paris Motor Show doesn't take place.

Welcome to the motoring exhibition with the longest history – started way back in 1898 by automobile pioneer Albert de Dion of the deDion-Bouton company, which began making steam cars way back in the 1880s and was (very!) briefly a world leader. This enduring institution is definitely one to anticipate at leisure, as the amazing Mondial de l'Automobile (Paris Motor Show) only takes place every other year.

No major carmaker can afford to ignore this prestigious international showcase and they all invest big bucks and make the maximum effort to stand out from the competition. They all hope to impress Europe's car-buying public . . . though in truth the real target audience is, more significantly, the world's motoring press. To that end the Paris Motor Show is often chosen for the launch of new models, and the leading manufacturers often seek to trump the opposition by presenting a stunning concept car that grabs the headlines, even if it will never actually go into production.

Here, too, it is possible to review progress on automobile technologies of the future like hybrids, electric cars and fuel-cell vehicles. Any innovations remain closely guarded secrets until the press preview, in the hope of cranking up the frisson factor and securing the best coverage when those all-important motoring writers finally get to see the goodies.

But the biennial extravaganza is also a massive public attraction. It's one of the planet's sexiest 'carfests' and nearly 1,500,000 people flock to this chic event. Eager visitors include hordes of serious 'petrolheads', supported by many who are simply attracted by the certainty of seeing some real showstoppers. And of course everyone is seduced by the glamour (yes, pretty girls galore!) that invariably swirls around the shiny metal. All that and Paris in the autumn – unmissable!

The stunning Peugeot RC concept car was a typical star of the Paris Motor Show.

Mondial du Snowboard

Snowboarding is a relative newcomer to the winter-sports firmament, but already has a large following. France has eagerly embraced this new discipline and hosts the Mondial du Snowboard (Snowboard World) event at Les Deux Alpes, southeast of Grenoble. The country's second-oldest ski resort (after Chamonix) has the largest 'skiable' glacier in Europe. It also possesses one of Europe's best snow-parks that boasts two boarder-cross courses, a half-pipe and multiple kickers.

That's all the snowboarders need to do their thing, and they gather in force on the Friday to mingle with like-minded enthusiasts, see all the latest equipment displayed by manufacturers . . . and use it. The deal is simple. In return for completing a report card, skilled snowboarders can test all the new kit – boards, boots, bindings, masks and clothing. Meanwhile, juniors participate in an amateur contest and dream of joining the professional ranks.

On Saturday, the New Era Threestyle Clash sees top boarders demonstrating pro skills for an admiring audience until the mid-evening. The crowd then gravitates towards the centre of town, where a massive après-board party breaks out. It can get pretty wild – this is a young sport practised by young people, so uninhibited fun is a mandatory part of the package.

Sunday morning sees the badly hung-over staying in bed, whilst the marquee of trade stands becomes busy with kids seeking free posters and stickers, along with coveters of the best brand-name snowboarding goods doing their shopping and those who have come to watch the latest boarding films in the video suite. Outside, there are mini-board competitions and the day ends with the Ranking Riders Ceremony for invited guests, which honours the year's top French and international riders. It's an event that's about a little snowboarding, lots of style and serious socializing.

A boarder flies through the air with the greatest of ease.

WHEN:
October/November
WHERE:
Les Deux Alpes, Isère
BEST FOR:
Getting in with the snowboard crowd
YOU SHOULD KNOW:
The Avalanche is the nightclub to be seen in at Les Deux Alpes – arrive early or the doors may already be closed on a full house.

Jan/Feb/March/April/May/June/July/Aug/Sept/**Oct/Nov**/Dec

Festival du Vent

WHEN:
October/November
WHERE:
Calvi, Haute-Corse, Corsica
BEST FOR:
Wild and wacky alternative culture
with a serious streak
YOU SHOULD KNOW:
This is primarily an event attended by
dedicated young people from outside
the island, often bringing their
children (for whom there are
numerous special activities).

Some things might not seem to blend seamlessly – for example technology, sport and art. But in the case of Corsica's Festival du Vent (Festival of the Wind) that's precisely what's been happening since 1992, with impressive results. Hundreds of scientists, athletes, artists and environmental campaigners gather at Calvi's Balagne Hotel every autumn to share their specialist interpretations of the theme, which is that wind can be taken to mean nature, freedom of expression, untrammelled thought, excitement and adventure. It's a vibrant alternative event with a difference, offering five days of uninhibited *joie de vivre* with a social conscience.

There's really no limit to the type of activity undertaken during the festival. Clearly, wind sports such as hang gliding, wind surfing, sailing, ballooning and kite flying play a prominent part, supported by imaginative artistic efforts that create unexpected 'Identified Flying Objects' (who says chairs and pigs can't fly?) that float down the wind. To that may be added daring extras like bungee jumping for inveterate thrill seekers who prefer to fly through the air personally.

But that's the fun and frolic part. There's also a strong measure of *avant-garde* intellectual input, with serious emphasis on good ecology, environmental awareness and saving the planet. This element of the festival is becoming increasingly important as awareness of the negative consequences of global warming grows apace. There are recycling workshops, demonstrations of energy-saving inventions and launches of environmental campaigns.

The human-rights element is served by seminars, chat cafés where like-minded people can meet and exchange radical ideas, thematic evenings and film shows. Add to that street theatre, concerts and way-out artistic installations and the unique formula is complete. No doubting it – the Festival du Vent is a real breeze for participating eco-warriors, and exhilarating for those who also serve by merely watching!

Monaco Grand Prix

Formula One racing has always been about glitz and glamour, and nowhere is this more evident than around the street circuit of Monaco. Since its inception in 1929, the Monaco Grand Prix has been the spiritual home of motor racing, where great bravery has been rewarded by even greater material wealth. The Principality exudes opulence, with huge yachts lining the harbour and lavish cliff-top homes providing a fitting backdrop to the race.

Movie stars and celebrities from around the globe gather to sip champagne and pose for the cameras, whilst man and machine are primed and ready to tackle the most demanding course in motor racing. Those sturdy enough to complete the 78-lap race have to change gears thousands of times and negotiate a total of 1,482 corners; all this whilst reaching speeds of over 300 kph (188 mph). One mistake and at best you are out of the race. The tight circuit makes overtaking nearly impossible, so the race develops into a true test of speed and endurance. It is perhaps for this reason that it is loved and hated in equal measure by the drivers who take part in it.

The Monaco Grand Prix is more than just a race; it is a weekend carnival for the rich and famous. The noise of roaring engines is mixed with Hollywood glamour and French elegance. Monaco is a place where even having a light lunch can seriously affect your bank balance. Yet for motor racing enthusiasts the Grand Prix is the biggest draw in the sport and its international appeal ensures that it fills the pages of newspapers and magazines the world over.

WHEN:
Traditionally the last weekend in May
WHERE:
The Principality of Monaco
BEST FOR:
Sport and people watching
YOU SHOULD KNOW:
It is possible to watch the race relatively inexpensively. Tickets can be bought in advance from the race organizers – the Automobile Club of Monaco. More affordable hotels can be found outside the Principality, in France.

A Ferrari passes massed yachts in the famous harbour.

Cádiz Carnival

WHEN:
Usually in February, sometimes
early March
WHERE:
Cádiz, Andalusia
BEST FOR:
Fabulous music and dressing up
(everyone wears some sort of
costume on Saturday night
before Shrove Tuesday, be they
locals or visitors).
YOU SHOULD KNOW:
Pickpockets have a field day at the
Cádiz Carnival, where the press of
jostling humanity makes their work
simple – so leave your valuables
behind and the fun won't be spoiled.

It's big! It's bold! It's brash! It's breathtaking! It's also Europe's biggest
by far and said to play third fiddle only to Rio and Trinidad in world
carnival rankings. That's hardly surprising, considering the massive
effort that goes into preparing for the Cádiz Carnival – a spectacular
ten-day explosion that precedes the onset of Lent, engulfing this
ancient port city in a colourful and extravagant musical 'tsunami'.

There is music everywhere. Coros (choirs) perambulate on open
carts, singing to the accompaniment of lutes and guitars. The people
of Cádiz are renowned for sharp humour and this comes to the fore
at carnival time, with the famous chirigotas groups, each wearing a
sophisticated 'uniform', performing satirical pieces that poke fun at
targets ranging from politicians to current affairs. Comical cuartetos
(quartets consisting, with impeccable carnival logic, of anything from
three to five strolling players) make music with the help of no more
than kazoos and sticks to beat out the rhythm. Costumed
romanceros have done their solo acts from time immemorial, telling
amusing tales in verse with the help of poster images that unfold
with the story. There's even a classical dimension to carnival, with
masked comparsas singing about more serious themes.

Encouraged by this abundance of music and humour, the city
mounts one great big, excessive, raucous celebration that attracts
visitors from all over Spain and beyond. Flowers are hung in
abundance across narrow cobbled streets packed with people and
rock concerts explode in the Plaza de Catedral. There are costume
parades everywhere, traditional carnival rides in the Parque
Genrives, beauty pageants, dancing and thunderous daily La Toronda
fireworks in Plaza San Juan de Dios. The street party goes on day
after day, from dawn until dusk and far into the night.

*An amateur singing group,
called a* chirigota, *performs for
the crowd.*

Santa Cruz Carnival

The holiday island of Tenerife has plenty of lively fiestas, but the queen of them all is held in Santa Cruz de Tenerife, the capital. The action begins impressively with the election of a new monarch. Naturally, the queen of carnivals has its own monarch and she is chosen at a spectacular pageant known as the Gala de Elección de la Reina. Hundreds of performers take part and candidates for the top job wear awesome costumes known as fantasies, whose design and elaborate creation has taken months. This is the most prestigious and coveted prize on the island, and the glory goes not only to the newly crowned Queen, but also to the dedicated team who created the winning costume.

On the Friday a magnificent costume procession parades slowly through the streets, continuing far into the night. Thousands of excited carnival goers in fancy dress dance and party until the early hours. With brief morning pauses for batteries to be recharged, the revelry continues unabated until the night of 'Fat Tuesday'. Countless amateur performers provide entertainment – though after a year of practice these performances seem thoroughly slick and professional. There's plenty of variety to choose from, with various *comparsas* (dance troupes), *rondallas* (singing groups) and *murgas* (comic ensembles) hard at work.

Sadly, all good thing come to an end, and the official end of carnival comes on Ash Wednesday when the good people of Santa Cruz 'entierran la sardina', following the ancient custom of burying a sardine to mark the start of Lent. Happily, the piñata weekend follows, when the party starts up all over again.

Holidaymakers are welcome at the Santa Cruz Carnival – nay, encouraged to attend, for this is officially a Festival of International Tourist Interest.

Tenerife's Carnival Queen waves to the crowd during the opening parade.

WHEN:
Usually in February, sometimes early March
WHERE:
Santa Cruz de Tenerife, Canary Islands
BEST FOR:
Colourful costumes and unusual holiday happenings
YOU SHOULD KNOW:
When dictator Francisco Franco banned such wanton celebrations throughout Spain, the resourceful people of Santa Cruz de Tenerife merely changed theirs to a 'serious' Winter Festival and carried on as usual.

The carnival is a riot of colour and noise.

Sitges Carnival

Sandwiched between mountains and the Mediterranean, the small Catalan city of Sitges is southwest of Barcelona. During the iron-fisted conservative rule of General Franco it was pretty much the only place in mainland Spain where counterculture flourished, having enjoyed a reputation as a bohemian hangout since the painter Santiago Rusiñol worked there in the late 19th century.

Today, Sitges is renowned for popular beaches and vibrant nightlife – also for hosting major events (a famous film festival, renowned carnival, jazz festival and summer concert series), which ensure its pre-eminence as a lively cultural centre that pays little heed to convention. As such, it has been described as 'one of Europe's most popular gay resorts', with thousands of gay men and women arriving for holidays in the sun during July and August.

The *carnestoles* (carnival) is a long-standing highlight of the Sitges calendar, putting those populous summer months into the shade. It begins on Dijous Gras (the Thursday before Ash Wednesday) with *arribo* – the grand entrance of the Carnival King. Thereafter the pace of life in the city quickens dramatically, with much drinking, eating (especially *xatonades*, the traditional local salad served with various omelettes) and general merrymaking enjoyed by up to 250,000 enthusiastic celebrants.

There are special *ruas* (carnival parades) for kids on Sunday and Tuesday afternoons, with the main events taking place on those same evenings. First comes the Rua de la Disbauxa (the self-explanatory Debauchery Parade), followed by the Rua de l'Extermini (Extermination Parade, don't ask) featuring 50 floats and 3,000 costumed masqueraders in extraordinary outfits. The final day also sees some amazing drag shows, before Spain's wildest party ends on Ash Wednesday when the inevitable sardine is ceremonially interred (it's not the sort that comes out of a tin, or even the fish market, but a large effigy).

WHEN:
Usually in February, sometimes in early March
WHERE:
Sitges, Catalonia
BEST FOR:
Uninhibited fun and frolics
YOU SHOULD KNOW:
For four days before the regular carnival begins, Sitges is taken over by the Gay Carnival – complete with Pink Night, Mantilla Night, Tourist Night and Widows' Night.

Las Fallas de Valencia

For four days in March, giants invade Valencia. For months, over 350 different *fallas* (communities) have put their hearts into the construction of *falla*-sculptures made of wood and papier maché (two each, for a total approaching 800). These magnificent confections are paid for by public subscription and constructed by professionals. Each consists of various brilliantly crafted *ninots* (figurines) that combine into a multi-faceted sculpture.

These can be up to 25 m (80 ft) tall, each making a satirical comment on some aspect of human experience. They are transported to Valencia, assembled and planted throughout the city on March 15, which is the signal for the start of a manic street party that will last for four days, with little pause for minor distractions like sleep.

There's a constant cacophony of firecrackers, supported by huge firework displays twice daily. Guardians of *falla*-sculptures camp out to honour-guard their big babies, cooking paella in the streets and proudly parading in local costume to the accompaniment of marching bands. Every evening there's a carnival in the central square, featuring folklore (March 16) and an offering of flowers to the Virgin (March 17 and 18). There's an infinite variety of nightlife provided by concerts and mobile discos to entertain Valencia's citizens, who abandon all else and celebrate in vast numbers.

Despite the frenetic atmosphere, nobody forgets the stars of the show – the *falla*-sculptures. Thousands of people stroll around looking at these monumental works, admiring the craftsmanship and delighting in appreciating the message implicit in each. It is an ephemeral opportunity – all that fine work goes up in smoke on the final night, with every *falla*-sculpture simultaneously torched to the accompaniment of wild cheering during the climactic Carnival of Fire. As the ashes cool, Valencia has once again welcomed spring.

WHEN:
Mid March
WHERE:
Valencia
BEST FOR:
Pyromaniacs with a good sense of humour
YOU SHOULD KNOW:
One *ninot* each year – voted for by the people and removed from its falla-sculpture before the all-consuming Night of Fire – is preserved for posterity in the Museo Fallero.

Hundreds of firecrackers engulf the proceedings in smoke.

La Feria de Abril

WHEN:
Two weeks after Semana Santa
(Easter Holy Week)
WHERE:
Seville, Andalucia
BEST FOR:
All things typically Spanish, from
flamenco to bullfighting
YOU SHOULD KNOW:
This isn't just an Andalusian affair –
people travel from all over the
country to enjoy this famous
occasion and accommodation is
sold out well in advance, along
with bullfight tickets.

Seville's Spring Fair is a great gathering where Andalusians put on their finery and come together to meet, talk, dance and have fun, beginning at midnight on Monday, two weeks after Easter. Celebrations continue until the following Sunday when the Feria de Abril ends with a massive firework display – again commencing at midnight. This timing highlights a key characteristic shared with many similar festivities throughout Spain – some of the most dramatic action takes place after dark, often lasting until dawn.

Which is not, of course, to say that there isn't plenty going on during the hours of daylight. This is a very Spanish affair, with no imported rock music or demented DJs. Instead, it's about tradition – like daily processions called the Paseo de Caballos (horse ride) consisting of high-stepping horses and carriages carrying beautiful women in stunning flamenco costumes, or the famous bullfighting festival that sees the season's best corridas take place each evening at the Real de Maestranza, Spain's oldest bullring (with the country's most critical fans).

Important though these high-profile activities may be, the beating heart of the Spring Fair is the Real de la Feria – a dedicated area outside the city centre, opposite Maria Luisa Park. It has a magnificent gilded entranceway and contains hundreds of colourful casetas (marquees), each one erected by a local organization, business, family or individual as a place to entertain. It is here that Seville parties the night away, with casetas dispensing liberal quantities of food and drink along with loud music, which encourages numerous wild flamenco dances – official or otherwise.

Right next door to the Real de la Feria is a huge fairground with all the usual rides and carnival attractions, which is also awash with sound, light and revelry far into the night.

Traditional bullfighting still draws in vast crowds.

San Isidro Bullfighting Festival

Spain's bullfighting season runs from March until October, with most cities having one event per week, usually on Sunday. But there are also major festivals such at the annual San Isidro Bullfighting Festival – Spain's most prestigious, held in Madrid.

This activity is not for everyone, as bulls suffer horribly, but many visitors feel it is part of Spanish culture and that they should see what bullfighting is really like. One thing's certain – huge crowds are drawn to Madrid's Las Ventas for the San Isidro Festival, and there couldn't be a better place to experience this dramatic Spanish tradition. So what do first-timers actually see?

Spanish matador Serafin Marin performs a daring routine.

These ritualized encounters are conducted by a *cuadrilla* (team) consisting of a matadore wearing a fabulous 'suit of lights', two mounted *picadores* (lancers), three *banderilleros* (flagmen) and a *moza de espada* (sword carrier). Each fight has three *tercios* (phases), announced by a trumpet blast and accompanied by pasodoble music.

After the *paseíllo* (opening parade) in which the presiding dignitary is honoured ('we who are about to kill salute you'), comes the *tercio de varas*, where the matadore sizes up the bull as it is weakened by attacking and lifting padded horses, plus loss of blood from lance-wounds. In the *tercio de banderillas* barbed flags are planted in the bull's shoulder, further weakening it. In the final *tercio de muerte* the matadore skilfully works the bull with his red *muleta* (cape), making a series of daring and dangerous passes before trying to kill the enraged animal with a single sword thrust.

Every fight takes a long time, with every aspect of the prolonged ritual evaluated minutely by the passionate crowd – who are not slow to make their vociferous approval (or disapproval) known. Like it or not, nobody can deny a bullfight is an extraordinary spectacle.

WHEN:
Mid May
WHERE:
Madrid
BEST FOR:
Those who enjoy an amazing traditional experience – and are not squeamish
YOU SHOULD KNOW:
The red cape is used by tradition – bulls are colour blind and attack the cape's movement, so it may be that red was originally chosen to hide any bloodstains.

A rider shows off his advanced equestrian skills.

Fiesta de Sant Joan

This extraordinary festival in Minorca dates back to the 14th century, so visitors are treated to a genuine slice of history. The Fiesta de Sant Joan is one of the most original religious celebrations in Spain, following strictly defined rituals that would be recognized by medieval participants. Everyone wears formal attire, especially *caixers* who represent all levels of traditional Minorcan society – the *caixer senyor* (nobility), the *caixer capellà* (clergy), *caixers menestrals* (artisans) and *caixers pagesos* (farm workers). During the fiesta a herald relays their orders with the help of a simple cane flute and small drum.

It begins on the Sunday before St Joan's Day, called 'The Day of the Lamb'. The *caixers* progress around Ciutadella's ancient streets, accompanied by the Homo des Be, a countryman dressed in sheepskins and carrying a live lamb who represents John the Baptist. In the evening a hazelnut party is held, with the municipal band playing, until the *caixers* arrive to be greeted.

On St Joan's Eve (June 23), the herald mounts an ass and rides to the home of the *caixer senyor* to ask permission to begin the celebrations, which commence with a procession of riders to the rural chapel of St Joan de Missa. The day's programme is completed by – amongst other activities – another hazelnut party, the Caragol de Santa Clara (three tours of the street) and formal farewells to the *caixers*.

The Saint's Day sees a *qualcada* (cavalcade) that proceeds to Plaza de Sant Joan for heats of games to be played in the afternoon before undertaking another Caragol de Santa Clara, followed by a solemn mass in the cathedral. In the afternoon the games commence – an amazing spectacle in which horsemen gallop full-tilt in all directions. Eventually the *qualcada* returns to Santa Clara and the *caixers* disperse, ending this moving fiesta.

WHEN:
Late June
WHERE:
Ciutadella, Minorca, Balearic Islands
BEST FOR:
The liveliest face of conservative Minorcan tradition
YOU SHOULD KNOW:
The handsome equine stars of the fiesta are the indigenous black Minorcan horses – these muscular animals were never required to labour in the fields (that was donkey work) so this local breed has retained its agility and slenderness.

Batalla del Vino

Spain's northern province of Rioja is synonymous with wine production, so it's entirely appropriate that the annual Batalla del Vino (wine battle) should take place here. However, this is a relatively recent development in an argument between Haro and nearby Miranda de Ebro over mountain pasturage that has been ticking on for a thousand years – they have long memories in rural Spain.

Whatever the cause, the modern-day expression of old grievances is unusual and highly entertaining. On the morning of St Pedro's Day a procession sets out from Haro, led by the mayor on horseback. He is followed by a large throng on foot and in assorted vehicles – dressed in white with red scarves, ominously carrying all sorts of containers.

It's quite a trek up to the hermitage of San Felices on Bilibio Crag, where mass is said. A banner is placed on the rocks, a rocket fired and the brass band strikes up to mark the start of a short but intense battle in the disputed fields below. Wine flies everywhere, with part of the fun being the use of bizarre containers like old boots. But there are plenty of *botas* (wineskins), water pistols and squeezy plastic detergent bottles wielded by serious wine snipers, whilst others whirl wine bottles and flagons until empty, soaking anyone in the vicinity. The action is fast and furious until the combatants run out of ammunition – which doesn't happen until tens of thousands of litres have been spilled.

Then it's time for picnic lunches as clothes dry in the sun, before the procession returns to Haro for music in the Plaza de la Paz (yes folks, the war's over for another year) and some gentle heifer-running in the bullring. It's a day full of tremendously good-natured entertainment.

WHEN:
St Pedro's Day (June 29)
WHERE:
Haro, La Rioja
BEST FOR:
Serious alcohol abuse
YOU SHOULD KNOW:
This one is not for the faint-hearted – there are no prisoners taken in the Batalla del Vino, with would-be pacifists who stay on the sidelines fully drenched by the time the last litre of wine is precipitated.

Heifer-running ends the day.

269

Granada International Festival of Music and Dance

They start young in Spain!

It's a mouthful, but the Festival Internacional de Música y Danza de Granada (Granada International Festival of Music and Dance) is one of Spain's most prestigious cultural events. Granada is a fabulous city, which fills with the sound of music every summer as concerts and dance performances are held within the courtyards and grounds of the stunning 14th century Alhambra – surely one of the world's most beautiful and famous locations – and in the Generalife Gardens, Cathedral and Monastery of St Jerónimo.

This is a festival with history and substance behind it – dating back to symphony concerts first performed at the Palace of Charles V during the Corpus Christi holidays in 1883 and re-energized when Falla, García Lorca and other intellectuals convened a major Cante Jondo (flamenco-singing) contest at the Alhambra in 1922. Today's official repertoire features over 60 major shows concentrating on classical music, ballet and Spanish dancing, but the festival also encompasses a wide assortment of concerts and activities including medieval and contemporary music, flamenco, exhibitions and master classes in all sorts of interesting venues.

Quite apart from the formal concert and dance programme, the streets come alive with the sound of Spanish guitars and castanets as flamenco dancers twirl, whilst churches, chapels, community centres, cafés, clubs, bars and open spaces see a huge variety of performances, from classical ensembles to jazz bands, popular singers to string quartets. There's even a dedicated children's festival.

The cumulative result is a vibrant atmosphere that attracts music lovers to southern Spain from all over Europe – and while the festival has the clout to attract the world's greatest conductors, soloists and classical dancers (and does), it also takes pride in picking musical supernovas of the future to give audiences in Granada the chance to see them at the start of their distinguished careers.

WHEN:
June/July
WHERE:
Granada, Andalucia
BEST FOR:
Serious culture in a stunning setting
YOU SHOULD KNOW:
Granada's climate blows hot and cold in summer, with daytime temperatures averaging 24°C (75°F) whilst the nights cool sharply thanks to the proximity of the Sierra Nevada.

Fiesta de San Fermín

There are too many fiestas, fetes and religious festivals in Spain to list – but the one everyone knows is held in Pamplona to honour St Fermín. Once, this may have been just another event in a provincial city, but that changed when macho American writer Ernest Hemingway lauded its most striking feature – the running of the bulls – in his book *The Sun Also Rises.*

In fact, there's a lot more to the nine-day Fiesta de San Fermín than headline-grabbing *encierros* (bull runs) and Pamplona prides itself on welcoming outsiders to celebrations where anything legal goes. The event, known locally as Los Sanfermines, begins at noon on July 6 with an elaborate opening ceremony (inevitably including music and fireworks) and ends at midnight on July 16, with a chaotic miscellany of activity in between.

The official face of the fiesta is seen on July 7 when a huge procession accompanies the effigy of St Fermín through the streets of Pamplona, accompanied by carnival giants, dancers and street entertainers. The festival involves many folkloric activities and traditional events such as the Riau-Riau (a symbolic parade by city councillors obstructed by dancing youths) and endless parties by night. But the daily *encierro* is undoubtedly the highlight. These dangerous events (causing occasional deaths and frequent serious injuries) take place each morning along cobbled streets in the old town.

White-clad runners wearing red kerchiefs and sashes gather before a statue of St Fermín to sing a chant begging for protection. At eight o'clock a rocket announces the release of the bulls. Mayhem ensues as beasts and men hurtle along the narrow course towards the Plaza de Toros, where the bulls will be penned to await the afternoon's corrida whilst young cattle with padded horns toss runners who challenge them – to the general amusement of spectators.

WHEN:
July 6-16
WHERE:
Pamplona, Navarre
BEST FOR:
The world's most dangerous running race
YOU SHOULD KNOW:
Anyone tempted to take part in the *encierro* should know that a critical point on the course is the sharp Mercaderes turn, where more participants are injured on slippery cobbles after colliding with fellow-runners than by the bulls' worst efforts.

Red scarves mark the start of the San Fermín Fiesta.

Festival de la Sidra

WHEN:
July
WHERE:
Nava, Asturias
BEST FOR:
A certain bubbly beverage
YOU SHOULD KNOW:
As cider is the Asturian drink of choice, it will come as no surprise to learn that the National Cider Museum is located in Nava.

Every year the small town of Nava in northwest Spain sees the population triple (or should that be 'tipple'?) when the three-day Festival de la Sidra (Cider Festival) comes around. Locals and visitors alike take every aspect of the national drink of the old kingdom of Asturias very seriously – its manufacture using traditional methods, its bottling in suitably champagne-like bottles, its ritual pouring . . . and of course its copious consumption. Most cities and towns have dedicated cider bars and Nava in particular is cider-crazy.

The town's annual homage to cider is open to all, providing only that the green scarf that shows allegiance to (and proper respect for) the alcoholic apple juice is worn. This homage to cider takes place in July, and consists of exhibitions, discussions, seminars, bowling championships, street dancing, singing, concerts, bagpipe and drum parades, mobile discos, a cider route offering free drinks and tours of the numerous regional *sidrerias* (rustic cider factories), all building inexorably towards prize-giving for the best brew made in Asturias.

Next up are prestigious pouring contests, where expert wrists decant fizzing cider from bottle to glass over the dangerous distance of 1 m (3 ft). Thereafter there's a mass tasting with thousands of litres of free cider available to those with the palette to appreciate subtle differences of taste or texture – and those who simply like quaffing refreshing booze.

Whisper it if you dare, but in truth this event is of fairly recent origin and cynics might suggest it has something to do with attracting revenue to the town – but if so, those who are duly tempted will have no regrets. The Spanish are great at celebrating, and the Festival de la Sidra doesn't disappoint, offering three party-packed, cider-filled days of festivities like no other.

Benicàssim International Festival

Does it always rain at the mighty Glastonbury Festival, creating the seemingly inevitable mud bath? Probably not, but Glasto has an increasingly important Spanish cousin that absolutely guarantees sounds, sun, sand and all-night partying – a very tempting combination. The Benicàssim Music Festival has only been going since the early 1990s, but has already earned the nickname Glastonbury-on-Sea and every summer attracts thousands of young music fans from all over Europe (especially Britain) to this small resort town between Valencia and Barcelona.

With a top attendance around the 150,000 mark, this is a major event on the music calendar – with the added bonus of a laid-back Spanish holiday thrown in. Hotels in town are booked out well in advance of the four-day festival (officially the Festival Internacional de Benicàssim, FIB for short). But the campsite opens for nine days and has room for all.

On festival days tents empty early (along with the site) as the morning sun starts to sizzle and the occupants head *en masse* for the cooling sea, beach and pavement cafés to laze away the scorching day until the musical action kicks off in the evening. The festival slowly starts returning to life from late afternoon, with the first acts venturing on stage around nine o'clock in the sultry night air.

By midnight the place is really starting to swing, and by the time the headliners appear to a rapturous reception at two o'clock in the morning it's really rocking, with music blaring from every stage and a sea of dancers gyrating the night away. Even when the live music is over, disco sounds pound out until dawn and the dancing continues, though gradually the numbers thin as exhausted dancers finally collapse on the grass or retreat reluctantly to their tents. It's a wild one!

Glastonbury's Spanish cousin is a spectacular event.

WHEN:
July
WHERE:
Benicàssim, Valencia
BEST FOR:
Music mania, Mediterranean style
YOU SHOULD KNOW:
After it's all over, hardy survivors consolidate Benicàssim's reputation as the world's wildest music festival by throwing an epic all-night farewell beach party on the Monday.

273

Pilgrimage of Near-Death Experiences

WHEN:
July 29
WHERE:
Las Nieves, Galicia
BEST FOR:
A weird combination of the bizarre and the brash
YOU SHOULD KNOW:
For many centuries Galicia was an isolated backwater where the Catholic Church never quite managed to overcome primitive beliefs in witchcraft and evil spirits – the Pilgrimage was an attempt to reconcile the two belief systems.

This is spooky. Although religious pilgrimages have long been an essential part of Spanish life, and it would be possible to spend years trying to attend them all, there's only one Pilgrimage of Near-Death Experiences. In late July thousands of people pour into the small northwestern town of Las Nieves – many devout believers and others who just come for the ghoulish spectacle.

This strange mixture of Paganism and Catholicism honours the patron saint of resurrection, Santa Marta de Ribarteme. Family members carry those who claim a near-death experience to the Saint's granite church in ornate open coffins, whilst elderly 'risen again' men without family carry their own. Mass is then celebrated (broadcast to crowds outside and subsequently replayed for latecomers).

After mass the church bells ring and the procession starts again, this time going uphill to the cemetery before returning to circle the church, with people solemnly chanting 'Virgin Santa Marta, Star of the North, we bring those who saw death'. The Saint herself makes an appearance in the form of a large statue, arm raised to encourage money offerings to help protect those who have recently escaped death.

If that sounds sombre, the surrounding swirl of activity in the packed town is anything but. The genetic Spanish urge to have fireworks with everything is given full expression, as is the national love affair with stirring music – brass bands play pasodobles in the main square and Gypsy music and dance entertain the crowds. Street vendors sell every sort of religious memorabilia from plastic angels to elaborate illuminated tableaux of the Last Supper, whilst food vendors are everywhere, many offering the local dish of octopus cooked in huge copper pots. Not everyone can be reborn, but nobody alive to experience it will forget this extraordinary day.

Feria del Málaga

WHEN:
August
WHERE:
Málaga, Andalusia
BEST FOR:
Culture and tradition
YOU SHOULD KNOW:
The fair has been celebrated since 1491, paying tribute to the city's patron saint (the Virgen de la Victoria) and commemorating the forcible expulsion of the Moors.

Naturally, the sun-loving inhabitants of Málaga choose the hottest month of the year for their nine-day annual fair (Feria del Málaga). Perhaps the idea is to share their festivities with some of the tourists who flood into the area for their annual sun-sea-and-sand holidays, along with sangria and anything else that may be on offer. In the case of the Málaga Fair, that's quite a lot – and a visit to this festival of Spanish culture and history is a memorable experience by day or night.

Long, hot days see the streets fill with casual strollers watching

274

processions of horses with haughty riders, often with a señora or señorita perched behind, and fine carriages carrying elaborately costumed occupants. There are ample opportunities to sample the wide range of local delicacies offered by decorated food stalls, and these tasty snacks must be washed down with sherry or a sweet local wine to the accompaniment of continuous loud music and impromptu dancing. Street entertainment (notably the magic fair for kids and a folklore festival) is everywhere, with amusing stiltwalkers on regular patrol. Late afternoon sees the city's main bullfighting season in full swing at La Malagueta bullring near the very beach where fabulous fireworks signalled the fair's opening.

Málaga cools down with the darkness – and the action hots up, switching to Cortijo de Torres, southwest of the city centre. Here, at the Real de la Feria, over 200 assorted pavilions may be found where many thousands gather nightly for more food and drink, dancing and all the fun of fairground rides and games. Different nights are dedicated to flamenco dance and music, pop and traditional bands and peña music groups, all competing for glory – until finally a gala performance and yet another firework display ends the Feria del Málaga for another year.

Women in traditional flamenco dress head for the fair.

Children dodge the Bull of Fire during the festival.

Aste Nagusia

Bilbao lights up for ten days in the month of August when the Aste Nagusia (Big Week) celebrations bring a wide variety of entertainment to the city. It all happens following the festival of Nuestra Señora de Begoña and is built around the strapping form of a rather less spiritual lady. Marijaia is a large, rosy-cheeked blonde who is constructed of papier maché and serves as the fiesta's mascot. She is joined by a bizarre army of grotesque effigies, stiltwalkers with huge heads and the fearsome Gargantua who eats children alive before returning them safely to the real world.

Over 100,000 people join the non-stop fun as the Basque capital comes alive with parades, theatre, street entertainment, film shows, comedy, traditional strongman games and bullfighting. Music plays a huge part in the festivities, with free performances in churches and on open-air stages throughout the city. Noteworthy amongst these are the amphitheatre behind the Town Hall and the stage in Plaza Nueva, where daily concerts begin at midnight.

This really is a fiesta for night birds – as darkness falls the vantage points on the city's bridges become crowded with spectators, waiting for the firework spectaculars that are mounted by surrounding communities desperate to outdo each other and win the prize for best display. Once the fireworks are over, huge quantities of food and wine are served from txosnas (marquees) that line the crowded streets, to the accompaniment of accordions and the prancing of costumed dancers.

Plenty of bleary-eyed revellers are still on the go as dawn breaks and street cleaners appear to prepare for another day's exuberant action, generated by the very best of Basque tradition and festive spirit – which will remain undimmed until the end of Aste Nagusia is marked by the ritual burning of Marijaia outside the Arriaga Theatre.

WHEN:
August
WHERE:
Bilbao, Biscay
BEST FOR:
Joining a whole city at play
YOU SHOULD KNOW:
Many of Bilbao's trendiest shops close down during Aste Nagusia, so 'shopaholics' should look for alternative sources of satisfaction.

Basque Rural Games

When it comes to brute strength, you have to go a long way to beat the Basques – as time spent at the three-day Herri Kilorak (Basque Rural Games) will swiftly confirm. They're brave and strong all right, producing extraordinary feats in primitive strength contests that stem from the agricultural work done in these parts since time immemorial. The traditional Herri Kilorak take place in Bilbao's central stadium as an integral part of the city's flamboyant Aste Nagusia (Big Week) celebrations, offering well-muscled giants the opportunity to impress the ladies and shame puny seven-stone weaklings.

Their achievements are awesome, particularly when it comes to stone-lifting contests, where weights weighing up to 325 kg (715 lb) are heaved aloft with much grunting, as whipcord veins stand out and faces redden. Other lifting displays involve rolling a 100-kg (220-lb) ball around the neck as many times as possible in a minute (expect over 35 revolutions) and repeatedly hoisting a 150-kg (330-lb) stone to the shoulder in a 10-minute spell (over 50 lifts).

A host of other games and activities also takes place, entertaining cheering crowds all day long. Basque specialities like the lightning-fast pelota ballgame are played, along with monumental soka-tira (tug-of-war) contests. There are woodcutting challenges with saws and axes, with massive tree trunks being dismembered with relentless endurance. Hay bales are tossed, full milk churns are transported as if empty, men with huge sacks of corn race each other, massive stones are dragged as far as possible in a set time by humans and oxen, grass is scythed at speed, carts are lifted and rams fight.

After marvelling at these unique games it's easy to understand why the Basques see themselves as a race apart – a race that fiercely guards its special character and traditions.

WHEN:
August
WHERE:
Bilbao, Biscay
BEST FOR:
Rural traditions that refuse to die
YOU SHOULD KNOW:
Like many a South American footballer, the star stone-lifters become known by a single *nom-de-guerre* – some famous examples being Arteondo, Aritza, Ondartza and Goenatxo. But the latest top dog goes by his own name, Iñaki Perurena.

Female competitors put their backs into a log-sawing contest.

EUROPE/SPAIN

La Tomatina

WHEN:
Late August
WHERE:
Buñol, Valencia
BEST FOR:
Watching rather than participating
YOU SHOULD KNOW:
It's necessary to get up early in order to secure a place in the central square where the tomato fight takes place – La Tomatina is now so well known and popular that latecomers get marooned a few streets away from the serious action. There is limited accommodation in Buñol so most people who wish to enjoy La Tomatina stay in nearby Valencia – 38 km (24 mi) away – and travel in by bus or train.

This is not an event likely to be enjoyed by those who wince at the price of fresh tomatoes in the supermarket, for La Tomatina sees literally millions of the plump red fruits wantonly destroyed. But what entertainment! Whilst the 'Battle of the Tomatoes' rages on the last Wednesday of August the celebrations start beforehand, creating a wonderful festive atmosphere in the small Valencian town of Buñol.

Indeed, La Tomatina has become one of Spain's most famous fiestas, with thousands of people arriving to join the general brouhaha that lasts for a week before the tomatoes fly. It's all in honour of the town's patron saints, St Louis Bertrand and the Mother of the God of the Defenceless (aka the Virgin Mary). If that sounds a little serious, the style in which these worthies are saluted is anything but. There are street parades, music, dancing and fireworks. On the night before the big fight a serious paella-cooking contest takes place, with the tasty results much appreciated by hungry festival goers.

The next morning, shop fronts are covered in plastic sheeting and lorries loaded with over-ripe tomatoes arrive in the town square, Plaza del Pueblo. As brave souls try in turn to climb a greasy pole and claim the prize ham that waits on top, a water cannon fires and the mayhem begins. Health and safety regulations demand that combatants should wear goggles and gloves, and that tomatoes must be squished before being used as missiles. These are ignored, along with the injunction that no clothing may be ripped, and it's a case of every man (or woman) for himself (or herself). After an hour the water cannon fires again and La Tomatina is over for another year as the fire trucks move in for the big hose-down. Mouth-watering!

The battle of the tomatoes gets rather messy!

Vuelta a España

The pack rides past vineyards in perfect single file.

On your bike – but only if you're a top professional rider willing to undertake this gruelling three-week race in search of glory. The Vuelta a España (Tour of Spain) is one of Europe's three great grand tours, the others being France and Italy, that together represent the world pinnacle of cycle road racing.

Inaugurated in 1935 and held annually since 1955, this pedalling marathon generates extraordinary media interest – indeed, as with the other grand tours, it was instigated by newspapers intent on boosting circulation – in Spain's case the daily *Informaciones*. It was a successful ploy because – then as now – nobody can see all the happenings during a long-distance cycle race, so dedicated followers need a media overview.

Today's lucky (or well-connected) fans secure VIP passes that give access to the race enclosures at start and finish points and to special viewing boxes that overlook the finishing straight of each stage. Densely packed crowds watch each start and finish, too, whilst scattered groups may be found spread out along the route to watch the race go by (along with its accompanying fleet of cameramen on motorcycles and the cavalcade of support vehicles). It's a hugely impressive sight that generates tremendous excitement.

Some enthusiasts like to follow every stage – and of course be part of the vast crowd that awaits the exhausted riders as they summon up the energy for a final sprint when the tour comes to a dramatic climax in Madrid. For visitors who wish to experience this Spanish institution for themselves, various companies offer Vuelta tours – for cyclists who want to follow the tour and cycle some of the route, or for those who merely wish to have an interesting holiday that covers a lot of ground and includes frequent opportunities to observe the race action.

WHEN:
Late August/September
WHERE:
Countrywide (the route varies from year to year)
BEST FOR:
A carnival on wheels
YOU SHOULD KNOW:
If you're interested in identifying the overall race leader as the race flashes by, look for the Jersey d'Oro (Gold Jersey). If you spot someone in a blue jersey with a fish on it, he's the star sprinter.

279

Folk dancers twirl.

La Festa des Vermar

At grape-picking time, the important wine-growing area around the historic town of Binissalem on the island of Majorca puts on an impressive harvest festival, offering bibulous festivities that are celebrated by locals and incomers alike. It's called La Festa des Vermar (The Harvest Party) – and what a party it turns out to be!

The decorated streets of Binissalem vibrate for nine days with an extensive range of entertaining activities, attracting energetic participants and large crowds of enthusiastic spectators. It all begins with the grape harvesters being welcomed at the Town Hall to the sound of traditional Majorcan musicians (*xeremiers*). Thereafter the town is engulfed in a whirl of open-air gatherings, dancing, music, speech making, chess contests, a procession of floats and wine-tasting challenges. A musical contest pits satirical songs relating to local issues against each other, each containing a minimum of eight verses.

There are frantic grape-treading competitions and an extraordinary grape battle between hundreds of children on the outskirts of town. On a more serious note, the grape harvesters take the season's young *mosto* (unfermented grape juice) to be blessed by the Virgin of Robines, who receives an offering. That done, there's yet another celebration in the square with all present invited to drink and be merry.

Another vital element of the fiesta is the consumption of large quantities of Fideus de Vermar (Grape Harvest Noodles). Made in vast iron vats, this flavoursome mutton dish traditionally contained the oldest sheep in the flock, which had been carefully fattened for months by the shepherd. Nowadays it often contains rabbit. Needless to say, whatever the content every portion is washed down with copious draughts of local wine, serving as a liquid reminder of what this very special occasion is all about.

WHEN:
September
WHERE:
Binissalem, Majorca, Balearic Islands
BEST FOR:
The joys of traditional viticulture
YOU SHOULD KNOW:
Binissalem is officially an 'Historical-Artistic Monument' – those who take time out from the festivities can see why by visiting the magnificent marble church with its Norman bell tower and looking at the impressive houses in Pere Estruch and San Vicente de Paúl Streets.

Festivals of Valls

The sociable Catalans have an infinite capacity for local celebrations, and one of the best places to appreciate this fact is the unassuming inland town of Valls, perennially overshadowed by Tarragona. But don't hurry through on the road south from Barcelona, for Valls is interesting. The centre consists of quaint streets winding towards the church and main square and is worth exploring in its own right. But to appreciate how special this place really is, the time to visit is late October when two festivals take place that laud the double-barrelled contribution that Valls has made to local culture.

In a nutshell, we're talking Human Castles and Calçots. Valls is called 'The Cradle of the Castles', for here the Valencian Dance that was a staple of country fiestas in the 17th century evolved into the Human Castle tradition that has become synonymous with Catalan identity. Today's Human Castle Festival in Valls sees rival groups (La Colla Jove Xiquets and La Colla Vella dels Xiquets) compete for supremacy, seeking to create ever-bigger and more impressive human towers to the distinctive music of the oboe-like gralle. Vast crowds throng the town to watch the battle of human beanstalks, packing every balcony and cheering progress . . . or booing heartily if an edifice wobbles. The main event is preceded by a celebration dedicated to St Ursula, with giants making a folkloric procession through town.

The following week Valls is transformed for the communal Calçotada (Calçot Festival), which also attracts thousands. Long tables appear in the streets, vine-wood fires are lit and the delicious aroma of cooking calçots fills the town. The festival marks the start of the season, when these special vegetables dear to the massed taste buds of Catalonia will start life as humble onion seeds.

A traditional human tower reaches for the sky.

WHEN:
Late October
WHERE:
Valls, Tarragona
BEST FOR:
Traditional Catalan culture
YOU SHOULD KNOW:
The method for producing calçots was discovered by a farmer from Valls at the end of the 19th century. Autumn-sown onion plants are lifted and stored, before being subsequently replanted half-out of the ground. Earth is heaped around as they grow on, so when harvested they have a leek-like appearance.

Ecce Homo, Braga

WHEN:
Holy Week
WHERE:
Braga
BEST FOR:
Religious ceremonies
YOU SHOULD KNOW:
The Portuguese say that 'Lisbon plays, Braga prays and Porto works'. Just outside town is the Sanctuary of Bom Jesus da Monte. It has an extraordinary Baroque stairway beloved of pilgrims, who still come to climb it on their knees. Less religious folk take the water-powered funicular to the top, where the view is superb, and walk back down.

Throughout Portugal, Braga is considered to be the nation's spiritual heart. An ancient city, it overflows with handsome buildings and monuments, including about 35 churches. Its splendid 12th century cathedral was built on the site of an earlier church that had been destroyed by the Moors. This is Portugal's oldest cathedral and its Archbishop remains Primate of Portugal. Braga's religious significance in this very Catholic country makes the events of Holy Week – culminating in Easter – particularly interesting, attracting up to 50,000 tourists from across the country as well as from Spain and France.

Solemn ceremonies take place to mirror the days prior to Easter. There are well-attended processions: the most imposing is the Procession of the Burial of Our Lord, the most unusual the Thephorical Procession, and the most popular the Procession of Our Lord Ecce Homo. The latter takes place on Holy Thursday, and represents the agony of Christ in Gethsemane, his betrayal and arrest.

The Ecce Homo procession was established by Queen Leonor in 1498, and it is well worth observing regardless of your religious views. Hundreds of devotees known as Farricocos, all wearing black, hooded habits and carrying lanterns or flaming torches, escort an effigy of Christ, tied, bound and wearing his crown of thorns, from the cathedral through the streets and finally back to the cathedral again.

Many of these hooded penitents are barefoot, adding an extra frisson to the proceedings. Others dress as Palestinians in robes and head-dresses, priests display their finery and are followed by their congregations; everyone walks slowly to a marching band. The streets are lined with onlookers and the atmosphere is sombre. Look above the heads of the Farricocos, however, and the incongruous sight of neon signs advertising pharmacies and restaurants reminds you that Braga is very much a city of the 21st century.

A torchlight procession wends its way through Braga's historic quarter.

Holy Spirit Festival in The Azores

More than 1,200 km (760 mi) from the coast of Portugal, way out in the Atlantic Ocean, is the archipelago known as The Azores. Comprised of nine islands, the largest and most populated is Sao Miguel. The Festival of the Holy Spirit is celebrated throughout the islands, but thousands of people, including those who live abroad, come to Ponta Delgada, Sao Miguel's capital city, for the main event.

In the 1430s, Henry the Navigator sent expeditions to find and take possession of the Azores, and by the 16th century settlers from both Portugal and Flanders were farming the fertile, volcanic earth in a climate that remains mild throughout the year. In the 14th century, Queen Isabel of Portugal was a devotee of the Holy Spirit and vowed to give her crown to the eponymous church in Lisbon if God would bring an end to a terrible drought that had left thousands dead. He did, and she both donated her crown and gave a feast for the poor every year for the rest of her reign.

The celebrations begin on the Sunday after Easter and continue for seven weeks. Families bid for the honour of sponsoring a Sunday, and are given the Holy Spirit's crowns and flags to care for at home for a week. The highlight is the three-day festival starting on the Friday night before the seventh Sunday. A special meal of meat and bread blessed by a priest is eaten, and food is given to the needy. Saturday evening is devoted to decorating the statues and on Sunday a huge procession takes place after Mass.

Each year a young woman from every community on the islands is chosen to represent Queen Isabella, and all the 'Queens' gather in Ponta Delgada to join a procession through the town with everyone else. Singing, dancing, feasting and fireworks end the day and are enjoyed by everyone.

A decorated ox cart is part of the procession.

WHEN:
The 7th weekend after Easter
WHERE:
Ponta Delgada, Sao Miguel, The Azores
BEST FOR:
Religion and Portuguese culture
YOU SHOULD KNOW:
The Holy Spirit Festival marks the miracle of Queen Isabel, who was married to the unfaithful King Dinis and dedicated herself to the poor. One day when secretly carrying an apron full of bread to give to the poor, Dinis stopped her and asked what she was carrying. She replied, 'Roses'. When she opened her apron for him to see, it was full of roses. Isabel was canonized by Pope Urban VIII in 1625.

Students in traditional yellow hats and sticks run the gauntlet.

Qeima das Fitas, Coimbra

WHEN:
May
WHERE:
Coimbra
BEST FOR:
Fado, student revelry and drinking
YOU SHOULD KNOW:
In 1960, during the dark days of Portugal's Salazar regime, Peter Benenson, a lawyer, opened his paper whilst travelling on the London underground. There he read that two Portuguese students had been jailed for seven years for the terrible crime of having drunk a toast to liberty. This proved to be the start of Amnesty International, which began as an appeal on behalf of several prisoners of conscience in July 1961, and became a permanent organization in September 1962. Peter Benenson died in 2005, but his legacy was the birth of human rights' activism, which led to human rights being enshrined by law in many countries.

Coimbra is probably Portugal's third most important city, after Lisbon and Porto. Once the country's capital, in 1255 Alfonso III decided that Lisbon should hold that honour. Coimbra lies on a hill rising above the River Mondego. Known for its two beautiful cathedrals, its churches, palaces and mansions, Coimbra's main claim to fame are the magnificent buildings of its ancient university and the ancient traditions (the Praxe) that are still upheld by the students.

Sometimes known as the City of the Students, Coimbra's university, founded in the 13th century, is one of the oldest in the world. At the start of the academic year, the Tin Can Parade is held to welcome new students but the month of May sees one of Europe's largest student parties when Qeima das Fitas (the Burning of the Ribbons) takes place. It lasts eight days, to represent the University's eight faculties.

Altogether there are some 35,000 students in higher education in Coimbra and life here is inevitably coloured by their presence. One tradition is that each faculty has its own colour and each student wears a ribbon indicating their faculty. During the Qeima das Fitas, a ceremonial burning of the ribbons and gowns takes place, and wild and raucous festivities are held to celebrate the end of the academic year and those students who are leaving. Black suits and capes are a Coimbra University tradition – one which has been adopted by virtually all Portugal's higher education students.

Thousands of students, all dressed in their black capes, take to the streets, filling every narrow, cobbled lane and every square. Bands of roving Fado artists from the University can be found performing on the steps of churches and every street corner. Large numbers of students fill every nook and cranny in order to watch and join in. More stylized, less fatalistic and with an emphasis on complex lyrics, Coimbra Fado, a specific genre, differs from that of Lisbon Fado, and the students' songs are optimistic about their futures. Speeches are made, great cheers ring out, the music is loud, but the students are louder – it's claimed that more beer is imbibed during this eight-day festival than during Munich's fabled Octoberfest.

St Anthony's Day

The month of June in Lisbon is very merry indeed because there are three saints' feast days to celebrate. They are known collectively as the Festas dos Santos Populares – the Feast Days of the Popular Saints – and, of these, the biggest celebration marks St Anthony.

St Anthony of Lisbon, better known as St Anthony of Padua, was born in Lisbon in 1195, studied in Coimbra, became a Franciscan missionary and ended his life, well known and loved, in Padua. The site of the house in which he was born – close to the cathedral – was turned into a small chapel in the 1400s. Over the centuries the church of Santo Antonio was rebuilt several times, the last in 1767 after it was destroyed in the earthquake of 1755. St Anthony is known as a matchmaker and as a protector of young brides. On his feast day mass weddings take place, with financially strapped couples given free hospitality afterwards at the city hall.

For the whole of June Lisbon is decked out with streamers, paper-chains, paper lanterns, tinsel and fairy lights. On the evening of June 12, every neighbourhood tries to outdo the next by putting on costumed parades complete with floats and marching bands. The biggest parade, with countless followers, takes place along the Avenida da Liberdade. The air is full of the smell of sardines grilling over hundreds of fires that virtually line the streets, and liberal quantities of delicious Portuguese wines and Sangria are available to wash them down.

You can party until the early hours, watching the street entertainers and listening to wonderful Fado music, playing everywhere you go. The wildest parties in the city on St Anthony's night are to be found in the bohemian areas of Alfama and Mouraria – there you'll still be dancing when the sun comes up.

WHEN:
June 12-13
WHERE:
Lisbon and all over Portugal
BEST FOR:
Portuguese culture
YOU SHOULD KNOW:
One of St Anthony's miracles occurred when he was a preaching in Rimini, Italy. No one wanted to listen so, depressed, he went down to where the river meets the sea and began to talk to the fish. Immediately a vast multitude of fish swam towards him, raised their heads from the water to see him better and, all perfectly ranked in size, bowed in reverence. Hearing about the miracle, people rushed to see it and acknowledged Anthony's holiness. Fortunately, the sardine season opens at this time, and the tonnes that are eaten during his festival represent this miracle. It is also customary to exchange little pots of sweet basil with lovers and friends.

St John's Festival, Porto

WHEN:
June 23-24
WHERE:
Porto and throughout Portugal
BEST FOR:
Traditional culture
YOU SHOULD KNOW:
No one knows where these traditions came from, but they possibly belong to an earlier pagan tradition of celebrating the summer solstice which was later superseded by the Catholic feast day of St John the Baptist.

Porto's reputation as a city full of serious-minded citizens is completely reversed each year when it hosts one of Europe's most exuberant parties. While St John's Festival – Festa de Sao Joao – is a national holiday in Portugal, Brazil, Quebec and Newfoundland, the rest of the world makes little of it.

This is Porto's major festival. For days beforehand communities construct models depicting religious scenes or their own villages, string bunting across streets, build stages and stalls. The party begins on the evening of June 23, when it seems that everyone in Porto, both young and old, is on the streets, heading towards the city centre. Avenida dos Aliados, the main square, is packed with people drinking and eating traditional foods – grilled sardines, delicious *bifanas* (spicy pork sandwiches) and Portuguese doughnuts.

There are carnival games to play, live performances to see, and some unusual traditions in which to participate. People throw leeks at one another and hold garlic under each other's noses. Bonfires are lit and must be leapt over whilst making a wish. Perhaps the most

Competitors in the barcos rabelos race on the River Douro.

curious ritual is bashing strangers, young women in particular, with squeaking plastic hammers.

At midnight, the Ribeira area is the place to be, by the edge of the River Douro, for a superb firework display. For many this is just the start of the evening. The party moves on to the beach at Foz for loud music, dancing and drinking until the light of many bonfires is overtaken by the light of day.

In the morning, Mass is held for the saint and the city is quiet. By the afternoon, however, it's off to the waterfront again to watch the *barcos rabelos* – the old wooden sailing boats that were once used to transport port wine – in a regatta.

Avante! Festival

To thousands of people living in and around Lisbon, the first weekend in September signifies the date of the *Avante!* Festival. The venue is only a short drive, 22 km (14 mi), south of Lisbon. Held each year since 1976, the festival is named after the Portuguese Communist Party's official newspaper. To begin with, the festival took place in different locations around Lisbon, but as its popularity grew, the owners of these locations boycotted *Avante!*. The Communist Party therefore set up a huge and successful fund-raising campaign, which culminated in the acquisition of the Quinta da Princesa in Amora.

The *Avante!* newspaper was founded in 1931 but was published and distributed irregularly because of the harsh measures taken against communists by Salazar's right-wing dictatorship. During World War II, *Avante!* denounced the Nazis; during the 1960s, it voiced the Portuguese people's opposition to the wars being conducted in Angola, Mozambique and Guinea Bissau. In 1974, democracy was restored to Portugal and *Avante!*'s first legal edition was published. Thirty years later, the paper is still going strong.

The first festival was held in celebration of the end of the dictatorship – today it is a big party for people of all ages, all backgrounds and all political persuasions. There are, of course, speeches, but there is also a sports festival, a book and music fair, and fantastic live music that showcases both Portuguese and international musicians on five different stages – the music encompassing everything from classical to African. Many different regions of Portugal and their food and drink are represented here and various foreign communist parties participate too. *Avante!* is free to attend, although a pass is sold giving visitors access to everything going on in the smaller venues, as well as showing support for *Avante!*.

WHEN:
The first weekend in September
WHERE:
Quinta da Princesa, Amora
BEST FOR:
Music, left-wing politics and a great party
YOU SHOULD KNOW:
Over the years, artists as varied as Buffy Sainte-Marie, Charlie Haden, Johnny Clegg, Richie Havens, The Band, the Chicago Blues Harp All Stars and Vieux Farka Touré have all played here.

287

Lusitano horses are the main feature of the fair.

Golega Horse Fair

For most of the year, Golega is a small, sleepy town of some 5,500 souls, about a one-and-a-half-hour drive northeast of Lisbon, lying in fine agricultural countryside. However, every November, thousands of people from the equestrian world visit the National Horse Fair that takes place here. It's a noisy, colourful and thoroughly Portuguese affair that you don't even have to be horse-mad to enjoy.

Originating in the 1800s in order to promote the region's agricultural trade, horses quickly became a feature because several Lusitano horse breeders lived around Golega. Before long they were the main attraction. As Lusitanos became known further afield, horse lovers and breeders from across Portugal and many other countries came to trade. Golega remains a major centre for breeding and training Lusitanos, and many of the estates in the surrounding countryside hold events on their land during the fair.

Lusitanos are majestic creatures: very strong, beautifully balanced and highly intelligent, they have an even temperament and make superb mounts. Particularly suited to dressage, which requires disciplined and elegant movements, they were also used on battlefields in the past, and are still used in bull fighting.

The days are filled with events such as dressage, show jumping, demonstrations, horse-ball, displays of working horses, a horse-driving Derby and endurance riding. Many of the riders wear traditional Portuguese costume – flat, wide-brimmed hats and bolero jackets – while the animals themselves are beautifully turned out with traditional saddles and decorative bridles.

There's also a fantastic market selling locally produced wines and delicacies – roast chestnuts feature strongly. In the evening, bars, restaurants and food stalls come into their own, and sometimes horsemen will ride straight into a bar for a drink, *en route* from the show ring to the stable.

WHEN:
Usually mid November
WHERE:
Golega, Ribatejo
BEST FOR:
Seeing Lusitanos in their natural habitat and enjoying the spectacle of a genuinely Portuguese event
YOU SHOULD KNOW:
Lusitano horses are descended from the original Iberian horses. Cave paintings prove that their earliest ancestor evolved c. 25,000 BC. The name is thought to refer to Lusitania, which was the Roman name for what is now Portugal. Lusitania was derived from Luso, son of Bacchus, the Roman god of wine.

New Year's Eve in Funchal

Although the Madeiran archipelago lies closer to the West African coast than it does to Lisbon, Madeira is one of Portugal's autonomous regions and is very definitely European. Blessed with a benign climate, this mountainous island attracts thousands of visitors every year, not just for the beaches or the 2,000 km (1,250 mi) of footpaths that wind through the interior by the side of the levadas (irrigation channels) that were dug to bring water from the rainier north to the drier south, but also for New Year.

Madeira was uninhabited when the Portuguese first discovered it in 1419 but it was soon settled, largely by farmers. Funchal, the capital, lies on the south coast, in a fabulous location. An amphitheatre of hills rise gently from the harbour to almost 1,200 m (4,000 ft), providing a well-protected harbour and the perfect spot for a city.

Several festivals take place on Madeira annually, and one of the best known is on New Year's Eve. At about 21.00, thousands of people begin to gather in and around the town, which already has just about every house, garden, tree and street decorated with coloured lights. In the harbour several cruise ships will have moored for the night and, as the night draws on, more and more boats go out to join them. At the stroke of midnight, the cars all honk their horns, the ships' sirens blare out and a huge firework display begins across 16 sq km (5 sq mi). This is a fantastic spectacle: literally tons of fireworks are exploded. In *Guinness World Records 2007* it was pronounced the world's largest display. When it's all over, people fill the restaurants and bars, or go home to party through the night, toasting each other with the local speciality – Madeira wine.

WHEN:
December 31
WHERE:
Funchal, Madeira
BEST FOR:
Fireworks like you wouldn't believe
YOU SHOULD KNOW:
Madeira, meaning wood in Portuguese, was so called because the island was covered in indigenous laurisilva sub-tropical rainforest when the first settlers arrived. Most of this was cleared from the south of the island, while the undisturbed forests in the north are now a UNESCO World Heritage Site. Funchal was supposedly named for the masses of fennel (*funcho*) that was found growing there.

The world's largest firework display is spectacular.

Giant characters delight the crowd.

Viareggio Carnival

In 1873, Viareggio's most important dignitaries thought to celebrate their civic worthiness with a big parade. The townspeople were delighted – and ambushed the event with well-rehearsed, masked protests about local political issues and a series of huge, colourful puppets satirizing the mayor, the tax collector and other politicians. Civic pride got the joke, and the point. Now everyone in the town gets involved, either as a 'romantic' (devoted to building ever more ambitious and beautiful floats) or a 'verist' (powered by the constant search for more amusing ways to satirize politicians). United by laugh-out-loud humour and the rebellious, 'anything goes' spirit of Martedi Grasso (Mardi Gras), there's enough competitive spirit between different areas of the town to underwrite the parades with fizzing spontaneity. Visitors may not understand some of the local references, but the ambience of laughter and goodwill is irresistible.

Viareggio's official clown, Burlamacco, leads the parade. He's a mobile grotesque, a composite of Harlequin's checked outfit and Pierrot's white pom-pom, with a red hat and black cloak. Prancing between the monster caricatures – giant blue cows 4 m (15 ft) tall, leering rag dolls, etc – on floats that weigh up to 40 tons and loom 20 m (65 ft) high by 14 m (46 ft) wide, Burlamacco whips up the crowds to song or hoots of derision at politicians' papier-maché portrayals. Burlamacco's shock troops are the *libecciata*, intricately made up and caparisoned 'messengers from the world of allegory'. In concert with instrumentalists and comics from the Commedia dell' Arte tradition, the *libecciata* flit between parade and watchers, dancing and playing games full of teasing provocations, but sealing the bond between performers and audience with the democracy of laughter. You expect a carnival to be raucous, irreverent, saucy, and pushing acceptable limits. Viareggio's is intelligent as well; updated and refreshed every year, it's a perfect Italian gem of public revelry.

WHEN:
January/February/March. The floats are paraded on five or six separate days, chosen according to the date of Shrove Tuesday.
WHERE:
Viareggio
BEST FOR:
Humour, exuberant revelry, Italian folklore and culture
YOU SHOULD KNOW:
Since 2002, the Viareggio Carnival has taken the splendid title 'Carnival of Italy and Europe'. Although its size (some 800,000 people participate in the parades) might justify the new name, the self-perception is akin to the grandiose observation that motivated the very first carnival.

The Battle of the Oranges

In the 20th century, the ancient Piedmontese town of Ivrea in the Aosta Valley was dominated by the Olivetti Typewriter Company – to the extent that, from the air, the factory actually looks like a portable typewriter, set among buildings as much as 2,000 years old. Now, with Olivetti in decline, the town is more famous for the Battle of the Oranges that makes Ivrea's pre-Lent carnival unique. Ivrea uses its carnival to tell an allegorical version of its history. After well over 1,000 years of being subjugated politically (by Lombards, Savoyards and Napoleon) and economically (as a company town), the Battle of Oranges tells of the abduction of a 'Mugnaia' ('miller's daughter' – the carnival queen chosen each year) by an 'evil duke' seeking to exact his *droits de seigneur*. A train of wagons full of the tyrant's men tries to escape town, while being pelted with oranges by 'revolutionaries' dressed in the livery of nine official revolutionary 'clubs' representing different sections of the town. Visitors may not throw oranges unless they sign up with the 'duke' or one of the clubs – but if you wear a red Phrygian cap (a legacy of Napoleonic rule) no one will target you, because the cap displays your revolutionary sympathy against authority.

The battle is messy and hilarious as it weaves round town – but its historically costumed chaos is only the climax of a series of solemn parades, blessings and ceremonies that take place during the previous month. The more you know about the symbolism of Ivrea's brilliant sense of theatre, the more you'll cheer when Mugnaia finally spears an orange to represent the duke's head; and understand about the intense emotions that Ivreans invest in their atavistic 'battle for freedom'. It feeds your sense of purpose, so you can really let rip in the orange-smashing free-for-all.

WHEN:
February, on the Sunday, Monday and Tuesday of Martedi Grasso (Mardi Gras) every year. Orange throwing begins at 14.15 on each day.
WHERE:
Piazza di Citta, Ivrea; and in all the major squares of the historic quarter
BEST FOR:
History, culture and folklore
YOU SHOULD KNOW:
Citizens of Ivrea are known in Italian as 'eporediesi' (Eporedians), from the town's Latin name of Eporedia (place to change horses), acquired when it was a cavalry post guarding one of the traditional invasion routes across the Alps from the north.

Wear a red cap if you want to dodge the barrage.

The ornate face masks are a particular feature of the Venice Carnivale.

Venice Carnivale

Surely one of the world's most glorious cities at any time of year, Venice during carnevale is truly a sight to behold. For two weeks in winter its citizens, together with thousands of visitors from around the globe, take to the streets dressed in elaborate, fantastically masked costumes, providing Europe's most visually stunning event.

First recorded in 1268, carnival season originally began on December 26. The word itself is thought to derive from the Latin *carne vale* (farewell to meat), a reference to the Catholic tradition of Lenten fasting during the weeks before Easter. In Venice, carnevale reached its peak during the 18th century, fading away after Napoleon's victory over the Republic. Banned by the fascists, it was finally fully revived in the late 1970s, in an effort to attract tourism.

Made mainly of papier maché or leather, masks were always worn, allowing those who wore them complete anonymity and therefore a freedom of behaviour inconceivable during everyday life. Mask makers had their own guild and nowadays an enormous variety of masks, from simple plastic to the most fantastical of hand-made creations, can be bought from numerous outlets.

During carnevale, hundreds of festivities take place around the city – processions and traditional ceremonies, masked balls and sumptuous private parties. The piazzas are full of theatrical troupes, acrobats and musicians, through which move groups of people sporting stunning 18th century costume, each year inspired by a new theme.

During winter, Venice is often cold and shrouded in mist, ensuring the dramatically coloured costumes glow against a ghostly background to surreal, sometimes almost frightening, effect. Clutches of highly decorated gondolas glide through the canals to loud cheers from the crowds on the bridges above. The grand finale of fireworks over the lagoon, shooting upwards in a triumphant display of noise and colour, is quite unforgettable.

WHEN:
The two-week period leading to Shrove Tuesday
WHERE:
Venice
BEST FOR:
Fabulous costumes and street entertainment
YOU SHOULD KNOW:
Carnival festivities take place all over Italy during this time, but Venice has taken carnevale to new heights. Don't forget your camera – masqueraders love to be admired. If you want to attend a masked ball, buy your tickets well in advance.

Sa Sartiglia Oristanese

When Oristano, on the west coast of Sardinia, lost its independence to the Kingdom of Aragon in the 14th century, its aristocracy was already thoroughly familiar with Aragonese traditions of knightly chivalry. Sartiglia was a widespread form of tournament learned from the Saracens in Spain, in which mounted knights used the tip of the sword to pick off a star suspended in mid-air. Success depends on the highest skills of sword- and horsemanship. The Oristanese knights loved it, and Sartiglia took root in the city. Inevitably, tournaments were a feature of public holidays, and Sartiglia became associated with the Sunday and Tuesday of Oristano's pre-Lenten carnevale. It was later opened to all comers, and has evolved into its present, highly ritualized form.

Sartiglia flourishes because you've never seen anything like it and if you had you'd go back and see it again. Oristano pours its soul and all its arcane magic spells, individual obsessions and superstitions into it. Dressing *su Componidori* (the tournament's MC) is a sacred rite that takes place on a real altar, conducted by handmaidens and many others with names and functions defined by tradition; once dressed (in white, androgynous mask, black top hat, veiled, and bearing *sa pippia de maju* – periwinkle wrapped in a green cloth with a bunch of violets at either end – a 'sceptre' with which to bless the crowd) he may not dismount until the whole joust ends with him riding, flattened backwards against his horse's rump, the entire course. By then you'll have seen huge costumed parades of people and masked equestrians, bands blaring to rolling drums, superb demonstrations of equo-batics, daredevil racing on the sand and straw-covered streets, and breathtaking swordsmanship at the full gallop, in mid-air, and quite often backwards too. It's weird, exhilarating, and one of a kind.

WHEN:
The Sunday and Tuesday before Lent, usually between mid and late February

WHERE:
Oristano, Sardinia. Sartiglia's equestrian and jousting course includes Via Duomo, where the stars are hung for the riders to pierce.

BEST FOR:
Folk customs, culture and history – and Sardinian enthusiasm

YOU SHOULD KNOW:
Sartiglia is not a re-enactment. It is an annual appeal for omens for a good harvest (the more stars the riders can pick off, the better), and the Oristanese take it very seriously indeed. That doesn't mean they (and you) won't have enormous fun, drinking and feasting. It does mean that if you talk at the wrong moment during one of the many rituals, you will get vigorously 'shush'-ed (not a good idea in Sardinia).

A masked rider speeds through the enthusiastic crowds.

Sant' Agata di Catania

WHEN:
February 3-5
WHERE:
Catania, Sicily
BEST FOR:
Religious ceremony, local culture, traditional folk customs
YOU SHOULD KNOW:
When Sant' Agata was executed, she is said to have dropped a red veil. The volcanic eruption a year later in 252 was apparently halted when the veil was held up in supplication. The veil has preserved Catania on several occasions, most recently in 1886, when it was carried in procession by Cardinal Dusmet to stop the lava before the walls of the town of Nicolosi – where you can see it to this day.

Votive candles are lit in readiness for the Luminaria procession.

The Feast of Sant' Agata in Catania, Sicily, is one of Italy's most important and biggest religious celebrations. Agata, a local girl martyred in the city in AD 251, is credited with miraculously halting eruptions on nearby Mount Etna in 252, 1444, 1669 and 1886, saving Catania each time. No wonder that each February more than a million people squeeze into Catania to show their devotion according to a strictly observed series of formal rituals, parades, processions, games, races and religious rites. It's a three-day affair, its present format scarcely changed in 500 years. The first day is the Luminaria, the solemn, candle-lit procession of civic, military and religious dignitaries to the cathedral, and the presentation of the 11 *candelore* (large candle-shaped biers) bearing the insignia of the ancient guilds. Then Sant' Agata's 'cross-country race' sees a costumed melée hurtling round Catania's streets before the evening's firework display.

Few sleep. At dawn on the second day, tens of thousands see the saint's effigy brought from the high altar to the silver carriage on which she will be pulled by devotees around Catania. The route is fraught with emotional significance for local people, who follow, yelling '*Cittadini, viva Sant' Agata!*' to remind everyone that they are on holy ground where the saint was born, tortured and killed. All night, houses, shops and kiosks stay open and brightly lit. Before dawn, more fireworks mark Sant' Agata's return to the cathedral – but after Pontifical High Mass she's off again, this time with the liveried *candelore* and a huge crowd. After more fireworks in Piazza Borgo, there's a final race up the incline of Salita di S Giuliano between the teams of *candelore*. Exhausted afterwards, these teams try to return Sant' Agata's *vara* to the cathedral 'in one pull' (without stopping). Success means good fortune for the coming year – a deep superstition as potent as Sant' Agata's miracles.

Easter Mass in St Peter's Square

Pope Benedict XVI conducts Holy Easter Mass.

Within Christianity no date is more significant than that of Easter and, for Roman Catholics, there is no finer place to be than the Vatican City, where the Pope celebrates Mass on Easter Sunday. In fact, the ceremonies of the *triduum*, (Latin for three-day period) begin on Holy Thursday and continue on Good Friday and Holy Saturday, when the Easter Vigil Mass commences at night in St Peter's.

Thousands and thousands of pilgrims and tourists from all over the world come to Rome for the Easter celebrations, the culmination of which is the Mass held in St Peter's Square on Easter Sunday morning. People begin to congregate hours in advance, passing through the security checks in a steady stream. Although there are seats, most people stand in a friendly, multi-national crowd. As the hour approaches, there are bursts of hymn singing and flag waving, and a general atmosphere of contained excitement.

Finally, the Pope arrives, wearing magnificent vestments, at the head of a splendid procession of cardinals, bishops and priests all in their finest robes. The splendidly attired Swiss Guards stand to attention. A canopy stands over the steps up to the Basilica, beautiful flowers adorn every inch of space, the choir launches into song and Mass begins. A huge screen enables even those standing far away from the altar to see this dignified ceremony, which concludes with a papal blessing.

However, this is not the end: some minutes after his departure, the pontiff reappears on a balcony to deliver his annual *urbi et orbi* (to the city and the world) speech, each year drawing attention to problems in different parts of the globe and offering greetings and blessings in scores of languages, in acknowledgement of the global reach of the Church.

WHEN:
Every Easter
WHERE:
St Peter's Square, in the Vatican City, Rome
BEST FOR:
Religious observance
YOU SHOULD KNOW:
Tickets must be obtained well in advance if you wish to attend the Easter Sunday Mass.

295

Religious procession is a vital part of the festival.

Corsa dei Ceri

Northeast of Perugia, Gubbio perches on the steep slope of Monte Ingino. It's a walled town of Gothic austerity, dark-grey stone, narrow streets and alleyways, developed to defend the wealth and power it acquired as a city state. There is a sense of community that binds Gubbio, which has sustained the town and outlasted feudal, regional and national allegiances. The people of Gubbio guard the soul of the region of Umbria, and the Corsa dei Ceri is their communal expression of the honour they defend with a heady mixture of solemnity, passion and raw enthusiasm.

The Ceri are three octagonal wooden 'candles', 5 m (16 ft) high and weighing 400 kg (882 lb), surmounted by figures of the saints Ubaldo, Giorgio and Antonio. They represent the medieval guilds of bricklayers, traders and farmers; and Ubaldo, once Gubbio's Bishop, is also the town's patron saint. Everyone in Gubbio holds allegiance to one of the three, and watches in enthralled silence as the three teams of *ceraioli* (identified by yellow, blue and black shirts) follow a careful ritual of assembly. Then, with bells ringing, bands blaring and the crowd cheering raucously, they race the Ceri through the streets and up the mountainside for 2 km (1.24 mi) to the Basilica of St Ubaldo.

The *ceraioli* make a tough 'race', vigorously backed up by supporters (loyalties pass from father to son in Gubbio), but St Ubaldo always wins – he's everybody's patron saint – and the race in fact ends in prayer.

The strong civic and devotional elements of the Corsa dei Ceri turn history and tradition into living folklore. The race is colourful and exciting, but the collective solemnity of the rituals surrounding it is truly inspirational. It's a privilege to witness such atavistic faith, and also a pleasure to share the communal glee of the secular party that follows afterwards.

WHEN:
May 15
WHERE:
Piazza Grande, Gubbio
BEST FOR:
History and local culture
YOU SHOULD KNOW:
The Ceri – which represent building, trading and farming – form the regional symbol of Umbria.

Festival of Sant' Efisio

Efisio was a senior Roman soldier sent to persecute Christians in Sardinia. Converted by a vision, he arrived to do God's work instead. His success brought him martyrdom on the beach at Nora, north of Cagliari in AD 303; and a church was later built over his grave. He was a local folk hero long before the people of Cagliari invoked his intercession during a plague epidemic. When it was over, in May 1657, they carried Efisio's statue from Cagliari to Nora in thanksgiving. They have done so every year since, but the festival has grown into Sardinia's most solemn and important public occasion, reflecting its importance as the fulfillment of a sacred vow. The Festival of Sant' Efisio is an epic of dazzling colour, exotic music, dancing and equestrian skills, driven by the compelling excitement of a community absorbed by its own arcane rituals.

WHEN:
May 1-4
WHERE:
Cagliari, Sardinia
BEST FOR:
Tradition, folklore, history, religion
YOU SHOULD KNOW:
In the principal ceremonies and most solemn processions, the great crucifix and statue of Sant' Efisio are preceded by 'Alter Nos' – a figure on a white stallion wearing 19th century frock coat, top hat and gold chain and medal. He represents the community, 'officially' expiating their vow for another year.

Sant' Efisio provides the only occasions where you'll see everyone in traditional dress. In the processions of fabulously decorated *traccas* (ox-drawn carts), you see that every village has its own style of costume and embellishment; and the haunting melodies of *launeddas* (hollow reed flutes) are often specific to tiny areas of the island. There is symbolism in the number of horsemen riding shoulder to shoulder at any given moment, or doing astonishing acrobatics at the gallop. You need to keep your wits about you not to confuse sudden shifts in the ceremonies from gay abandon to religious solemnity. You don't have to share the 60 km (36 mi) round trip on foot to Nora and back with the saint's reliquary, as many thousands of Sardinians do (spreading flower petals on the road the whole way) – but it's a good gauge of the festival's potency as an authentic demonstration of public worship and communal celebration that is increasingly rare in mainland Europe.

Local women in traditional Sardinian dress take part in the procession from the comfort of an ox-drawn cart.

Maggio Musicale Fiorentina

WHEN:
May and June (with occasional performances in April and/or early July)
WHERE:
Teatro Comunale, and several other venues, in Florence
BEST FOR:
Music, history, architecture and culture
YOU SHOULD KNOW:
Maggio Musicale is frequently themed to promote a particular composer, like the Rossini Maggio of 1952, or to highlight the influence on music of different international cultural movements, like Expressionism in 1964, the early 20th century in 1994, and early Romanticism in 1995. The festival is unfailingly full of surprises.

As though Florence didn't already offer the world far more than its share of aesthetic pleasure and cultural riches, the city likes to present itself anew every springtime. The Maggio Musicale Fiorentina (Musical May in Florence) is primarily an opera festival but, since its beginnings in 1933, it has included ballet and a series of carefully chosen concerts. The hallmark of all its productions has been the vision of the festival's founder, the conductor Vittorio Gui. He chose Verdi's *Nabucco*, then staged very rarely, to open his first season because it fulfilled his long-term intention to restore forgotten or little-known works to proper esteem, and to give contemporary opera a chance to attract an international audience. Gui's energy attracted the best conductors, musicians, and (where possible) composers, and turned inspiration into reality. Maggio Musicale has gone from strength to strength.

Most performances take place in the 2,000-seat Teatro Comunale, the smaller Teatro Piccolo, and the historic Teatro della Pergola. But none of them can contain the entirety of Gui's vision: when the festival's principal conductor, Zubin Mehta, wanted to make a point in 1993 (to demonstrate solidarity following the terrorist attack on the Uffizi), he staged a concert in the Piazza della Signoria, open to the air and the public, and free. Now there are regular open-air performances in both the Piazza and the Boboli Gardens, utilizing the architectural nonpareil of their settings. Staging has always been innovative and exploratory in Maggio Musicale, and so successful that Florence now boasts a school of technical stagecraft inspired directly by the festival.

Conceived each year with intelligence and curiosity, and performed by virtuosi, Italy's most important and oldest music festival achieves the near impossible – of actually enhancing the glory that is Florence. Maggio Musicale Fiorentina is the cognoscenti's dream made manifest.

Zubin Mehta conducts the orchestra and chorus in the Teatro Comunale.

Calcio Storico

Festa di San Giovanni Battista (the feast of St John the Baptist), its patron saint, is pre-eminent in the calendar of the Tuscan city of Florence. It explains why the many celebrations include the eagerly awaited final of the city's oldest sporting contest – Calcio Storico (historic football), sometimes described as a cross between Graeco-Roman wrestling, football and rugby. It's a tradition that began in 1530, when Florentines, exhausted by a long siege, played football in full view of their besiegers (the Medici). It was a calculated insult. Swaggering Florence lost the battle but won perpetual moral advantage for its arrogant insouciance. Now, Florentines practise on each other. Four teams (Blues, Reds, Greens and Whites) of 27 strapping young men represent the four quarters of Florence. Their pitch is the Piazza San Croce, a mess of sand and mud surrounded by protective netting, with the whole of each end as the 'goal' over which players tip, throw or boot a special leather ball (particoloured with the combatants' colours) to score *caccie* (goals); and there are penalties for missing or hitting the side netting.

It might sound like football, but it isn't. Anything goes. To begin with, everyone is in lavish Renaissance costume, including the team captains, who sit in a magnificent tent in the centre of the goal mouth, stirring only to fire a gun when a goal is scored, while their standard bearer runs up and down the pitch waving his flag. Referees wear doublets and hose, with ostrich plume accessories and swords. While players get their clothes ripped off ('playing the ball' is an unheard-of concept), referees ignore the strangling, biting, chopping and kicking unless death is imminent. It's a primeval, exhilarating contest, as authentically bloodthirsty as its historic origins.

Players of the teams of Santa Maria Novella or Rossi (Reds) and Santa Croce or Azzurri (Blues) in action during their Calcio Fiorentino final match in Florence's Piazza San Croce.

WHEN:
June 24
WHERE:
Piazza San Croce, Florence
BEST FOR:
History, culture and local folklore
YOU SHOULD KNOW:
No one with a criminal record is allowed to play Calcio Storico. And although many players view the Calcio as an opportunity to wreak revenge on rivals for a particular girlfriend, the actual prize is a live cow – now interpreted as Bistecca Fiorentina served up for everyone.

299

Festa di San Giovanni Battista

WHEN:
June 24
WHERE:
Florence. The *fochi* (lights) of St John are best seen either close to the Piazzale Michelangelo, or from somewhere along the banks of the Arno (get it right and the water reflects the fireworks for extra visual fizz).
BEST FOR:
History, culture, folklore and entertainment
YOU SHOULD KNOW:
In Christian theology, St John the Baptist is the harbinger of the Messiah and the age of the Kingdom of God. He represents a threshold of moral rectitude and new possibilities to which medieval Florence aspired, at the moment when Florentines perceived themselves as the vanguard of a 'renaissance' in culture, the arts and government. No wonder they enthuse about their patron saint.

In Florence, June 24, Midsummer's Day, is the feast of the city's patron saint, John the Baptist. For Florentines, it's the most important day of the year. Their devotion to St John has been marked down the centuries by the dedication to him of the most significant civil and military events. It became the custom on June 24 for Florentine nobility and gentry to process from the Palazzo Vecchio with votives of lighted candles. By the late Renaissance, when the Baptistery was complete, the candles were so huge and richly decorated that they kept the Baptistery lit and in funds for the whole year. By then, celebrations for St John were assuming their current shape, with a procession of boats, street games of football, fireworks and city-wide merrymaking.

The big difference is the democratization of the good times. The whole of Florence dresses up, dances and goes to the feast. All kinds of people form the procession that goes from the Duomo (cathedral) to the Baptistery (the door is marked 'Paradise') with the traditional offerings of wax – even if they are still preceded by the entire cathedral clergy and city dignitaries. There are rowing races on the Arno, fiercely contested by crews from the city's districts. Nearly everyone makes some effort to wear Renaissance costume, or the colours of their teams, which can make for exciting encounters anywhere in the city.

Local rivalries culminate in universal camaraderie for the day's finale. At 22.00, a dazzling explosion of colour erupts from the Piazzale Michelangelo, high on the hill overlooking the river and the old city proper. Every year, it's one of the best firework displays in Italy; and it sets you up for the city-wide communal party that follows.

Gioco del Ponte

The beautiful city of Pisa was ancient long before it gained its iconic 'Leaning Tower'. In Roman times, its heart was defined – as it is still – by the Ponte di Mezzo, straddling the river Arno between what are now the Piazza Garibaldi and Piazza XX Settembre. Since 1568, when Pisa revived a 9th century tradition in a new form, the Ponte di Mezzo has been the location for the Gioco del Ponte (Game of the Bridge), the focal point of a city-wide jamboree of stunning colour, Renaissance costume, heraldic splendour and raucous parades with authentic music. The river divides Pisa into two halves, called the Mezzogiorno and the Tramontana. For centuries the Gioco pitted the men from opposite banks of the Arno against each other, fighting for the 'honour' of pushing their opponents off the bridge in a spirit of fiercely contested goodwill.

Extreme violence got the Gioco banned for nearly 130 years; but since its restoration in 1935, it has evolved into an ever more glorious, flag-twirling pageant, dazzling the senses with regiments of *alberdieri* (pikemen) clad in the 'sailboat' curved helmets of the Spanish Renaissance mode; fifes and bassonets; and a rainbow-costumed cast of tens of thousands of local partisans. For the Gioco proper, teams of 20 representing the six districts on each side of the river compete, one-on-one, to push a 70-ton steel 'wagon' on rails over the opposite end of the banner-draped bridge. Each contest is fiercely fought, among supporters as well as over the water. Men do fall in, to howls of laughter and jeers. The Gioco is still very much a local occasion. For visitors, that's its rare charm. It isn't a re-enactment. Its highly charged parochial loyalties are the glue of living history. The Gioco del Ponte is an enthralling spectacle that cements the sense of belonging between individuals and every level of the Pisa community.

WHEN:
The last Sunday in June
WHERE:
Ponte di Mezzo, Pisa
BEST FOR:
Interactive history and folklore
YOU SHOULD KNOW:
You'll see many of the Gioco team-members and costumed guards in the parades carrying a *mazzascudo* (club/shield). It's the traditional weapon of Pisa, made of wood, wide and flat at the top, and tapered at the bottom. 'Mazzascudo' was the name of Pisa's 9th century version of the Gioco (more like a battle than a game); and the now (principally) ornamental weapon is named after it.

One of the many highly coloured uniforms worn for the Gioco del Ponte.

EUROPE/ITALY

Genzano Infiorata

WHEN:
June (even when Corpus Domini Sunday falls in May, Genzano holds its Infiorata in June).
WHERE:
Genzano
BEST FOR:
Culture and community folklore
YOU SHOULD KNOW:
Sometimes the Infiorata has a theme, anything from 'the 500th anniversary of Columbus and America' (1992) to 'the 60th anniversary of the Italian Constitution' (2008) – but you will always see religious 'paintings' like the Martyrdom of St Lawrence, and secular subjects drawn from myth, like Diana the Huntress.

In the Catholic religion, the holy day of Corpus Christi commemorates the 'Miracle of Bolsano', a 13th century Eucharistic miracle when a priest broke the communion host and it apparently bled. Pope Urban IV named the Thursday after Trinity Sunday to be Corpus Christi, and the following Sunday to be the feast of Corpus Domini. It is a major holy day in Italy, and because it falls in late spring/early summer, it is celebrated with 'Infiorata' (flower festivals) across the country. Nowhere does it bigger or better than Genzano, one of the medieval hill towns in Lazio, southeast of Rome.

Genzano's Infiorata began in 1778. The whole community is involved. For days beforehand, adults and children scour the countryside and raid private gardens to collect flower petals, leaves, and greenery, and sort them into a hundred shades of colour. On the Saturday morning, teams work quickly to sketch out their different designs on the road. By early Sunday, the petals have been arranged into a series of giant artworks, stretching the length of three football pitches from Genzano's main piazza all the way up Via Belardi to the church of S Maria della Cima. The effect is mesmerizing. Floral carpet or tapestry, the intricate patterns – geometrical, biblical, folkloric and representational – are works of art. Collectively, the rainbow assemblage (stems, petals, coffee grounds, pine cone seeds, whatever) is an outstanding synthesis of natural beauty and human inspiration, and after the Blessing and church services, the community gathers on the garlanded pavements to admire it and make serious group merriment.

Be sure to stay in Genzano until Monday for the 'spallamento'. At a given signal, the children of Genzano stampede into the display, crushing the petals underfoot in a spectacularly amusing floral kaleidoscope that gives off the divine fragrance of rose, lavender, violet and cyclamen.

Floral decorations 'carpet' the main street of Genzano.

Festival dei Due Mondi

Spoleto is a gem of an ancient Umbrian hill town. Medieval buildings are visibly melded to Roman remains: the Rocca Albornoziana on the hilltop is a 14th century castle built on the Roman acropolis; the Casa Romana was once lived in by Emperor Vespasian's mother; the Roman Theatre really was built in the 1st century AD; and the nearby Piazza del Duomo and the cathedral itself are 12th century additions to buildings 1,000 years older, along with one of Italy's very first theatres, the Teatro Caio Melissa. All of these are venues for the Festival dei Due Mondi, a two- to three-week programme of music, opera, theatre, art and sculpture that fills the town with some of the world's most illustrious artistes.

Spoleto's most dramatic sight is the Ponte delle Torri (Bridge of Towers), spanning the steep gorge beside the Rocca like the Roman aqueduct it replaced. Its grandeur emphasizes the intimacy of the old town, clustered on the hilltop. Intimacy is Spoleto's trump card. From dawn to dusk, every open space is liable to exude beautiful music, or reveal a new aesthetic delight; and the magnificent churches and old theatres enable you to hear first-class orchestras and soloists in informal proximity unparalleled in modern festivals. Since 1958, when the late composer Gian Carlo Menotti first realized his dream, the festival has sought to bring the 'Due Mondi' (Two Worlds) of European and American culture closer together. Menotti was canny enough to foresee that continual expansion can wreck a good idea, and chose Spoleto because it is beautiful, and can't get any bigger.

Menotti lived to see his inspiration threatened by competitive managements, as music festivals like his proliferated; but Spoleto's quality remains unrivalled – it's one of the most joyous musical occasions in the world.

The cast of the opera Ercole su'l Termodonte *take their bow.*

WHEN:
June and July, for two to three weeks
WHERE:
Spoleto, southeast of Perugia, Umbria. Head for the tourist and festival offices in Piazza della Liberta in the upper town.
BEST FOR:
Music, art, culture and history
YOU SHOULD KNOW:
The Ponte delle Torri links the castle to the once-untamed woods of Monteluco beyond the gorge. Goethe crossed the bridge in the 1780s, 'declaring that the awesome vistas he encountered reminded him of the importance also of our inner spirit and life'. Spoleto inspires both musing and the Muse.

303

Opera Festival in Verona

One of Verona's many minor delights is the enthusiasm with which its citizens urge you to admire the 'original houses' of the fictional Montagu and Capulet families, and even 'Juliet's Balcony' where Romeo achieved immortal fame as a lover. They gain real pleasure from Verona being considered a place where poetry, drama, music and most of all opera have always been taken very seriously. The Opera Festival is just the most dramatic of all Verona's pro-active initiatives, combining its stupendous architectural heritage with arts programmes.

Every festival performance takes place in the Arena, purpose-built by the Romans in AD 30 just beyond the walls on the city's south side. It's colossal, seating up to 22,000, and the Romans designed it to stage almost anything from Greek tragedy to gladiatorial showdowns and sea-battles. Sets have to be to scale. For grander operas like *Aida* or *Tosca*, massive constructions are wheeled through Verona from hangar-like workshops; assembled inside the Arena, they instill a befitting sense of grandeur that electrifies audiences when they first see it.

Already entranced by the special beauty of Verona at sunset, and at a fever pitch of noisy anticipation when the performance begins, people are stunned into a sudden silence as they understand the Arena's 2,000-year-old secret: it is acoustically perfect. No microphones are used or needed. It sets you a new standard of purity for the timbre and quality of voices and instruments. It is the genius of the festival and the main attraction for the best international orchestras, conductors and soloists who have so often turned a performance at the Verona Opera Festival into a night of musical history.

Great music sounds magical in the Arena – and the special atmosphere of the magnificent setting will transport your imagination as much as it did Shakespeare's.

The open-air Arena in Verona provides a wonderful setting.

WHEN:
Late June to August. Performances are usually on the same dates every year.
WHERE:
Verona
BEST FOR:
Music, history, literary fiction and architecture
YOU SHOULD KNOW:
The *poltrone numerate* in the middle are the most expensive seats – but aficionados recommend the 'numbered steps' (a ticket designation meaning the numbered seats on the lowest two or three raised tiers). Be on time – Italian opera-lovers do not take kindly to late arrivals.

Giostra del Saracino

Folk memory dies hard in Arezzo, an important Etruscan city a full thousand years before serious threats from Saracen (the term once used throughout the Mediterranean to refer to Muslims) incursions inspired the city fathers to establish regular military training for its young men. The exercises became Giostra del Saracino (Joust of the Saracen). In its current form it is a 16th century ceremony, with rules that have resisted amendment since 1677; and since its restoration in the 1930s, it has inspired a living link between Arezzo and its history.

The 'Saracen' is a painted wooden head on a greased, swivelling pole. An armoured knight charges, seeking to hit the Saracen and ride off, ducking to avoid the counterweight before it swings round and wallops him. Local pride is at stake. Competing 'knights' represent Arezzo's various districts; and all the tournament officials, along with the city dignitaries and most of the town, are dressed in full Renaissance costume. Squadrons of caparisoned cavalry, grim crossbowmen, and heralds in tabards accompany the processions to the sloping rectangle of Piazza Grande, at Arezzo's historic heart. Amid fanfares, proclamations, and beating drums, jousters charge down a raised plinth, lances tilted to smash the Saracen.

The panting horses, clash of steel as weapons hit the ground, and clamour of the crowd raise the atmosphere to fever pitch – but the visual spectacular takes on special local significance when the knights are blessed by Arezzo's Bishop. This blessing, as much as the Municipal Herald's Proclamations, confirms the Giostra as a local event which visitors are in fact privileged to witness. It's enormously entertaining for everyone, but of real importance to the people of Arezzo. Twice a year at the Giostra, they proclaim their complicated allegiances to church, state, city and district.

WHEN:
The third Sunday in June and the first Sunday in September
WHERE:
Arezzo – the actual Giostra takes place in Piazza Grande and the parades and pageantry throughout the city's historic centre.
BEST FOR:
History and culture
YOU SHOULD KNOW:
Petrarch's house is just around the corner from the Piazza Grande. Arezzo is famous for Guido d'Arezzo, a medieval Abbot who devised 'solfeggio', the mnemonic for music notation given expression by the song *Doe, a deer* . . . from *The Sound of Music*.

Renaissance costumes are worn to celebrate the killing of the dreaded 'Saracen'.

The Palio

WHEN:
July 2 and August 16
WHERE:
Siena
BEST FOR:
Historic local culture
YOU SHOULD KNOW:
The race can be dangerous for
participants and audience alike.

Built between 1280 and 1350, the Piazza del Campo – Siena's magnificent central square – is the site of The Palio, the renowned, adrenaline-filled, bare-backed horse race that takes place twice a year. Shaped more like a shell than a square, the Piazza has resounded to the sounds of The Palio since 1656.

This is a race between the city's 17 *contradas* or districts, made even more competitive as only ten are able to participate. Three days beforehand, jockeys in place, the chosen *contradas* select the ten best available horses, drawing lots to decide which will run for whom, and six trials are run, morning and evening. The night before the race, each district holds a festive street dinner. The big day begins with the Jockeys' Mass, celebrated by the Archbishop. Later, the horses receive blessings in their respective district churches, being told '*Vai, e torna vincitore*' – 'Go, and return victorious'.

Some 70,000 spectators throng the sloping piazza, which has been transformed into a racetrack with protective crash barriers as jockeys and horses frequently skid and fall. A crowd of 28,000 people stand squashed into the centre, with many more seated around the outside. They also stand on every balcony and hang out of every window, waiting for the grand parade – a fabulous medieval pageant featuring banners, the flags of the contradi, armoured horsemen, pages, drummers, buglers and a magnificent war chariot carrying the Palio – the victor's banner – drawn by two white bulls.

Tension rises, the crowd reaches fever pitch, the horses and jockeys arrive and the place erupts into pandemonium. It takes just 90 seconds to gallop wildly round the piazza three times, but it is some gallop. Jockeys use whips on their own mounts and any others in their way. The defeated mourn. For the victors, a month of celebrations is due, and the party begins immediately.

The contradas *race one another around the Piazza del Campo.*

Regata Storico

The Regata Storico is like stepping inside a giant Canaletto picture of 15th century Venice. The most important and one of the oldest of Venice's celebrations, it's a pageant of awesome magnificence in which flags and drapery emblazon the palaces lining the Grand Canal, and every terrace and balcony is alive with gesticulating, velvet-turbanned, silk-swathed crowds come to cheer the mighty parade of liveried boats. With the 'Bucintoro' (State Barge) of La Serenissima at their head, carrying the Doge and the most eminent of the Venetian Magistracy, the boats re-enact the glorious occasion in 1489 when Caterina Cornaro, Queen of Cyprus, arrived in true majesty to seal an alliance.

Ever since, the regata has survived as an annual expression of Venice's power and wealth, and it's the one day you can glimpse the fabled imperial city of universal legend. The Grand Canal and the Lagoon are crammed with spectators, dressed like their boats in every bright colour of the rainbow or heraldic invention. But this kaleidoscope of gilded splendour is just the beginning: the procession is only the prelude to a programme of races rowed down the Grand Canal.

You need cunning, intimate knowledge of the currents, and technical mastery as well as mere strength to row in the 'Storico'. Contestants have survived rigorous eliminations just to reach the start. By race time, Venetians' partisan excitement is at fever pitch. Aware of every subtlety within the strictly traditional rules governing the boats and methods of rowing, locals vent storms of rage and triumph. Their mounting intensity will blow you away – the races are dramatic and picturesque enough on their own. In the heart of Venice, with no obvious, visible points of modern reference, you can easily believe you've been transported to a parallel, Renaissance world. You'll love it.

A traditional Venetian vessel with trumpeters and oarsmen adds to the magnificence of the Regata Storico.

WHEN:
The first Sunday in September
WHERE:
The Grand Canal, Venice
BEST FOR:
History, culture and sport
YOU SHOULD KNOW:
The final race of the Regata Storico is between Venice's champion *gondolieri*, who race in pairs in a *gondolino* – a racing version of a normal gondola, specially created for the race and never used otherwise. Unlike gondolas, which must by law be painted black (to avoid over-ostentatious embellishment), *gondolini* can be eye-poppingly technicoloured.

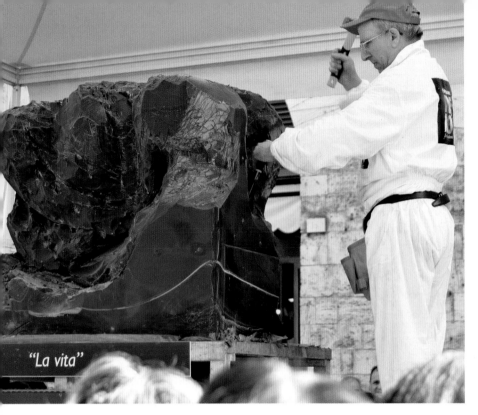

A sculptor goes to work on a cube of chocolate.

Perugia's Chocolate Festival

The beautiful, hilltop town of Perugia is famous for its university and for its *baci* (kisses) – little chocolates made by Perugina, one of Italy's most important confectioners, in a local factory. In 1994, the chocolate manufacturer inaugurated a chocolate festival in the knowledge that the huge community of students was a captive audience, ready and willing to join an experiment to see how many ways chocolate could be enjoyed. What an invitation! From the start, other manufacturers and devotees of chocolate clamoured to participate, and 'Eurochocolate' was born. An instant success, it has outgrown all its early objectives. Now, over a million 'chocaholics' come to laugh at chocolate jokes, wonder at chocolate art and chocolate applications in the home, in health and in entertainment, ponder questions of chocolate ethics, and to revel in the 'food of the gods' in each of thousands of forms.

Perugia's historic centre swarms with devotees sampling the wares of over 150 designers; admiring the chainsaw-wielding sculptors carving mammoth blocks of dark chocolate into graceful nudes or famous buildings (one year, five tons went into a chocolate igloo); enjoying the 'Choco-Farm', a real beauty clinic using chocolate-based treatments and aromatherapy; or just throwing caution to the winds with a chocolate sandwich, chocolate cocktail or chocolate-and-pepper snack. Not even pasta, salami or cheese is safe from chocolate additives – but nobody cares. Music is everywhere: 'Cioccolata Movida' (chocolate nightlife) takes over the town, with 'Cioccolata con l'Autore' (chocolate with authors) as an alternative for literary folk. 'Eurochocolate' even created a chocolate building site for one festival, and gave away thousands of chocolate trowels to visitors who contributed their labour. The festival demonstrates that chocolate can improve just about anything on the planet. As a visitor, all you have to do is like it.

WHEN:
Nine days in mid October
WHERE:
Throughout the streets and squares of Perugia's historic centre
BEST FOR:
Indulging a sweet tooth or an obsession, and imaginative entertainment
YOU SHOULD KNOW:
You can save money, and still experience some of the finest, hand-made chocolates on the planet (made while you watch) by acquiring a 'ChocoCard' – a festival credit card that enables you to sample dozens of different, small items for minimal expense.

Giro di Lombardia

The Giro di Lombardia (Tour of Lombardy) provides a real flourish to the end of the professional cycling calendar. This one-day, 230-km (144-mi) ride around Lake Como is in a class of its own. Like the Paris-Roubaix or the Spanish Vuelta, winning is a matter of personal triumph as much as team strategy – a difference of emphasis that reflects the Giro's venerability and the patina of its traditions. It started in 1905 and the route has varied greatly, but essentially it threads through the alpine foothills whose steep, wooded flanks form the shores of Lake Como. These are among Italy's most beautiful landscapes.

Since the 1920s, the Giro has always included the vicious ascent out of Bellagio (where the two arms of Como's Y-shape meet, providing some of the most enchanting vistas in the world) to Madonna del Ghisallo. After some 185 km (116 mi) of tactical racing, the world's best cyclists set off on 12 km (7-8 mi) of narrow switchbacks, many with an incline of 14 per cent, rising 554 m (1,817 ft). At the summit is a genuine shrine to cycling: as long ago as 1949, the ancient chapel was already so full of cycling memorabilia (pennants, programmes, team jerseys, *maillots jaunes* from the Tour de France, and famous bicycles nailed to the walls and ceilings) that Pope Pius XII declared the Madonna del Ghisallo the patron saint of cycling. This is where the views are divine and the race gets critical. It's also one of the handful of places in any race, anywhere, where it's easy to see the event and get close to understanding the nature of the special thrill that has gripped fans of the Giro di Lombardia for over a century.

WHEN:
October
WHERE:
Lake Como, north of Milan – the exact route varies each year, but almost always ends at Como itself.
BEST FOR:
Sport and natural beauty
YOU SHOULD KNOW:
Though it's one of the loveliest towns in Italy, it's best to avoid Como just before and during the Giro itself. On the other hand, it's the place to share the excitement of the motorcades, paparazzi, back-up cars and buses, and paraphernalia of besotted fan-dom. Because it's the end of their season, many professional stars are prepared to spend time meeting and greeting fans.

The competitors race through the village of Dizzasco.

EUROPE/SWITZERLAND

Vogel Gryff

WHEN:
Either January 13, 20 or 27
(on a three-year cycle, each guild
takes its turn organizing the rites).
WHERE:
Mittlere Brucke and Kleinbasel
district, Basel
BEST FOR:
Folklore and redemptive partying
YOU SHOULD KNOW:
Vogel Gryff, the leader of the dance
whose bird-head costume is
crowned with the awesome hook of
a beak sticking out of yellow, blue
and red tufts of wiry hair, has been
compared to Big Bird from TV's
Sesame Street.

*The Wild Man shows contempt
by keeping his back to
Grossbasel.*

Vogel Gryff is a one-day pagan revel evolved since the 13th century by the three venerable Guilds of Kleinbasel, the city wards on the right bank of the Rhine facing Basel proper (Grossbasel) on the left. If you stand on Basel's Mittlere Brucke (Middle Bridge) on a January morning, you can join the Dionysian fun.

The heraldic figures from the Guilds' three standards have leapt into life. Floating down the Rhine is an oversize, hairy ragamuffin brandishing an uprooted pine sapling, jigging up and down on his makeshift raft to the accompaniment of on-board drummers, flag-waving standard bearers, and the din from two guns firing non-stop salutes. He is 'Wild Maa' (Wild Man), the ancient symbol of fertility, and he dances with his back to Grossbasel in traditional contempt. Waiting on the bridge are 'Leu' (Lion) and 'Vogel Gryff' (Griffin) himself, shaggy of mane and hooked of beak respectively. Together, the three apparitions perform a very precise ritual, a surreal dance every step of which has been documented since the Middle Ages. Afterwards, they lead a huge and growing crowd back into Kleinbasel for the formal Guilds' lunch, the 'Gryffemahli'. Then, since nothing succeeds like excess, they just carry on being grotesque and fabulous for the rest of the day and night, interspersing their own prescribed moves with leading the increasingly overheated crowd in a hilarious scrum-conga through the streets and bars.

The generations-old folkloric subtleties of Vogel Gryff may be hard for visitors to grasp, but the communal geniality distinguishes it from other hard-partying, traditional festivities. For all its magnified caricature, hooting, singing and mayhem, it's underscored by real gentleness and neighbourly concern. Wild Maa, Leu and Vogel Gryff represent organizations that help their community all year round. Indulge yourself by thanking them on the one day they go public.

Polo World Cup on Snow

Graceful polo is played on the frozen lake at St Moritz.

The pitch is smaller but the surface is thrillingly different. Polo, one of the roughest and toughest sports on earth, becomes a triumph of optimism over danger, on snow. Only the very best even contemplate playing, and they like their skills to be matched to a location and circumstances worthy of their prowess. The Polo World Cup on Snow guarantees them the quality adventures they crave.

St Moritz and polo are both synonymous with glamour. The Engadine Valley in eastern Switzerland is famously beautiful in all seasons. Polo was first played here (informally) around 1897 by British subalterns looking for new excitement after founding the Cresta Run (in 1885). The playground of the rich and famous for more than a century, St Moritz is in some ways more exclusive than ever – and polo is necessarily so, because players must invest fortunes to maintain their strings of ponies. The World Cup on Snow allows only five ponies to each player for the four-chukka matches (instead of ten, for six chukkas); but the acclimatized ponies have studded shoes and special plastic 'over-bootees' against the ice and cold. Matches are fast, furious, and astonishingly graceful. Instead of the usual thunder on turf, you hear and see more acutely in the sharp air – the whinnied, snorting breath and creaking leather, and the swirling pillars of mist wherever players and ponies tangle in the cold. The razmatazz of parties during the tournament creates much the same impression.

Polo has been called the sport of kings, emperors and princes. It is, but the old-world charm of St Moritz makes the rarified social whirl of this competition feel inclusive to all comers. All you need to join in is a taste for madcap exhilaration, a pair of sunglasses for the evening, and a glass of champagne.

WHEN:
The last weekend in January
WHERE:
The lake, St Moritz
BEST FOR:
Dangerous sports, jet-set culture
YOU SHOULD KNOW:
Each of the four-man teams at the Polo World Cup on Snow carries a combined handicap in the range of 20 to 22 goals. According to the sport's stringent handicapping procedures, that's super-World Class.

311

Jan/Feb/March/April/May/June/July/Aug/Sept/Oct/Nov/Dec

*Colourfully garbed flute players
join in the festivities.*

Fasnachts-montag

Fasnacht in the city of Basel means the three-day carnival that – uniquely in the world – takes place after Lent has begun. It is Switzerland's biggest carnival, often called *die drey scheenschte Dääg* (the three most beautiful days) because it is meticulously organized with the sole (and somewhat contradictory) aim of creating space for maximum anarchy. It lasts exactly 72 hours, during which Basel's old town is completely surrendered to Fasnächtler (the participants) and whatever misrule and havoc they can wreak; but the biggest surprises, sprung with the most energy, take place on the first day, the Monday after Ash Wednesday, *Fasnachstmontag*.

At exactly 04.00 on *Fasnachstmontag*, the whole of Basel is plunged into darkness for *Morgestraich*. A moment later, thousands of lanterns flare to reveal a huge parade moving off. It consists of 'cliques', who later on will wear carnival uniforms illustrating different themes, but who now sport head-mounted lanterns of fabulous wit, colour and invention. Typically, each clique heads in a different direction with their drummers and musicians. The polite chaos when they converge is ably assisted by the bars and cafés, which never close. *Morgestraich* only ends so that *Fasnachtler* can prepare for 'Cortège', the second major parade of the day when the now-uniformed cliques are joined by brilliantly decorated floats from which treats are thrown at spectators by *Waggis* – traditional grotesques of local farmers. Spectators should beware of *Schyssdräggziigli* – who dress like benign *Waggis*, but sneak up on you and stuff confetti down your neck.

Unusually, there's a clear distinction between participants and spectators – but get a carnival badge and you'll be spared the *Schyssdräggziigli*. Among many conventions (like no flash-photography, and – if you wear a mask – remaining incognito throughout Cortège), confetti is never thrown at *Fasnachtler* – but they'll make sure you're having as much fun as you can take anyway.

WHEN:
The Monday following Ash Wednesday, either late February or early March
WHERE:
Basel
BEST FOR:
Folk traditions, political and social satire, and exhaustive revelry
YOU SHOULD KNOW:
Despite its name, Fas(t)nacht is celebrated a week later than anywhere else in the German-speaking Christian world because when a 16th century Pope changed the calendar, Protestant Basel took no notice. Fasnacht ends at exactly 04.00 on the Thursday – music and conversation stops in mid flow, and the huge crowds disperse in silence.

Montreux International Jazz Festival

It started as pure jazz. Claude Nobs from the Swiss Tourist Office, and his fellow devotees Géo Voumard and René Langel, initiated Montreux as a three-day festival of the music they loved in 1967. Now that Montreux is a demonstrably world event, it seems like heresy to remember that, back then, jazz was being ousted by rock and pop music. The eastern end of Lake Geneva, in a small, historic city set between the Alps and the water, seemed a suitable backwater for a vibrant – but unfashionable – culture to be nurtured and appreciated. From the start, Montreux attracted the biggest names. The megastars of an earlier generation came because they knew they would perform for cognoscenti; and the young musicians who came to sit at their feet also brought the first crossover influences of rock. The catalyst for all of them was the knowledgeable enthusiasm of the organizers and audiences. After the gigs, they could sit down, talk serious music, and jam.

They're all still at it. Montreux gradually expanded via rock and blues to Brazilian and World music; and now you can expect to see the best exponents of just about anything musical worth hearing. The venues have shifted only slightly in response to crowds and technical necessities, but you still get marvellous music in a stunning setting. Best of all, and the reason the festival goes from strength to strength, you still get the opportunity to meet and talk to some of the world's greatest musicians, who certainly don't come for the money. Montreux is about peer-group respect and the kind of inspirational intimacy you only get when everyone parks pomposity at the door. Claude Nobs, the acclaimed founder of this event that now attracts over 200,000 people, can't last forever but The Montreux Festival almost certainly will.

WHEN:
Two weeks in July
WHERE:
Montreux
BEST FOR:
Music
YOU SHOULD KNOW:
The Festival has its own currency – the 'Jazz' – so swap your Swiss Francs before you reach the bar. In recent years, Montreux has spawned a great 'Off-Festival' including lots of free, open-air concerts with the lake and mountains as backdrops, and musical cruises specializing in salsa and samba.

British Indie band The Ting Tings perform on the banks of Lake Geneva.

Combat des Reines

WHEN:
October
WHERE:
The Roman Amphitheatre, Martigny,
Canton Valais
BEST FOR:
Folk culture, sport
YOU SHOULD KNOW:
Spectators are far more passionate
about the Combat des Reines than
the cows, who despite being trained
like sumo wrestlers on massage,
'special' oats and (allegedly) wine,
never quite seem to get the point. A
winning cow gets a cowbell for a
prize. A winning owner gets a small
fortune in breeding fees.

Each October, hundreds of Swiss farmers come together at the
Roman amphitheatre at Martigny, in Canton Valais on the French
border, for the finals of the Combat des Reines (the Battle of
Queens) between Switzerland's most ornery cows. And only cows
– bulls are banned. The contestants at Martigny are already 'Queens'
– proven champions that have fought their way up through village
and regional contests, held on Sundays throughout the spring. In
fact, the Combat des Reines developed from the scuffling push and
shove between the senior matrons of every herd that takes place
each spring to decide which cow will lead the herd to its Alpine
grazing. Long, long ago farmers noticed that Eringer cows bred in the
Val d'Herens were regularly more aggressive and generally more
feisty than others, and began to breed them specifically for fighting.
The centuries-old tradition was formalized in 1923, and now it is the
sport of thousands in the Swiss Alps.

Cows are never forced to fight. Horns are filed and contests are
bloodless to the extent that most of them consist of psyching the
opposition with aggressive cud-chewing and bovine mean looks. A
bellow, a leery looming of the front haunches, and perhaps a jabbing
sort of shove; then if it escalates, much pawing of the ground (cue
cheering of the spectators and the bookies holding their surprisingly
large bets) followed by a solid head-butt does the trick. Cows that
funk it get a prod with a stick from a *rabatteur*, before being
returned to pasture. But in the close, slightly foetid, carnival-like
atmosphere of shouting, drinking and cheering, with the earthy smell
of animals and dung-soaked straw, you reach far past the Switzerland
of Victor Hugo ('The Swiss milks his cow and lives in peace') to the
atavistic Helvetian celebration of its own, too-well hidden world.

*Two cows go head to head
during the Battle of the Queens.*

Faschings-Dienstag

In most of Germany it's called the familiar Karneval, but in Munich it's called Fasching. Though it actually begins as early as November, effectively Fasching refers not so much to *die närrische Saison* (the foolish season) of giant fancy-dress parties, parades and white-tie balls, as to its culmination on the three days before Ash Wednesday. The pace really hots up. Everyone wears exotic costumes and masks – everything from chic dominoes to grotesque fantasias – and huge papier-maché caricatures on floats, lampooning local politicians and celebrities, idle through the crowds. Intoxicated by music, dance and colour, people abandon themselves to the lawless pleasures of the incognito moment. As lords of misrule, everyone gets ready for the climax of the festivities – Faschings-Dienstag, Shrove Tuesday.

Carnival soldiers take a break.

Anything goes as the fabulous party moves from the Gothic magnificence of Marienplatz around the corner to Viktualienmarkt (the Food Market). The whole area of cobbled streets is crammed with laughter and music, and the air is filled with the tantalizing aromas of doughnuts – traditional on this day – filled with vanilla, marmalade or chocolate. They are the prelude to one of Faschings-Dienstag's oldest and most bizarre traditions, the 'Dance of the Market Women'. The women who run the market stalls perform a series of complicated ritual dances, made hilarious by their exotic fancy dress. Gradually, women and girls from the crowd join in, as do many others dressed like women. At some point in the uproarious melée, a procession forms for 'Sweeping Out The Fool' – carrying an effigy of the Fasching 'Fool' in a coffin to the Lowenbrau beer cellar.

It's not over. By nightfall Munich's heart is jammed with masked merrymakers going to and from any of a thousand *Kehraus* (last dance) parties held in bars, beer halls and palaces. You bop until you drop at midnight (sharp) – and that's Faschings-Dienstag.

WHEN:
February
WHERE:
Munich
BEST FOR:
Drinking, dressing up and having fun (incognito's best)
YOU SHOULD KNOW:
Visitors are often surprised how readily Bavarians (and Muncheners in particular) embrace the notion of 'anything goes' during Fasching, and especially on Faschings-Dienstag (when they're masked). Try not to be offended by differing norms of behaviour in public.

The Town Hall is stormed during the festival.

Dusseldorf Carnival

Dusseldorf is the holder of the flame of the Rhineland Carnival tradition. Other cities might hold bigger or more licentious carnivals, but it's in Dusseldorf that you'll find the most arcane rituals and the most respect for age-old conventions. Dusseldorf is also famous for encouraging the most politically incorrect behaviour during carnival, often so outrageous (and funny) that it scrambles your brain as much as the beer does. Between Hoppeditz' Erwachen (Jester's Awakening) on November 11 (at the 11th minute of the 11th hour), the official start of the entire German carnival season, and Ash Wednesday, Dusseldorf hosts more than 300 balls and carnival costume parties. They get increasingly wild in anticipation of the street carnival proper, which begins on Altweiberfastnacht (Old Hags Festival), the Thursday before Ash Wednesday. The women of the city – and many of the men – use wigs, period costumes and grotesque masks or make-up to look old and spiteful. Then they storm the Town Hall, 'seizing' government for the day. Expect your tie to be chopped off, and to be roundly kissed on demand, anywhere in the Altstadt.

All weekend, Dusseldorf plays open house to costumed revellers. Clowns, harlequins, pierrots, cowboys and milkmaids shout the traditional 'Helau' Rhineland greeting to walking tubes of toothpaste and fairy princesses. By Monday, perhaps a million people line the streets or march in the Rosenmontagszug (Running Monday Parade), and visitors are expected to make an effort to dress or wear make-up too. Rosenmontag is the climax of the festivities. Lead by Hoppeditz with his pig's bladder on a stick, and the Carnival Prince and Princess, the huge parade is a masterpiece of anti-pomp and misrule. You'll enjoy it most if you just let yourself get swept away – you have a whole year to recover.

WHEN:
The main celebrations take place around Ash Wednesday (February/March) but the carnival season starts on November 11.
WHERE:
Dusseldorf
BEST FOR:
Political and social satire, folk traditions and riotous assembly
YOU SHOULD KNOW:
Dusseldorf retains its pre-eminence among the Hochburgen (principal carnival cities) of the Rhine. Its Rosenmontag parade – the mock uniforms screaming with colour and the raucous bands – is a parody of royalty and Prussian militarism, still valid satirical targets after 125 years.

Cologne Carnival

As one of the Hochburgen (principal carnival cities) of the
Rhineland, it's no surprise that Cologne follows certain carnival
traditions, or that it adds its own twist to them. Cologne's Carnival
Prince, for example, is called *Seine Tollitat* (His Craziness), and
instead of a Princess, he has a carnival trinity including the
Jungfrau (the Virgin, always played by a man in a dress) and the
Bauer (Peasant). These *Dreigestirn* (Three Stars/Triumvirate) by
their very existence cock a snook at the hierarchy of normal
government; and most of the costumed balls and hundreds of street
parties held by the city's 105 historic carnival associations are
conceived as fresh opportunities for lampoon, parody and satire.
However spirited, they are also mere rehearsals for the five *Tolle
Tage* (Crazy Days) prior to Ash Wednesday, which culminate in
Cologne's version of the Rosenmontag Parade.

Most of the legends associated with Cologne's carnival originated
from Rosenmontag. The parade is Germany's biggest, wildest, most
colourful, best costumed and definitely naughtiest. One and a half
million people crowd the beautiful Altstadt to watch His Craziness
preside over a 6 km (4 mi) column of snazzily uniformed 'regiments'
(whose only 'duty' is to
disobey orders), and to
admire satirical floats,
bands and marching groups
co-ordinated under fantasy
themes (you might see two
dozen teapots dancing
down the street). It's open
house on mischief – but
you deserve everything you
get by way of confetti down
the neck if you don't make
the effort to dress up for
the day. In any case,
Cologne is the only city to
host a completely
Alternative Carnival at the
same time. Begun as a
refuge for carnival-
disaffected youth, it's
grown to supply all the
party elements felt to be
missing in the traditional
craziness. You choose.
Cologne parties, and
parties some more.

WHEN:
February/March
WHERE:
Cologne
BEST FOR:
Street partying, costumed spectacle,
social subversion
YOU SHOULD KNOW:
At any time, be prepared to receive a
Carnival *butzje* – a kiss made with
pursed lips. It usually just means the
bestower is happy, ebullient and
feeling generous. Learn to give them
back, and a *butzje* could be the start
of a beautiful friendship.

*Clowns make merry in front of
the cathedral.*

Rhine In Flames

WHEN:
The first Saturday in May (Bonn); the first Saturday in July (Rudesheim/Bingen); the second Saturday in August (Koblenz); the second Saturday in September (Oberwesel); the third Saturday in September (Lorelei)
WHERE:
Middle Rhine Valley
BEST FOR:
Magnificent spectacle, natural beauty and history
YOU SHOULD KNOW:
In-the-know Germans have a fondness for medieval Oberwesel's 'Rhine In Flames' – for the music, for the wine festival in progress, and for the phenomenal staging of the town 'in flames' (Oberwesel is the only town to use its Bengal Fire to commemorate a historical incident – the burning of the town in the Middle Ages).

On five occasions each summer, at five different locations along the World Heritage Site of the Middle Rhine Valley, over half a million people gather to be amazed by firework displays so spectacular that the Rhine itself appears to be in flames. The secret is 'Bengal Fire' – a particularly long-lasting flare whose spreading jet of intense (usually red) colour can be exploded to create what looks like sheets of flame. Fired from a fleet of 50 or 60 boats, a river of fire a kilometre long illuminates some of Germany's most beautiful castles and churches on their rocky crags. As each is engulfed by the hellish glow, it adds its own fireworks to the technicolour spray arcing across the gorge, its drama doubled by reflections in the water, and redoubled by the violence of the echoing explosions in the gorge. It's breathtaking, and each of the 'Rhine In Flames' celebrations is structured to a glorious finale – in Koblenz, for example, on the promontory where the Rhine meets the Moselle the huge bulk of the Ehrenbreitstein fortress suddenly explodes into (Bengal!) flames.

The Rhine In Flames series begins in May, with the 'Night of the Bengal Lights' when a fleet of over 60 ships sails between Linz and Bonn. The 'Night of Fire Magic' in July takes place at the truly beautiful southern bend of the river between Rudesheim and Bingen. This is followed by the 'Procession to Koblenz' (the biggest, dating back to 1766) in August. 'Night of a Thousand Fires' in September is orchestrated to wonderful music, including the 'Symphony of Fire' which you can hear as you sail past the Lorelei on your way from St Goar to the wine festival at Oberwesel. Finally, the fleet gathers on 'Lorelei Night', also in September, for the statue's adulatory fireworks – and just this once, Lorelei is lit by green Bengal fire.

The Rhine Valley is set alight.

The Oberammergau Passion Play

In 1633 the villagers of Oberammergau in the foothills of the Bavarian Alps prayed for deliverance from the scourge of the bubonic plague. Following their collective appeal, not even one more person died of the plague. In gratitude, the surviving community pledged to re-enact the 'Play of the Suffering, Death and Resurrection of Our Lord Jesus Christ' every ten years. They kept their word. Now, the village of little more than 5,000 people is world famous for its communal dedication to an act of faith which requires between 700 and 1,800 performers (drawn exclusively from Oberammergau) to perform the 18 acts and numerous tableaux that constitute a single, day-long performance. There are no short cuts or theatrical sleights of hand. Oberammergau's original, solemn vow of 1633 is renewed publicly every decade, and each Passion Play is informed by this fresh declaration, and by the intense competition for major and minor roles in each production. Each time the script, casting and staging are subjects of lively debate – but the result for both cast and audience is always a feeling of being involved in something fundamental to human existence in a material and dangerous world.

The Passion Play has been criticized for 'amateurism' and theatrical cliché, but technical innovations backstage have only enhanced the play's gift to a sophisticated audience of intimacy with the deeply rooted fervour of the villagers' faith. It finds its universal echo in every creed and culture. It shames cynicism with the honesty of its colourful spectacle. The major change of the new (1999), purpose-built auditorium was to provide shelter and comfort for the 4,720-strong capacity; the 'stage' is still open-air, so the transforming drama and pageantry of the Passion takes place against the vast skies, forests and mountains of its original backdrop. Oberammergau is about watching ordinary people striving for an extraordinary spiritual fulfillment, and succeeding.

This scene depicts the crucifixion of Christ.

WHEN:
May to October, every tenth year
(2010, 2020, 2030, etc.)
WHERE:
Oberammergau, in the Bavarian Alps,
close to Garmisch-Partenkirchen
and the Austrian border
BEST FOR:
Religious and cultural history
YOU SHOULD KNOW:
The Passion Play is always
oversubscribed by at least half a
million people. Register with the
Passion Play Office as early as you
can – they will keep you informed
about when and how you can
actually make a reservation.

319

Jan/Feb/March/April/**May/June/July/Aug/Sept/Oct**/Nov/Dec

Riflemen fire a salute during Schutzenfest.

Schutzenfest Hannover

Every village and town in Germanic Europe subscribes to the tradition of Schutzenfest. The term means Shooter's (or Marksman's) Festival, and it harks back to the archery (and later, shooting) competitions that were already popular 500 years ago. Fairs grew round the actual shooting matches, but then the tournaments got lost in the rides, entertainments and heroic drinking bouts that gradually dominated the event at local and regional levels. Schutzenfest Hannover began in 1529 and was no different from the others, except for the increasing numbers of genuine marksmen who wanted to compete at shooting and to promote their shooting clubs by parading with their comrades. Now, Schutzenfest Hannover is the biggest Marksmen's Festival in the world, and one of Germany's biggest summer events.

The centerpiece of Schutzenfest Hannover is the Marksmen's Parade. Five thousand marksmen are joined by seven thousand or so friends, marching in the hunting 'uniforms' of their local marksmen's clubs. Interspersed with dozens of huge floats and more than 100 bands from various countries playing everything from 'oompah' to reggae, they form a parade some 12 km (7 mi) long – one of the longest march-pasts in the world. It's full of good cheer, amplified by a throng of more than a million, who come for the colour and spectacle, the universal appeal of over 250 rides and sideshows, one of Europe's highest Ferris wheels, and the five gigantic beer tents sponsored (and subsidized) by various breweries.

Children love it, because the sponsors also make sure that there's plenty to keep them occupied when their parents run out of steam. Adults love it because the whole tradition of Schutzenfest promotes the *gemütlichkeit* (warm friendliness) fundamental to German families and communities. Visitors love it because it's a great parade and a better funfair.

WHEN:
June/July
WHERE:
Hannover
BEST FOR:
Folk traditions, spectacle and entertainment
YOU SHOULD KNOW:
Probably the most famous of all Schutzenfest traditional rites is 'Luttje Lage'. You hold a glass of Weissbier (wheat beer) tightly against a tiny (shot) glass of schnapps – using only the fingers of one hand – and try to drink both simultaneously, without spilling. You can guess the forfeit for failing.

Kieler Woche

Piqued by the success of his royal English cousins' regatta at Cowes, Kaiser Wilhelm II transformed a local regatta created by Hamburg's sailing club. The club's members had done all the hard work, but imperial backing gave the new 'Kieler Woche' (Kiel Week) instant international clout. After 1892, Kiel rapidly became not only a mecca for the world's best yachtsmen, but also (because of the Emperor's presence) a mandatory sojourn for the diplomatic corps, whose families and entourages needed entertaining. So Kiel Week has always developed on twin axes – and now, as well as being the world's biggest sailing event, it's also the biggest summer festival in Northern Europe.

Five thousand sailors race two thousand ships and boats in over 100 class divisions; and three million people come to watch or participate in a staggering mixture of street festivals, rock, pop, and classical concerts, political and social events, and the world-famous 'Spiellinie' (Play Line) of children's entertainment. So much happens – from the city centre for miles along Kiel's beautiful fjord – that Kiel Week is nine days long.

All of it is world class and Olympic sailors come to Kiel first. The Olympic harbour at Schilksee is the centre of the fast and furious sporting action and when no race is in progress, there's a non-stop programme on the water – including cutter racing between various navies whose warships are visiting, trips on windjammers, and the heart-stirring Tall Ships parade. At intervals along the shore massive stages hold bands of every description. Music fills the clear sea air, reinforcing the atmosphere of benevolent expectation that makes popular festivals truly great. Kieler Woche applies Germanic intensity to the giving and receiving of a good time. At this exalted level, nobody does it better.

WHEN:
Nine days, from the Saturday preceding the last full week of June
WHERE:
Kiel, Schleswig-Holstein
BEST FOR:
World-class sport, music, family entertainment and festival fun
YOU SHOULD KNOW:
In the less complicated days of 1882, when the very first race took place, the only announcement made was: 'Start at 10.30 am'. But the 23 yachts entered for the race didn't cross a starting line – they started from their individual moorings.

Just a few of the 2,000 boats that take part in Kiel Week.

DOM Festival

The history of Hamburg's DOM Festival dates back to the 14th century, when the town's St Mary's Cathedral (St Marien Dom) followed the medieval tradition of offering shelter to those who needed it, including travelling merchants, itinerant craftsmen and strolling players. The result was much worldly merry-making somewhat at odds with the cathedral's religious role, but the action continued there until – with the development of steam-powered fairground attractions towards the end of the 19th century – it moved from the cathedral precinct to Heiligengeistfeld (Holy Ghost Field), becoming an extravaganza that still retains the name that testifies to its origins.

The summer DOM Festival (known as Hummelfest) is the largest fun fair in North Germany, taking place for most of August. The action gets into its stride in the early afternoon and continues until late, seven days a week. This vast event, dominated by a giant ferris wheel, has a huge variety of entertainment including an apparently endless choice of thrilling rides traditional and modern, stalls offering a wide variety of fairground amusements, family-friendly activities, musical happenings, assorted special attractions that vary from year to year (such as a Wild West town with lots of cowboy action), numerous beer tents and bars, a choice of food ranging from tasty snacks to fine dining . . . and much more besides.

Anyone who wants to see everything will have to walk for at least 3 km (2 mi) up and down the packed fairground. The Hummelfest is a magnet for locals and tourists alike, and it is estimated that over three million visitors enjoy this spectacular festival every summer. And if you can't make the summer festival, there are also DOM events in spring (starting in late March) and winter (starting in early November), both also lasting for a month.

A fun fair ride not for the faint hearted!

Kulmbach Bierfest

The Kulmbach Bierfest is heaven on earth for serious beer drinkers. Kulmbach, in Franconia (the northern region of Bavaria, near the Thuringian Forest) is often called Germany's Capital of Beer. There's evidence that beer was brewed in Kulmbach in 3000 BC, and in medieval times every one of its inhabitants was entitled to brew the stuff. The town is still a major brewing centre, and although its traditional expertise is concentrated in a few surviving breweries, they still make a huge variety of beers. For nine days, starting from the last weekend in July, the Kulmbach Bierfest puts the fruit of its local skills on display – and the combination of the rare, the subtle, the traditional, the historic and the mouth-wateringly delicious brings the international cognoscenti, panting, to its door.

Beer drinking is a serious business!

The bierfest takes place in the square in front of the rococo façade of the Rathaus – a proper match for the hoppy elegance in your glass. Bands play, banging and crashing with infectious enthusiasm, and people dance with a contented glow in their eyes. There's less of the unrestrained exhibitionism you sometimes see in Bavarian beer festivals, and much more sense of intense discussion in the huddled groups of beer professionals and gifted amateurs. It's marvellous for visitors. Your interest is welcomed, and new friends join you (usually with conflicting advice!) with every round. Among others, Kulmbach is internationally famous for its Schwarzbier, a *dunkel* (dark lager) first brewed in the town by monks around 1349; its Pilsener (voted by Germans as the best in their country); its Eisbock, made by freeze-distilling a doppelbock (double-strength beer) to concentrate the flavour and raise the alcohol to as much as 14 per cent; and – if you can cope – Kulminator 28, one of the strongest beers in the world.

WHEN:
The last weekend in July
WHERE:
Kulmbach
BEST FOR:
Serious beer-drinking and technical analysis
YOU SHOULD KNOW:
The Kulmbach breweries create at least three new beers especially for each bierfest. They may not be the strongest of brews, but they are always among the most complex and delicious.

323

Christopher Ventris plays the role of Parsifal in Richard Wagner's opera of the same name.

Bayreuth's Wagner Festival

The blazing anthems of Richard Wagner's music are part of Germany's cultural soul. Drawing on the vast treasure chest of Teutonic history and legend, masterpieces like *Parsifal* or *Tannhäuser* made Wagner the willing standard-bearer for the wild beauty of Romanticism. In fact, he was so passionate about his mythical vision that he himself created the festival which celebrates it annually. He even designed a special opera house exclusive to his own music (it opened with the premiere of *Der Ring des Nibelungen*). It is the ark of Wagner's musical legacy, and the heart of the festival which makes Bayreuth's name synonymous with the composer.

Hearing the glories of Wagner performed in the place and conditions of his prescription can be emotionally powerful. The Festspielhaus' auditorium is an amphitheatre where the wooden floor is uncarpeted and the wooden seats lack both cushioning and armrests in order to meet Wagner's exacting acoustical specifications. It only seats 1,925 people, so every performance is charged with the compressed excitement of aficionados who have often travelled huge distances to fulfil a lifetime dream. Every summer, the Bayreuth Festival presents ten of Wagner's works, alternating giants like the *Ring* and *Tristan und Isolde*. Each performance is literally heralded from the Festspielhaus balcony with a fanfare based on a theme from the opera about to begin, and played by a brass section from the evening's orchestra. Wagner decreed every detail of this unique ceremony, and it's one of Bayreuth's proudest traditions. Of course, not even Wagner could anticipate the interpretations of his music by the world's leading conductors and orchestras, and the festival's productions are often fiercely controversial. What never changes is the depth of passion and commitment to the composer's original spirit: shared by the performers and a typically international audience of cognoscenti, it is the essence of the Bayreuth Festival.

WHEN:
Late July/August
WHERE:
Bayreuth, in northern Bavaria close to the Czech border
BEST FOR:
Music, opera, and cultural insight
YOU SHOULD KNOW:
Bayreuth's Wagner Festival has been sold out since 1876, and confirmed reservations can run over a year ahead. Unconfirmed bookings entered as late as the previous October may get lucky in a draw for the small number of tickets held back to give everyone a reasonable chance.

Oktoberfest

Each year, Munich hosts the world's biggest folk festival. Oktoberfest began in 1810 as a city-wide wedding party thrown by Ludwig I of Bavaria for his bride, and developed as an annual harvest hootenanny and carnival incorporating Bavaria's traditional codes of dress, folk customs and sense of mischief. Now it's a raucous, rip-roaring celebration of Bavarian beer, food and good fellowship that attracts enthusiastic international participation. While it lasts, over six million people take their turn at 100,000 seats in 14 hangar-sized tents to drink super-strong beer specially brewed for the occasion, and to carouse for as long as they can remain conscious to brass 'oompah' bands. Anything goes – as long as you observe the strictly enforced etiquette that, believe it or not, really works in diffusing even the most eye-poppingly alcoholic confrontations into good-humoured rowdiness.

Oktoberfest (known as d'Wiesn, short for Theresienwiese, the name of its traditional site) is slowly becoming more sophisticated and more specialized. Around the main 'party' tents are 100 smaller ones offering specific food and beer varieties; and around them, dozens of carnival rides and sideshows attract happy families in the daytime, and foolhardy drunks by night. Every tent creates its own atmosphere. The Hacker-Festzelt's rock bands attract a whooping, younger crowd; the Schutzen-Festzelt's relaxed (brass) folk music appeals to older people; and everywhere groups of Italians, Australians, New Zealanders and other nationalities bring their own interpretations of Bavarian drinking customs to the party. But whatever the type of music or size and mood of the tent, every ten minutes the band plays *Ein Prosit der Gemutlichkeit*. This short tune ends in a loudly shouted 'Eins, zwei, drei, g'suffa!' (One, two, three, drink!), and then you must take a swig. It's simply to remind you why you came to Oktoberfest.

WHEN:
September/October. Oktoberfest lasts for the 16 days before the first Sunday in October, its traditional close.

WHERE:
Theresienwiese, nearr Goetheplatz in central Munich

BEST FOR:
Guilt-free beer drinking and cultural exchange

YOU SHOULD KNOW:
During Oktoberfest, the kind people of Munich understand the frequent occurrence of acute *Gedachtnisverlust* (memory loss), and are usually happy to help you track down your hotel, or even name.

A waitress carries beer to eager drinkers during Oktoberfest.

EUROPE/AUSTRIA

New Year's Day Concert

WHEN:
January 1
WHERE:
Vienna
BEST FOR:
The sounds of Strausses
YOU SHOULD KNOW:
Addicts of Viennese music can get a double fix, by attending the splendid New Year's Eve concert put on by the Hofburg Orchestra.

This magnificent hall is where the New Year Concert is held.

The year 1939 may not have been the most auspicious in which to lay the foundations for an enduring Austrian tradition, but that's nonetheless when the first New Year Concert of the Vienna Philharmonic Orchestra took place – actually on December 31. But the regular date has been January 1 ever since, and this magnificent musical occasion has become a much-loved international institution.

The lively morning classical music concert lasts for two-and-a-half hours and has always taken place in the Large Hall at the Wiener Musikverein, decorated for the occasion with flowers gifted by Sanremo in Italy (home of a famous music festival). The repertoire invariably includes numerous pieces by the talented Strauss family (Johan I, Johan II, Josef and Eduard). The programme also includes the works of other Austrian composers, plus the occasional honoured outsider. One piece is always accompanied by dancers from the Vienna State Opera Ballet.

There are plenty of marches, polkas, waltzes and mazurkas to set pulses racing and toes tapping, coming to a wonderful climax with three traditional encores – a fast polka, then Johan Strauss II's *Blue Danube Waltz*, finally Johan Strauss I's *Radetzky March* . . . the latter with the conductor (a different baton-wielder each year) turning to the audience to lead a thunderous clap-along.

This is not an easy event to attend – demand for tickets is so great that would-be concert goers have to register their names for a ballot one year in advance, with no guarantee of a ticket even then. But there is a fall-back position – it's probably the world's most-watched classical concert, with an estimated television audience of one billion people in nearly 50 countries – Vienna's New Year's Concert really is that good, so it's worth making a serious effort to experience the rousing live atmosphere.

Hahnenkamm Race Weekend

With the big jump in the background, a skier competes during the prestigious Men's Downhill event.

Oh to be in Austria, now that January's here! And three days towards the end of the month are an especially good time for winter sports aficionados, for then the world-famous ski resort of Kitzbühel has a little something extra to offer – the three-day Hahnenkamm Race Weekend.

Continuing a tradition dating back to 1931, when the Hahnenkamm Alpine Downhill Ski Race was first held, dozens of top professional skiers arrive in Kitzbühel to contest the most prestigious races in the FIS (Féderation Internationale de Ski) World Cup calendar – itself the blue riband competition for downhill racers. They all desperately want to win at Kitzbühel, for this is the toughest race of all. That being the case, tens of thousands of spectators gather in this tiny Tyrolean town to watch them trying and (for all but one supreme performer) failing heroically in the attempt.

This is a true festival of winter sports, with giant screens showing each run complete with split times, blaring music, national flags waving and excited fans screaming. But all good races come to an end so once the result is decided and medals have been awarded, everyone's thoughts turn to celebrating a great occasion. Soon, the entire town takes on the aspect of one giant party, with hyped-up revellers carousing in the streets and packing every restaurant, club and bar in Kitzbühel. The whole thing is illuminated with a brilliant display of fireworks, adding to a carnival atmosphere.

And for those daring souls who manage to wake up next morning without a hangover, there's the chance to follow in the ski tracks of their heroes – the resort's most demanding run has been closed all winter as it is prepared for the Hahnenkamm Downhill Race, but now the awesome Streiff is opened to the public.

WHEN:
January
WHERE:
Kitzbühel
BEST FOR:
Superlative ski and super-abundant après
YOU SHOULD KNOW:
The place to go after the race is the Londoner Pub – for tradition has it that the race winner will show up late at night and become an honorary barman into the wee small hours.

327

Vienna Life Ball

The rich and often famous are able to buy an expensive ticket to attend one of Austria's most glittering social occasions – the fancy-dress Life Ball in Vienna's impressive neo-Gothic City Hall that is restricted to 4,000 prestigious partygoers. The title comes from the event's purpose – to raise money for AIDS charities. This is a good cause dear to the hearts of many international celebrities, so the ball is prominently supported by the likes of Sir Elton John and Hollywood stars, who in turn attract the jet set.

But that's just the tip of the iceberg. For any big hitters who are unable to get in to the main event there are numerous after parties, exclusive gatherings and gala dinners that make the Life Ball a major entry on the international social calendar, encouraging the great and good to mingle and open capacious wallets in a good cause.

But this is by no means an exclusive occasion, having steadily expanded to include

The Red Ribbon Stage offers a variety of top entertainment.

events that provide some splendid free entertainment for everyone else. Following a grand opening ceremony that takes place on the giant Red Ribbon Stage in Rathausplatz outside City Hall, each year sees a stunning catwalk fashion show featuring the work of a leading designer, with clothes invariably modelled by a mixture of professionals (like Naomi Campbell) and stars (like Kylie Minogue).

Vienna's credentials as a cosmopolitan, tolerant and liberal metropolis are not only underlined by the loan of its finest civic building, but reinforced by the street parties, extraordinary costumes and general entertainment that are becoming an important part of the Life Ball, widening the appeal of an increasingly well-known charity event that is making an enormous contribution to the worldwide fight against AIDS.

WHEN:
May
WHERE:
Vienna
BEST FOR:
Star-gazing in a good cause
YOU SHOULD KNOW:
The fabulous Vienna State Opera Ballet may be seen performing on the Red Ribbon Stage as part of the festivities.

Lange Nacht der Musik

No sooner has the colourful Vienna Life Ball faded from the radar for another year than the Lange Nacht der Musik (Long Music Night) appears to brighten the city's cultural firmament. This innovative event is of fairly recent origin (launched in 2000 to greet the forthcoming new millennium) and brings one night in the city alive with music, music, music – some 60 venues present mainly Austrian musicians performing everything from classical music to electronic sounds, folk to jazz, pop to rock, band sounds to musicals, DJ performances to cabaret. It's even possible to listen to historical instruments being played.

The beauty of this unusual occasion is that a single reasonably priced ticket permits access to each and every one of the venues, which are as diverse as concert halls, theatres, churches, museums, clubs, bars and cafés. At one end of the spectrum, a popular venue is St Stephen's Cathedral, which regularly hosts more than 5,000 visitors on this busy night, whilst at the opposite end the Moulin Rouge nightclub offers standing room only for Viennese songs. Symbols at each venue indicate the style of music on offer within, and there are widely displayed 'Long Night' master plans showing the entire programme and exact location of every performance.

Although the various venues in Central Vienna are easily accessible on foot, they are also connected by regular free shuttle buses from Herbert von Karajan Square that run every 15 minutes, with stops clearly marked by special posters. This service permits music lovers to plan a packed itinerary and hustle round as many performances as possible, starting in the early evening and continuing far into the small hours. It's an occasion that really does justify that old boast 'something for everyone'.

WHEN:
June
WHERE:
Vienna
BEST FOR:
Night owls with wide-ranging musical tastes
YOU SHOULD KNOW:
If music isn't your thing, an appealing alternative might be Austria's Lange Nacht der Museen (Long Night of Museums) in early October, when a single ticket gives access to over 600 museums connected by a hop-on-hop-off bus service.

329

Donauinselfest

WHEN:
End of June
WHERE:
Donauinsel, Vienna
BEST FOR:
Beautiful people and sensational sounds
YOU SHOULD KNOW:
Be aware that there are extensive official nudist beaches at each end of the Donauinsel – make of them what you will.

If you're young, fit, love music, are intent on having a good time and happen to be passing anywhere near Vienna in June, be sure to make a hot date with the Donauinselfest (Danube Island Festival). This rip-roaring event is the largest dedicated youth festival and biggest open-air event in all Europe, attracting hordes of fun-seekers from all corners of the globe to an awesome party.

The Donauinsel is an ideal venue. This extensive island lies in the River Danube where it passes through the elegant Austrian capital and is 21 km (13 mi) long but only 70-210 m (230-690 ft) wide. It is already the city's recreational paradise with numerous clubs, bars and restaurants along with assorted sports facilities. To that add 20 stages in the central area to showcase the musical talents of local DJs, cabaret acts, bands and top international stars and it's easy to understand why nearly three million visitors turn up each year for a fabulous weekend of free entertainment.

This vast assembly is looked after by 1,500 volunteer stewards and prevented from going completely berserk by a highly visible police presence. But that doesn't prevent plenty of fireworks – literally (there's a magnificent display of pyrotechnics on the Saturday night) and musically. A wide range of tastes is catered for, with up to 2,000 performers strutting their stuff during the three days of pulsating action, collectively delivering over 600 hours of compelling entertainment.

Needless to say, the bopping festival goers cannot live by music alone, so an equally wide range of culinary tastes can be satisfied, with the grounds containing countless food outlets offering a huge range of international cuisine. Vienna in summer, terrific music, fine food and great company . . . what more could anyone want?

Donauinselfest is the biggest open-air event in Europe.

ImPulsTanz

In common with many headline events that underpin Vienna's first-rate cultural credentials, ImPuls Tanz is of fairly recent origin. This prestigious modern dance event – full title ImPulsTanz Vienna International Dance Festival – was started in the 1980s as a modest workshop week but has grown and grown. The festival now offers a five-week programme of performance, workshops and experimental research projects that bring thousands of teachers, choreographers and professional dancers to the city. It is still run by joint-founder Karl Regenburger.

Some 4,000 direct participants are drawn by the opportunity to learn from the best and work with their contemporaries to push the dance envelope in new and innovative directions. The event offers around 200 workshops conducted by 80 of the world's top teachers, all seeking the latest trends and breakthroughs in contemporary dance. During ImPulsTanz lovers of the dance can enjoy a vast array of productions at many different venues – an opportunity to see the world's finest contemporary dance troupes and individual dancers that is enjoyed by a collective total of at least 30,000 modern-dance enthusiasts each year.

One unique aspect of ImPulsTanz is its laid-back atmosphere, based on the fact that everyone – be they audience members, students, teachers, choreographers or professional dancers – is encouraged to interact. Performances are scheduled with rest days so the artists are in town for a while, permitting them to become involved in interactive sessions.

A spin-off from ImPulsTanz is danceWebEurope – a scholarship programme founded in 1996 to foster the exchange of ideas and dance knowledge and further the careers of participants, whereby 50 emerging dancers and choreographers from many countries are encouraged to play a full part in every aspect of the festival. For those chosen, it's a terrific way to see and do it all.

This is modern dance at its finest and most innovative.

WHEN:
July/August
WHERE:
Vienna
BEST FOR:
Seriously motivated dancers and those who really appreciate cutting-edge modern dance
YOU SHOULD KNOW:
To get a real feel for the festival's objectives and character, be sure to pay a visit to the free-entry ImPulsTanz Festival Lounge at the Burgtheater. It's also possible to attend amazing opening and closing parties for a modest fee.

Salzburg Festival

WHEN:
July/August
WHERE:
Salzburg
BEST FOR:
The uplifting talent of
Wolfgang Amadeus
YOU SHOULD KNOW:
Salzburg was the film location of
The Sound of Music . . . and the
Trapp Family Singers who were the
inspiration for that much-loved
musical and movie actually
performed on stage at the Salzburg
Festival in 1936.

The annual Salzburg Festival is a world-famous 'culturefest' devoted to
opera, drama and classical music. It was founded in 1877 and – with
interludes before World War I and during World War II – has been held
annually in the fairytale Austrian city of Salzburg ever since. The
birthplace of Wolfgang Amadeus Mozart is rightly proud of its cultural
heritage and the festival's modern incarnation began in 1920, inspired by
the composer Richard Strauss, poet Hugo von Hofmannsthal and theatre
director Max Reinhardt.

This delightful city is worth an extended visit in its own right and
summer visitors would be entirely justified in exploring Salzburg for its
numerous historical delights, but many thousands arrive with something
else in mind – attending world-class performances at the festival's three
main venues. The two Grosses Festspielhäuser were created on the site of
the Archbishop's extensive stables and provide a magnificent principal

venue, ably supported by the Felsenreitschule. The main emphasis is always on Mozart's operas and the music of Strauss, though tradition dictates that Hofmannsthal's play *Jedermann* (Everyman) is always performed on the steps in Cathedral Square, serving as a reminder that this is not an event for classical music alone.

Indeed, from late July to the end of August some 200 assorted performances are given in Salzburg, enjoyed by around a quarter of a million spectators. In addition to great classical works, the festival provides a showcase for challenging modern music and drama. A recent innovation is the digital transmission of some of the top opera performances to cinema screens in many countries . . . but there's no substitute for being there and experiencing the festival's live delights in the magical atmosphere of Salzburg.

There is also a Salzburg Easter Festival that presents opera and orchestral concerts over Whitsun weekend.

Spectacular performances take place in Salzburg's squares.

Cow's Ball

WHEN:
Mid September
WHERE:
Lake Bohinj, Gorenjska province
BEST FOR:
Folklore and country pursuits
YOU SHOULD KNOW:
While you are here you should on
no account miss the stunning 15th
and 16th century frescoes in the
tiny church of St John the Baptist
in Ribcev Laz at the other end of
the lake.

Traditionally, Alpine farming communities have always marked one of the most important events in their calendar – the return of the cattle from their summer pastures in the mountains to the lower valleys. Few places celebrate the homecoming of the bovine beauties with more gusto than Lake Bohinj in the Julian Alps of northwest Slovenia. This beautiful, unspoiled glacial lake lies a short distance south of the country's highest peak, Mount Triglav, and is the setting every September for the Kravji Bal or Cow's Ball.

Local residents from all the villages around the lake gather with visitors and tourists in the hamlet of Ukanc at the western end to watch the returning cows being paraded through the streets. Richly decorated with garlands of flowers and bells, the cows are escorted by their herdsmen and by dairymaids and cheese-makers, all wearing traditional dress.

The Cow's Ball is an excuse for a weekend of feasting, drinking and outdoor merrymaking. There is lots of music and folk dancing, and light-hearted contests in traditional country pursuits such as sawing logs, sling shooting and casting horseshoes. Although the dairy farming that the area is famed for has suffered a marked decline from its heyday at the end of the 19th century, you will still find plenty of local produce on sale in the many market stalls at the Cow's Ball, including delicious local cheeses.

A month previously, Lake Bohinj also provides the setting for Slovenia's equivalent of bonfire night, when flotillas of candle-lit boats on the lake and a huge fireworks display commemorate the Feast of the Assumption.

Cows are escorted through the streets by herdsmen during Cow's Ball.

Bridge Jumping at Mostar

The historic town of Mostar is enchantingly situated in a green valley surrounded by hills covered with deciduous trees, mountains rising in the distance. Mostar's famous Stari Most bridge, built in 1567 to boost trade between Turkey and Europe, towers above the greenish-blue waters of the River Neretva as it thrashes through the centre of town. Historically, on July 31 each year, local men competed in diving from the bridge into the chilly waters beneath. Today, the interest in extreme sports brings people from many different countries to try their luck here.

Mostar's history is long, complex and, recently, tragic; it suffered appallingly during the Balkan civil war of the 1990s, when it was bombed, shelled and laid siege to by both Bosnian Serbs and the Croats. Much of the town was razed, including Stari Most, and the scars of war are still visible. Today, in a spirit of reconciliation, Mostar is governed by both Croats and Bosnian Muslims, and a huge reconstruction project is ongoing. Psychologically, its most important work was the rebuilding, stone for stone, of Stari Most. Partially funded by UNESCO, it is now listed as a World Heritage Site.

Protected at each end by fortified towers, the bridge stands some 21 m (70 ft) above the river – an Olympic high-diving platform is a mere 10 m (33 ft). During the summer, many young men earn themselves extra money by collecting payment from passing tourists. When a small crowd has gathered, off they leap, usually feet first. At the diving competition, however, the river banks are crowded with locals and tourists alike. All watch with their hearts in their mouths as more and more perfectly executed dives, including somersaults and backflips, are performed to wild cheers and applause.

WHEN:
July, but check with the Tourist Board
WHERE:
Stari Most Bridge, Mostar
BEST FOR:
Local tradition – young men have been jumping from this bridge for centuries – and extreme sport
YOU SHOULD KNOW:
This feat must be taken very seriously. It is extremely easy to get hurt if you are not an experienced high-diver. The local lads are very territorial about their bridge – pay up if you want to have a go, or risk being hurt by both the river and the lads.

A head for heights and plenty of courage is needed for this jump.

Winged Dragon International Street Theatre Festival in Nyirbator

WHEN:
July
WHERE:
Nyirbator
BEST FOR:
International street theatre
YOU SHOULD KNOW:
The Bathory family produced several Transylvanian Princes, one King of Poland and 'Blood Countess' Elizabeth. She and four collaborators were accused of the torture and murder of hundreds of young women. Found guilty as charged, her assistants were all executed and she was bricked into a suite of rooms in Cachtice Castle where she died four years later.

Hungarians don't need much of an excuse to hold a festival, and you'll find they take place in towns and villages all over the country, throughout the year. Nyirbator, in the northern Great Plain region of eastern Hungary, is no exception. Its Winged Dragon International Street Theatre Festival draws thousands of people both from around the country and much further afield.

With a population of little more than 13,000, Nyirbator is an historic town. First recorded as a settlement in 1279, the Bathory family owned the land. They were a highly influential, noble family and the town became the administrative centre for all their interests and estates. Istvan Bathory built the town's two churches, one of which – St George's Church – is perhaps the most important Gothic building in the country. The Bathory family coat of arms, granted in 1325, refers to a legendary victory by a member of the clan against a marauding dragon – hence the name and logo of Nyirbator's street-theatre festival.

For a week in July, Nyirbator is over-run with extravagantly costumed street performers, both individuals and troupes. You'll see human statues, operettas, morality plays, Punch and Judy shows, fire eaters, clowns, assorted puppeteers and chainsaw jugglers, as well as any number of musicians playing weird and wonderful instruments.

There are so many shows to see, often performed by international artists, that in order to enjoy one you'll have to forego another, simultaneous event. As well as all the street theatre, there are kite-flying exhibitions, arts-and-crafts stalls, fabulous firework displays and a huge, traditional feast. If you want to get away from it all for a moment, you can relax in the healing thermal baths, or take a walk by beautiful Lake Szenaret.

Puppeteers perform during the Street Theatre Festival.

Sziget Festival, Budapest

A huge crowd enjoys the opening concert.

Budapest, Hungary's capital, is widely acclaimed as one of Europe's most beautiful cities, welcoming over 20 million visitors each year. Located in the centre of the country, the city is divided by the River Danube, with hilly Buda on the western bank and the flatter Pest on the east. There are seven islands in the river, including Obudai-Sziget, a man-made entertainment centre, and it is here that the Sziget Festival takes place each year.

In comparison with many other festivals, Sziget is not particularly expensive.

Lasting for a week each August, it is one of the largest music festivals in existence, showing over 1,000 performances to about 400,000 people, some of whom stay in town and some of whom camp on the island in a temporary city complete with bank, post office, shops, bars and restaurants. This is a well-run event, made simpler to police by the fact that there is only one way in or out – across the bridge connecting it to the city. While security is visible, it is neither overwhelming nor inhibiting.

Every sort of music can be enjoyed here, even classical concerts and opera. You can watch theatre, cinema, cabaret and dance, bungee jump, play football, try table tennis or swim – though not in the Danube, as it is both against the law and dangerous. You can dance all night and sleep all day – if you have earplugs; this is a fantastic party. You'll meet like-minded souls from all over Europe, eat well and cheaply, over-indulge and wake up to discover you had a tattoo done while you were on another planet. Your first sight of the crowds queuing to cross the bridge may make your heart sink, but people are friendly and the pounding music is so exciting that you'll be through the gates and into Szigetland before you know it.

WHEN:
August
WHERE:
Obudai-Sziget, Budapest
BEST FOR:
Music, dancing and partying 24/7
YOU SHOULD KNOW:
If you plan to come to Sziget, do your homework well in advance; you'll find it pays off. Try to stay for a few extra days so that you can explore and enjoy this absolutely gorgeous city

337

Festival floats come in all shapes and sizes.

Flower Festival and St Stephen's Day in Debrecen

Debrecen, Hungary's second-largest city, is the regional centre of the area known as the Great Hungarian Plain, some 220 km (137 mi) east of Budapest. Debrecen's physical location, close to Romania, Slovakia and Ukraine, ensures that it will continue to grow, not just in size but in importance as good transport links bring more international trade.

Debrecen is an ancient town, formed from a number of small villages. It was sufficiently important to choose its own judge and council by 1361; by the early 17th century it had become a large market town; and in 1849 it was briefly Hungary's capital city. Debrecen went from strength to strength until being almost totally destroyed in World War II, only recovering its second-city status in the 1990s. It hosts a number of splendid festivals during the year, the most significant and spectacular of which is the Flower Festival.

This week-long fiesta, which has been celebrated for 100 years, attracts about 500,000 visitors to its climax on August 20, which is also St Stephen's Day and a national holiday. After days of concerts and performances by Hungarian and international musicians and dance companies, events culminate in the most stunning parade of hundreds of flower floats. Accompanied by flag-waving majorettes and marching bands, it moves through the city to the stadium. It is said that up to 1,000,000 flowers are used for one float, and certainly the intricate and colourful designs are so detailed that it could be true. There's a festive, carnival atmosphere: stalls fill the main square, selling food, crafts and other bargains. Pay a small entrance fee and go into the stadium where you can admire the floats at leisure and enjoy the Folk Dance Show. The festival closes on a high note – more music and an excellent firework display.

WHEN:
August, during the week leading up to St Stephen's Day (August 20)
WHERE:
Debrecen
BEST FOR:
Hungarian culture and flowers
YOU SHOULD KNOW:
If you are planning on sampling this festival, be sure to book your hotel well in advance. The city also hosts a major choral competition – the Bela Bartok International Choir Competition.

Lajkonik Festival, Krakow

Krakow, Poland's second city, stands at the foot of the Carpathian Mountains, on the River Vistula. Dating back to the 7th century, this ancient city which was once the capital has always been a major player in the country's artistic and creative life, its charms drawing over seven million tourists each year.

Krakow escaped the worst ravages of World War II, but the postwar Communist government changed it from being a university town to an industrial one. Today academe is thriving once again, with over 20 universities, academies and colleges educating almost 200,000 students. Consequently Krakow is vibrant, awash with restaurants, cafés, bars and nightspots, and hosting numerous festivals and artistic events.

Visit the city's UNESCO-listed historic centre during June and catch the Lajkonik Festival, which has taken place for centuries in remembrance of the defeat of the Tartars in 1241. Although its origin is probably mythical, thousands of people turn out to cheer a man costumed as a Tartar warrior riding a white hobbyhorse for a couple of hours through the cobbled streets to the famous Market Square. This colourful figure, sporting a highly decorated pointed hat, wields a golden mace.

Street entertainers and followers accompany Lajkonik Man, some wearing traditional Krakowian costume and others flowing Oriental garments. Musicians play loud, high pitched music and Lajkonik Man collects donations and touches people with his mace for good luck, whilst prancing and dashing about. In the Market Square the mayor awaits with a symbolic heap of ransom money and a goblet of wine with which to toast the city and all its inhabitants. Music and merriment continue in the square until the participants decide it's time to move into the many nearby bars – Poles don't need an excuse to drink vodka, but the Lajkonik festival offers a good one.

WHEN:
June – the date varies, so check in advance.
WHERE:
The historic centre of Krakow, starting at the Convent of St Norbert and ending at the Market Square
BEST FOR:
Traditional Krakowian culture and a night out on the town
YOU SHOULD KNOW:
The Mongol invasion is remembered in another tradition in Krakow. The Hejnal trumpet call, which rings out every hour from a church tower in the Market Square, is abruptly cut off at the end. This is in memory of the trumpet player shot through the throat with an arrow as he tried to warn the city's inhabitants of the approaching Tartar horde.

Lajkonik Man rides a white hobbyhorse and dispenses good luck with his mace.

International Highland Folk Festival, Zakopane

WHEN:
August
WHERE:
Zakopane
BEST FOR:
Folk music, dance, song and costumes from around the world
YOU SHOULD KNOW:
Zakopane has hosted the Nordic World Ski Championships three times, the Biathlon World Championship, several ski jumping world cups and the 1939 Alpine World Ski Championship – the first to be held outside the Alps.

Zakopane, which is some two hours south of Krakow, is a delightful Alpine resort in the Tatra Mountains. Renowned for its beauty since the 1800s, the town itself is charming, boasting unusual and marvellously decorated wooden buildings. In winter the skiing is fabulous and in summer many people hike the mountain trails. Those less energetic can take the funicular to the viewpoint at the top of Mount Gubalowka or stay put at a café table, drinking coffee and people watching.

Every year since 1968, Zakopane has held an International Highland Folk Festival. Modest to begin with, the festival's popularity has grown so much that it now presents four categories of competition, taking place over eight days, each category offering a golden, silver and bronze Highlander's axe. Since its inception, about 500 folk groups from over 60 countries have competed here, as well as over 200 Polish groups, all singing, dancing and playing the music of their own highland territory, and wearing their own traditional dress. Classic Zakopane dress has women wearing vividly coloured, flowery dresses and scarves, and men wearing white shirts, embroidered breeches and a round black hat.

The festival kicks off with a joyful street parade, in which all the contestants participate. Groups come from all over the world, and it's a fantastic sight – you're as likely to see a team from China or Bolivia as from Russia or Hungary. Concerts are held in the tented town that appears in the valley and the programme traditionally includes a Highland Wedding and a Coachman of the Year competition. Bored with folk music? Sample the umpteen other delights on offer – try Highlander food from around the world, learn a folk dance, visit the museum, craft market or local artists' studios, and always enjoy the wonderfully clean air and the glorious scenery.

Traditional folk dancers perform at the festival.

Prague Spring International Music Festival

Renowned as one of Europe's most glorious cities, Prague's cultural and architectural heritage is second to none. Beautifully situated on the Vltava, the Czech Republic's longest river, the city welcomes millions of visitors each year. The Prague Spring International Music Festival, one of the most famous classical music festivals in the world, attracts quantities of people to its almost three-week long extravaganza.

Coinciding with the 50th anniversary of the Czech Philharmonic Orchestra, the festival was first organized on May 11 1946 by President Edvard Benes. In recognition of the high esteem in which the orchestra was held, it performed all the orchestral concerts. In 1952 the date of the festival was moved forward by one day to honour the death of Bedrich Smetana, the country's most significant composer, and so it has remained ever since.

The show begins with a ceremony at Smetana's grave, followed by a procession to Smetana Hall. It always opens with his composition *Ma Vlast* (My Country) and, until a few years ago, ended with Beethoven's Ninth Symphony. Since 2004, however, a different work by Antonin Dvorak provides each year's finale. Opera, chamber music, soloists and symphonies can be heard in various venues, most traditionally in the neo-Renaissance Rudolfinum concert hall and the Art Nouveau Municipal House. Czech composers feature heavily, as does Mozart, who visited Prague and composed several pieces relating to the city. The festival celebrates musical anniversaries and premieres new works by contemporary composers.

Prague Spring International Music Festival also hosts a major competition for young musicians, showcasing two disciplines per year. The winners can expect a glittering career – in the past they have included Mstislav Rostropovich, James Galway and Maurice Bourgue. If you love classical music, Prague is a truly magical city in which to enjoy it.

WHEN:
Three weeks in May
WHERE:
Various venues in Prague
BEST FOR:
Classical music
YOU SHOULD KNOW:
Rostropovich, the world-famous Russian cellist, was the first winner of the competition and he met his wife-to-be at the festival. When Russia invaded Czechoslovakia in 1968, Rostropovich vowed not to perform in the country again until it was free. In 1991, after the Velvet Revolution, he accepted a personal invitation to come and perform again from the new Czech president Vaclav Havel, himself a distinguished playwright.

Israeli violinist Gil Shahan performs at the festival.

World Roma Khamoro Festival

Festivals and cultural events take place throughout the year in the Czech Republic's glorious capital city, Prague, and every May since 1999 it has hosted the exciting Khamoro festival, celebrating Roma music and dance, and highlighting Roma culture from a different country each year.

Roma history is hard to pin down, partly because, traditionally, there was no written language. However, the Roma are believed to have originated with groups migrating from northern India c. 1000, and were recorded in Czechoslovakia by the 1300s. These semi-nomadic people have been persecuted, enslaved, discriminated against and murdered throughout the centuries by the indigenous people of the countries to which they migrated. Almost all Czech Roma are descended from Slovakian Roma, as the authorities virtually wiped them out during World War II. The Khamoro Festival, sponsored by the government, Slovo 21 (an NGO), the City of Prague and media partners, aims to promote a greater understanding of the Roma among the Czech population.

During this week-long shindig, you can enjoy Roma jazz, traditional music or classical music. You can attend films, theatre, dance, workshops and exhibitions, all presenting different aspects of Roma culture from around the world. Simultaneously, an international ethnomusicology conference takes place, with seminars open to all.

Roma women perform traditional dance in the streets.

WHEN:
May
WHERE:
Various venues in Prague
BEST FOR:
Worldwide Roma culture
YOU SHOULD KNOW:
In August 2008, the European Commission condemned a new Italian law ordering the fingerprinting of all Roma in the country, noting that it 'is very similar to the one used by Nazis and fascists before the mass killings started in the '30s and '40s'.

The festival opens with a colourful parade that moves from Mustek to the Old Town Square. After that, it's up to you: there is such diversity here, both in the music itself and the performers' countries of origin. You can see world-class jazz, or possibly Spanish flamenco, maybe music and dance from northern India – all totally different, all exciting and made even more so by the astonishingly dramatic traditional dress that is worn. If you are in town and can only catch one event, try to make the grand finale: a gala concert featuring all the musicians who have performed during the week.

World Festival of Puppet Art

May is a great month to be in Prague, the Czech Republic's stunning capital city. Always lively, with events and festivals thick on the ground, Prague hosts seven major events that occur annually in May. One of the best of these is the World Festival of Puppet Art, entrancing adults and children alike with both traditional and utterly innovative shows from around the globe.

Puppeteering is an ancient art that is far more complex than might first appear, and puppetry in the Czech Republic is world class. It was first used in 12th century religious ceremonies and became a staple of the population's cultural diet in the 1700s. For centuries, people all over the world have been both entertained and informed by the different types of puppet show – around 20 different types of puppets exist, from the simplest finger puppets to complicated marionettes made of many different materials, and Wayang Kulit – the intricately cut-out shadow puppets native to Indonesia.

The festival, which takes place in several theatres as well as in the Old Town Square every evening, is also a competition. It is, to the world of puppeteers, the equivalent of the Oscars. An international jury awards prizes for Best Actor, Best Director, Best Scenery and Puppet Design, Best Original Performance, Best Artistic Creation, Best Performance, Best Scenario, Best Puppet Film, Best Animation, and various special awards.

One of the joys of the medium is that language is not as much of a barrier as it might be with theatre or film – and every year troupes come from English-speaking countries, so the chances are you'll find something you want to see. What's more, the inevitable Puppet Parade through the streets is a good deal more fun than watching movie stars walk the red carpet to the Kodak Theatre in Hollywood on Oscars night.

WHEN:
May, but check the dates before you go.
WHERE:
Prague
BEST FOR:
Puppet shows, old and new
YOU SHOULD KNOW:
Many unlikely people famous in other walks of life practised puppetry, such as Howard Stern (US broadcaster), Henrik Ibsen (Norwegian playwright), Jean Cocteau (French writer/film maker), Pete Seeger (US folk singer) and Johann Wolfgang von Goethe (German writer/artist/scientist).

Pohoda Music Festival

WHEN:
July, but check for the exact dates.
WHERE:
Trencin Airport, Trencin
BEST FOR:
Music of all genres
YOU SHOULD KNOW:
In 2008, Vaclev Havel, former
President of the Czech Republic and
playwright, attended Pohoda, where
two of his plays were being
performed. Here he met singer Joan
Baez for the first time since a
concert held in Bratislava in 1989.
That was prior to the Velvet
Revolution, when Havel was a
dissident. When Baez boldly greeted
him from the stage, the organizers
reacted by turning off all the
electricity in the concert hall.

The beautifully situated city of Trencin lies in the Vah River valley, surrounded by the Strazov Mountains. With its historic city centre and a stunning medieval castle perched above, it provides a fantastic backdrop for Slovakia's number one music festival. Inhabited since forever, there's a fascinating Roman inscription adorning the rocks beneath the castle, dating from AD 179. In 1790 the town and castle were burnt down. Used as the Gestapo's headquarters during World War II, Trencin was captured by Soviet troops in 1945. Both the historic centre and the castle, now a national monument, have largely been restored.

Pohoda Music Festival was started in 1997 in an attempt to redress the balance between the many festivals held in the Czech Republic, and the few offered in Slovakia. Although about 2,000 people attended, only 140 tickets were sold. Since then Pohoda, which means 'relaxation', has grown exponentially. In 2008, attendance at the two-day festival surpassed 30,000 for the first time, and international as well as national musicians played on seven main stages.

Pohoda prides itself on its celebration of all the arts, its broad mixture of music, and the fact that it attracts people of all ages as well as many nations. You can enjoy anything from rock and techno to folk and world music, or opera and classical music. Watch films or theatre, take workshops, paint, bungee jump, chill out on beanbags in the shady Tuli Zone, record your own music and dance the night away at the Silent Disco, where you'll be given headphones and a choice of music to dance to. Pohoda is a laid-back affair: there's plenty of room to camp, people are friendly, food and drink are plentiful and cheap, there's a huge choice of music, the surroundings are gorgeous and the sun almost always shines.

You can listen to many different types of music at Pohoda.

EXIT Music Festival

Novi Sad, Serbia's second city, is set in a bend of the Danube. Its 19th century centre, ringed by modern tower blocks, lies over the river from an old town built around a massive 18th century citadel. Petrovaradin Fortress towers over its surroundings and is known as 'the Gibraltar of the Danube', for it never fell to invaders. Usually a peaceful place with galleries and museums, since 2001 it has been besieged every summer by an army of exuberant music lovers, surrounded by a riverside city of tents, bombarded by a heavy barrage of sound.

The EXIT Festival (Exit out of Ten Years of Madness) started in 2000 and was a thinly disguised protest against Milosevic. Organized by three university students and lasting 100 days, it mixed music, discussion groups, drama and workshops. The general election held the day after after the festival finished marked the beginning of the end for the dictator and EXIT was firmly established, with left-wing support and funding. Since its relocation to the Fortress in 2001 it has grown and now has more commercial input. Performers and audiences are international, and, despite a background of continuing political intrigues, EXIT is now very much a summer music bash and indeed won a 'Best European Festival' award in 2007. A dozen or more stages in the Fortress accommodate hundreds of acts playing Hip Hop, Reggae, Metal, Electronica, Latin, Rock and more. Big names in recent years have included Wu-Tang-Clan, Iggy Pop, Neneh Cherry, Billy Idol and Paul Weller, while bands from all over the former Yugoslavia appear. Around 150,000 fans enjoy the music, long nights of unrestrained drinking, pogo-ing and other pleasures.

WHEN:
Three days in July
WHERE:
Novi Sad
BEST FOR:
Music
YOU SHOULD KNOW:
Around the Fortress, an extreme sports arena and open-air cinema provide alternative entertainment and in 2006 big screens allowed football fans to catch up with the World Cup.

Music lovers flock to the popular EXIT Music Festival.

EUROPE/CROATIA

Rijeka Carnival

WHEN:
January/February/March
WHERE:
Rijeka, Primorje-Gorski
BEST FOR:
Magnificent masquerade
YOU SHOULD KNOW:
The first Rijeka Carnival Parade in 1982 had just three performing groups and attracted no attention beyond the city. From little acorns . . .

Croatia's largest seaport is located in an impressive natural setting on an inlet of the Adriatic Sea. This busy transport hub is not an automatic tourist destination, though it has fine buildings and plenty of visitors do pass through in summer. But the highlight of Rijeka's year for locals and tourists alike is undoubtedly the Latin-style carnival. This has been established in its current form for barely a quarter of a century, but has already become a massive occasion that attracts attention far beyond Croatia's borders.

Despite its youth, the Rijeka Carnival follows the long-practised Slav tradition of Maskare where people gather to fight evil, banish winter and look forward to the fertility of spring. Local folklore calls for the wearing of grotesque masks that scare away evil spirits whilst the Zvoncari (bellringers) are attired in sheepskins and sport rams' horns as they prance symbolically to protect the nation.

To this traditional mix has been added more conventional elements like Rijeka's mayor delivering the city's keys to the Master of the Carnival, followed by a Carnival Queen contest and victor's crowning. The following days are filled with exhibitions, concerts, parties and general festivities . . . including a Children's Carnival Procession with 20 allegoric floats attended by 5,000 incredibly excited youngsters.

It all leads up to the main event. The International Carnival Parade sees 100 brightly decorated floats from many countries progress through the city, accompanied by 10,000 masked participants, with the whole extravaganza watched by well over 100,000 enchanted spectators. The atmosphere is competitive, with each float seeking to outdo the others in terms of originality and humour. After the parade comes the Burning of Pust on a boat in Rijeka harbour – he is a puppet blamed for everything bad that happened in the preceding year, which hopefully burns with him.

Bell ringers dressed in sheepskins ward off danger.

Dubrovnik Summer Festival

The ancient trading centre of Dubrovnik on the Adriatic rivalled Venice for power and influence in the Middle Ages, and this fascinating city certainly merits its UNESCO World Heritage Site status – with ravages caused by a Serbian-inspired siege in the early 1990s now happily (and invisibly) repaired.

The civilized character of this delightful port is emphasized by the annual Dubrovnik Summer Festival, which always opens with the words of the 17th century Croatian writer Ivan Gundulic, who predicted the downfall of the mighty Ottoman Empire and his country's eventual freedom. The keys of the city are then ceremonially handed to actors, artists and performers who make a ceremonial entrance to the walled city in anticipation of entertaining the people of Dubrovnik and their visitors for over a month.

A rapt audience enjoys a concert in front of St Blaise Church.

This dramatic opening ceremony concludes with fireworks and music, heralding the series of theatrical performances, concerts, operas and dance that takes place on open-air stages and in assorted indoor venues throughout the city. Notable sites are the Baroque Dubrovnik Cathedral, the beautiful Gunduli Square, Luza Square before the magnificent 18th century St Blaise's Church, the now-uninhabited wooded island of Lokrum with its ancient Abbey and Annunciation Church, the monumental Lovrjenac Fort built in the 11th century to repel the Venetians, the atrium of the stunning Sponza Palace and the 15th century Rector's Palace, now a splendid museum. These and other historic locations add a unique dimension to the performances they host.

When conceived in the late 1940s, the festival was intended as a musical platform for local composers, orchestras and soloists, but it has subsequently developed into a truly international occasion that has broadened its cultural remit to offer music, theatre, dance, poetry and folklore, often featuring significant premieres and attracting prestigious performers (and visitors) from all over the world.

WHEN:
July/August
WHERE:
Dubrovnik, Dubrovnik-Neretva
BEST FOR:
Cultural excellence in incomparable settings
YOU SHOULD KNOW:
Most of the festival's major events start in mid-evening, allowing ample time to enjoy this fabulous Renaissance city during the day.

The Pageant of the Juni

WHEN:
April/May
WHERE:
Brasov
BEST FOR:
Mounted festivities
YOU SHOULD KNOW:
Brasov's Lutheran Black Church is not in fact black – a fire in 1689 gave it that name. It is one of the largest Gothic churches in Europe and its interior is hung with a large collection of fine Turkish carpets, brought home from their travels by Transylvanian Saxon merchants.

Transylvanian Saxons built defensive walls around Brasov during the 13th century, when it became a wealthy centre of trade, and it is now one of the largest and best-preserved medieval towns in Romania. Long stretches of the walls, complete with towers, gates and bastions, surround a fascinating network of residential streets, the huge, brooding Black Church and – the heart of the city – Piata Sfatului (Council Square), which is lined with splendid Renaissance and Baroque buildings. In the 13th century native Romanians lived in Schei, a town just southwest of the city, and were only allowed inside the walls on certain dates. One of these, usually the first Sunday in May, is remembered with the Pageant of the Juni.

This is a glorious piece of drama. 'Juni' comes from the Latin for young men, and it is unmarried men who don superbly elaborate costumes encrusted with beading, embroidery and applied silverwork, and ride in groups named after famous regiments, each with its own 'uniform'. Some of the costumes are over 150 years old. On the day of the pageant the bachelors, on horses harnessed with fringes and tassels, ride sword in hand from Schei, through the city to Piata Sfatului. They are closely followed by the 'old Juni' (married men) and exuberant brass bands. The cavalcade returns to Shei and then continues to Solomon's Rocks on the lower slopes of the imposing Mount Tampa.

Elaborately dressed bachelors ride into the city of Brasov.

Unmarried men are the stars of the show but this was never a matchmaking event, rather a coming-of-age celebration. Some 'trials', such as 'throwing the mace', are retained, but the modern pageant ends with music and dancing. The hora circle dance with its hypnotic, rhythmic swaying and stamping forms the centrepiece of the hillside party.

The Maidens' Fair

Part of the Western Carpathians, the Apuseni Mountains with their steep crags, sheer gorges and spectacular caves, have some of Romania's most dramatic scenery. The extensive limestone uplands are home to a scattered people (the Mots); the rugged terrain that separates the villages also unites their inhabitants, who gather from their isolated communities at the annual Targul de Fete (Maidens' Fair) on Mount Gaina, a flat-topped massif surrounded by glorious countryside. Now largely an opportunity to meet, socialize and celebrate, this fair was originally a marriage market. Young women, after long preparation and surrounded by watchful relations, would display their charms – and their dowries in elaborately carved chests; subsequently, engagements and marriage contracts were formalized. Though matchmaking is no longer an official part of the fair, it seems probable that couples do still meet, talk, dance and fall in love.

The modern fair is essentially a folk festival, though it also offers shopping opportunities; farming paraphernalia and local crafts are displayed and traded. Early in the morning, the opening of events is heralded by the amazing sound of a group of alpenhorns, played by women who, like many of the Mots, wear beautiful traditional costume. Colourful, thickly embroidered waistcoats and long overskirts are worn over white shirts and dresses, heavy with hand-made lace. Dances always include the hora; dancers form a large circle and stamp, sway and clap to a chanted rhythm. Food and drink are copious and usually include spit-roasted lamb and mamaliga, a dish of polenta with bacon and onions; liquid refreshment may be local wines or tuica, a fiery plum brandy. Music, dancing and feasting continue all day and, round a huge bonfire, late into the night.

WHEN:
The weekend closest to July 20,
St Elijah's Day
WHERE:
Mount Gaina, about 30 km (19 mi)
west of Campeni village, 100 km
(62 mi) east of Arad
BEST FOR:
A traditional fair
YOU SHOULD KNOW:
Mount Gaina (Hen Mountain) was
home to a legendary hen which laid
golden eggs. Once a year,
transformed into a beautiful
goddess, she handed out her
precious eggs to couples who were
truly in love. A greedy man spoilt
things by trying to trap the hen; he
was swallowed by a crevasse. The
hen flew off, never to return.

Pes Ponedelnik – Kukeri Festival in Shiroka Luka

WHEN:
The first Sunday in March
WHERE:
Shiroka Luka – 12 km (7.5 mi) from
the ski resort, Pamporova;
24 km (15 mi) from Smolyan
BEST FOR:
Fertility rites
YOU SHOULD KNOW:
Delightful Shiroka Luka is known for
its Folk Instrument and Music School,
where local musicians play, and the
naif frescoes in its church. It is built
in a narrow valley along a river
crossed by hump-backed bridges and
its attractive old houses are solidly
built and roofed with stone.

The origins of Bulgaria's remarkable Kukeri festivals are ancient and obscure – disputing folklorists have suggested Dionysian, Orphic, Thracian, even Egyptian – but it is clear that they concern death, rebirth and fecundity. These age-old rituals are enacted in a number of villages and vary a little, but in essence they are sympathetic magic – fertility rites – for these isolated farming communities depend on the cycle of the sun.

The dancers are men, and the massive costumes are spectacular and terrifying. Heavy under-layers are covered by a huge outer robe, sometimes covered in seed heads, reeds or scarves, tassels and ribbons, but usually with very longhaired goat- or sheepskins. It is built up into a towering headdress surrounding a carved mask, often a goat-like face, its curling horns twined with ivy, ribbons and beads. Jangling bells may complete the outfit.

Dancers visit village homes, collecting 'taxes' of food to ensure a successful harvest, and frightening away the lingering evil spirits of winter. In the square, villagers watch as the Kukeri leap over fires and perform dances which portray mock marriages and births or ploughing and sowing, and honouring the rotation of the seasons. This is magic for the last days of winter, a prayer to the god of vegetation and the sun. In most villages now it takes place around New Year, but in Shiroka Luka it is still celebrated to coincide with the ancient New Year, at the beginning of spring. Some Kukeri festivals close to large towns have been somewhat diluted by the modern world, but here, deep in the Rhodope Mountains in a place inhabited since pre-history, tradition is still very powerful.

A masked dancer performs his magic at the opening ceremony.

Valley of the Roses Festival

Roses have been grown commercially in Bulgaria's Valley of the Roses since the 18th century, when the Ottomans realized that the soil and climate (regular light rain combined with cloud-tempered sun) were perfect for the heavily scented varieties which produce attar (extract) of roses, the highly prized base of so many expensive perfumes. The lush green foothills of the Balkan Range form the Valley of the Roses. The area extends east from Karlova to Kazanlak, the 'Rose Capital' and centre for distillation where a museum explains the history and processes of the industry.

The roses – rosa alba and the red damask rose – are grown on small farms, for this is a labour-intensive business. The blooms must be picked very early, before the sun dries the dew – this limits oil evaporation and prolongs the flowering season. The painstaking work is done by women and children, usually from the farmers' extended families. The slow distillation process was originally a cottage industry; now countless sacks of petals are transported to commercial plants. It takes thousands of kilos of petals to produce one litre of attar, which is sold for huge sums all over the world. Growers are currently concerned that the hotter, drier weather experienced recently is causing the roses to become sparse.

At the end of the harvest, the Festival of the Roses celebrates not only the flowers, but youth and beauty. It was originally held at the beginning of the harvest, when the growers organized parades of rose-clad workers. Now, workers and villagers from the whole area, all dressed in traditional costume, join in a street parade with music and dancing, watch the symbolic harvesting of roses by children, and honour the newly elected Queen Rose.

The Queen of the festival encourages her entourage to throw roses in the air.

WHEN:
The first Sunday in June
WHERE:
Kazanlak
BEST FOR:
Roses
YOU SHOULD KNOW:
Much rose oil now goes to Japan, where it is used to produce edible capsules. The Japanese like to smell flowery – one (presumably very expensive) capsule a week perfumes the whole body.

Patras Carnival

WHEN:
January 17 until the last weekend before Lent (Greek Orthodox dates)
WHERE:
Patras
BEST FOR:
Carnival
YOU SHOULD KNOW:
The popular Bourboulia, now held in the Apollo Theatre, began in the 19th century when masked and robed society ladies escaped their chaperones at an afternoon dance where, alone and incognito, they could choose their own partners.

Known chiefly as the principal port for Italy and the Ionian islands, Patras is a big, mainly modern town also famous for its exceptionally high-spirited carnival. This can be traced back to the 19th century, when a wealthy merchant threw some famously lively carnival parties and balls. Later, with the introduction of floats and parades, it expanded to include all the inhabitants of Patras. Two World Wars, the bitter Civil War and the years of Junta rule effectively curtailed the event, but since the 1970s, Patras Carnival has flourished and now the exuberant festivities attract visitors from all over Greece.

This is a very long party; irrespective of the date of Easter, it begins in January, on the feast of St Anthony, with an opening ceremony, music and dance. Much of the time between this and the last wild weekend before Lent is taken up with 'The Treasure Hunt Game'. This – part talent contest, part quiz and part initiative test – involves the city's young people in tradition; they form large groups, which then take part in competitions and create elaborate floats. Other regular events are the Children's Carnival and Tsiknopempti – Smoky Thursday – when, all over town, fat is thrown onto the coals of the many barbecues to produce huge clouds of smoke, before the serious business of cooking, eating and drinking. The final weekend is one of processions and fun. The torchlit Saturday Night Parade moves through the town accompanied by bands, while the Great Sunday Parade has so many floats and marchers that it takes hours to pass through the packed streets. On the waterfront, amid music and dancing, formalities conclude with the burning of the Carnival King, fireworks and more partying.

Huge elaborate floats are created for the parade.

Skyros Goat Dance

The isolated island of Skyros is known for its family 'museums' (open-fronted rooms packed with folk art), its tiny wild ponies (thought to be identical to those carved on the Parthenon friezes), its goat meat and milk – and the Goat Dance in Hora, Skyros' main town. This very traditional island has many lively festivals, but the

The bells of the goatmen, or Yeri, *ring out as they walk the streets.*

Horos tou Tragou (the word tragedy comes from *tragoudia*, 'goat songs'), though thinly Christianized as the Apokries (pre-Lenten) Carnival, remains a mysterious, potent and undeniably pagan celebration.

The dancers, all men, wear goat masks; these were in the past cut from the skin of a kid, and became so unpleasantly smelly they needed frequent spraying with ouzo – now they may well be made of plastic. Their costumes represent three distinct characters: the *Frangi* (Westerners) scare children by hooting down conch shells, while the *Korelles* (maidens) dress as Skyrian brides and the most important of the trio are the *Yeri* (the old men). The *Yeros* is a real bogeyman; his nightmarish costume combines shepherd's dress – white cross-gartered leggings and breeches and a very hairy coat – with a hump made of rags and a weighty harness of copper goat bells. He carries a shepherd's crook partly to threaten onlookers but also to balance himself – the bells are very heavy and the *Yeri* are played by strong men who often become local celebrities – while he performs the swaying, clanging 'dance' and lurches through the steep narrow streets. Women and children, also in fancy dress, follow the dancers and join in the singing, dancing and feasting.

WHEN:
The last weekend before (Orthodox) Lent begins (usually February)
WHERE:
The island of Skyros
BEST FOR:
Primitive abandon
YOU SHOULD KNOW:
Skyros has a long tradition of cross-dressing. Following the prophecy that Achilles would die at Troy, his mother sent him to King Lykomedes' court disguised as a girl. Suspicious Odysseus visited with gifts; the ladies of the court seized baubles and trinkets but Achilles chose sword and shield – and went to meet his destiny.

Priests of the Orthodox Church walk through the town.

Greek Easter in Corfu Town

Easter, the most important festival of the Greek year, is observed similarly all over the country. Formal proceedings begin on Good Friday with Epitaphios, when processions leave every church accompanying Christ's garlanded funeral bier. Late on Saturday, crowds gather in and around churches for the Anastasis mass, celebrating Christ's triumph. At midnight, every light is extinguished; the priest announces 'This is the Light of the World' and starts a chain of candle lighting until the church is radiant. A great chorus of 'Christ is risen' and 'Truly He is risen' fills the streets and fireworks burst into the night.

There are regional variations, and Corfu has a few of its own. One is the participation of several 'philharmonic bands', whose members wear different-coloured uniforms and play an established repertoire. On Good Friday, Epitaphios from all over town, moving with great solemnity to funeral marches, converge on the Liston. Easter Saturday starts with a parade for the patron saint, Spiridon, commemorating his saving the town from famine. Next, the sound of smashing china fills the air, as pots and jugs of water plummet from balconies into the streets (probably a Venetian legacy, symbolizing a new beginning) accompanied by rather more up-tempo music from the bands. In the evening, the Catholic cathedral welcomes Orthodox worshippers before they attend their own churches. Then all the congregations flood down to the esplanade to hear the Bishop proclaim the joyful news. A huge firework display is followed by jubilant music from the massed bands as good tidings are spread through the wakeful town. The Lenten fast is broken and celebrations continue all night. After an early morning parade of icons, the faithful sleep before Easter feasting.

WHEN:
Orthodox Easter
WHERE:
Corfu Town
BEST FOR:
Exhilarating faith
YOU SHOULD KNOW:
Greek Easter has its special foods. In Holy Week, restaurants serve 'fasting dishes', such as salt cod. A rich Easter soup of lamb offal, lemon and eggs breaks the fast, and on Easter Sunday, red-dyed eggs are cracked together like conkers. In Corfu, columbines – Venetian bread rolls in the shape of doves – are eaten.

354

The Anastenaria

A sheep is slaughtered to the sound of music; later, barefoot devotees cross a bed of glowing embers. Surprisingly, this is rural Greece, most of the fire-walkers are women, and they carry icons. The ritual takes place in several villages north of Thessaloniki, supposedly in honour of saints Constantine and Helen.

Families who came to this area with the 1923 exchange of populations from Turkish Thrace, originated in Kosti – now in Bulgaria – where fire-walking still takes place. In each village a special shrine (*konaki*) houses icons and the large red handkerchiefs (*simadia*) are considered to have special powers. On the eve of the saints' day, the *astenaridhes* (groaners) engage in hours of devotional dancing. The next day a sheep is sacrificed and, at dusk, after more dancing in the *konaki*, the fire-walkers parade through the village carrying *simadia* (draped icons) accompanied by drum and lyre. They circle the raked coals and dance across them in a state of ecstatic trance until the ashes cool. During the next two days they process round the village, finishing with another fire-walk.

For years this ritual was performed in secret, and the church still refuses to hold services on the day. Now, however, visitors are welcomed at the first fire-walk. The origins of these rites are disputed. While villagers claim they began after icons were saved from a blazing church in 1250 and that faith protects them from the fire, there is much in common with the revels of Dionysus and his god-intoxicated Maenaeds, while the sacrifice – an intact animal whose blood is allowed to drain into the soil – surely has links with fertility rites.

WHEN:
May 20-21
WHERE:
Langhadas, 20 km (12.5 mi) north of Thessaloniki, is the most easily accessible village for visitors.
BEST FOR:
A strange experience
YOU SHOULD KNOW:
The dancers' feet are never burned; scientific tests suggest merely that their brain waves show an altered state. One sceptical visitor leapt into the coals and suffered bad burns.

A fire walker holds icons of St Constantine.

The Miaoulia

WHEN:
The Saturday closest to June 21
WHERE:
The island of Hydra
BEST FOR:
Watery pyrotechnics
YOU SHOULD KNOW:
Miaoulis did in fact use fire-ships to terrorize the Ottoman fleet; Ibrahim Pasha had so much grudging admiration for the admiral and his brave seamen he nicknamed Hydra 'Little England'.

Hydra, with its pretty harbour and tiers of pale mansions stacked on a semi-circle of grey rocks, is outrageously photogenic. It has long been a favourite with visitors: Athenian weekenders, artists, film makers and day trippers are captivated not only by its looks, but also by its peace – donkeys are the only form of transport on the island.

But seafaring, not tourism, lies at the true heart of Hydra. This barren island was settled by those who could make a living from the sea, and by the late 18th century it supported a large population whose wealth came from merchant shipping – and a little piracy. The Ottomans never occupied Hydra, but levied heavy taxes – including sailors, as a tribute to the Sultan. When Hydra joined the War of Independence, merchants quickly converted 130 of their vessels into warships, which became the backbone of the Greek navy. One of a number of fine Hydriot commanders, Admiral Andreas Miaoulis became Commander in Chief, and his integrity and superb seamanship eventually led to the successful blockade of the Turkish fleet.

One of Hydra's most famous and well-loved sons, he is honoured by the Miaoulia, part of the annual Navy Week celebrations. Days of athletic competitions, regattas, swimming races and song and dance culminate in a 'naval battle' in the harbour. Brass bands entertain the crowds until all the lights go out; then, under cover of darkness, a boat is rowed quietly out and the crew ignites a firework-filled replica of an Ottoman flagship. The ship explodes in a rainbow of fire and rockets, then cannons roar – a prelude to more fireworks and general merrymaking. On Sunday, a splendid parade precedes the laying of a wreath at the statue of Miaoulis.

Athens Festival

Performing arts have always been central to Greek culture. Modern theatre has its roots in Greek drama and the folk dances which are an essential part of social gatherings in Greece can be traced to the temple dances of antiquity. Cycladic figures dating to 2000 BC hold musical instruments and, while Western 'pop' thrives and classical music is mostly mainstream, traditional music flourishes. In 1955, the first Hellenic Festival based in Athens was held, featuring international stars and Greek artists at the Theatre of Herod Atticus on the southern slopes of the Acropolis. The military coup in 1967 effectively cut Greece off from the arts world, but after the fall of the Junta big names returned to Athens for a festival which lasted the whole summer.

Over the years, limited by its conservative programming, the festival lost its appeal to a wider public, but a new and visionary director has completely revitalized it. The festival now lasts just two months and uses locations across the city more suited to young and contemporary artists from home and abroad. Orchestral concerts, ballet and opera can still be found at the Herodeion, while popular music, experimental theatre, jazz, modern and world dance take place at venues which include the spectacular setting of Lykavittos Hill and the newly converted warehouse complex – Pireos 260 – which comprises small theatres, outside spaces and cafés and is perfectly suited to the new, cosmopolitan festival.

With its wider scope and excellent innovative programming, the Athens Hellenic Festival is once again one of Greece's most important and enjoyable cultural events.

The festival uses many locations across Athens.

WHEN:
June and July
WHERE:
Athens
BEST FOR:
Performing arts
YOU SHOULD KNOW:
The Herodeion was built by a wealthy Roman in memory of his wife. It seats 6,000 and, with a backdrop of the floodlit Acropolis, is a magnificent venue, though extra cushions are recommended and, while the acoustics are excellent, binoculars are useful in the top tiers.

357

Epidaurus Festival of Greek Drama

Epidaurus is one of Greece's most famous sites. It was originally the hilltop sanctuary of an unknown Mycenaean god; Olympian Apollo followed and was in turn superseded by his son Asklepius, the god of healing. The Asklepeion became the most famous healing centre in the ancient world, renowned for treatment of both physical and mental illness with cures ranging from diets and herbs to dreams and the lick of a serpent. In the Sanctuary are fragments of temples, a circular tholon, and a hostel for pilgrims. After the establishment of the Festival of Asklepeia, held every four years, a stadium and a theatre were added, and the latter is the main attraction today.

One of the best preserved in the world, it was built in the 3rd century BC to seat 6,000, and then extended. Now, its 54 tiers of limestone seats can accommodate 14,000 and, for more than 40 years, it has been the location for a festival of Greek classic drama. This is a superb place to see a play. With its gentle, wooded hills the site is beautiful and the air is soft with the scent of pine trees and wild herbs. The theatre's acoustics were famous when it was new, and they remain remarkable – a whisper on the traditional packed-earth circular stage can be heard from the top tier (acoustic scientists suggest that high-frequency sounds are magnified by the precision of the seating arrangement). Traditional and modern productions of the 'greats' – Euripides, Sophocles, Aeschylus and Aristophanes – are performed in modern Greek; the programmes include translated synopses. Even without a full translation, the power and emotion of Greek drama in this peaceful and extraordinary setting is thrilling.

The famous open-air theatre at Epidaurus has perfect acoustics.

EUROPE/GREECE

Night of the Full Moon, Athens

WHEN:
August, the night of the full moon
WHERE:
Athens and sites nationwide
BEST FOR:
Moonlit magic
YOU SHOULD KNOW:
Monuments, churches and castles open all over Greece. Some of the outstanding sites (the long list may change from year to year) are the Sanctuary of the Great Gods on Samothrace, the Temple of Poseidon at Cape Sounion, the monasteries of Meteora, the Byzantine city Mistras and the Island of Delos.

Summer days in Athens are suffocating. The sun hammers down through a blanket of pollution and the dusty streets are chaotic with traffic. With nightfall, the city comes alive and floodlit hilltop monuments seem to float above the urban sprawl. Moonlight particularly becomes the city and recently the Hellenic Ministry of Culture has arranged free, late-night (usually up until 22.00) openings and performances at many sites on the night of the beautiful August full moon. This nationwide initiative aims to familiarize everyone with the archaeology, history and culture of Greece.

In Athens, it is possible to enjoy a piano recital in a museum, jazz among fallen marble columns, folk dance in an open-air theatre, music on a rocky hill. Locations vary, but late-opening museums include the National Archaeological Museum, with its vast collections, and the Numismatic Museum, which is housed in the splendid neoclassical mansion once home to Heinrich Schliemann. Both may stage performances. Other concert venues include the Herodeion, the theatre on Lykavittos Hill, and the Hill of the Pynx, once a platform for famous orators. Outstanding archaeological sites are the Temple of Olympian Zeus (the largest temple in the Greek world), with its 15 massive standing columns, and the Acropolis. A leisurely stroll among marble ruins kissed by the silvery moonlight, high above the city beneath a sky scattered with stars clustering round the huge moon, is unforgettable. As the moon sinks and first light starts to brighten the east, the spirit of place is bewitching.

Festival of the Panagia

The splendid neoclassical church Our Lady of Tinos was built to shelter a miraculous icon. It was found in 1922 by Pelagia, a nun directed to it by the Virgin Mary in a dream – a chapel marks the spot. The island quickly became a place of pilgrimage, especially for the sick, and is known as the Greek Lourdes. Inside the church the icon of the Virgin is surrounded by gold and silver, gifts and offerings. Outside, pilgrims make the ascent from the harbour along a special padded rubber mat on hands and knees all year round. But two days in the calendar are special: the Feast of the Annunciation which coincides with Independence Day on March 25 and August 15, the Dormition of the Virgin. Pilgrims arrive in their thousands.

The harbour is crammed with boats, the hotels are overflowing – many visitors camp out – and the big day starts with uproar. Firecrackers, cannons, and brass bands augment the booming bass of the Orthodox liturgy, broadcast around town. Shopkeepers do a roaring trade in icons, candles, votives and incense – bundles of it are lit, filling the streets with thick, fragrant smoke. To the pealing of bells, the icon, borne aloft beneath a gilt canopy, leaves the church escorted by resplendent crowned clergy and a forest of glittering crosses and candlesticks. The procession sweeps downhill under packed balconies, jostled by joyful pilgrims. At the harbour, speeches are followed by commotion: cheers, ships' sirens, fireworks, bands, and every bell in Tinos competes to honour the Virgin. As the pilgrims disperse and the icon is carried back to the church, optimistic elation mingles with the incense drifting in the air.

WHEN:
August 15
WHERE:
Tinos
BEST FOR:
Religious pageantry
YOU SHOULD KNOW:
On August 15 1940, the light cruiser *Elli*, at anchor and decked with bunting, was sunk by an Italian submarine. This ignoble act drove Greece towards war. Nowadays, the navy frigate *Elli* moors to honour the Virgin and the dead sailors, who are buried at the original chapel.

Orthodox clergy head for the harbour in procession with pilgrims.

Kataklysmos

Pentecost and the Day of the Holy Spirit (Whit Monday) are celebrated throughout Greece, but in Cyprus they are combined with Kataklysmos, the Festival of the Flood. Stories of a great cleansing deluge and of life beginning anew are found in many cultures, and Orthodox festivals are often tightly entwined with pre-Christian myths. Noah's Flood blends with the tale of Deukalion, spared by Zeus so that he and his wife – they took to the waters in a wooden box – might re-populate the world. Cyprus is Aphrodite's Island, however, and it is also possible that the festival may be linked to the goddess's birth – she arose from the waves off the south coast, and drifted to land, where flowers sprang up beneath her feet.

Several coastal towns organize concerts and games near the waterfront on the Sunday and Monday but in Larnaca the festival lasts about a week. After a procession to the sea, revellers walk into the water and happily splash each other, to symbolize purification. The palm-lined promenade is packed with food stalls and kiosks and the crowds watch swimming contests, beach volleyball, a regatta and water polo. Here and around the town, stages are set up for a wide range of amateur and professional performances – Greek and Cypriot folk singing and dancing, magic shows, comedians and shadow puppets. One very popular and unique event – with echoes of the music and poetry competitions of ancient Greece – is chatista, a contest for groups who perform rhyming songs in Cypriot dialect, vying to improvise more and more verses. Torch-lit processions and fireworks bring the evenings to a close.

Imnarja – the Feast of St Peter and St Paul

Fireworks punctuate Maltese summer nights. Every town and village dresses up for its festa – saint's day – when prayers precede a lively procession of the saint's statue through the lavishly decorated streets, accompanied by brass bands. At dusk, fireworks start. The Feast of St Peter and St Paul is a major event. St Paul brought Christianity to Malta; he was shipwrecked here and then hidden from the Romans in a cave in Rabat, where the first feasts were held. The Knights of St John called this feast 'luminaria', for the lighted cathedral façade, and the Maltese adapted this Italian name to Imnarja.

Now essentially a country festival lasting two days, it takes place mainly in Buskett Gardens outside Rabat. The largest green space in Malta and a popular picnic spot during the parched, scorching summers, this is actually a park – an extensive area of mixed woodland and citrus, once used by the Knights for falconry. On the eve of the feast, marquees are erected for produce and livestock shows, the animals are blessed and crowds from all over the island arrive to settle in groups under the trees for a night of socializing and merriment. Against a background of bonfires, bands, folk singing and fireworks, the Maltese national dish *fenkata* (rabbit stew) is eaten in large quantities, washed down with local wine.

Next day, the agricultural show is judged before everyone heads for the road to Saqqajja Hill to enjoy an afternoon of horse and donkey races, the bareback riders cheered on by supporters. Prizes are presented from a stone loggia outside Mdina, built for the Knights. The trophies are ornate banners, *palji*, which are carried triumphantly back to the winners' villages to hang proudly in their churches until the following year.

WHEN:
June 28-29
WHERE:
Buskett Gardens and Rabat
BEST FOR:
Horse racing and all-night picnics
YOU SHOULD KNOW:
The British Governor of Malta, Sir William Reid, brought the agricultural fair to Buskett Gardens in 1854; before that, 'carousing' was forbidden in the park. The British also introduced the Maltese to brass bands – now every village has one.

Fireworks light up the sky around Buskett Gardens.

EASTERN
MEDITERRANEAN
& MIDDLE EAST

Fireworks are just one of the entertainments at the Dubai shopping festival.

Dubai Shopping Festival

Since its inception in 1996 the Layali Dubai (Dubai Shopping Festival, DSF for short) has boomed as a tax-free magnet that attracts serious shoppers from all over the globe. It's easy to understand why. This leading member of the United Arab Emirates is not oil-rich, instead developing as a trade and financial services centre that has also set out to become a tourist hotspot. With its fabulous setting on the Persian Gulf and ultra-modern developments everywhere it's worth a visit at any time. But when a host of special activities are added to create a month-long shopping festival, Dubai in the spring becomes a tempting proposition indeed.

So what's on offer at the DSF, apart from an incomparable selection of merchandise to suit every need and taste? The action is multinational, with participants from assorted countries showcasing their wares, combining to give the event a truly cosmopolitan atmosphere. Shops determined to do serious business offer worthwhile discounts during the festival, there are daily raffles for great prizes like new cars and later fireworks illuminating the night sky, whilst free entertainment such as concerts, fashion events and laser shows is on offer in public open spaces, contributing mightily to the carnival spirit. There's even a jazz festival.

DSF's focal point is the Global Village, where many countries gather to display their culture and heritage through the medium of handicrafts, music, dance and clothing, creating a genuinely international flavour. The choice for shoppers is almost limitless, with over 40 shopping malls and many traditional souks to tempt myriad visitors. This may be an event dreamed up to boost Dubai's tourist profile – but it actually delivers in spades, with bargains galore to be purchased, great entertainment for free . . . and all the welcoming advantages to be found at one of the world's most seductive holiday destinations.

WHEN:
January, February or March
WHERE:
City of Dubai
BEST FOR:
Shopping until you drop . . . or just a great holiday
YOU SHOULD KNOW:
Anyone who has any energy (and cash) left can return to enjoy Dubai's awesome Summer of Surprises – 65 days between mid June and August when a new fun-filled event is held every other day.

Dubai World Cup

If there's one sport Dubai's ruling Al Maktoum family takes seriously it's horseracing, and Sheikh Mohammed's Darley Stud and Godolphin Racing is one of the world's leading breeding and racing operations. Initially, Godolphin delighted in trying to win Europe's most prestigious races – often succeeding. Then this well-funded organization extended its ambitions to the world stage, taking especial pleasure when their own-bred horses triumphed, as opposed to one of Godolphin's many expensively purchased four-legged flyers.

As Dubai continued to develop as a commercial powerhouse and popular international tourist destination, the Al Maktoums decided that they would create the world's richest horse race at their recently refurbished hometown racecourse, and did just that. From 1996 the Dubai World Cup (current prize value $6 million) has been the top target for Godolphin itself (the shrewd Maktoums have won their own prize more often than anyone else) and owners of leading thoroughbreds in countries like America where top horses race on dirt. This does exclude most European horseracing nations, though European horses do take part (thus far without notable success) and English-based jockeys have ridden several winners of 'the big one'.

But there are other prizes to strive for – the Dubai World Cup is one of seven races on the meeting's evening card, with massive purses on offer for turf races (the Europeans love those) and a race for pure-bred Arabian horses. Participation is by invitation only to ensure that only the finest from all over the globe compete for total prize money of over $21 million and the racing fraternity enjoys generous subsidies to attend. So do over 50,000 spectators, who are drawn to this friendly Gulf Emirate by the unique opportunity to see the world's finest racehorses do battle (for free from the public enclosure) – and are duly rewarded with an equine spectacular.

WHEN:
March
WHERE:
Nad Al Sheba Racecourse since 1996; in 2010 the race moves to the new Meydan Racecourse, City of Dubai
BEST FOR:
Thrilling encounters between million-dollar racehorses
YOU SHOULD KNOW:
One driving force behind the desire of owners and breeders in the Arab world to increase their profile in international horseracing stems from the fact that all the world's top thoroughbreds are descended from three 18th century stallions that originated from the Arabian Peninsula – the Godolphin Arabian, Darley Arabian and Byerly Turk.

Fifty thousand spectators enjoy the Dubai World Cup.

EASTERN MED & MIDDLE EAST/JORDAN

Dead Sea Ultra Marathon

WHEN:
The second Friday in April
WHERE:
Amman
BEST FOR:
Masochistic runners and sadistic spectators
YOU SHOULD KNOW:
All that pain is endured for a very good cause – sponsorship monies go to a local medical charity that has successfully treated hundreds of neurological patients.

This charity event is of relatively recent origin, but the DSUM has already established a reputation as one of the world's 'must do' charity running races. Its unique selling point is the fact that the event begins 900 m (2,950 ft) above sea level, and finishes 400 m (1,300 ft) below sea level. Runners in the Ultra Marathon therefore descend through 1,300 m (4,265 ft), amply justifying the slogan 'run to the lowest point on earth'. But be warned that gravity won't be helping all the way – there's plenty of up-and-down stuff before the long descent to the Dead Sea and level run-in along the shore.

Over 3,000 runners from around 50 countries currently participate, with numbers increasing each year. The most demanding option they can choose is the 48.7-km (30-mi) Ultra Marathon, followed by the 42-km (26-mi) Marathon. Then there's the Half Marathon at 21 km (13 mi), a Fun Run that clocks up 10 km (6 mi) and a Junior Marathon for Under-15s at a mere 4.2 km (2.6 mi). The start point is at the Amman International Motor Show Hall, with buses taking all competitors who are not in the Ultra Marathon to their respective start points. The races start early, allowing participants to head for the finishing point on Amman Tourist Beach beside the Dead Sea before the heat builds up to intolerable levels – temperatures of 35 °C (95 °F) or more are the norm.

There are options for those who do not actually feel up to tackling this gruelling test of stamina. It's possible to enter as a team of four or (better still!) pitch up as a spectator and watch everyone else going through physical agonies, before gallantly joining in the beach party that greets weary finishers.

Ultra Marathon runners compete below sea level in Jordan.

The Feast of Tabernacles

This is one of three major holidays known collectively as the Shalosh Regalim (Three Pilgrim Festivals) when Jewish people traditionally made a pilgrimage to the Temple in Jerusalem. The Feast of Tabernacles (known in Israel as Sukkot) occurs on the 15th day of the month of Tishri in the Hebrew calendar.

The word *sukkah* (plural sukkot) translates as 'hut' and represents the type of simple dwelling in which the Israelites lived during 40 years of desert wandering after the flight from Ancient Egypt. The major characteristic of the Sukkot festival is the erection of temporary structures large and small, that appear everywhere as if by magic, in which families spend time during the festival eating, entertaining or simply relaxing. Those in synagogue grounds are used for study or religious ceremonies.

Today, the Sukkot holiday lasts for seven days in Israel. The first day is celebrated with holiday meals and special services, the last day is Hoshana Rabbah (Great Hoshana) which also sees a special service, in which worshippers make seven circuits of the synagogue. The festival days in between (Chol Hamoed) are for enjoyment and relaxation, with menial and labour-intensive tasks prohibited. In practice, this is a time to eat well, visit relations and neighbours, entertain visitors and take family outings.

During the festival, seven symbolic guests are invited into the *sukkah* – they are the Seven Shepherds of Israel (Abraham, Isaac, Jacob, Moses, Aaron, Joseph and David). A different one enters first each day, bearing a spiritual message for the occupants. Living guests are also encouraged. Despite the religious nature of The Feast of Tabernacles, there are no restrictions that prevent non-Jews from entering the *sukkah* and hospitality is encouraged. So this is a happy time when anyone can – and will – be welcomed inside for a snack or a meal.

WHEN:
September/October
WHERE:
Everywhere in the country
BEST FOR:
Meeting people
YOU SHOULD KNOW:
A number of Christian churches – mainly minority denominations – also celebrate The Feast of Tabernacles.

Worshippers gather for the special blessing.

Orthodox Jews observe the Hanukkah candles in Jerusalem.

Festival of Lights

The Festival of Lights (Hanukkah) is a traditional Jewish celebration that begins on day 25 of the month of Kislev in the Hebrew calendar. The Jews never forget, and Hanukkah recalls a victory won by the Maccabees around 160 BC. Those freedom fighters defeated Syrian Greek occupiers and succeeded in ritually cleansing and rededicating the defiled Second Temple in Jerusalem. It is said that when the Maccabees relit the sacred flame there was enough concentrated olive oil for just one day – yet miraculously it burned for eight, allowing fresh oil to be prepared and consecrated.

Thus, the Festival of Lights lasts for eight days during which time families, loved ones and friends socialize, eat generously and play traditional games involving the use of a dreidel – a four-sided spinning top inscribed with Hebrew letters forming an acronym that means 'a great miracle happened there'. The lighting of the eight-branch menorah (another branch each day, ignited using an extra light called a shamash) remains the central ritual, usually taking place at sunset with the menorah often placed near a window where it can be seen from outside. Other customs include the eating of food fried in olive oil and dairy produce, plus the exchange of gifts (often small coins).

This is a deeply religious occasion, which is seen as an annual reaffirmation of the Jewish faith's enduring strength and continued survival. However, it is not an official religious holiday, and there is no prohibition of activities that are forbidden on the Sabbath, such as going to work. Neither are there religious reasons to close schools, though in Israel they are shut for the entire Hanukkah week. So this becomes an annual holiday that provides precious time for old-fashioned togetherness amidst the hustle and bustle of modern life.

WHEN:
Late November/December
WHERE:
The whole of Israel observes the Hanukkah holiday.
BEST FOR:
Visiting family and friends
YOU SHOULD KNOW:
It is becoming increasingly common to identify 'the miracle of the oil' that is central to Hanukkah with modern environmental concerns regarding conservation and the efficient use of energy.

Eid al-Fitr in Damascus

The feast of Eid al-Fitr signals the end of the holy month of Ramadan, the ninth month in the Muslim calendar, during which the Quran was revealed to Mohammed. Throughout Ramadan, every day is spent fasting. Nothing is permitted to pass the lips between dawn and dusk – nothing to eat or drink, no smoking and no sexual relations. The annual Ramadan fast is one of the precepts of Islam, to be practised by everyone unless they are excused on health grounds. It is meant to teach patience, self-restraint and humility; the three-day Eid holiday at the end of the fast is a recognition of the material reward granted to those who have completed their religious penance. Eid is for 'eating, drinking and remembrance of God' and, after the self-enforced discipline of Ramadan, it comes as an only too welcome relief.

Eid is held throughout the Islamic World, but Damascus is perhaps the most flamboyant in its celebration, an especially good place to experience the festival not just on account of the city's atmospheric winding streets, wonderful food and breathtaking World Heritage architecture but, more importantly, for the Damascenes' open-hearted hospitality. At Eid, the city erupts in an ebullient display of goodwill, encouraging visitors to join in. Everyone dresses up to the nines and families hit the town, showering relatives and friends with gifts and sweets and giving alms to the poor. The streets are festooned with decorative ribbons, food stalls are piled high with mouth-watering sweetmeats, there are fairs and fireworks, and music blares out from every direction. Visitors who witness the Eid celebrations here invariably retain fond memories of Islamic hospitality and culture.

WHEN:
First day of Shawwal, the 10th month of the Islamic year, based on the lunar calendar (11 or 12 days shorter than the solar year).
WHERE:
Damascus, or anywhere in the Islamic world
BEST FOR:
Traditional Middle-Eastern hospitality and food
YOU SHOULD KNOW:
While you are in Damascus, the experience of going to a hammam (bath house) should not be missed. The hammams are open at Eid.

Shoppers admire the tempting sweets for sale during the feast.

Chahar Shanbeh Suri

WHEN:
The last Tuesday night of the year
WHERE:
Tehran, or anywhere in Iran
BEST FOR:
Traditional culture and food
YOU SHOULD KNOW:
To really become part of the
celebrations, you need to be invited
into somebody's home. This is not in
the least difficult as Iranians are
extremely hospitable.

Despite the best efforts of the Ayatollahs to stamp out any non-Islamic practices in Iran, they have never managed to eradicate Chahar Shanbeh Suri (Festival of the Last Wednesday). Even though almost no Iranian any longer knows or cares what this spring festival is about, nobody is prepared to forego the freedom to light their annual bonfire and eat a symbolic family meal, a tradition of such long-standing that all attempts to ban it had to be abandoned.

Chahar Shanbeh Suri is celebrated at the vernal equinox, the start of the new agricultural year, as an exorcism of all the bad luck from the previous year. It is pre-Islamic in origin, probably Zoroastrian, the ancient light-worshipping religion of Iran that is the wellspring of the world's great religions. Fire was integral to Zoroastrian religious practice and would certainly have been lit at the approach of the spring to symbolize the health and prosperity that the sun would bring in the coming year. The festival was overlaid by Islamic folklore, in which Wednesday is a day of bad luck, so Chahar Shanbeh Suri had to be celebrated on the night before the Wednesday of the equinox to banish the demons that would otherwise surely blight the start of spring.

Youths jump through the flames.

Today the festival has absolutely no religious significance; it has evolved into an occasion for a family party. Two traditional foods are always prepared: a hearty bean and noodle broth and a sweetmeat of seven dried nuts and fruit. Firecrackers are set off, children bang on pots and pans and bonfires twinkle all over Tehran. It is customary to jump over the flames chanting a traditional verse that roughly translates as 'Your fiery red is mine; my sickly paleness is yours', a wish that the coming year should be fuelled with abundant energy and good health.

The Hajj

Muslim pilgrims walk around the Kaaba during the sunset prayer at the Grand Mosque in Mecca.

Hajj is the largest annual pilgrimage on earth, a spiritual journey that is a central tenet of the Islamic faith. More than two million Muslims from all round the globe converge on Mecca to perform a complex set of holy rituals that symbolize events in the life of Abraham and his wife. They must make seven circumambulations of the Kaaba, the holy cube-shaped building that is the most sacred site of Islam, in the Great al-Haram Mosque; make the ritual walk between the hills of al-Safa and al-Marwah seven times; drink holy water from the Zamzam Well in the Mosque; hold a vigil at Mount Arafat; and throw stones against the pillars that mark the place of the Temptation of Abraham, symbolically casting out the devil. On completion of these rituals, which are performed *en masse* over several days, everyone buys a lamb to sacrifice, and the men shave their heads and women cut their hair in preparation for the festival of Eid al-Adha,

Believers may endure a great deal of hardship in order to accomplish Hajj. It can take years to save up enough money to make the journey and a pilgrim must often travel for thousands of miles from his home only to spend days in the heat of the desert in desperately uncomfortable and overcrowded conditions. Every year people are injured and killed in the crush despite the constantly overhauled safety procedures put in place by the Saudi authorities. But none of this puts anyone off. Pilgrims experience the Hajj as an intense spiritual emotion, the holiest occasion of their lives. They return to their families with a renewed sense of meaning and an expression of joyful calm in their faces. The piety and passion with which the Hajj is performed is truly impressive.

WHEN:
8th to 12th day of Dhu al-Hijjah, the twelfth month of the Islamic calendar
WHERE:
Mecca
YOU SHOULD KNOW:
Only people of the Islamic faith may enter Mecca. It is a very serious offence, deserving of the death sentence, for any non-believer to take part in the Hajj.

373

Two bull camels are watched closely by their handlers as they battle for supremacy.

Camel Wrestling Championship

Once widespread among the semi-nomadic herdsmen of Anatolia, camel wrestling is nowadays confined to the villages along the Aegean coast. The grand championship is held in an open field near Selçuk, a tourist town best known for its proximity to the ruins of Ephesus.

For the visitor, perhaps the best part of camel wrestling is the pomp and pageantry of the parade, held the day before the competition.

Accompanied by pipe-and-drum music, some hundred specially-bred Tülu camels, dripping with decorative tassels, their humps saddled with brilliant-coloured blankets and embroideries, are led through the town by their owners, who are dressed in traditional costume. It is all wonderfully festive with lively crowds lining the streets to gawp at the stately procession of beasts swaying sedately down the road.

Normally docile creatures, the male camels are stirred into wrestling with each other by the stimulus of a female on heat. Each round lasts a maximum ten minutes and often much less; it is won as soon as a camel makes his rival retreat, scream or fall. The animals barge against each other, getting entangled while attempting to trap their rival's head under their chest, all the time salivating heavily, until one of them runs off – it is not uncommon for a spectator to be hit by flying sputum or, worse, a sudden jet of urine. Serious injuries are rare because camels can only really hurt each other by biting and they are muzzled throughout a fight. The subtleties of the sport are way beyond the comprehension of the casual observer, apparently involving an intricate set of penalty regulations announced by motley arbiters on the sidelines. Surrounded by the commentary and cheers of crowds of spectators, all you can really be certain of is that you are witnessing a genuine slice of Anatolian heritage.

WHEN:
January
WHERE:
Selçuk
BEST FOR:
Traditional cultural activity and colourful procession
YOU SHOULD KNOW:
The Tülu camel used in camel wrestling is a cross between a Bactrian and a Dromedary, which results in a sturdy breed larger and stronger than either.

The oil wrestlers struggle for a hold during a bout at the Kirkpinar.

Kirkpinar Oil-Wrestling Festival

Oil-wrestling is a favourite Turkish sport that harks back to the Ottoman Empire when it was a military pastime to fill the gaps between battles and keep the soldiers fit. It is from this tradition that the Kirkpinar (Forty Springs) Festival stems, deriving its name from a legendary 14th century match in which a unit of 40 soldiers took part.

Today's Kirkpinar is held in a field, once the site of the Sultan's summer palace, just outside Edirne, the former capital of the Ottoman Empire on the border of Turkey and Greece, a beautiful city famed for its elegant mosques.

The *pehlivans* or 'brave warriors' wear only a pair of buffalo-hide leather breeches, emulating the costume of the Janissaries (an elite band of Ottoman imperial bodyguards) and fight barefoot, their bodies heavily oiled to make it harder for their opponents to get a grip on them. About a thousand *pehlivans* attend the Kirkpinar, ranging in age from young boys to 40-year olds, all competing for the coveted title of Head Wrestler, the overall champion. His prize is a golden belt which he gets to keep if he wins for three consecutive years. There are few rules and victory is achieved by either pinning one's opponent to the ground or lifting him above the shoulders. Despite the ferocity of the fighting, there is a warm camaraderie among the wrestlers: they oil each others' backs, help opponents to their feet, and generally display an extraordinary degree of courtesy towards each other.

The Kirkpinar is surrounded by festivities and ceremony. The *pehlivans* warm up to the accompaniment of folk musicians, each match is announced with a prayer and Romany gypsies set up a fair to add to the entertainment of this most macho of sports events.

WHEN:
June/July
WHERE:
Edirne
BEST FOR:
Turkish wrestling and traditional festivities
YOU SHOULD KNOW:
The Kirkpinar is supposedly the oldest officially sanctioned sports event in the world, having been held somewhere in Thrace, western Turkey, since 1362.

Seb-i-Aruz – Whirling Dervishes

The ancient city of Konya, south of Ankara, has a long religious tradition. Here is the tomb of Jelaleddin Rumi, a 13th century Sufi dervish (Islamic monk), mystic and poet, the initiator of whirling as a form of worship. He was born in Afghanistan but came to teach and study in the religious seminaries of Konya, where he wrote his renowned love poetry to Allah and formed an intense friendship with an older mystic called Semsi Tebrizi. When Tebrizi was killed by some disapproving disciples, Rumi was bereft and retreated into himself for some years before finding another route to divine harmony: in later life he was often seen whirling down the street, transported into a religious ecstasy. Thus a whole new way of worshipping God was invented. After his death, the Sufi sect of the Mevlevi was founded by his son, Sultan Veled, and the practice of the Whirling Dervishes was formalized.

After the fall of the Ottoman Empire, the new anti-religious government of Turkey clamped down on the Mevlevi; their *khanqah* (monastery) was closed and became a museum. By the 1950s, the authorities were persuaded that the Sufi version of Islam presented no political threat and permitted the traditional Mevlevi practice of whirling again as part of Turkey's cultural heritage.

At the Mevlana Cultural Centre, the main Mevlevi khanqah, Rumi's death is commemorated annually at Seb-i-Aruz (Wedding Night With God) with a special *sema*, or religious performance. The *sema* is a combination of dance, music and chanting which represents man's journey to the oneness of perfect truth through the power of divine love. The spectacle of the dervishes in their pristine white gowns whirling and chanting themselves into a trance is absolutely mesmerizing. It is an utterly unique and outstandingly beautiful religious ceremony.

WHEN:
December
WHERE:
Mevlana Cultural Centre, Konya
BEST FOR:
Religious dance
YOU SHOULD KNOW:
The Mevlevi believe that everybody is equal in the sight of Allah and, unlike many Islamic zealots, welcome non-Muslims to their *sema*. There is also a Mevlevi khanqah (monastery) in Istanbul where you can see performances of the *sema*.

The whirling dervishes wear white gowns for their sema *in Konya.*

ASIA

White Moon Festival (Sagaalgan)

WHEN:
Late January or early February
WHERE:
Ulan Ude, or anywhere in Buryatia or Mongolia
BEST FOR:
Traditional Buddhist religious celebration
YOU SHOULD KNOW:
The lunar new year is celebrated in one form or another all over Asia.

It is customary to throw vodka over stones for good luck.

Despite nearly a century of communist rule, Buryatia, the Siberian republic east of Lake Baikal, is still a land steeped in its ancient pastoral mythology. At the collapse of the Soviet Union, when open religious worship was allowed again, there was a massive revival of the ancient Tengri (shamanic) and Buddhist beliefs that are such an integral part of Buryat culture, and the lunar new year Sagaalgan festival was immediately declared a public holiday.

The lunar new year is one of the most important of the ancient oriental holidays, traditionally a time for forgiving and forgetting and getting the new year off to a good beginning. Everyone prepares for the festival by cleaning out their houses and making traditional dairy food dishes to share with their relatives and friends, then at the new moon they build a fire to burn their old clothes and household waste, signifying a symbolic purging of the past and a resolve to make a fresh start. In the *datsan* (Buddhist monasteries) a special

new year fire is lit and complicated rites are performed for the spirits of the dead as well as the living, a ceremonial occasion which visitors are welcome to watch.

This is a great time to be in Ulan Ude. An old merchants' town with a distinctive oriental charm, it is one of the most pleasant cities in Siberia; but especially so at Sagaalgan when everyone's front door is lit up with candles, the scent of incense wafts through the air and people dress up in traditional costume to pay their respects in the *datsan*. The whole city gets into the celebrations, with offerings of food, innumerable vodka toasts and the warm hospitality to guests that is customary in Central Asia.

Pole of Cold Rally and Festival

Game for an extreme adventure? How about a daredevil drive to the coldest inhabited spot on the planet? The annual five-day Pole of Cold Rally starts at Yakutsk, capital of Yakutia (Sakha Republic) and ends in the village of Oymyakon – otherwise known as the 'Pole of Cold'. The 1,270-km (790-mi) route goes through a spectacular frost-bound region of rivers and lakes, forests, mountains and reindeer pastures, where at night the stars shine with a piercing surreal brilliance and the Northern Lights dance on the horizon. Despite the overwhelming natural beauty, this is one of the most inhospitable regions in the world, where Stalin disposed of millions of his countrymen in the Siberian gulags (prison labour camps) and where, on the infamous 'road of bones', one prisoner is said to have died for every metre of road built.

The rally attracts more entrants every year, and at the millennium Oymyakon held the first Pole of Cold Festival to coincide with it. The festival was such a hit that tourists started pouring in to this picturesque village in the middle of nowhere specially to join in the Pole of Cold celebrations, a Siberian extravaganza complete with ethnic music, reindeer sleigh rides, ice-fishing, fireworks, a visit from Chis Khaan – Frost Lord of Yakut mythology and, not least, ice-carving – a craft that is enjoying a renaissance throughout the Russian Federation. The Yakutians, renowned for their skill in the traditional craft of woodcarving, are far and away the most talented ice sculptors and, at the Pole of Cold, a disused gold mine has been transformed into an art gallery. The underground permafrost acts as a natural refrigerator where the ephemeral sculptures are exhibited, beautifully illuminated under changing coloured lights. It's hard to believe that these exquisite crystalline structures are, after all, only water.

WHEN:
March
WHERE:
Oymyakon, Sakha Republic (Yakutia)
BEST FOR:
Ice sculptures, the Northern Lights and reindeer
YOU SHOULD KNOW:
The thermometer regularly plunges below –50°C (–58°F) in Oymyakon. The lowest temperature ever recorded in the area was at the nearby village of Tomtor when the thermometer hit –71.2°C (–96.2°F) in January 1926.

381

The Sun Vibes Festival takes place in idyllic surroundings.

Siberia Sun Vibes Festival

WHEN:
July
WHERE:
Chemal, Altai Mountains
BEST FOR:
New Age spiritualism and electronic music
YOU SHOULD KNOW:
It is easy to find a room to rent in local houses in Chemal, or you can camp at the festival site where there are cafés and facilities.

In the heart of Central Asia, the *taiga*, the steppe and the desert all meet at the Altai Mountains. According to Siberian mythology, this spectacular mountain range rises from the earth's spiritual node, radiating mystical power and healing energy. The region is so hauntingly beautiful that even the most cynical traveller can believe it. The local inhabitants certainly do, for if you look carefully you see signs of shamanism all around you: morsels of food or a coin left on a wayside rock for the spirits and coloured prayer cloths fluttering from the trees. Every summer, eco-tourists, outdoor adventurers and 'new-agers' are drawn to this nature lovers' paradise by the mind-blowing mountain scenery, white-water rafting, horse riding and good vibrations.

Where 'new-agers' congregate, DJs are bound to follow and in the past few years an electronic dance music festival has sprung up near the tourist town of Chemal. The three-day festival is held in idyllic surroundings – a lush meadow of soft grass surrounded by forest, overlooking the grey cliffs and foaming waters of the Katun River. There has been an explosion in new age spiritualism throughout the former Soviet Union and every year since 2002, when it was first held, Sun Vibes has grown in size. Several thousand idealistic young people now come flocking from all over the Russian Federation to revel in nature and celebrate a new-found freedom to express themselves through trance dancing. The festival has begun to be noticed on the international scene and while it is still small enough to feel uncommercialized, those of a mystical bent and a pioneer spirit can get a huge buzz from the natural vibes here, at the wild heart of the planet.

Tabyk Ethnic Music Festival

Frozen wastes, prison camps, the occasional preserved mammoth tusk – Siberia doesn't sound exactly inviting. Yet returning travellers from the Siberian Sakha Republic tell another tale – of an elemental landscape so vast as to be almost unimaginable, of an ancient nomadic culture steeped in mythology and magic, of myriad flora and fauna and unending human warmth. Even though this remote part of the world has been accessible to foreigners for only two decades, it has made its mark on the map as an eco-tourist wonderland. Its capital, Yakutsk, has always attracted adventurers – from the 17th century Cossacks navigating the mighty River Lena into the back-of-beyond to the 19th century prospectors sniffing for diamonds and gold and 20th century entrepreneurs who transformed Yakutsk from a remote settlement into a wealthy commercial centre.

For a snapshot of Siberian heritage, it's worth timing a visit to Yakutsk to coincide with the city's music festival. The *tabyk* is a traditional Siberian tambourine and the eponymous festival was established in 1990 with the aim of reviving the ancient animist mythology, shamanist rituals and musical traditions of the Yakuts, descendants of the tribal nomads of Central Asia, and the Evenks, Arctic Circle reindeer-herders. Under the Soviet communist agenda, the culture of both these minority ethnic groups had been almost entirely suppressed.

From small beginnings the Tabyk Festival has grown increasingly international with performers from all over Central Asia and even the Baltic and the UK. There are exuberant displays of epic singing, shamanic chanting and traditional ethnic music and dance as well as 'ethnic rock', a hypnotic variant of Western rock music played on traditional instruments. The festive mood is infectious, with impromptu jamming sessions in venues all over town.

WHEN:
December
WHERE:
Yakutsk, Sakha Republic (Yakutia)
BEST FOR:
Ethnic music and shamanic chanting and dance
YOU SHOULD KNOW:
Siberia is almost equal in size to the whole of Europe; the Sakha Republic is by far the largest of the Siberian republics, covering an area of over 3,000,000 sq km (1,000,000 sq mi) with a population of only 1,000,000.

Nooruz

WHEN:
March 21
WHERE:
Bishkek
BEST FOR:
Traditional music, warm hospitality
and spectacular mountain scenery
YOU SHOULD KNOW:
The spring (vernal) equinox is a major
celebration throughout Central Asia.

A timeless pastoral land of mountains, nomads and yurts, Kyrgyzstan well deserves its growing reputation as the most beautiful country in Asia. It is a superb destination for trekkers and climbers. By Western standards life is hard here and holidays are few and far between, so it's no wonder that at Nooruz everyone is set on having a jolly good party.

Nooruz literally means 'New Day'. It is one of the most ancient festivals in the world, probably Zoroastrian (sun worship) in origin, a celebration of the spring equinox and the start of the sowing season, a time for optimism when everyone dresses in their most colourful clothes and shares food with their neighbours. Although there is no formal religious ritual, there is a spiritual dimension to the festival in that it is a time when everyone snatches a breather from the mundane realities of the daily grind, a chance to mull over their lives, dream of romance and pray for the fulfilment of their hopes in the coming months.

Girls dressed in traditional costumes take part in the celebration.

The capital of Kyrgyzstan, Bishkek, is a small but lively ex-Soviet city which compensates for its rather glum architecture with masses of green space and glorious views of the Tian Shan Mountains. At Nooruz the inhabitants easily revert to their rural roots, turn out onto the streets and mill around the central Ala-Too Square for a vibrant New Year show of singing, traditional *komuz* (lyre) music, dancing and fireworks. Mouthwatering smells of sizzling meat waft from the street vendors' stalls and all over town people indulge themselves in the festive spirit – eating, drinking and making all visitors feel thoroughly welcome.

At Chabysh Horse Games

The skills of the Central Asian horseman are legendary and nowhere is this more apparent than in Kyrgyzstan where the nomad's relationship with his horse is almost symbiotic and children start to ride at the same time as they learn to walk. Horse games have always been an integral part of Kyrgyz culture, providing an opportunity to hand down equestrian expertise from one generation to the next and encouraging healthy competition between riders.

The people of this breathtakingly beautiful rural backwater, where daily life has remained unchanged for centuries, have to find a way of adapting if they are to hold their own in a post-modern world. At Chabysh was conceived several years ago with the aspiration of attracting tourists to a showcase of Kyrgyz culture, and with the spin-off effect of reviving the value of the Kyrgyz horse in the local economy.

The games are held in spectacular hiking country on the shore of Lake Issyk-Kul, the second largest mountain lake in the world, once a stopover on the Silk Road and now one of Kyrgyzstan's major natural attractions. Local horsemen perform incredible feats of trick-riding, and play traditional games such as *Oodarysh* (wrestling on horseback) and *Kyz-kuumai* or 'Catch the Girl', in which a female rider has to escape being kissed, as well as the national sport of *Kok boru*, a sort of super-violent, frenetic version of polo, whacking a goat's carcass instead of a ball. There are also horse races and displays of archery and falconry as well as ethnic music, a folklore exhibition and crafts stalls. The festival is unashamedly aimed at tourists but that makes it no less enthralling – participants and spectators all get equally caught up in the thrill of the moment. At Chabysh is an exceptional opportunity to observe the Kyrgyz equestrian tradition up close.

WHEN:
October/November
WHERE:
Near Karakol, Lake Issyk-Kul
BEST FOR:
Equestrian displays and traditional culture of yurt-dwelling nomads
YOU SHOULD KNOW:
The famous Central Asian sport of *Kok boru* is also known as *Ulak Tartysh* or *Buzkashi*, depending on where you are and whether the local language is Persian-based or Turkic in origin.

Naadam

The midsummer Naadam sports festival dates from Mongolia's 12th century glory days under Genghis Khan, when a man was measured by his prowess in martial arts – the 'three manly games' of wrestling, horse racing and archery. More recently, under the thumb of both Soviet Russia and China, the Mongolian people suffered severe hardship, and the Naadam sports have enormous significance in the public consciousness as a ritual reminder of the country's ancient heritage and successful bid for independence.

In the capital, Ulaanbaatar, Naadam kicks off at the central Sukhbaatar Square with a spectacular parade of athletes, monks, musicians and splendid-looking mounted men dressed and armed as Mogul warriors. The games are held at the city's main sports stadium, which at Naadam looks more like a fairground, bedecked with coloured banners and souvenir stalls while touts and food vendors mill around amongst the thousands of spectators plying them with endless supplies of the national diet – fermented mare's milk and meat pancakes.

The start of the Naadam festival

Popular as horseracing and archery are, it is the wrestling that really gets the crowd going. The passion it stirs is comparable to soccer fever in the West and there is an atmosphere of febrile anticipation when the burly bare-chested wrestlers, wearing clumping great boots, tiny shorts and brightly coloured, tight little embroidered silk jackets, make their appearance. Before each fight the wrestlers perform an 'eagle dance' – an almost incongruously graceful, balletic movement with arms outstretched like wings. There are no weight divisions, no time limits and, apparently, few rules. The loser is the first to fall. Each wrestler has a *zasuul*, a personal sidekick who acts as protector and referee, chanting encouragement, and who, if his man wins, sings a victory song. You won't see a sports event like this anywhere else in the world.

Golden Eagle Festival

The Kazakh ethnic minority of Mongolia is one of the last horse-riding nomadic cultures in the world. The tribes migrated about 200 years ago into the foothills of the Altai Mountains of northwest Mongolia, a beautiful wilderness lake region of wooded hills and open meadows. Unlike native Mongolians, the Kazakhs are Muslim, and have their own language and customs. At one time they were renowned throughout Central Asia for their skill in falconry, taming golden eagles to catch rabbits, foxes and even wolves for their fur – vital for surviving the bitter winters.

WHEN:
October
WHERE:
Bayan-Olgii Province
BEST FOR:
Falconry; tribal heritage
YOU SHOULD KNOW:
You can only attend this festival by pre-arrangement with the organizers. Visitor numbers are limited and you should be prepared to rough it a bit and preferably have been on a horse before. All profits from tourists go towards conservation projects in the Altai.

The Golden Eagle Festival was first held as a millennial cultural celebration to resuscitate enthusiasm for this dying art, and it was a great success. Even though the three-day event has only been going a few years, hunters turn up from all over the region to take part in the competition near the remote town of Olgii, sometimes riding for several days across the steppe with their birds.

The festival is held about 20 km (12 mi) outside town and opens with a wondrous display of pageantry – a posse of savage-looking Kazakh huntsmen on horseback in traditional costumes of fur and leather, their saddles tooled in silver, parading with their birds perched on their arms.

A handler launches his eagle into the air.

Golden eagles have a wing span of up to 2 m (7 ft) and eyesight eight times more acute than a human's; they are truly awesome creatures to watch soaring through the skies, chasing after fox carcasses dragged by galloping huntsmen and swooping off narrow mountain ledges onto their trainer's arm. For an outsider it feels a real privilege to be on the receiving end of Kazakh hospitality, staying with a tribal family in their *ger* (yurt tent), mingling with the huntsmen and watching performances of music, dance and traditional games.

387

Basant Kite-Flying Festival

Before the partition of India and Pakistan, the ancient Punjabi capital of the Mughal Empire – Lahore – was a multi-cultural city and the Hindu spring festival of Basant Panchami was one of its many festivals. In 1947 the Hindus were forced to resettle across the border in the Indian part of Punjab, but Basant lived on – far too deeply ingrained as a Lahore custom for its religious origin to bother anyone.

Preparations for the biggest kite-flying festival in the world start weeks ahead. In the bazaar the kite-makers are kept busy building new models in every conceivable shape, size and colour while fathers and sons spend hours earnestly pondering the aerodynamic potential of their prospective purchase. Basant takes place inside the walls of Old Lahore, in the maze of narrow streets around the landmark 16th century Badshahi Mosque where families gather on the roofs of their homes, which serve as a giant arena. The men peer into a sky thick with fluttering, darting coloured-paper birds, studiously planning their battle campaigns, while the women supply copious amounts of food to sustain them.

A kite is launched from a roof-top.

WHEN:
January/February
WHERE:
Lahore
BEST FOR:
Traditional festivities
YOU SHOULD KNOW:
Unfortunately, at the time of writing, due to the threat of terrorism, a visit to Lahore is not recommended except for essential business.

The aim of the competition (as anyone who has seen the film *The Kite Runner* will know) is to cut opponents' lines until yours is the only kite in the sky. Each victory is greeted with trumpet blasts, drum rolls, firecrackers, gunshots and a dance of delight as the loser's kite spirals down into the city's gutters. The competition continues throughout the night – people rig up floodlights so that the whole of Old Lahore is lit up. It is a truly spectacular scene.

Although kite-flying may sound the most innocuous of activities, it is more dangerous than it seems. Every year there are terrible accidents when over-excited kite-flyers tumble off roofs, are cut by strings sharpened with shards of glass or are hit by stray gunfire.

The Sibi Mela

Sibi is the 'hot spot' of Baluchistan, Pakistan's largest province – summer temperatures here can reach 50°C (122°F). But this ancient town is famous for rather more than its sizzling heat; it is where history might be said to have started. Sibi is strategically situated at the southern end of the renowned Bolan Pass, the gateway between Central and South Asia through which both Alexander the Great and the Mughals led their armies into India. But that's the least of its claim to fame. Here in 1974 archaeologists unearthed Mehrgarh, one of the most important Neolithic sites in the world. The evidence suggests that it was in the environs of Sibi around 7000 BC that mankind first practised agriculture – growing grain and farming animals – a cultural revolution that was to fundamentally alter man's relationship with nature forever.

It is out of this ancient agrarian heritage that the Sibi Mela (Fair) originated, in response to the needs of the semi-nomadic Baluch tribes who still drive their herds of sheep and cattle through the town every spring, escaping the heat of the plains for summer pastures up in the high mountain valleys on the borders of Iran and Afghanistan. Sibi is a central junction where disparate tribes cross paths. For at least the past 600 years, the *mela* has provided an opportunity to trade animals, stock up with supplies, swap news, arrange marriages and bride-prices, and hold the *Jirga* (tribal assembly) for settling inter-tribal feuds.

Today the Sibi Mela is as important an event as ever, and in recent years has become a popular tourist attraction. For the *mela* is as much about entertainment as it is about the important business of herdsmen showing their prize horses and cattle and women selling their exquisite embroidery work. It is a full-blown celebration of Baluch culture.

WHEN:
February
WHERE:
Sibi, Baluchistan
BEST FOR:
Ancient traditional culture, crafts and music
YOU SHOULD KNOW:
At the time of writing much of Pakistan is not safe for foreign travellers because of the terrorist risk. The area around the Bolan Pass is particularly dangerous since Quetta, the provincial capital, is a known base for insurgents.

Tribesmen gather around their camels to discuss prices.

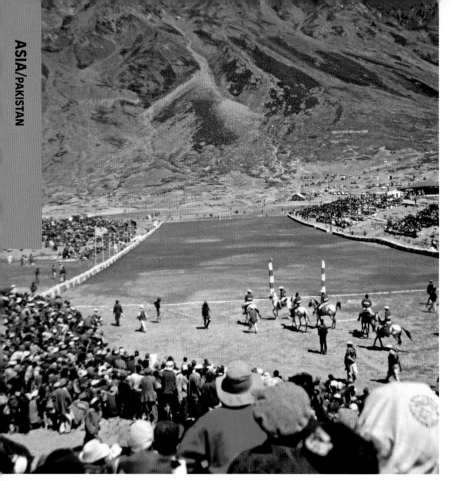

Riders get ready for the opening game of polo in the Shandur Pass.

Shandur Polo Tournament

High in the Hindu Kush Mountains is the remotest polo ground in the world. For more than 70 years rival teams from the valleys of Chitral and Gilgit have been competing in the annual Polo Tournament held at 3,700 m (12,000 ft) above sea level at the Shandur Pass, 'on the ridge between Heaven and the descent to Hell'.

The first official tournament was organized here in 1936 by the local British political agent at the time, a fanatical aficionado of this 'game of kings and king of games' which has its origins in ancient Persian cavalry exercises. The matches are played according to the old rules of Ali Sher Khan (a descendant of Genghis Khan): teams of six play an hour-long game with no stoppages allowed apart from a short midway break; players have only one horse apiece throughout the match; if anyone is forced to stop through injury his opposite number must also withdraw. The lack of any other rules means that the games are played at an astounding pace, with players wildly whacking not only the ball but also their opponents. Injuries are inevitable, and there is even the occasional death!

During the tournament the shore of Shandur Lake is transformed into a bustling tent town with sleeping accommodation and a marquee bazaar where local traders and musicians can grab a rare opportunity to spin a fast buck from the thousands of spectators. The tournament has become so popular that it is now televised. Just getting to Shandur is an achievement in itself; it's a hair-raising two-day drive up crumbling hairpin mountain roads. But the journey is more than worth it for the breathtaking views and the stark beauty of the mountain scenery, let alone the thrill of watching the polo.

WHEN:
July
WHERE:
Shandur
BEST FOR:
Polo matches; local colour; hiking and fishing; spectacular mountains
YOU SHOULD KNOW:
The far north of Pakistan has been relatively untouched by recent political events but anyone thinking of travelling in this beautiful, remote region should seek advice regarding the security situation before setting out.

The Thimphu Tsechu

Bhutan, the ancient 'Land of the Thunder Dragon' in the eastern Himalayas, is a veritable Shangri-La of snowy mountains, wooded hills and fast-flowing rivers, of temples, shrines and awesome dzong architecture (monastic fortresses), of a simple pastoral way of life based on Buddhist spiritual beliefs. Instead of measuring his country's success in terms of economic expansion, the King has declared that 'Gross National Happiness is more important than Gross National Product', and through his adept political skills has managed successfully to secure a unique place for this extraordinary culture in the globalized world, preserving the country's distinctive Tantric Buddhist cultural heritage, at the same time as introducing the benefits of Western technology and healthcare.

The religious *tsechu* festivals are compelling spectacles held in the local dzong of each district, the biggest being in the capital, Thimphu. The annual *tsechu* is a time for riotous celebration when people come home to their families, dress up in their finest silk clothes and congregate in the dzong for the traditional Cham dance-dramas – morality tales in which the performers, wearing outlandish costumes and grotesque masks, whirl and leap and contort themselves in a wild, atavistic display designed to exorcize evil spirits, bring spiritual merit to observers and celebrate the triumph of good. The crowd of thousands responds rapturously by chanting incantations until the *tsechu* reaches its climax with the ritual unfurling of a huge and exquisite silk *throngdrel* (sacred embroidered or painted cloth banner) depicting Guru Rinpoche, the founder of Tantric Buddhism.

Any visitor attending the *tsechu* cannot help but feel an overwhelming sense of awe at witnessing the marvel of this ancient religious festival, so full of colourful ritual and so utterly alien to Western culture.

WHEN:
September
WHERE:
Thimphu
BEST FOR:
Incredible costumes; Buddhist culture
YOU SHOULD KNOW:
Bhutan is the only country in the world to have made the sale of tobacco illegal. The government has been cautious about encouraging tourism, fearful of the effects it may have on the environment and tourists are only allowed in on pre-organized tours and are not permitted to travel independently.

Buddhists outside the temple in Thimphu.

Maha Shivaratri

WHEN:
February/March
WHERE:
Kathmandu
BEST FOR:
Hindu religious celebrations
YOU SHOULD KNOW:
Only Hindus are permitted inside the Pashupatinath Temple.

Maha Shivaratri is a festival to celebrate the birthday of Lord Shiva, the most worshipped of all the Hindu gods. More than 100,000 devotees from all over India and Southeast Asia flock into Kathmandu, the capital of Nepal, for a day of fasting and a night of vigil at the beautiful pagoda-roofed Pashupatinath Temple, one of the most sacred of all Hindu shrines, and to bathe in the holy water of the Bagmati River.

No food is consumed but there is much smoking of *charas* (hashish) and drinking of *bhang* (milk spiced with marijuana leaves). The drug is legalized just for use on Shiva's special day, because He is said to be pleased by the signs of intoxication. The shrines and *ghats* (river steps) around the temple are packed with pilgrims. *Sadhus* (holy men) squat round fires smoking *chillums* (pipes) and meditating, musicians play their sitars and tabla drums, while street vendors try to earn a few pence selling religious tat and beggars importune likely looking pilgrims for a single coin. As darkness falls, thousands of oil wicks are lit and the sound of chanting echoes out across the river throughout the night.

At any time Kathmandu, with its hundreds of ancient oriental temples, must be counted among one the world's most amazing cities but at Maha Shivaratri it is nothing short of magical. The semi-naked *sadhus,* smeared with ash, gaze into the distance seemingly in a trance, priests in ochre robes chant and make offerings, the air is thick with the sweet sickly fumes of incense and hashish and everywhere there is the hypnotic murmur of music and prayer. It is a spectacle that will last in your mind's eye for years to come.

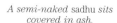
A semi-naked sadhu *sits covered in ash.*

Dashain

There are more than 50 festivals celebrated in Nepal every year but Dashain is the biggest, a national holiday lasting for 15 days. It takes place throughout the country, starting at the new moon straight after the monsoon season, as a celebration of the ferocious Hindu mother goddess, Durga, who slew the demon Mahisasur, enabling the gods to triumph in their terrible battle against the power of evil.

A devotee rings the bell while worshipping.

In preparation for the festival everyone cleans and decorates their houses, absent relatives arrive home and the bazaars are packed with people buying new clothes and food. The livestock market is stuffed with animals for sacrifice, a ritual which may seem bloodthirsty to Westerners – until they are reminded that in a country as poor as Nepal, the Dashain slaughter is often the only time of the year that people get to eat meat.

Each day of the festival different religious rituals are observed and, in Kathmandu, on the seventh day, there is a huge procession to Hanuman Dhoka Gate accompanied by brass bands and cannon fire. On the eighth day devout Hindus fast and take their animal – a goat, sheep, buffalo, duck or chicken, according to their means – to the temple, where it is slaughtered and the blood collected to be daubed all around the walls and floor as an offering to the bloodthirsty goddess. The meat is blessed and taken home to be eaten the following day at a special auspicious family meal. On the tenth day vermilion paint mixtures are prepared for the *tika*, a red mark that the elders daub on their young relatives' foreheads as a blessing. The atmosphere throughout Dashain is chaotically jolly. Everyone is in a good mood and gets into the holiday spirit, having fun at the city's fair, flying kites, and generally fooling around.

WHEN:
Late September/early October
WHERE:
Kathmandu, or anywhere in Nepal
BEST FOR:
Religious rituals and festive atmosphere
YOU SHOULD KNOW:
Nepal's national flag is the only one in the world that is not a quadrilateral. It is shaped like a sideways W with symbolic representations of the twin virtues of peace and courage.

Pongal in Tamil Nadu

WHEN:
Mid January – the auspicious date is
calculated by the solar calendar and
does not vary much.
WHERE:
State-wide in Tamil Nadu
BEST FOR:
Rice pudding and decorated cows
YOU SHOULD KNOW:
Kolams are seen outside homes and
temples in Tamil Nadu all year.
Coloured rice flour is carefully
applied in intricate floral and
geometric designs, inviting good
fortune into the house. Their absence
may indicate misfortune. The rice
flour becomes food for ants and
other small creatures, a mark of
respect for life.

In Tamil Nadu, a state of towering temples, cool green hills and fertile farmland, the four-day harvest festival, Pongal, is a joyful time. Each day has its own rituals. Bhogi Pongal is a day of renewal when old cooking utensils are thrown out and discarded items are burnt on communal bonfires to symbolize a new beginning. A first harvest of rice, turmeric and sugarcane, cut using sickles consecrated with sandalwood paste, is brought in from the fields.

Surya Pongal is a day of rejoicing because the granaries are full, the sun shines and birds sing in blossoming trees. Surya the sun god is worshipped, then *pongal* (a dish of rice, sugar and milk) is cooked outside in streets decorated with flowers and rice-flour patterns – *kolams* – marked out by the women. To symbolize prosperity, the *pongal* is allowed to boil over, prompting happy cries of '*Pongal-o Pongal!*'

Maatu Pongal is a day for honouring the cattle. Washed and garlanded with wheatsheaves and flowers, horns painted and festooned with bells, the herds are led around the villages to receive homage. The animals are bowed to, touched respectfully on head and feet, and given a food offering of *pongal*.

Although a dangerous sort of bull fight takes place in some villages, the last day – Kaanum Pongal – is essentially a day for family visits and games.

This traditional rural festival is a particularly cheerful one, when country people welcome the sun and give thanks to God, earth and their cattle. Visitors are welcomed and the tourist office in Madurai (a city surrounded by rich agricultural countryside) provides information and can arrange visits to nearby villages where Pongal is celebrated traditionally and enthusiastically.

A bull races through a Tamil Nadu village.

Dover Lane Music Festival

Sitar player Ravi Shankar performing at the festival.

The chaotic metropolis of Kolkata leaves no visitor indifferent. Though its Western image is of a place of poverty and desperation, it bursts with life and culture. Kolkata has produced great thinkers, political heroes and artists. Over 50 years ago, a group of music lovers gathered in Dover Lane (a modest residential area) to enjoy recitals of classical music. One aim of this small festival was to introduce the art form to a new generation, which at that time had little knowledge of, or enthusiasm for, their musical heritage. It has since become one of Kolkata's most important cultural events, attended by eminent performers and musicologists from all over the country. Still called the Dover Lane Festival, it now takes place in a 3,500-seat auditorium in Rabindra Sarovar, a lovely swathe of parkland surrounding a large, scenic lake.

Classical music is one of India's oldest and most respected art forms. Carnatic (southern) music and the northern classical style, Hindustani, have much in common. Both use *raga*, melodic form, and *tala*, rhythmic meter, as a basis for composition and improvisation. Carnatic vocalists usually sing unaccompanied, while Hindustani singers are often accompanied by a small hand-pumped harmonium, but for instrumental music both use similar small groups – strings (*sitar*, *sarod* or *sarangi*), a wind instrument, and *tabla* (drums).

Great maestros from all genres of classical music appear at Dover Lane and, in the spirit of the original, young musicians also perform. Some daytime concerts are staged and in the evenings stars play to packed houses of knowledgeable listeners in marathon recitals. Concerts last for hours, as long as musicians provide improvisations and audiences demand encores, and often continue until dawn.

WHEN:
During the fourth week of January
WHERE:
Nazrul Mancha Auditorium,
South Avenue, Kolkata
BEST FOR:
Indian classical music
YOU SHOULD KNOW:
Music training in India is long and demanding. Students – selected on talent, dedication and capacity for hard work – may spend up to 12 years at an academy, working and living with a musical guru.

Indian soldiers parade on their camels during the Republic Day celebrations.

Republic Day

India became independent on August 15 1947 but the Constitution did not come into effect until 1950 and this date, January 26, is now Republic Day. Though celebrated as a public holiday nationwide, New Delhi puts on the most magnificent parade, and the presence of the President, Prime Minister and VIPs and foreign dignitaries adds solemnity to this military and cultural jamboree.

The Prime Minister lays a wreath at India Gate, where the names of thousands of soldiers who died for India are inscribed. The President – also Supreme Commander of the Armed Forces – receives a 21-gun salute and then unfurls the national flag before reviewing the march past. The parade, which sets off from Raisini Hill near the Presidential Palace, sweeps down the spacious Rajpath, between government buildings and thousands of cheering onlookers, past India Gate and on to the historic Red Fort.

Winners of gallantry awards head the parade, followed by representatives of all branches of the armed services, marching in dress uniform to the sound of brass bands. All the latest military hardware is displayed, as well as divisions of the para-military and civil forces and an army motorcycle display team which performs some thrilling stunt riding. This impressive military show is followed by floats and tableaux depicting regional cultural heritage and a brightly costumed Children's Pageant. This section is led by children who have won National Bravery Awards, proudly riding caparisoned elephants. The finale is a spectacular low-level formation flypast, after which the National Anthem rings out, followed by the release of thousands of balloons.

WHEN:
January 26
WHERE:
New Delhi
BEST FOR:
Military pomp and circumstance
YOU SHOULD KNOW:
It can be difficult to get tickets for Republic Day – and even harder to reach the front of the crowds. However, Republic Day ceremonies are brought to an official close on January 29 with the Beating of the Retreat, which also entails military pageantry and is easier to get to see.

Kavadi

Kavadi is the most powerful propitiatory rite a devotee can perform for Murugan, the second son of Shiva, and takes place wherever there is a shrine to the god. The *Kavadi* is a yoke-cum-altar; pilgrims traditionally carried a long pole with baskets for food offerings at each end, and this remains the base of the *Kavadi*. The elaborate structures are built round half moons of bamboo, wood or steel and adorned with flowers, brass bells and peacock feathers (the peacock is Murugan's 'vehicle'). *Kavadi* bearers – *Bhakta* – wear robes of saffron-dyed cloth, red caps and religious insignia over their bare chests. Some carry the *Kavadi* on foot from village to village collecting alms, but many impose self-mortification. Metal spikes often pierce tongues and cheeks, and some devotees walk through a pit of burning coals (Agni Kavadi); for Vel Kavadi, the altar hangs on hooks from the flesh of the chest and back. This is a physical trial by which devotees seek aid from Murugan; all reach a state of religious ecstasy, which allows them to endure agony.

The town of Palani lies amidst fertile rice fields, backed by the forested Western Ghats. Its hilltop temple, dedicated to Murugan, is visible for miles over the plains and here, during an exuberant post-harvest festival, hundreds of *Kavadi* bearers converge. As they approach, dancing in a hypnotic trance to the rhythm of drums, their chanting becomes more frenzied. They dance around the base of the hill before carrying their precious burdens up the hundreds of steps to the temple, exhilarated by the knowledge that their blessings will infinitely outweigh any self-inflicted pain.

WHEN:
The ten-day festival at Palani takes place in January. Kavadi happens at other times at various shrines to Murugan.
WHERE:
Palani, Tamil Nadu
BEST FOR:
Religious ecstasy
YOU SHOULD KNOW:
Murugan is Ganesh's younger brother; their mother Parvati promised a golden mango to the first to circle the universe and Murugan set off on his peacock. When he returned, he found that Ganesh had simply walked around his mother, saying 'You are my universe', and won the prize. His mother tried to comfort Murugan, saying 'You are the fruit' – 'Pala nee' – but he left home in a rage and settled in Palani. The temple here is a major pilgrimage destination all year round.

An Indian woman walks on hot coals while carrying a pot of milk as an offering.

Teppothsavam Float Festival

The fascinating old town of Madurai, its narrow streets packed with pilgrims, garland sellers, *sadhus* (holy men) and elephants, clusters around an enormous temple complex dedicated to Meenakshi (the beautiful goddess with fish-shaped eyes) and Sundareshwarar (an incarnation of Shiva), her consort. The Meenakshi Temple covers about six hectares (15 acres) and its soaring *gopurams* (multi-pillared halls) are covered in coloured carvings of gods, goddesses and animals. Within the temple there is also a museum. One of the entrances to the temple is through a bazaar where the thousands of pilgrims who arrive every day purchase garlands and food offerings, and sometimes camp.

Madurai is known as the 'City of Festivals', and there is a major one every month except monsoon. Most important are the Chithrai Festival, celebrating the wedding of Shiva and Meenakshi, and the Float Festival in which, after 11 days of ceremonies at the temple, images of Meenakshi and Sundareshwarar are placed on floats and taken in a parade of elephants, musicians and thousands of pilgrims to the Mariammam Teppakkulam Tank on the eastern outskirts of town. This huge artificial lake, with an island and temple at its centre, is filled through underground channels from the river.

The holy couple are towed twice around the lake on a splendid raft, garlanded with flowers, by men on the shore and on the island pulling on ropes. The raft is then moored at the central island with its temple to Ganesh. At dusk, the five towers of the island temple are illuminated, and the brilliantly lit float makes a third circuit of the lake, whose waters dance with reflected light beneath a perfect moon. After prayers, pageantry and fireworks, the deities are returned to their temple home at Madurai in a glittering and joyful cavalcade.

*The raft carrying images of
Lord Sundareshwarar (Shiva)
and Meenakshi is towed around
the Mariammam Teppakkulam
Tank by ropes.*

Jaisalmer Desert Festival

The massive golden citadel of Jaisalmer towers above the Thar Desert. Historically a powerful and wealthy city state whose position gave it command of trade routes from Central Asia, it remains strategically important – it lies close to the border with Pakistan – and is a popular tourist destination. The walled city is still inhabited and very much alive; the ring of massive bastions encloses a warren of busy streets, palaces, temples and fine merchants' houses, all carved from glowing yellow sandstone, and its bazaars overflow with the famous crafts of Rajasthan. It also makes a base for trips to the desert, though the Thar is not an endless sea of golden sands but mostly a wilderness of barren scrub, isolated villages and wandering flocks. However, the smooth undulations of the Sam sand dunes, west of the city, are a lovely location for the finale of Jaisalmer's Desert Festival. This event is promoted by the State Tourist Board to allow visitors a chance to experience the exuberant life and culture of Rajasthan.

The three-day festival begins with a scintillating procession through the town which includes a camel-mounted band, dancers, musicians and decorated camels as well as the local people who wear flame-coloured turbans and saris. In the stadium, enthusiastic crowds watch competitions such as turban tying and 'best moustache' and the flamboyant 'Mr Desert' contest.

Camels star in the second day's events at the polo ground, with races, polo and tugs-of-war. Both evenings conclude with an excellent programme of Rajasthani music and dance.

Day three's evening show – hypnotic music, singing and the swirling mirrored skirts of tribal dancers against a background of moonlit dunes and flickering bonfires – makes a fine end to this glorious festival.

A dance group performs at the festival.

WHEN:
January/February
WHERE:
Jaisalmer and the Sam sand dunes, 42 km (26 mi) to the west, Rajasthan
BEST FOR:
Rajasthani culture
YOU SHOULD KNOW:
Rajasthanis always look as if they are dressed for a party, but on high days and holidays their costumes dazzle. All over India turban colours often indicate caste, but the popular saffron dye of Rajasthan signifies chivalry.

Khajuraho Dance Festival

Every spring, India's most famous and talented classical dancers perform in the dreamlike setting of the illuminated temples of Khajuraho, a remote little town in northern Madhya Pradesh. No evidence of a large-scale settlement exists, but this was once the religious capital of the Chandela empire. Of the 85 temples built between AD 950 and 1050, 25 survive – each a masterpiece. The pointed towers and spires are balanced by ornate bands of carving which are some of the world's best temple sculpture, portraying all aspects of life. The temples of the western group make a perfect backdrop for dance. Among the carved gods and goddesses, real and mythological beasts, the 'courtly arts' – particularly music and dance – figure large. This sculptural evidence underlines the flourishing tradition of dance in India, where it remains not just a very skilled entertainment (dancers train for many years) but a symbol of spirituality in a land where Shiva (as Natraja, the Lord of Dance) danced the universe into creation. Now, costumes reflect ancient carvings and movement breathes life into the myths.

Indian classical dance has many distinct disciplines, each with its own splendid costumes and music, and may be performed solo or as group dance-dramas. Some of the many dance forms seen at Khajuraho, such as *Kathakali* with its ornate make-up and stylized battles of good and evil, and *Kathak*, with its lively rhythms and story-telling, are well known in the West. The many other genres on show include the dynamic and sophisticated *Bharatnatyam*, delicate, beautiful *Manipuri* and *Odissi*, a lyrical, flowing temple dance. This, one of India's most prestigious cultural events, highlights the richness of classical dance and the glory of these temples – undisputedly works of sculptural and architectural genius.

A Bharatnatyam dancer

WHEN:
Late February/early March
WHERE:
Khajuraho, Madhya Pradesh
BEST FOR:
Dance and temples
YOU SHOULD KNOW:
The Khajuraho carvings include energetic erotic scenes. It is possible that these were educational, a stone *Karma Sutra*, or Tantric images, as seen elsewhere in India, or even to prevent lightning strike by entertaining Indra, the rain god. Whatever the original purpose, they portray a life where, along with music and dance, joyous sexual expression is a celebration.

Goa Carnival

When the Portuguese arrived in Goa in the 16th century, they found a tiny, lush area of well-watered lowlands and, importantly, mountains producing spices. They stayed almost 500 years and their legacy can still be seen in a state best known today for its gorgeous, palm-fringed beaches and easy lifestyle. Many names are Portuguese, skirts are worn as often as saris and, in the vegetarian south, Goan cuisine is unusual in its plentiful meat –including pork – dishes. Architecturally, there are colonial homes with deep roofs and shaded verandahs, towns with ancient warehouses and narrow streets of balconied terraces and, everywhere, churches. Many are elaborately gilded and carved and Old Goa, once the hugely wealthy capital and a city rivalling Lisbon, is an enthralling ghost town – a tiny, rural village dotted with dozens of enormous baroque religious buildings.

Christianity remains a major faith and Goa holds India's only pre-Lent carnival. Now primarily a secular three-day spring party, it begins with a riotous procession through the streets of Goa's capital, Panaji, on Sabado Gordo (Fat Saturday). 'King Momo', glorious in red and gold, sets things in motion, proclaiming his three-day rule and urging his 'subjects' to eat, drink and be merry. A huge parade of floats and tableaux, ranging from ecological themes and scenes of traditional Goan life to Portuguese galleons and gods and goddesses, accompanied by dancers, bands, clowns, and thousands of masked and costumed revellers, is watched by vast crowds – and even government officials don paper hats and lick ice creams. Throughout Goa, towns and villages stage parades, cultural events and competitions, music and dancing. Everywhere, days end with bonfires, music and spectacular firework displays. Goans take King Momo's instructions to heart!

WHEN:
March or April (three days before the start of Lent)
WHERE:
Goa, particularly Panaji
BEST FOR:
Fun and fireworks
YOU SHOULD KNOW:
Goan Christianity incorporates elements of Hinduism and some saint's day festivals have been adapted to life in India. The monsoon is important – if it has not arrived by the feast of St Anthony, statues of the saint are lowered into the dry wells; the feast of St John the Baptist is a thanksgiving for the rains and young men, fuelled by the local spirit *feni*, leap into wells newly filled with water.

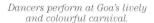
Dancers perform at Goa's lively and colourful carnival.

Holi

WHEN:
Usually March (at the full moon of the Hindu month Purnima)
WHERE:
Jaipur and all over northern India
BEST FOR:
Elephants and colours
YOU SHOULD KNOW:
Huge quantities of pink powder fly around Jaipur on Holi Day. Pink is, for Indians, the colour of hospitality. Maharaja Ram Singh had the whole city of Jaipur painted for the Prince of Wales' visit in 1876 and the colour scheme of this big, chaotic and fascinating city remains unchanged.

Holi, also called the Festival of Colours, is a celebration of the end of winter and one of northern India's most exuberant festivals. Although this is a Hindu festival, people of all faiths participate. On the eve of Holi (Purnima Day) bonfires are lit in the streets to destroy the evil demon Holika and on Holi Day itself everyone throws coloured powders and water at each other.

In Jaipur, the annual Elephant Festival is held on Purnima Day. A fabulous procession of elephants, dressed in fringed silks and brocades, tusks wound with beads and garlands, toenails painted and ankles circled by jingling bracelets, skins painted with geometric patterns and psychedelic flowers, heads proudly out to the sports ground. After a grand parade, huge crowds watch Rajasthani musicians and dancers in fabulous costumes, an elephant beauty contest and elephant polo matches and races. After firework displays, everyone heads back to the city. Bales of hay are burnt in the streets to consume the ills of winter, and partying continues late into the night.

With its dusky pink streets and rosy palaces, the old city is always colourful; on Holi Day it becomes dazzlingly polychromatic. For visitors venturing out, old clothes are essential – though some groups of revellers ask permission to dab colours on face, hair and hands, most loose blizzards of powder and fountains of coloured water at tourists and friends, men and women, old and young – even at bank managers! 'Bombs' – balloons filled with water and powder and dropped from roofs – explode all around. The Festival of Colours is joyful, good-natured and very, very messy.

Coloured powder is thrown to celebrate Holi.

Holla Mohalla

The Punjab is known in the West for its bhangra music, tandoori cooking and its turbaned and bearded men, the Sikhs. Sikhism was founded by Guru Nanak, a saintly mystic who believed in equality and sought to combine the best of Hinduism and Islam. In 1699, Guru Gobind Singh created the Khalsa, a brotherhood of holy soldiers whose distinctive insignia still makes them recognizable. Two years later, in the face of Mughal hostility, he introduced a ceremony to display their battle-readiness. This occasion is commemorated by Holla Mohalla, which takes place at Anandpur Sahib, now one of the holiest Sikh sites, and at *gurdwaras* (Sikh temples) all over the world.

A young man shows off his sword skills.

Sikhs travel long distances to attend this three-day community festival. Local people eagerly organize accommodation and work in the communal kitchens, for this is a time for re-dedication to the service of others – an important aspect of Sikh belief. During the first two days, thousands join in prayer, singing hymns and telling tales of the Ten Gurus, music and dance and shared meals. Although the festival has lost much of its original military significance, the last day is a showcase for horsemanship and feats of arms by the Nihangas, the 'Guru's Knights', famous for courage in battle and self-discipline. After early devotions and a procession to all the town's temples, the Nihangas, armed to the teeth and distinctively dressed in dark-blue robes and conical turbans, lead a glittering cavalcade to the site of the first festival, the river bed just outside town. Here they thrill the huge crowds with dazzling displays of swordsmanship, bareback riding and mock battles. Celebrations end with a great feast; in accordance with tradition, everyone sits together on the ground to eat, with no social distinctions.

WHEN:
First of lunar month Chet, usually March (the day after the national spring festival of Holi)
WHERE:
Anandpur Sahib – about 80 km (50 mi) north of Chandigarh, Punjab
BEST FOR:
Galloping horses and twirling moustaches
YOU SHOULD KNOW:
The distinctive 'five K's' of the Sikhs are *kesh* (uncut hair), *kangha* (comb), *kachh* (shorts – more convenient for battle than robes), *kara* (steel bracelet) and *kirpan* (sword – nowadays usually an emblematic miniature). From the time the Khalsa was founded, all Sikhs have had the surname Singh (lion).

Volunteers hold colourful umbrellas above the elephants.

Thrissur Pooram Elephant Festival

WHEN:
April/May (the Malayalam month of Medom)
WHERE:
Thrissur, Kerala
BEST FOR:
Elephants and drums
YOU SHOULD KNOW:
Thrissur and its surrounding towns and villages have dozens of temple festivals, including Thypooya Maholsavam, a procession of dancers carrying huge decorative structures, an elephant race at Guruvayur, and Uthralikavu Pooram, where elephants circle a shrine with an entourage of chanting worshippers.

Thrissur, known as a cultural and religious centre, is built around the Vadakumnathan temple, one of Kerala's largest. In a state famous for temple festivals, the biggest and best known takes place here. Although non-Hindus may not enter the temple, all are welcomed at the festival and it is popular with tourists and Keralites of all faiths. *Pooram* means 'meeting', and it is believed that all the gods and goddesses gather for this day of celebrations at Thrissur.

The 36-hour festival starts at 06.00, when decorated elephants from outlying village temples parade the streets with their divinities. In the temple grounds, hundreds of drummers play for hours in the Elanjithara Melam, a day-long percussion show which provides insistent rhythms, while onlookers perform wild, spontaneous dances.

The main event is the arrival of two 15-elephant processions from the temples of goddesses Paramekkavu and Thiruvambadi. The elephants are absolutely magnificent, adorned with jewels and silks,

404

silver and gold, palm leaves and peacock feathers. Team supporters spend a great deal of time and money creating this regalia and the ornate parasols which the *mahouts* hold on immensely tall bamboo poles, sheltering the images of their goddesses. The resplendent elephants also carry riders with fans like huge feather dusters. To the music of temple orchestras of drums, cymbals and horns, the teams line up to face each other outside the Temple and conduct a 'pass the parasol' competition, while the roars of approval from the crowds indicate winners. Later, a massed cavalcade of elephants is followed by huge firework displays and festivities, which continue all night and well into the next day.

Kodava Hockey Festival

A delightful and prosperous region of rolling hills, forests, coffee plantations and scattered villages in the Western Ghats, Kodagu only became part of Karnataka in 1956. As a tiny independent state, it was remarkable for avoiding subjugation by successive imperial powers, and its proud people were famous warriors. Nowadays they are renowned for their sporting prowess, and Kodagu is known as the 'cradle of Indian hockey' – many Kodavas have played at national and international level over the years. In 1997, Pandanda Kuttappa, a hockey referee himself, launched the Kodava Hockey Festival as a way to showcase Kodavan hockey, bring villages together and encourage young players.

Teams consist of members of extended families (women may play for their own family or for their in-laws) and the winning family becomes responsible for organizing and hosting the next year's tournament, which bears their name. They are partly responsible for costs, though these are largely covered by sponsorship. The first festival attracted around 60 family teams; now over 200 enter, making this one of the world's largest field hockey events.

The opening ceremony is splendid: the organizing family is accompanied by musicians and Kodavas in colourful national dress; after speeches and flag raising, a visiting celebrity starts the festival by hitting a silver ball with a silver hockey stick. Between games, the crowds are entertained by brass bands, jugglers and acrobats. But this is more than a sporting fixture: it is a time for family reunions (Kodavas living elsewhere return home), socializing with other villages, and shopping – the sports grounds are surrounded by stalls, and profits from the recent coffee harvest are spent on clothes, consumer durables and agricultural equipment.

WHEN:
Late April/early May
WHERE:
Several locations around Kodagu, depending on the home of the organizing family
BEST FOR:
Hockey
YOU SHOULD KNOW:
The customs and ceremonies of the Kodavas include marvellous weddings – which usually do not involve dowries – with mock battles. Although they worship a range of deities, including the holy River Cauvery (Kodava means 'blessed by Mother Cauvery') they do not recognize any heads of religion.

405

Rath Yatra

WHEN:
June or July
(end day of the bright half of the
Hindu month of Asadha), annually
WHERE:
Puri, Orissa
BEST FOR:
Juggernauts and crowds
YOU SHOULD KNOW:
Rath Yatra takes place all over
Orissa. In Baripada, the deities
parade separately over three days
and Subhadra's chariot is pulled by
women, who travel long distances to
be part of this show of spiritual
emancipation.

The seaside town of Puri is popular with holidaymakers from Kolkata and further afield; it is also one of the four 'Cardinal Points' of Hinduism and home to the Lord of the Universe. With his sister Subhadra and brother Balabhadra, Lord Jagannath (an incarnation of Vishnu) resides in Jagannath Mandir, a majestic temple built in the 12th century, tended by about 6,000 priests. Non-Hindus may not enter, but tiny replicas of the image of Jagannath, with his black face and round white eyes, are seen everywhere, and the triad can be glimpsed when they leave their home in the famous Rath Yatra procession, when over a million pilgrims of all castes inundate the town.

The enormous, temple-like chariots – *raths* – which bear the deities are built anew each year (last year's become temple firewood). Hundreds of people are employed in their construction. Lord Jagannath's chariot is 14 m (46 ft) tall and travels on 16 gigantic wheels (this is the origin of the English word juggernaut), the other two *raths* are only slightly smaller. Every few years, temple astrologers decree the renewal of the images and the old ones are buried in the temple graveyard.

After ceremonies in the temple, the divinities leave, to journey to Gundicha Mandir for a short holiday. In the heat and humidity (and often monsoon rain) of mid summer, the vast crowds clamour and cheer, push and shove – just touching the ropes or structure brings countless blessings, which is why people are still sometimes crushed under the massive wheels, despite contingents of security guards. Thousands of devotees pull the ponderous chariots along Grand Road to choruses of hymns and prayers, the beating of drums, the wailing of conches and pipes.

The crowds attempt to touch the raths *as they make their journey.*

Hemis Festival

With its deep, green valleys, towering ranges and colourful rituals of Mahayana Buddhism, Ladakh seems closer to Tibet than to India in spirit. It is a great place for trekking and Leh, the main town, makes a relaxing and pleasant base. The hillsides of Ladakh are scattered with whitewashed *gompas* (monasteries) and many of these centres of Buddhist life welcome interested visitors. Buddhist festivals are frequent and pilgrims come to pray and watch the masked dances, though most take place during the winter months when all the mountain passes are closed and temperatures are very low.

Lamas at the festival dance wearing glorious robes and grotesque masks.

One of the liveliest summer festivals is at Hemis. The largest and wealthiest of the *gompas*, it is a large, rambling 17th century building, fluttering with coloured flags and richly frescoed. The two-day Tse Che Festival of Hemis honours the birthday of the monastery's patron sage, Padmasambhava, who introduced Buddhism to Tibet. Lamas wearing glorious coloured silk and brocade robes and extraordinary, grotesque masks which represent demons and divinities, gather round the flagpole in the large courtyard and perform slow dances symbolizing the triumph of good over evil. Music is provided by drums, cymbals and long horns, whose haunting notes echo around the peaceful valley. These dance-dramas are performed as ritualized offerings to guardian divinities by selected lamas and choreographed by the 'mystic dance master'. At the end of the last day, a grotesque human figure made of dough is cut into pieces and scattered in the four cardinal directions; this figure represents the evils of the human soul – ignorance, jealousy and hatred.

Summer festivals are a valuable opportunity for people to come together, trade, socialize and worship, for communities in the Indus Valley are very scattered and isolated by many months of snow.

WHEN:
July
WHERE:
Hemis, 40 km (25 mi) from Leh, Ladakh
BEST FOR:
Buddhism and mountains
YOU SHOULD KNOW:
Every 12 years (in the Year of the Monkey) the monastery's *tanka* is unfurled during the festival. This huge banner (four storeys high) depicts Padmasambhava, and is embroidered with pearls and precious stones; it will next be unfurled in 2016.

Young girls carrying silver pots during the festival loved by women.

Kajli Teej in Bundi

Bundi is an enchanting town of hills, lakes, bazaars, palaces and narrow lanes of blue houses. In one corner of the towering Taragarh Fort stands the fairytale Bundi Palace, whose interior walls are famous for their exquisite murals of 18th century court life. The town is scattered with water features – lakes, tanks and *baoris* (stepped wells).

Teej, the 'Festival of Swings', celebrates the wedding of Shiva and Parvati and the arrival of the monsoon. It symbolizes married bliss and is beloved by women, who pray for a long and happy married life, decorate their hands and feet with henna in honour of the goddess, and receive gifts. Rajasthan is a parched, desert state for most of the year, and the monsoon brings its own sensuous pleasures – the soft sound of rain, the sweet smell of damp earth, and, during Teej, the singing of girls on flower-decked swings suspended from trees.

Teej is celebrated all over the states – in Bundi, the festival starts later than most and lasts for two days. It begins with a vibrant traditional procession from Nawal Sagar Lake; the goddess is borne by ornamented elephants, accompanied by camels, horses, performers and women who, in their finery, seem to have stepped straight out of the Palace murals. The crowded streets are busy with stalls selling folk art, jewellery and a tempting array of sweets and savouries. In the Stadium, performances during the festival include folk dance, music competitions and Qawwali evenings.

WHEN:
July/August (the third day of the month of Bhadra)
WHERE:
Bundi, Rajasthan
BEST FOR:
Delightful feminine imagery
YOU SHOULD KNOW:
Sukh Mahal, a small palace on Jait Sagar Lake, was for a time home to Rudyard Kipling who wrote part of *Kim* while he stayed there. Now the Irrigation Rest House, it is open to the public.

Naga Panchami

Regarded with both fear and veneration, snakes, particularly cobras (*nagas*), have a very important place in Indian culture and religion. Because they shed and renew their skins, they are a symbol of immortality; their worship is thought to bring wealth and wisdom, and many shrines and temples are dedicated to snake deities. During Naga Panchami, all over India flute-playing snake charmers carry cobras in baskets from house to house and women who offer milk are blessed. Snakes are painted on walls and floors, modelled from cloth, dough and clay, while cow-dung images guard doorways. In rural areas, live snakes (which leave the flooded fields during the monsoon and move nearer villages) are captured, kept in clay pots until the festival, and fed with rats and milk.

Naga Panchami is very important in Maharashtra and hundreds travel to honour the vast collection of snakes assembled in the remote village of Baltis Shirale. On the festival day, an enormous parade of worshippers, many with cobra-pots on their heads, others dancing alongside bands or riding in decorated bullock carts, progresses to the temple of the snake goddess, Amba Mata. Here, the released snakes are blessed and sprinkled with flower petals, then offered milk and honey. They are returned to their pots and the procession visits outlying hamlets, freeing snakes wherever offerings are made. In the evening, during a lively fair around the temple, the cobra-pots are placed on a platform and the lids removed. Snakes and crowds – who come from all over the state – gaze at each other. Whether lulled by the melodic flutes, the burning camphor, or overeating, the cobras remain calm and reputedly never bite those seeking their divine protection. Next day, they are set free in the forest.

WHEN:
July/August (fifth day of the moonlit fortnight of the month of Shravan)
WHERE:
Baltis Shirale, 70 km (44 mi) from Sangli, southern Maharashtra
BEST FOR:
Snakes
YOU SHOULD KNOW:
There are several major snake gods in India, including the thousand-headed cosmic serpent often depicted sheltering Shiva. Cobra veneration is second only to that of the cow, and most Hindu homes possess a snake idol. During Naga Panchami, no ploughing is undertaken, to avoid injuring snakes.

A snake charmer keeps a watchful eye on his snakes.

ASIA/INDIA

Onam in Kerala

WHEN:
August/September (Malayalam
month Chingham)
WHERE:
All over Kerala
BEST FOR:
Dances and boat races
YOU SHOULD KNOW:
The revered King Mahabali ruled
over an earthly paradise, with no
poverty, sorrow or disease, and no
caste system (Communism remains
popular in Kerala). The gods became
jealous of so much happiness and
tricked him into sacrificing himself to
save his beloved people. But they
granted his wish to visit his country
once a year, and now people strive
to show him how joyful and
prosperous they still are.

Kerala's biggest festival, Onam is celebrated throughout the state
over ten days to mark the homecoming of King Mahabali and the
Malayalam New Year. Many of the rituals take place in homes, for this
is a time for new clothes, treats for the children, family gatherings
and present giving.

Atham, the start of the festival, is a holy and auspicious day when
work starts on the *pookalam* in front of each house. Children collect
flowers and girls and women make them into elaborate floral carpets,
which are added to during the festival. On the last day, Thiru Onam,
Kerala celebrates, with all faiths and castes joining in. After prayers
at the local temple, extended families enjoy a vegetarian feast,
onasadya. Much care is taken over the preparation of the many
courses and even over the arrangement of colours on the banana-leaf
plates. After this beautiful meal, women dance and games are played.

Across the state, the people greet their mythical ruler with feats
of valour in archery contests and martial arts displays. Spirited
performances of Pulikali are staged, with dancers, bodies painted in
yellow, black and red, representing tigers; and at the Kathakali
Training Centre in Cheruthuruthy, enthusiastic crowds enjoy
fabulous epics. A few days before Thiru Onam, at Alappuzha,
spectators line the banks to cheer the 'snake boat' races – Vallamkali.
The long, beautifully decorated boats with curved prows carry
hundreds of oarsmen, and drummers to beat time as they row.
Everywhere, Onam ends with fireworks.

*Performers dressed as tigers
perform the Pulikali, or
tiger dance.*

Ganesh Chaturthi in Maharashtra

Elephant-headed, pot-bellied Ganesh is a popular Hindu deity. His appearance seems comical to Westerners, but he is an old and powerful deity and, as the god of wisdom and prosperity, he is invoked at the start of any auspicious enterprise. In legend he is the son of Shiva and Parvati; she made him from sandalwood dough, breathed life into him, and left him to guard her door while she bathed. Shiva returned and, angered by a challenge from the strange child, chopped off his head. Distraught Parvati begged him to bring the child back to life, so Shiva lopped off the head from an elephant, fixed it on the child, and Ganesh was born.

Ganesh Chaturthi is celebrated all over India, but with particular enthusiasm and pageantry in Maharashtra. Statues of Ganesh (some are enormous) are installed on street corners, and shrines in temples and homes are decorated. Small clay models of the god are brought home on the day before Chaturthi, when women fast and invoke blessings from Parvati. The festival starts on Ganesh's birthday, when prayers and sticky confectionary (he was very fond of sweets) are offered to the statues, and continues for several days. On the last day of the festival, all the images, from huge street statues to clay figurines, are carried through the streets in joyful procession to be immersed in water, be it sea, river, lake or tank. Chaturthi, the largest Hindu festival in Mumbai, sweeps the entire city as families and communities bear their images of Ganesh down to the seafront. Thousands of processions converge on Chowpatty Beach, where Ganesh sand-sculptures are also consigned to the waves as millions throng to submerge all the images, with resounding calls to the god to return soon.

A statue of Lord Ganesh is carried through the streets.

WHEN:
August/September (full moon, Hindu month of Bhaarapada)
WHERE:
Maharashtra
BEST FOR:
Processions
YOU SHOULD KNOW:
A great deal of Hindu symbolism is tied up with Ganesh; the whole cosmos is in his round belly, held together by cosmic energy (the snake he wears around his middle). He rides on a mouse, which represents the ego, and only has one tusk because he threw the other at the moon when it mocked him; looking at the moon on his birthday is forbidden.

Phang Lhabsol

WHEN:
August/September (15th day of the
seventh month of the lunar calendar)
WHERE:
Gangkot (and other monasteries),
Sikkim
BEST FOR:
Mountain worship
YOU SHOULD KNOW:
Sikkim is known as the 'Garden
Kingdom' and is particularly famous
for its orchids. Literally hundreds of
varieties can be seen in the Orchid
Sanctuary on the mountain slopes
around Gangkot's fascinating
Institute of Tibetology.

The tiny state of Sikkim, until 1975, was an independent kingdom. Originally settled by the Lepchas, a tribal people, it became an extensive Buddhist kingdom after the arrival of the Bhutias from Tibet in the 15th century. Later, the British encouraged the Nepalese to immigrate and they now make up the majority of the population – though religions, cultures and customs intermingle freely and Buddhist ceremonies are fundamental to Sikkimese life. This is a peaceful and beautiful country, with unspoilt hillsides clothed in rhododendron forest and, everywhere, glimpses of massive, snow-capped Khangchendzonga, India's highest peak and the presiding deity of Sikkim. It was on the lower slopes of the mountain that the Lepchas and Bhutias made a treaty of blood-brotherhood, witnessed only by the magnificent peak, and Phang Lhabsol commemorates this occasion and pays homage to the mountain with prayers for continued brotherhood and good fortune.

In 1700, the third Chogyal (Buddhist king) had a divine vision of the Pang Toed dance, which he then introduced as part of the festival. It is still performed in important monasteries, in particular outside the Royal Chapel Tsuklakhang in the capital Gangkot – a pleasant hillside town with fine views of Khangchendzonga. The Royal Chapel is open during the festival; its interior is lavishly carved and painted and it houses an important collection of Buddhist treasures. Prayers to the protective deity for peace and prosperity begin a week beforehand and, on the day of the festival, lamas perform the spectacular war-like dance. The choreography and costumes are marvellous; jesters entertain onlookers with comic routines and 'warriors' with swords, shields and helmets whirl and leap. The dancer representing Khangchendzonga wears a fierce, fiery red mask, with a crown and regalia of skulls and flags, and rides a 'snow lion'. This serious but lively and colourful celebration is greatly enjoyed by people of all faiths.

Dussehra in Mysore

Dussehra in Mysore commemorates the victory of the goddess Chamundeshwari (a warlike incarnation of Durga) over the buffalo-headed demon Mahishasura who ruled Mysore, and symbolizes the triumph of good over evil. The days leading up to the festival are dedicated with prayer and fasting to Chamundeshwari, the nights to feasting, song and dance. It is celebrated in many places and is also known as Navrati, Festival of Nine Nights. But the festival is most magnificent in Mysore, whose name traditionally comes from Mahisura – the place where the demon was slain by Chamundeshwari.

An attractive city of wide avenues lined with Raj-era buildings and lively narrow lanes (the market is one of India's most colourful), Mysore is known for fine silks, incense and sandalwood products, and for its fantastically elaborate Palace. This, an Indo-Saracenic complex of sumptuous rooms full of mirrors, stained glass, gilding, mosaics and carving, was built for the Maharajas of Mysore State – the Wodeyars – respected rulers who still play an important part in their city's ceremonial life. Chamundeshwari is the family deity, and Dussehra begins with their visit to her temple on Chamundi Hill. During the festival, Mysore enjoys a programme of events, from food and craft fairs to dancing and wrestling. By night, musicians perform in front of the Palace which, along with other public buildings, is brilliantly illuminated.

On Vijaydashami, the tenth day of the festival, a dazzling procession has all the pomp and pageantry of the age of the Maharajas. The image of the goddess Chamundeshwari, carried in a golden palanquin on a caparisoned elephant, leads a glittering array of camels, cavalry, dancers, liveried retainers, garlanded idols and brass bands. A glorious torch-lit parade and fireworks bring events to a close.

WHEN:
Late September/October
WHERE:
Mysore, Karnataka
BEST FOR:
Pomp and illuminations
YOU SHOULD KNOW:
Around 1,000 steps lead to the top of Chamundi Hill, where the towering temple of Sri Chamundeshwari stands. Outside the temple is a lively polychrome statue of the demon, brandishing a sword in one hand and a long snake in the other. Halfway up the hill, the huge, monolithic statue of Nandi, Shiva's bull, is visited by many pilgrims.

Ornately painted elephants take part in the parade at the Dussehra festival.

Pushkar Camel Fair

WHEN:
Usually November (around the full
moon of the Hindu month, Kartika).
About five days of trading precede
the four-day festival.
WHERE:
Pushkar, Rajasthan
BEST FOR:
Camels
YOU SHOULD KNOW:
There are very few Brahma temples in
the world. According to legend,
Brahma, after waiting impatiently at
the lake for his wife Savitri,
impulsively married another woman.
Savitri, enraged, vowed that he would
not be worshipped anywhere else.

The crowds gather for the fair.

Pushkar is a lovely little town, clustered round a lake and sheltered
by hills and sand dunes from the harsh Thar Desert. This is a very
important place of pilgrimage for Hindus, and among its 400 temples
is one dedicated to Brahma. The sacred lake, formed where he let
fall a lotus petal, is surrounded by 52 bathing *ghats*, from one of
which the ashes of Mahatma Gandhi were scattered.

Just before the November full moon, the atmosphere of religious
contemplation changes to intense excitement as the Pushkar Camel
Fair (with up to 50,000 camels and 200,000 visitors, the world's
largest) begins. A vast funfair-cum-market springs up as villagers
from all over Rajasthan pitch their tents in the dunes west of town
and settle down to buying and selling camels, worshipping in the
temples, bathing in the lake and shopping for goods ranging from
cooking pots to magnificent ceremonial camel harness. Visitors are
welcome at this huge event and often get involved in cricket

matches, but it retains the atmosphere of a rural fair.

After a few days of trading, the camels are washed and dressed in pom-poms, silver bells and beads, while some are shaved into intricate patterns, in preparation for a camel beauty contest and races. The size and animation of the show grounds – a glorious jumble of musicians, dancers, magicians, traders, acrobats, fortune-tellers and snake charmers – are intoxicating. This is also a very important religious occasion and every day the town is full of incense, chanting and processions; when the races finish, everyone crowds to the lake and enters the purifying water.

Poush Mela

Poet and polymath Rabindranath Tagore (1861-1941) was the first Asian writer to win the Nobel Prize for Literature. As a passionate educationalist and social reformer, he set up a school on his much-loved family land – his father had named it Shantiniketan (abode of peace) because of its rural tranquillity. When the Shantiniketan school first opened in 1901 there were just five students and classes were held outside under the trees to encourage a spirit of harmony with nature. Out of these small beginnings grew the university of Visva Bharati, a renowned centre of excellence for the study of Bengali culture, music and the fine arts, and the tradition of the annual Poush Mela (harvest fair).

Poush Mela commemorates the founding of Shantiniketan. It was devised by Tagore as a way of stirring townspeople's interest in the many different aspects of Indian rural culture, for he was only too aware of the frightening inequalities embedded in Indian society and the lack of understanding between different sectors of the community. Although by Indian standards Poush Mela is a festival of very recent origin, in existence for only around a hundred years, it always attracts thousands of people, both from home and abroad.

For three days Shantiniketan is turned into a massive fairground with any number of arts and crafts stalls, performance artists and musicians, all celebrating Bengal's rich folk heritage. The highlight of the fair is the Baul music. The Bauls are a mysterious sect of mystical Hindu and Muslim wandering minstrels, instantly recognizable by their distinctive orange clothes and ancient musical instruments. Tagore was attracted to their philosophy as well as their distinctive melodies, through which they transmit the power of divine love. Their high profile at Poush Mela ensures that their unique musical tradition will be kept alive for future generations.

WHEN:
Late December (usually at Christmas)
WHERE:
Shantiniketan, Birbhum District, West Bengal
BEST FOR:
Baul music and Bengali folk heritage
YOU SHOULD KNOW:
The Baul tradition is listed as a UNESCO Masterpiece of the Oral and Intangible Heritage of Humanity. Rabindranath Tagore has a special place in both the Indian and Bangla Deshi national consciousness. He wrote the lyrics and composed the music for both countries' national anthems.

415

Vesak

WHEN:
Starting on the full moon in May
WHERE:
All across southern Sri Lanka, but
most lavish in Colombo
BEST FOR:
Culture
YOU SHOULD KNOW:
Recently there has been tension
between those who see the holiday
as a time for great devotion and
mainly younger people who see it as
a chance to have a good time. It
should be noted that alcohol sales
are banned.

Due in large part to its great ethnic diversity, Sri Lanka has a staggering 25 national holidays, averaging almost one per fortnight. Buddhism, Hinduism, Islam and Christianity all have their holy days but, for the majority Sinhalese population, the week-long festival of Vesak is the most revered time of the year. Commencing on the day of the first full moon in May, Vesak commemorates the anniversary of the birth, enlightenment and death of the Lord Buddha Jayanthi.

For many it is a time to show devotion, and many of the population dress in white, to symbolize purity of mind and spirit, and congregate at the temple bearing gifts of food. The country's capital, Colombo, becomes the focal point for celebrations, as trains and buses bring crowds from outlying towns and villages to the festivities. Vesak is also known as the Buddhist Festival of Light and the whole city centre is illuminated by intricate decorations. Colourful lanterns known as Vesak *koodu* are hung outside shops and houses, creating a wonderful luminosity to complement the moonlight. Panels of colourful lights called *toranas* are put up all across the city, each depicting a scene from the life of Buddha. Months of work are put into their construction and the best ones draw huge appreciative crowds.

Vesak is a time to reflect on the teachings of Buddha and displays of kindness and charity are commonplace. Free nourishment is handed out along the city's streets by *dansalas* (Buddhist devotees) and birds are released to represent liberation from incarceration. Vesak is a wonderful time to be in Colombo and the goodwill on display is infectious. It is a time when people can take a break from their often hectic lives and forget for a moment the country's troubles to rejoice in the generosity of the human spirit.

Buddhist devotees light coconut-oil lamps at Vesak.

Esala Perahera in Kandy

Male dancers add to the vibrancy and colour of Esala Perahera.

There are certain souvenirs one brings back from holiday that looked so perfect when you were away, but look so wrong when you get them out of the suitcase. You are then faced with two options: you can try to foist them off as a present or put them at the back of a cupboard. The Kandyan mask is one such item. There is something magical about the light in Sri Lanka's second city that means it can get away with a garish clash of colours like few other places.

The ten-day festival of the Esala Perahera is possibly the most vibrant show on earth, bombarding the senses with noise, light and, above all, colour. The festival starts with the ceremonial cutting down of a jack tree, which is then offered to four deities in order that the people will be blessed in the year ahead. For the next five nights intimate gatherings (Kumbal Perahera) take place at the shrines (*devales*) dedicated to these guardian gods.

The following five nights see the Randoli Perahera – processions that get bigger each night, building up to an unmissable last night spectacular. Anticipation mounts under the milky light of the full moon and the crowd falls silent as the cracking of whips symbolically clears the path for the parade. Flag bearers follow, carrying pendants of all shapes and colours, soon to be succeeded by astonishingly gymnastic fire dancers, who writhe and leap to create an amazing pyrotechnic show. More sedate dancers follow, before the centrepiece of the parade is revealed: the Maligawa Tusker – a carriage conveying a replica of the casket that holds the tooth of Lord Buddha. The pounding of drums builds to a crescendo, heralding the arrival of the parade of elephants. Each of these magnificent beasts is adorned with intricately woven silk costumes and the sight of so many walking in harmony is stunning to behold.

WHEN:
For ten days leading up to the full moon in July or August
WHERE:
Kandy
BEST FOR:
Religious spectacle
YOU SHOULD KNOW:
The final parade lasts for four hours, so if you wish to come and go without losing your pitch, several hotels and restaurants will reserve you a seat as long as you eat there.

The procession of kavadi *bearers moves through the fields.*

Thaipusam Kavadi Parade

The Hindu festival of Thaipusam commemorates the birthday of the god Murugan (or Subramanian), the youngest son of Lord Shiva and Parvati (the mother goddess in Hindu mythology). Murugan is the patron deity of the South Indian Tamil people, who worship him as the incarnation of nature's beauty and the source of all spiritual wisdom. The cult of Murugan is especially widespread on the island of Mauritius in the Indian Ocean where the large immigrant Tamil community, settled here since the 18th century, has steadfastly clung to its ancient cultural and religious heritage and has dedicated more than a hundred temples to its god.

Thaipusam is an occasion for penitence, thanksgiving, and transcendence of the material world. For ten days before the festival, devotees purify themselves by fasting and abstaining from sex and on the day itself, after shaving their heads, they set off *en masse* to their local Murugan temple, each carrying a *kavadi* (literally 'burden') – an enormous wooden crate or frame, bedecked with flowers, in which a pot of milk is placed as an offering to their god. These *kavadi* are carried aloft as the procession of penitents dances its way toward the temple to the accompaniment of chanting, bell-ringing and rhythmic drumming. As if the heavy load were not the cause of enough discomfort, the *kavadi* bearers also pierce their forehead, cheeks and tongue with *vel* (spikes) and attach hooks weighted with chains to their chest and back in the belief that the greater the mortification of the flesh, the more spiritual merit earned. Many of them go into trances or frenzied fits of religious ecstasy. Onlookers can only gaze in wonderment at this truly awesome display of mass religious masochism, in which the participants are apparently capable of rising above any amount of pain.

WHEN:
January/February
WHERE:
Port Louis (or any of the Murugan temples in Mauritius)
BEST FOR:
Extraordinary religious rituals
YOU SHOULD KNOW:
Mauritius was the home of the proverbial dodo – a large flightless bird that was endemic to the island and which became extinct in the late 17th century.

Harbin International Ice and Snow Sculpture Festival

It will take the accelerating process of global warming some time to disrupt the Harbin International Ice and Snow Sculpture Festival in northeast China. Under the influence of biting winds from Siberia, winter temperatures can sink to –38°C (–100°F). This permits the month-long Harbin International Ice and Snow Sculpture Festival – one of the world's top such events – to proceed without any fear of meltdown. Human interference is another matter – the festival was banned during China's infamous Cultural Revolution, but was resumed in 1985.

The range of chilly attractions is impressive. There's a huge selection of amazing ice sculptures, centred on Sun Island in the Songhua River but found throughout the city, that are crafted by artists from all over the globe using both traditional techniques (chisels) and more modern tools like chainsaws and lasers. Ice lanterns are created by the thousand to decorate Harbin's streets and parks, many of which offer enchanting lantern trails and the added bonus of trees and shrubs that have been artistically iced. On a more physical note, for hardy souls there's alpine skiing, skating, sledding and winter swimming in the Songhua – even fun-hating Chairman Mao must surely have approved of the latter after his famous dips in the Yangtze River.

A simple description of the festival's scope does no justice at all to the magnificence of extraordinary works of art. As many thousands of visitors from all over China wander by night through a wonderland of brilliantly lit visions in ice, they can only wonder at the creative vision that produced such a wide range of ambitious work, knowing that the spring thaw will sweep it away. It may be a cliché, but this event really does deserve the description 'must be seen to be believed' – the whole thing is simply breathtaking.

WHEN:
January (though some exhibits are created earlier and remain for longer)
WHERE:
Harbin, Heilongjiang
BEST FOR:
A winter wonderland like no other
YOU SHOULD KNOW:
The festival reflects the traditional practice of making ice lanterns – a bucketful of water would be allowed to part freeze before being tipped out, whereupon a hole would be cut in the top, the remaining water poured out and a candle placed inside to make a perfectly windproof outside winter light.

Ice dancers perform at the festival in front of a huge ice sculpture.

Crowds walk under a row of trees decorated with fans and lanterns.

Chun Jie Spring Festival

The oldest and most sacred festival in the Chinese calendar is Chun Jie, known in the West as the spring festival, lunar new year or Chinese new year. This important annual occasion is a time to reaffirm the family and kinship ties that are so important in Chinese society, put old grudges aside and make a fresh start in life.

In the run-up to Chun Jie any debts are paid, hair is cut, new clothes are purchased and the house is diligently swept. Doors are decorated with vertical scrolls of red paper, covered in text whose characters praise nature and seek good fortune. Incense is burned in homes and temples as a mark of respect to ancestors. On New Year's Eve families feast together in brightly lit houses, with dinner including traditional dishes like *jiaozi* (steamed dumpling) or *nian gao* (sweet rice pudding).

At midnight, fireworks explode all over China to drive away those unfriendly devils and greet the arrival of another year and all that it will bring.

Many Chinese families then spend New Year's Day visiting neighbours, family and friends to extend the general feeling of goodwill that pervades the entire community during the period of Chun Jie. Visitors are always made welcome and invited to be a part of the vibrant party atmosphere that illuminates streets everywhere, from great cities like Beijing, Shanghai or Hong Kong down to the smallest provincial town.

In the vast Chinese countryside, Chun Jie is an affirmation of a timeless way of life that is changing but slowly, whilst cities and towns celebrate a modern urban lifestyle that still remembers its traditional roots. But wherever you are, this is a great time to visit China and start to appreciate the enduring influence of its age-old culture.

WHEN:
Between late January and the middle of February
WHERE:
All over China and wherever established Chinese communities are found.
BEST FOR:
Seeing China's happiest face
YOU SHOULD KNOW:
The hanging scrolls widely seen at Chun Jie descend from the custom of hanging peach-wood charms to ward off ghosts and evil spirits, a practice that still persists in remote areas.

Lisu Knife-Pole Festival

On the eighth day of the second Chinese lunar month, an extraordinary event may be observed in southwestern China. The Lisu tribe spreads across four countries (Burma, Thailand, India and China) and consists of some 60 different clans that have largely maintained their traditional culture and way of life. The Knife-Pole Festival celebrated by the Chinese clans has been held annually since 1644, commemorating a decisive victory that validated their wise decision to join the upwardly mobile Qing Dynasty in its fight against the fading Han Chinese Ming Dynasty.

On the eve of the festival there is much singing and dancing, with hardened warriors proving their bravery with courageous acts like leaping through flames or walking barefoot over hot coals. The main event consists of well-practised menfolk climbing a dangerous 20-m (65-ft) 'ladder' whose rungs consist of knives jammed into a pole. The climber's feet and hands have no protection, so it requires great skill to make the ascent and descent without allowing razor-sharp steel to inflict serious gashes. These courageous feats reflect the old Chinese saying that bravery is 'climbing the Knife Mountain and diving into the Fire Sea'.

During the festivities the women wear their brightest dresses and decorate themselves with elaborate silver jewellery, shells, coral and pearls whilst the men carry knives, bows and arrows at all times. The Lisu people have their unique gwa-che dance and music is made using the Lisu guitar and *fulu jewlew* (a flute-like instrument consisting of bamboo tubes and a gourd). Every occasion in the Lisu calendar, from harvest to the homecoming of hunters, has its own distinctive songs and dances, but the Knife-Pole Festival is the event that draws spectators from all over China, who are warmly welcomed by these hospitable people.

WHEN:
March
WHERE:
Yunnan Province
BEST FOR:
The colourful culture of one of China's 56 officially recognized ethnic groups
YOU SHOULD KNOW:
Every traditional Lisu village has a sacred grove where offerings are left for the Sky God and other important spirits – look but don't intrude.

Climbers make their way up the razor-sharp pole.

Weifang International Kite Festival

WHEN:
Late April
WHERE:
Weifang, Shandong
BEST FOR:
Kites, glorious kites
YOU SHOULD KNOW:
The finest kites ever made may be inspected at leisure in the extensive Weifang Kite Museum, which has a remarkable collection of flying confections collected over the years.

It may sound like an overblown boast, but isn't – Weifang really is the world's kite capital, celebrating this lofty status with a high-flying festival that proves the point beyond doubt. The whole place goes kite-crazy, with participants and spectators arriving from all over China and the wider world for a number of organized activities.

These include an International Kite Competition, Character Kites and the local Weifang Competition, supported by numerous opportunities for spectators to try their hand at the noble art and a mass flight which sees thousands of kites aloft simultaneously. Meanwhile, the city is decorated with coloured streamers and traditional lanterns that provide a fabulous light show after dark. Many traditional artistic performances and firework displays are staged during the festival, adding another dimension to the magical miscellany of soaring kites.

The festival opens with a grand parade of participants marching to the sound of firecrackers, drums and gongs, each proudly displaying the creation that carries high hopes of a prestigious prize. The imagination that has gone into these cutting-edge kites is extraordinary, as is the variety of styles. Though they may all be visually stunning, ultimately it's performance that counts – so the festival highlights are undoubtedly the flying competitions.

These take place on Fuyan Mountain, on the beach beside the Bohai Sea or in Weifang's romantically named Municipal Government Square. The International Competition attracts over 100 teams from many countries and all China's principal cities. The Character Kites are presented by invited Chinese teams, each flying ten kites representing aspects of traditional mythology. Finally, each of Weifang's counties puts up a 20-person team with 30 kites apiece for the most ferocious contest of all. The cumulative result is a dazzling display of fabulous kites soaring against the blue sky to the delight of appreciative spectators.

A panda kite lifts into the sky.

Guizhou Azalea Festival

Though of fairly recent origin (it was held for the first time in 1993) and paying more than passing respect to China's burgeoning internal holiday market and the international tourist dollar, the Guizhou Azalea Festival in China's southwest offers incomparable displays of 'garden royalty'. The azaleas that grow hereabouts are certainly fabulous, and local people have taken with rare enthusiasm to this shrewd opportunity to enhance their province's great natural resource. In consequence, the festival has grown to present a diverse selection of traditional activities that are designed to complement the dramatic azalea show.

There are thousands of named varieties of these wonderful plants and this area is home to a huge number of them. Heavily wooded Qianxi and Dafang counties in Guizhou Province provide a dramatic showcase and this wild flower garden becomes a riot of colour in spring, now formally recognized after the creation of Guizhou Baili Azalea National Forest Park. The azaleas start to bloom in March, reach a spectacular peak in April and continue flowering into May.

To take advantage of a floral phenomenon that brings thousands of visitors to Guizhou every year, the festival itself is held over five days in April at various locations. The opening features brightly clad performers conducting an extended ceremony of worship to the flower goddess. This includes daring acrobatics, much blowing of horns, waving of flags and the giving of solemn offerings. Subsequently, there are further folk performances by the Yi, Miao and Buyi peoples, bell dancing, Lusheng dance, the music of reed pipes, festive lantern shows, mountain ball rolling, bull and cock fighting and a bonfire carnival with fireworks. The festival is also notable for the fact that local people prepare and serve a wide range of delicacies for the duration of this unusual event.

WHEN:
April
WHERE:
Qianxi and Dafang counties, Guizhou
BEST FOR:
Billions of blooms
YOU SHOULD KNOW:
Most festival visitors also take the opportunity to see the impressive Huangguoshu waterfall and extraordinary Zhijin cave.

Acrobats add their own colour to the Azalea Festival.

Fireworks explode on the tower of mock buns.

Festival of the Bun Hills

Also known as the Cheung Chau Festival, after its location on a small island to the southwest of Hong Kong, the Festival of the Bun Hills begins on the eighth day of the fourth moon in the Chinese calendar. Such is the spectacle that many thousands of visitors are attracted to Hong Kong each year to share in the fabulous fun and games.

Once a ritual during which fishing communities gathered to ward off evil spirits and pray for deliverance from pirates, the festival's specific origins have been forgotten as it has changed over time into a general celebration of Chinese culture. The centrepiece may be found at the island's Pak Tai Temple, where three gigantic bamboo towers are erected and covered in the buns, thus providing the festival's name. There used to be a race where young men competed to grab the highest (and therefore luckiest) bun possible. After a collapse that injured many people this ritual is restricted to one climber per tower, though the 'bun-snatching' tradition is maintained with a climbing race on a specially constructed steel-framed tower in a nearby park where (sadly for traditionalists) the buns are made of plastic.

But there's a lot more to the festival than buns. A procession of floats is headed by the image of Pak Tai, Spirit of the North and God of Water. He is followed by a noisy parade whose loudly beaten gongs and drums scare away ghosts and ghouls, whilst the stars of the show are children who seem to glide through the air, suspended above the crowds on paper fans and sword tips (actually rigid frames). Chinese operas, dragon dances and lion dances are staged and paper effigies of the King of the Ghosts burn as the island enjoys an uninhibited week-long bunfight.

WHEN:
Usually early May
(very occasionally late April)
WHERE:
Cheung Chau Island, Hong Kong
BEST FOR:
A lively display of Chinese culture
YOU SHOULD KNOW:
Only vegetarian food may be
served on Cheung Chau Island
during the festivities.

Sanyue Jie in Dali

The festival of the third month (Sanyue Jie) has been taking place in the former Kingdom of Dali in the northwest of China for over a thousand years. The city of Dali in the scenic foothills of the Cangshan Mountains has been redeveloped of late, but the new centre is some distance from the Ming Old Town built in the 14th century, that retains many ancient buildings and a timeless atmosphere.

A human dragon gets ready to perform.

Originally a Buddhist festival, Sanyue Jie became rather less spiritual as the centuries rolled by. At its heart is a vast open-air street fair and market that lasts for between five and seven days, organized by the Bai people. The Bai are joined by other ethnic minorities, who travel considerable distances from all over Yunnan to attend, mostly wearing colourful clothing to create a fabulous collective display of traditional costumes.

Everything imaginable is on sale from laden stalls and there's always plenty of horse-trading going on (we're talking about buying and selling horses rather than haggling for a bargain, though that's worth trying too!). The local marble is famous throughout China and a huge variety of carved objects is on offer during Sanyue Jie. When simply cut and polished to reveal 'pictures' on the surface, marble *chushi* are framed to make attractive wall decorations. Other specialities include beautiful embroidery, often created by the Miao minority from Guizhou Province.

Serious shopping is enlivened by a great festive atmosphere. There is much feasting (don't miss the delicious local fried cheese) whilst acrobats, musicians and dancers entertain the crowds. Meanwhile, skilful competitors demonstrate their prowess at various sports like wrestling, horseracing and dragon-boat contests. Dali is always worth a visit in its own right, but being there at festival time greatly enhances the experience.

WHEN:
Usually April (sometimes early May)
WHERE:
Dali, Yunnan
BEST FOR:
The unchanging face of old China
YOU SHOULD KNOW:
This festival was first held well over a thousand years ago to honour Guanyin, the Goddess of Mercy.

ASIA/CHINA

Sisters' Meal Festival

WHEN:
Usually early May (very occasionally late April)
WHERE:
Shidong, Guizhou
BEST FOR:
Unspoiled ethnic tradition
YOU SHOULD KNOW:
It is possible to book special tours that include a visit to the Sisters' Meal Festival, rather than trying to organize a solo trip.

The age-old boy-meets-girl (or girl-meets-boy) quest takes many forms, none more interesting that the annual homage conducted by the Miao minority in rural Guizhou Province. Legend has it that lovesick girls at the riverside met the God Zhang Guolao, who told them to prepare coloured rolls of glutinous rice filled with fish and shrimp. When young men came down from the mountain the rice was offered and the girls found marriage partners – a delightful way of saying that the way to a man's heart is through his stomach.

The Sisters' Meal Festival stemming from this legend is a very special event that celebrates love and the arrival of spring. Miao people from remote villages come together in Shidong in a colourful kaleidoscope of customs and local traditions, ostensibly for girls to seek partners. To that end, they wear beautifully embroidered clothing and huge amounts of silver. Dressed to kill, these exotic creatures are at the heart of a festival that does indeed see much flirting amongst the group of youngsters that gathers but once a year.

But the Sisters' Meal Festival is for everyone, and the day starts with meals featuring rice dyed using leaves, berries and flowers. This may be formed into balls concealing tokens with a message that may be presented to a suitable recipient (strangely, a thorn means 'you're the one'!). Later, the Qingshui riverside where the legend was born comes alive with music and dance, while the elders attend cockfighting as well as bullfighting competitions, haggle in the market or paddle dugout canoes along the river. It's a wonderful opportunity to meet, greet and catch up on a year's gossip. As night falls the party really begins, with dragon dances, music and fireworks entertaining the packed crowds far into the night. Next morning, it's a case of begin again!

Miao girls wear traditional silver headdresses and embroidered clothes for the festival.

The Great Wall Marathon

Nowadays, everywhere that's anywhere has to stage a marathon – so where better than the mighty Great Wall of China? Luckily for runners in The Great Wall Marathon, they only have to cover the same 42.195-km (26-mi 385-yd) distance that applies to every other marathon, rather than The Wall's full 6,400-km (4,000-mi) length. That doesn't mean that this race is an easy touch, though the usual 5-km (3-mi), 10-km (6-mi) and half-marathon options are available for those who don't want to (or who are not capable of) tackling the real thing.

Competitors are bussed in to the course in rural Tianjin Province, three hours from Beijing. It's so demanding that experienced marathoners expect to add at least an hour to their normal time. Despite an early start, searing heat becomes a factor as the race unfolds, though drink stations serve bottled water at regular intervals. The first (and last, for it is repeated) section of the course takes runners up to and along the Great Wall. This part consists of steep ascents and descents that include thousands of steps, some shallow, some knee-high. The rest of the course is along flat gravel and asphalt roads that pass through rice fields and picturesque villages. The race takes place in breathtaking mountain scenery that provides huge compensation for the additional physical effort and cost (that includes medical insurance) required to participate.

For those tough enough to tackle all or part of it, The Great Wall Marathon is the running experience of a lifetime. Better still, it's possible to be one of the first – only a couple of thousand currently compete, but this number is sure to rise rapidly over the years as the dramatic quality of this race becomes more widely known.

Super-fit competitors tackle the Great Wall Marathon.

WHEN:
May
WHERE:
Tianjin
BEST FOR:
Super-fit sightseers with serious stamina
YOU SHOULD KNOW:
Those whose ambitions exceed their athletic abilities will be saved from themselves – the race must be completed within eight hours and there's a six-hour cut-off point at kilometre 32 that prevents stragglers entering the final, demanding Great Wall section of the course.

Dragon Boat Festival

On day five of the fifth moon, a long-ago death is remembered in style. Over 2,000 years ago a popular Chinese hero – government minister, poet and Confucian scholar Qu Yuan – drowned himself in despair after the powerful state of Qin conquered his beloved state of

Teams of rowers battle for the lead during the race.

Chu. Local people threw food into the river to stop fish eating him, and launched boats in a frantic attempt to recover his revered body.

From this legend spring the principal activities that characterize today's Dragon Boat Festival (Duanwu in Mandarin or Tuen Ng in Cantonese). It sees people cooking and consuming large quantities of *zongzi* (substantial rice wraps), washed down with *realgar* wine. Offerings of food are carefully placed in the water and many participants dip their hands or even swim. The second part of the ritual consists of passionate dragon boat races that give the festival its name, which see these brightly painted craft competing to the beat of heavy drums.

The boats are elaborately decorated and have ornately carved dragon heads at prow and stern. The drummer sits up front and the helmsman at the back, with 20 well-trained paddlers sitting in pairs providing the motive force. As several of these amazing beasts power through the water at high speed engaging in mortal combat, they make a spectacular sight.

Sadly, traditional cultural holidays were abolished by the People's Republic and have only just been reinstated in mainland China. Over time, the recently neglected Dragon Boat Festival will surely recover its former glory in all parts of the country. But for now the best places to see truly uninhibited Dragon Boat Festivals are Hong Kong and Macau, where this important day has always been a public holiday (Tuen Ng Jie) that allowed activities associated with the festival to flourish unchecked.

WHEN:
Late May or early June
WHERE:
Hong Kong or Macau
BEST FOR:
No contest – it must be the dramatic Dragon Boat racing!
YOU SHOULD KNOW:
Not everyone subscribes to the Qu Yuan theory – some argue that the festival has always been about dragon worship, with *zongzi* put in the water as an offering to the Dragon King and dragon boat racing a further tribute. But maybe the origin hardly matters when the end result is so impressive . . .

Yi Torch Festival

Yunnan Province is home to 25 ethnic minorities so the place is a hotbed of fascinating folk festivals. One of the most interesting is the Torch Festival mounted by the fire-worshiping Yi people, who gather annually at the Stone Forest known in China as 'The First Wonder of the World'.

Such festivities provide a great opportunity to get together and exchange news and views, do business . . . and let young men and women pursue suitable marriage partners. The latter aspect of the Torch Festival is highly ritualized. Women signal availability by wearing triangular pieces of stiff fabric on either side of their headdresses, plus an embroidered belt. If a young man is attracted he snatches the belt, at which point the 'victim' will either return his interest or don another belt to reject his suit. Meanwhile, everyone has fun. Men play stringed instruments while women clap and dance. Stunning costumes compete for honours. There's horseracing and animal fights featuring bulls, rams and gamecocks, whilst wrestling tests human prowess.

The serious business begins when night falls. Massed spectators watch as the sacred site is illuminated and hundreds of blue-clad women wearing black aprons enter the arena, beating drums and writhing to represent the hard life lived before the advent of fire. They kneel as an army of black-turbaned men appear, accompanied by a shaman and images of the God of Fire. The shaman advances to an elevated shrine, prays for a good harvest and points to the shrine, which ignites into a fireball. After more wild cavorting, the women fetch burning torches and fireworks explode in the sky, whilst bonfires are lit for excited revellers to dance around. The Torch Festival really is an extraordinary event that will excite anyone fortunate enough to witness it.

WHEN:
Late June
WHERE:
Shilin, Yunnan
BEST FOR:
Fabulous fiery happenings in the wonderful setting of the Stone Forest
YOU SHOULD KNOW:
Never reach out and touch a young woman's triangular headdress during the festival – this causes great offence and the culprit is expected to labour (unpaid!) in her household for three years.

The Yi people perform one of several rituals at the Torch Festival.

Qingdao International Beer Festival

WHEN:
Mid August
WHERE:
Qingdao, Shandong
BEST FOR:
Chinese hospitality at its most welcoming
YOU SHOULD KNOW:
Karaoke fans can test their tonsils in front of a huge and appreciative crowd – and even buy a CD of the result to remind them of an epic visit to Asia's best beer festival.

This is not a beer festival of the sort to be found offering warm ale in a marquee on an English village green, but an altogether more impressive occasion. Sponsored by the coastal city where it takes place and supported by national government, the Qingdao International Beer Festival proudly bills itself as an event that integrates tourism, culture, sports and business activities with all the beer you can drink thrown in for good measure. The event was launched in 1991 by the local Tsingtao Brewery, producer of China's most famous amber nectar.

The main venue is Qingdao's International Beer City, an amusement park with rides, theatres for a variety of shows . . . plus the fabulous Beer Palace for tastings and drinking contests. Additional events are held in the city's recently renovated HuiQuan Square, whilst most visitors also find their way to Dengzhoulu Beer Street, reconstructed beside the old Qingdao Brewery as a bar and restaurant haven. It is decorated with huge inflatable beer bottles and a giant incarnation of festival mascot Jiajia, an appealing dog. In fact, the whole city takes on a festive atmosphere for two weeks.

The festival's opening ceremony is followed by some serious beer drinking, punctuated by a variety of entertainment that includes laser shows and concerts. Hordes of Chinese drinkers surround vast tables, sampling a variety of national brews and beers imported from all parts of the world. Foreigners are made welcome, and rarely have to buy their own drinks. A huge choice of food is on offer, too, to ensure that the sin of drinking on an empty stomach need never be committed. This has become one of China's most important events and is a festival to savour – as millions of visitors each year will (very) happily testify!

Happy drinkers imbibe in Dengzhoulu Beer Street.

Birthday of Confucius

Knowledge is for everyone, and this simple philosophy of Confucius (Chinese name Kong Fuzi) has influenced learning and scholarship for more than 2,500 years. Like the English monarch, he has two birthdays that are celebrated. China's National Teacher's Day coincides with his birthday in the Western calendar – September 28 – whilst traditionalists remember the great thinker on day 27 of the eighth moon in the Chinese lunar calendar (late September to mid October).

Qufa City, birthplace of Confucius

In order to appreciate fully the esteem in which Confucius is still held in modern-day China it is necessary to visit his charming home city of Qufu, where the magnificent Confucius Temple stands in his memory, dominating the town. This amazing structure ranks second only to Beijing's Forbidden City and has numerous elaborately roofed pavilions, halls and shrines surrounded by a wall with 53 imposing gateways.

Every time his birthday comes round, many thousands of people from all over China and the world gather in and around the Temple to celebrate his enduring influence. There is much pomp and ceremony, with people in traditional red costumes enacting rituals that go back to the Qing Dynasty in the 17th century, including a sacrificial ceremony that sees a cow, sow and mountain goat swiftly dispatched in succession to the rhythm of brown-capped drummers (animal lovers look away). The ceremony includes lots of music and dance but is of relatively brief duration – perhaps lasting an hour. Members of the Kong family who can claim direct descent from the sage attend and are treated with due deference.

Unfortunately, the birthday celebrations not only attract large numbers of international visitors, but also hordes of street vendors selling food and souvenirs. They are prone to overcharge when they snare a foreigner, so it's wise to ascertain a price before buying.

WHEN:
September 28
WHERE:
Qufu, Shandong
BEST FOR:
An opportunity to see the fabulous Confucius Temple and appreciate the soul of old China
YOU SHOULD KNOW:
For those who are unable to make the official birthday, there are now special 'Confucian' days in Qufu on the 28th of each month between April and October when the traditional birthday rituals are enacted, reflecting the new importance of internal and external tourism to the Chinese economy.

431

Mooncake Festival

*One of the many floats
that parade during
Mooncake Festival.*

Along with the Chun Jie Spring Festival, the Mooncake Festival is one of the two most important holidays in the Chinese calendar. This harvest festival has been celebrated in China for over three millennia, dating back to moon worship under the Shang Dynasty. Known as Zhongqiu Jie in China, it has alternative names – Mid-Autumn Festival and Lantern Festival.

The 'Mooncake' title is derived from the food most commonly eaten during the festival. There are many versions of the legend that inspires continued consumption of this traditional treat, but most involve worship of the Moon Goddess Chang'e and the search for a magical pill that confers immortal life, enabling her to be reunited with her murdered lover, Hou Yi. Mooncakes symbolize this quest, and are eaten with pomelo, the huge pale-yellow Chinese grapefruit that represents the moon.

Families gather to eat mooncakes beneath the bright harvest moon, often placing pomelo peel on each other's heads for good luck. Lanterns are carried, placed on towers and floated into the night sky. Incense is burned in tribute to Chang'e, dandelion leaves are collected, trees planted and fire-dragon dances held. Customs vary from place to place, but basic principles remain the same everywhere.

However, there are certain places where there is a special tradition of viewing the moon on the night of the Mooncake Festival. One of the most famous is the West Lake in Hangzhou, at a spot lyrically described as Three Pools Mirroring the Moon. Towers set in the shallow lake have apertures that beam shafts of light onto the water from candles within, whilst the most fortunate watch the moon rise from boats. Thousands more festival goers stroll around the lake, munch mooncakes and other tasty snacks and enjoy this magical moment.

Shaolin Martial Arts Festival

The Shaolin Temple in Dengfeng has stood for 15 centuries or more, and over time it has become widely known as a monument to the martial arts. During the Tang Dynasty (618-907) fierce warrior monks had already devised scores of hand-combat styles and developed advanced cudgel-fighting skills. Shaolin martial arts went on to reach an incomparable zenith during the Ming Dynasty (1368-1644). As with many ancient and honourable Chinese traditions, a combination of national pride and hard-nosed commercial acumen has led to the establishment of an annual tribute to the icon in question, with a principal objective being the attraction of visitors with money to spend.

That doesn't mean that such festivals are tacky, as the Chinese have a knack for staging dramatic events – and this is definitely the case with the Shaolin Martial Arts Festival, which was established in 1991. Visitors may be bombarded with the usual tourist temptations but dedicated followers of high-kicking action will not be disappointed. The festival showcases a wide variety of martial arts displays and contests, and also provides an important forum for the exchange of ideas and new techniques amongst serious martial artists who are drawn to the festival from all over the globe.

The world's premier martial arts event sees well over a thousand fighters converge to compete in Shaolin Wu Shu, Kung Fu and Tai Chi disciplines, with six awards in each category and also for the best demonstrations. In addition to the vast array of fighting techniques and exotic weapons, the festival caters for those who appreciate the wider picture – Chinese culture and heritage, natural health practices, spiritual and mental discipline.

Another fascinating dimension can be added to the festival experience – those who tear themselves away from the martial arts arena for half a day can enjoy a wonderful cruise on the mighty Yellow River.

Shaolin martial arts experts perform during the festival.

WHEN:
September
WHERE:
Dengfeng, Zhengzhou, Henan
BEST FOR:
Enthusiasts of the featured sports or lovers of those fabulous films featuring extraordinary Chinese martial arts fight scenes
YOU SHOULD KNOW:
Since 2001 there has been another annual martial arts festival at the newly authenticated and recently reconstructed Southern Shaolin Temple in Fujian.

National Day

WHEN:
October 1
WHERE:
All over the country
BEST FOR:
Relaxed revelry, everywhere in China
YOU SHOULD KNOW:
Anyone viewing the moving National Day celebrations in Tiananmen Square can add to the experience by visiting the National Museum of China along the east side of the Square.

The People's Republic of China was proclaimed in Beijing's Tiananmen Square on October 1 1949 and that date remains the PRC's National Day, celebrated with all sorts of government-sponsored festivities and concerts. It is now part of one of two 'Golden Week' national holidays (the other is Chinese New Year) when red lanterns appear everywhere, serving as potent symbols of luck and happiness. One special venue at which to appreciate this great occasion at its most impressive is the place where it all began, Tiananmen Square.

The world's largest urban plaza has great symbolic importance and for many years the Chinese Communist state made a vigorous annual statement here with an awesome military parade. They may be a thing of the past except for grand re-stagings on every fifth anniversary of Mao Zedong's original declaration of the Republic (next in 2014, 2019, etc), but China's National Day Flowerbed Festival has its most beautiful expression in Tiananmen Square. Over 400,000 potted plants form a wonderful creation around a tall palace lantern decorated with fine paintings and topped with a life-like dragon. Many tens of thousands of people gather around this extraordinary floral

A boat cruises along the Jinghang Canal during night-time celebrations.

display at dawn on National Day to watch the ceremonial raising of the national flag with full military honours.

This activity is repeated across the country, with flag-raising and stunning flowerbeds in all major cities serving as centrepieces for public demonstrations of patriotic fervour. Most celebrations end in firework displays, and the place to see the most spectacular of these is in Hong Kong, where National Day has seen major activity since the former British colony reverted to China in 1997. It culminates in 25,000 brilliant fireworks bombarding the night sky above Victoria Harbour, creating an unforgettable display of pyrotechnics and national pride.

Kurban Bairam

This is a hard one to catch, though well worth the effort. The Kurban Bairam Festival is celebrated by Muslim communities right across China and begins 70 days after the end of the fast of Ramadan – an event that happens 11 days earlier each year. For those familiar with the Islamic calendar, Kurban Bairam commences on the tenth day of Dhul-Hijjah (the 12th month) and lasts for four days.

Kashgar is the very best place to witness this moveable feast. Located west of the Taklamakan Desert at the foot of the Tian Shan Mountains at China's western extremity, this oasis city is the meeting point for many ancient trade routes. The Muslim faith arrived with Arab invaders in the eighth century and – with occasional setbacks – has thrived ever since, enriching the varied tapestry of Chinese culture. The huge Idkah Mosque, China's largest, is situated at the heart of Kashgar. Equally grand is the 17th century Abakh Khoja Tomb of a powerful ruler considered locally to be a prophet second only to Mohammed in importance.

Kashgar is worth exploring in its own right for the old town with its bazaars, Sunday market and livestock trading provides a fascinating opportunity to see life much as it has been lived on the Silk Road for many centuries. But planning a visit to coincide with Kurban Bairam adds an extraordinary dimension to the experience. The whole city is in festive mood, with much exchanging of gifts, begging family and friends for the forgiveness of sins and feasting on rich food. But the visual highlights are undoubtedly wonderful feats of tightrope walking seen daily in the main square, and the non-stop uninhibited dancing by colourfully clad celebrants in front of the Idkah Mosque.

WHEN:
70 days after Ramadan
WHERE:
Kashgar, Xinjiang Uygur
BEST FOR:
Spectacular acrobatics and wild dancing
YOU SHOULD KNOW:
Kurban Bairam, which is known in the Arab world as Eid al-Adha, celebrates Abraham's willingness to surrender everything to God, including his son Ishmael.

435

Tsongkhapa Butter Lamp Festival in Lhasa

WHEN:
December or January – the precise date depends on the phase of the moon.
WHERE:
Lhasa
BEST FOR:
Spectacle, music and dance
YOU SHOULD KNOW:
Tibet is a notoriously difficult place to visit and once there travel can be ponderous. Tourists must obtain visas from their local Chinese Embassy and visitor numbers are strictly controlled, especially close to culturally sensitive events like New Year. Having said that, it is an amazingly beautiful place and it is probably best to take the advice of the Dalai Llama when he says, 'Go to Tibet and see many places. Then tell the world.'

Few human-animal relationships are as symbiotic as the one between the Tibetans and their Yaks. Life in this mountainous region revolves around the yak, as it has done for over two millennia. Inhabitants build fires fuelled by yak dung, light their homes with yak butter lamps, eat the animal's meat, drink and preserve its milk, wear its hide and even make boats out of its hair. In return the yak is treated like one of the family, albeit an ultimately expendable one.

The most precious produce gleaned from this very versatile beast is butter. It is pounded together with tea to make the staple dish of *tsampa*, which is also rubbed into the skin for warmth and to repel insects. That it is so valuable makes the Tsongkhapa Butter Lamp Festival all the more poignant. The celebration dates from 1409 when the Buddhist theologian Tsong Khapa dreamt of Lord Buddha surrounded by beautiful flowers and trees. He then commissioned monks to make replicas of his wondrous floral vision out of butter.

Though held throughout Tibet, the place to go for the best spectacle is Barkhor Street in downtown Lhasa. The whole street is lit with thousands of elaborately designed butter lamps and singing and dancing lasts well into the evening. When the sun finally sinks behind the mountains and the multitude of flickering flames becomes more iridescent, you are left with the feeling that there can be no better place on earth to burn the midnight oil.

Losar

Those whose New Year festivities involve no more than raising a glass a few minutes before midnight on New Year's Eve, may be shamed for their lack of stamina by the Tibetans' marathon three-day New Year celebration. The festival of Losar has its origins in pre-Buddhist Tibet, when locals practised the animistic Bon religion and used the blossoming of the peach tree as a symbol of the changing of the years. As time passed the ceremony was integrated into the Buddhist faith and it is now a time of great devotion as well as wild partying.

On the first day the emphasis is on the home and the family. Buildings are whitewashed and new clothes are worn to symbolize purity and renewal. A visit to the monastery to make offerings of ornaments and Chang beer is followed by an intimate family meal.

Day two is heralded by the noise of people exchanging *Tashi Deleks* ('may everything be well') as Tibetans journey out to visit friends and relatives. It is now that the feasting and partying get more lavish, as gifts are exchanged and the Chang beer flows. Once the men have had their fill, many slope off to gamble on dice and mahjong, while the women and children gather round to sing traditional ballads.

The final day is more subdued, with many nursing bloated stomachs and hangovers. Year-old roof-top prayer flags (*tar-choks*) are replaced and the air is filled with the scent of burning bunches of *sang* (fragrant grasses), before the locals get their second wind and start feasting and partying again. After so much gorging it is little wonder that Tibetans take more than a few days off after the revelry in order to recover.

WHEN:
February, although the exact dates depend on the phase of the moon
WHERE:
All over Tibet, but most lavish in Lhasa
BEST FOR:
Culture and religious ceremony
YOU SHOULD KNOW:
Nearly all shops and businesses close for the three days of festivities. If you book a hotel check that food is available during your stay and make sure that you exchange any currency before the New Year.

Labrang monastery during the Losar festival

The Saga Dawa Festival

Held on the full moon of the fourth lunar month the Saga Dawa Festival is the most important religious day in Tibet, as it celebrates the date on which the Lord Buddha Sakyamuni was born, achieved enlightenment and died. Pilgrimages are made to the foot of Mount Kailash – a peak so central to the faiths of Buddhism, Jainism and Hinduism that climbing it is forbidden. In a ceremony that stretches back over one millennium, the Tarboche flagpole is replaced by one bearing new prayer flags, asking for blessings in the year ahead.

Pilgrims on the Barkhor circuit, Jokhang Temple

In the capital city, Lhasa, crowds gather to watch a procession of prayer wheel turners before partaking in a vegetarian picnic by the side of Dragon King Pond in the grounds of Potala Palace – a palace built by the sixth Dalai Lama in the 17th century. After lunch it is customary to take to the water in colourful paddleboats. All around the centre of town folk entertainers perform traditional Tibetan songs and dances in homage to Lord Buddha.

Rather like Ramadan in Islam or Lent in Christianity, Saga Dawa is a time of abstinence and devotion. It is tradition that no animals are slaughtered during the month and only simple meals are taken. It is also a time for charity and sharing and many of the region's poor are drawn to Lhasa as alms are given. When viewed as a whole, Saga Dawa is a charming festival. It is largely without ostentation or razzamatazz, instead offering the visitor insight into the lives and belief systems of the people of this magnificent mountainous region.

WHEN:
Around April and May, though timings are based on the lunar calendar
WHERE:
Lhasa
BEST FOR:
Religious ceremony
YOU SHOULD KNOW:
Because of the religious prohibition on climbing Mount Kailash, it stands as one of the most significant unclimbed peaks in the world.

Nagchu Horse Racing Festival

Perched at the dizzying height of 4,500 m (14,750 ft) above sea level, on the lip of the Changtang Plateau, Nagchu is one of the highest towns in the world. This home to a population of 70,000 is bitterly cold and windswept for most of the year, and oxygen levels are little more than half those to be found at sea level. It is little wonder, then, that when what passes for summer in these parts does arrive, they go a little bit wild. Up to 10,000 hard-bitten nomads descend on the town, where an *ad hoc* tented village is set up. They bring not only their horses with them, but also produce to trade and, most importantly, their skills to test as well.

Mexico City in 1968 may be considered the 'Altitude Olympics', but Nagchu sits at almost double Mexico's elevation, making the lung-bursting feats of strength and agility on display here all the more remarkable. The horse racing always takes centre stage, with great jockeyship and equine muscularity on show, but there are several other events, sporting and cultural, some of which would not look out of place at an English village fete. The more burly tribesmen test their strength in tug-of-war and stone-lifting contests, while mounted and standing archery test stillness of hand and sharpness of eye.

Culture is also high on the agenda and there is often a recitation of the world-famous Gesar Epic Ballad – a work of around 20,000,000 words which tells the triumphs and struggles of the fearless King Gesar who ruled over these lands 1,000 years ago. Tibetan singing and dancing fills the evenings around the tented village, while the herdsmen regain their strength for the next day's contests.

WHEN:
August
WHERE:
Nagchu
BEST FOR:
Sport and culture
YOU SHOULD KNOW:
Because of Nagchu's high elevation it is advisable to stagger your journey there so as to avoid altitude sickness. There are also very few hotels in town, so camping may be a better option.

Changpa nomads race flat out at the festival.

Lantern Festival in Tainan

WHEN:
February
WHERE:
Tainan
BEST FOR:
Spectacle
YOU SHOULD KNOW:
Some Taiwanese are beginning to
question the wisdom of releasing
lanterns into the night sky. Aside
from the incredible amount of smoke
they generate, the returning lanterns
often cause large fires. One year the
country's airport was endangered by
a nearby blaze.

It is interesting to note the subtle differences in New Year
celebrations across the Chinese diaspora. Although there is great
commonality, for instance dragons and the zodiacal animal of the
new year are central to the celebrations, each region or country that
plays host to the festivities brings to the table its own characteristics.
Tainan is an industrial town rather like Pittsburgh or Newcastle and
has the same rough-and-ready feel. The people of Tainan work hard
and they certainly know how to play hard too.

A spectacular laser show illuminates the sky to herald the start
of festivities. Blazing lanterns light the ground and revellers are
greeted by giant illuminated sculptures, many depicting stories
associated with the emblem of the
year ahead. You need not worry if
you have missed anything, as these
shows run every 30 minutes between
07.00 and 23.00.

The final stage of the festivities
requires the tourist to check
carefully the details of their travel
insurance. The firework 'display' at
the Yanshuei Beehive Rockets
Festival in Tainan's Yanshuei
Township is a unique experience.
Fireworks are fired at figures of
deities mounted on palanquins
while onlookers, who are mainly
dressed in protective gear, take
cover. The noise is incessant and
the sight all too quickly resembles
a battle scene with fireworks
landing amongst the scattering
crowd. It seems that the people of
Tainan have their own firework
code and view them as less
dangerous than do the rest of us. It
is for this reason that the firework
display in Tainan is best viewed
from a distance.

*Fireworks light up the
lantern festival.*

Wakakusa Yamayaki

As one of Japan's most important festivals, Wakakusa Yamayaki's origins are surprisingly obscure. In essence, it is a simple agricultural ceremony of clearing the land by burning the old grass ready for the new growth of spring. In fact it is a highly ritualized event evolved during the Kamakura Period (1185-1333). Ever since, on January 14, monks and priests set fires that engulf Wakasuka Hill at Nara, the ancient capital of Japan and still one of its most beautiful and historic cities.

The ceremony begins at 17.30 with a procession of monks from the Kasuga shrine complex nearby. Dressed as medieval warriors, and carrying torches lit from the sacred flames of Kasuga, they assemble at the foot of the hill to perform purification rites and say prayers. In the last of the twilight, to the sound of drums, the solemn figures flickering in the fires belong to a timeless drama. Beyond the circle of light you sense rather than see the multitude of over 100,000 people, a deeper shadow in motion, silently shifting for a better look. The tension is simultaneously shattered and exalted. Fireworks explode across the sky in a dazzling display of colour and light, that stops dead when the monks blow a fanfare of conch horns. It's exactly 18.00 and the signal for the priests and their assistants to fire the grass on Wakakusa. The crowd's murmur rises to a clamour of primeval joy. In a few minutes the entire 342-m (1,121-ft) hillside is ablaze and a single enormous flame jets into the winter sky. It transforms an already spectacular 'rebirth' into a visceral phenomenon.

The best views of Wakakusa Yamayaki are from Nara-koen, outside Todaiji, the middle of Heijo-kyo, or (especially for photographers wanting the reflections) along the lake towards Yakushiji.

The whole hillside of Wakasuka becomes engulfed in flames.

WHEN:
January 14
WHERE:
Wakakusa-yama, Nara
BEST FOR:
Religious rites, historic rituals and primeval spectacle
YOU SHOULD KNOW:
Should the night prove chilly away from the conflagration, food and drink are available from a whole shanty town of stalls set up for the evening around the base of Wakakusa.

A group of women dance in front of Sakura trees.

Hanami (Cherry Blossom Viewing)

Only those born and raised within Japanese culture can fully comprehend the significance of Hanami in Japan. The cherry blossom is Japan's national flower. The cherry tree, *Sakura*, is sacred; and though *hanami* means 'flower-viewing', it is reserved for reference to *Sakura*. In Japan the cherry tree produces no fruit. It produces, or inspires, an aesthetic of transience – equivalent in many ways to the *memento mori* of Western art and culture. The lovely *Sakura* bursts into extravagant and beautiful blossom, each petal a paragon of intense colour and scent. All too soon they drift with careless grace to the ground, ousted by the fresh budding leaves of the *Sakura's* urgent life cycle. The metaphor is fundamental to the Japanese psyche, as it is to Japanese poetry, painting and even kimono design. As spring progresses from south to north, the whole country follows the *Sakura Zensen* (cherry-blossom front), and signs are posted at railway stations, predicting *mankai* (full bloom) in the region. Many businesses close to give their staff a chance to enjoy a traditional *Sakura Matsuri* (festival) – a simple enjoyment of the clouds of pink perfection with friends and family, that invariably turns into a party beneath the trees in a park or by a river.

Hanami arrives first in Japan's southernmost island of Okinawa and, rather than wait (in Hokkaido it doesn't happen until May!), over 200,000 people gather at Nago in central Okinawa for the first and most spectacular of all Hanami, in late January. Nago hosts a big *matsuri* of rides, parades, folk music, *eiso* drumming, dancing and special food – but it's among the 20,000 hot pink *Higan Sakura* which line the 700 steps up the hill to Nago Castle that you come closest to the spirit of Japan. Looking across the bay, the deep-pink sea of petals mocks the grey January sky in an annual triumph of hope in renewal.

WHEN:
Late January/early February
WHERE:
Nago, Okinawa
BEST FOR:
Natural beauty, folk legend and party picnics
YOU SHOULD KNOW:
Hanami originated among the aristocrats of the Japanese Imperial Court of the Heian Period (794-1192). Glamorous scenes recorded on porcelain show ladies dressed in kimonos swooning at beauty (and their Samurai swains) over their medieval *bento* (lunch) boxes, and languorously composing poetry while drinking improbable amounts of *sake*.

Sapporo Snow Festival

Sapporo is the capital of Hokkaido, the northernmost of Japan's main islands. Ever since it hosted one of the most successful Winter Olympics, the city has been synonymous with winter entertainment; and nowhere knows better how to make the most of what it's got – snow. Sapporo's Snow Festival (Yuki Matsuri) is purely about having fun with snow in as many different, creative and playful ways that you can think of. With plenty of the stuff almost guaranteed every year, the festival can indulge in ever bigger, more inventive and spectacular ideas. What began in 1950 with six snow statues by high school students now attracts over 2,000,000 visitors to marvel at over 300 constructions in snow and ice, spread over three distinct sites. The biggest can be palaces, shimmering with internal light. A group of ice pyramids, pulsing with hazy colour, might conceal a huge stage for a rock band or orchestra. Ice sculptures of famous sports stars and politicians grin between enormous fantasy carvings. You can lose yourself in a giant ice-maze (while your friends laugh from the observation tower!), watch ice-carving competitions between chainsaw-wielding artists, and admire crabs or salmon incorporated into the intricacies of ice-sculptures.

The International Snow Statue Contest takes place in Odori Park, a vast space in Sapporo's centre that is the heart of the festival. It's where you find the biggest and most spectacular creations. But the most dramatic are often among the hundreds of smaller fantasies displayed in the Susukino district, which is also Sapporo's 'red light' and bohemian quarter. Families may prefer Satoland (Sapporo Satorando) on the edge of the city. There's a 100-m (328-ft) long slide, a snow maze, hot-air balloon rides and snow-rafting on special boards.

WHEN:
Second week of February
WHERE:
Sapporo City, Hokkaido
BEST FOR:
Winter sports and games, entertainment, ice-art and architecture
YOU SHOULD KNOW:
One of the best (unofficial) views of the enormous sculptures in Odori Park is from above – at the Sapporo TV Tower. It's at the east end of the park, and there's a small charge to get to the observatory deck at the top of the tower.

Visitors view the snow and ice sculptures at Sapporo.

ASIA/JAPAN

Hounen Matsuri

WHEN:
March 15
WHERE:
Komaki, Aichi Prefecture,
near Nagoya
BEST FOR:
Religion, history, folklore and
authorized insobriety
YOU SHOULD KNOW:
Hounen festivities at other penis-
venerating shrines in Japan are pale
imitations of Komaki. Mostly they
seek to capitalize on the ribaldry and
drinking associated with the
occasion. Only one – Kanamara
Matsuri held in Kawasaki in April –
has sought, admirably, to make the
link between ancient Shinto
principles and modern Japan's
society. Drawing on its own local
history, it seeks *hounen* of a kind by
raising money for AIDS victims, and
to promote protection from STDs.

Nothing expresses the robust earthiness of Shinto beliefs better than the spring fertility rites of Hounen Matsuri. *Hounen* actually translates as 'abundant harvest' – the annual objective of ceremonies that re-enact symbolically the introduction of the male to the female procreative principle. It is celebrated to some degree all over Japan on March 15, roughly the time of the spring equinox. All the ceremonies have one thing in common: the use of graphic illustrations and sculptures to represent the penis and the vagina, the yang and yin of creation in the broadest sense.

The biggest Hounen Matsuri is held at the Tagata Shrine in Komaki, north of Nagoya. It is also the oldest and most 'folklorically' authentic. Essentially it's a procession. A 2.5-m (13-ft) long wooden phallus (carved out of cypress under strict rules of purification) is carried from the Kumano shrine for 1.5 km (1 mi) to the Tagata Shrine, home of a powerful female deity. Although everything about the parade – costumes, music, prayers, behaviour and ritual – is dictated by established rules with a deeply serious meaning, it's a very jolly occasion fuelled by barrel-loads of free *sake* (doled out by the gold-swathed Shinto priests), and food and souvenirs all fashioned like phalluses. But the predominance of male fetishes is not to glorify the phallus. The entire Hounen ceremony is in honour of the female principle. Only the 'mother' can give birth to bounty and prosperity, and Shinto recognizes this in a subtle and profound way. Not least, Shinto restores the notion of pure, guilt-free joy to the union of male and female.

Hounen Matsuri at Komaki is one of the most fascinating Japanese celebrations of all, and most deeply revered. To Western eyes, it can be shocking; but if you hope to understand Shinto, it's the festival you cannot and should not miss.

Bearers carry a huge wooden penis to the Tagata Shrine.

Takayama Matsuri

Isolated in the beauty of the Japan Alps of the Chibu region in Gifu Prefecture, Takayama has survived most of the ravages of 20th century technology and design. Set near the natural wonders of the Shirakawa-go World Heritage Site, Takayama's old town is a perfectly preserved Edo-style surprise, as dramatic as Carcassonne in France or Williamsburg in the USA. The town is a symbol of the continuum of Japanese history, religion and culture – and its 500-year-old festival is officially one of the three 'most beautiful' in the country.

Takayama Matsuri takes place in the spring and autumn. The autumn festival follows the spring pattern, but takes place in the north part of Takayama's old town. The spring, or *sanno* festival, is more important, and takes place in the south part, based on the Hie Shrine. Joy pervades the town. With the mountain snows melting, it's time to celebrate planting the new rice crop, and renewal in general. Warehouse doors are thrown open to reveal gigantic floats (*yatai*) supporting mechanical dolls (*karakuri ningyo*) that move and dance. After lengthy display, they are pulled through the streets in support of the portable shrine (*mikoshi*) containing a specific Shinto deity on its annual excursion. Ritual is more or less confined to the continuous processing itself – but somewhere in the incense, colour, drumming, chanting and singing, the carnival grotesques on the *yatai* weave a spell that entwines the tens of thousands of visitors into a single consciousness. Everyone feels the great rhythm of renewal and shares its release, as optimism.

Takayama families certainly do. Since the 17th century, the town's wealthiest residents have shared their fortune by commissioning local craftsmen to build fabulously ostentatious *yatai*. Discernible through the infrastructure for visitors, this ongoing sense of community is what makes Takayama Matsuri so rare and special.

The decorated floats are called Yatai.

WHEN:
April 14-15
WHERE:
Takayama Old Town (south section as far as Kokobunji), Chibu region.
BEST FOR:
Folklore, history, religious rites, colourful spectacle and natural beauty
YOU SHOULD KNOW:
The master-craftsmen who produce the splendid intricacies of the *yatai* are known as *Hida no Takumi*. They, and the *yatai*, and indeed the whole Sanno Matsuri (Takayama's spring festival) are officially designated as 'Significant Intangible Folk Cultural Assets'.

*Mongolian grand champion
Hakuno, right, sweeps away
his opponent's foot.*

Tokyo May Basho

Exclusively Japanese, steeped in history, tradition and Shinto ritual, sumo wrestling is the most exciting contact sport in the world. It is blindingly quick. Two super-heavyweights face each other across a 4.5-m (15-ft) diameter clay *dohyo* (ring). After a lengthy exchange of stamping, stretching and tossing salt – purification rites shared by a referee holding a fan as an emblem of authority, and whose every action is prescribed by Japan's most ancient history – they hurl themselves at each other in a blur of action. There are about 80 recognized ways of forcing an opponent out of the *dohyo* (if any part of the body other than the soles of your feet touch the ground, you lose), and top sumo wrestlers can attempt several in the few seconds that most bouts last. Their speed, skill and aggression make it look like whole-body fencing.

There are just six, two-week-long Hon-basho (tournaments determining ranking) in the sumo calendar, and Natsu Basho, held in Tokyo in May, is one of the most splendid. The best *rikishi* (wrestlers) in the sumo world meet in the 11,000-seat Kokugikan. You'll see the action up close if you get there early at 09.00, but the top ranks don't fight until 16.00, when the best seats are taken by aficionados in traditional Japanese dress. The constant ceremony and ritual creates an atmosphere of timeless history by the time the top ranks of all – *yokozuna* (grand champion) and *ozeki* (champion) – step forward. Each is already a national hero, and known by a special sumo nickname. Their fights are the stuff of legend and scandal. In 2008, when the first foreigner (the Bulgarian *ozeki*, known as Kotooshu) won the Emperor's Cup at the Natsu Basho, the national shame was overshadowed by the failure of the defeated *yokozuna*, Asashoryu, to behave with the decorum demanded of his exalted rank.

WHEN:
Two weeks in mid May
WHERE:
Ryogoku Kokugikan
(sumo wrestling hall), Tokyo
BEST FOR:
Sport, history, religion and culture
YOU SHOULD KNOW:
When the *rikishi* clap violently before a bout, they are demonstrating they are unarmed. By contrast, the referee in his splendid traditional dress carries a small dagger. It symbolizes his willingness to commit ritual suicide if his impartiality is called into question. Honour is everything in sumo.

Sanja Matsuri

Forget preconceptions about Japanese sobriety and reticence. Sanja Matsuri is a three-day debauch in Tokyo's Asakusa district to rival the wildest excesses of Munich's Fasching or Rio's Carnival. The Shitamachi area of Asakusa is one of Tokyo's oldest, and its medieval flavour is enhanced by the 1,300-year history of the festival, which consists of parading the *kami* (deities) of some 50 major and minor local shrines through 'their' territory in small *mikoshi* (portable shrines) as an invocation to prosperity. Men, women and children carry these small *mikoshi*. There are also three large shrines which need about 40 men to carry them but they only appear on the Sunday.

Each day, the processions are joined by musicians and drummers on floats, and by the famous Asakusa geishas in all their finery – the only time they appear *en masse*. But the fabulous parades quickly become a violently jostling scrum of hundreds of thousands of extremely boisterous, heavy-drinking well-wishers. People 'ride' the large *mikoshi* – and in the process reveal tattoos showing some of them to be *yakuza* (members of Japan's criminal gangs), as well as scandalizing Shinto adherents, who see it as offensive to the on-board deity. Fortunately, increasingly vigilant *kashira* (stewards associated with individual *mikoshi*) are helping diminish the sporadic outbursts of violence.

In fact, the deities love to be shaken up, and the *mikoshi* jostling is the whole point of the exercise. It brings luck. It's huge fun to be accepted as a temporary community member, and wear its uniform (visitors just need to register to participate), knowing that the racket and the din – and indeed the pageantry, the geishas and the *taiko* drumming – is validated by Shinto and by history. You've never seen Japan like this before. Sanja Matsuri is a wild marathon in which normal rules just don't apply.

WHEN:
The third Friday, Saturday and Sunday in May
WHERE:
Asakusa district, Tokyo
BEST FOR:
Good-humoured drunken revelry, folklore, culture
YOU SHOULD KNOW:
Sanja Matsuri means 'Three-Shrine Festival', and refers to the three *kami* of the men who in 628 found a statue of the Buddhist Goddess of Mercy (Kannon) in the river, and consecrated it in a small temple. The temple is now called Senso-ji. It's the oldest temple in Tokyo, the reason for Sanja Matsuri's existence, and its focal point. The *mikoshi* of the three *kami* are the biggest of the festival, and only appear on the final day.

Gods are paraded in portable shrines at the festival.

ASIA/JAPAN

Yamaboko Junko at Gion Matsuri

WHEN:
July 17 (Yamaboko Junko) Gion
ceremonies take place
throughout July.
WHERE:
Yasaka-jinja Shrine, Higashiyama-ku,
Kyoto City
BEST FOR:
Religion, history, folklore and
carnival spectacle
YOU SHOULD KNOW:
On Yoiyama days only, the Byobu
Matsuri (Folding Screen Festival) is
when families living close to Yasaka
Shrine open their doors to all visitors.
This is a very rare opportunity to see
inside traditional Japanese houses, so
it's important to observe the
appropriate etiquette. The same goes
for the Tea Ceremonies, traditional
dancing and other events that take
place at Yasaka-jinja itself.

*A large ornate float is pulled
through the streets.*

Kyoto's Gion Matsuri (July Festival) is one of Japan's three most
important celebrations. It's also one of the biggest, longest and the
oldest *goryo-e* (protective) festivals, first held in the early Heian
period (794-1192) to appease the deity of pestilence. By the 12th
century religious ritual provided the opportunity for people to show
off their wealth by investing in elaborate floats and, over 1,000
years, the highlight of the whole Gion Matsuri has become the
Yamaboko Junko – the procession of floats on July 17. The floats are
two-storey giants of 6 m (20 ft) or more, weighing upwards of ten
tons, hugely elaborate and colourful – and made entirely without
nails or metal. There are about 30 of them and two sorts: *yama*
floats illustrate Japanese history and legend, and may carry *mikoshi*
(shrines) and Shinto musicians; *hoko* floats have evolved into
dazzling individual circuses, art shows, museums of antiques, and
music hall stages. Pulled by teams of 50 men in traditional dress
(as is a large proportion of the crowd), and with a full complement
of surrounding musicians, drummers and chanting choruses,

the procession fills the streets
with dramatic spectacle and
cheerful noise.

Prior to Yamaboko Junko on
July 17, the subsidiary festival of
Yoiyama between July 14 and 16
offers visitors the chance to see
the parked floats up close at
night, when their fabulous designs
and genuinely valuable artefacts
(paintings, rugs) are beautifully
lit. Many of the floats represent a
deity with a specific benefit
(longevity, easy childbirth, plague
avoidance, etc), which you can
invoke by buying a *chimaki*
(amulet) made of bamboo grass.
Others offer hilarious
entertainments (a wind-up
praying mantis was very
successful one year). Yoiyama
familiarizes everyone with the
floats before the festival climax of
Yamaboko Junko – strengthening
the communal sense of wellbeing
on the big day.

Miyajima Kangensai

Kangen is the music of the ancient Japanese Imperial Court. Flute, drums and stringed instruments unique to the genre combine with poetic grace and subtlety according to rituals and etiquette that make its performance rare. At Miyajima Kangensai, its exquisite textures form the sound track to a spectacular sea pageant in honour of the sea goddesses of the Itsukushima Shrine on Miyajima Island, just south of Hiroshima. It is one of Japan's most sacred places, and so beautiful it is protected as a World Heritage Site. Just looking at it is one of the 'Three Views of Japan' (each view is a 'National Treasure') – and you'll recognize the towering, vermilion Torii gate apparently floating on the water, like the shrine itself.

If any single event encapsulates the 'soul' of Japan, it is this one. It engages all the senses, all four elements, and references to the zenith nodes of Japanese history and Shinto religion – and presents them in the outward trappings of the rarest courtly formality with the paradoxical (and successful) aim of freeing your mind to join the river of natural consciousness. In an age of devalued superlatives, this is 24-carat wonder.

The boat carrying the *mikoshi* (portable shrine) is called *gozabune*. It is decked for the *Bugaku*, ancient courtly dances performed with gentle solemnity, and for the *Gagaku* – a form of *Kangen*. Richly decorated, and illuminated by exotic paper lanterns at dusk, it is led by the brightly lit fishing fleet through the Torii to the mainland Jigozen Shrine, and on to several of Miyajima's smaller shrines, before returning triumphantly back through the magnificent Torii to Itsukushima Shrine. The studied, courtly grace of the ceremonies induces peace and wellbeing. Drift away on the ethereal layers of *Kangen* into the best waking dream of your life.

Ancient traditional instruments are played at the festival.

WHEN:
Late July (the date is always June 17 according to the lunar calendar, so it sometimes falls at the beginning of August).
WHERE:
Itsukushima Shrine, Miyajima, Hiroshima Prefecture
BEST FOR:
Music, history, religion, natural beauty, optimism
YOU SHOULD KNOW:
Miyajima is sacred to both Shinto and Buddhism. Itsukushima is its primary shrine, but the sacred geography includes a further seven scattered round the 30-km (19-mi) island circumference, and the 16-m (53-ft) tall Torii whose main camphor-wood pillars, 10 m (33 ft) in circumference, are all free-standing on the sea-bed. No nails or metal are used, and no part of them is buried – but they survive even the worst typhoons.

449

Soma-Nomaoi

The head of the Soma clan, a minor feudal lord in Japan's Samurai society, 1,000 years ago released a herd of wild horses on his estates and ordered his entire army of bannermen (warriors bearing his crest) to catch and train them to military standards. His action, legendary as a proven method of raising *esprit de corps* by rigorous military training, has acquired a deep spiritual patina. Soma-Nomaoi (wild horse chase in Soma) is a Samurai cavalry display and competition spread over three days, dedicated to the *kami* (spirit deities) of the tenth century clan chief. His descendants devised the festival as a way of rehearsing their often-needed fighting skills. Today, led by the current Soma clan chief, 600 Samurai cavalry in full armour (including their brightly coloured company banners on poles strapped to their backs), parade with huge pomp and pageantry to the mournful boom of medieval conch horns. On the second day the parade is far bigger. Even the horses are fully caparisoned, weapons gleam, and squads of traditionally costumed marchers – burly pikemen, children dressed as Samurai, girls and women with fans and umbrellas – create the impression of a medieval army on the march.

The magnificence of the parade is subsumed into the excitement of the horse races that follow. They become increasingly boisterous, until the yelling and gesticulating resolves into a full-scale Samurai cavalry charge. Expertly drilled and presented, it's the real thing, and really blood-curdling. Whirling and stamping in the dusty grass, they compete for crested banners, which after the battle they dedicate to a Soma family shrine. On the third and final day, Samurai horsemen corral a herd of unsaddled and untrained horses inside the temple precincts of Soma Odaka Shrine for Nomaoi itself. Young Samurai initiates dressed in white capture them barehanded, and present them to the Shinto *kami*.

Samurai riders dressed in full medieval armour take part in Soma-Nomaoi.

WHEN:
July 23-25
WHERE:
Hibari-ga Hara, Haramachi, Fukushima
BEST FOR:
History, culture, religion, pageantry and spectacle
YOU SHOULD KNOW:
During the Sengoku (Warring States) Period, the Soma clan was already famous in the Tohoku region of northern Japan for breeding and training excellent horses. By 1622, in peacetime, the wild horses of Soma were being illustrated in paintings on teacups and other pottery.

Tenjin Matsuri

One of Japan's 'top three' summer festivals, Osaka's Tenjin is the most spectacular. It celebrates the deities of learning and art, typified by the courtier and scholar-poet Sugawara Michizane (845-903), whose *kami* (spirit) is revered at the Tenmangu Shrine, the centre of the ceremonies. As the god of academic achievement, Tenjin Tenmangu attracts especially large crowds of nail-biting students, fearful of Japan's rigorous examination system but willing to have a good time until then. The first day of the festival is preparatory. Across Osaka, performances of traditional Japanese arts include *bunraku* (puppet theatre), *taiko* drumming, lion-dancing and *kagura* music.

The real show comes on the second day. It starts with the Rikutogyo – a procession of thousands of people dressed in the Imperial Court style of the eighth to 12th centuries who carry *mikoshi* (portable shrines) from the Tenmangu Shrine to Tenjinbashi Bridge. They arrive at dusk and board over 100 specially decorated boats, which blaze into light for Funatogyo – the torchlit boat pageant down the Okawa River through Sakuranomiya and Kawasaki Parks. With hundreds of unofficial skiffs darting between the principal barges like fireflies, the drama intensifies as bonfires (on boats and on the banks) light their way, and Suito-sai Hono Hanabi (a firework display) begins. These ceremonial fireworks add their fizz, sparkle and brilliant colour to the music and drums accompanying the palanquins and *mikoshi* on the barges.

It's an image from ancient Japan, and from ancient Osaka in particular. As Funatogyo returns to its finale at Tenmangu Shrine, the million-strong crowd begins the special, rhythmic handclapping and shouting that proclaims '*Osaka iki*', the charming lifestyle said to be typical of Osaka during the Edo period (1603-1867), and quite distinct from that of Tokyo or anywhere else.

A little girl takes part, wearing festival costume.

WHEN:
Late July (note that Tenjin Matsuri rituals and events take place throughout the month).
WHERE:
Tenmangu Shrine, Osaka
BEST FOR:
Religion, history, culture, folklore, and brilliant waterborne spectacle
YOU SHOULD KNOW:
During Funatogyo, hundreds of pavilions line the riverbanks to provide visitors with food, drink and other entertainments. When the spotlit golden *mikoshi* carrying important deities go past, the pavilions and any unofficial small boats nearby go quiet and dark out of respect for the deity; and there is no clapping, chanting or cheerleading until they pass. It's a reminder of the deeply religious foundations of the festival.

Tetsuya Odori at Gujo Hachiman

WHEN:
The *O-bon* days are August 13-16 throughout Japan, but Tetsuya Odori generally refers exclusively to Gujo Hachiman. (NB. The dates of *Bon Odori* and the *O-Bon* days vary widely in Japan, thanks to historic variations in the adoption and application of various calendars.)

WHERE:
Gujo Hachiman, Gifu Prefecture

BEST FOR:
Dance, folklore, history, religion (Tetsuya Odori is officially a 'Significant Intangible Cultural Folk Asset')

YOU SHOULD KNOW:
Tips for getting involved include wearing a *yukata* (light cotton kimono) and *geta* (wooden Japanese flip-flops that make a great noise when dancing); also, watch the dancers in the innermost circle, who will certainly have practised the steps since childhood.

Gujo Hachiman is a beautiful medieval town set in the forested mountains north of Nagoya and Gifu City. Its steep cobbled lanes are lined with wood-and-plaster houses of the Edo Period, and a magnificent 17th century castle looks down on myriad streams and river courses gurgling through the town. Naturally, such a magic place has the festival it deserves. It has remoulded in its own image the midsummer *Bon Odori* (summer dance) festival widely celebrated throughout Japan. As long as 400 years ago, the feudal lord of Gujo's castle took the democratic initiative of encouraging everyone in the town, regardless of status or birth, to take part in a summer-long hoedown. The result is Gujo Odori, a six-week period when the town's versions of *Bon* dances are performed 30 times; and which includes the four-day Tetsuya Odori (all-night dancing) over the mid August *O-Bon* period. Those four days are an exhausting, exhilarating marathon of rhythmic clapping and movement, when local residents (and visitors) from every walk of life communally welcome the spirits of their ancestors back home for a visit.

Anyone can join in, and thousands come to whirl and twirl outside the twin circles formally dancing round the *odori yagura* (dance scaffold), a bamboo structure containing the musicians, drummers and singers (there's one in every town or village, the focal point of the dancing). Gujo has ten *Bon* dances, which you can learn by imitation (or by taking the free lessons on offer each morning), rhythmically varied to stave off exhaustion. In fact, the dancing energizes you. The lanterns and flickering lights, the timeless music and *taiko* drumming that guide the ancestral spirits home will encourage you as much as the beaming locals pulling you into the circle. In Gujo, at Tesuya Odori, people make you feel you belong.

Tetsuya Odori welcomes back ancestral spirits.

Owara Kaze-no-Bon Matsuri

Traditionally dressed women perform their dance.

Obon is the Shinto-Buddhist observance of honouring your ancestors by inviting their spirits back to visit their homes and families. During the summer, all over Japan fires are lit in welcome and prayer. Special food and drink is prepared. Most important of all, *Bon Odori* (dances) combine individual family ceremonies with those of the community – and most towns and regions have evolved their own variations. The most famous of these is the Owara Kaze-no-Bon Matsuri, peculiar to the stunning mountain community of Yatsuo. Isolated by its geography and history, Yatsuo's *Bon Odori* reach their apotheosis in the first three days of September, when dancers from 11 local neighbourhoods tour the vicinity of Yatsuo's Monmyo-ji Temple, performing the most extraordinary, colourful and stylish exercises in rural dance chic. Already over 300 years old, the dances (and dancers) could be futurist masterpieces of styling and choreography. The miracle is that despite the growing crowds of spectators, the ceremonies appear to be uncorrupted by exposure to modern common denominators.

The key to the *odori* is the local hand-me-down folk song called *Ecchu Owarabushi*, a synthesis of high-pitched vocals, plucked *shamisen*, and the mournful *kokyu*. It covers both the traditional *Kyu Odori* (which is more or less familiar elsewhere) and the newer *Shin Odori* in which the men dance out themes drawn from farming, and the women combine expressing rustic tasks with the elegant motions of Japanese classical dance. Men wear *happi* (very short) jackets; women the traditional *yukata*. Both wear *amigasa* hats, like little straw roofs tilted forward over the eyes. They come down the steep cobbled streets in a long, doubled chain, flashing out the extremely stylized steps like a crazed marching band. It's magnificent, moving, and utterly without self-consciousness or cynicism. It is a glimpse of ancient Japan at its unique best.

WHEN:
September 1-3
WHERE:
Suwa-machi, Yatsuo, Toyama Prefecture
BEST FOR:
Folk culture, religion, history, world music
YOU SHOULD KNOW:
Unusually, Owara Kaze-no-Bon combines the *Bon* rituals of homage to ancestors with rites to invoke a good harvest. Typhoons often hit the Yatsuo region, and September 1, according to the ancient Japanese calendar, is considered propitious for appeasing the deities of the wind (*Kaze*, as in *Kami-kaze* – divine wind).

453

Lanterns adorn the festival floats.

Chichibu Night Festival

The western part of Saitama Prefecture, northwest of Tokyo, rises to a series of forested mountains within the protection of Chichibu-Tama-Kai National Park. Chichibu itself is a larger version of the typical small towns ranged along the river terraces of the Arakawa River, and it owes its prominence to the existence of Chichibu-Jinja, an important shrine some 1,700 years before the town sprang up around it. It is one of the 100 Sacred Kan'non Temples of Japan (with a pilgrimage path exactly 100 km long between the first (Simabu-ji) and the 34th (Suisen-ji) minor shrines surrounding it); and the Chichibu Yomatsuri (Chichibu Night Festival) is its most significant annual ceremony.

Chichibu Yomatsuri is one of Japan's supreme *hikiyama* (float) festivals, ranking alongside Gion Kyoto and Takayama in spring. What it lacks in numbers it compensates for with float size, complexity, aesthetic beauty, detailed craftsmanship, dazzling illumination and breathtaking surprise.

December 2, the first day, is a day of preparation and purification. The real action is on December 3. At dusk, six teams of roughly 100 people in ritual dress heave six gigantic floats – weighing 20-30 tons and 11 m (36 ft) high – through the crowded streets. Festooned with lanterns, and ridden by *taiko* drummers and musicians with horns and flutes, the floats are miniature gilded palaces of ornate wood carvings, ancient tapestries, and ingeniously modelled interiors that flash and sparkle – and swing open either side to create a stage on which *Kabuki* plays are performed. As a prolonged finale, the procession resumes its progress to the Chichibu Shrine. For more than two hours, fireworks sparkle, zip and crackle in the clear winter sky, while the floats bearing the local *mikoshi* (portable shrines) are dragged with enormous enthusiasm up a steep incline to their destination. That's when the spectacular ceremonies transform into an equally wonderful street party.

WHEN:
December 2-3
WHERE:
Chichibu Shrine, Chichibu, Saitama Prefecture
BEST FOR:
Culture, religion, pageantry, folk crafts, fireworks (very rare in Japan in winter)
YOU SHOULD KNOW:
You can encourage the teams heaving on the ropes by chanting *Ho-ryai! Ho-ryai!* (Heave-ho! heave-ho!). For some years, the people of Chichibu have considered their community to be the inspiration for Gilbert & Sullivan's famous 1885 comic opera, *The Mikado*, chiefly because the fictional setting of 'Titipu' is pronounced 'Chichipu' in Japanese.

Hi! Seoul Festival

Ever since it staged the Olympics in 1988, Seoul has been a city with big ambitions. Founded in 2003, the Hi! Seoul Festival has the twin aims of attracting visitors from overseas and making the city more accessible to its ever-growing number of citizens. The festival replaced the drably named Seoul Citizens' Day and it has grown into a truly international event, providing a window to the world for Korean culture.

Each year sees a different theme and past events have been framed around such diverse motifs as the four seasons, the colour red and miracles. The main events take place in the historic City Hall but there is also a large fringe at venues throughout the city. A formal opening ceremony sees dancing and music, before a spectacular evening fireworks festival over the Han River.

From then on, and with programme in hand, you can take your pick of the assorted entertainments on offer from dawn until dusk. Both classical and local folk music are well represented. There are traditional art exhibitions as well as more *avant-garde* sculpture and design on show. Children can marvel at the sleight of hand at the Seoul Magic Festival, while all can feast at the food festival. If one had to choose a time to visit the South Korean capital it would be this. The festival is held in perfect
T-shirt weather and it provides a good insight into what makes Seoul's inhabitants tick. The compactness of the venues for the events on show also makes what can at first seem a chaotic urban sprawl manageable, as nearly all the performances are within easy walking distance of the centre.

WHEN:
Over nine days in May
WHERE:
Seoul
BEST FOR:
Music, dance, theatre, food, magic and art
YOU SHOULD KNOW:
Koreans are wonderfully creative with the English language. Very often shop signs will only offer cryptic clues as to what you may find inside. A favourite for tourist snaps is the sign for 'Born to be Chicken', a restaurant in the downtown area.

Performers dressed as traditional civil ministers in a re-enactment of the King's march.

455

ASIA/SOUTH KOREA

Jindo Sea Parting Festival

WHEN:
The main festival takes place in May – there are other partings in March and July.
WHERE:
Jindo Island
BEST FOR:
Mass participation, music and culture
YOU SHOULD KNOW:
The sea parts fully for only one hour, so if you do not want to end up wading back you need to time it right. If you have not made it halfway across within 15 minutes, it is probably wise to head back. For those who just want to watch, several nearby hills offer great views of the spectacle.

It takes a great leap of faith to just walk out into the sea hoping that the tide has parted sufficiently to make your journey safe. This is something thousands of Koreans do each year by walking along an exposed sandbar that links Hoedong on Jindo Island in the southwest of the country with the island of Modo. Legend has it that an old lady was left behind when the rest of the villagers took flight and swam away from an attack by tigers. Now alone, she prayed to the Sea God to reunite her with her kith and kin and her prayers were answered by the parting of the waves.

Thankfully, the exposure of the seabed is no longer in the lap of the gods and can easily be predicted with the aid of tide charts. This seemingly supernatural parting of the waves was little known outside Korea until Pierre Randi, the French Ambassador, visited the area and eulogized about it in the French press. This led to a worldwide interest and a festival soon grew up around the event, bringing much-needed revenue to this remote corner of the country. Folk singing, a dog show, dancing and local straw crafts all add to the charm of the main occasion.

The sea-walk itself stretches for around 3 km (1.9 mi) and the passageway is some 40 m (130 ft) wide. At the allotted time, usually in the early evening, locals and tourists alike take the first few steps along the exposed seabed, quickly forming an amazing serpentine line out into the sea. Progress is at a brisk pace, halted only by locals taking the opportunity to bend down and harvest the fruits of the sea – seaweed and molluscs. Over 1,000,000 people now visit the festival and it is a uniquely uplifting experience to be part of such an extraordinarily human chain.

People walk briskly along the 2.8 km sand bar before it floods.

Chingay Parade of Dreams

Multi-cultural Singapore enjoys a great many festivals, celebrations and cultural events during the course of each year, and the Chingay Parade of Dreams, a celebration of the country's unified cultural identity, is probably the greatest extravaganza of them all.

A city-state and Southeast Asia's smallest nation, Singapore lies at the southern edge of the Malay Peninsula. Once a Malay fishing village, Singapore became a British trading post in 1819, and the Empire's centre of power in the region. Captured by Japan in World War II, it reverted to Britain in 1945, becoming part of Malaysia in 1963, and fully independent in 1965.

The Chingay Parade was a Chinese religious festival that originated in Penang, Malaysia, in the late 1800s. It was not introduced to Singapore until 1973, after the government banned the traditional firecrackers of Chinese New Year. Chingay quickly became multi-cultural, and by 1987 the first foreign participants joined the fray. The Downtown Core, containing the most expensive real estate in the country, is situated around the mouth of the river, and this is where the parade is held.

Chingay is a night-time spectacular, a vibrant, noisy, colourful and unmissable occasion. This being Singapore, stands and viewing platforms are available to those who buy tickets, but it's far more fun just to watch from the side. The floats are extraordinary, vast and flashing with lights. In 2008, the President's float was escorted by 36 gleaming Ferraris. There are huge structures that require between 100 and 300 people to move them along the route, lion dancers, stilt walkers, marching bands, Chinese opera singers, boy bands, flag bearers, lantern carriers, and street performers from around the world. It's a riot of cymbals clashing, drums drumming, and sequins glittering, and if the post-parade party doesn't appeal, drop into Raffles for a complete change of atmosphere and a quiet Singapore Sling.

WHEN:
February – check for the exact date
WHERE:
The route of the parade has changed over time: today it runs from City Hall to Raffles Avenue.
BEST FOR:
Extravagant spectacle, fantastic floats, multi-cultural performers and family-friendly fun
YOU SHOULD KNOW:
Lee Kuan Yew, who was Prime Minister of Singapore from 1959-1990, ran the officially democratic country in a very authoritarian way. His successor, Goh Chok Tong, was replaced in 2004 by Lee Kuan Yew's oldest son, Lee Hsien Loong.

Chingay is a night-time parade.

A spectator touches the head of a dragon lantern for good luck.

Singapore Lantern Festival

Just a few decades ago the name Singapore conjured up visions of the tropics in all their glory: junks and pearl luggers bobbing about in the harbour, narrow, winding streets full of shop-houses, dark, mysterious opium dens, rickshaws, ceiling fans 'whoomphing' lazily above romantic-looking bedsteads draped in white mosquito netting. Today's Singapore is a world away from its past – a thoroughly modern, sparklingly clean city of concrete, steel and glass, complete with traffic jams, department stores and banks, its harbours full of container ships and oil tankers.

The Lantern Festival, or Moon Cake Festival, takes place across East Asia in the autumn, traditionally over the full moon of the eighth lunar month. This being Singapore, the festival has become part of the wider, mid autumn festival, but lanterns are still the highlight – indeed every street and every Chinese household hangs lanterns for the occasion. The three main venues are the river, with its decorated embankments, Chinatown, where there are still a few original buildings and street bazaars, and the Chinese Garden in Jurong. This 13.5-ha (33-acre), beautifully landscaped garden, with its 17-arch bridge, pagoda, tea house and pavilions, is completely decked out with lanterns in over 20 themes, and thousands of Singaporeans come here with their families to marvel at their artistry and to float their own lanterns on the lake.

Children particularly love this festival – they get to stay up late, eating moon cakes and special Chinese pastries while enjoying the fireworks and watching the lion dancers dip and twirl to the sound of clashing cymbals and beating drums. For adults, a trip to the Chinese Garden to enjoy the Lantern Festival harks back to earlier times. Despite the full moon, at night much of Singapore's modernity fades into the background, allowing ancient and time-honoured traditions to shine through.

WHEN:
September/October – check the exact dates in advance
WHERE:
Singapore – and especially the Chinese Garden in Jurong
BEST FOR:
Lanterns, traditional and modern
YOU SHOULD KNOW:
The festival can be traced back to 2000 BC in China, when the Xia and Shang dynasties worshipped the moon. Moon cakes are made of lotus-seed paste and sesame seeds in a type of dough. Traditionally, but no longer, the centre was the yolk of a salted duck egg.

ZoukOut Dance Festival

Gleamingly modern Singapore is in many ways a success story. Its businesses boom, its harbours are some of the busiest in the world, millions of tourists visit each year, the streets are litter free and the crime rate enviably low – but the price is the many authoritarian laws under which the population lives. This may be one of the reasons Singaporeans love the ZoukOut Dance Festival, because it is an occasion when everyone can really let their hair down.

Held on Sentosa Island, ZoukOut is Southeast Asia's biggest dance festival, attracting people from across Asia as well as some dedicated clubbers from Australia, Europe and the USA. Sentosa, connected to the mainland by a causeway, is a popular holiday resort boasting a 3.2-km (2-mi) strand of glorious white sand. Siloso Beach lies at the western end of the island's southern coast, and it is here the party takes place.

ZoukOut is organized by Singapore's most famous club, Zouk, which opened in 1991, introducing dance music culture to the whole region. An instant success, it has grown to be recognized as one of the world's leading dance clubs. ZoukOut was dreamt up in 2000, and 9,000 people turned up. Today the numbers are nearing 30,000, and it really is a must-visit event.

Beginning at sunset and ending at dawn, clubbers dance to techno, hip hop, trance, indie, mash up, house and Mambo Jambo, played across four arenas on the beach by some of the best DJs in the world. Just like every other music festival, there are also umpteen food stalls, massage tents and fringe events for those who need a break, but there aren't many festivals where you can dance with bare feet, while the sea rustles over the shoreline beside you and palm trees sway in the breeze.

WHEN:
December – but check the exact date
WHERE:
Siloso Beach, Sentosa Island
BEST FOR:
All kinds of dance music
YOU SHOULD KNOW:
A few examples of Singapore's more unusual laws are: the sale and chewing of gum is forbidden; you could be heavily fined for failing to flush a public loo; it is an offence to enter the country with cigarettes; it is illegal to cross the road anywhere other than at a pedestrian crossing; it is illegal to bungee jump.

Clubbers dance the night away on Siloso Beach.

Idul Adha in Yogyakarta, Java

Idul Adha, or Eid al-Adha, is celebrated by Muslims all over the world. It falls on the third day of the Hajj, the obligatory pilgrimage to Mecca that every Muslim should take, and the largest annual pilgrimage on earth.

Idul Adha commemorates the day that Ibrahim (Abraham) accepted Allah's will that he should sacrifice his son. Withstanding temptation by the devil to disobey this cruel demand, Ibrahim was about to kill Ismail (Isaac) when Allah replaced the boy with a sacrificial ram. Idul Adha necessitates sacrificing an animal and sharing the meat with family, friends and the poor. It is extremely important in the Muslim calendar, and has different names in different countries.

In Yogyakarta, a special ceremony called Grebeg Besar dating back to the 12th century is held on Idul Adha, during which the Sultan shows his affection and respect for his people with offerings of food. Preparations begin in the Kraton (palace) four days beforehand – this is not just any food, this is artistic food. Thirty vast cones, known as *gunungan*, of superbly presented fruits, vegetables, rice and sweet cakes are prepared, each cone needing 16 palace officials to carry it.

On the morning of Idul Adha, after special prayers at the mosque, thousands of people go to the Kraton for Grebeg Besar. Shots ring out and, through clouds of incense, courtiers and nobles in their finery, traditionally dressed soldiers carrying banners and the *gunungan* appear. With drums banging, trumpets blaring and wildly cheering crowds, they process to the Grand Mosque, where prayers and blessings are said. Finally the *gunungan* are up for grabs, and a mad scramble takes place to snatch just a tiny piece of food, believed to bring good fortune. Back at home, animals are slaughtered, cooked and shared in a major three-day celebration.

Muslims take part in special prayers to mark the start of Idul Adha.

Pasola Festival, Sumba

Riders get ready to do battle.

To the south of Flores and Komodo in Indonesia's Nusa Tenggara, lies the remarkable island of Sumba. Unusually, Sumba remained uncolonized until the Dutch arrived in the early 1900s. As a result, animism and ancient traditions retain their influence here, despite a veneer of Christianity. East Sumba is arid and sparsely inhabited; West Sumba is green, undulating and home to 65 per cent of the population. Nine separate local languages reflect the various war-like tribes who once fought each other endlessly.

The Pasola festival is unique, and begins with a ritual that could easily come from a book by J R R Tolkien – the search in the wet sand at dawn by *Rato* (traditional spiritual leaders) for multi-coloured *Nyale* (sea worms). Once a year, after the full moon in early spring, *Nyale* appear in their thousands, mating furiously. Seen as a sign from the gods, their numbers and size indicate the success or failure of the rice harvest.

Sumba was famous for sandalwood, slaves, horses and head hunting. Nowadays the Sumbanese expend their violence during Pasola, in a series of battles involving the flinging of (usually) blunted wooden spears at one another. Preceded by prayers, incantations and the sacrificing of chickens, teams of traditionally garbed, bareback riding warriors practise this unusual form of jousting, accompanied by frenzied cheering and screaming from the crowd.

The explosive ritual battles of Pasola are both skilled and dangerous. Some catch the spears flying towards them and hurl them back. Some get knocked off their mounts and others spill their blood onto the field of play. Blood is good – the more spilled, the better the harvest. Although the battles are refereed, and police are on hand to prevent the crowd from having battles of their own, there are still occasionally serious woundings and deaths – but no one is culpable during Pasola. Go see.

WHEN:
February or March – the Rato determine the exact start date each year
WHERE:
West Sumba, in several venues. Try Lamboya, Kodi, Gaura or Wanukaka
BEST FOR:
Traditional culture
YOU SHOULD KNOW:
The Sumbanese traditional religion is called Marapu, and almost everything in the island relates to it, from the shape of the houses with their high peaked roofs, to the megalithic tombs. Sumbanese weddings and funerals are just as extraordinary as the Pasola.

A woman takes offerings to the temple.

Galungan, Bali

Unlike the rest of Indonesia, Bali is a Hindu island, and it's famous for its myriad festivals. Working to the Western calendar and two others, the *saka* and the *wuku*, festivals take place at some temple or village every day. The most important, however, is Galungan, celebrated throughout the island.

Galungan takes place every 210 days – once during the *wuku* year. Symbolizing the victory of good over evil, it is when all the Balinese gods come down to earth to celebrate. The festivities are made even more special by the construction by each household of a *penjor* – a tall, curved bamboo pole, intricately decorated with young coconut leaves woven together, fruit, vegetables, sheaves of grain, cakes and 11 Chinese coins. There is also a small shrine, with offerings of flowers, rice and incense. These are placed to the right of every front gate, producing a beautiful arched effect over every street.

Barong dances are traditional at Galungan, and troupes move from village to village, and temple to temple, to perform this classic dance that also describes the fight between good and evil – *Barong* and *Rangda*. The dancers' masks are sacred, and the local priest makes blessings and offerings to them before they are brought out and worn.

As all the family temples must be visited, there are always a great many people dashing about the island. You'll see families all decked out in their finest clothes, riding five to a motorbike, the woman modestly sitting side-saddle, clutching at least two children, with not a helmet between them. Offerings are taken in procession to every temple, and a great deal of feasting with family and friends takes place on this family orientated national holiday.

WHEN:
Every 210 days (In 2010 – May 12 and December 8; in 2011 – July 6; but check the dates in advance.)
WHERE:
All across Bali
BEST FOR:
Traditional Balinese religion, culture and dance
YOU SHOULD KNOW:
Penjor represent Mount Agung, Bali's holiest mountain and symbol of the universe. The decorations constitute man's basic needs and the care that must be taken of them. The festivities require the sacrifice of much livestock, but it is believed that those sacrificed for Galungan will become higher creatures in their next life.

The Waisak Festival at Borobudur, Java

The Waisak Festival at Borobudur is a great, three-in-one celebration of Buddha's birth, enlightenment and death. It is a majestic, moving occasion, regardless of your personal religious affinity, and it is the only day during the year when Borobudur is once again used as a temple – the rest of the time it is a much-visited monument, where pilgrims must meditate on their own.

Borobudor was officially re-opened by President Suharto in 1983, after complete restoration. Later that year the government proclaimed Waisak a national Buddhist holiday, enabling thousands of Buddhists from all over Indonesia to go there each year.

Starting in the afternoon, pilgrims and monks in saffron robes gather at nearby Mendut temple, which houses the country's largest statue of Buddha – on this day decorated with gold leaf, flowers and incense sticks. To the sound of a *gamelan* orchestra, the procession starts out, everyone carrying yellow or orange flowers. Monks from Mendut monastery carry sacred relics, including a piece of Buddha's bone, in special containers. Slowly, the crowd of more than 15,000 walks the 5 km (3 mi) to Borobudur under the hot sun, sharing water, sweets, smiles and words.

At Borobudur, a huge red carpet has been laid out in front of a specially built dais; monks sit to the right. The carpet is soon completely covered with seated pilgrims, who are completely dwarfed by the huge and magnificent temple before them. Around 15,000 voices chant mantras in unison and fall silent in meditation. This is powerful stuff. It is believed the energy of Borobudur is channelled into the earth beneath and sent back to the heavens by the power of prayer, and as you watch the full, yellow moon rise behind the *stupa*, you feel that circle is complete.

WHEN:
May, but check on the date of the full moon
WHERE:
Borobudur, 40 km (25 mi) northwest of Yogyakarta, Central Java
BEST FOR:
Buddhist religious rites
YOU SHOULD KNOW:
Borobudur is the world's largest Buddhist monument. Built in the ninth century, it was deserted in the 14th century when the Muslim faith became dominant in Java, and it was swallowed up by the surrounding rainforest. Rediscovered in 1814 by Sir Stanford Raffles, it was finally restored by UNESCO and the Suharto government. It is now Indonesia's biggest tourist attraction and a World Heritage Site.

Buddhists release paper lanterns during the Waisak Festival.

Sriwijaya Festival in Palembang, Sumatra

WHEN:
June – check up on the precise date in advance
WHERE:
Palembang, south Sumatra
BEST FOR:
Sumatran culture
YOU SHOULD KNOW:
The name Palembang probably derives from the word *limbang*, which means panning for gold – an activity that continued in the Musi River until the end of the 19th century.

In ancient times, Palembang, set on both banks of the broad, brown Musi River, was the capital of the wealthy and powerful kingdom of Sriwijaya, effectively controlling the straits through which ships had to pass to get from India to China. Culturally, too, its glory days were during the 13th century – there were already more than 1,000 monks there in AD 671.

Sometimes known as the Venice of the east, Palembang today continues to be industrial, dominated as it has been for a century by the trappings of the oil business. Oil has attracted many other industries here, all of which are spread out along the riverbanks on the outskirts of town, perfectly placed to move their goods to the South China Sea and the wider world. Several festivals take place here, and the Sriwijaya Festival aims to promote both the ancient and modern culture of the region.

Thousands of visitors come to Palembang for the week-long festival. Many arrive from other parts of Sumatra, but also from Java, Malaysia and Singapore, to enjoy a programme of traditional and contemporary dance, theatre, exhibitions of art and history, boat-decorating competitions, story telling, and live music. Here you can try food from many different regions, look at and learn about regional textiles and weaving skills, and even go in for an international fishing contest. As if you needed reminding that Palembang is on a river, there are even noisy and dangerous looking speed-boat races, which draw huge crowds of cheering enthusiasts.

Sumatra is home to a number of extraordinary tribes and unique cultures. Visiting the Sriwijaya Festival gives you the chance of meeting and learning about some of them without having to travel to hard-to-reach places on terrible or non-existent roads.

Pangandaran Kite Festival, Java

Pangandaran lies on a teardrop-shaped peninsula. It is joined to the southwest coast of Java by a narrow isthmus, ending in rainforest that covers the whole of the headland. The town lies on the isthmus, both sides lined with dark, volcanic sand, and it is here that Pangandaran hosts an international kite festival.

Java, while it can't compete with Bali in the beach department, does have a few seaside destinations, and Pangandaran is one. Originally a small fishing village, the waves on the western side proved popular with the surfing fraternity. In July 2006 a *tsunami* hit this area, killing about 700 people and devastating parts of the town. Although much has been rebuilt, Pangandaran, like all of Indonesia, is not as touristy as it was before recent man-made and natural disasters hit the country.

Kite flying is extremely popular here – people spend months designing and decorating the most wonderful kites, many of which can be seen in action during the competition. Teams arrive to compete from across Indonesia, as well as from Malaysia, Singapore, China and other countries. There are several different categories, including kites of two and three dimensions, which require up to ten men to control them. Kite fighting is *de rigueur* – the lines are all carefully treated with a mixture of glue and ground glass, the better to sever the lines of rival teams.

Of course there is plenty of other activity on the beach, including live music and stalls selling all sorts of food and drink. On a sunny day, this is an amazing spectacle – the blue sky provides a perfect backdrop for hundreds of colourful kites, some modest others vast. Batik motifs, squid, butterflies and dragons, all with sparkling tail extensions that can be up to 300 m (990 ft) long, swoop, swish, dance and glitter in the air above.

WHEN:
July – check in advance for the exact date.
WHERE:
Pangandaran, southwest Java
BEST FOR:
Kite flying
YOU SHOULD KNOW:
Many adults use their kites to catch bats at dusk, some of which are eaten – apparently they taste rather like venison – and some of which are used in traditional medicine.

A pair of water buffalo thunder round the track.

Negara Buffalo Races, Bali

Negara is the capital of Bali's western Jembrana regency, the least populated and most Islamist area of the island. Most people here are farmers or fishermen, and few speak any English. Although thousands of tourists pass through Jembrana, en route to and from Gilimanuk, the ferry terminal for Java, they don't stay to explore the rocky coastline with its lonely sea temples, or the local culture with its unique *gamelan* and dance style.

Jembrana is best known for the water-buffalo races that take place at Perancak, a small town on an estuary to the south of Negara. Races take place between July and October, but the championships are held each August. Originally a Madurese sport, racing quickly became popular locally. Today people arrive from Java as well as other parts of Bali, though there are very few foreign tourists – a pity, as this is such unexpectedly good fun.

Admission is free, and the area crowded. Hawkers of food, drinks and baubles shout out their wares, loudspeakers blare, friends chat animatedly, punters bet ferociously, and when the sleek, fit animals appear, the noise rachets up. These are the *crème de la crème* of buffalo bulls, and they look it. Infinite effort goes into dressing them – the horns are painted with different colours or striped, the animals draped in silk, bells hang around their necks and harnesses are highly decorated. Each pair, and there are many, pulls a two-wheeled wooden cart with a flag flying from the yoke.

After the bulls have been paraded, their ornaments are removed, the jockeys stand in their carts and, two at a time, to a roaring crowd, they thunder around an uneven oval track, desperately trying to keep their balance, while the bulls reach speeds of up to 50 km (30 mi) per hour.

WHEN:
The Sunday before August 17, Indonesia's Independence Day
WHERE:
Perancak, near Negara, western Bali
BEST FOR:
Local culture and tradition
YOU SHOULD KNOW:
Indonesians are not known for their sensitivity towards animals. The faint of heart beware – jockeys whip their animals' hindquarters with a nail-studded lash, and use chilli paste on the anus to pepper up their speed. Winning bulls, however, will go to stud and be well cared for.

Procession of the Black Nazarene

The revered occupant of the Minor Basilica of the Black Nazarene in Manila is Santo Cristo Jesús Nazareno, the most famous religious relic in the ultra-Catholic Philippines. Carved by an Aztec craftsman, this life-sized representation of Jesus carrying the cross is indeed dark – legend suggesting it was blackened by a shipboard fire on the galleon that brought it from Mexico in 1606, along with a group of Augustinian friars bent on converting the locals. The charmed image also survived earthquakes in 1645 and 1863, and fires that destroyed the Basilica in 1791 and 1929.

Such a hardy survivor is held to have great powers and has a huge following amongst the devout populace. The statue is paraded thrice yearly, but the largest procession is on the feast day of the Black Nazarene in January. For more than two centuries the Black Nazarene has been drawn through the streets of Quiapo (Manila's old town) on a gilded carriage pulled (and guarded) by barefooted men who constantly shout '*Viva Señor*'.

This grand occasion is a mad rough-and-tumble, with numerous injuries and occasional deaths. Around 80,000 devotees join the procession, whilst the vast crowd that watches it passing along a 5-km (3-mi) route is estimated at 2.5 million. It is believed that those who touch the Nazarene may be miraculously cured or have wishes granted, so there's a constant scrum as people hurl themselves forward in an attempt to reach the statue, whilst those who can't get that close throw handkerchiefs or towels with a plea that they should be rubbed against the giver of miracles.

The day-long event is a great spectacle, but those intent on witnessing this breathtaking procession would be well advised to find a safe vantage point rather than getting sucked into the general melee.

WHEN:
January 9
WHERE:
Quiapo, Manila
BEST FOR:
Being part of the world's largest crowd
YOU SHOULD KNOW:
The statue used in the procession has been a replica since 1998 – the original was being damaged by too many eager hands and now remains enshrined in the Basilica.

Devotees parade replicas of the Black Nazarene.

Sinulog Festival

WHEN:
January
WHERE:
Cebu City
BEST FOR:
The happy marriage of religious ceremony and that irrepressible Filipino festive spirit
YOU SHOULD KNOW:
The central figure in the Grand Parade who dances with Baby Jesus in her arms to cast out evil spirits from the sick, represents Queen Juana, wife of the local ruler who embraced Christianity after Portuguese explorer Ferdinand Magellan arrived in 1521 and claimed the Philippines for Spain.

The festival Queen holds up an icon.

This celebration honours Cebu City's patron Santo Niño (the Holy Child). Despite that patently Christian orientation – and the devout character of most people in the Philippines – the Sinulog Festival has some distinctly pagan elements, harking back to the time before proselytizing Spaniards swiftly converted the population to Catholicism way back in the 16th century.

At the festival's heart is the traditional *Sinulog* dance (two steps forward, one step back), which symbolically recalls that life-changing transition. Brightly costumed dancers progress through the streets, moving to a rhythm beaten out on native gongs and drums accompanied by trumpets. This Grand Parade actually represents every aspect of Cebuano society and is a fitting climax to nine days of festivities. It first took place in 1980 and has undoubted tourist appeal, which is further enhanced by a Sinulog Dancing Competition for contingents from all over the Philippines that takes place in the Cebu City Sports complex.

But the religious aspect of the festival has not been forgotten, and pilgrims still travel to Cebu as they have for generations to pay their respects to Baby Jesus. The most dramatic manifestation of that piety is the Fluvial Procession at dawn on the day before the Sinulog Grand Parade. The image of Santo Niño is carried from Mandaue City to Cebuon on a pump boat bedecked with flowers and surrounded by hundreds of candles. He is met by devotees and escorted to the Basilica, where the Christianization of Cebu is re-enacted. Later, a solemn procession circulates through the city at snail's pace, slowed by eager crowds who want to pay their respects.

On the feast day itself, many worshippers attend a Pontifical Mass at the Basilica, conducted by the Cardinal and his bishops, before flooding out onto the streets to watch the fun-packed Grand Parade.

Ati-Atihan Festival

On a Sunday in January the town of Kalibo comes to vibrant life as the wildest fiesta in the Philippines reaches a pounding climax. The Ati-Atihan is proudly known as 'The Mother of all Philippine Festivals' and traces its origins back to the 13th century when immigrants arrived from Borneo and were granted land by the local Ati people. The incomers celebrated by darkening their faces in respect for their benefactors and holding a great feast, which became established as a pagan festival.

A fire-breather performs for the crowd.

Today, this uninhibited event has become a volatile mixture of Catholic ritual, local traditions and social gathering. It is staged in honour of the Holy Child (Santo Niño) and two weeks of general partying culminate in an explosive three-day period. The festival's religious aspects are highlighted by masses before the event and a formal opening mass on day one. After that, the drums hammer out an insistent rhythm and Kalibo's streets fill with dancing revellers. Day two begins with a rosary procession at dawn, followed by another mass. After that anything goes, with participants blackening their faces with soot in an echo of the festival's origins and donning outlandish costumes before indulging in some seriously devil-may-care collective action.

On day three, a feverish festive atmosphere engulfs the town. The black-faced participants split into groups representing different tribes, each competing for a coveted award that goes to the group with the best and brightest costumes. These are truly splendid, artfully created from sugar-cane flowers, plant leaves, bamboo, feathers and shells. The winners are announced after a final procession lit by bamboo torches, where the faithful carry images of Santo Niño. The masquerade ball that follows extends seamlessly into a wild all-night extravaganza that matches anything Rio's Carnival or New Orleans' Mardi Gras can offer.

WHEN:
January, concluding on the third Sunday
WHERE:
Kalibo
BEST FOR:
Tumultuous merriment
YOU SHOULD KNOW:
There is relatively little accommodation in Kalibo, so those bent on attending this stimulating celebration should book well in advance.

A Morione dressed as a Roman soldier.

Moriones

The week before Easter sees the most unusual of many festivals in the Philippines taking place on the island of Marinduque. It is named after Moriones – men and women who dress in helmets, painted masks and bright costumes to represent Roman soldiers, for this quasi-religious event is built around the legend of the half-blind Longinus. After the crucifixion, he is said to be the one who pierced Christ's side with a spear. Spurting blood touched his blind eye and sight was miraculously restored, causing Longinus to become a believer – much to the dismay of fellow centurions.

Though portraying events said to have happened nearly two millennia ago, the custom of dressing as helmeted Romans to seek Longinus only dates back to the early 19th century and was first organized by an imaginative parish priest. For seven days colourful cohorts of Moriones roam the streets of Marinduque's towns seeking Longinus, starting on Holy Monday and culminating on Easter Sunday. They constantly engage in ambushes, pranks and outlandish antics designed to attract attention whilst continuing their search. The quest comes to a dramatic finale with a re-enactment of the Longinus story that ends with his capture and execution for those newly acquired Christian beliefs.

WHEN:
March or April (Holy Week)
WHERE:
Buenavista, Boac, Gasan, Mogpog and Santa Cruz
BEST FOR:
Brilliant masquerade and traditional religious ceremony
YOU SHOULD KNOW:
The name Moriones derives from the Spanish *morión*, the wide-brimmed steel helmet worn by Conquistadors who arrived in the Philippines during the 1560s, thus becoming the military headwear enshrined in local lore.

But there's much more to the Moriones festival than that. This extraordinary activity forms an important part of the island's Lenten celebrations, which include *pabasa* (recitation of Christ's passion in verse) in the various towns. On Good Friday the Santo Sepulcro is observed, as old women exchange biblical verses standing in the wake of the dead Christ. Another major re-enactment sees a recreation of the Via Crucis – Christ's journey to the cross. Men whip themselves and carry a heavy cross as atonement for their sins. It's a moving climax to this unique festival.

Santacruzan

The festival of Flores de Mayo (Flowers of May) is held throughout the month in question. All over the Philippines extra religious observance takes place regularly, often on Wednesdays and Saturdays. Whatever form this may take, the conclusion is always a traditional Santacruzan parade in honour of Reyna Elena (Queen Helena).

This pageant depicts St Helena's quest for the Holy Cross with her newly converted son, Emperor Constantine. After the sacred relic was recovered in Jerusalem and brought to Rome there was great thanksgiving and prolonged celebration – now replicated in towns and villages all over the Philippines. Though introduced by Spaniards, Santacruzan has become part of Filipino culture and is identified with youth, love and joy.

It is preceded by a *novena* (nine days of prayers), then a procession that presents a succession of symbolic characters who tell the story of Christianity's virtues and influence on Filipino life. These include Methuselah (dust to dust), Aetas and Queen Mora (the pagan Philippines), Queen Banderada (the coming of Christianity), Queen Fe (faith), Queen Esperanza (hope), Queen Caridad (charity), Queen Abogada (defender of the poor), Queen Sentenciada (the martyrs), Queen Justicia (justice), Queen Judith (saviour of her city), Queen of Sheba (the wisdom of Solomon), Queen Esther (saviour of the Jews), Samaritana (the woman Christ spoke to at the well), Veronica (who wiped the face of Jesus), three Marys (Magdalene, Mother of Christ, Mother of James), eight angels (together spelling out *AVE MARIA*) . . . and finally Queen Helena herself, escorted by son Constantine.

Naturally, there is plenty of May blossom in evidence and the costumes are stunning. The Santacruzan procession marches to the beat of musicians singing and playing *Dios Te Salve* (Hail Mary), a chant taken up by following devotees holding candles. The whole thing is an awe-inspiring sight.

WHEN:
End of May
WHERE:
Everywhere in the Philippines
BEST FOR:
Spectacular pageantry
YOU SHOULD KNOW:
The identity of the young woman chosen to be Queen Helena is a closely guarded secret until the procession gets underway, surprising and delighting the massed spectators.

471

Regada Water Festival

WHEN:
Late June
WHERE:
Cavite City
BEST FOR:
Waterproof fun-lovers
YOU SHOULD KNOW:
Visitors to the Philippines in June are spoiled for choice when it comes to festivals – around 60 take place but perhaps those who like the Regada Water Festival might also be tempted by Mucia's Mudpack Festival, a symbolic return to primitive times when people were closer to nature.

Although the tourist-orientated Regada Water Festival is nominally dedicated to St John the Baptist (traditionally associated with the sprinkling of baptismal water), a more suitable patron might be Neptune. This unusual annual fiesta was only instigated in 1996, but has rapidly become an enduring tradition, whose fame has spread far beyond the Calabarzon Region.

Regada is an anarchic mixture of religious, environmental and cultural themes, but in truth it's all a great excuse for a week-long knees-up that turns the city of Cavite (itself surrounded by water) into a carnival venue – a pretty wild and wet one. In the run-up to the saint's day there are numerous entertaining events – a bike rally, water sports, music and dance competitions, concerts, cultural presentations, fashion shows, cookery demonstrations, art exhibitions and a whole variety of colourful themed parades and intriguing processions, including one by youthful eco-warriors dressed in herbage to underline the festival's 'green' credentials.

It all comes to a splashy climax on St John's Day. In order to maintain Regada's self-proclaimed status as the world's largest water festival, the entire main thoroughfare of P Burgos Avenue is equipped with sprinklers and powerful sound systems. It becomes a festival centrepiece with townsfolk, students and adventurous visitors getting soaked as they indulge in the prolonged wet-dancing session. Faint-hearted visitors can watch – and be highly amused – from the safety of the sidelines.

This extraordinary sight is complemented by a reminder of the festival's more serious aspect – the Caracol, which sees an image of St John paraded through the city streets to remind the many devout onlookers to give thanks for the year's blessings. It's the final piece of a colourful jigsaw and makes a vibrant picture that anyone visiting the Philippines in June should be sure to see.

Kadayawan sa Dabaw

Countless annual celebrations in the Philippines are colourful occasions that serve as authentic expressions of this island nation's interesting history and culture, but some stand out as being very special indeed. One such is the Kadayawan sa Dabaw in Davao, surely amongst the most impressive (and famous) of them all.

This massive occasion sees 'business as usual' suspended as Davao City transforms itself into a playground for a week-long celebration with many faces. The time-honoured rationale is to give thanks for the bountiful harvest provided by the area's forests,

fertile land, rivers and seas, though Kadayawan sa Dabaw itself is of fairly recent origin, created in the 1980s to unite the people after a dark period of dictatorship. As such, it formalized the village ritual of giving thanks to the gods with offerings of food, flowers and farming implements, whilst indulging in feasting, singing, dancing and general merriment.

But Kadayawan sa Dabaw has always included other objectives, notably the preservation of indigenous peoples and their way of life on ancestral lands. As such, the festival also serves as a showcase for the arts, crafts, cuisine and culture of the local tribes, providing visitors with fascinating insight into these traditional communities, how they live and the ways in which they have influenced contemporary life. This is an important multi-faceted strand woven through the entire event.

The end result is a truly spectacular fiesta that keeps Davao rocking for seven days (and nights!). Extensive activities include parades featuring the civic, military and tribal aspects of local life, flower and produce shows, a trade fair, traditional sports, horse races, native rowing races, powerboat races, music and dance contests and a glittering beauty pageant. Highlights are the stunning Floral Float Parade and the constant Indak indak sa Kadalanan – street dancing in breathtaking tribal costumes.

Street dancers re-enact traditional legends.

WHEN:
Third week in August
WHERE:
Davao City
BEST FOR:
The uninhibited *joie de vivre* of Davao's friendly people
YOU SHOULD KNOW:
Davao's official tagline as a City in Bloom is amply justified by the intricate Floral Float Parade's extraordinary variety of orchids, shrubs and flowers . . . with the bonus of assorted vegetables and local fruits like bananas, *durian*, pomelos, papaya and mangoes.

473

Street dancers on the final day of the festival.

MassKara Festival

There are any number of long-established festivals and fiestas of various sorts in the Philippines, so that very profusion tells its own tale – the good-natured Filipino people love celebrating and are never slow to seize the opportunity to launch a new event. In fact, the MassKara Festival had somewhat sad origins in the 1980s – created when the local sugar industry was in crisis and Negros Occidental Province was in mourning for 700 people lost in a disastrous ferry sinking. Determined to dispel the gloom and try to live up to its nickname of 'The City of Smiles', Bacolod came up with the MassKara concept.

Taken to mean a multitude of smiling faces, MassKara sees hordes of citizens wearing masks that always smile – a reminder to the population of Bacolod and the surrounding area that this resilient region will always pull through the toughest of times and emerge triumphant. Indeed, the very creation of MassKara duly helped to generate tourist revenue that contributed greatly to the local economy's revival.

Bacolenos are lovers of the good life – and they're delighted to share their sunny optimism with all those welcome visitors. It's not always easy to predict what will happen during MassKara, as all sorts of surprising *ad hoc* events are organized each year. But the main ingredients are always the same, providing great entertainment for participants and spectators alike.

As with most celebrations in the Philippines this one is incredibly colourful, with all those smiley masks being teamed with fabulous headdresses and dazzling costumes for prolonged street dancing competitions to Latin rhythms, the MassKara beauty pageant and carnival parades. Other activities include flower and produce shows, concerts, drum and bugle-band contests, sports events and ethnic-food festivals. It's a great time to be in Bacolod and be happy.

WHEN:
Mid October
WHERE:
Bacolod City
BEST FOR:
Putting a smile on your face
YOU SHOULD KNOW:
MassKara sends performers to festivals in China, Hong Kong, Japan and Singapore and the exceptional quality of their displays may be judged by the fact that they are frequently invited to give exhibitions and often win awards – but the best place to see the complete show is, of course, on home soil.

Giant Lantern Festival

The 'Christmas Capital of the Philippines' is San Fernando, and the title is well merited. Traditionally, the nine-day *novena* (prayers) before Christmas was accompanied by the making of small lanterns from locally available materials. These were carried around each area and brought together at church for midnight mass on Christmas Eve. This humble seed has grown into the Giant Lantern Festival that illuminates the city on the Saturday before Christmas Eve, creating a unique spectacle.

The first event to feature these gigantic lanterns was held in honour of President Manuel Quezon in the 1930s, with his wife presenting the inaugural prize. The competitive spirit has never dimmed, and skilled fabricators compete passionately for top honours, with each *barrangay* (district) represented. These impressive round lanterns are up to 6 m (18 ft) across and are paraded through the darkened streets of San Fernando to the stirring music of marching bands and lithe movement of dance troupes, with the entire population of the city turning out to watch enthusiastically. After a late-night mass the winner is announced to wild acclaim.

The lanterns themselves are amazing. Their intricate designs require both imagination and technical skill, as the key to each is a complex lighting plan that switches thousands of coloured bulbs on and off in quick succession, controlled manually by a spinning rotor that determines the sequence. The rapidly changing interplay of light thus created gives each giant lantern stunning visual impact and the collective display is quite simply   fabulous – but perhaps the most impressive feature is that each lantern keeps time with the music, and after each 'set' the rotors are changed and an entirely different lighting sequence reacts to the next tune. Visitors can only marvel at this extraordinary sight, which is guaranteed to get Christmas off to a brilliant start.

WHEN:
Last Saturday before December 24
WHERE:
City of San Fernando
BEST FOR:
The dazzling light show
YOU SHOULD KNOW:
Smaller versions of the famous San Fernando Giant Lanterns are highly prized in the Philippines, and local makers have been quick to meet demand for household-size versions of these unique creations.

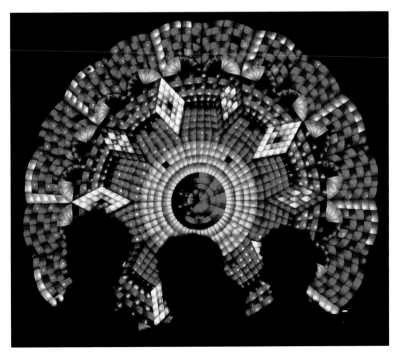

Spectators marvel at the huge intricate lanterns.

475

Flower Festival, Chiang Mai

WHEN:
The first weekend in February
WHERE:
Chiang Mai, northern Thailand
BEST FOR:
Everything concerning flowers
YOU SHOULD KNOW:
Chiang Mai was founded in 1296, rapidly becoming the capital of the Lanna kingdom. Frequently occupied either by the Burmese or Thais from Ayutthaya, it has had a very chequered history, only formally becoming part of Siam (as Thailand was then called) in 1774. Today, Chiang Mai is Thailand's second city.

The floral floats are quite magnificent!

Northern Thailand is renowned for its flowers, and Chiang Mai, its historic capital, is often referred to as The Rose of the North. The city's location is perfect, enjoying a tropical climate that suits plants such as orchids and Bird of Paradise flowers, while the surrounding hills are high – the highest peak in Doi Suthep-Pui National Park, just outside the city, is 1,685 m (5,561 ft) – and cool, allowing blooms such as carnations and chrysanthemums to thrive.

February is probably the best month for enthusiasts to visit – the gardens of Chiang Mai are laden with flowers, and many more grow wild in the countryside and foothills around the city. This is when the Flower Festival takes place, a carnival that attracts thousands of visitors, both Thai and foreign. For days beforehand, Chiang Mai's main streets are busy with workers setting up pots and troughs of flowering plants. Shopkeepers, too, place plants outside their doors, and even the moat around the historic city centre, the bridge and the embankments are all decorated.

The festival takes place over three days, with traditional music shows, beauty contests and flower arranging competitions. Prize blooms are displayed in Nong Buak Hat Park, including over 3,000 species of wild and cultivated orchid. However the main event is the parade, where huge floats, decorated with flowers and topped by beautiful girls in traditional northern costume, roll through the streets in a seemingly never-ending stream. Each float tells its own story: perhaps an event from history, or from Buddha's life. Some floats are modern and abstract, and many have written messages. They are quite remarkable, each flower, petal, and shade of colour is chosen with care and arranged with love, and the pleasure and admiration on the faces of the crowds that line the streets to watch and cheer says it all.

King's Cup Elephant Polo Tournament

Elephants are revered in Thailand, indeed one of the highest honours that the King can bestow is the Order of the White Elephant. Renowned for their intelligence, strength and good nature, elephants helped shape the country, from being ridden into battle, to carrying valuable hardwoods out of the most inaccessible areas of mountainous rainforest.

Now, however, Thai elephants are in dire straits. In the late 1980s, deforestation due to excessive and often illegal logging across the country, resulted in the worst floods Thailand had ever seen. Thousands of people drowned and new legislation on logging left 300,000 domesticated elephants and their keepers with no means of support.

In 2001 the elephant polo tournament was introduced to Thailand, since when it has grown from a modest affair to a week-long event featuring seven or more teams from 15 countries. The King's Cup attracts big-name corporate sponsors and raises badly needed money for the National Elephant Institute in Lampang.

The basic rules are simple: two teams of three elephants play two ten-minute chukkers, with a half-time break. Elongated mallets are used with normal polo balls. The elephants are directed by their *mahouts*, since the pith-helmeted players know how to play polo but not how to direct elephants, and the whole spectacle is both amusing and charming. During half-time, the players consume sandwiches and 'G and Ts' in their VIP tent, the spectators do much the same, the *mahouts* have a smoke round the back and the elephants lumber off to squirt pond water over themselves. At the end of the tournament, the winning team enjoys a prize-giving ceremony, and their name is inscribed on an ornate silver cup. Spectators can enjoy the Elephant Orchestra, and watch elephants painting, before putting in bids for elephant polo memorabilia at the well-attended auction.

The polo tournament was started as a way of helping to pay for the upkeep of the elephants.

WHEN:
March/April – check for exact dates
WHERE:
Anantara Resort Golden Triangle, northwest of Chiang Rai
BEST FOR:
All things elephantine, and having a good look at Thailand's wealthy ex-pats
YOU SHOULD KNOW:
The new logging laws obliged some elephants to be used for tourism. Some wound up begging in the streets, others were used to continue illegal logging, braving landmines on the Burmese border. Their plight inspired the setting up of sanctuaries, but more help is needed. There are only about 2,500 domesticated and 1,500 wild elephants remaining in Thailand, down from 50,000 in 1950.

Poi Sang Long Festival at Mae Hong Son

Buddhist men are expected to join a monastery at least once during their lives, if only briefly. The annual festival of Poi Sang Long, which takes place only in Burma's Shan State and Thailand's northern provinces, is a colourful, three-day ordination celebration for boys

Members of the Thai Buddhist Yai tribe celebrate novice ordination.

becoming Buddhist novices. In Mae Hong Son, Thailand's most mountainous province, most people have Shan ancestry and the eponymous city is the perfect place to enjoy this festival.

Day one sees the boys assemble in the monastery courtyard and beg their parents' forgiveness for past wrong-doing. After having their heads shaved clean by their fathers, they all return home. Day two involves bathing, anointing and being lovingly dressed as a prince from ancient times. Splendidly adorned in headdresses, sequined jackets, vivid satin trousers, bedecked with jewellery and fully made up, the boys are now Sang Long – jewelled sons – and until their ordination, their feet stay off the ground.

Carried to the monastery by their fathers, and showered with jasmine petals, prayers are said. Then, asking for blessings from the community for their new life, the Sang Long are carried shoulder high around town, musicians banging gongs and cymbals alongside. Decorative parasols shade them from the sun – the carriers have no such luck, relying instead on beer. That night, the families of the soon-to-be monks throw lavish feasts while the boys lie around on raised platforms, playing at being princes.

Day three sees the main procession, but this time the boys are carried to pray at various temples en route. The whole town celebrates increasingly wildly until finally the procession reaches the main temple. Inside, the boys strip off their finery, make their vows and put on their new orange robes. While feasting and merrymaking continues outside, the new novices begin a very different life.

WHEN:
March/April – check the exact dates in advance
WHERE:
Mae Hong Son and the other northern Thai provinces
BEST FOR:
Buddhist religion and culture
YOU SHOULD KNOW:
Buddhist monks and nuns rely entirely on what is given to them by the faithful. Monks are allowed to collect, receive and consume food between dawn and midday only. They may drink water at any time. Although monks live on whatever they are offered, vegetarianism is encouraged.

Songkran

Probably the best known of Thailand's festivals, Songkran, the Water Festival, marks the Thai New Year and is when everyone tries to return to their family homes for three days of celebration. Songkran begins on April 13, slap in the middle of the hottest time of year, so it is perhaps not surprising that, in recent times, the water element of the celebration has overtaken everything else.

The festival begins with firecrackers exploding at dawn, intended to drive away any lurking evil spirits, then everything is cleaned in readiness for the New Year. On day two people prepare food for the main event and build pagodas of sand in the temples. Thais believe they take sand away on their feet each time they go to pray, so at Songkran they return a bag of sand to the monks. The third day is for feasting and, after an early visit to the temple, families get together to ask for forgiveness from their elders for any transgressions, and for blessings for the future. This ceremony ends with the sprinkling of a little water on the heads and hands of respected older relatives, and it is this that, some say, has got out of hand.

Everyone – locals, tourists, policemen and soldiers – gets soaked when they venture out at Songkran, and this must be taken with good grace. Children and young adults arm themselves with talcum powder, water pistols and buckets full of water. Water is tipped from windows, hosepipes see plenty of action and young men load pick-up trucks with huge barrels of water, hurling it indiscriminately at those walking or driving by. Roads become slippery and treacherous. Most revellers get very drunk, and a lethal combination of alcohol and water in the face has traffic accidents reaching their annual peak at this time.

It is essential to enter into the spirit of Songkran.

WHEN:
April 13 for three days
WHERE:
All over Thailand. The festivities in parts of Bangkok and Chiang Mai are the best known
BEST FOR:
Being drenched with water
YOU SHOULD KNOW:
Be careful with your possessions during Songkran. You may want to photograph or video the festivities, but keep your cameras, videos, passports, etc, sealed in plastic bags. Drenched means drenched, and no amount of pleading can prevent it.

Bun Bang Fai Rocket Festival in Yasothon

WHEN:
May, but check the exact dates in advance
WHERE:
Yasothon, northeast Thailand
BEST FOR:
Traditional culture, music and rockets
YOU SHOULD KNOW:
An average rocket holds 20-25 kg (44-55 lb) of gunpowder and is 9 m (30 ft) long.

Isan is Thailand's poorest and most rural area. The population here speaks a variation of Lao, and is rightly proud of its distinctive culture and heritage. The Bun Bung Fai Rocket Festival, believed to have evolved from ancient fertility rites, is celebrated across the region, and the festivities in Yasothon are renowned.

May brings the start of the rains, and therefore rice planting, and this festival is held to ensure the rains do their job. Taking place over three days, the festival is bawdy and high-spirited, reflecting its origins. Cross-dressing, phallic symbols, dirty jokes, gallons of alcohol and lots of flirting is the name of the game – theoretically, there will be too much hard work to do in the coming weeks to have the time or strength for much *sanook* (fun).

Throughout the weekend there are processions and floats, beauty competitions and stalls, as well as rockets. The festival kicks off with a display of all the fabulously decorated rockets and a folk dancing contest, followed by *mor lam* – traditional music, song and dance – interspersed with raunchy comedians. Saturday brings processions, marching bands, a traditional Isan dinner of many courses and a firework display.

Sunday is the big day, with launches starting early in the morning. Highly competitive, the home-made rockets are so huge and so packed with gunpowder that they have to be launched from specially built platforms. Many have the heads of *nagas* – mythical serpents that inhabit the Mekong – which, thanks to concealed mechanisms, spit water on the crowds. Rockets are judged on height achieved and distance travelled, and the owners of those that misfire jump into, or are dumped into, mud. The crowds cheer and shriek, or jeer and groan, music plays loudly, the noise of the launches is terrific, and a good time is had by all.

A rocket with a serpent's head is mounted on a traditional cart and carried on poles.

Khao Phansa Candle Festival in Ubon Ratchathani

The Candle Festival is probably Ubon Ratchathani's best-known event, bringing thousands of visitors – both Thai and tourist – into the eponymous city and providing a boost for the local economy. This is Isan's largest province; to the south lies Cambodia and to the east, across the Mekong River, is Laos.

Historically part of the Khmer Empire, which is reflected in its architecture, Ubon Ratchathani only became part of Siam in the late 18th century. The province is renowned for having the most temples of any Thai region, many of which are ancient Khmer marvels. Buddhism is strong here, and the Candle Festival marks the start of Buddhist Lent, when monks are confined to their temple compounds for three months. It is also a very popular time for young men to be ordained as novices.

The festival stems from the tradition of presenting candles and other useful offerings to the temples at this time. Today, the temples still receive the candles (in reality, light bulbs are more practical and last longer) but only after a day of festivities and a truly impressive parade.

Throughout the province, groups of villagers, wider communities, parts of government and the private sector co-operate in the designing, making and transporting of these magnificent creations on highly decorated vehicles. For days beforehand, local artisans carve elaborate and intricate beeswax candles, usually one of four basic design types, and many of them several metres in length and height.

Each float is accompanied by representatives of its sponsor, and often by beautiful young women, dancers and musicians, too. Naturally there are competitions for the most artistic offering in several different categories, the winners earning themselves serious prize money. The fame and popularity of this festival is underlined by the fact that the first candle in the procession is given by the King of Thailand.

An ornately carved candle is paraded around Ubon Ratchathani before being presented to a local temple.

WHEN:
July – check for the exact date
WHERE:
Ubon Ratchathani city
BEST FOR:
Isan culture, a fantastic parade and Buddhism
YOU SHOULD KNOW:
Ubon's imaginative native sons are constantly dreaming up ways of making this pageant larger and more exciting, and it has been suggested that the candles should be paraded on the Moon River, upon which the city lies.

A boat illuminated by thousands of lanterns glides down the Mekong River.

Ok Phansa Illuminated Boat Procession

The festival of Ok Phansa takes place each autumn, and celebrates the end of Buddhist Lent and of the rainy season. Buddhist monks have spent the previous three months confined within their temple compounds, studying *dharma* (Buddhist doctrine) and meditating. At the end of this retreat, people celebrate the return of the monks to their normal duties with lavish offerings and joyous festivities.

Ok Phansa is celebrated across Thailand, but notably in Nakhon Phanom, which lies on the banks of the Mekong River, where it is called Lhai Ruahfai. Groups (*khum*) from each of the many temples organize the celebrations. Processions take place as well as traditional performances of music, dance and theatre. Boat races are held along a 3-km (2-mi) stretch of the Mekong River, in front of the city's embankment. These races are a cause of major excitement and are fervently supported, but the main focus of Lhai Ruahfai – which literally means fire-boat – is the wonderful illuminated boat procession.

Historically the boats were 10-12 m (33-39 ft) long rafts made of lengths of bamboo, or hollowed-out trunks of banana palms, filled with offerings. Today, they are much larger and far more extravagantly decorated with flowers, candles, lanterns, fruits, sweet sticky rice wrapped in banana leaves and great bunches of fragrant incense sticks. As darkness falls, the boats are illuminated and launched, gliding gently down river in a magical stream of light.

Ok Phansa coincides with the phenomenon of the *naga* fireballs. Thousands of glowing reddish balls, about the size of an egg, can be seen rising from the Mekong, climbing high into the air before vanishing. The scientific cause of the fireballs is unknown, but locals on both sides of the river believe them to come from the *naga*, the mythical serpents that live in the water.

WHEN:
October/November – check for the exact date
WHERE:
Nakhon Phanom, Isan, northeast Thailand
BEST FOR:
Traditional culture and religion
YOU SHOULD KNOW:
Buddhist Lent comes at the time when, it is believed, Lord Buddha retreated to Heaven for three months to preach to his mother, who had died a week after his birth. When his mission was completed, he returned to Earth by means of a triple staircase of gold, silver and precious stones, escorted by angels. People were so happy he had come back that they celebrated with special gifts and offerings.

Lopburi Monkey Banquet

Lopburi, the ancient capital of the province that bears its name, is located about 150 km (94 mi) northeast of Bangkok. Known as Lavo in the 6th century, it was part of the Dvaravati Kingdom, but was conquered by the Khmers early in the 11th century. Today, the oldest architecture that can be seen is all Khmer. However, these ancient ruins are no longer the town's main claim to fame – that is reserved for the couple of thousand macaque monkeys that inhabit them.

The two main macaque hang-outs are in and around San Phra Kan and the larger and more extensive Prang Sam Yot, a Khmer shrine and temple. Both are very central and within easy walking distance of the railway station. At first sight, the monkeys are charming – sweet little babies clinging to their mothers, adults bounding about, or communicating together. However, with no fear of humans at all, thanks to being fed by the locals, they can be quite alarming and even threatening. Talented thieves, they'll leap onto your back or shoulders as you try to take a photograph, or rip your purse from your hands as you try to buy peanuts to give them – so keep your distance.

The macaques bring so many tourists that local businesses now put on an annual Monkey Banquet as a thank you, and this is without doubt a most unusual and entertaining sight. A vast array of food is beautifully prepared and arranged in front of the temple. Tables groan beneath the weight of jellies, ice cream and fruit. Mangos, papayas, rambutans, grapes, apples, oranges, bananas, *longans*, even expensive *durian* fruit, are offered. The macaques, whose table manners are appalling, wander amongst this largesse, stuffing food into their mouths, squabbling, chucking fruit at one another and generally causing mayhem.

WHEN:
November – check the exact date in advance
WHERE:
Lopburi, central Thailand
BEST FOR:
Khmer ruins and an extravagant food fest for macaques
YOU SHOULD KNOW:
During the 17th century, King Narai briefly moved his capital from Ayutthaya to Lopburi, building a summer palace here. Today, most tourists are Thais coming on a day trip from Bangkok to enjoy not only the macaques and the ruins but also the vast fields of sunflowers all around.

Monkeys help themselves to food.

Loy Krathong, Chiang Mai

WHEN:
Usually in November, but check the exact date
WHERE:
Chiang Mai, northern Thailand
BEST FOR:
Traditional culture and a huge, noisy party all over the city
YOU SHOULD KNOW:
What goes up must come down, sometimes still burning. Every year several shop houses burn down and the emergency rooms fill with those injured by lighting or being hit by rockets. Most people, however, have a really good time.

Chiang Mai, northern Thailand's major city, is situated on the Ping River against a backdrop of some of the country's highest mountains. In many ways the loveliest of Thailand's festivals, Loy Krathong falls on the full moon of the 12th month of Thailand's traditional lunar calendar. This Festival of Lights is known here as Yi Peng. It venerates Buddha and it also heralds the end of the rainy season.

Highly decorative papier-maché floats, each sponsored by a different company, are paraded along the embankment before being launched onto the river to be towed downstream. Throngs of revellers crowd the riverside, bars and cafés are packed, people buy drinks, snacks and fireworks from hawkers and temporary kiosks.

As night falls, everyone seems over-excited – no doubt due to excess alcohol consumption – and fireworks explode indiscriminately, often apparently aimed at those on the opposite bank. Local citizens and tourists launch their own little boats (*kratongs*), which are traditionally fashioned from banana leaves and decorated with flowers, a candle, an incense stick and a sparkler. Sadly these days many people cheat and buy a *kratong* made from polystyrene, but in the gloaming the Ping becomes a river of light as they float away downstream. This is symbolic of letting go the worst parts of oneself, enabling a new and better chapter to begin.

The custom of sending fire balloons up into the night sky is peculiar to northern Thailand. As soon as darkness falls, paper and bamboo cylinders with firecracker tails, powered by paraffin wax, are launched in their tens of thousands – if you don't launch at least one you haven't really participated. At about 1 m (3.3 ft) tall, these lanterns drift up to great heights, catching the breeze and wafting across the night sky in long, spectacular skeins of light that look utterly amazing.

Thousands of floating lanterns are released into the sky.

Surin Elephant Round-up

An elephant steps carefully over brave volunteers.

Today Surin Province shares its southern border with Cambodia, but once it was part of the Khmer empire. Its ethnic population is largely Suay, who for thousands of years have been recognized for their tradition of capturing and training the elephants that lived in the forests near the border. Sadly, many years of war and cross-border incursions have left these forests inaccessible, so the Suay elephant handlers have gone into entertainment. Northeast Thailand – Isan – has some wonderful festivals, and if you are keen on elephants, you must see the Round-Up, held in Surin City each November.

Traditionally, a *mahout's* skill is passed down from father to son and young boys grow up with baby elephants, forming extraordinarily strong, deep, life-long relationships. Unlike the elephants in northern Thailand, that have long been considered working animals, in Surin they are as close as family.

The Round-Up is a celebration of the intelligence, skill, agility and strength of these gentle creatures, and it begins with several hundred animals carrying local bigwigs, a few tourists, and *mahouts* in traditional battle dress, plus many people on foot, processing through the town to a massive elephant banquet of elegantly displayed fruit. The festival, which was inaugurated in 1960, is now widely known and there may be as many as 50,000 spectators enjoying the proceedings.

During the course of two days there are many shows, such as elephant football matches and elephant tug-of-war against 100 men, demonstrations showing how to capture a wild elephant, how to train them for working in the logging industry, even a demonstration of their use in battle. All of this is interspersed with performances by school children, and traditional music, which is played throughout. The grand finale features about 2,000 costumed performers and several hundred elephants and is a magnificent sight to behold.

WHEN:
Usually the third weekend in November, but check to make certain

WHERE:
Surin City, northeast Thailand

BEST FOR:
Traditional elephant culture, costumes and music

YOU SHOULD KNOW:
Surin is an interesting and not much visited province. Apart from its elephant culture, it is famous for its Khmer ruins, including the oldest in Thailand, its extremely high-quality silk, and hot, spicy food such as grilled meat or fish salads (*laaps*), green papaya salad (*som tam*), various fried insects and sticky rice. As Isan people travelled seeking work, their food became famous throughout Thailand.

Tet Nguyen Dan

WHEN:
Late January or early February
WHERE:
Throughout Vietnam
BEST FOR:
Culture, folklore, religion, food
and drink
YOU SHOULD KNOW:
Lucky Nguyen Dan presents to give
are rice wine in a gourd (for a
wealthy and comfortable life) or
anything coloured red (red is the
symbol of happiness and good luck).

The Vietnamese lunar new year (Tet Nguyen Dan) is the country's most important festival. After frantic preparations, shops and offices shut down to allow as many people as possible either to go to their family or ancestral home, or to share the celebrations in the house of a relative. Family, including especially the ancestors, comes first. The living and the dead are regaled with food and drink, and so are the household deities governing crafts (like plumbing and carpentry), the land (including chickens and livestock), and the kitchen (the family hearth). Spotlessly clean houses, new clothes and haircuts emphasize the optimism of renewal – and it helps that in Vietnam, blossoming peach trees (in the north) and apricots (in the south) seem to show that nature itself is in tune with aspirations to abundance.

Happiness abounds, because it's lucky to be with family members even if you avoid them the rest of the year. To be a guest is an enormous privilege; and you need to be hypersensitive to the hundreds of minor rituals and taboos that, confusingly, vary with family, community or region. For example, the first person to cross

Incense burning at Thien Hau Temple during Tet Nguyen Dan

the threshold on Nguyen Dan is considered the arbiter of the entire year's family fortunes. In case that person be some rapacious devil, the head of the household often takes a turn round the house at midnight to make sure he's the first through the new year's door. There are special foods and special drinks. Everyone gives the children some trifling 'lucky money'. The children buy lucky firecrackers to frighten away putative 'devils' (and adults). Whichever part of Vietnam you may be in, the five days of Nguyen Dan provide privileged insight into the core Vietnamese characteristics of generosity, courtesy, playful spirituality and inherent charm.

Lieu Doi Wrestling Festival

Martial arts are of supreme significance in Vietnam. They represent the country's illustrious history of resolute self-defence against myriad invaders – a defence which only succumbed completely to the 'hot' weapons of 19th century gunpowder. There are wrestling competitions all over the country for sport and entertainment, but Lieu Doi, a small village in the Liem Tuc commune of Ha Nam, south of Hanoi, guards the soul of Vietnam's ancestral martial spirit. From the fifth to the tenth days of the first lunar month (February in the Western calendar), Lieu Doi holds a highly ritualized wrestling festival in honour of its tutelary spirits – the hero and heroine of historical events so glamorous that they have been mythologized into local religion. Their story is a mixture of Beowulf, Romeo and Juliet and the Celtic Sword in the Stone legend: a local man called Doan moved mountains to rid his country of invaders, using a sacred sword and a pink sash found with it, but at the cost of his life. Approaching his grave, his warrior lover, as courageous as she was beautiful, collapsed and died of grief. Their selfless defiance of the enemy is immortalized in the festival's series of ritual wrestling matches.

Preliminary ceremonies re-enact the legends. Sword, sash and the hero's palanquin are brought to the wrestling ring. Ritual dances, drumming, firecrackers and the bells and gongs of nearby pagodas introduce the first bouts of wrestling between toddlers. They represent the future, but are symbolically represented by the past (their fathers or grandfathers). Nobody 'loses' these fights – they are a metaphor for communal resistance to oppression. Formal etiquette governs even the later, serious wrestling. It's not just great sport – it's the historic spirit of Vietnamese independence being celebrated with passion. And that's why, simultaneously, the spectators go wild with food and drink.

WHEN:
Early February
WHERE:
Lieu Doi, Liem Tuc commune, Thanh Liem district, Ha Nam
BEST FOR:
Sport, history, folklore, culture, food
YOU SHOULD KNOW:
The festival includes a cooking competition of local specialities like eels, frogs and snails.

487

ASIA/VIETNAM

Lim Festival

WHEN:
February
(During the week before the actual Lim Festival, the rehearsals – when people are effectively auditioning each other – can be equally musically entertaining.)
WHERE:
Lim Village, Bac Ninh province
BEST FOR:
Music, folklore, culture, religion
YOU SHOULD KNOW:
Among the blossoming peonies of northern Vietnam's spring, *Quan Ho* offers a ready means of romantic encounter. Because *Quan Ho* itself treats both sexes as equals in the great game of life, women may approach men with the offer of a *quid* of betel by way of an introduction. The exchange continues as a *Quan Ho* dialogue of song – which must make the genre one of the world's most arcane mating rituals.

The festival that culminates on the 13th day of the first lunar month (February on the Gregorian calendar) at Lim village, just north of Hanoi, brings together the best performers of *Qhan Ho* music. *Quan Ho* is the most highly prized manifestation of the regional culture of Bac Ninh province, the heartland of Vietnamese Buddhism and famous for its proliferation of beautiful temples. Lim Pagoda is where a local woman attained enlightenment. Her later intervention saved the village from drought and the festival is held in her honour. Since its inception in the 13th century, *Quan Ho* music has evolved throughout the area and its practitioners have always come to Lim to pray through song, to show off their skills and to share them in a flurry of local cultural exchange.

Quan Ho is an antiphonal singing tradition requiring *lien anh* (a male part) and *lien chi* (a female part). These may be a man and a woman, or two entire villages, or any four or six people. It consists of improvised exchanges (a form of 'cry and response') based on an agreed canon of melodies and subjects. Mostly they are songs of intimacy and yearning, using the homespun imagery of the fields, rivers and nature. Very strict rules and taboos govern this dialogue.

Quick wits and a deep knowledge of *Quan Ho* traditions are at a premium; but grace and courtly elegance are vital. The *Quan Ho* singers at Lim Festival are drawn from some 49 regional villages devoted to preserving and extending their craft. They share multiple *Quan Ho* relationships between individuals and groups, and the festival is where they make and break partnerships. It gives real piquancy to the ethereal music; and a thrilling undercurrent to the other, less subtle festival entertainments on offer.

Money is given to the singers as a mark of appreciation.

Elephant Races

In the central highlands of Vietnam's Dak Lak province, the many different ethnic groups who share the forested hills and fertile river valleys also share – passionately – the cult of the elephant. Elephants still roam wild as they always have; yet they willingly respond to human partnerships in the tasks of farming, logging, and transport. They have also been famously effective in combat, and the M'Nong people in particular have a strong history of fighting with elephant cavalry. Indeed, M'Nong martial traditions are the hallmark of the spring Elephant Race festival at Don Village, by the Serepoc River near Buon Ma Thuot. In the third lunar month (April in the Gregorian calendar), hundreds of elephants crowd a racing ground some 500 m (1,640 ft) long, and wide enough for ten elephants to line up together. Each elephant has two handlers, magnificently dressed like traditional military generals. One uses a *kreo* (iron stick) to prevent the elephant from dawdling; the other uses his *koc* (wooden hammer) to guide its headlong dash. Before each race, the elephants pirouette and whirl their trunks to a fanfare of *tu va* (horns carved into musical instruments) and crashing gongs and drums. Between the thundering beasts and the crowd pressing forward in the clouds of dust, the excitement, the bazaar of stands serving festive food and drink, and the exotic music in the heat, the atmosphere peaks in a glorious frenzy.

After the racing, you'll see elephants splashing about in impromptu swimming competitions, in tugs-of-war and even football games. For visitors who may never before have seen a single elephant up close, it's sheer magic to see them apparently enjoying themselves *en masse*. And you needn't have any doubts about the symbiosis between elephant and handler – the better elephants are fed and treated, the better they respond.

All the fun of the elephant race!

WHEN:
April
WHERE:
Don Village, Buon Don district,
Buon Ma Thuot
BEST FOR:
Grand spectacle, culture, folklore
YOU SHOULD KNOW:
Some of the M'Nong racing elephants are celebrities in their own right, earning nicknames as young contenders, or reverence as veterans. Recently, one elderly elephant was still competing at the age of 67. Called Y Trut, he's a genuine warhorse famous for army service, carrying ammunition during the two wars of resistance against France and the USA.

Thay Pagoda Festival

WHEN:
April
WHERE:
Thay Pagoda, Thuy Khe,
Sai Son Mountain, Quoc Oai, Ha Tay
BEST FOR:
Folklore, history, religion, culture,
music and traditional games
YOU SHOULD KNOW:
Tu Dao Hanh used water-puppets to
impart his wisdom. The stories are
still usually short and silent (with
perhaps a brief introduction or
musical accompaniment), but always
directly relevant to daily village life.

The Thay Pagoda Festival celebrates the Buddhist monk Tu Dao Hanh. His exploits helped establish the Ly Dynasty (1010-1225), the first Vietnamese power to challenge Chinese rule successfully, and brought him legendary status as a folk hero. The festival takes place at Thuy Khe village, one of four participating villages near Hanoi.

After due ritual preliminaries, the festival's climax has two parts. On the seventh day, the four villages take the tablets representing their Spirit Protectors in procession with the tablets of Tu Dao Hanh. Every detail of cloth colour, precedence and ritual variation is formal and exact. Buddhist nuns chant narratives from the hero's life and a huge crowd follows the procession round the villages with music and singing.

Save most of your wonder for the next day. Tu Dao Hanh was the original master of the art form peculiar to the paddy fields of the Red River Delta: water puppet shows. Puppeteers remain semi-submerged, hidden behind figures they operate with sticks and strings – the artistry is in using the reflections (of trees and sky as well as the puppets) in the water to double the effects and expand the narrative. The stories tell of weaving, fishing and cultivation; of history and the struggle against civil and natural calamity; and of fire-spouting dragons and legends.

Oc Om Boc Festival

WHEN:
Usually in October
WHERE:
Soc Trang City, My Tu district,
Soc Trang province
BEST FOR:
Spectacle, sport, religion,
folklore, culture
YOU SHOULD KNOW:
The *Ngo* boats (*tuk ngua* in Khmer)
with their elevated sterns and
sharply raised and pointed prows
are shaped and decorated to
symbolize the *naga* (snake), sacred
to Khmer culture. The boats are only
used for festival racing, which with
its accompanying music, gongs and
drums, is always part of a greater
ceremony.

One of Vietnam's most revered festivals, Oc Om Boc (Festival of Worshipping the Moon) is unique to the Khmer minority of the Nam Be region in the Mekong Delta. Kho Me people come from 600 villages to gather in the My Tu district at Soc Trang. They come to honour and thank the moon for the past year, and to ask for its blessing on the crops, fish and their own family health for the next. As the full moon appears, everyone sets out little feasts of rice cakes, bananas and other delicacies to attract 'the Rabbit in the Moon', a folkloric hero of generosity and self-sacrifice. At the same time they fly beautiful illuminated kites and free-flying lanterns, and release paper boats carrying lit candles and incense into the river's current.

Next morning, everyone is jumping with excitement in anticipation of the *Ngo* boat racing. Sanctified by the pagodas in which they are built, hollowed from a single sao tree, *Ngo* racing boats are 24 m (80 ft) *pirogues*, lozenge-shaped, with an upturned prow. Precarious in the extreme, rowed by 40 men and women, the boats are elaborately carved or decorated with the motifs of Khmer culture. You might think that the happy hysteria of spectators on the riverbank is caused by the drama unfolding on the water, and the huge betting involved. Much of it is; but the *Ngo* boat races are a fundamental part of Oc Om Boc, the manifestation of thanks and honour to the water deities.

Bun Nam

The end of the Buddhist three-month rains retreat, when monks leave their monasteries at full moon and travel in search of alms, is known as Awk Phansao. It is marked by people making offerings at the temples and holding candlelit evening processions, before hundreds of banana-leaf boats carrying candles, incense and flowers are launched onto the water in honour of river spirits.

Next day the Bun Nam (Water Festival) takes place, a massive annual occasion built around intensely competitive boat races (*suang heua*) on the Mekong River held in the bigger towns such as Vientiane, Savannakhet and Luang Prabang. Some smaller places also celebrate Bun Nam at this time, though many reschedule their races to coincide with National Day on December 2, thus avoiding the expense of two major events in two months.

Although the races attract rowing teams from all over Laos – plus China, Myanmar and Thailand – and are watched by passionate supporters, Bun Nam is also an excuse for a serious party that leaves few revellers standing after three days of non-stop action. The banks of the river are lined with discos, beer gardens, carnival attractions and food stalls, whilst all manner of goods from brightly coloured straw hats to giant umbrellas are on sale. The idea is to generate as much general mayhem as possible, with water fights breaking out between races and everyone hell-bent on having a great time.

The isolation of Laos from foreign influence for many decades offers visitors an opportunity to see a traditional Southeast Asian way of life that has yet to be unduly shaped by the demands of modern tourism, and Bun Nam offers a perfect opportunity to see the locals letting their hair down in a big way . . . and to join the fun.

WHEN:
October
WHERE:
Larger river towns
BEST FOR:
Uninhibited local celebrations beside a great river
YOU SHOULD KNOW:
Sexism has no place at Bun Nam – some of the boat crews that race frantically on the Mekong River are all female.

Competition is intense at Bun Nam.

ASIA/LAOS

That Luang Festival

WHEN:
November
WHERE:
Vientiane
BEST FOR:
Traditional Lao culture in
stunning settings
YOU SHOULD KNOW:
The Vat Phra Kaeo in Vientiane was
once the lavish temple of the Lao
Royal Family, but it is now a museum
housing some of the finest Lao
Buddhist sculpture.

In November The Buddah's faithful followers come together at full
moon for a moving climax to the year's religious calendar. The
festival begins with offerings at the Vat Simuong in Vientiane – a
temple containing the venerated pillar dedicated to Nag Si, the city's
guardian. Hundreds descend at sunset, bearing *phasats* (banana-
stem towers decorated with wax flowers), money and offerings for
saffron-clad monks. For all its religious significance, this is a happy
occasion, with drums beating and cymbals clashing as the
procession circles the Vat three times, bearing candles and incense.
It ends in a homage of fire as rockets soar into the night sky.

Next day the action shifts to the gilded That Luang (the Great
Stupa, a repository for relics) for continuing celebration of Buddhist
teachings – and Lao nationalism, for this magnificent temple
complex contains many references to local culture and identity.
Another procession – more solemn this time –journeys from Vat
Nongbone to That Luang. Once more numerous *phasats* are in
evidence and most people wear traditional costume. Dancers and
musicians accompany three circuits of That Luang before devotees
recite prayers and make offerings to massed monks.

At dawn on the following day a crowd gathers in the grounds to
pray and prepare further offerings to be made during the ceremony
that follows, usually attended by the country's leaders. Then there's
a mass picnic where families and friends meet and greet, before an
afternoon game of *tikhee* (hockey played with bamboo sticks and a
bamboo-root ball) that provides great entertainment, with a hugely
colourful
procession to the
playing grounds
and back. There's
another procession
around the *stupa*
before a
spectacular
firework display
ends this special
day. The festival
concludes with yet
another *phasat*
procession the next
evening, ending a
wonderful event
that effortlessly
combines solemn
observance and
joyous celebration.

Buddhists gather at the festival.

Khmer New Year

The locals know it as Chaul Chnam Thmey, but to many international visitors who arrive in Cambodia to enjoy this splendid annual celebration it's simply Khmer New Year. This three-day holiday coincides with the end of harvest and provides the opportunity for relaxation, frolic and fun before the start of the rainy season . . . with some rather more serious activities mixed in.

First, the formalities: on day one (Moha Songkran) people don their best clothes, light candles and burn incense at their shrines before bowing and prostrating themselves three times before the Buddha's image to give thanks for his teachings. Faces (morning), chests (noon) and feet (night) are washed in holy water to bring good luck in the year ahead. Day two (Wanabat) is reserved for open-hearted charity directed at the less fortunate, plus monastery visits for dedication ceremonies to honoured ancestors. Day three (Tanai Lieang Saka) is for ritual cleansing. Statues of the Buddha are carefully washed with perfumed water, symbolizing the vital role water plays in everyday life, whilst children wash their parents and grandparents in the hope of bringing longevity, happiness and prosperity.

Second, the fun bit: for all the seriousness with which the religious aspect is taken, New Year is a time when families can set aside the cares of everyday life and simply enjoy themselves. The streets are full of music and people dancing, whilst every corner sees light-hearted but boisterous Khmer games in progress. There is a huge number of traditional outlets for surplus energy, from *Klah Klok* (a gambling game played on a mat with dice) to *Chab Kon Kleng* (where an evil 'crow' tries to catch 'chicks' protected by the 'mother hen'). These activities are guaranteed to provide some memorable entertainment.

WHEN:
April
WHERE:
All over Cambodia
BEST FOR:
Watching the extraordinary variety of uninhibited Khmer games played throughout the New Year celebrations
YOU SHOULD KNOW:
The mounds of sand erected in temple grounds during New Year represent the *stupa* at Tavatimsa where's Buddha's hair and diadem are buried.

A girl bites plant bulbs in a street game.

493

Bonn Om Touk

WHEN:
November
WHERE:
Phnom Penh
BEST FOR:
The fabulous festive atmosphere
YOU SHOULD KNOW:
Sadly, the climax of the festival is often symbolic – it's impossible to predict the exact moment when the Tonlé Sap River starts flowing downstream . . . but everyone seems too busy having fun to care.

Twice a year a phenomenon vital to Cambodian life takes place – the Tonlé Sap River changes direction. This combined river and lake system drains into the Mekong River in dry season but during the monsoon it flows back up into the great Tonlé Sap Lake, which triples in size. With the reversed flow silt is picked up and washed along to enrich rice paddies after the lake drains once more, and huge shoals of fish that provide much of Cambodia's protein.

The Tonlé Sap meets the Mekong at Phnom Penh and Bonn Om Touk, also called The Water and Moon Festival, marks its change of direction after the monsoon season. The three-day event sees a combined campground and market spring up in bankside meadows to house and sustain thousands of people who travel from all over Cambodia for this joyful occasion. Friendly monks in burnt-orange robes circulate among the crowds, adding to a kaleidoscopic and colourful picture.

A brightly lit float moves slowly along the river front at Phnom Penh.

Excitement builds as boat races begin, with beautifully decorated boats around 14 m (45 ft) long doing battle. Spectators go mad as crews of 60 or more paddlers drive them through choppy water in search of glory. On the night of full moon a midnight celebration sees lighted floats sailing by before and after a flashy firework display, whilst meals of pounded rice are eaten to give thanks for abundance brought by the life-giving waters.

The festival ends with a final day of races, culminating in the two lead boats heading for a finishing line that consists of a stretched vine. A sword is used to cut the vine and slice open this symbolic barrier that holds back the waters, thus allowing them to flow back downstream. At this point, a massive cheer goes up from the massed audience that lines the banks and fills the many boats on the river. It's a spine-tingling moment.

494

Thaipusam at Batu Caves

Thaipusam is a Hindu festival of purification and atonement. Originating in southern India, it's celebrated all over the world – but it is observed with the greatest fervour at the Batu Caves outside Kuala Lumpur. It commemorates the gift from Shiva's wife, Parvati, of an invincible *vel* (lance) to their youngest son, Murugan, so that he could vanquish the evil army of *asura* (demons). A silver chariot bearing Lord Murugan's image is feted with smashed coconuts, fruit and flowers strewn in its processional path. Devotees wear yellow and orange, Murugan's favourite colours, and many carry a *Kavadi* (literally 'burden'), a metal yoke decked with tinsel, flowers, fruit and streamers, with little pails of milk or honey attached. Borne on the shoulder, they are attached by steel hooks to the body. In extreme cases (and there are many among the million people who come to the Batu Caves), penitents pierce cheeks, tongues and even backs or chests, to drag their *Kavadi* up the final 272 steps to the Waterfall Temple. Pain fosters the trance, which enables them to concentrate fully on the god.

For visitors it's not so straightforward. The frenzied dancing, incense, bells, dazzling colours and vibrant music make Thaipusam an extraordinary event by any standard, and the Batu Caves are in addition one of Southeast Asia's great natural wonders. Don't let the thought of so many different forms of exquisite torture and self-mutilation put you off. The imagination recoils, but in context you'll find yourself inspired by the trance-like drumming and chanting of '*vel vel shakti vel*' to the point where instinctive horror is replaced by intense empathy with the pilgrims. Thaipusam at Batu Caves offers you a spectacular intuitive insight into the nature of total religious commitment.

Batu caves at Thaipusam

WHEN:
End of January/beginning of February
WHERE:
Batu Caves, outside Kuala Lumpur
BEST FOR:
Religion, ceremonial pageantry and spectacle
YOU SHOULD KNOW:
The Batu Caves are both a natural wonder and a Hindu shrine. The Temple Cave alone – where pilgrims bring their *Kavadi* and personal *vel* (body-piercing skewers) – has a vaulted ceiling 100 m (328 ft) high. The 'Art Gallery' Cave is full of wall paintings of Hindu mythology. At a deeper level, the Dark Caves are a 2-km (1.2-mi) network of caves famous for the unique species that flourish there.

Water Festival

WHEN:
April
WHERE:
Pantai Cenang, Langkawi
BEST FOR:
Water sports, beach games, family entertainment
YOU SHOULD KNOW:
The event has been known as the Langkawi Water Festival. Since its success, the government has taken it over as the Malaysia Water Festival, and there are plans for the event to be held in Labuan or elsewhere because, according to the tourist authorities, 'there are so many other attractions in the country that need more exposure'.

Langkawi, the Malaysian island resort at the entrance to the Strait of Malacca, is a tropic paradise of mythic beauty. Inevitably, the building developments that demonstrate its success have challenged the environmental wonderland that is its chief attraction. The Water Festival, part of the problem when it began, has evolved over a decade into a paradigm of environmental and commercial balance. Now it concentrates on harnessing its fabulous natural surroundings by promoting (at the most recent count) 155 activities in a single, three-day event based on water sports and beach games. The fun – particularly for families or groups of friends – is to register for as many activities as you think you can rush between, on and off shore. The athletic events (like kayaking, swimming vast distances and running on dunes) tend to be dominated by teams of enthusiasts from a dozen different countries. They contribute just as much to the spirit of the Water Festival as anyone, but you can be as athletic or as flippant as you like.

The Water Festival takes place on two distinct levels. At their most dramatic, some activities like jet-ski sprinting, Wet & Wild, or Beach Sumo are (perhaps) spectator sports. Others demand participation, like the kayak-capsizing, sandcastle competition, Duck Walk and Beach Treasure Hunt. Wonderful family activities include the cross-country Sack Race, Water Guns, Giant Clogs and Creative Family Picnic. Aficionados of the weird and marvellous will enjoy the Sampan Tug-o-War and the Power-Boat Pillow Fight.

With a continuous accompaniment of music from bands and karaoke stages, and exhibitions by local dance troupes, the Water Festival continues into each night; yet each morning you wake to a pristine Langkawi, lapped by a pristine Andaman Sea. It's a sight worth competing for – and every activity has a cash prize.

Gawai Dayak

Sarawak is the Malaysian part of the island of Borneo. Although it is home to many ethnic groups, Sarawak's lowlands belong to the Dayaks, the fabled headhunters of history, who live among the myriad steaming watercourses of the jungle rainforest. Gawai Dayak is, literally, the Festival of Dayaks, celebrating the completion of the rice harvest and anticipation of bounty to come in the year ahead. In theory, Gawai Dayak is a national event. In fact, once the preliminaries are over, cities and towns empty for the two days of the actual Gawai, and people either return home or visit friends in the lowland jungle longhouses where the real action takes place.

Typically, around 25 families share each village longhouse, with family quarters ranged along either side of a communal hall where they eat, drink, and make merry.

Making merry is an art form among the Dayaks, and since Gawai Dayak effectively combines New Year, the harvest, religious ritual and family reunion, it's their highest expression of hospitality. The rituals may vary between the ethnic groups, but essential to all are copious *tuak* (rice wine), traditional dress and *ngajat* (semi-competitive dancing and revelry). You'll be offered *tuak* on arrival (make it clear from the start if your beliefs prevent you drinking alcohol), and honoured thereafter with constant attention. You'll be stuffed with delicious food and (if you go with the flow) full to the gills with *tuak*, warm beer, or *borak* (a homebrew of fermented wine). Pass out with confidence. The party will continue round you, until you're pulled back to bleary wakefulness and the manic dance that rages all day and night. There are stories, songs and recitations. The thick smell of the jungle, the sound of a gurgling stream and the smoky darkness of the longhouse envelop you in welcome. You'll never feel closer to magic, or more alive.

Gawai Dayak is a time to spend with family and friends.

WHEN:
June 1-2
WHERE:
Sarawak
BEST FOR:
Culture, folklore, natural beauty, wildlife, food, drinking and dancing
YOU SHOULD KNOW:
Try to arrive in Kuching a few days before the festival. Since everyone will be going somewhere outside the city, you're bound to meet and make friends with someone who will suggest a longhouse to visit. Such is the world-class hospitality and generosity of Sarawak.

497

A girl of the Kelabits tribe of Sarawak dances with feather fans.

Rainforest World Music Festival

WHEN:
July
WHERE:
Sarawak Cultural Village, near Kuching, Sarawak
BEST FOR:
Music, culture and folklore
YOU SHOULD KNOW:
You will hear music as you've never heard it before but don't let this stop you performing an Iban war dance or shooting darts from a Penan blowpipe. At the village you can also see Bidayuh bamboo carving, listen to Orang Ulu oral legends and get initiated into the mysteries of *tuak* and *borak* (*tuak's* yeast-fermented cousin). It's festival fun with attitude.

There are many excellent roots and world music festivals, but Sarawak's Rainforest World Music Festival is one of the few which truly matches locale to event. World music is as much about a socio-political manifesto as it is about pure musical curiosity and pleasure. Sarawak effortlessly combines the two by re-inventing the actual experience of listening. Instead of major and minor, indoor or outdoor stages, you stand among the trees of the living rainforest or sit in the longhouses of communities who actually live on the site. Instead of talking about ecological and environmental problems, you inhabit them. The festival takes place at the Sarawak Cultural Village, a community of traditional longhouses set round a lake in the jungle at the foot of Mount Santubong. Each building represents one of the major ethnic groups, who live there according to their own customs and crafts but share their quotidian lives as a collective.

The Rainforest World Music Festival fits right in. The audience is still very much from Malaysia itself, especially Sarawak whose peoples are genuinely interested in their neighbours' artistic achievements. You'll hear the *sape*, a traditional bamboo lute, and the traditional Penan songs called *sinui*; and infectious rhythms from Madagascar, Senegal, Ireland, Bulgaria, Cuba or wherever. All too often the songs speak of shared ancestral or gender longings buried by oppressive regimes. It's this empathy-in-common which makes any world music festival a joy and, in the rainforest, something incalculably greater. European visitors particularly, blasé with their wealth of access, learn during the three days of workshops, jamming, and near-mystical performances to listen with the innocence of local ears. The insistent rhythms of life in Sarawak's tropical rainforest actually restore authentic novelty to all kinds of music – which makes this one of the world's most successful events.

MME – the Merdeka Millennium Endurance

Conceived by the Malaysian motorsports industry as its tribute to Malaysian Independence Day, the Merdeka (Independence) Millennium Endurance car race was inaugurated in 2000 as a 12-hour marathon for four classes of production cars. The unusual length – half a Le Mans 24 – was (and is) intended to give local drivers who don't have the backing of corporate funds a real chance. It's been successful beyond its creators' wildest dreams, with competitors from all over the world clamouring to bring teams to the Sepang F1 track south of Kuala Lumpur. Each car has a team of three drivers who share one-hour stints for the duration. In the equatorial heat, the driver is strapped into a cockpit where the temperature can reach 60°C (140°F) even with a body-cooling suit. Fatigue, tension, and split-second concentration take their toll in the blazing glare and twilight shadows. Even 12 hours is a mighty test of car and driver: there are many more disasters than triumphs.

Aficionados of endurance racing study the signs – the inappropriate swerve or wisp of smoke from a locked wheel – as portents of their afternoon entertainment. Endurance races are something of an acquired taste. Without the duelling element of F1, MME has more subtle vital signs. You need to look into the paddock for pit preparations, study the registrations in each class to decipher the significance of on-track manoeuvres and note the various drivers' body language at change-overs, to share endurance racing's democracy of excitement. Yet after ten years, MME is turning out to be more in tune with racing fans than anyone could have imagined. People want more races like it, so that it can never be hijacked completely by big names and wealthy corporations. It's a great way to celebrate independence.

WHEN:
August
WHERE:
Sepang F1 Track, Kuala Lumpur
BEST FOR:
Sport and culture
YOU SHOULD KNOW:
With international entries in the O (Open) Class increasing, bringing more supercars and higher speeds to MME, there is less track room among the 77 maximum permitted starters for the much less powerful Class B and C production race cars. Were they to be elbowed out, without another race to accommodate the unique racing ambience they inspire, the MME's growing laurels would be terminally dessicated.

499

AUSTRALASIA & OCEANIA

AUSTRALIA

Australia Day Cockroach Races

WHEN:
January 26
WHERE:
Brisbane
BEST FOR:
Quirky sport
YOU SHOULD KNOW:
Dating from 1886 and built in the classic Queensland style, the Story Bridge Hotel is one of Brisbane's most iconic pubs and has been lovingly restored by the present owners to its original glory.

Where else but Australia would come up with the idea of celebrating its national day by putting one of its most unloved critters in the spotlight? Even by the standards of a nation that prides itself on adopting an original, if not downright eccentric, perspective on many aspects of life, the Cockroach Races held annually in Brisbane on Australia Day take some beating. On this day in the middle of summer the humble 'cocky' leaves its normal habitat behind the kitchen fridge and other dark, dank places to assume centre stage at the Story Bridge Hotel, a large pub with an award-winning restaurant tucked in beneath the southern approach road to the bridge.

Excited crowds gather around a boxing-style ring for a packed day of racing action, launched by a bagpipe band. There are normally 14 races on the card, with some 20 roaches competing in each. A race starts when a steward empties the insects out of a container onto the centre of the ring; the contestants generally scuttle off in all directions, with one or two remaining rooted to the spot, seemingly overwhelmed by the occasion. The winner is the one judged to be the first to reach the edge of the ring. You can enter your own cockroach for a modest fee, or else buy one at the hotel. The spectators become increasingly partisan as the day wears on, earnestly debating the relative merits of contestants with colourful names like Lord of the Drains, Cocky Balboa and Sir Roach-a-Lot.

With all proceeds going to a local charity, this is a relaxed and good-natured event, helped along of course by a steady flow of beer throughout the day.

Spectators and punters alike gather to watch the races.

Perth International Arts Festival

French group Ilotopie perform
Water Fools *on the Swan River.*

One of the world's more isolated cities, Perth sits happily on Australia's west coast facing the crystal-clear waters of the Indian Ocean. A fine climate, a string of magnificent beaches and a beautiful setting on the Swan River have helped to forge the city's reputation for relaxed outdoor living. In the early 1950s far-sighted officials at Perth's University of Western Australia, after a visit to the Edinburgh Festival, took a decisive step to counter the geographic remoteness by establishing an arts festival which aimed not only to bring to Western Australia some of the world's finest artists but also to provide a showcase for home-grown talent and creativity.

Held every summer since 1953, the Perth International Arts Festival is the oldest annual arts festival in the southern hemisphere, a record of which the city is justly proud. Today's programmes cover the full spectrum of theatre, music, opera, dance, film, visual arts, literature and street performance. Perth is now an established player on the international festivals circuit and actors, musicians and visual artists from all over the world come to show their work during the three weeks of the festival. The main event has spawned mini-festivals within its orbit: a season of open-air film screenings, for example, and a Writers' Festival on the university campus. There is also a healthy sprinkling of free events for those wary of committing their wallets.

Perth's isolation has fostered a spirit of self-reliance, which has helped generate a flourishing local arts scene. The regular injection of energy and ideas from abroad which the festival has brought has led to the creation of a number of permanent ensembles, including West Australian Opera, Perth Theatre Company and West Australian Ballet which now presents an annual festival programme in the spectacular outdoor setting of a disused quarry.

WHEN:
February/March
WHERE:
Perth, Western Australia
BEST FOR:
Arts and culture
YOU SHOULD KNOW:
With live bands, late-night music and DJs every night, Beck's Music Box and its open-air stage is the place for the festival goer to chill out.

503

A participant makes his way through the streets of Sydney.

Sydney Gay and Lesbian Mardi Gras

If you like your street parades loud, glitzy, irreverent and with an edge of unpredictability, then the annual Mardi Gras in Sydney has to be one of the best. Sydney has one of the most vibrant gay and lesbian communities in the world and it celebrates its pride and diversity in this late-summer jamboree. The parade's 10,000 participants and estimated half-a-million spectators belie the event's relatively short history. Mardi Gras originated in 1978 with a gay rights protest held in the wake of the Stonewall riots in New York. What was seen as the excessive police response to the protest led directly to the decriminalization of homosexuality in New South Wales and also saw the birth of a celebration of gay and lesbian culture that is now reckoned to be the world's largest.

The evening parade starts in Hyde Park and makes its loud and boisterous way along the so-called 'golden mile' down Oxford Street and Flinders Street, finishing in Moore Park. A succession of extravagantly decorated floats and outrageous costumes provides a feast for the senses. There are marching boys, disco lorries, drag queens in limos and, at the head of it all by tradition, the Dykes on Bikes. You will have to stake out your pitch early in the day if you want to make sure of a good street-side view of proceedings, although you may be able to buy tickets for grandstand seats. The parade is followed by an all-night dance party held at the Fox Studios in Moore Park.

The glittering Mardi Gras parade is in fact the culmination of a three-week arts festival promoting a huge range of gay and lesbian cultural events, including a film festival showcasing the latest in Queer Cinema.

WHEN:
Late February/early March
WHERE:
Sydney
BEST FOR:
Costumes, music and dancing in the streets
YOU SHOULD KNOW:
A particularly popular feature of the parade in recent years has been the contingent of gay lifesavers.

The Rip Curl Pro

The long Victorian coastline provides a dramatic location for some of Australia's greatest surfing spots. One of the best of the best is Bells Beach, fronting the Bass Strait along the walking trail between Torquay (Australia's Surf Capital) and Anglesea. Sitting beneath craggy cliffs, this jewel of the Surf Coast is reached by steep steps and is home to the world's oldest professional surfing contest – the Rip Curl Pro.

The surfing potential of Bells Beach was recognized around 1960 by local surfer and Olympic wrestler Joe Sweeney, who proceeded to drive a road along the cliff top with a hired bulldozer and recoup the cost by charging eager surfers to use it. The first competition was held there in 1961, and the event went professional in 1973.

Now, Round Two of the ASP (Association of Surfing Professionals) World Tour comes to town for ten days every year, pitting the planet's finest surfers against each other . . . and those sensational waves that roll in majestically from the Southern Ocean. The Rip Curl Pro action is spectacular, watched by thousands of enthusiastic spectators who pack the cliff top and beach to watch their athletic male and female heroes in action, battling against a high-performance right-handed reef break that tests even the most experienced surfers to the limit.

Young Aussies love an open-air party, and the Rip Curl Pro provides some entertaining *après-ski*. A concurrent music festival brings live sounds to the cliff top above Bells Beach as the surfing contest comes to a climax, enlarging the official title to the Rip Curl Pro Surf and Music Festival. A loud selection of local and national performers and bands light up the nights of Easter Saturday and Sunday, providing the perfect way to wind up after an easy day's bay-watching.

WHEN:
Easter time
WHERE:
Jan Juc, Victoria
BEST FOR:
Beach boys and girls
YOU SHOULD KNOW:
For those who like sinking a cold 'tinnie' (or ten) as they watch the surfing or groove to the music, there's a shuttle bus that connects Torquay, Jan Juc and the event site, allowing revellers to return to their hotels without risking a drink-drive charge.

Professional surfer Mick Lowe rides a wave.

AUSTRALIA

ANZAC Day Commemoration

WHEN:
April 25
WHERE:
Canberra (and towns and cities
throughout Australia)
BEST FOR:
Public ceremony
YOU SHOULD KNOW:
ANZAC Day is a public holiday
in Australia.

The most solemn day in the Australian calendar, ANZAC Day commemorates the ill-fated Gallipoli landings of World War I when in the chilly dawn light of April 25 1915 an expeditionary force of 50,000 Allied troops, including 17,000 soldiers of the Australian and New Zealand Army Corps – the Anzacs – attempted to capture the Gallipoli Peninsula on the Dardanelles. This strategically important Turkish peninsula controlled vital shipping routes to the Black Sea and was fiercely defended by Turkish forces. By the end of the day 2,000 Anzac men lay dead on the beaches, and by the time it was finally abandoned, the Gallipoli campaign had claimed in all 8,000 Australian lives.

The event had a traumatic effect back home on the young nation, whose states had only come together 14 years previously to form the Federation. The anniversary of the Gallipoli landings has been commemorated ever since and has now become Australia's principal act of remembrance for its countrymen killed in the wars of the 20th century. Ceremonies take place throughout the country, but the most important is held in the Federal capital, Canberra. The day begins with a simple dawn service at the Australian War Memorial, marking the actual time of the 1915 landings. Later in the morning the focal point of the main National Ceremony is the parade of veterans. Wreaths are laid at the tomb of the Unknown Australian Soldier by the Prime Minister and other civic and military leaders and the Last Post is sounded by a bugler as the signal for the one-minute silence.

A less formal act of remembrance takes place afterwards in pubs and clubs with the playing of 'two-up', a gambling game based on the spinning of two coins that was popular amongst the Diggers (as soldiers were known in former times).

Members of the Australian Light Horse Association take part in the dawn service at Bogan Gate, Sydney.

State of Origin Series

The midway point of the national rugby league season sees one of the fiercest contests in Australia's sporting calendar when the states of Queensland and New South Wales battle for supremacy in the State of Origin series. Rugby league recently celebrated its centenary 'down

Jonathan Thurston makes a break for the line.

under', having arrived in 1908 not long after the predominantly working-class clubs of northern England had broken away from the then amateur code of rugby union. The league game established itself quickly in New South Wales, especially in the industrial communities around Sydney, before spreading up the coast to Queensland. Although there has been a resurgence of interest in the union game, rugby league remains the premier code in Australia and its national team has long been the world's best.

Although there have been interstate games from the earliest days, the best-of-three State of Origin series was inaugurated only in 1982. As with international eligibility, players compete for the state from which they originate, rather than the club they currently play for. For weeks beforehand the contest between the 'Maroons' of Queensland and the 'Blues' of New South Wales is analysed exhaustively in the local sports pages and in bars and clubs throughout the states. The matches themselves alternate between the ANZ Stadium in Sydney's Olympic Park and the Suncorp Stadium in Brisbane. If you are lucky enough to get a ticket, the cauldron of emotions at each venue is an experience in itself – regardless of the quality of the game on the pitch.

State of Origin has remained a remarkably close contest over the years with Queensland, who have won it recently for three years in a row, just ahead in the number of series wins.

WHEN:
May/June/July
WHERE:
Sydney and Brisbane
BEST FOR:
Sport
YOU SHOULD KNOW:
Although the Melbourne Storm team from Victoria have dominated the national club competition in recent seasons, the State of Origin series seems likely to remain focused on its historical roots in New South Wales and Queensland.

Aboriginal boys perform at Laura.

Laura Aboriginal Dance and Cultural Festival

Australia has always had an uneasy relationship with its indigenous peoples, but the recent and long-awaited formal apology by the federal government for the mistreatment and mistakes of the past gives grounds for a more optimistic view of future relations. You cannot really claim to have taken the true pulse of the country if you have not immersed yourself at some stage in the culture of its original inhabitants. The biennial Dance and Cultural Festival at Laura in Far North Queensland is one of the best places to learn about and enjoy the many distinctive features of what is commonly regarded as the oldest surviving culture on the planet.

Laura is a small town on the Cape York Peninsula 300 km (190 mi) northwest of Cairns. Its relative remoteness makes the journey there very much part of the whole experience. Cape York is one of the few remaining areas in the country with a high concentration of Aboriginal settlements, and for the past 30 years these communities have come together in Laura for a vibrant celebration and assertion of their cultural identity. Here you can see traditional dances from across the region, including those of the Torres Strait islanders. Amidst the calls and foot-stomping of the dancers, the haunting sounds of the didgeridoo also resonate through the bush. Great emphasis is placed on passing on these traditions and children's groups feature prominently. The festival, which also includes spear- and boomerang-throwing competitions, opens with the traditional 'welcome to country' followed by the shield ceremony which heralds the start of the dance programme.

Laura is close to some of Australia's finest prehistoric rock art sites where you will see the mysterious Quinkan figures – depictions of spidery ancestral spirits.

WHEN:
June every other
(odd-numbered) year
WHERE:
Far North Queensland
BEST FOR:
Indigenous culture
YOU SHOULD KNOW:
The festival is a 'dry' event (no alcohol permitted) and is held on sacred land outside the town.

Imparja Camel Cup

The winner of the big race is likely to be unpredictable, grumpy, selfish, snarling and liable to spit without warning . . . and that's just the camel. The rider will be proud, tough and a little crazy, for camel racing Aussie-style is not for the faint-hearted. These who find themselves anywhere near the middle of Australia in July should make their way to Blatherskite Park in Alice Springs when the Imparja Camel Cup is taking place, to see this hilarious spectacle.

The tradition started when two mates raced camels along a dry riverbed in 1970 and has gone from strength to strength, now forming the centrepiece of an annual event that has its own arena and draws a large number of spectators from the town and surrounding outback for some wacky entertainment. Unlike ultra-serious camel racing that takes place in some Arab countries, with highly trained beasts ridden at high speed by child jockeys, this is pure mayhem. Every race is totally unpredictable, with up to 15 camels getting off to a chaotic start – some don't, others go backwards and a few even get off on a good stride. But once these temperamental beasts work up a head of steam they're an impressive sight, with riders hanging on for dear life.

There are serious heats before the big race – the Imparja Camel Cup – followed by fun races like the Honeymoon Handicap. There's a wonderful carnival atmosphere and between races there are all sorts of delightful distractions for all the family, like rickshaw races, Kids Kamel Kapers and a variety of stalls that cater to the every need of visitors, also offering an opportunity to meet friendly representatives of the voluntary organizations that make life in this remote town tick. It really is a terrific day out.

WHEN:
July
WHERE:
Alice Springs
BEST FOR:
Wacky races and outback fun
YOU SHOULD KNOW:
Camels were imported into Australia around 1840 to provide transport in the arid central regions (Alice Springs could not have been founded without them) and their descendents have thrived to this day as a feral population of dromedaries that is at least a million strong.

Off they go!

AUSTRALIA

Darwin Beer Can Regatta

WHEN:
A Sunday in mid July
WHERE:
Darwin, Northern Territory
BEST FOR:
Beach culture and family fun
YOU SHOULD KNOW:
Mindil Beach also has a large street market, with stalls selling crafts and all kinds of mouth-watering food, much of it Asian, and a reminder that Darwin is as close to Singapore as it is to Sydney.

Two great features of the Australian lifestyle – beach culture and the 'amber liquid' – combine in this wacky event held each year in the dry season on Darwin's famed Mindil Beach. Australia's northernmost city enjoys a tropical climate, so the cooler conditions found further south in July do not prevail in Darwin. With sunshine and heat guaranteed, the conditions are perfect for a day of relaxed competition and family friendly fun on the beach and in the water.

The main feature of the regatta is the races between homemade boats which have been constructed entirely of empty beer cans. All kinds of weird and wonderful vessels have been launched over the years, including Viking longships and floating ambulances, although the imagination shown in the designs is not always matched by their seaworthiness. Children have their own contest using soft-drink cans and there are also events on the beach for landlubbers, including tug-o'-war and thong-throwing competitions (flip-flops, not underwear). The climax of the regatta is the Battle of Mindil when teams take to the water in those boats still afloat and spray one another with water hoses and flour bombs, as they search for the prize hidden in the water.

The first Beer Can Regatta was held in 1975 in the wake of Cyclone Tracy which had devastated the centre of Darwin the previous Christmas. With no recycling schemes in existence at the time, someone made the novel suggestion that the litter problem caused by the vast quantities of beer cans which the reconstruction teams were consuming could be tackled by putting the empties to use as 'canstruction' materials. Nowadays the regatta is organized by the local Lions clubs with all proceeds going to charity.

Pirates ahoy!

The Ekka (Royal Queensland Show)

For ten days in August the country comes to the city when Brisbane hosts the Royal Queensland Show. The full title of the largest annual event in Queensland is The Royal National Agricultural and Industrial Association of Queensland's Exhibition, but in keeping with the Australians' inveterate love of abbreviations the show is known simply and universally as the Ekka. Since its first year in 1876 the Ekka has been held on the same site, the RNA Showgrounds in Bowen Hills, just north of Brisbane's central business district. Covering a site of 22 ha (54 acres), it is an agricultural show on a truly massive scale, a proud celebration of the wealth and vibrancy of working the land in all its many forms throughout this enormous state.

Every kind of farm animal is on display in the Animal Boulevard and you can see the top specimens in the prizewinners' parades in the main ring. There are sheep dog trials, show jumping, a hugely popular dog show, and demonstrations of rural and outback activities such as sheep-shearing, wood-chopping and chain-sawing. The Ekka is very much an event for the whole family and should the younger members tire of looking at the animals there are always the attractions of Sideshow Alley, a large collection of rides and other fairground entertainments. Nor does the action stop at night; the lights come on, the Cattleman's Bar continues to do a roaring trade, there are show balls, and a full programme of live bands under the big top in Nova Park.

A special feature of the Ekka, and a must-have souvenir for families, are the showbags – hundreds of bags containing varying combinations of food and novelty items at heavily discounted prices, and available in every category, from budget to luxury.

It's fun to look down on the crowds at the Ekka.

WHEN:
First half of August
WHERE:
Brisbane
BEST FOR:
Country show
YOU SHOULD KNOW:
The Wednesday towards the end of the Ekka is known as People's Day and is a public holiday in the Brisbane area.

511

Henley-on-Todd Regatta

Most regattas have water, but these boats would sink.

WHEN:
Late August or early September
WHERE:
Alice Springs
BEST FOR:
Sports day with a difference
YOU SHOULD KNOW:
Anyone can take part on payment of a small entry fee, or else you can watch the fun and frolics from under the shade of the gum trees on the banks.

The Red Centre may have been a name dreamt up by the marketing men, but it turns out to be a pithily accurate description of the heart of the vast Australian continent. This is where you will find Alice Springs – like Timbuktu, one of those places which is almost mythical in its remoteness. It remains a long way from anywhere, but thanks to the wonders of modern transport you no longer have to be a pioneer yourself to sample the special atmosphere of this outback town.

The very remoteness of Alice (as it is usually and more simply called) has meant that its residents have had to create their own amusements, displaying considerable ingenuity in the process. Nowhere is this better demonstrated than at the Henley-on-Todd Regatta, which both mimics and pokes fun at the renowned and decidedly more snobbish event back in the land of the 'poms' (England). Alice's regatta, now approaching its 50th birthday, is famous for being held on dry land, its course the usually dry bed of the Todd River. Indeed, it is almost certainly the only regatta in the world that has to be cancelled because of water (as has happened on a couple of occasions when rainfall has led to a flow of sorts in the river). If all goes according to plan, however, teams compete by running along the river-bed holding bottomless boats around their waists. All kinds of specially adapted 'watercraft' are involved, including yachts, canoes, washtubs and even human-sized hamster wheels.

Races have traditional names like Eights, Head of the River and the coveted Admiral's Cup, but other names like Bring Your Own Vessel and High School Chick of the Todd betray the essentially light-hearted nature of an event which crystallizes the eccentricity of the Australian outback.

AFL Grand Final

Australia has put a distinctive spin on many of the cultural and recreational pursuits imported by settlers from 'the old country', and nothing illustrates this more dramatically than Australian Rules football. The modern game is unique to Australia but has its historical roots in a combination of Gaelic football from Ireland, rugby and the native Aboriginal game of *marngrook*. Played since 1858, 'Aussie Rules' football is the country's most popular spectator sport, inspiring unrivalled levels of passion and partisanship amongst the clubs' supporters. As the premier ball code in Australia it was inevitable that the game would appropriate to itself the simple descriptor 'footy'.

The heartland of the game has always been Victoria, and nine of the 16 sides in the national club competition, the Australian Football League (AFL), are based in the Greater Melbourne area. In fact it was only in 1987, with the entry of the West Coast Eagles from Perth and the Brisbane Bears (now the Lions), that the first clubs outside Victoria were admitted to the League. It is appropriate, therefore, that the climax of the AFL season, which runs from March to September, takes place at the MCG, or Melbourne Cricket Ground, when the top two teams in the play-offs contest the Grand Final for the coveted AFL Flag. Tickets are notoriously hard to come by, but if you are in Australia at any time during the 'footy' season it is definitely worth going to a regular game; even if you only have a dim grasp of the rules (and they are not as complicated as sometimes assumed), the special atmosphere generated by this fast-paced, hugely physical game, both on the pitch and in the stands, is not to be missed.

WHEN:
Late September
WHERE:
Melbourne
BEST FOR:
Spectator sport
YOU SHOULD KNOW:
Because Aussie Rules football originated as an off-season activity for cricketers, games have traditionally been played on cricket grounds which has led to the distinctive feature of there being no standard-size playing area in AFL grounds.

513

AUSTRALIA

Birdsville Races

WHEN:
First weekend in September
WHERE:
Outback Queensland
BEST FOR:
Sport in an unusual setting
YOU SHOULD KNOW:
There are no rooms available in
Birdsville over the races weekend so
you will have to make your own
camping arrangements, or else sign
up for one of the special tour
packages.

In the far southwestern corner of Queensland lies the tiny township of Birdsville with a resident population of just over 100. This is the heart of the great Australian outback and is the place to come if you want to get away from it all and immerse yourself in the vast desert expanses. Not, however, if you choose the first weekend in September when Birdsville, like a desert flower after rain, explodes into brief and colourful life for the annual races – a two-day flat meeting which attracts thousands of spectators from across the country. Run on a dusty clay-pan track south of the town (you won't see any turf here), the races are a serious event in the Queensland racing calendar and have been held annually since 1882 (except for war-time and in 2007 when they were cancelled owing to an outbreak of equine flu).

The climax of the 13-race meeting, and the longest race on the card, is the coveted Birdsville Cup. The crowds of race goers come as much for the atmosphere and attendant amusements as for the racing itself and there is a full programme of live music, whip-cracking contests and other sideshows. Needless to say, beer oils the wheels and the serious drinking tends to be concentrated on the Birdsville Hotel, a classic outback pub that is as old as the racing and something of a legend in drinking circles. Another Birdsville institution is Fred Brophy's boxing troupe, the last of the old travelling shows, which pitches its tent opposite the hotel over the racing weekend.

Birdsville is a very long way from anywhere, but if you don't want to make the journey there part of the overall adventure, a number of flights land at the town's own airstrip, conveniently located just opposite the hotel.

Not the Melbourne Cup, but these races are in a class of their own.

Deni Play on the Plains Festival

Festival goers relax in a pool-in-a-pickup.

In just ten years the Play on the Plains Festival at Deniliquin, New South Wales, has imprinted itself on the national psyche as a place where some of Australia's most cherished icons are celebrated. Chief among these is the revered 'ute', or utility vehicle, the light pickup truck that is the traditional transport of choice in these rural parts. Play on the Plains is a two-day gathering of ute owners and drivers held over the Labour Day long weekend. The event first captured the attention of the nation's media when its Ute Muster was advertised as a record-breaking event. The world record for the most utes gathered in one place has been broken each year since and currently stands at 7,242. The muster is also an opportunity for owners to show off their lovingly customized vehicles and to enter them in competitions with categories such as Best Artwork Ute, Best Aussie Themed Ute, Furthest Travelled Ute and Ultimate Street Ute. The overall top entry is given the accolade Ute of the Year.

Their numbers and status may have declined, but the stockmen and station hands of the outback are still much in evidence at Play on the Plains in their trademark wide-brimmed hats and moleskin trousers. As well as various motorized competitions, which even include racing lawnmowers, Deni is a showcase for traditional outback activities such as bull riding, whip cracking and sheep shearing. The 'Grunt Off' is a contest to decide which team of five can pull a Holden ute the fastest over 40 m (131 ft). And when the sun goes down on the plains, the crowds are kept entertained by some of Australia's top country music acts.

WHEN:
Labour Day weekend (end of September/beginning of October)
WHERE:
Deniliquin, New South Wales
BEST FOR:
Custom cars and outback lifestyle
YOU SHOULD KNOW:
Deni also cultivates the world 'bluey' wearing record – the largest gathering of wearers of the blue singlet (sleeveless top), which is the unofficial uniform of the ute driver.

515

The track for the Gold Coast Indy 300 is on the urban streets of Surfers Paradise.

Gold Coast Indy 300

The Gold Coast is Australia's playground, the place to come for sun, surf and serious partying. At its heart are the golden sands that stretch in an almost unbroken sweep 35 km (22 mi) from south of Brisbane to the border with New South Wales. Commerce and pleasure reign supreme in this world of noisy bars, frenetic nightclubs and high-rise apartment blocks. The pace and pressure to enjoy yourself is intense here at the best of times, but everything goes into overdrive for four days in late October when the Gold Coast is host to the Australian leg of the world IndyCar series.

A 4.5-km (2.8-mi) racetrack is formed from the urban streets of the main resort, Surfers Paradise, and 300,000 spectators arrive to watch some of the world's fastest cars in action, their 650-hp engines reaching speeds in excess of 300 kph (190 mph).

The IndyCar race is the centrepiece of a racing carnival, which also includes events for Aussie Racing Cars and Formula Three. Almost as popular as the IndyCars is the V8 Supercar Challenge featuring a long-running battle for supremacy between the Ford and Holden brands. In between the serious racing, the spectators are kept amused by motorcycle stunt shows and custom cars and trucks. Clear blue skies and unrelieved sunshine are more or less guaranteed and, as you would expect, there is lots of off-track entertainment too: live bands, street parades, spectacular air shows (including the crowd's favourite, a 'dump and burn' by an F-111 jet), and the inevitable beauty contest all make sure this is one giant party to remember.

The meeting builds to its climax on the final day with the Indy 300 race itself, 60 ear-splitting laps around some of Australia's most expensive real estate.

WHEN:
Late October
WHERE:
Gold Coast, southeast Queensland
BEST FOR:
Motor racing
YOU SHOULD KNOW:
In 2008 Ryan Briscoe became the first Australian driver to win the Indy 300 in its 18-year history.

Melbourne Cup

To claim to be the best-known sporting event in a country as sports-mad as Australia takes some bravado, but few would dispute the confident boast made by the organizers of the Melbourne Cup. Not only is it one of the world's top horse races (and one of the richest), it also holds the entire country in thrall, its appeal extending far beyond the ranks of dedicated punters and race goers. Even more of a national occasion than England's Grand National, the 'race that stops a nation' sees a crowd of over 100,000 gather at Flemington Racecourse on the first Tuesday in November, whilst millions more watch the race on TV at home and in bars and clubs throughout the land.

The Melbourne Cup forms the climax of the month-long Spring Racing Carnival at Flemington run by the Victoria Racing Club. It is a flat race over a distance of 3.2 km (2 mi) and, unusually for a race of this calibre, takes the form of a handicap. With race day a public holiday in Melbourne and throughout Victoria, the Melbourne Cup is very much a social occasion and, as at Royal Ascot, provides an excuse for people to dress up in their finery. Out come the hats, heels and fascinators, and the competition amongst the 'fashionistas' is only a little less intense than on the turf itself. The frocks and frills, together with the manicured lawns and the spring roses in full bloom, make Cup Day at Flemington a true feast for the senses.

Although it is approaching its 150th anniversary, the Melbourne Cup saw no horses from the northern hemisphere until 1993, when the Irish-trained Vintage Crop beat the field. The home team retaliated in 2003-2005 when Australian mare Makybe Diva achieved the unparalleled feat of three successive wins.

WHEN:
First Tuesday in November
WHERE:
Melbourne
BEST FOR:
Sport and fashion
YOU SHOULD KNOW:
Some estimates suggest that a staggering 85 per cent of Australians have a flutter on the Melbourne Cup.

Fancy hats are the order of the day at the Melbourne Cup.

AUSTRALIA

Sydney to Hobart Yacht Race

WHEN:
December 26-29
WHERE:
Sydney and Hobart (for viewing)
BEST FOR:
Ocean-racing yachts
YOU SHOULD KNOW:
Safety measures have been tightened considerably since tragedy struck the race in 1998 when heavy seas and freak storms claimed the lives of six crew members and five yachts were lost.

Christmas in Australia means beach, swimming, 'barbies' (barbecues) – and the mighty yacht race which for over 60 years has left Sydney at lunchtime on Boxing Day, finishing three days later and 628 nautical miles (1,163 km) south in Hobart, capital of the island state of Tasmania. This is probably the world's most famous annual ocean race and thousands of 'Sydneysiders' line the cliffs and shorelines either side of Sydney Harbour for the unforgettable spectacle of 100 yachts in full sail making their way out to sea. The Heads which form the relatively narrow entrance to the enormous harbour provide particularly good vantage points; it is easy to see how Captain Cook failed to explore the opening further when sailing north from Botany Bay in 1770.

The course of the race takes the yachts out onto the Tasman Sea and down the southeast coast of Australia before crossing the Bass Strait which separates the mainland from Tasmania. The final leg is down the east coast of the island to Tasman Peninsula, which the boats round to enter Storm Bay and the home run up the Derwent River to the finishing line at Hobart's Battery Point. The finish also attracts large crowds of spectators and whatever time of day or night the racers complete their gruelling journey, they are assured of a warm and enthusiastic Tasmanian welcome on the quays at Sullivans Cove.

The race is a genuinely open one; anyone can enter who owns an eligible yacht and who meets the safety requirements. Weekend sailors regularly rub shoulders with seasoned professionals in vessels that range from a wooden 30-footer (9 m) built in 1932 (the year the Sydney Harbour Bridge opened) to state-of-the-art carbon fibre 'maxis' at 30 m (100 ft) in length.

Yachts jockey for position at the start in Sydney harbour.

Boxing Day Test

*There's usually a full house
for the Boxing Day Test.*

International test cricket may have a doubtful reputation for the levels of excitement it can generate in these days of short attention-spans, but that does not deter thousands of Melburnian cricket fans from shaking off the post-Christmas torpor and making the annual pilgrimage on Boxing Day to the Melbourne Cricket Ground for the first day's play in the Test match between Australia and that season's visiting overseas nation. 'Pilgrimage' is the right word, for the MCG is one of the world's great sporting shrines, and to immerse yourself in the whirl of emotions at a major game there is to enjoy one of the classic experiences that spectator sport has to offer.

From its opening in 1853 the MCG has always been run by the Melbourne Cricket Club which shares its initials with, but is not to be otherwise confused with, its northern-hemisphere counterpart – the Marylebone Cricket Club at its equally iconic London home, Lord's. Today's modern ground boasts a capacity of 100,000, which made it a perfect centrepiece for both the 1956 Olympic and 2006 Commonwealth Games.

The first Boxing Day Test match took place in 1950; since 1980 it has been an annual game. It is a special occasion whoever are the opponents of the boys in the 'baggy greens' (as the Australians' caps are known), but there is an extra edge to the Ashes series, contested every four years between Australia and England in one of international sport's most ancient and intense rivalries. Australia's recent domination of the Ashes was interrupted briefly in 2005 when England reclaimed the coveted urn on home soil, only to lose it once again in a swift and comprehensive act of revenge the following year with a 5-0 series drubbing.

WHEN:
December 26-30
(if the match lasts the full five days)
WHERE:
Melbourne
BEST FOR:
Sport
YOU SHOULD KNOW:
The most recent among the many memorable cricketing moments the MCG has witnessed occurred on the first day of the 2006 Ashes Boxing Day Test when Shane Warne, the great Victorian spin bowler, became the first man ever to take 700 test wickets, and did so in front of an adoring 90,000-strong home crowd.

Festival goers stroll around between performances and check out the stalls.

Woodford Folk Festival

The small town of Woodford is an unremarkable place, albeit one set in the beautiful rolling farmlands north of Brisbane, behind the Sunshine Coast. Mention the name to an Australian, however, especially one under 40, and it will almost certainly conjure up images – if not actual memories – of the Folk Festival held there each midsummer in the six days leading up to New Year's Day. The festival began in 1987 in nearby Maleny but has been on its current site, a former dairy farm, since 1994 when the Queensland Folk Federation which runs the festival acquired the land. Woodford is now the country's leading folk arts festival and one of the largest events of its kind anywhere.

Some 2,000 artists and over 400 performances are featured in a festival whose compass has broadened over the years to include an extraordinary array of traditional and world music, giving the lie to Australia's reputation in some quarters for a certain parochialism. Particular strands include blues and roots, and indigenous performance, showcasing the culture of the local Jinibara people who are the traditional custodians of this land. The music programme has more than enough to keep you entertained but if you want a change there are substantial offerings of dance, cabaret, stand-up comedy, circus, film, street theatre, and the chance to get involved yourself with any number of art, craft and performance workshops. Healthy and sustainable ways of living are also promoted at Woodford, with an extensive programme of talks and demonstrations devoted to complementary medicine and sustainable lifestyles.

Public ceremonies are an important element of the festival, including a three-minute silence shortly before midnight on New Year's Eve to honour absent friends and a spectacular closing fire ceremony on the following evening.

WHEN:
End of December
WHERE:
Southeast Queensland
BEST FOR:
Folk and world music
YOU SHOULD KNOW:
The organizers take their environmental responsibilities very seriously and have made a commitment to 'conserve and enhance the natural environment'. In the past ten years they have planted over 60,000 trees on the festival site.

520

Waitangi Day

New Zealand's founding document was the Treaty of Waitangi in 1840, between the British Crown and Maori chiefs. Subsequently, other copies were signed, laying the foundations for Britain's colonial administration. Unfortunately, the incomers largely ignored the land and citizenship rights Maoris thought they were acquiring and it is only in recent decades that the Treaty has been revisited with a view to undoing earlier wrongs. This new awareness saw Waitangi Day declared a public holiday and the country's national day. But there are no grand parades to celebrate statehood. Indeed, this is an occasion that sees a strange mixture of national pride and guilty conscience.

For those interested in New Zealand's history and hybrid culture, the place to be is Waitangi itself. The house where the first treaty signing took place was presented to the country in 1934 and now serves as the focal point for an annual ceremony – often accompanied, until recently, by angry protests about the unfair treatment of the Maori population. At dawn on Waitangi Day the New Zealand Navy hoists flags in the grounds. Subsequently there are displays of indigenous dance and song, a church service and re-enactment of the British landing that preceded the signing of the Treaty. Finally, the flags are lowered with due pomp.

Elsewhere, Waitangi Day is celebrated in many different ways. There are numerous educational presentations highlighting Maori culture, whilst all sorts of one-off events take place. These range from concerts to the sort of general public entertainment that can mark any official holiday. Wellington's One Love Festival celebrates national unity, whilst Groove in the Park at Western Springs has a similar remit. For most people, it's simply a day to relax and have fun.

WHEN:
February 6
WHERE:
At Waitangi in particular and throughout New Zealand in general.
BEST FOR:
Chilling out (maybe on the beach) with many other holidaying New Zealanders – it's the height of summer.
YOU SHOULD KNOW:
National celebrations often include concerts, and as Waitangi Day and Bob Marley's birth date are one and the same, reggae music often features prominently.

Rowers get ready to race on Waitangi Day.

NEW ZEALAND

Wellington Sevens

WHEN:
Early February
WHERE:
Westpac Stadium, Wellington
BEST FOR:
Rugger fans and all lovers of
top-level sporting competition
YOU SHOULD KNOW:
Ticket numbers are limited and
invariably sold out in advance, so
those who wish to watch this
top-line tournament are advised to
book well ahead of time.

The fearsome *haka* dance that precedes rugby matches featuring New Zealand's mighty All Blacks reminds teams from fifteen other countries of the challenge they face in the annual Wellington Sevens. The Sevens is one of the country's leading sporting occasions and this fast and furious rugger tournament provides fantastic entertainment. Thousands of spectators from the home nation are joined by visitors from all over the world who come to cheer on their own teams.

It is one of eight tournaments that make up the IRB (International Rugby Board) Sevens Series, with points won here going towards determining an overall winner. Each team has a dozen players – seven on the field and five on the bench – and a game consists of two seven-minute halves with a short break at half time (although the final is longer, featuring two ten-minute periods).

Day One sees round-robin matches between teams in four pools, each of four nations. Points are awarded that decide each team's position. After this phase is completed, first- and second-placed teams in each pool progress to the knockout Cup Championship on Day Two whilst third- and fourth-placed teams contest the consolation Bowl Championship. Both involve quarter-final, semi-final and final matches and the ultimate tournament winner is the team that wins all three in the Cup Championship.

For rugby union aficionados sevens are a delight, leading to lots of the sort of open running play that can often be absent from more congested 15-a-side contests. It's invariably action all the way, with a selection of games to watch within a short space of time. Better still, some teams that don't necessarily shine at full international level – notably Pacific nations like Fiji, Samoa and Tonga – are amongst the most exciting and successful at the Sevens.

Kenya's Kahuthia nails England's Cracknell.

Te Matatini Festival

Though general rugby-related perception suggests that the impressive Maori *haka* is a warriors' dance, it's actually a posture dance with shouted accompaniment performed by groups that may be all male, all female, mixed and include children. The reasons for staging a *haka* can be many, from welcoming honoured guests to celebrating great occasions, or simply for amusement and the pleasure of performing. It's an intricate art form, with various different types including *whakatu waewae*, *tutu ngarahu* and *peruperu* (the latter once actually being the aforementioned war dance).

The biennial four-day Te Matatini Festival is the leading celebration of Maori culture, and it is here that *kapa haka* teams that have come through a series of competitive regional heats compete for top honours. The *kapa haka* is a series of songs and dances that form a coherent whole, representing and celebrating the Maori identity. That theme is pursued at each festival with teams from New Zealand and Australia demonstrating sets with six disciplines – a choreographed *whakaeke* (entry), *moteatea* (traditional chant), *poi* (juggling), *waiata-a-ringa* (traditional song), *haka* and *whakawatea* (exit). Performances are judged by 26 *kaiwhiriwhiri* (judges) and prizes awarded. There are further contests for teams and individuals, delivering an impressive repertoire of traditional performance art throughout the festival.

The Maori cultural package is completed by supporting activities – including a thousand-dancer *powhiri* (welcoming ceremony) followed by massed pageants and a spectacular firework display. The 25,000 people who attend the festival each day can also shop at the tribal market with its wonderful display of handmade original crafts, plus traditional and contemporary art. There are also interesting demonstrations and workshops featuring *ta moko* (Maori tattooing), carving, rope weaving, plaiting and hand games. The Te Matatini Festival is a fascinating experience to be savoured by New Zealanders and international visitors alike.

WHEN:
Biennial, in February
WHERE:
Different locations; the 2011 festival will be in Te Tairāwhiti (Gisborne) and in 2013 the venue will be Te Arawa (Roturua).
BEST FOR:
Traditional Maori culture that has never been allowed to fade away – and is increasingly appreciated with every year that passes.
YOU SHOULD KNOW:
The festival was formerly known as the Aotearoa Traditional Maori Performing Arts Festival – Aotearoa is the name most commonly used by Maoris for the country of New Zealand, and is becoming more frequently used outside the Maori community.

Festival goers gather amidst the vines.

Marlborough Wine Festival

WHEN:
Second Saturday in February
WHERE:
Renwick, near Blenheim
BEST FOR:
The many tastes of fine
New Zealand wine.
YOU SHOULD KNOW:
Serious wine buffs attending the
festival should make time to visit the
permanent Wine Exhibition at the
Marlborough Museum in Blenheim,
to marvel at the tale of Kiwi
ingenuity that led from green
pastures to a viticulture success
story inside three decades.

Events that showcase the country's finest wine and food are not uncommon in New Zealand, but one of the best is the Marlborough Wine Festival. Set in the winelands around Blenheim, this summer event takes place amidst the huge expanse of vines at the Montana Brancott Estate, near Renwick, the first (and largest) commercial vineyard to be planted in the South Island's Marlborough district. This is not just for those who appreciate fine wine – this is a something-for-everyone festival day.

A tented village springs up on the festival site with large marquees used by around 50 wineries to present their wares, with free tastings that confirm the range and quality of the vintages produced by New Zealand's booming wine industry. This core activity is supported by tutorials that explore various aspects of the wine business – in depth! For those who like to cut a dash, there's a free-entry Fashion in the Vines contest that seeks out and rewards the festival's best-dressed man and woman, with style and originality the order of the day. There is also live music playing throughout to entertain visitors as they explore the alcoholic attractions, and delicious food on offer for those who never like to drink on an empty stomach.

It adds up to a great occasion for those with a serious interest in wine, or simply wanting a lively day out in good company. To satisfy visitors who want to make a long weekend of it, the all-round experience actually stretches to three days with build-up before the event and wind-down afterwards – offering an assortment of related activities that can enhance the festival experience, from special gourmet dining at local restaurants to Kenepuru Sound cruises complete with lunch and bubbly on the Sunday. Marlborough here we come!

Lion Red Snapper Classic

This is definitely one for snappy snapper-snappers – or those who might simply enjoy watching snapper-snapping or snap snapper-snappers-snapping in a fabulous natural setting. The location in question is Ninety-Mile Beach up from Waipapakauri Ramp and the week-long Lion Red Snapper Classic is a single-species beach-casting contest that attracts angling teams and individuals from all over the world, to the limit of 1,000 contestants. Many anglers take the opportunity to combine their participation with a family holiday, and one reason for founding this prestigious (and lucrative) contest was to generate tourist activity in the Far North.

The quarry is the highly prized red snapper (aka *Centroberyx affinis*) and the winners of this five-day fishing classic carry off huge cash prizes. There are prize draws and awards for teams and individuals, whilst the jackpot of $50,000 goes to the angler who lands the largest red snapper beached during the competition – a specimen that just may exceed 9 kg (20 lb) in weight. There are strict rules and these are rigorously policed. Cheats have tried to prosper but the organizers know all the tricks – for example, catches that have been weighed in are gutted to make sure no (heavy) foreign objects have mysteriously found their way into the fish.

Whilst participating in the Classic is a 'must' for serious Antipodean sea anglers (and those from further afield who feel compelled to attempt all the world's great fishing challenges), it's not the greatest of spectator sports for non-fishers – though plenty of competitors bring a support team of family and friends. No matter, it provides a wonderful excuse to visit New Zealand's remote northwestern tip, where some leisurely beach time spent watching the Classic can be coupled with rewarding exploration of the rugged Aupouri Peninsula, including that special visit to Cape Reinga.

WHEN:
March
WHERE:
Near Kaitaia
BEST FOR:
The easy camaraderie and fun-filled atmosphere that surrounds the Classic.
YOU SHOULD KNOW:
There is plenty of local accommodation available during the Lion Red Snapper Classic, from caravan parks through motels to a variety of hotels – but it's still advisable to book early.

Golden Shears

WHEN:
March
WHERE:
Masterton
BEST FOR:
Surprisingly gripping entertainment
YOU SHOULD KNOW:
They are tough all right – in the real world a skilled shearer regards well over 200 sheep as a good day's work (that's less than three minutes per shorn animal over the course of a punishing nine-hour day).

It's an old chestnut but true enough – there are lots more sheep than people in New Zealand. Sheep husbandry has always been an important plank of the national economy, which makes the annual Golden Shears ('The world's greatest shearing and wool handling competition') a major national occasion. Before television coverage, tickets to witness the sizzling shearing sessions first-hand were highly prized and sold out months in advance.

This three-day 'snipathon' has taken place annually since 1961 at Masterton in the North Island and covers the main woolshed disciplines – shearing, wool handling and pressing compressed fleeces into bags – with a huge range of competitions for men, women, juniors, novices, pairs and teams culminating in the prestigious Open Shearing Final with its magnificent trophy. There's even a triathlon for hardy souls who tackle all three activities in quick succession.

The success of the Golden Shears over the years has led to the establishment of numerous lesser shearing contests through New Zealand and Australia, often with generous sponsors, allowing a new breed of super-shearer to emerge – the semi-pro who regards shearing as a genuine sport that requires serious training and total dedication. There are international tests (New Zealand versus Australia is a real needle match) and a World Shearing Championship that moves around the globe.

But there's nothing like the sheer excitement of seeing the world's best in action live, and anyone lucky enough to get a ticket for the Golden Shears Open Shearing Final will find the swift work of these top operators hugely impressive. The winner is likely to shear 20 sheep in around 15 minutes using extraordinary skill and dexterity. But the lesser classes that take place earlier are also worth watching, and anyone who is interested in discovering the real New Zealand should consider the whole experience totally mandatory.

The judges keep a careful watch over the shearers.

Queenstown Winter Festival

Mountain bikers race in the snow.

It's one of the (quote) 'Leading Mountain Resorts of the World', so there couldn't be a better place to stage a Winter Festival. This ten-day extravaganza spans two weekends, running from Friday to Sunday, and offers a packed programme guaranteed to entice pleasure-seeking winter wonderlanders.

The Queensland Winter Festival kicks off with a wild free party and from the moment the thunderous noise of major-league fireworks echoes round the surrounding mountain peaks the action never slackens. The Festival Pavilion is in the centre of town, providing an admirable focal point for those sallying forth to engage in all (impossible!), most (demanding!) or some (good decision!) of the 60 events on offer – many free, some requiring tickets.

The Queenstown Winter Festival has everything that a seriously entertaining 'snowfest' could offer – including pro ice hockey matches, mountain bikes on snow, Frisbee golf, free entertainment at the Coronet Peak base building, an invitation ski race, various downhill snow races (comic or otherwise) and freestyle boarding displays. Those who prefer to do rather than watch can engage in a full range of winter sports – or even join those hardy swimmers who plunge into icy lake waters.

But this festival is mostly about having a great time and 60,000 people cheerfully hurl themselves into the buzzy spirit of things. In addition to all sorts of parties and sponsored goodies, there's also an arts-and-crafts market, a glittering festival parade and family fun day, jazz nights, a variety of concerts, assorted competitions, debates, a birdman contest (they never manage to fly, invariably ending up in the lake), jetboat races, gourmet dining sessions, comedy shows, a lakeside Mardi Gras party, a festival drag race (as in cross-dressing rather than smoking tyres!), a grand ball and riotous closing party. It's not for the prudish or faint-hearted.

WHEN:
June/July
WHERE:
Queenstown
BEST FOR:
Revellers young and old . . . providing they have the stamina to go at it 24/7.
YOU SHOULD KNOW:
The festival's mountain events are held at the Coronet Peak Skifield, whilst other major events are held in Queenstown's Earnshaw Park and at the lakeside, with plenty of extra activities taking place in town.

NEW ZEALAND

Jamis Day-Night Thriller

WHEN:
September
WHERE:
Taupo
BEST FOR:
Serious mountain bikers or lovers of
outdoor spectacle
YOU SHOULD KNOW:
Keen youngsters may enter the Little
Devils ride for under-13s, which
involves one supervised circuit of the
track and a prize giving to the
enthusiastic cheers of massed
spectators in 'Tent City'.

Magnificent Waikato River scenery surrounds the course created for one of New Zealand's most entertaining sporting challenges – the North Island's Jamis Day-Night Thriller, which is as near to Heaven as mountain biking enthusiasts can get. It's the world's largest mountain-bike endurance event, staged at a venue that becomes a tented city where thousands of like-minded mountain bikers, support crews and keen spectators set up camp from Friday, adding camaraderie and high jinks to the whole Day-Night Thriller experience. During racing, teams start and make changeovers from their own campsites at different points around the course.

This exhilarating Saturday relay event should be at the top of every competitive mountain biker's 'must try' list. A splendid 8-km (5-mi) course is prepared in Taupo's Spa Park that allows individuals or teams consisting of up to five riders to compete in a six-hour race (between 10.30 and 16.30) or the 12-hour race (between 10.30 and 22.30, giving four hours of dramatic racing in darkness). Both races takes place simultaneously on the same course, designed to accommodate all levels of ability. It includes fast, open park grounds, forest stretches, single tracks and awesome downhill runs. A circuit takes around 30 minutes.

The two Day-Night Thriller races each offer awards in numerous categories – including single-sex or mixed teams of two, three, four or five riders, junior teams, school teams, over-35 teams, cycle shop teams and individual male and female titles. The overall number of entries is limited to 750 teams and 50 individuals to ensure that the course doesn't become overcrowded. All entrants are accurately timed as they give the race their best shot, with winners in each category being determined by the fastest average speed. A host of prizes includes special awards for the Most Colourful Team and Most Interesting Campsite. Well worth watching!

Montana World of Wearable Art Awards

There's only one word for it – WOW. That's actually the official acronym for the Montana World of Wearable Art – a place where (are you ready for this?) 'art and the human form combine, where dance, music and lighting tell a story of the body as a canvas, where the lines of fashion and art blur and merge as one'. All this at once, in New Zealand . . . WOW!

It's not the most predictable aspect of a generally macho local

A world of wearable art is on view at WOW.

entertainment scene, but the WOW Awards Show is as spectacular a theatrical occasion as anything staged elsewhere in the world. The two-hour show takes place annually and is repeated ten times, allowing a combined audience of 35,000 to marvel at the fantastic costumes, music and movement that make for a unique event that has achieved significant artistic prestige and international fame within two decades.

Originally launched by sculptor Suzie Moncrieff as an innovative promotion for a rural art gallery in Nelson, WOW is not really about fashion, instead reflecting the founder's then-revolutionary concept of presenting art as a theatrical experience. Today, over 150 way-out garments from designers all over the world compete for a generous prize pot, with each outfit presented on stage with the help of striking sets, dramatic lighting, music, dance and stunning choreography. There is a Supreme Award winner (announced at the first Friday show), with further prizes for sectional winners and the best first-time entrant.

There's nothing quite like this extraordinary experience to be found anywhere else, and such a visual treat certainly gives the lie to any thought that New Zealand's cultural life begins and ends with rugby, bungee jumping and other extreme outdoor activities. Give it a try and be prepared to say one word . . . 'WOW!'

WHEN:
September/October
WHERE:
Wellington
BEST FOR:
A highlight of New Zealand's cultural calendar
YOU SHOULD KNOW:
If you're not around at show time, there's a World of Wearable Art gallery in Nelson, where it all began . . . along with a slightly incongruous bedfellow in the form of a large classic car and motorcycle collection.

Woodcutters compete at the show.

New Zealand Cup and Show Week

When is an umbrella not strictly an umbrella? In Christchurch's case the answer is stimulating – when it's the brolly that covers a series of several spectacular happenings that turn the place into a massive party shower.

New Zealand Cup and Show Week was created in 1996 to focus interest on disparate events that happened in the city around the same time. The intention was to express local pride and create a high-profile national occasion and both objectives have been amply fulfilled – 'The Week' has become something of a supercharged extravaganza.

Around 120,000 traditionalists head for the impressive three-day Royal New Zealand Show, which brings the very best of the country to town – with the Grand Parade, livestock, city farm, food, wine, music, demonstrations, competitions and hundreds of trade stands providing regal rural revelations.

Racing fans enjoy trotting and thoroughbred contests at Addington and Riccarton Park that present the country's best horseflesh (and greyhounds) in action. This major social occasion climaxes with the New Zealand Cup and 2000 Guineas on the final Saturday at Riccarton Park. Many racegoers enjoy leisurely picnics whilst keen fashionistas boldly strut their stuff, with numerous fashion events and competitions taking place at the tracks backed by designer fashion shows at Style Christchurch in town.

On a dramatic man-v-beast note, there's an International Rodeo at the Westpac Arena, though non-cowpersons are not forgotten – with a jumping music festival in town and the SOL (South of Lichfield) Square heritage precinct in the heart of Christchurch offering fashion retailers, great restaurants, busy bars and a wide choice of live entertainment for those who like partying into the wee small hours.

'The Week' provides an exciting all-round opportunity to have fun and experience the distilled essence of New Zealand life – putting a BIG tick in the be-there-if-you-can box.

WHEN:
November
WHERE:
Christchurch
BEST FOR:
Free 'n' easy wine, horse racing and song . . . with generous measures of the latest fashion and country living New Zealand style thrown in for good measure.
YOU SHOULD KNOW:
Specific events like fashion shows, the Rodeo and New Zealand Cup Day at Riccarton Park tend to sell out in advance, so don't expect to turn up on the day and get lucky.

Jetsprint Championships

New Zealand has lots of shallow, fast-flowing rivers – and in the 1950s inventor Sir William Hamilton developed a craft that overcame the problem of conventional propellers striking rocks, leaving boats disabled and many rivers thereby unnavigable. His elegant solution was a boat that sucks in water and uses a pump-jet to expel it from a nozzle in the stern, and the company he founded became the world's largest manufacturer of jetboats.

Bill Hamilton had practical applications in mind, and his new babies did indeed solve the problem of navigating shallow rivers. But New Zealand is besotted with outdoor activities, so it wasn't long before the racy potential of jetboats was appreciated and a new sport was born. These craft are incredibly manoeuvrable and capable of operating efficiently at high speed and Jetsprint boat racing was swiftly developed, subsequently spreading to Australia and the USA.

After initially taking place on rivers and lakes, Jetsprinting was formalized and is now held on purpose-built courses with lots of twists and turns. Two-person crews (driver plus navigator) hurl their powerful Jetsprinters round a series of shallow channels, following a complex predetermined route that requires some 30 gut-wrenching changes of direction in a run that lasts a minute or less. It makes for spectacular viewing and there is a North Island Championship, South Island Championship, several rounds of the New Zealand Championship and World Championships, so there are plenty of opportunities to thrill to this home-grown summer sport.

There are several courses, mainly in the North Island, and one of the best venues for spectators is the course at Wanganui, where the ones to go for are the North Island Championship in November or Round One of the New Zealand Championship in December. It's fast. It's furious. It's compulsive viewing.

WHEN:
Meetings from November to March
WHERE:
Various courses including Wanganui and Featherston
BEST FOR:
Thrills, spills and flying spray
YOU SHOULD KNOW:
Despite the growing international popularity of Jetsprint racing, New Zealand crews are still the best in the world, though Australians and Americans are starting to follow ever closer in their wake.

Jetsprint is a thrilling sport.

Aloha Festivals

WHEN:
September/October
WHERE:
Statewide in Hawaii
BEST FOR:
Massed hula dancing *par excellence*
YOU SHOULD KNOW:
The Aloha Festivals loosely coincide with the traditional Hawaiian time of Makahiki, when the harvest was in, tributes were paid to chiefs, war was forbidden and the people played games and rejoiced.

The whole community enjoys participating in the Aloha Festivals.

In the spirit of preserving Hawaiian heritage and culture, the collective Aloha Festivals are held over a six-week period on the Big Island of Hawaii, Kauai, Oahu, Maui, Molokai and Lanai and have become a single extended event. It all began in Honolulu as Aloha Week after World War II, the idea being to celebrate Hawaii's history, music, dance, arts and crafts and cuisine. There was always an intention to offer a rewarding tropical experience to tourists, and that perhaps explains the extended duration of the festivals and spread to the other islands. Festive activities are now attended by around a million people – mostly Native Hawaiians participating with infectious enthusiasm, ensuring that it remains their grand occasion.

In keeping with the original rationale, the festivals adopt an appropriate theme each year – past choices have included 'The Natives Endure', 'A Gift of Beautiful Leis', 'Honour the Voyagers', 'The Spirit of the Masters' and 'The Art of Hawaiian Dance'. However, the ingredients of Aloha Festivals remain much the same from year to year, and the fact that they are spread out over a long period ensures that – with around 300 assorted events taking place during the festivals – visitors are likely to find something entertaining happening during their visit, whichever island they choose.

The statewide celebrations begin with opening ceremonies that are dedicated to the now-vanished Hawaiian Royal Court and subsequent activities include parades, concerts, street parties, competitions and a variety of special events unique to each island. But the place to be for the opening of the festivals is where it all began – Honolulu on the island of Oahu. After the Royal Court Investiture and opening ceremony, one of the world's most impressive floral parades travels from the Iolani Palace, home of Hawaii's last reigning monarch, through Honolulu, Kakaako, Ala Moana and Waikiki. It's a flamboyant sight.

Ironman Triathlon

Over 1,800 participants take to the water.

Ironmen can also be Ironwomen nowadays (though actually 'Ironman' is taken to cover both genders) and Hawaii's Ironman Triathlon is the star in their punishing firmament. The Triathlon involves a 3.9-km (2.4-mi) swim, followed by a 180-km (112-mi) bike ride and finally a 42.2-km (26.2-mi) marathon run. This gruelling endurance test was first staged in Hawaii in 1978 and, though there are now many other triathlons, the Hawaii race is the most prestigious – and as such it also serves as the world championships.

It started with an argument between swimmers and runners as to who might be fittest, and the Triathlon challenge was devised to decide the point (cycling was added as equally applicable to both groups). Only 15 started that first race and the briefing paper that listed course details and rules bore the handwritten exhortation 'Swim 2.4 miles! Bike 112 miles! Run 26.2 miles! Brag for the rest of your life!' This started a tradition that merely finishing any triathlon is a major achievement.

Today, the Ironman Triathlon sees 1,500 competitors putting themselves through hell, after first going through qualifying competitions. The race is held in Kailua-Kona on the Big Island. The swim is in Kailua-Kona Bay, the bike ride goes across the lava desert to Hawi and back, whilst the run is along the coast from Keauhou via Keahole point to Kailua-Kona. Conditions are tough. No buoyant wet suits are permitted to help swimmers, bike riders are often subject to vicious crosswinds and the marathon is run in hot, sticky conditions. Gasp!

Spectators often gather on the seawall to watch the start of the Ironman Triathlon, before retreating indoors to watch television coverage whilst sipping cool drinks. Other excellent vantage points include the lawns in front of the Kona Inn or beside Bubba Gumps, both on Alii Drive.

WHEN:
October
WHERE:
Kailua-Kona
BEST FOR:
Schadenfreude in the sun!
YOU SHOULD KNOW:
The televised incident that brought the Ironman Triathlon to the attention of the world involved student Julie Moss in 1982 – she fell just short of the finish when leading, suffering from severe dehydration, and was passed by another runner . . . but then she somehow summoned the courage to crawl painfully over the finishing line.

533

Polynesian dancers perform during the festival.

Teuila Festival

WHEN:
August/September
WHERE:
Mainly in Apia
BEST FOR:
The very essence of the romantic South Pacific
YOU SHOULD KNOW:
The Teuila Festival is named after the bright national flower, the red ginger, which blooms vigorously around the islands.

Western Samoans are the friendliest of people and the annual Teuila Festival offers a perfect opportunity to extend their open-hearted hospitality to visitors, who are duly rewarded with a wonderful series of cultural events and entertainment that captures the spirit of this delightful island nation. The old *fa'a Samoa* (Samoan way) is maintained here, complete with associated customs and rituals, a fact that comes over strongly during the festival.

Week-long festivities are concentrated in the capital, Apia, on the main island of Upolu. Residents from outlying villages and islands travel in to play their part in the national celebrations, joined by expatriate Samoans who return for the occasion, plus visitors from all over the world drawn by the chance to experience Polynesian culture at its most exuberant.

The Teuila Festival takes place on land and sea. There are keenly contested *fautasi* races within the reef, featuring the longboats with 40 rowers that once provided inter-island transport. On shore, there are song-and-dance contests, with sinuous female performers doing the graceful *siva* (the local version of Hawaii's hula) to insistent drumbeats. Meanwhile youths try to climb a greasy pole to claim the lofty treasure and chaotic games of *kirikiti* take place (it's an extraordinary version of cricket with unlimited numbers on each side) – both activities generating much hilarity.

Music is everywhere. Church choirs sing their hearts out, bands play, community groups sing folk songs or modern hits. Numerous stalls offer a tasty selection of local fare, or interesting souvenirs. There's also fire-knife dancing and displays of traditional craft skills like weaving and carving. But the highlight of the week is undoubtedly the Miss Samoa Pageant, which is both a beauty contest and stunning floral parade that delivers a suitably kaleidoscopic climax to this colourful event.

Hibiscus Carnival

Flowers, flowers, glorious flowers all the way . . . at least that's what you might expect to find at Fiji's Hibiscus Festival, but actually this high-profile annual occasion lasting over a week is mostly about an incomparable variety of entertainment on the main stage in Suva's Albert Park and various related activities in the adjacent Hibiscus and Circus Tents. There is also an amusement park, food stalls galore and dozens of stands selling assorted goods. The festival is very much one for the locals, though visitors are welcome and can be part of the festive atmosphere as they join 250,000 joyous revellers.

On the opening Saturday the March of Youth parade to Albert Park takes place. The following week sees themed nights reflecting Fiji's diverse ethnic population, with a huge variety of events such as talent shows, musical competitions and concerts, fashion events, dance contests and demonstrations, acrobatic displays, puppet shows, cookery competitions, a police dog display, tug-of-war, a shoe-shining contest, wheelbarrow racing, baby shows, catapult competitions, traditional sports, arm wrestling and bodybuilding heats. It's undoubtedly the People's Festival, and the most tremendous fun.

The final Saturday sees everything come to a frenetic climax. A float procession proceeds from the Flea Market to Albert Park, with contenders for the year's many crowns showing themselves off. The afternoon sees an award for the best float and the ceremonial crownings of such luminaries as Miss Photogenic, Miss Personality, Miss Friendly Face, Miss People's Choice and Miss Charity Queen. The festival concludes with the most important coronations – of the Hibiscus King and Miss Hibiscus – before the really big one – the final determination of the year's Mr Suva in the Fiji Bodybuilding Competition. It ends with more music and a final Mardi Gras session.

WHEN:
August
WHERE:
Suva
BEST FOR:
Joining the locals as they have fun, fun, fun . . .
YOU SHOULD KNOW:
Fijians are generally fairly sober citizens – islanders consider it rude to even raise their voices – which perhaps explains why they love the opportunity to let their hair down and enjoy themselves at Fiji's various festivals.

Heilala Festival

WHEN:
June/July
WHERE:
Nuku'alofa
BEST FOR:
A fascinating glimpse of the real
South Pacific
YOU SHOULD KNOW:
Today, visitors really are welcomed to
Tonga, but when Captain Cook
arrived in 1773 he mistakenly named
the archipelago 'The Friendly Islands'
after receiving effusive greetings
from islanders who were celebrating
a festival – but in fact chiefs wanted
to kill him, but couldn't agree on a
plan to do so.

Until recently visitors to the Kingdom of Tonga faced a volatile situation, with serious tension between King Taufa'ahau IV and his people, who felt the island's resources were not being fairly shared. But following the elderly King's death in a California road accident, successor King George Tupou V ceded much of his power to Parliament and unrest subsided. Tonga remains one of the Pacific's least-developed tourist destinations, though belated attempts are being made to catch up.

As such, the country's biggest event – the two-week Heilala Festival – is more for the entertainment of locals than the sort of visitor-orientated fiesta seen in many tourist havens. It provides an opportunity for people to travel into the national capital of Nuku'alofa on the island of Tongatapu for an annual get-together, which also attracts many members of the Tongan diaspora – half of the country's population lives abroad and their remittances make a major contribution to the Tongan economy.

The festival is full of rather innocent and charming events: lots of traditional singing and song contests; a music festival; flower arranging; golf, basketball and tennis tournaments; special church services; a grand prize giving. More conventionally, there is a none-too-impressive float parade – and less conventionally an impressive military parade in honour of the King.

The most eagerly awaited 'regular' at the festival is the Miss Heilala Pageant. The winner has to survive a stern examination with half-a-dozen judging events throughout the festival that include Miss Heilala Tau'olunga and Miss Heilala Sarong, culminating in an on-stage interview in front of an appreciative audience. This isn't any old beauty contest – it's a beauty contest to find a roving ambassador for the tourist industry. Miss Heilala will be required to join delegations to overseas trade shows and represent Tonga at international pageants. It's tough, but someone has to do it!

Heiva i Tahiti

Tahiti's most flamboyant festival is Heiva i Tahiti (Festival in Tahiti), a major gathering of the clans from the scattered archipelago of French Polynesia. It attracts groups from the other Society Islands – Marquesas, Gambier Islands, Tuamatos and Australs. Anyone with an interest in Polynesian culture should be sure to visit Tahiti while this event is in progress, for they will see an incomparable range of traditional performances.

Tahiti is part of a self-governing French territory – and the three-week-long Heiva i Tahiti starts around the anniversary of autonomy and incorporates France's great national holiday on July 14 (Bastille Day), which sees a special military parade. The principal venue for Heiva i Tahiti is Papeete's paved waterfront area, To'ata Square, where an amphitheatre and stage provide a fabulous setting for performance art. There can be nothing more alluring than Tahitian dancing, with garlanded girls in colourful costumes singing melodiously as they dance, accompanied by lithe young men moving with incredible agility to the rapid beat of slit drums. There is keen competition between different islands, ensuring a virtually continuous spectacle.

The Square is also the venue for an impressive craft village. French Polynesia has a great tradition of arts and crafts and an incredible variety of carving in many materials (wood, stone, bone, mother of pearl, coral), woven goods, ornaments, *pareo* cloth, stunning *tifaifai* (hand-sewn quilts) and more besides may be inspected at leisure. Better still, artisans may be seen at work creating ethnic masterpieces and practising traditional skills like tattoo art. Another dimension is the sporting field, with javelin throwing, archery, canoe racing, stone lifting and banana races, where burly islanders charge around carrying great bunches of bananas on poles. Is this the best festival in the South Pacific? See for yourself!

WHEN:
June/July
WHERE:
Mainly in Papeete
BEST FOR:
The heart and soul of enduring Polynesian culture
YOU SHOULD KNOW:
It doesn't matter when you go – Heiva i Tahiti buzzes each and every day, with endless competitive dancing, sidewalk bazaars, fire walking, carnivals, historical re-enactments and elaborate processions . . . it's one long party!

Competitors get ready to run with their bananas.

Hawaiki Nui Va'a Race

WHEN:
Early November
WHERE:
Huahine to Bora Bora via Raiatea
and Taha'a
BEST FOR:
The *bringue* – that traditional
Polynesian celebration at the finish
in Bora Bora with lots of joyous
laughter, music and drink that
flows freely
YOU SHOULD KNOW:
Those who prefer to watch their
sport in the comfort of an
air-conditioned bar with the help
of a cold drink will be pleased to
know that the Hawaiki Nui Va'a
is extensively covered on
local television.

A boat is needed to see it all, but that doesn't stop the three-day Hawaiki Nui Va'a outrigger canoe race making grand viewing for those lucky enough to be in the Leeward islands of Huahine, Raiatea, Taha'a or Bora Bora when it takes place. The serious spectator can island-hop after watching each day's start to be there for the finish, but many visitors are happy just to be on one of these idyllic islands while Hawaiki Nui Va'a is taking place to witness this dramatic contest.

Around 2,000 racers gather for this unique event, coming from Tahiti, the Marquesas, New Caledonia, the Tuamotus, Hawaii . . . and even France. It pits the world's best canoe teams against each other, with over 100 boats lining up for this ultimate Pacific challenge. Day One sees a 45-km (28-mi) crossing from Huahine to the sacred island of Raiatea, a trip that takes about four hours. Day Two is reserved for a sprint race, inside the reef, between Raiatea and Taha'a that lasts a lung-bursting 90 minutes. Day Three sees the final ocean crossing between Taha'a and Matira Beach in Bora Bora – a 52-km (32-mi) leg accomplished in something over four hours. The racing canoes are accompanied by a motley flotilla of official launches, support teams, fishing boats and anything to which an outboard motor can be fitted.

Needless to say, a large and enthusiastic crowd is awaiting the first canoe's arrival in Bora Bora, with excitement reaching fever pitch as anticipation builds. The winners are greeted with wild cheering and are presented with flower *leis* (garlands) to the sound of singing and the beating of drums. It's a wonderfully festive occasion, with the party gathering pace as successive canoes and their support crews arrive to join the action.

*Boats head for the
finishing line.*

Mount Hagan Cultural Festival

There are hundreds of tribes in Papua New Guinea (PNG), and at least 50 of them converge on the Kagamuga Showgrounds every August for the Mount Hagan Cultural Festival. Missionaries created this extraordinary event in the early 1960s – hoping to improve relations between tribes that had often been enemies for centuries, stress common cultural experiences and celebrate the individual differences from one tribe to the next. It proved to be an inspired – and successful – initiative.

PNG's Highlanders remain proud and competitive people, but rivalries are now expressed in fantastic displays as each tribe seeks to outdo the next. The people wear *bilas* (traditional costumes), which have elaborate feather headdresses and shell breastplates. The full, fearsome impression is completed by elaborate face tattoos and bright body paint. As dancers whirl and caper to the rhythm of pounding drums, performing their unique 'sing-sings', the effect is almost mesmeric. To avoid conflict between tribes that would echo former times, all revenues collected are split between the performing groups, rather than being awarded to 'winners'.

Taken as a whole, with various other musical performances, cultural demonstrations and modern entertainments, the Mount Hagan Festival is a stunning visual treat – sufficiently colourful to (almost) put Rio's Mardi Gras in the shade. Though its ethnic foundations remain firmly based on tribal culture, the festival has evolved over time into a major visitor attraction, with up to 50,000 spectators from elsewhere in PNG arriving to enjoy the two-day show, supported by international tourists whose numbers increase every year as the fame of the Mount Hagan Cultural Festival spreads around the globe. Sadly, this may be one of those cases where commercial exploitation destroys the very thing that attracts visitors, so the time to experience this unique occasion would ideally be as soon as possible.

A tribesman wears traditional face paint at the festival.

WHEN:
August
WHERE:
Mount Hagan, Western Highlands Province
BEST FOR:
A vibrant display of traditional ethnicity
YOU SHOULD KNOW:
In the 1970s tribesmen told organizers of the Mount Hagan Festival that they would happily return to cannibalism if it helped to draw in more tourists – adding that they weren't savages and had no wish to kill anyone, so would make do with a corpse from the local mortuary. Their offer was politely declined.

COUNTRIES AND REGIONS

Africa 102–50
Argentina 76–9
Asia 380–499
Australia 501–20
Austria 326–33

Bahamas 73
Barbados 68–9
Belgium 239–43
Belize 62
Benin 123
Bhutan 391
Bissau 109
Bolivia 86–7
Bosnia Herzegovina 335
Brazil 80–5
Bulgaria 350–1

Cambodia 493–4
Canada 10–20
Cape Verde Islands 139
Cayman Islands 72
Central America and the Caribbean
    58–73
Chile 97–8
China 419–36
Colombia 96
Croatia 346–7
Cyprus 361–2
Czech Republic 341–3

Denmark 165–8
Dominica 70–1
Dominican Republic 70

Eastern Mediterranean and Middle East
    366–77
Ecuador 99
Egypt 102–3
England 182–208
Estonia 175
Ethiopia 148–9
Europe 154–363
European Russia 176–8

Fiji 535
Finland 169–73
France 244–61

Germany 315–25
Ghana 124
Greece 352–60
Guatemala 63
Hawaii 532

Holland 232–7
Hungary 336–8

Iceland 154
India 394–415
Indonesia 460–6
Iran 372
Irish Republic 222–31
Isle of Man 215
Israel 369–70
Italy 290–309

Jamaica 64–5
Japan 441–54
Jordan 368

Kenya 143–7
Kyrgyzstan 384

Laos 491–2
Libya 104
Lithuania 174
Luxembourg 238

Madagascar 128
Malawi 129
Malaysia 495–9
Mali 106–8
Malta 363
Mauritius 418
Mexico 58–61
Middle East and Eastern Mediterranean
    366–77
Monaco 260–1
Mongolia 386
Morocco 112–18

Namibia 130–1
Nepal 392–3
Netherlands 232–7
New Zealand 521–31
Nigeria 110–11
Northern Ireland 219–21
Norway 155–59

Oceania 532–9

Pakistan 388–90
Papua New Guinea 39
Peru 88–91
Philippines 467–75
Poland 339–40
Portugal 282–9

Republic of Ireland 222–31
Romania 348

Russia, 176–8
Russian Federation 380–1

St Lucia 66
Samoa 534–5
Saudi Arabia 373
Scotland 209–15
Serbia 345
Seychelles 150–1
Singapore 457–9
Slovakia 344
Slovenia 334
South Africa 132–8
South America 76–99
South Korea 455–6
Spain 262–81
Sri Lanka 416
Swaziland 126–7
Sweden 160–4
Switzerland 310–14
Syria 371

Tahiti 536–7
Taiwan 440
Tanzania 140
Thailand 476–85
Tibet 436–9
Togo 104–5
Tonga 536
Trinidad and Tobago 67
Tunisia 119–22
Turkey 374–7

Ukraine 179–81
United Arab Emirates 366
Uruguay 92
USA 20–55

Venezuela 94–5
Vietnam 486–90

Wales 216–18

Zambia 142–3
Zanzibar 141

EVENTS

Aalsmeer Flower Parade 237
Aarhus Festival 167
Abu Simbel Festival 102
Accompong Maroon Festival 64
Addo Elephant Trail Run 133
AFL Grand Final 513
Albuquerque International Balloon Fiesta 49
All-Ireland Hurling Final 227
Aloha Festivals 532
American Birkebeiner 25
Amsterdam Canal Parade 236
Anastenaria 355
ANZAC Day Commemoration 506
Appleby Horse Fair 199
Argentine Polo Finals 79
Argungu Fishing Festival 111
Ashes Series (cricket) 201
Assumption of the Virgin 60
Aste Nagusia 276
At Chabysh Horse Games 385
Athens Festival 356–7
Ati-Atihan Festival 469
Australia Day Cockroach Races 502
Avante! Festival 287
Avignon Festival 250

Ballinasloe Horse Fair 231
Barranquilla Carnival 96
Basant Kite-Flying Festival 388
Basque Rural Games 277
Bastille Day 252
Batalla del Vino 269
Battle of the Oranges 291
Bayreuth's Wagner Festival 324
Benicàssim International Festival 272–3
Binche Carnival 239
Birdsville Races 514
Birthday of Confucius 431
Bissau Carnival 109
Bloomsday 223
Boat Race, England 184–5
Boca Juniors v River Plate 76
Boi Bumbá 82
Bonn Om Touk 494
Boston Tea Party 54
Boxing Day Test, Australia 519
Bridge Jumping at Mostar 335
Buenos Aires Tango Festival 77
Bun Bang Fai Rocket Festival in Yasothon 480
Bun Nam 491
Burning Man Festival 45

Cádiz Carnival 262
Calcio Storico 299
Calgary Stampede 16–17
Camel-Wrestling Championship 374–5

Canada Day 13
Cannes Film Festival 247
Cape Breton Celtic Colours International Festival 19
Cape Town International Comedy Festival 137
Casimir's Fair 174
Celebration of Light Festival 18
Chahar Shanbeh Suri 372
Chelsea Flower Show 191
Cheltenham Festival 182
Cheyenne Frontier Days 39
Chichibu Night Festival 454
Chingay Parade of Dreams 457
Chocolate Festival, Perugia 308
Chun Jie Spring Festival 420
Cinco de Mayo 31
Círio de Nazaré 83
Cologne Carnival 317
Combat des Reines 314
Common Ridings 210
Comrades Marathon 134–5
Confucius, Birthday of 431
Cooper's Hill Cheese Rolling 188
Corsa dei Ceri 296
Cow's Ball, Slovenia 334
Cowes Week 205
Crop Over 68–9
Crufts Dog Show 183
Cucurbitades Festival 256

Dancing Procession of Echternach 238
Darwin Beer Can Regatta 510
Dashain 393
Day of the Dead 61
Day of the Gaucho 78
Dead Sea Ultra Marathon 368
Deegal – Crossing of the Cattle Festival, 108
Deni Play on the Plains Festival 515
Derby Day 195
Día del Descubrimiento de Dos Mundos 97
DOM Festival 322
Donauinselfest 330
Dover Lane Music Festival 395
Dragon Boat Festival 428
Dubai Shopping Festival 366
Dubai World Cup 367
Dubrovnik Summer Festival 347
Durbar Festival 110
Dussehra in Mysore 412–13
Düsseldorf Carnival 316

Easter Mass in St Peter's Square 295
Ecce Homo, Braga 282
Edinburgh Festival 211
Eid al-Fitr, Damascus 371
Eisteddfod 217
Ekka (Royal Queensland Show) 511
Ekstremsportveko 157
Elephant Races, Vietnam 489

Epidaurus Festival of Greek Drama 358–9
Equinox at Chichen Itza 59
Erfoud Date Festival 118
Esala Perahera in Kandy 417
Ethiopian Music Festival 149
European Medieval Festival, Horsens 168
Evala Festival 104–5
EXIT Music Festival 345

FA Cup Final 190
Famadihana 128
Faschings-Dienstag, 315
Fasnachtsmontag 312
Feast of Tabernacles 369
Feria del Málaga 274–5
Fes Festival of World Sacred Music 113
Festa di San Giovanni Battista 300
Festival of the Bun Hills 424
Festival in the Desert 106
Festival of the Dhow Countries 140
Festival dei Due Mondi 303
Festival of Giants 251
Festival of Kings 85
Festival of Lights, Israel 370
Festival on the Niger 107
Festival of the Panagia 361
Festival of the Sahara 120–1
Festival of St Thomas 63
Festival of Sant' Efisio 297
Festival de la Sidra 272
Festival du Vent 260
Festival du Voyageur 11
Festivals of Valls 281
Fiesta de la Cultura 98
Fiesta de la Mama Negra 99
Fiesta de la Patria Gaucha 93
Fiesta de la Virgen de la Candelaria 86
Fiesta de Merengue 70
Fiesta de San Fermín 271
Fiesta de Sant Joan 268
Finlandia Hiihto Ski Marathon 169
Flower Festival, Chiang Mai 476
Flower Festival and St Stephen's Day in Debrecen 338
Flushing Meadow: US Tennis Open 42–3
Four Days Marches 235

Galungan, Bali 462
Galway International Oyster Festival 228–9
Galway Races 224–5
Ganesh Chaturthi in Maharashtra 411
Gathering of Nations Pow Wow 28
Gawai Dayak 496–7
Genzano Infiorata 302
Ghadames Festival 104
Giant Lantern Festival 475
Gioco del Ponte 300–1
Giostra del Saracino 305
Giro di Lombardia 309

Glastonbury Festival 196
Glorious 12th 212
Glyndebourne Festival Opera 189
Gnawa World Music Festival 114
Goa Carnival 401
Gold Coast Indy 300 516
Golden Eagle Festival 387
Golden Shears 526
Golega Horse Fair 288
Gothenburg Book Festival 164
Gotland Medieval Week 163
Grahamstown National Arts Festival 136–7
Granada International Festival of Music and Dance 270
Grand National 186
Great Wall Marathon 427
Greek Easter in Corfu Town 354
Guizhou Azalea Festival 423

Hahnenkamm Race Weekend 327
Hajj 373
Halloween in New York City 47
Hanami (Cherry Blossom Viewing) 442
Harbin International Ice and Snow Sculpture Festival 419
Hawaiki Nui Va'a Race 538
Hay-on-Wye Festival of Literature and Arts 216
Heilala Festival 536
Heiva i Tahiti 536–7
Helsinki Festival 173
Hemis Festival 200
Henley Royal Regatta 202
Henley-on-Todd Regatta 512–13
Hi! Seoul Festival 455
Hibiscus Carnival 535
Highland Games 203
Hogbetsotso 125
Hogmanay 214
Holi 402
Holla Mohalla 403
Holmenkollen Ski Festival 155
Holy Spirit Festival in the Azores 283
Homowo Festival 124
Hounen Matsuri 444
Humorina 179

Icarus Cup 255
Iditarod Dog Sled Race 27
Idul Adha in Yogyakarta, Java 460
Iemanjá in Olinda 84–5
Imilchil Marriage Moussem 115
Imnarja – the Feast of St Peter and St Paul 363
Imparja Camel Cup 509
ImPulsTanz 331
Independence Day, USA 35
Indianapolis 500 32
International Festival of Carthage 119
International Highland Folk Festival, Zakopane 340

International Sand Sculpture Festival 233
Inti Raymi 89
Ironman Triathlon 533
Isle of Man TT Races 215
Ivan Kupala 180

Jaisalmer Desert Festival 399
Jamis Day-Night Thriller 528
Jetsprint Championships 531
Jindo Sea Parting Festival 456
Jokkmokk Winter Market 161
Junkanoo 73
Just For Laughs Festival 14
Jutajaíset Festival of Nightless Nights
 170

Kadayawan sa Dabaw 472–3
Kajli Teej in Bundi 408
Kataklysmos 362
Kavadi 397
KaZantip 181
Kentucky Derby 30
Khajuraho Dance Festival 400
Khao Phansa Candle Festival in Ubon
 Ratchathani 481
Khmer New Year 493
Kieler Woche 321
King's Cup Elephant Polo Tournament
 477
Kirkpinar Oil-Wrestling Festival 376
Kiruna Snow Festival 160
Knutsford Royal May Day 187
Kodava Hockey Festival 405
Kreole Festival 150–1
Kulmbach Bierfest 323
Kuomboka 142–3
Kurban Bairam 435

La Diablada 90–1
La Feria de Abril 266
La Festa des Vermar 280
La Fête des Gardiens 245
La Flèche Wallonne 240–1
La Tomatina 278
Lajkonik Festival, Kraków 339
Lake of Stars Music Festival 129
Lamu Dugong Festival 143
Lange Nacht der Musik 329
Lantern Festival, Tainan 440
Las Fallas de Valencia 265
Laura Aboriginal Dance and Cultural
 Festival 508
Le Mans 24 248
Lewes Bonfire Night 207
Lieu Doi Wrestling Festival 487
Lim Festival 488
Lion Red Snapper Classic 525
Lisdoonvarna Matchmaking Festival 230
Lisu Knife-Pole Festival 421
London-to-Brighton Veteran Car Run 208
Lopburi Monkey Banquet 483

Lorient Inter-Celtic Festival 253
Los Diablos Danzantes 94–5
Losar 436–7
Loy Krathong, Chiang Mai 484

Macufe – Mangaung African Cultural
 Festival 138
Macy's Thanksgiving Day Parade 51
Maggio Musicale Fiorentina 298
Maha Shivaratri 392
Maherero Day 130–1
Maidens' Fair, Romania 349
Maine Lobster Festival 41
Maitisong Festival 131
Maralal Camel Derby 144–5
Mardi Gras, São Vicente 139
Marlborough Wine Festival 524–5
Maslenitsa in Moscow 176
MassKara Festival 474
Mazatlán Carnival 58
Médoc Marathon 254
Melbourne Cup 517
Miaoulia 356
Miyajima Kangensai 449
MME – the Merdeka Millennium
 Endurance 499
Mombasa Carnival 147
Monaco Grand Prix 260–1
Mondial du Snowboard 259
Montana World of Wearable Art Awards
 528–9
Monterey Jazz Festival 46
Montreux International Jazz Festival 313
Mooncake Festival 432
Moriones 470–1
Moulid of Abu El Haggag 103
Mount Hagan Cultural Festival 539
Mwaka Kogwa 141

Naadam 386
Naga Panchami 409
Nagchu Horse Racing Festival 439
National Day, Belize 62
National Day, China 434–5
National Finals Rodeo 53
National Vodun (Voodoo) Day 123
Ncwala 127
Negara Buffalo Races, Bali 466
New Year's Day Concert, Vienna 236
New Year's Eve in Funchal 289
New Year's Eve in Times Square 54–5
New York Marathon 50
New Zealand Cup and Show Week 530
Niagara Falls Festival of Lights 20–1
Night of the Full Moon, Athens 360
Nobel Peace Prize Concert 158–59
Nooruz 384–5
Norwegian National Day 156
Notting Hill Carnival 206

Oberammergau Passion Play 319
Oc Om Boc Festival 490
Ok Phansa Illuminated Boat Procession
 482
Oktoberfest 325
Old Settler's Music Festival 29
Ommegang Pageant 242
Onam in Kerala 410
Opera Festival in Verona 304
Orange Day Parades 219
Oshkosh Air Show 37
Ould Lammas Fair 221
Owara Kaze-no-Bon Matsuri 453

Pageant of the Juni 348–9
Pageant of the Masters 40
Palio 306
Pangandaran Kite Festival, Java 465
Paris Fashion Shows 244
Paris Motor Show 258
Pasadena Rose Parade 22
Pasola Festival, Sumba 461
Patras Carnival 352
Perth International Arts Festival 503
Perugia's Chocolate Festival 308
Pes Ponedelnik – Kukeri Festival in
 Shiroka Luka 350
Phang Lhabsol 412
Pikes Peak International Hill Climb 38
Pilgrimage of Near-Death Experiences
 274
Pinkpop Festival 234
Pirates Week 70–1
Pistes de Lancement Circus Festival 240
Pohoda Music Festival 344
Poi Sang Long Festival at Mae Hong Son
 478
Pole of Cold Rally and Festival 381
Polo World Cup on Snow 311
Pongal in Tamil Nadu 394
Poush Mela 415
Prague Spring International Music
 Festival 341
Prix de l'Arc de Triomphe 256–7
Procession of the Black Nazarene 467
Proms 203
Pukkelpop 243
Pushkar Camel Fair 414–15

Qeima das Fitas, Coimbra 284–5
Qingdao International Beer Festival 430
Quebec Winter Carnival 10
Queen's Day, Netherlands 232
Queenstown Winter Festival 527
Quema de Judas 94

Rainforest World Music Festival 498
Rath Yatra 406
Rayne Frog Festival 52
Regada Water Festival 472
Regata Storico 307
Reggae Sumfest 65

Republic Day, India 396
Rhine in Flames 318
Rijeka Carnival 346
Rio Carnival 80
Rip Curl Pro 505
Roma Pilgrimage and Festival 246
Rose of Tralee Festival 226
Roskilde Festival 166
Royal Academy Summer Exhibition 192
Royal Ascot 194
Royal Nova Scotia International Tattoo 15

Sa Sartiglia Oristanese 293
Sabantui 178
Saga Dawa Festival 438
St Anthony's Day, Portugal 285
St John's Eve 175
St John's Festival, Porto 286–7
St Lucia Jazz 66
St Olav's Day, Norway 158
St Patrick's Day Parade, Dublin 222
St Patrick's Day, Boston 26
Salvador Carnival 81
Salzburg Festival 332–3
San Isidro Bullfighting Festival 267
Sanja Matsuri 447
Sankt Hans Bonfires 165
Sant' Agata di Catania 294
Santa Cruz Carnival 263
Santacruzan 471
Sanyue Jie in Dali 425
Sapporo Snow Festival 443
Savonlinna Opera Festival 171
Schutzenfest, Hannover 320
Seb-i-Aruz – Whirling Dervishes 377
Semana Santa 88
Shandur Polo Tournament 390
Shaolin Martial Arts Festival 433
Siberia Sun Vibes Festival 382–3
Sibi Mela 389
Sidi Ben Aissa Moussem 112
Singapore Lantern Festival 458
Sinulog Festival 468
Sisters' Meal Festival 426
Sitges Carnival 264
Skyros Goat Dance 353
Soma-Nomaoi 450
Songkran 479
Splashy Fen Music Festival 132
Sriwijaya Festival in Palembang, Sumatra
 464
Stanley Cup 33
Stars of the White Nights Festival 177
State of Origin Series (rugby league) 507
Stellenbosch Wine Festival 135
Stonehenge Summer Solstice 198
Storytelling Festival on Cape Clear Island
 228
Sturgis Motorcycle Rally 44
Sundance Film Festival 23
Super Bowl 24
Surin Elephant Round-up 485
Sydney Gay and Lesbian Mardi Gras 504

Sydney-to-Hobart Yacht Race 418
Sziget Festival, Budapest 337
Tabyk Ethnic Music Festival 383
Takayama Matsuri 445
Te Matatini Festival 523
Tenjin Matsuri 451
Teppothsavam Float Festival 398
Tet Nguyen Dan 486–7
Tetsuya Odori, Gujo Hachiman 452
Teuila Festival, 534–5
Thaipusam at Batu Caves 495
Thaipusam Kavadi Parade 418
That Luang Festival 492
Thay Pagoda Festival 490
Thimphu Tsechu 391
Thrissur Pooram Elephant Festival 404–5
Timket 148–9
Tinku Festival 87
Tissa Horse Festival 116–17
Tokyo May Basho 446
Toonik Tyme, Iqaluit Spring Festival 12
Tour de France 249
Trinidad Carnival 67
Trooping the Colour 193
Tsongkhapa Butter Lamp Festival, Lhasa
   336
TT Races 215

Umhlanga 126
US Independence Day 35
US Open Golf Championship 34
US Tennis Open, Flushing Meadow 42–3

Valborgsmassoafton (Walpurgis Night) 162
Valley of the Roses Festival 351
Venice Carnivale 292
Vesak 416
Viareggio Carnival 290
Vienna Life Ball 328–9
Vienna New Year's Day Concert 236
Viking Fire Festival 209
Virgen del Rosario Festival 90
Vogel Gryff 310
Vuelta a España 279

Wagner Festival, Bayreuth 324
Waisak Festival at Borobudur, Java 463
Waitangi Day 521
Wakakusa Yamayaki 441
Walpurgis Night (Valborgsmassoafton) 162
Water Festival 496
Weifang International Kite Festival 422
Wellington Sevens 522
West Belfast Community Festival 220
Westman Islands Festival 154
White Moon Festival (Sagaalgan) 380–1
Wimbledon Tennis Championships 197
Winged Dragon International Street Theatre
   Festival, Nyirbator 336
Wodaabe Geerewol and the Cure Salée
   Festival 122

WOMAD Festival 204
Woodford Folk Festival 520
World Bog Snorkelling Championship
   218
World Creole Music Festival 72
World Festival of Puppet Art 343
World Roma Khamoro Festival 342–3
World Series (baseball) 48
World Stinging Nettle Eating
   Championship 200
World Wife-Carrying Championship 172

Yamaboko Junko at Gion Matsuri 448
Yi Torch Festival 429

ZoukOut Dance Festival 459

Alamy/42pix 530; /Rami Aapasuo 173; /Rubens Abboud 10; /Idris Ahmed 403; /Bryan & Cherry Alexander Photography 161; /Jake KY Anderson 125; /Jon Arnold Images Ltd. 476; /Claudio H. Artman 361; /Richard Ashworth/Robert Harding Picture Library Ltd. 398; /Gaspar Avila 283; /AWPhoto 482; /Bill Bachman 6 picture 4, 519; /Mark Baynes/Basque Country 276, 277; /John Baxter 199; /Paul Bernhardt 282; /Barry Black/All Canada Photos 13; /Barry Bland 500 inset 3, 526; /Tibor Bognar 338; /Jean Du Boisberranger/Hemis 3 right, 112; /Marion Bull 200; /Demetrio Carrasco/Jon Arnold Images Ltd. 75 inset 2, 80; /Angelo Cavalli/Robert Harding Picture Library Ltd. 378, 391; /C. Christodoulou/Lebrecht Music & Arts Photo Library 203; /Bernhard Classen/vario images GmbH & Co.KG 317; /CLEO Photo 26; /Iain Cooper 212; /Roger Cracknell 10/Pagan Festivals 353; /Rob Crandall 23; /Sue Cunningham Photographic 84; /DK 118; /Ros Drinkwater 230; /Chad Ehlers 160; /Sindre Ellingsen 511; /estancabigas 468; /David Ewing/INSADCO Photography 364 inset 1, 377; /Michele Falzone 5 picture 3, 113; /Stuart Forster 394; /Stéphane Frances/Hemis 301; /Gallo Images/Daily Sun 138; /Kevin Galvin 319; /Paul Gapper 139; /Bertrand Gardel/Hemis 7 picture 1, 521; /Kenneth Garrett/Danita Delimont 382; /Gimmi/CuboImages srl 290; /Michel Gotin/Hemis 437; /Johnny Greig TR 365 inset 1, 367; /Hackenberg-Photo-Cologne 330; /Juergen Hasenkopf 335; /Dallas and John Heaton/SCPhotos 237; /Heiner Heine/imagebroker 320; /Gavin Hellier/Jon Arnold Images Ltd. 156; /Christoph Henning/Das Fotoarchiv/Black Star 124; /Holger Heue/LOOK Die Bildagentur der Fotografen GmbH 168; /Christopher Hill Photographic/scenicireland.com 231; /Terence Hogben 136; /Hendrik Holler/Bon Appetit 254; /Andrew Holt 520; /Philippe Houze/Hemis 153 inset 1, 251; /India Images/Dinodia Images 399; /Minako Ishii/Photo Resource Hawaii 501 inset 2, 532; /Javed Jafferji/Imagestate Media Partners Limited/Impact Photos 141; /jameshj 497; /Bo Jansson/Pixonnet.com 162; /JazzSign/Lebrecht Music and Arts Photo Library 167; /Maurice Joseph 308; /JTB Photo Communications, Inc. 71, 441; /Wolfgang Kaehler 9 inset 1, 12; /Marion Kaplan 140; /Richard van Kesteren 481; /Tom Kidd Photography 211; /Terrance Klassen 11; /Christian Kober 102; /Christian Kober/John Warburton-Lee Photography 430; /Ton Koene/Picture Contact 236; /Juraj Kovacik 344; /Rob Lacey/vividstock.net 188; /Æ. Laue/Arco Images GmbH 316; /Jason Laure/Danita Delimont 28; /Graham Lawrence 288; /Frans Lemmens 235; /Sheldon Levis 503; /Yadid Levy 45; /Yan Liao 421; /Lightworks Media 363; /Riccardo Lombardo/CuboImages srl 294; /Craig Lovell/Eagle Visions Photography 46; /David Lowe 461; /Sabine Lubenow/FAN Travelstock 304; /Ludovic Maisant/Hemis 100 inset 3, 146; /Makno 209; /Luz Martin 114; /Neil McAllister 187; /Bernd Mellmann 318; /Mira 438; /Giles Moberly 101 inset 2, 110, 111; /Jeff Morgan Rural Environment 218 bottom; /Adrian Muttitt 226; /Robert Noyes 196; /Original Images 7 picture 6, 215; /Oso Media 264, 264; /Werner Otto 289; /Panorama Media (Beijing) 18, 429; /PhotoBliss 340; /Photo Japan 451; /Pieder 315; /Shane Pinder 56 inset 2, 73; /Constantinos Pliakos 352; /Lincoln Potter/Danita Delimont 439; /Emil Pozar II 346; /An Qi 425; /R1 31; /Nicolas Randall/Expuesto 280; /Randolph Images 275; /Simon Reddy 401; /Todd Reese 100 inset 1, 105; /RIA Novosti 152 inset 2, 178; /Robert Harding Picture Library Ltd. 7 picture 5, 509; /Mick Rock/Cephas Picture Library 286; /Peter Schickert/imagebroker 151; /Vittorio Sciosia/CuboImages srl 291; /Alistair Scott 142; /Alex Segre 189; /Neil Setchfield 297; /Paule Seux/Hemis 378 inset 3, 400; /Mark Shenley 116; /Shenval 213; /Marco Simoni/Robert Harding Picture Library Ltd. 75 inset 1, 86; /Peter Skinner/Danita Delimont 539; /Jonathan Smith 174; /Stefan Sollfors 163; /Paul Souders/Danita Delimont 469; /South America Photos 91; /South West Images Scotland 210; /Marmaduke St. John 40; /Stormcab 538; /Bjorn Svensson 491; /Homer Sykes/CountrySideCollection 217; /Luca Tettoni/Robert Harding Picture Library Ltd. 480; /Julia Thorne/Robert Harding Picture Library Ltd. 500, 514; /Kube? Tomá?/isifa Image Service s.r.o. 109; /Angelo Tondini/CuboImages srl 305; /Travelscape Images 268; /Travelshots.com 307; /travelstock44 312; /Masa Uemura 445; /Untrodden Path 407; /V1 6 picture 1, 69, 238; /Patrick Ward 242; /Chris Wayatt 269; /way out west photography 224; /Christine Webb 296; /Henry Westheim Photography 440; /Tim Whitby 74 inset 3, 99; /David White 172; /Jochem Wijnands/Picture Contact 165; /Wilmar Photography 322; /Rob Womad 204; /Adam Woolfitt/Robert Harding Picture Library Ltd. 5 picture 2, 50; /wronaphoto.com 351; /Liu Xiaoyang 431; /Ian Macrae Young 214; /Ivan Zupic 345

Artemis Images/Jay Bonvouloir 38

Austrian National Tourist Office/Österreich Werbung/Lammerhuber 326; /Österreich Werbung/Markowitsch 332

Celtic Colours International Festival/Ralph Dillon 19

Corbis/Peter Adams/JAI 81; /Atlantide Phototravel 246; /Carl Auer/NewSport 27; /Ballesteros/EFE 257; /Arno Balzarini/epa 311; /Charles Baus/Icon SMI 34; /Remi Benali 245, 462; /Amit Bhargava 411; /Walter Bibikow/JAI 419; /Gene Blevins 53; /Tibor Bognar 495;

/Christophe Boisvieux 339, 486; /Jean-Christopher Bott/epa 314; /Jacques Bourguet/Sygma 14; /Everett Kennedy Brown/epa 444; /Manuel Bruque/epa 265; /Paul Buck/epa 6 picture 5, 8 inset 3, 24; /Geoff Caddick/epa 206; /Sebastien Cailleux 106; /Car Culture 258; /Domenech Castello/epa 273; /Erik de Castro/Reuters 470; /Matthew Cavanaugh/epa 35, 48; /David W Cerny/Reuters 342; /Tim Chong/Reuters 457; /Tim Clayton 518; /Gil Cohen Magen/Reuters 370; /Revoli Cortez/epa 474; /Alan Crowhurst/epa 194; /Maurizio Degl'Innocenti/epa 299; /Alexander Demianchuk/Reuters 177; /Tomasso DeRosa 42; /Vinai Dithajohn/epa 379 inset 2, 478; /Kieran Doherty/Reuters 152 inset 3, 201; /Sergey Dolzhenko/epa 180; /Vassil Donev/epa 350; /Julio Donoso/Sygma 266; /Benoit Doppagne/epa 239; /Juan Echeverria 100, 130; /Maxi Failla/Pool/epa 76; /Carlo Ferraro/epa 306; /Helmut Fohringer/epa 328; /Peter Foley/epa 9 inset 2, 51; /Andrew Fox 183, 216; /Owen Franken 39; /Franz-Marc Frei 47; /Thomas Frey/epa 533; /Marcus Fuehrer/epa 324; /Albert Gea/Reuters 281; /Laurent Gillieron/epa 313; /Christophe Gin 74 inset 2, 82; /Philippe Giraud/Goodlook 83; /Philip Gould 52; /Russell Gordon/ZUMA 7 picture 3, 36; /David Gray/Reuters 420, 506; /Peter Guttman 418; /Barry Harcourt/Handout/Reuters 527; /Tobias Hase/epa 325; /John Van Hasselt 222; /Lindsay Hebberd 417; /So Hing-Keung 428, 432; /Dave G. Houser 8 inset 1; /Jon Hrusa/epa 126; /Yorick Jansens/epa 243; /Alfred Cheng Jin/Reuters 427; /Tan Jin/Xinhua Press 434; /Jen Judge/Aurora Photos 8, 49; /Michael Kai 517; /Sergei Karpukhin/Reuters 176; /Ed Kashi 44, 389; /Kham/Reuters 489; /Manjunath Kiran/epa 404; /Peter Kollanyi/epa 337; /Earl & Nazima Kowall 148; /Jeff Kowalsky/epa 33; /Olaf Kraak/epa 232; /Bob Krist 534; /Ludo Kuipers 5 picture 1, 501 inset 1, 508; /Dai Kurokawa/epa 488; /Kim Kyung-Hoon/Reuters 455; /Russell LaBounty/ASP Inc./Icon SMI 2 centre, 32; /Frank Leather/Eye Ubiquitous 448; /Jason Lee/Reuters 422; /Floris Leeuwenberg/The Cover Story 255; /Barry Lewis 386; /Michael S. Lewis 108; /Anuruddha Lokuhapuarachchi/Reuters 416; /Villar Lopez/epa 270; /Joshua Lott/Reuters 55; /Liam Ludbrook/epa 132; /Ricardo Maldonado/epa 74 inset 1, 96; /Enrique Marcarian/Reuters 79, epa 6 picture 2, 121, 244, 397; /Sterba Martin/epa 341; /Leo Mason 182, 186, 190, 197, 205; /Lea Meilandt Mathiesen/epa 166; /Toby Melville/Reuters 207; /Kimimasa Mayama/epa 443; /Gideon Mendel 128, 198; /Andrea Merola/epa 152, 292; /Pierre Minier - Ouest Medias/epa 248; /Gail Mooney 250; /Bruno Morandi/Hemis 293; /Nabil Mounzer/epa 350; /Nyein Chan Naing/epa 479; /James Nazz 20; /Herbert Neubauer/epa 327; /Alain Nogues 252; /Kazuyoshi Nomachi 88; /Paulo Novais/LUSA/epa 244; /Richard T. Nowitz 223; /Dwi Oblo/Reuters 463; /Matthieu Paley 387, 390; /Douglas Peebles 500 inset 2, 537; /Anthony Phelps/Reuters 522; /Alessia Pierdomenico/Reuters 302; /Pool/Immaginazione 295; /Cornelius Poppe/epa 159; /Ben Radford 202; /Andy Rain/epa 192; /Carsten Rehder/epa 321; /Stephane Reix/For Picture 247; /Mak Remissa/epa 379 inset 1, 493; /Reuters 2, 3 centre, 5 picture 4, 87, 144, 193, 233, 278, 402, 485, 498, 504; /Michael Reynolds/epa 378 inset 2, 380; /Robert Harding World Imagery 16; /Ramon de la Rocha/epa 153 inset 2, 263; /Henry Romero/Reuters 57 inset 1, 61; /Jeffrey L. Rotman 364 inset 2, 376; /Gus Ruelas/Reuters 22; /Anders Ryman 115; /Dennis M. Sabangan/epa 467, 475; /Narong Sangnak/epa 477; /Faith Saribas/Reuters 374; /Sangdao Sattra/epa 484; /Schlegelmilch 261; /Jayanta Shaw/Reuters 395, 409; /Narendra Shrestha/epa 393; /Andrea De Silva/epa 57 inset 2, 66, 67; /Seppo Sirkka/epa 152 inset 1, 171; /Tyrone Siu/Reuters 424; /Richard Hamilton Smith 25; /Frédéric Soltan/Sygma 406; /Wang Song/Xinhua Press 433; /James Sparshatt 77, 262; /Hubert Stadler 74, 78; /Benjamin Stansall/epa 218 top; /Andres Stapff/Reuters 2 left, 92; /STR/Reuters 134; /Stringer/epa 119; /Stringer/India/Reuters 410; /Stringer/Mexico/Reuters 59; /Keren Su 89; /Sukree Sukplang/Reuters 483; /Rudy Sulgan 18; /David Sutherland 414; /Jane Sweeney/JAI 5 picture 5, 378 inset 1, 392; /Jason Szenes/epa 30; /Takeshi Takahashi/amanaimages 454; /Liba Taylor 408; /Pierre Tostee/ASP/Reuters 500 inset, 505; /Tuul/Hemis 100 inset 2, 122; /Harish Tyagi/epa 396; /Robert Vos/epa 234; /Tim De Waele 241, 249, 279, 309; /Patrick Ward 101 inset 1, 120, 195, 208, 512; /Scott Wensley/Handout/Reuters 502; /Nik Wheeler 492; /Clifford White 516; /Nevada Wier 426; /Howard Yanes/Reuters 95; /Ronen Zvulun/Reuters 364 inset 3, 369

Dubrovnik Summer Festival/Damil Kalogjera 347

Ekstremsportveko.com/Nils-Erik Kjellman 7 picture 4, 157 top right, 157 bottom left

Getty Images/AFP 303, 456, 460; /Juan Barreto/AFP 56 inset 3, 58; /Louai Beshara/AFP 371; /Milos Bicanski 355; /BWP Media 219; /Anthony Cassidy 413; /Johannes Eisele/AFP 357; /Wilbur E. Garrett/National Geographic 60; /David Greedy 473; /Koichi Kamoshida 450; /Keenpress 154; /Christopher Lee 184; /Frans Lemmens 56 inset 1, 63; /Salah Malkawi 368; /Mark Nolan 507; /Vyacheslav Oseledko 7 picture 2, 384; /Christopher Pillitz 129; /Insy Shah 366; /William West/AFP 515; /Wireimage 29

ImPulsTanz/Christian Ganet 331

Iulian Cozma 348

Jetpro.co.nz 531

JNTO/Y. Shimizu 447

Maine Lobster Festival/Kelly Woods Photo 41

OnAsia/Darren Ruane 442; /Tom Vater 494

Photolibrary/Francois Le Divenah 253; /JTB Photo 449; /Kicca Tommasi 103

Photoshot/De Agostini 354; /Designpics 229; /Carlo Ferraro/UPPA 298; /Marcus Führer/UPPA 323; /Alois Furtner/UPPA 6 picture 3, 169; /Igor Kubedinov/UPPA 181; /Egmont Strigl/World Pictures 8 inset 2, 15; /UPPA 452; /World Pictures 358; /WpN 365 inset 2, 372; /Hiroyuki Yanada/G-PHOTO/WpN 453;

Polly Manguel 6 picture 6, 191 centre right, 191 bottom

Press Association Images/AP 446; /B.K. Bangash/AP 388; /Niall Carson/PA Archive 227; /Firdia Lisnawati/AP 466; /Wong Maye-E/AP 458; /Collin Reid/AP 56, 64; /Michel Spingler/AP 257; /Song Zongli/Landov 179

Rex Features/Newspix 510; /Tommy Noll 164

Scenicireland.com/Chris Hill 220, 221

South African National Parks/Megan Taplin 133

The Montana World of WearableArt./Liina Gruener & Marjorie Cox, USA 529

Vogel Gryff 310

Wine Marlborough New Zealand (www.wine-marlborough.co.nz) 524

www.bohinj-info.com 334

www.mondialdusnow.com Nico Lafay 259

www.szarnyas-sarkany.hu 336

www.travelbelize.org, Image Copyright 2008 · Tony Rath of Tony Rath Photography www.tonyrath.com 62

Xinhua News Agency 423

Zouk (www.zoukout.com) 459